D1336691

THE PLACE-NAMES OF ROMAN BRITAIN

THE PLACE-NAMES OF ROMAN BRITAIN

BY

A. L. F. RIVET AND COLIN SMITH

B. T. BATSFORD LTD
LONDON

This edition first published 1979

ISBN 0713420774

Printed in Great Britain at the
University Press, Cambridge
for B. T. Batsford Ltd,
4 Fitzhardinge Street,
London W1H 0AH

UXORIBUS
NOSTRIS
BENEMERITIS

Leucece veut dire en grec blanchette, pour les blanches cuisses des dames dudit lieu.

(Rabelais)

FLUELLEN.—I think it is in Macedon where Alexander is porn. I tell, you, captain, if you look in the maps of the 'orld, I warrant you sall find, in the comparisons between Macedon and Monmouth, that the situations, look you, is both alike. There is a river in Macedon, and there is also moreover a river at Monmouth; it is called Wye at Monmouth; but it is out of my prains what is the name of the other river; but 'tis all one, 'tis alike as my fingers is to my fingers, and there is salmons in both.

(*Henry V*, iv. 7)

CONTENTS

Preface
Abbreviations and References
Glossary of some Technical Terms

PART ONE

CHAPTER I: INTRODUCTION 3
1. A Brief History of the Subject 3
2. The Languages of Roman Britain (in relation to the place-names) 10
3. Textual and Linguistic Problems 29

CHAPTER II: THE LITERARY AUTHORITIES 37
1. The Nature of the Literary Evidence 37
2. Names for Britain 39
3. Names for Ireland 40
4. The Orkneys, Hebrides and other Islands 40
5. Islands described but not named 42
6. Thule and the Cassiterides 42
7. Seas around Britain 44
8. Capes and Promontories 44
9. Forests and Mountains 44
10. Rivers 45
11. Names of Roman Provinces 46
12. Peoples, Tribes and Districts 46
13. Towns and Forts 48
14. The Texts 49

CHAPTER III: PTOLEMY'S GEOGRAPHY 103
1. Ptolemy's Aims 103
2. Ptolemy's Methods 105
3. Earlier Studies of Ptolemy's Britain 108
4. The 'Turning' of Scotland 111

5. The Sources of Ptolemy's Britain 114
6. The Coastline 116
7. The Smaller Islands 117
8. The Interior of the Southern Part of Britain 117
9. The Interior of the Northern Part of Britain 123
10. Textual Questions 129
11. The Text 131

CHAPTER IV: ITINERARIES 148
1. The Nature of Roman Itineraries 148
2. The Peutinger Table 149
3. The Antonine Itinerary 150
4. The Crossing from Gaul to Britain 154
5. Iter I 155
6. Iter II 157
7. Iter III 160
8. Iter IV 160
9. Iter V 162
10. Iter VI 164
11. Iter VII 166
12. Iter VIII 167
13. Iter IX 168
14. Iter X 170
15. Iter XI 172
16. Iter XII 173
17. Iter XIII 175
18. Iter XIV 176
19. Iter XV 178
20. The Maritime Itinerary 180
21. Appendix: The spurious *De Situ Britanniae* of 'Richard of Cirencester' 182

CHAPTER V: THE RAVENNA COSMOGRAPHY 185
1. General 185
2. The Cosmographer and his Aims 187
3. Sources in general 188
4. Nature and Sources of the British Section 190
5. Linguistic Considerations 200
6. Errors of Copying 202
7. The Text 204

CHAPTER VI: THE NOTITIA DIGNITATUM 216

CHAPTER VII: INSCRIPTIONS 226
1. General 226
2. Formal inscriptions on stone 227
3. *Instrumentum domesticum*, coins, graffiti, etc. 230
4. The Rudge Cup and Amiens *patera* 232

PART TWO

ALPHABETIC LIST OF NAMES 237

Index of modern names in Britain 518

List of Illustrations

1. Ptolemy's map of the British Isles	107
2. Possible evolution of the map of the British Isles	110
3. Scotland	113
4. Southern Britain after Ptolemy	118
5. The Flavian occupation of Scotland	121
6. Agricola's campaigns in Scotland	122
7. An interpretation of Ptolemy's map of southern Scotland	121
8. An interpretation of Ptolemy's map of northern Scotland	122
9. The evidence of the Peutinger Table laid on a modern map	151
10. The extent of the Antonine Itinerary	162
11–24. The courses of Iter I–XV inclusive	156–179
25. Islands near Britain listed in Maritime Itinerary	182
26. River-names derived from *Abona*	239
27. River-names derived from *Alauna* or *Alaunos*	243
28. River-names derived from *Derventio*	333
29. River-names derived from *Deva*	336
30. River-names derived from *Isca*	376
31. River-names derived from *Ituna*	380
32. River-names derived from *Trisantona*	477
33. Map of Great Britain	516–17

Plate I Part of the Peutinger Table	*facing* p. 150
Plate II Manuscripts of the *Ravenna Cosmography*	

PREFACE

This book is offered with the confidence that at least there is no other of the same title or in which the same material is treated. It is perhaps surprising that the task has not been undertaken by others earlier, for both the sources and the number of names provide a corpus of manageable size, and the matter – the earliest stratum of the toponymy of Britain which is known to us – has enormous interest. It may have seemed to others that the material was in some ways intractable, and that to work on it was to risk incurring the dissatisfaction of at least one interested group, whether archaeologists or historians or linguists; the risk is recognised, and accepted, in the hope that any dissatisfaction – with what is offered as a basic survey for general use, rather than a highly specialised account – will not to be too great. This is in any case a good moment at which to attempt the task, for the last thirty years have seen great progress in both archaeological and linguistic studies, and one can now draw on the work of many others with confidence because of its excellence. Our debt to them (most notably to Professor Kenneth Jackson) will be apparent on many pages, and bibliographical references will take the serious reader and research worker to specialised publications in a variety of languages. Further reading is in any case advised, because often the etymology of a name or the identification of a place is the subject of controversy.

Our aim has been to be economical rather than discursive, despite the temptation to wander into large speculations and to toy with problems because of their inherent fascination. The framework of the book has been constructed with practical, informative ends in mind. The technical material is sometimes dense but is, we hope, presented in a plain style that neither complicates an issue nor makes it seem simpler than it is. In the linguistic discussions, we have avoided the tendency to use an excess of abbreviations which in saving a little space can also make for difficult reading.

Our sources are those from the earliest times up to the end of Roman rule in Britain in about A.D. 410, together with the writings of those who, after 410, continued to record for us in relatively pure form the toponymy of the Roman province as they knew it from classical sources. There is, for example, no doubt that in the early eighth century the Ravenna Cosmographer used, for Britain, materials which dated from the fourth century at the latest. When an ancient name appears in Gildas, Bede or Nennius, we cite it but without conceding it the prominence accorded to the wholly classical sources; their information is often most valuable, but is of a different nature from that defined above.

The compilation of the work has inevitably entailed much correspondence and we wish to thank all those who have answered our persistent enquiries (whether or not we have always followed their advice), among them Messrs G. C. Boon, A. P. Detsicas, D. Elkington, Miss Margaret Faull, Messrs J. Fox, I. Fraser, Dr Margaret Gelling, Mr M. Hassall, Professor G. D. B. Jones, Messrs O. Padel, H. G. Ramm, Drs W. Rodwell, K. A. Steer, Professor A. C. Thomas and, in respect of the Channel Islands, Mr and Mrs C. G. Stevens.

A special debt of gratitude is owed to Professor D. Ellis Evans of Oxford (formerly of University College, Swansea). Despite pressure of work and of many commitments, he very kindly reviewed a large number of our name entries in draft form and offered guidance, opinions (never dogmatic) and in particular bibliographical indications of the greatest value. We have not cited his opinions conveyed *in litt.* because we are not entitled to use them in support of an argument as one would be if they had appeared in print, and because we would not wish to embarrass a generous man if it should happen that controversy flows from some of our views; suffice it to say that his advice has greatly improved our work, but that remaining deficiencies are our responsibility alone.

We are grateful to the editors of *Bonner Jahrbücher* and *Caesarodunum* and to the Council of the Society for the Promotion of Roman Studies for permission to repeat some passages in Chapters III and IV which have appeared in *Studien zu den Militärgrenzen Roms* II, *Caesarodunum* IX*bis* and *Britannia* I.

Our collaboration arose from the discovery some six years ago that we were both working on what was essentially the same book, though our approaches to it were different. In the event, C.C.S. has been primarily responsible for Chapters I, V, VI and VII and for the linguistic discussions, A.L.F.R. for Chapters II, III and IV and for the identifications and cartography; but since we have criticised and revised each others work at every stage, what we now offer is to be seen as a joint production.

ABBREVIATIONS AND REFERENCES

A *Original geographical sources, itineraries, etc.*

AI	*Antonine Itinerary*, ed. O. Cuntz in *Itineraria Romana*, I (Leipzig, 1929)
IM	*Maritime Itinerary, ibid.*
ND	*Notitia Dignitatum*, ed. O. Seeck (Berlin, 1876)
Ptolemy	*Claudii Ptolemaei Geographia*, ed. C. Müller, 2 vols. (Paris, 1883–1901) for Books I–V; ed. C. F. A. Nobbe (Leipzig, 1845; repr. Hildesheim, 1966), for Books VI–VIII
Ravenna	*Ravennatis Anonymi Cosmographia*, ed. J. Schnetz in *Itineraria Romana*, II (Leipzig, 1940) with reference also to the edition of
(R&C)	I. A. Richmond and O. G. S. Crawford in *Archaeologia*, XCIII (1949), 1–50
TP	*Tabula Peutingeriana*, ed. K. Miller, *Die Peutingersche Tafel* (new edn, Stuttgart, 1962)

B *Epigraphic sources*

Burn	A. R. Burn, *The Romans in Britain* (2nd edn, Oxford, 1969)
CIIC	R. A. S. Macalister, *Corpus Inscriptionum Insularum Celticarum*, 2 vols. (Dublin, 1945–49)
CIL	*Corpus Inscriptionum Latinarum* (1863–); especially vol. VII, ed. E. Hübner, *Inscriptiones Britanniae Latinae* (Berlin, 1873)
EE	*Ephemeris Epigraphica* (Berlin, 1872–1912)
ILS	*Inscriptiones Latinae Selectae*, ed. H. Dessau, 3 vols., (Berlin, 1892–1916)
Mack	R. P. Mack, *The Coinage of Ancient Britain* (2nd edn, London, 1964)
RIB	R. G. Collingwood & R. P. Wright, *The Roman Inscriptions of Britain*, I, *Inscriptions on Stone* (Oxford, 1965)

C *Literary sources*

MGH(AA)	*Monumenta Germaniae Historica* (*Auctores Antiquissimi*), (Berlin, 1877–1905)

Migne	J.-P. Migne (ed.), *Patrologia* (Series Graeca, Series Latina), (Paris, 1844–)

(For texts of individual authors see Chapter II, 14, Texts)

D *Linguistic, archaeological, historical*

ANRW	*Aufstieg und Niedergang der Römischen Welt* (Berlin, 1972–)
CPNS	W. S. Watson, *The History of the Celtic Place-names of Scotland* (Edinburgh, 1926; repr. 1973)
DAG	J. Whatmough, *The Dialects of Ancient Gaul* (Cambridge, Mass., 1970); reference is by page-number
EIHM	T. F. O'Rahilly, *Early Irish History and Mythology* (Dublin, 1946)
Elcock	W. D. Elcock, *The Romance Languages* (2nd edn, London, 1975)
ELH	*Enciclopedia lingüística hispánica*, ed. M. Alvar and others, I (Madrid, 1960)
EPN	E. Ekwall, *The Concise Oxford Dictionary of English Place-names* (3rd edn, Oxford, 1947)
EPNS	English Place-name Society
ERN	E. Ekwall, *English River-names* (Oxford, 1928)
ETP	C. Rostaing, *Essai sur la toponymie de la Provence* (Paris, 1950; repr. Marseille, 1973)
Frere, *Britannia*[2]	S. S. Frere, *Britannia* (2nd edn, London, 1974)
FT	M. Förster, *Der Flussname Themse und seine Sippe*, in *Sitzungsberichte der Bayerischen Akademie der Wissenschaften*, 1941 (Munich, 1942)
GPC	*Geiriadur Prifysgol Cymru*, ed. R. J. Thomas (Cardiff, 1950–)
GPN	D. Ellis Evans, *Gaulish Personal Names* (Oxford, 1967)
Holder	A. Holder, *Alt-celtischer Sprachschatz*, 3 vols. (Leipzig, 1896–1907)
LG	G. Dottin, *La Langue gauloise* (Paris, 1920)
LHEB	K. Jackson, *Language and History in Early Britain* (Edinburgh, 1953; repr. 1971)
Margary	I. D. Margary, *Roman Roads in Britain* (3rd edn, London, 1973)
Miller	K. Miller, *Itineraria Romana* (Stuttgart, 1916)
Ogilvie & Richmond	R. M. Ogilvie and I. A. Richmond, *Cornelii Taciti de vita Agricolae* (Oxford, 1967)
Pokorny	J. Pokorny, *Indogermanisches etymologisches Wörterbuch*, 2 vols. (Berne and Munich, 1959, 1969)
PP	F. T. Wainwright (ed.), *The Problem of the Picts* (Edinburgh, 1956)
P.-W.	*Paulys Real-Encyklopädie der Klassischen Altertumwissenschaft*, ed. G. Wissowa and W. Kroll (Stuttgart, 1893–)

R&C	I. A. Richmond and O. G. S. Crawford, 'The British Section of the *Ravenna Cosmography*', *Archaeologia*, XCIII (1949), 1–50
Rhys (1904)	J. Rhys, *Celtic Britain* (3rd edn, London 1904)
Rivet *AI*	A. L. F. Rivet, 'The British Section of the Antonine Itinerary', *Britannia*, I (1970), 34–68; with Appendix II by K. Jackson on the place-names, 68–82
RNNB	I. A. Richmond (ed.), *Roman and Native in North Britain* (Edinburgh, 1958)
Ross (1967)	A. Ross, *Pagan Celtic Britain* (London, 1967)
TCRB	A. L. F. Rivet, *Town and Country in Roman Britain* (2nd edn, London, 1964)
TF	A. Dauzat, *La Toponymie française* (Paris, 1960; repr. 1971)
TRB	J. S. Wacher, *The Towns of Roman Britain* (London, 1975)
VCH	*Victoria History of the Counties of England*
W.-P., Walde-Pokorny	A. Walde & J. Pokorny, *Vergleichendes Wörterbuch der Indogermanischen Sprachen*, 3 vols. (Berlin & Leipzig, 1928–32)
Williams	I. Williams, linguistic notes to the study of Richmond & Crawford, in *Archaeologia*, XCIII (1949), 1–50
Vincent	A. Vincent, *Toponymie de la France* (Brussels, 1937); reference is by section number
Zachrisson	R. E. Zachrisson, *Romans, Kelts and Saxons in Early Britain* (Uppsala, 1927)

E *Journals*

Ant.J.	*Antiquaries' Journal*, 1921–
Arch.	*Archaeologia* (London), 1770–
Arch.Ael.[4]	*Archaeologia Aeliana*, 4th Series, 1925–
Arch.J.	*Archaeological Journal*, 1845–
BBCS	*Bulletin of the Board of Celtic Studies*, 1921–
BZN	*Beiträge zur Namenforschung*, 1949–
CW[2]	*Transactions of the Cumberland and Westmorland Antiquarian & Archaeological Society*, 2nd series, 1901–
EC	*Etudes Celtiques*, 1936–
EHR	*English Historical Review*, 1886–
JBAA	*Journal of the British Archaeological Association*, 1845–
JHS	*Journal of Hellenic Studies*, 1880–
JIES	*Journal of Indo-European Studies*, 1973–
JRS	*Journal of Roman Studies*, 1911–
N&Q	*Notes & Queries*, 1849–
PSAS	*Proceedings of the Society of Antiquaries of Scotland*, 1855–
RC	*Revue Celtique*, 1870–1934 (continued as *EC*)
REA	*Revue des Etudes Anciennes*, 1899–
REL	*Revue des Etudes Latines*, 1923–
RIO	*Revue Internationale d'Onomastique*, 1949–
VR	*Vox Romanica*, 1936–

ZCP	*Zeitschrift für Celtische Philologie*, 1896–
ZFN	*Zeitschrift für Namenforschung*, 1938–
ZOFN	*Zeitschrift für Ortsnamenforschung*, 1925–37 (continued as *ZFN*)

Other journals are cited in full: *Antiquary*, 1871–1915; *Antiquity*, 1927–; *Arctos*, 1930– *Britannia*, 1970– ; *Celticum*, 1961– ; *Ériu*, 1904– ; *Hermes*, 1866– ; *Latomus*, 1937– ; *Ogam*, 1948– ; *Studia Celtica*, 1966– .

GLOSSARY

OF SOME OF THE TECHNICAL TERMS USED IN THIS BOOK

Canabae. The officially authorised settlement (literally 'huts') beside a legionary fortress.

Castellum. Properly a diminutive of *castrum* (q.v. sub *castra*), the word is regularly used for a fort, such as was occupied by a unit (*cohors*, *ala* or *numerus*) smaller than a legion. From the fifth century, however, it is sometimes used as a synonym for *vicus* (q.v.) in its colloquial sense.

Castra. Either a camp (of a temporary nature) or a fortress (of a permanent nature) occupied by a large body of troops, especially a legion but occasionally no more than a cohort. The singular *castrum* is hardly ever used in classical Latin, but from the fifth century onwards approximates in meaning to *vicus* (q.v.) in its technical sense.

Civitas. This word has a wide variety of meanings – citizenship, the citizen body, a state (whether a city state or a tribal state and whether or not incorporated in the Roman Empire), the physical city which embodied the state and finally, as in the Ravenna Cosmography, any town or place (cf. Ptolemy, who uses the Greek equivalent, πόλις, with similar looseness). In our index it is used in the third sense, to mean one of the tribal states which made up the Roman province of Britannia and which were initially *civitates peregrinae* (i.e. 'foreign states', whose members were not Roman citizens).

Colonia. A settlement of Roman citizens established by law (in the first century primarily of legionary veterans), consisting of a city and its dependent *territorium* and thus constituting a separate *civitas* within the province. The *colonia* represented the highest grade of *civitas* and communities which proved worthy of it by their cultural development could be promoted to it (as happened in Britain in the case of the settlement which grew up near the legionary fortress at York).

Gnomon. A vertical staff of a particular length whose shadow was used to measure the angle of elevation of the sun and so to compute latitude (also called a *sciotherum*).

Latin Rights (*Ius Latii*). Originally the rights enjoyed by the *populi Latini* of Italy, but in imperial times conferred on *civitates* rather than individuals. In such cases a local magistrate (with his family) was granted Roman citizenship, if he did not already possess it, on completing his year of office.

Mansio. A stopping-place on a road where there were facilities not merely for changing horses but also for an overnight stay.

Municipium. A chartered settlement either of Roman citizens or of people enjoying 'Latin rights' (whereby magistrates and their families were granted Roman citizenship); similar in organisation to a *colonia* (q.v.) but different from it in that the status was conferred on an already existing community, which was thus 'taken in' to the Roman commonwealth, while a *colonia* was an offshoot from it. *Municipia* ranked next to *coloniae* in dignity and *civitates peregrinae* might hope to be promoted to this grade.

Mutatio. A stopping-place on a road where there were facilities for changing horses.

Pagus. A subdivision of a Celtic tribe and the territory occupied by it and so, in Roman terms, a subdivision of a *civitas peregrina*. The inhabitants of a *pagus* were *pagani*, 'country-dwellers', whence the word 'pagan'.

Praesidium. Properly a garrison, but often used as an alternative to *castellum* or *castra* (qq.v.).

Praetorium. Properly the tent or dwelling of the *praetor*, or commander, and hence the commander's house in a fort or fortress, but also a governor's residence elsewhere and occasionally even more generally any magnificent residence. The word is also sometimes used for the Praetorian Guard (properly *Cohortes Praetoriae*).

Roman Mile. The *mille passus* consisted of a thousand *passus* (double paces of five Roman feet) and measured approximately 1,618 yards (1,480 metres). In some parts of Gaul, and possibly also in Britain, the *leuga* (league), equal to 1½ Roman miles, was sometimes used for measurement.

Stadium (*Greek* στάδιον). A measure of distance equal to one-eighth of a Roman mile (i.e. 202¼ yards or 145 metres).

Statio. Any post or station, but especially a post of the fiscal officers of a province, concerned with the collection of dues and taxes.

Territorium. The land attributed to, and subject to the jurisdiction of, a city.

Vicus. This has both a colloquial and a technical meaning. Colloquially it means any village or insignificant town. Technically it means a town which, though possessing some administrative organisation of its own, is yet subordinate to a higher authority, whether civil (a *civitas*) or military (as in the case of *vici* attached to forts) or the administrator (*procurator*) of an imperial estate; in this technical sense it was also applied to the internal wards of large cities.

PART ONE

CHAPTER ONE

INTRODUCTION

1. A BRIEF HISTORY OF THE SUBJECT

Our work is concerned with two aspects of Romano-British names: their identification, and their linguistic aspects. The first was naturally of no concern to the ancient world, for the names were 'alive' and the identifications current. It is likely that a certain small amount of research had to be undertaken into Romano-British names in the early medieval centuries by Augustine and his colleagues as they sought to christianise the Anglo-Saxons and make the 'Celtic' church conform, for which purpose the names of ancient episcopal sees might be important, and in all cases where we can check they seem to have done their work well. The instances in which Bede gives the Romano-British name, the Saxon name and the British name of his own day show, beyond the strictly necessary equation, an awareness of the problem and possibly an interest in names for their own sake, and certainly provide us with a valuable and unique record. Later medieval writers were for the most part incurious about the matter, though naturally for ecclesiastical, legal and historical purposes they used either genuine or newly latinised forms of place-names constantly in their work.

A curiosity about the etymology and meaning of place-names is probably very ancient. We do not know if Roman officials and educated Romans questioned native Britons about these matters, but it is by no means unlikely, and the same would apply to personal names, divine names and ethnic names, and to the British language as a whole. We have no information about this, not even of an anecdotal kind. What is clear is that a number of classical Latin writers often indulged in etymological and semantic speculation. Some of these were concerned in any case with words and names on a large scale, such as Pliny and Varro; an example of Pliny's work is mentioned under our *Bannaventa*[1]. Other cases are mentioned by Dottin (*LG* 23–24). In the Latin poets, of whom Dottin quotes three, etymologising seems almost to have become a sort of rhetorical *topos*, a periphrastic adornment surrounding mention of a name. Various Celtic names in *-dunum* and *-magus*, together with *Eporedia* and especially *Mediolanum* (Milan) are analysed – often fancifully – in this way. It remains, perhaps, curious that no classical Latin writer produced a catalogue or full study of place-names, despite the continuous interest in the grammar and sounds of the Latin language shown by many, and the authentic scholarly interest shown by such as Pliny in animal names, in the technical parlance of Spanish mining, and so on.

The first such toponymic catalogue, on a modest scale within a vast work, seems to have been that produced by Isidore of Seville (*c.* 560–636), in Book xv of his *Etymologiae*. It is probable that by this time the needs of Christian scholars, writers and preachers to know how to analyse and understand Biblical proper names and concepts stemming from Hebrew and Greek provided the essential stimulus, for Isidore includes a range of Old and New Testament place-names beside those of the pre-Christian Middle East and Mediterranean worlds. Failing at the outset to find any etymology for the name *Roma*, beyond the fact that it was connected with that of its founder Romulus, he explains (in terms that all subsequent students of the matter will echo):

> Si igitur tantae civitatis [*Roma*] certa ratio non apparet, non mirum si in aliarum opinione dubitatur. Unde nec historicos, nec commentatores varia dicentes imperitiae condemnare debemus, quia antiquitas ipsa creavit errorem. (xv, 193, 2)

Much of his information is derived from earlier writers. From Strabo and St Jerome he holds that

> *Saguntum* Graeci ex insula *Zacyntho* profecti in Hispaniam condiderunt. (xv, 206, 68)

while for the name of Lisbon he goes, via Solinus and others, to Homeric epic:

> *Olyssipona*, ab Ulysse est condita, et nuncupata. (xv, 206, 70)

Sometimes, however, the guesswork seems to be his own, as in the case of his native Seville:

> *Hispalis* autem a situ cognominata est, eo quod in solo palustri suffixis in profundo *palis* locata sit. (xv, 206, 71)

The name of Milan preoccupied Isidore as it had done others:

> Galli. . .*Mediolanum*. . .condiderunt. Vocatum autem *Mediolanum*, ab eo quod ibi sus *medio lanea* perhibetur inventa. (xv, 204, 57)

The modern student of toponymy feels at times that his speculations, even if expressed in more scientific terminology, are not fundamentally different from what Isidore says about Seville, for example, though we should probably not venture as far as he did in talking about half-hairy sows. Moderns are hardly permitted his flights of poetic fancy, nor the kind of dignification-by-association which he expresses with his mention of Ulysses. We may today be more accurate, but are undeniably the poorer too. Isidore's work, a fundamental text for the education of Europe in the early Middle Ages, was echoed and improved upon by many writers, doubtless encouraged by nominalist beliefs.

Renaissance humanism, nowhere greater than in its textual, antiquarian and linguistic achievements, put a sudden end to the medieval tradition in this as in other respects. Our prefatory squib from Rabelais sums up, probably, the many hours he had spent in agreeable discussion, part-serious but often ribald, on these matters, with new-found Greek serving to elucidate or befog amusingly the sense of rediscovered *Lutetia*, Lutèce. The Continental scholars, especially Germans, during the sixteenth century produced printed texts of the works on which we still depend today for most of our toponymic material of the ancient world – the literary authors, Ptolemy, *AI*, *TP*, and *ND* – and had begun the study of inscriptions; only *Ravenna*, among texts of importance to us, awaited publication (1688). In Britain the work of the sixteenth-century scholars in the fields of Roman, topographical and linguistic studies culminated most splendidly in William Camden's *Britannia* of 1586 (quotations here are from the 6th edition, 1607). This work, superior to anything of the kind produced by Continental scholars about their own countries at the time, astonishes us by its grasp of historical fact, topography and cartography, and especially of linguistic matters. Here is Camden on the name of the British:

> Britannos enim se glasto (*Glass* caeruleum etiamnum illis significat) depinxisse gravissimi quiqui authores Caesar, Mela, Plinius, &c. doceant; quid si a depictis corporibus Britones dictos fuisse coniectarim? Quicquid enim depictum & coloratum, *Brith* patria & antiqua lingua appellant. Nec est cur quis hanc duriusculam aut absurdam esse Britonum etymologiam existimet, cum quae in etymis maxime requiruntur, & voces consonent, & nomen, tanquam rei imago, rem ipsam exprimat. *Brith* enim & *Brit* optime consonant, & *Brith* illud Britonibus denotat, quod Britones re ipsa erant, i. *picti*, *depicti*, *infecti*, *colorati*... (p. 19)

He was not far from the accepted modern truth, and his method of argument is impeccable. Even when partly wrong, he is so for good reasons, misled into thinking (as most did, long after) that *Camboritum* must be Cambridge; but he still goes to the British root and has comparative material from Gaul:

> *Camboritum* etenim *Vadum ad Camum*, vel *Vadum flexuosum* significat, nam *Rith* '*Vadum*' Britannis nostris significat, quod eo adnoto, ut Galli facilius videant, quid sit *Augustoritum*, *Darioritum*, *Rithomagus*, &c. in Gallia. (p. 256)

When Camden is wrong, he is never nonsensical. In the following, about *Venta* (Winchester), a name which is still doubtful for us today, he gently dismisses at the start some unlikely notions of others and proceeds to a solution which is at least reasonable, and is securely founded upon comparative material in three languages:

> Ventae huius etymum alij a *Vento*, alij a *Vino*, alij a *Wina* Episcopo petunt, qui omnes Bonae menti litarent. Potior mihi videtur Lelandi nostri opinio, qui a *Guin*, sive *Guen* Britannorum, i. *albo* deduxit, ita ut *Caer Guin*, Albam urbem significet. Et qui non? cum ab albedine prisci Latini *Albam Longam*, & *Albam Regiam* civitates denominarint, Graeci itidem *Leucam*, *Leucada*, &c., & alia ab albedine loca nominata habuerint. Haec etenim *Venta*, uti & aliae duae eiusdem cognominis, *Venta Silurum* & *Venta Icenorum*, in solo ex creta, & argilla albicanti collocatur. (p. 190)

More gentle progress over the next century and a half ensured the success of John Horsley's *Britannia Romana* (London, 1732; reprinted, with introduction by E. Birley, at Newcastle in 1974), an equally splendid work which includes editions of Ptolemy, *AI*, *ND* and for the first time *Ravenna*, in their British sections. This textual basis, extremely sound for its time, allowed Horsley to be firmer than Camden in his identifications and sometimes in his linguistic discussions also, and he reproduced many inscriptions, including a large number discovered since Camden's day. Since we have already mentioned British *Venta*, it is worth quoting Horsley on the same theme (p. 443), noting that he concludes with a mention which today seems entirely relevant in our own Alphabetic List:

> I shall only farther remark, that the same place which is called *Bennavenna* in the second *iter*, and *Isanavatia* in the sixth, is here [VIII] called *Bannavantum*. Dr Gale prefers *Bennavenna*, or *Pennavenna*, as the true name; I know not but *Bannavantum* may be as near to the truth. This name however brings the Italian *Beneventum* to mind...

Horsley was puzzled by *Ravenna*, as anyone might be:

> I shall not stay to criticize on the several barbarous words and expressions in the introduction, nor to enquire who *Anschis* was. I would only leave it to the reader to consider, whether the whole passage, and particularly *olim gens Saxonum in ea habitare videtur*, does not strongly imply, that not only our author himself, but even those he consulted and borrowed from, must have been considerably later than the Saxon invasions. And indeed I did not intend at first to have concerned myself with this geographer... (p. 497)

Horsley explains that he was persuaded to take the Cosmographer seriously when the discovery of the Rudge Cup (1725) showed that for its list of Wall-forts at least the Cosmographer had some inklings of sound ancient information. Some of Horsley's hints, both about identifications and about etymologies or other linguistic matters, are still highly relevant today; and since he regularly cites Camden and other scholars, and seems to command all the available bibliography, it is proper to pay tribute to his achievement.

Our last eighteenth-century landmark is the *Itinerarium Curiosum* of William Stukeley (2nd edn London, 1776). This is a mine of essential information for archaeologists in particular, because Stukeley saw and recorded – in maps and drawings – so much on the ground which has since been lost or damaged. In identifications and etymologies he was, however, an inventive romantic who represents a step backward from the place reached by Camden, Horsley and others. He follows Geoffrey of Monmouth in insisting, for example, that

> The name of *Trinobantes* is derived from *Trinobantum*, the most ancient name of London. (I, p. 9)

and, neglecting the comparative method of his illustrious predecessors and their relatively great care with British elements, Stukeley has many entries like the following:

> *Lemanis*...Stone-Street...such it literally signifies, *via lapidea*...*Lhe* signifies a way in British; *maen*, a stone. (I, p. 132)

Yet he could do better than this, in terms which are relevant both semantically and topographically for our discussion of *Bannovalium*:

> Horncastle was undoubtedly the *Banovallum* in *Ravennas*; the latter part of the word is Latin, so that it signifies the fortification upon the river Bane. It is of a low situation, placed in the angle of the two brooks meeting here, the Bane and Waring; whence the modern name Horncastle, which signifies an angle, all this country over...I will not venture to conceit it came from the ancient way of painting rivers horned, from their windings and turnings; of which we may find a hint in Burton's Comment on Antoninus's Itinerary, pag. 56, and they that please may consult Bochart's *Phaleg*., II.22, where are many proofs of the ancients expressing an angle by the term *horn*. (I, p. 30)

Stukeley, alas, was an enthusiastic victim of the spurious *De Situ Britanniae* of 'Richard of Cirencester'; he was the prime propagator of this fiction, and by his authority in his otherwise valuable book served to establish the text as part of the canon of our toponymy. The effects of this were extraordinarily long-lasting (see pp. 182–84).

While identification of names had already made great progress by Horsley's day, and continued to advance slowly in local and national studies, the linguistic study of names could not go forward until the revolution which was brought about by the establishment of philology as a discipline in the early nineteenth century, largely by Germans, in the fields of Romance, Germanic, classical and above all comparative Indo-European studies. In this, specifically Celtic scholarship made a late start, but benefited from the methodology and principles established in related fields. Alfred Holder's great *Alt-celtischer Sprachschatz* of 1896–1907, though by now capable of improvement in some respects, remains not only an indispensable collection of data but also a monument to the breadth and vigour of nineteenth-century scholarship, still mainly in Holder's day German and French. When one seeks analogues for British names, it is to Holder's volumes that one turns first, especially since he has the merit of recording names not only from ancient sources but from medieval ones too, many of them local in nature. Holder was able to build on the work of such scholars as Glück, Zeuss, d'Arbois de Jubainville and Stokes. In our own century the work of G. Dottin (1920), Whatmough (1970, etc.) and many others on aspects of Continental Celtic has been most valuable to us, and in particular the studies of the toponymy of Gaul and of France by Vincent, Rostaing and Dauzat. There is a full survey of onomastic work on Gaulish by Professor D. Ellis Evans in *GPN*, 2–15, and a masterly (and frank) commentary by Professor Jackson in *Modern Language Review*, LXXI (1976), xxiii–xxxvii ('Fifty Years of Celtic Philology': The Presidential Address to the Modern Humanities Research Association, 1976).

The progress in philological studies and in Celtic work might have meant little for our immediate purposes had it not been accompanied by good editions of the texts of those ancient works which list our names. The editions of *Ravenna* by Pinder and Parthey (1860; now superseded by that of Schnetz, 1940), of *ND* by Seeck (1876) and of Ptolemy by Müller (1883, for the part which includes Britain), have all provided solid bases for work, as has Cuntz's edition of *AI* (1929), together with good texts – many also of the later decades of the nineteenth century – of literary writers whose work is important for toponymy and ethnic names, e.g. Caesar, Pliny and Tacitus.

When we turn to Britain in particular, we are conscious of the great improvement in our essential tools in recent decades, as a result of steady progress in relevant disciplines. One of these, scarcely mentioned so far in this account, is archaeology, whose methods – largely introduced in the late nineteenth century, but constantly enhanced by scientific invention – provide factual information about the nature of our sites and serve to limit the wilder speculations. A special type of scientific analysis of materials has been responsible for the deletion of one inscription – should one say alas? – from the corpus of our materials (see *Anderitum*). It is unlikely that any others are suspect. The information on inscriptions is now readily available in *The Roman Inscriptions of Britain*, I (Oxford, 1965), supplemented by annual reports of discoveries in *JRS* and more recently in *Britannia*; for an example of the importance of some, but unfortunately rare, inscriptions for our purposes, see our entry for *Velunia*.

Among British and Irish Celticists of our century, among the older generations, we have relied much on the work of Rhys, Watson, O'Rahilly and Ifor Williams, together with much else published in article form. The books of Ekwall are of course fundamental; his handling of Celtic materials in *English River-names* (1928), where they are naturally strongly present, is – to our eye – not only competent but sympathetic, but in *The Concise Oxford Dictionary of English Place-names* (1936, and later editions) seems somewhat reluctant, even perfunctory, no doubt because in this context the great mass of names is Germanic and Ekwall was unable to give any undue emphasis to the earliest stratum of our toponymy, the Celtic one, despite its altogether exceptional interest. The same criticism may be made of most of the volumes so far published in the County Series of the *EPNS*; but perhaps we are expecting too much in the interests of a rather sectional enthusiasm. Two contemporary Celtic scholars have by their publications put us very greatly in their debt. Professor Ellis Evans's book *Gaulish Personal Names* (Oxford, 1967) is a near-inexhaustible mine of information for Insular Celtic as well as Continental, particularly as it includes where relevant a great deal on toponymy and on ethnic and divine names; its bibliographical apparatus is superb. For a personal note, see also our Preface. An altogether special word is warranted by Professor Kenneth Jackson's *Language and History in Early Britain* (Edinburgh, 1953; reprinted 1963, 1971). Jackson allows himself only four lines on this in his 1976 *Address* mentioned above, but on any assessment of Celtic studies about or in Britain this great book claims pride of place. It is not only fundamental for the history of British and early Welsh, its main subject, but contains a great deal relevant to other aspects of Celtic, and a good deal of it concerns Latin in Britain, the Latin element in Welsh, and Anglo-Saxon. We have used *LHEB* constantly, both for what it tells us about place-names and other names in a specific way, and for its essential guidance on points of phonology. Our instinct has been to cite Jackson's etymologies, opinions and caveats not quite unquestioningly, but certainly in a spirit of near-total confidence in their general excellence. On phonological facts and processes, it has seemed to us that he is hardly ever open to challenge, and we can only hope that we have succeeded in understanding him on what are often difficult subjects. Our only major disagreement with him is that expounded in our Chapter 1 (2), on the nature of the Latin records of Romano-British names, which is in any case hardly at the core of his work. It is regrettable that *LHEB* is not more widely known as the national monument which it is; its form and content are inevitably daunting, and the work by its nature is probably incapable of being presented in the form of an abridgement or semi-popular digest. Professor Jackson's Appendix on the names of *AI* in *Britannia*, 1 (1970), has naturally had the same authority for us, as have other publications of his where appropriate.

On the subject of Romano-British toponymy, the most ambitious publication of recent decades has been that of Richmond and Crawford on the British section of *Ravenna*, in 1949. We have cited this for every relevant name, both as a source for forms and as a source of data and opinions. Since it was the first serious study of this difficult text it deserves high praise, but its defects have become apparent as we have reworked the same material. The main problem is that Richmond and Crawford placed far too much trust in the accuracy of the conflated text on which they worked, itself built up from a study of the main manuscripts; as a result, they scarcely allowed for duplications, wildly aberrant forms, and so on. This made them proceed to identify as valid places names which are in various ways non-names. On the linguistic side they sometimes attempted their own commentary and sometimes submitted forms to Professor Ifor Williams, but the latter, great Celtic philologist though he was, seems to have worked in the dark in that he had no access to comparative materials and had no reason to distrust *Ravenna* as he ought to have done. All three are further open to the criticism that, although they employ topographical arguments about the nature of sites, they seem to have little feeling for processes of place-name formation and employ semantic arguments that are distinctly weak. The work of Richmond and Crawford, with that of Williams, has (because of the general authority of the scholars) become something approaching canonical truth with archaeologists and other students of Roman Britain, but we hope they they will tolerate, even welcome, our sometimes disturbing rectifications. Other recent work by British scholars and others, on both identifications and linguistic matters, much of it of high quality, will be acknowledged in its place.

It would be a lengthy and difficult task to try to assess the importance of recent work by foreign scholars on aspects of toponymy, especially Celtic, of relevance to us here. This ranges from indispensable and massive works of reference such as Pokorny's *Indogermanisches etymologisches Wörterbuch* through books down to, for example, articles about a single group of names or notes (some perhaps a few lines in extent) of E. C. Hamp on a question of Indo-European phonology which may, almost in passing, give us the explanation of a British name. Our debt to these becomes apparent most clearly in the Alphabetic List, though citations there could have been multiplied many times. It cannot be doubted that access to these specialised books and articles in journals that are often not easy of access is an essential in research; one feels that occasionally British writers on these topics have taken a limited or unduly insular stance, or have not been prepared to read the languages in which important work is published. It may be true, for example, that Pokorny's 'Illyrian' thesis is open to the gravest doubt, but his assembly of names and forms on a pan-European basis, whatever the reasons for the similarities, is something that cannot be allowed to pass unacknowledged.

In the Alphabetic List, we have not attempted to do justice to all or even to most of the previous studies in which a point of view is expressed or data given, and the entries are not overloaded with bibliographical material. In very many cases a reference to *LHEB* or *GPN* or Pokorny is intended to suffice for the purposes of the entry; the inquirer should, in addition to finding sound doctrine in Jackson or Ellis Evans, be guided to further specialist information by our references to these general works. This seems consonant with our exposition here of no more than a 'brief history of the subject'.

Subjects that have a past and a present also have a future. It seems doubtful whether progress in philology could provide greater certainties about our names, though no doubt some problems will be resolved and new etymologies proposed. It is on the side of further identifications that progress may be made. New epigraphic discoveries are bound to occur, and although inscriptions rarely mention place-names, some do, and those from the military zones might well provide key information. Perhaps the **Vicani Uxelodunenses* will provide a stone, most desirably at Stanwix, or a milestone unearthed near Lancaster might give us the full name of the place. There might easily come to light pairs of sheets from lost medieval copies of works that interest us, for parchment from dismembered manuscripts was often used in the late medieval centuries and in the Renaissance for stiffening the binding of books; in this way two sheets of the *AI* which had formed part of the Codex Spirensis have appeared in the present century. We hardly need a new text of *AI*, but a better text of *Ravenna* would be invaluable. Perhaps, in some minor ecclesiastical library, lurking anonymously behind the spine of a manuscript labelled *Tractatus* or *Leges*, there is a pristine copy of a **Notitia Britanniarum*, protected by a layer of dust that began in the fifth century.

2. THE LANGUAGES OF ROMAN BRITAIN (IN RELATION TO THE PLACE-NAMES)

At the time of the Roman invasion, the inhabitants of the greater part of Britain spoke British, a language of the Brythonic (or Brittonic) group of Celtic speeches. British had reached these shores with migrants and invaders who brought their distinctive grades of Iron Age culture in movements from the eighth century B.C. onwards. These incomers shared language and culture with the Brythonic-speaking peoples of areas which are today France, Iberia, northern Italy, Switzerland, the Rhineland, and the Low Countries, the whole making up the group of *P*-Celtic speakers. There were also the Galatians in Asia Minor, an amalgam of tribes which had taken a route different from that which ranged generally westward from Central Europe. Place-names also prove an early Celtic penetration to the Upper Danube and eastward from the Alps as far as Belgrade (*Singidunum*). The modern representatives of these *P*-Celtic speeches are Welsh, Cornish and Breton. *Q*-Celtic or Goidelic is represented in modern times by Irish, Manx and Scots Gaelic, the last having been introduced into

Scotland by Irish settlers from the fifth century A.D. There are traces of Q-Celtic peoples also in Iberia.

There is no reason to suppose that at the time of the Roman invasion British was much different from the language of the nearer Continental areas. Gaulish, in particular, from which the language of most of Britain had derived, offers us many useful parallels in toponymy and in other ways, and is moreover better recorded and more accessible by conjecture than is Insular speech of the early centuries. Before the end of the Roman period in Britain, regional and dialectal features were beginning to emerge within British speech, but these hardly concern us here.[1] The place-names recorded in our Latin and Greek texts are of an entirely uniform kind within Britain, and in many cases are uniform also with corresponding names in Gaul, Iberia, and other parts. This is scarcely surprising when we recall the comparatively recent date of the migration of some peoples from Gaul to Britain, the fact that some British tribes were offshoots whose brethren remained on the Continent (e.g. Atrebates, Parisii and Belgae), the constancy of contacts before and after the Roman invasion, and the presence of military units, traders, etc., of Continental Celtic blood in Britain under Roman rule.

In what is now Scotland the linguistic situation is less clear. South of the Clyde–Forth line the Dumnonii (recorded as *Damnonii* by Ptolemy) were presumably related to the Dumnonii of south-west England, and the Cornovii (*Cornavii* in most Ptolemy MSS) of north-east Scotland were related to the Cornovii of Shropshire and Cheshire, these and other south Scottish tribes speaking British. The inhabitants of Scotland north of the Clyde–Forth line (marked in the second century by the Antonine Wall) were designated Caledonii by the Romans, and are thought to have been a partly Celtic people whose speech had Brythonic elements superimposed upon an older, non-Indo-European language. In the fourth century they were known as Picti, and their language and culture, which persisted down to the ninth century, are known as Pictish. Place-names from this northern region sometimes present difficulties of a kind not found elsewhere and may indicate the presence there of originally non-Celtic peoples. It is possible that elsewhere in Britain, pre-Celtic and even non-Indo-European elements may underlie place-names, i.e. that the latter are based on words taken from an older language into British, but there is no absolutely firm evidence of this; students of Gaulish seem more ready to accept the possibility of this in their work.

The number of Latin speakers who came in A.D. 43 was a small one in proportion to the number of native Celtic speakers, but the Latin speakers were disproportionately influential. Latin was the language of the Army, the administration, the law, of some trade, of officially approved religious cults. Above all, it was the language of the victors and of a greatly superior culture. At once, pressures of romanisation and hence of latinisation must have been considerable. They were natural and inevitable rather than artificially imposed. As time went on and units of Britons were raised to serve in the Army abroad, these must have acquired a minimal competence in Latin, as

[1] Jackson, *LHEB* 3–5, 24 and *passim*.

must any Briton who (later still) joined an Army unit stationed in Britain. In religion, the major Celtic deities were early associated with the Graeco-Roman pantheon and given cults in Latin; the devotees of even very local Celtic gods seem to have conformed to the Roman habits of the votary tablet, the small altar, etc., and to have used only Latin in writing on them. For the rest, the degree to which pressures of romanisation affected the Celtic population varied according to the class, ambitions and geographical situation of the latter.[1] The old tribal ruling families, if throwing in their lot with Rome, must have had a strong reason to latinise themselves promptly if they wished to continue in positions of authority, and a few individuals may even have been groomed in this way, at Rome, before A.D. 43 (e.g. Cogidubnus?). Once schools were established in the chief towns, especially during Agricola's governorship (*Agricola*, 21), the elements of a classical literary education could be added to basic latinity for the sons of upper- and middle-class Britons, with Greek also in some instances. From this class came the officials of each *civitas* and, in the towns, the magistrates, members of the *ordo*, and dignitaries of the religious cults; and, in the countryside, the romanised owners of the villas of Lowland Britain. After a time any young Briton who wished to get on in the world as soldier, craftsman, trader, or in any other way, must have needed some Latin to do so, not so much in order to ingratiate himself with new masters, or because of any official encouragement, but simply because conditions of life favoured it. Among a smaller number literacy in Latin must also have meant rising in the world, whether by handling the tools of new technology, measuring and building things, or simply by buying and selling produce in a market run on the Roman system of weights and measures.

As for geographical location, this made for a very clear linguistic division. The cities – every one of them being a Roman creation, whatever the status of any pre-existing Celtic settlement on the site – had much Latin spoken in them at all times; the countryside very little in early times and probably not a great deal, except among the villa-owning gentry, in later periods. However, in both cases there are distinctions to be made. The three *coloniae* of the first century – Colchester, Lincoln and Gloucester – were by definition Latin-speaking, since they were founded for legionary veterans who were all Roman citizens, and they must have remained strong centres for the diffusion of Latin throughout their existence. The same is true of the *colonia* of York (early third century?), whose latinity, opulence and Continental trading links are demonstrated in a remarkable series of inscribed tombs and other texts. London, as an administrative and trading centre, with a strong element of cosmopolitanism, must also have been Latin-speaking in a high degree, and the same must have been true, for different reasons, of the spa at Bath. For the typical *civitas*-centre, we have no possibility of guessing accurately its linguistic make-up. It is likely that inhabitants who spoke Latin only were not numerous. Those who were of Celtic blood and advanced up the social scale may have needed to use a good deal of Latin, but can have had no reason to renounce or forget their Celtic speech, even by the third and fourth centuries. The urban proletariat probably had some Latin for practical needs

[1] For a complementary discussion, see S. S. Frere, *Britannia* (2nd edn London, 1974), especially 350–53, with a reference to views of Haverfield. *LHEB* throughout is obviously of the utmost relevance.

though no doubt remaining largely Celtic-speaking; more of them than one might expect were literate – to judge by names scratched on pots, craftsmen's tallies of production, curses, etc. – and of course this means literate in Latin, probably the fruit of elementary education in the towns. Hence a large measure of very varied bilingualism is implied. In the rural areas, the villas were centres of romanised taste in many (but far from all) cases, and it is likely that their owners spoke Latin regularly, enjoyed literary culture (witness scenes from the *Aeneid* and mythological themes in mosaics and on wall-plaster),[1] but had to maintain Celtic speech for communication with servants and estate workers. On native farms even in the most settled and civilised parts of lowland Britain, Celtic speech remained dominant, and in remote areas of northern and western Britain its domination must have been total.

Yet some reservations have to be made in those northern and western areas. The military zones are a special case. From the first, especially in the legionary fortresses, the soldiers spoke Latin. Their liaisons with native British women, and eventually their marriages to them, must inevitably have produced a situation in which the pressure was on the woman to 'convert' (as it were) to Latin, and for children to be brought up principally in Latin, especially if in the larger *vici* attached to the forts there was some elementary schooling. This is likely to have given a predominantly Latin character to the numerous *vici* which grew up near the forts along Hadrian's Wall, in other northern areas and in Wales, and even for a time in southern Scotland. One such *vicus* grew eventually into nothing less than a *colonia*, at York, and those at Chester and Caerleon must have been substantial; their latinity would have increased as elements of local government were introduced into them, while continuous involvement with the adjacent fort ensured awareness of *romanitas*.[2]

Opinion about the degree of romanisation, and with it on the extent of latinisation of the British population, has varied widely. Celtic scholars have tended to regard both as superficial, and to write of Roman rule as the military occupation of a subject people, whereas the more classically minded portray a Britain which was a province as fully a part of the culture of the Empire as any other, citing the Panegyrists of Autun who, at the end of the third century, rhetorically welcomed Britain back into the fold after the quelling of revolt. It serves no purpose to quote Roman writers against this on the theme of 'remote and barbarous Britain', for this was merely an enduring literary *topos*. In support of the 'Celtic Britain' view is, however, the fact that, when Roman authority was withdrawn in the early fifth century, the latinity of the province was too weak to survive for long, and what emerged – after a decade or two and until the irruption of the Saxons – was a largely Celtic-speaking Britain with Latin remnants. As a spoken language this Latin must have been restricted to a rapidly dwindling class whose economic base was vanishing as towns and villas decayed. As a literary language this Latin still had much vigour in it, in part because of the classical and educational tradition, but now mostly because Latin – in the somewhat simplified style of the Vulgate, the Mass and the Church Fathers – was

[1] See D. J. Smith in A. L. F. Rivet (ed.), *The Roman Villa in Britain* (London, 1969), 94 ff. and conclusion, 118.

[2] On the culture of such *vici* see I. A. Richmond, *Roman Archaeology and Art* (London, 1969), 70–71.

the language of Christianity in a strongly proselytising phase. Not only did Latin remain the sole language for funerary inscriptions in the fifth and later centuries, it remained the sole literary language too, and in a fair state of correctness; so strong a British patriot as Gildas, about A.D. 540, still writes of Latin as *nostra lingua* without needing to add any explanation.[1] None the less, even without the *adventus Saxonum*, Britain would not have emerged speaking a Romance language. This state of affairs contrasts with that of the western Continental areas, notably Gaul and Spain, in which, when Imperial authority collapsed, Latin speech was almost universal and has evolved into modern French, Spanish, etc. In Iberia it is thought that all native languages were extinct before about A.D. 100, except in the Basque country (somewhat larger then than it is today). In Gaul, the best modern opinion is that Celtic speech continued strongly in the early centuries of Roman rule and became extinct only shortly before the collapse of the Empire.[2] In Gaul it seems that 'The progress of Christianity, with Latin as its language, was the determining factor which finally suppressed the use of Celtic in outlying regions' (Elcock), a progress which was evidently slower and less effective in Britain in the fourth century, and which was seriously interrupted in the early fifth, in part by reductions of contacts after A.D. 410, in part perhaps by the confusion introduced by Pelagianism.

Some support for those who believe in a through romanisation of at least parts of Britain comes from the fact that all the written texts and fragments, down to the slightest jotting on tile and pot and lead, from A.D. 43 until long after 410, are in Latin (rarely Greek). In all that time, not a single word of British seems to have been written down in these islands. The written record is thus a severely distorted one. Professor Jackson comments upon it that: 'It should always be borne in mind that British was not a written language, and that the *only* language of writing was Latin; it would not occur to anyone to write in British, nor would they know how to do so...In Roman Britain those who had enough education to know the alphabet had enough to know some Latin, and those who had none did not write at all.'[3] This is a statement about an observed fact, but it leaves questions about the reasons for the fact. In Gaul the Gaulish language had been written for certain purposes in

[1] The context is Gildas's description of the arrival of the Saxons: *tum erumpens grex catulorum de cubili leaenae barbarae, tribus, ut lingua eius exprimitur, cyulis, nostra longis navibus*... Three of the MSS have *nostra*; one has *nostra lingua*, and one *latina*, perhaps showing that copyists felt the point needed emphasising (*De excidio*, 23).

[2] There seems to be general agreement about this. However, there is no agreement about the force of the remark of St Jerome († 420) about Celtic speech. W. D. Elcock says: 'The latest and clearest testimony which we possess concerning its persistence in Gaul is contained in an epistle of St Jerome to the Galatians, in which he compares the speech of the latter to that of the Treveri. From this it would appear that towards the end of the 4th century A.D. a Celtic idiom was still in use in the neighbourhood of Trèves (now the germanised Trier), despite the fact that this town became the site of an important Roman school' (*The Romance Languages*, 186–87). A. Vincent thought otherwise: 'Un passage de St Jerome..., interpreté jadis comme montrant le gaulois encore parlé à Trèves, doit se rapporter à un état antérieur' (*Les Noms de lieu de la France* (Brussels, 1937), 114). See also Dottin, *LG* 69–70; A. H. Krappe in *RC*, XLVI (1929), 126–29.

[3] *LHEB* 99–100. On the use of Greek writing for Gaulish, see Dottin, *LG* 45–54.

Narbonensis in Greek characters, these having been learned from the Greeks of Massilia, and Greek lettering on coins is found much further north. Professor Frere speculates: 'When we remember the close connections between Gaul and Britain and that schools existed in Britain at which Druids from the Continent acquired a higher learning, we may accept the probability that the British language could be, and was, written and read.'[1] Presumably Jackson would deny this probability. In Roman times in Gaul, despite the relatively greater intensity of romanisation, the Gaulish language was written, now in Latin characters, for a variety of purposes, though not in all very extensively: formal inscriptions, the Coligny Calendar, records of industrial production (notably graffiti on *terra sigillata* fragments at La Graufesenque), etc., in addition to the frequent occurrence of personal names on potters' stamps. In Iberia Celtic was written not uncommonly in very early times, and from Cisalpine Gaul two texts are known in Etruscan characters. It is hard to see why no attempt was made to write British in ways similar to these, particularly when Celtic went on as a much more important factor in British life than did Gaulish in Gaul. In addition to Frere's speculation, there is the fact (which he also mentions) that in the century before A.D. 43 the tribes of southern Britain, in imitation of the Continental practice introduced here by the Belgae, wrote names of rulers and places in abbreviated form and in Latin characters on their coins. Although Jackson dismisses this as of no significance (*LHEB* 100, note), the fact remains that an early effort was regularly made to write British sounds in Latin characters, over a long period of time and a wide geographical area. It is hard to see why this practice did not continue – not on coins, of course – especially since no great problem existed in equating most (not all) of the Celtic phonemes with those of Latin and hence in writing them down in Latin letters.[2] A further point is that the Celtic languages did eventually become fully written languages, using the Latin alphabet: in Old Welsh from the eighth century, for any kind of continuous text, though isolated names had been written much earlier, and Jackson believes that the devising of a regular written system for Brythonic names was the work of the sixth century (*LHEB* 72 ff.). If this was done then, there is no inherent reason why it should not have been done much earlier, under Roman rule when the degree of literacy must have been much greater. That it was not remains, we repeat, something of a puzzle. Possibly some British writing was done on perishable materials, these being the cheaper ones available to the poorer classes, but the record in Gaul and elsewhere shows that this was by no means exclusively the case there. To the factors mentioned above we must add that the ready adaptation of hundreds of personal names and place-names to Latin, the transfer of loanwords

[1] *Britannia*², 350–51.

[2] 'On the whole, the phonetic and morphological systems of Latin and British were unusually similar to each other. Consequently it was easy for Britons to adopt Latin words into their speech with very little change' (*LHEB* 80–81). This is the same point made the other way round within Jackson's line of argument. In the following pages he details the few ways in which the two sound-systems differed. Even the British coins show up at times the problem of representing awkward sounds in Latin letters: the father of Cunobelinos is usually *Tasciovans* on his coins, but once *Taxci-* (Mack No. 150); his name seems to mean 'slave of the god *Taxis*', this deity also appearing in a diversity of spellings in Continental records.

from Celtic (mainly Gaulish) to Latin, and the transfer of hundreds of loanwords from Latin to British, all with the minimum of phonetic adjustment that was necessary, should all have provided hints of the ease with which Celtic could be written once it was in contact with Latin. The surviving written record is a distorted one, certainly; but after discussion we can see that the distortion, against logical expectation, is evidence of the total domination of Latin literacy.

The written texts of Roman Britain are of very diverse kinds. None is a contribution to classical literature, and no son of the province made his name in the literary or scientific fields, though Pelagius and Patrick did in religion. The texts which make up the sources of our Chapters II–VI were naturally compiled from materials ultimately gathered in the province, but largely in the form of lists or maps. The epigraphic evidence (Chapter VII) ranges from magnificent formal inscriptions on stone in the strictly classical language down to single names scratched on pots. There survive hundreds of tombstones, some giving details in a personal language, others having nothing but the name and age of the deceased. Altars and votive tablets dedicated to a wide range of deities both Roman and Celtic (also Germanic and oriental) provide many different kinds of text. More extensive and personal documents are the rare surviving letters and the *defixiones* or curses and imprecations, on lead, whose language is colourful in the extreme. Other texts are the stamps of oculists and apothecaries, rare texts set in mosaics or on wall-plaster, a variety of graffiti sometimes amorous (Caerwent), jocular and obscene (Leicester), writing exercises (whole or partial alphabets, presumably schoolboys' homework), Christian messages, and even the Virgilian tag *Conticuere omnes*... (Silchester).[1] The best-explored site in this respect, Silchester, has produced over fifty names on potsherds and thirteen comments on tiles, all in legible cursive hands. Much else written on papyrus, wood and other materials has perished, and much that must have been painted on stone and other substances has vanished also. Some texts found in this country are of course of Continental origin (e.g. graffiti on imported *amphorae*); equally, a few texts found abroad originated in Roman Britain (notably the Amiens *patera* and the Thorigny Marble). The losses of epigraphic material on stone from the civil centres of lowland Britain, discussed in Chapter VII, have much impoverished our knowledge. On the other hand, archaeological research each year produces a store of fresh materials, mostly minor but sometimes of the utmost importance (e.g. the *Vindolanda* texts). The impression left by the minor materials collectively – by all those personal names cut on vessels, by workmen's production tallies, by *defixiones* and epistles, is – as mentioned above – of a degree of literacy and fluency in Latin which extended to the urban proletariat and to some country areas, a degree which would have surprised nineteenth-century students of these matters.[2]

[1] These details and discussion of them are readily accessible in J. Liversidge, *Britain in the Roman Empire* (London, 1968), 315–16.

[2] All this is still the subject of controversy, and the reader should consult a variety of authorities. Chapters 4 and 5 of *TCRB* set the scene. Professor Jackson's Chapter 3 of *LHEB*, especially pp. 94–121, is an admirably full and conscientious discussion, not fundamentally affected by our occasional disagreements with it. One should also see: M. P. Charlesworth, *The Lost Province* (Cardiff, 1949), Chapter 4, especially pp. 64–67; R. G. Collingwood and

Latin in Britain was, as everywhere, of different kinds. Literary classical Latin was known to an educated minority of administrators and Army officers in A.D. 43, and it was the language taught in schools when these were established under Agricola, by schoolmasters brought in from (presumably) Gaul for the most part. Among those natives who learned it were the sons of the tribal aristocracy, the country landowners; these, Jackson thinks, actually came to speak this rather stilted Latin, whose phonetic ultra-correctness is reflected in the loanwords for domestic and agricultural items picked up from them by the Celtic-speaking workers on the estates and eventually transmitted to Welsh and Cornish.[1] Some Romano-Britons were capable of writing reasonably classical metrical compositions for funerary purposes and others (e.g. *RIB* 265, Lincoln). This kind of Latin, without the literary flourishes, was also that used for formal inscriptions, and was the basis for all kinds of writing at whatever level, though often performed incorrectly by the less well educated (see, for example, the London *defixiones RIB* 6 and 7, which have errors of spelling and intrusions of the spoken language).

The spoken Latin of the province, at first brought in by the Army and those who came in its wake (perhaps 60,000–75,000 persons in all) and picked up by Britons as contacts developed, was the ordinary Vulgar Latin of the Western Empire. Whether this was spoken here sufficiently widely and distinctively to justify the notion of a 'British Latin' is doubtful. The evidence recorded in writing during the Imperial period in Britain is too thin for us to say, though what there is does show many features in common with the Vulgar Latin of the Continent, especially Gaul. Jackson, on the evidence of Latin loanwords taken into the surviving Celtic languages, thought that 'British Latin' did exist as an entity possessing notable conservative features, the result – as mentioned above – of Latin having been acquired as an artificial second language learned in schools from grammarians. But his evidence is open to challenge in several respects, and his conclusions equally. In view of a number of recent studies[2] in which epigraphic evidence of Imperial times is massively assembled and

I. A. Richmond, *The Archaeology of Roman Britain* (London, 1971), Chapter 11 (on inscriptions); and for notes on the social significance of some of the epigraphic evidence, A. R. Burn, *The Romans in Britain: An Anthology of Inscriptions* (2nd edn Oxford, 1969). The work of Professor Frere, with comments on Jackson's views, is mentioned in note 1 on p. 12 above.

[1] The ultra-correctness of some of the loanwords in the Celtic languages is a fact; the circumstances in which they were taken from Latin is a matter for debate. Many, not recorded in Celtic in writing until a suspiciously late date (twelfth century and later) may have been borrowed from Latin not during the Imperial period, but later, from written Latin and from Church sources, in which case their ultra-correctness is natural. Moreover, such learned influence (which is discussed but dismissed by Jackson) could have served to restore ultra-correctness to some loanwords which had been borrowed earlier in more vulgar form. The Romance tongues provide complementary evidence for these processes at all stages. For discussion, see Colin Smith's study in *ANRW*, forthcoming.

[2] J. C. Mann, 'Spoken Latin in Britain as Evidenced in the Inscriptions', *Britannia*, II (1971), 218–24; N. Shiel, 'The Coinage of Carausius as a Source of Vulgar Latin forms', *Britannia*, VI (1975), 146–49; E. P. Hamp, 'Social Gradience in British Spoken Latin', *ibid.*, 150–62; and Colin Smith, 'Vulgar Latin in Roman Britain: Epigraphic and other Evidence', forthcoming in *ANRW*. In the studies of Mann and Shiel there are simple listings of deviant spellings for

studied, we now have much more information than was available to Jackson in 1953, and while retaining a number of Jackson's ideas, we are able to conclude that Vulgar Latin in Britain was not noticeably different from that of Gaul, though lagging a little behind it in pace of development. Where we do have a certain body of written evidence from one locality, as we have from the civil *colonia* of York (mainly from the third and fourth centuries), we can say that the spoken Latin of this wealthy community was in most respects similar to the spoken Latin of urban areas in other parts of the Western Empire.[1] However, since the epigraphic evidence of many localities, especially military sites, may record the speech-habits of persons who were not native-born Britons, it still seems safer to talk of 'Vulgar Latin in Roman Britain' rather than of 'The V.L. of Roman Britain'.

When we turn to toponymy the balance is heavily tilted towards Celtic. Only some forty of our toponyms (not counting names of provinces and seas) are wholly Latin. The rest were British in origin, or in a few cases were perhaps pre-Celtic names which had been accepted and assimilated by Celtic speakers.

In examining the names of Latin origin, one can begin by separating clearly from them those which in Ptolemy's text consist of a name of British origin plus the Greek word for 'river', 'promontory', etc. In these cases the Greek word is an official or scientific defining element, almost in apposition, and is hardly to be reckoned as part of the name (compare our normal usage 'a trip on the Thames', 'a bridge over the Ouse', 'Views of the Grampians', where the addition of 'River', 'Mountains', etc., is needed only on rare occasions). A few names in Ptolemy do require us, however, to take both elements into account and to see behind his Greek a fully Latin name for a British place; such are compound names in which one element is an adjective, as in *Magnus Portus*, *Novus Portus*, which even if descriptive of new developments and perhaps lacking in currency as full place-names could have become so ('Newport') and perhaps did. A name like *Prominentia Litoris*, however, is probably no more than a description of a seafarer's mark made *ad hoc*. Among military stations we find *Castra Exploratorum*, *Horrea Classis* and *Pinnata Castra*, and it is perhaps surprising to find so few Latin names for Roman Army establishments; even in very remote areas, where one feels it is unlikely there was already a named British settlement, a native name seems to have been adopted, that is, coined. We discuss the mechanism of this process further under *Durobrivae*[1] in the Alphabetic List. The *Litus Saxonicum* is a later creation of the Army high command. A name such as *Herculis Promontorium* in honour of a deity is likely to have had little real currency, although such names survive abroad in areas that were fully Latin-speaking.

The other Latin names are diverse and interesting. There are administrative terms both military – *Praesidium* and *Praetorium*, *Victoria* – and civil, such as *Colonia*,

the most part, and the casual errors of engravers are not separated from forms which show phonetic developments; consequently, these studies need to be handled with great caution, but they are very useful as assemblages of material. The paper by Hamp adds much of the linguistic commentary to the materials provided by Mann and has some admirable sections on the social background, grades of bilingualism, etc.

[1] It is strange that no linguistic study of this remarkable series of texts has been made. They range from the Greek of Demetrius and the long metrical text of *RIB* 684 down to such Vulgar Latin forms as *Sepronie Martine* (686), *que* (690), *Audes* (653), *possuit* (670), *posit* (689).

**Terminus* and the honorific *Augusta*. The two *Statio* names, **Derventio*[6] and *Devionissum* relate, it is thought, to offices of the taxation system, and were obviously Roman creations, but the second element in each case is a British name in Latin guise. Only four names are known to us which contain the Latin name of a person, the owner of the villa or estate (a contrast with Gaul, where such names are very frequent): the straightforward *Villa Faustini*, *Epiacum*, built on *Ep(p)ius* with the Latin–Celtic suffix *-ācu*, a common means of formation in Gaul, **Albiniano* (in *Ravenna*, *Albinumno*), and *Anicetis*, a locative plural perhaps denoting 'at (the villa of) the family of Anicetus'. Presumably every villa had a name, that of the owner, as many modern farms do; but since few lay on main roads mentioned in itineraries, or figured in other kinds of record, their names are scarcely known to us. Nor do the villas seem to have grown into villages as they often did in medieval France, preserving their names. A further category consists of a few names indicating exploitation of minerals – *Calcaria* and the two *Salinae* – and new technology: *Ad Pontem*, *Pontibus*, *Pons Aelius*, *Tripontium*, with which we may associate *Trajectus*. Finally there is a category of names descriptive of a topographical feature: *Ad Ansam*, *Cana* (?), probably **Concavata*, *Ripa Alta*, *Spinae*, *Saponis* (?), *Trimontium*, and the fanciful or poetic *Susurra*. In some of these instances, it is hard to believe that the Latin name was the original one. This may have been the case for *Ad Ansam* if a wholly new settlement on a Roman road, and for **Concavata* if new eyes saw the area for the first time in that way when the fort was built; but a name like *Trimontium* is strongly suggestive of a translation into Latin of a pre-existing Celtic name. It is hence hardly possible to take *Ravenna*'s *Velox* seriously as a genuine Latin river-name, for it would be a unique case; nor is it likely to be a translation of a Celtic name, for this would have been somewhat pointless and certainly rare. Of *Trimontium* it can be said that it was not merely an *ad hoc* translation but had real currency over a long period, being recorded by Ptolemy, on an Antonine milestone and in *Ravenna*. Its currency, however, would have been limited to the Roman military establishment and the garrison of this and neighbouring forts, while the surrounding native tribe, the little-romanised Selgovae, presumably went on calling both the distinctive 'triple peaks' (of the Eildon Hills) and the Roman fort by a Celtic name not known to us, but almost certainly one signifying equally 'three hills'.

The final point to note about the Latin names is that many of them applied to small places or unimportant features. Most of them did not continue long in use in post-Imperial times and have left no later trace. Among places of importance, *Colonia* survives in the names of Colchester and Lincoln, but *Augusta* (a fourth-century honorific title of London) never displaced *Londinium*. Only three other Latin names survived: *Cataracta* > Catterick, *Calcaria* > Kaelcacaestir in Bede's time[1] (these two in an area which remained ungermanised into at least the early seventh century), and one which is hard to account for, *Spinae* > Speen.[2]

Next comes a group of composite Latin + Celtic names in which the Latin element

[1] *Secessit ad civitatem Calcaria, quae a gente Anglorum Kaelkacaestir appellatur* (IV, 23). Bede, surely akin to modern philologists in spirit and a man who has put them much in his debt, makes a number of other comments of this kind.

[2] See now M. Gelling, *Signposts to the Past* (London, 1978), 34 and 58.

is not merely an explanatory addition or a definition (as with the *Statio* names above), but more essential. Such are the names with *Portus – Abonae, Lemanis*, etc., in which the second element is the name of a river, and *Portus Setantiorum* in which the second element is the name of a sub-tribe. Two religious names of the same formation are *Locus Maponi* and *Fanum Cocidi*, in the second of which one suspects that a British word for 'temple' has been translated into Latin. In the names of the spa establishments, *Aquae Sulis* and *Aquae Arnemetiae*, the same type of formation is used. Only one name in Britain is a true Latin–Celtic compound: *Caesaromagus*, by which a new foundation was named by adding the ruling Imperial dynasty to a Celtic common noun. In the Continental provinces many more names are known of this type: *Augustodunum, Juliobriga, Claudiomagus*, etc.

The names of wholly British origin are so numerous and diverse that few general remarks can be ventured about them. In the mass they look much like the mass of names from Gaul, Spain and other areas, and many of our names have precise Continental parallels. A few elements common in Gaulish names are not found in our records, though they may well have existed in fact: such are **ialo-*'clearing' and **nant-* 'valley'. Equally, many British names are unique, and many lack an assured etymology even when we are reasonably sure of their correct form. Analogy with forms in the modern Celtic speeches and in early medieval documents is often illuminating, and in some cases, of course, a name has survived from Romano-British times until the present on Celtic lips (for example, the name which is *Segontium* in the Latin records, or perhaps rather the name of its river, > modern *Saint* or *Seiont*, the latter with false learned regression). But it must be recalled that before the earliest Celtic written texts lay more than a thousand years (that is, from Celtic settlement in Britain from the eighth century B.C.) during which the language evolved and words were lost, altered and confused, and during which the etymological track of place-names (often very ancient) could be obscured. *Camulodunum* is an easy, self-revealing name, consisting of elements widely used and for long on Celtic and even Latin lips. *Verulamium* bristles with problems, even though well recorded. A name such as *Birila*, of who knows what island (perhaps not even British at all), retains its mystery, perhaps because it has become corrupted in its sole recorded form, perhaps because it is Celtic but consists of elements already archaic by Roman times and not paralleled elsewhere, perhaps because although used in a largely Celtic country it consists in fact of pre-Celtic elements.

Among names that are well understood, categories can be distinguished (as in any language) according to the type of reference made in them.[1] The first category – first in point of size and perhaps in antiquity also – consists of names that refer to water. It is most noteworthy that almost all our river-names recorded in ancient sources are of clear Celtic origin, in such a strong proportion that one tends to assume that the few cases which are not readily explicable must be Celtic also. Such are *Abona, Abus, Dubris, Isca, Ituna* and others, based on words which mean simply 'water, river'. Their variety surprises; even though all were used contemporaneously in Romano-British times as place-names, they may have owed their origin to common nouns used by

[1] For a complementary survey, with excellent discussion of the distinctive features of the Celtic system, see Chapters 2 and 4 of the book of M. Gelling mentioned above, n. 2 to p. 19.

each group of immigrants which left its mark in succession upon toponymy. At the time of Saxon contacts with Celtic speakers, it seems likely that inquiry by the incomers about the name of a river may have produced an answer **abona* or **isca*, that is vaguely 'river, water' in general; these, on being taken by the Saxons as proper names, produced what are now Avon and Axe (etc.) rivers, but it is entirely possible that the 'proper' names of such rivers in Romano-British times were quite different, e.g. **Uxela* for the river Axe of Somerset. Some such explanation seems to be needed for the very numerous Avons on the modern map. Other names describe water: *Novius* perhaps 'fresh, lively river', *Stuctia* 'winding river'. The *Lindum* names refer to a 'pool' or lake or broad part of a river. *Condate* is a 'confluence' of streams. In rare instances a simple adjective is substantivised, as in *Leuca* 'shining one'. River-names are often transferred to settlements on their banks, apparently without confusion arising. This happened sometimes without change of form, as in *Alauna* (several cases) and *Tuesis*, but more often with the addition of a suffix, as in *Bremenium* (British **Bremenįon*) 'settlement on the **Bremįā* river', *Rutunium* 'settlement on the **Rutūnā* river'. The survival-rate of these Celtic water-names on the map of modern Britain is extraordinary, even in those southern and eastern regions which have been germanised linguistically from the fifth and sixth centuries; moreover, there are many other water-names of British origin on the map which were not recorded in Roman times but must be of equal antiquity with those that were.

A second category of almost equally ancient names includes those that refer to geographical features. 'Hill' names of various kinds include *Mamucium*, *Mona*, *Verteris*, and others; *Regulbium* is the 'beak' or 'headland', and the two *Magnis* are 'at the rocks'. *Mediolanum* is probably '(place) in the middle of the plain', *Magis* is 'at the plains'. *Glannoventa* includes British **glanno-* 'bank, shore'. *Calleva* is probably '(town in the) woods', *Letocetum* 'grey wood', and there may be botanical references in *Blatobulgium* and *Bocrandium*. *Delgovicia* has **delgos* 'thorn' as its first element, but the whole name may employ this in a metaphorical function as a tribal designation (see the Alphabetic List). On the whole these geographical names, especially those for 'hill' and 'wood', are much less common than would be anticipated from the abundance of such names in Romance and in Germanic territory. However, this impression may be deceptive. Ptolemy and *Ravenna* conscientiously list rivers, but (except that Ptolemy lists many promontories) no text notes hills or forests in a systematic way.

A few animal names make a third category. Common nouns are recognisable: in *Bibra* the beaver, in the first element of *Branodunum* and *Branogenium* the crow, horses of various kinds in *Eposessa*, *Manduessedum*, *Marcotaxum* and *Voreda*. See also entries for *Tarvedunum* and *Orcades*. However, the references may not in all cases be directly to animals. Although *Bibra* does mean 'beaver', as a river-name 'brown one' rather than 'beaver-river' might be implied. *Branogenium* in full is 'place of Branogenos' (a personal name), and he in turn is '(he who is) born of the crow' (or 'raven'), with some ulterior reference which is lost to us. The 'horse' names, on the other hand, seem fairly literal.

Divine names, in a fourth group, require separate study in terms of comparative religion and of the whole Celtic pantheon. Some of those represented in our place-names, such as Camulos, Lugos and Belisama, were worshipped on the Continent as well as in Britain; others, such as Cocidius, had more local cults. The equation of Celtic gods with Graeco-Roman, well attested in British inscriptions, is illustrated by what seems to be the entry for Bath in *Ravenna*, **Aque Sulis Minerve* (cf. *RIB* 150). Other deities represented in our toponymy are, in their Latin guise, Arnemetia, Maponus and Verbeia. *Deva* means simply 'the goddess', her name forming the basis of several names in Britain and others abroad. Many other river-names, including *Verbeia* and others mentioned earlier, may contain names of deities also. Celtic *nemet-*, *nemeton* in various combinations in place-names indicates 'sacred grove', later perhaps more generally 'shrine, temple', and is found all over the Celtic regions.

A fifth group of what one may loosely call 'technical' names may be deemed relatively recent, in that they imply a development of activities well beyond the primitive. Agriculture is probably implied in *Aballava*, *Bovium*, perhaps iron-working in *Gobannium*. Here too belong the names involving British **briu̯a* 'bridge' and **-ritu* 'ford'. The names *Ratae* 'ramparts' and *Vindocladia* 'white (i.e. chalky) ditches' refer to fortifications.

These lead us to a sixth and final category of names which *per se* imply human habitation (i.e. they are not borrowed improperly, as it were, from other kinds of reference). These correspond to periods of highly organised social activity, political groupings, defensive measures, etc. Here belong the numerous names which (rarely) use alone, or have as elements in second place for the most part, **brĭga*, **dūno-* and **dŭro-*, all well represented in Britain. We discuss the range and implications of these exceptionally interesting names in the Alphabetic List (respectively under *Briga*, *Branodunum* and *Durobrivae*[1]).

The names retained by, or newly given to, the *civitas*-centres as organised by Rome after A.D. 43 are of special importance within the sixth category. Where a *civitas*-centre continued upon an existing tribal centre, the name naturally continued: *Calleva*, *Ratae*, with the addition of the tribal name in the genitive plural as a matter of official definition and perhaps of local pride too. Where a British tribe had no real centre, a new town had to be created and named, e.g. *Isca Dumnoniorum*, simply '(the town on the) river of the Dumnonii' (Exeter). Where the inhabitants were gathered to a lowland site the name might be transferred, as perhaps at *Moridunum*[2] (Carmarthen), or a new one used as being more appropriate, e.g. *Durnovaria* (Dorchester), which can hardly have applied to the older settlement of the Durotriges at Maiden Castle (this would almost certainly have had a *-dunum* name). *Noviomagus* 'new place', a common name in many Celtic regions, was the new capital of the Regini at Chichester, after their move from Selsey. The three *civitas*-centres called *Venta* seem to bear mildly artificial names newly imposed under Roman rule, and the naming seems to be new whether or not archaeologists find evidence of pre-Roman habitation on their sites.

One general impression which emerges is that the Roman invaders were not linguistic imperialists. When a place had a name, the Roman Army, administration and settlers adopted it without question, merely latinising its form and fitting it into a declension. When a new habitation-name was needed because a new or transferred settlement was involved, the name in nearly all cases was Celtic in Latin guise. This was true not only of the civil settlements but also of the *coloniae* for legionary veterans (*Camulodunum*[1], *Glevum*, *Lindum*). Moreover almost all the names of purely military establishments were Celtic also, including that of the Roman fort at Slack, *Camulodunum*[2], whose name is thought to have been transferred from a native hill-fort. Even more extraordinary, this was the case also with the forts of Hadrian's Wall (except *Pons Aelius*), most of which were built in sparsely inhabited areas, but for which native, not Latin names were devised, including two in *-dunum*. We know of no instance in which an older British name was replaced by a Latin one, as occasionally happened elsewhere in the Empire. It seems that once the conquerors were firmly in command, they felt no more need than did Henry V to emphasise their victory by linguistic action;[1] and even though no special benevolence is implied, this policy, like the *interpretatio romana* in religious matters, may have been of some importance in the process by which most of the Britons accepted their new masters.[2]

In the Latin takeover of British names after A.D. 43, it is clear that the Romans were prepared for it to a great extent by their long acquaintance with such names in the Celtic areas of N. Italy, Iberia and Gaul. Much of the mechanism, phonetic and morphological, by which British sounds were adapted to Latin spelling and by which British names were fitted into the declensional system (further discussed below, p. 33) was already in existence by A.D. 43. Even so, a certain amount of care seems to have been used. An example is the British name of Dover, **Dŭbrās*. This in British is a plural, 'waters, stream'. It would have been possible, perhaps more natural, for Latin to adopt this as a first-declension feminine singular, but in fact Latin carefully echoed the plural of the original with a notional nominative plural **Dubrae* and a locative plural *Dubris* by which the port appears in all our sources. This is not an isolated case; others of the names known to us in *-is*, perhaps all of them, belong with it. Evidently Latin speakers acquainted themselves from the first with the meaning and structure of British names. That this did not always remain the case in later times is shown by certain reinterpretations of Celtic names in terms of Latin in communities which were predominantly Latin-speaking, for example *Campoduno* and *Luguvallo* (see *Cambodunum*, *Luguvalium*); the most interesting possible instance of this is discussed under *Cataractonium*.

This brings us to a fundamental question. In discussing the toponymy of Roman Britain as it appears in our third- and fourth-century sources, that is as an established system, are we dealing with a few Latin names and a mass of Celtic names, or with a corpus of names which had become Latin? Celticists may resist the latter notion. Professor Jackson says: 'The *Antonine Itinerary*, presumably going back to a road-book made up on the spot, is probably the most useful to us in this respect [that is, in tracing sound-changes in British], as well as being textually the best preserved, but even here

[1] *King Henry*: What is this castle call'd that stands hard by?
Montjoy: They call it Agincourt.
King Henry: Then call we this the field of Agincourt. (IV. 7)

[2] This makes an agreeable contrast with more recent history. Older *Fiume* became *Rijeka* (a translation) in 1945, and at the same time there was widespread renaming throughout Eastern Europe.

we cannot be sure that the compilers did not use (particularly for very well-known and important places) forms of town names as they had been taken into official government Latin early in the history of the Roman administration, and not the contemporary pronunciation of the British natives' (*LHEB* 37). Our impression is that on the other hand *it was natural* for the compilers to use the Latin forms of the town names, because by this time – indeed, much earlier – they were deemed Latin. It is not merely a matter of their use in 'official government Latin', but of their everyday use in spoken and written Latin by many thousands of Latin speakers, whose status and influence we have tried to establish in the earlier discussion. Furthermore, it was entirely natural for the *AI* in particular to record Latin forms, since the document deals with the romanised settlements of the province – towns, posting-stations and military centres – and because it was drawn up to be used by Latin-speaking officials. This would also be true of *ND* in the military sphere, but less true of *Ravenna* taken as a whole, since sections of this record many names of little-romanised regions. There is, then, a radical difference of view between Professor Jackson and ourselves, which is worth arguing further. That names pass from the language of a subject people into that of the conquerors, become established there and no longer follow the sound-developments of their original language, seems obvious and natural. Contact rather than conquest may be involved. In English, *Paris* is sounded with final *-s* because it was so sounded when the English adopted the name; we take no account of the fact (except jokingly, 'gay Paree') that the French have long ceased to pronounce it. Germanic invaders of these islands in the fifth century took over their Latin and Celtic names and made them English, paying no heed to further changes in Celtic, and freely interpreting the elements to suit themselves, even when a clear memory of the original name was preserved by the Church.[1] The result might have been different in Roman Britain if Celtic names had resisted latinisation, but they did not, since both phonetically and morphologically the names fitted easily into the Latin system and were thereafter treated as Latin by Latin speakers.

This proposition can be supported (hardly proved) if the evidence of place-names, which is scanty, is set beside that of the personal names and of the language in general. Here a few instances, drawn from a more comprehensive survey,[2] must suffice. Among the vowels, one notes *Esica* on the Amiens *patera* (and in *Ravenna* 107_{27}) for *Aesica* of *ND*, which shows the typical Vulgar Latin reduction *ae* > *e* (or, if *E-* is the proper form, that with *Ae-* represents a hypercorrection which results from the same process). In Vulgar Latin unstressed *ŭ* > *o* eventually, a change apparent when we find *Eboracum* for older *Eburacum* (see the details in the Alphabetic List); this is a *Latin* development, for the corresponding change did not happen in British until the sixth century, and then only in one region. It is paralleled by – for example – *Viboleius*

[1] There are numerous instances of Celtic-Latin elements being assimilated to more meaningful elements in Germanic. *York* provides a notable example. Bede illustrates the Anglo-Saxon mania for eponymous coinings and explanations which fly (one would have thought) in the face of a simple logic which any available Briton could have explained if asked: *in civitate Durobrevi, quam gens Anglorum a primario quondam illius qui dicebatur Hrof, Hrofaecaestre cognominat* (II, 3).

[2] See the papers of Hamp and Smith mentioned in note 2 on p. 17.

(for *Vibu-*: *RIB* 1052) and possibly by *Camoloduno* in *AI* 480_4. Among final vowels it appears when we find *-om* for *-um* in genitive plural endings in the recently discovered Caves Inn (*Tripontium*) text, which has what seems to be an ethnic name in *-orom* (for *-orum*) and probably two third-declension genitive plurals in damaged words,]*niom* and]*cesom* (for *-nium*, *-cesum*); thus *Venta Velgarom* in *Ravenna* 106_{18} could be a genuine Romano-British form rather than the adjustment of a later Continental compiler or copyist. The syncope of the unstressed vowel was common in Vulgar Latin (recorded at Pompeii, before A.D. 79), and there are numerous examples of it from Latin in Britain, including among names originally British *Congennccus* (for *-iccus*: *RIB* 1053, South Shields) and the ethnicon *Catvallavna* (for *Catvva-*, that is, *Catuva-*: *RIB* 1065). This elision did not occur in British speech until the sixth century. The assimilation *ns* > *ss* is typical of Vulgar Latin, and it is no surprise to find it in the two adjectival forms *Banniess(es)* (*RIB* 1905) and *Vindolandesses* (*RIB* 1700). The form *Conventina* for *Cov-* (*RIB* 1522, 1523) seems to show either the influence of the Latin prefix *con-* or a hypercorrection; one may compare *Conlegio* (for *coll-*) in *RIB* 70. Other variations in the names *Coventina* and *Belatucadrus* seem to be due to Latin rather than to Celtic changes, for the most part, though the latter are certainly present also.[1]

There are rare indications of the possible influence of Celtic phonology upon what we have described as the largely Latin system of Romano-British toponymy *as it is recorded in our sources*. One inscription of *Vindolanda* shows a Vulgar Latin development (above). But the name appears as *Vindolana* in *ND*, with assimilation of *nd* > *nn*. If this is a spoken form and not a scribal error (one cannot be sure), it represents an assimilation which is common in the Vulgar Latin of some regions, but for which a non-Latin cause has to be sought: in some regions it is attributed to Oscan influence, in others to Celtic. There is also the hypercorrection *Gabaglanda* (*Ravenna* 107_{11}), which is most unlikely to have resulted – in its second element – from scribal error. After emendation this is *Camboglanda*, the true form of the name (*Camboglanna*) having British **glanno-* as its base; the hypercorrection is equally indicative of the process *nd* > *nn*, and there is other possible evidence from Britain.[2] However, the matter is not clear, because Jackson dates the *nd* > *nn* assimilation within British to the late fifth and sixth centuries. Rather different are the cases of the forts called *Alone* by *AI* 481_3 (our *Alauna*[3]) and *Alauna Ravenna* 107_4 = *Alione ND* XL_{43} (our *Alauna*[4]). The *-au-* diphthong was maintained in Latin until long after the Imperial period in Britain, so that *au* > *o* is not open to us as an explanation in terms of Latin. In British, however, '*au*, *ou* and *eu* fell together in *ọ̄* in the late first century, at least in part' (*LHEB* 313). Other *Alauna* and *Alaunus* names were taken into Latin from British speech which still had *au* in the first century, and in the above cases this happened also with *Alauna*[4] as set down on the Flavian military map (we may assume) which was one of *Ravenna*'s sources. But the same fort's name does seem to have responded

[1] On *Belatucadrus*, see *LHEB* 430–31, and the discussion of all recorded forms by Smith in *ANRW*, forthcoming.

[2] Possibly *V(e)recunn* for *Verecundus* on a pot from London, *CIL* VII, 1338. 29; *cod(itum)* for *conditum* 'spiced' on an amphora from Chester, *Britannia*, II (1971), 294; *caled(ae)* for *calendae* on a bone counter from Wroxeter, *JRS*, LVIII (1968), 210.

to the British *au* > *o* process by the time it was set down in the source for *ND* (later fourth century); one may speculate that this happened when a new garrison moved in after a period during which the fort was not occupied, and took the name anew from British speakers in the area. As for *Alauna*[3] as recorded with *-o-* by *AI*, the *linguistic* assumption (further dependent upon archaeological data and subject to them) would be that the fort was not an early one, and was not built and named until after the *au* > *o* process was accomplished in the British speech of the area. These seem to be the only pieces of evidence in favour of Jackson's view *that appear in our sources.* It is naturally the case that a complete system of Romano-British names *as spoken by British speakers* existed, and that this, in the natural evolution of the Celtic languages, produced the forms of names which are known from the documents of early and middle Welsh, etc., and which are set down occasionally in Latin by Bede, Nennius, etc.

In all this it must be said that the value of *all* our sources – epigraphic as much as itineraries, etc. – for a study of sound-changes both Latin and British, is very limited. In part this results from the fact that most of our sources consist of 'official government Latin', but in the main it results from the conservative nature of any system of writing. This system for Latin was perhaps not so rigidly fixed as that of the modern languages whose uniformity is maintained by the printing press, universal education, etc., but it was relatively rigid and was also propagated by education, public inscriptions, potters' stamps, and so on. In modern English we persist in writing *Gloucester* out of a sense of conformity and respect for tradition, but have for long pronounced [ˈglɔstə]. It would be eccentric (or American) to pronounce *Balham* as anything other than [ˈbæləm]. Moreover, spelling can actually put the phonetic clock back, restoring the sound of written *-d-* in *London*, whose standard (not vulgar) pronunciation in the eighteenth century was [ˈlʌnən], and making us pronounce *Birmingham* more or less as written, against older *Brummagem*, now humorous-vulgar. This is a further reason for asserting that such names as *Alauna* went on being pronounced as such in most cases (that is, except the two studied above), both because *-au-* was maintained in Vulgar Latin (without regard for Celtic *au* > *o*), and because Latin written authority was so powerful. To put the matter another way, respected traditional spelling in Latin without variations must often conceal changes in pronunciation that took place within Imperial times, and in some cases this respected spelling may have retarded sound-changes in place-names. As we saw above, the *ŭ* > *o* change was recorded, but this is a rare instance. An equally typical example is provided by Latin *ĭ*, both stressed and unstressed, which in spoken Latin was sounded *ẹ* by the third century in most regions (much earlier in some: *veces* for *vĭces*, etc., at Pompeii). That this occurred in the Latin of Britain is shown in numerous inscriptions: *baselicam* in *RIB* 978 (Netherby, A.D. 222), *demediam* in *RIB* 306 (Lydney, late fourth century), *ella* for *ĭlla* at Leicester (*JRS*, LIV (1964), 182), *Felicessemus* in *RIB* 988 (Bewcastle, third century), among others. But our place-name sources offer no case whatsoever of this *ĭ* > *e* in any of our numerous names containing this sound (although one would like to argue it for *Isca* > **Esca*, it is not so recorded). Such a statement as that by Jackson about another change is hence open to question: 'On the date of *g* > *ụ* in all these cases, the presumption is that it happened after *g* had been lenited to ʒ . . . The forms *Luguvallum* in the *AI* and *Lagubalium* in *Ravenna* show, in effect, that it had not yet occurred in the third and fourth centuries; and since Latin words undergo the change equally with British, it was subsequent to the borrowing period' [i.e. the period when Latin words were being taken into British] (*LHEB* 444). Here Jackson's phonetic fact is not in doubt, but the place-name evidence which he quotes will not serve, first because *AI* and *Ravenna* were citing the name of what must have been a strongly Latin-speaking town which had early adopted *Luguvalium* into Latin, and second because even if those speakers pronounced it with a Vulgar Latin change, as is likely, this change would not show in writing because of the conservative and retarding nature of the written tradition.

In view of this, it is likely that a variety of pronunciations was tolerable in the case of many of our place-names. Inscriptions and itineraries almost always recorded the official, traditional name, usually British in origin but long treated as a fully Latin name. This written form would have been spoken in its classical form only by officials, by the educated, by those used to seeing the name in writing. Literate traders, craftsmen and other ranks would have spoken it with whatever Vulgar Latin features were current in ordinary speech; not *Eburacum*, but **Eboracu*, **Eboraco* and perhaps also *Eb'raco* (cf. *Ebruduno Ravenna* 63_{47} for *Eburoduno AI* 342_{1}, now Embrun in the Alps; also *Ebriacus* and *Eburiacus* > Yvré and Evry in France). That applies to towns and military stations. The class of very carefully spoken villa-owners defined by Jackson would obviously have pronounced place-names as did the officials and the educated of the towns. But a third category of pronunciation for each name must also have existed: that of those who were mainly speakers of British among the urban proletariat, perhaps also in some Army units. These, as we suggested earlier, had some basic Latin for their needs, but any Latin they did pronounce would have been influenced by their dominant Celtic speech. It is in this class that scant regard would be had to established Latin *Alauna* (for example) and that *Alona*, in line with developments within British, would be heard. Nothing much is known about their preferences because they could not write, though a good deal can be deduced about them, as has been done so brilliantly by Professor Jackson in *LHEB*. The further class of rural, purely British speakers, hardly enters into the discussion here.

The importance of our third category of speakers was in a way small for our purposes, since their spoken Latin habits hardly affected the place-name record. However, they, together with the rural British population, were to have their moment. Any small latinity they had must have been quickly lost during the fifth century when Roman authority was withdrawn and the towns decayed. But it was their pronunciation of town-names and river-names which survived and evolved to give the names we eventually know in Welsh for places far outside Wales: thus Carlisle is *Cair Ligualid* in Old Welsh, now *Caer Liwelydd*. Moreover, since it is far from certain that Germanic settlers in the fifth and sixth centuries heard any of our place-names from speakers of Latin, the Celtic (not the Latin) tradition of these names was the vital one in the further development of our toponymy. This can be illustrated even in the name of our capital, Jackson thinks. Whereas most of our Latin and Greek sources (including inscriptions) agree upon *Londinium*, Jackson points out that the Anglo-Saxon forms of this name demand derivation from a British **Londoni̯on*.

There must have been a variation in the suffixes attached to this difficult name in its British form of the first century, *-inion* being that adopted in official and spoken Latin usage (as *-inium*), while *-onion* was favoured by those who remained speakers of British in and around the city.[1] Following our earlier view of the near-exclusive latinity of our Latin (and Greek) place-name sources, a view argued against that of Jackson, it is clear from what we have said later that in other respects we must think in terms of Latin and British enjoying a coexistence, a symbiosis. While at all times there remained in the individual a consciousness of speaking either Latin or British, or of course both in different situations, and a consciousness that the written tradition (including that of place-names) was a Latin one only, there must have been a great deal of linguistic interaction. Speakers may have found it hard to tell whether many of the words they used were really Latin or British. Latin in Iberia and in Gaul had absorbed a number of Celtic words, those which appear in Latin as *betulla, bracae, camisia, capanna, carpentum, carrus, cerevisia, leuca, salmo, vassallus*, to cite only the best-known. Latin speakers who came in A.D. 43 probably used these as though they were fully Latin already. *Essedum* 'two-wheeled war-chariot' was used by Caesar and Cicero, even Virgil, and was so well established that the derivative *essedarius* is found in several writers. No doubt an educated Roman could have defined the term, even when well established, as relating primarily to a Celtic object, but it had its declensional forms and was used by writers without the equivalent of the inverted commas or italics as it were, that characterise the neologism.[2] British also absorbed a great many latinisms, their number remaining large even after we have discounted the numerous learned (especially religious) terms that can only have been borrowed into the Celtic languages long after the Imperial period.[3] Many conversations between Latin and British speakers, for example orders about agricultural tasks, dealings between tax-officials and peasants, proceedings in law-courts involving witnesses who spoke British only, must have mixed the two languages to some extent. In personal names Celtic habits of course continued, but there was probably a tendency for Latin names – and later Latin-Christian names – to be given to many of British stock, e.g. upon marriage of manumission. At York, in the numerous texts on tombs and altars, the only Celtic names seem to be those of *Julia Brica* and *Julia Velua* (*RIB* 686, 688), though there must have been much British blood even in the class which could afford altars and tombstones in the civil *colonia*. Place-names in Latin were freely formed from Celtic personal names, with suffix added. Many of the suffixes, indeed, seem to have operated as genuinely Celtic-Latin items, thus providing further evidence of that mixing or symbiosis mentioned earlier. The *-aco-*,

[1] *LHEB* 308; also in *Britannia*, I (1970), 76. Jackson seems to be mistaken in remarking in the latter that 'There is some support for *-onion* in Greek and Latin sources, including the *AI* itself.' We know of none until Stephanus of Byzantium and Bede (who regularly has *Lundonia*). In the ancient sources it is the *first* vowel of the name which varies (*Lundinio* in vars. of *AI*, *Lundinium* in Ammianus).

[2] But there was some uncertainty: against general *essedum -i* there is a feminine *esseda -ae* in Seneca. One may compare general *bracae -arum*, feminine plural, found once as a feminine singular *braca* in Ovid, and as *braces* in an edict of Diocletian.

[3] See note 1 on p. 17 above, and Smith's paper in *ANRW*, forthcoming.

-acu- suffix was originally Celtic and appears abundantly in Gaul, where it could eventually be attached to any personal name, whether Celtic, Latin, Ligurian or even Etruscan, to denote the ownership of land.[1] Other suffixes which eventually count (whatever their origin) as Celtic-Latin include *-atia* (*Bannatia*), *-ava* (*Aballava*, *Galava*) and *-avum* (*Brocavum*), *-eia* (*Arbeia*, *Seteia*), *-arum* (*Lutudarum*), *-ona* (*Abona*, *Othona*), etc., and most commonly of all, *-io-*. Some British elements also perhaps functioned as suffixes and were readily adapted into Latin, for example *-isso*, *-magus*, *-sessa*, *-vicia*. Finally it has to be remembered that certain nouns which are frequent elements in place-names of Celtic origin are known to have passed into the Vulgar Latin of Gaul, and although Britain has no surviving Romance language which could prove the point, it is likely that the same happened in the Latin of Britain. Examples are *briga*, *dunum* and *verna*. It is possible that these could be used, by Latin speakers, to form new names for new places, that is those having no pre-existing British settlement or name. An obvious case of this is *Branodunum* (Brancaster, Norfolk), a Saxon Shore fort of the late third century which stands on no sort of a hill (*dunum* in its strict sense). The case would not be so extreme as the continued use of Norman-French *ville* in modern English namings, or of Greek *polis* in America.

Lastly, one may suspect that in the symbiotic situation in Britain there existed a divergence similar to that which existed in Gaul with regard to the stress on names. *Condate* 'confluence' is both Gaulish and British. In French one can distinguish those names that derived from *Cóndate* stressed according to the habit of Gaulish (> Condes, etc.) from those that derived from *Condáte* stressed in the Latin way (> Condat, Condé, etc.), and a few other names show a similar dichotomy. In Gaul the persistence of a Gaulish stress clearly shows the continuation of Gaulish long enough to impose itself in the regions concerned upon Latin speakers. We have no information on which to base any guess about either type in Britain, but presumably names of Celtic origin were stressed in the Latin way by Latin speakers if that suited their speech-habits; the cases of difference would have been few, however.

It is not our purpose to contribute directly to the study of the survival of names from Roman Britain into later times, though the whole book is a contribution in a way because it provides a full corpus of names in accurate forms and with variants. Occasional notes are however appended to entries in the Alphabetic List on this subject. Several studies on this difficult question of name-survival are available.[2]

3. TEXTUAL AND LINGUISTIC PROBLEMS

Although the special features and problems of each type of source will be discussed in relation to that source, some general remarks are proper here. The only 'pure' source is the epigraphic one (Chapter VII) in the sense that its texts have reached us

[1] A. Vincent (1937), 70. He notes that 'Les noms de lieu en *-acus* forment à peu près le vingtième du total des noms de lieux habités de la France'. The suffix is found all over Gaul except in the extreme south-west, and is common in N. Italy but infrequent in Iberia.

[2] There is a good deal in the work of Zachrisson (1927), but this needs to be handled with caution. A. H. A. Hogg in *Antiquity*, XXXVIII (1964), 269–99, discusses the principles of such study and offers a classification. M. Gelling (1978) has much on these matters in early chapters.

without being subject to intermediate copying. However, the inscriptions (including those on coins, graffiti, etc.) give us relatively few place-names, and these are sometimes so abbreviated that they tell us little. In texts on vessels a certain nonchalance seems to have been allowable, for these were not the product of any official act (see discussion on the Rudge Cup and Amiens *patera* in Chapter VII, and of the *Vases Apollinaires*, below). In all these cases there is no difficulty about restoring classical spellings which better represent the original names.

In other cases the linguistic habits of the medieval scribes to whom we owe surviving texts of Ptolemy, *AI*, *Ravenna* and *ND*, which give us the great majority of our names, are of vital concern to us, since through an awareness of them we can see how changes and corruptions arose and can then proceed by detailed conjecture back towards the original forms. In some instances we cannot tell whether the Vulgar Latin and Romance speech-habits of copyists have influenced their written Latin, or whether a vulgar form proceeding from Britain in Imperial times is being recorded. Among the vowels, this is so when we find *ae* reduced to *e*, as in *Cesaromago* (*AI* 480_6, *Ravenna* 106_{51}), *Abone* (*AI* 486_1), *Brige* (*AI* 486_{12}), and unstressed *ŭ* > *o*, as in *Camoloduno* (*AI* 480_4), and other uncertainties over unstressed vowels, as in *Celunno* (*Ravenna* 107_{36}; for *Cil-*), *Virolanium* (*Ravenna* 106_{50}; for *Veru-*), etc. Among the consonants it seems certain that disturbances were the fault of the copyists, because we have very little documentation of such changes in the spoken Latin of Britain before the end of Roman rule. Examples are provided by the common confusion of *b*/*v*, as in *Aballaba* (*ND* XL_{47}) for *Aballava* (Rudge Cup) and *Caleba* (*Ravenna* 106_{32}) for *Calleva*; the copyists' assibilation of *c* before *e* and *i* is shown when by hypercorrection *c* appears in *Gabrocentio* (*Ravenna* 107_3) for *Gabrosenti* (*ND* XL_{50}); and the further Vulgar Latin equivalence of /kj/ with /tj/ is shown in the *-itia* variants of both *AI* and *Ravenna* for the name *Delgovicia*, and in many other examples. The form *Canza* of *Ravenna* 106_{11}, for **Cantia*, and several parallel cases, show the further assibilation in the late Vulgar Latin of the Continent of /kj/ and /tj/. The most distinctive feature of *Ravenna* in this category, *-on* for *-um*, is discussed on p. 201. For the corresponding changes which have to be borne in mind in dealing with Ptolemy's Greek, see p. 130 and the full exposition in *LHEB* 34–5.

In the second place there is simple miscopying, not only in texts and lists but on maps such as *TP* and those used as sources by *Ravenna*. The nature of the problem can be judged from the photographs which we reproduce of *TP* and *Ravenna* (plates I–II). In some scripts *c* and *g* readily suffered confusion; thus, within *AI*, there is *Galleva* 478_3 against the correct *Calleva* in three other itinera; there is *Glota* for *Clota* in *IM* 509_1 (one MS), and the reverse, *Clevo* for *Glevo* (*AI* 485_4) and *Clanoventa* for *Glan(n)oventa* (*AI* 481_1). Similarly *c* and *t* were often confused; the frequency of this enables us to say with confidence that *Camborico* of *AI* 474_7 should be *Camborito*, even though *AI*'s record of this name is the only one we have. In copying *n* and *v* (*u*) were often interchanged, as in *Convetoni* of *TP* for the better *Conbretovio*, with *v*, of *AI*, and considerable confusions developed when *n*, *m* and *v* (*u*) were in association with *i*. A full analysis of such confusions, together with cases of scribal metathesis, dittography, wrong division of names and also the conflation of names, is undertaken for *Ravenna* (the most corrupt of our texts) on pp. 202–204. Other instances of serious miscopying are illustrated by our entries in the Alphabetic List for *Bannaventa*[1], *Bremetenacum*, and many others. Sometimes there is a lacuna because the eye of some early copyist has strayed one or more lines below the one he should have followed; we discuss a lacuna of *AI* on p. 176, and another of *ND* on p. 221. There is repetition of many names (by no means useless for our purposes) in *AI*, when because of the presence of two *Moriduno* names a part of Iter XV was copied improperly into Iter XII. Miscopying of numerals in the mileages of *AI* and *TP*, and in Ptolemy's bearings, has to be borne in mind when distances are important for identification of places; thus the Roman numeral *ii* was seemingly liable to confusion with *v*, and *v* with *x*. A further problem which concerns Ptolemy's text alone is that his information for Britain, gathered in the official Latin of the province in the late first century, was transposed into Greek; however, any resulting corruptions are perhaps balanced by the advantage of having the quantity of certain vowels represented by Greek letters.

It is plainly of no great moment that a well-recorded name such as that of Colchester, *Camulodunum*, should appear in one source – *Ravenna* – as *Manulodulo*; the text adds that it is *Colonia*, so all is clear. But we learn from this that the compiler of *Ravenna* or one of his copyists was capable of representing *c* as *m* (possibly via *ch*, according to Schnetz), and the *-dunum* or *-duno* element as *-dulo*. It is worth collecting the instances in which this common element is misrepresented in our texts, as an indication of the dimensions of our problem and as a guide to possible new identifications. In *AI* we find only *-dono* 482_9 and *-doni* 486_{13}. In *Ravenna*, *-moni* 106_2, *-onio* 106_{13}, *-dulo* 106_{52}, *-dono* 106_{59}, *-dino* 107_{17} (MSS B and C), *-damo* 107_{28}, *-danum* 108_9 (= *-xana* in MS C), *-xaua* 108_{10}. In this way one can build up a feeling for likely confusions which is invaluable in the task of trying to repair the copyists' errors in cases where we have only a single record of a name, or two between which we must decide. A case in point is that of *Veromo* of *Ravenna* 108_2; one can argue that its *m* may represent *ni* (as often), and hence that **Veronio* could, in view of *-onio* in 106_{13}, really be **Verdunum* or some similar form. The Rudge Cup's *Uxelodum* may be an abbreviation of *Uxelodunum* rather than an error, but its existence allows us to take *Subdobiadon* of *Ravenna* 107_{55} as possibly another *-dunum* name. Often comparisons with non-British sections of *AI*, *Ravenna* and other texts provide illumination. Even so, and however good the instinct one acquires, many names continue to defeat us. Names such as *Minox* (*Ravenna* 108_{18}) and *Intraum* (*Ravenna* 108_{34}) do not look right, offer no Celtic or Latin roots, and remain wholly resistant to correction on scribal grounds. The problem may be illustrated from comparative material in non-British sections of our texts, where *Castra Herculis* (a site near Huissen, Holland) appears unbelievably as *Coadulfaveris* (*Ravenna* 60_{19}), *Confluentes* of *TP* becomes *Conbulantia* in *Ravenna* 62_{14}, and *Fano Minervae* of *AI* appears (via an abbreviation **Fano Min*) as *Tanomia* in *TP*. Moreover, this happens with such extremely well-known Latin nouns as *castra*, *confluentes*, *fanum*, and divine names such as *Herculis*, *Minervae*, whose accurate copying, one might think, was assured. If scribes so corrupted easy names, it is small wonder that they corrupted difficult names, those of Celtic origin whose elements were meaningless to them. At all times we must remember that the copyists were of various Continental nationalities, not natives of Britain, and that they were dealing with lists of names of often small and unknown places in a country which had ceased to be part of the Continental political system in the early fifth century. They were moreover for the most part Benedictine monks, whose sense of classical and Imperial affairs, and often of good latinity, became increasingly shaky. It was not their job to show any special regard for Hercules or Minerva.

In the third place, it has to be recalled that although British was the language of the majority throughout the Roman period, the official language and only written language of the province was Latin, and place-names as official items are known to us only in the form in which they were set down in Latin documents or in Latin and Greek literary and scientific works. We seem to have no case in which one form of a well-recorded name leans more towards British than another (on **Alona*, which is not precisely such a case, see p. 25); any phonetic variants shown seem to be those of Latin. On the whole, as mentioned above (p. 15), British names were readily latinised in pronunciation and in writing. Once it was accepted that **dūnon* was accurately represented by Latin *dūnum*, no problem existed in saying and writing *Camulodunum*. However, there was an inbuilt tendency for Celtic elements in place-names to be assimilated improperly to better-known Latin elements. In some cases this assimilation is entirely the work of Continental scribes and is of scant importance to us, as in *Ravenna*'s *Condecor* 107_{24} and *ND*'s *Procolitia* XL_{39} (which may show respectively assimilation to Latin *decor* and *pro-* or *procul*). Much more important are cases which probably show such assimilation to Latin elements by speakers of Latin in Britain, for these are indications of Latin-speaking communities which knew little or no British. A good instance is that of *Luguvallo* of *AI* 467_2 (Latin *vallum*; the correct form has *-valium*), and another is provided by forms of *Cambodunum*; see also, in the Alphabetic List, *Canonium*, *Letocetum*, *Leucomagus*, *Noviomagus*[1], both *Moridunum* names, and especially *Durovernum*, which in one form has the picturesque folk-etymology *Duro Averno*. Such forms are equally common in records of the Continental and other provinces. There one finds just as many miscopyings or assimilations of such standard Celtic elements as *-briga*, *-dunum*, *-durum* and *-magus*, in which Gaul and some other areas were as rich as Britain; the memory of a Celtic past had become utterly remote in those areas by the time our texts were copied. We may speculate that if any MSS of *AI*, *ND* or *Ravenna* had been copied in Britain, in the Latin-using but 'Celtic' Church, or even in the early Saxon Church, our proportion of accurately known names would have been much greater than it is. For Gaul, Dottin *LG* 54–67 provides a very full survey of these matters.

A fourth problem concerns the Latin case-endings of our names and the form in which they should ideally be cited. Sometimes there is no problem. *Abona* is a first-declension nominative, and when we find *Abone* in *AI* we know that this is a vulgar form of *Abonae*, either locative, 'at *Abona*', or a genitive from which the element *Portus* has been dropped (*Ravenna*'s entry shows it still present). *Londinium* is amply recorded in that form and we take it as a straightforward second-declension neuter. *Ratae* is a plural name, first-declension feminine, and is so recorded by Ptolemy and *Ravenna*; we also find the accusative, *Ratas*, in *AI*, and the ablative *Ratis* on a milestone and in a decree of citizenship. This is a well-recorded name with a range of declensional forms. But in many instances our texts offer forms in *-um* (*-on*) and *-o*, and we have no means of knowing if they are masculine accusatives or neuter nominatives and accusatives. In general it seems that names in *-briga*, *-sessa* and *-venta* and others in *-a* were first-declension feminines, *-magus* was second-declension masculine, and *-dunum* and *-durum* were second-declension neuters. Continental analogues help here. The numerous *-magus* names often appear in this form, and the equally common *-dunum* names always appear in this form also (that is, never **-dunus*); the *-durum* names nearly always appear as neuters, though there is one example – *Octodurus* in Caesar *BG* III, 1 – which shows that at an early stage there was an attempt to decline these names as masculine before they settled down as neuters. Many of the common suffixes, whether Celtic or Latin originally, also sort themselves readily into genders and declensions: I, feminine, *-ava -eia -ica -ara*, etc.; II, neuter, *-acum -anum -arum*. Third-declension names present a problem. They seem to have been few. *Meletio* (the corrected form of *Ravenna*'s *Melezo* 106_{16}) is probably not a third-declension nominative (of which *Ravenna* has none that is certain) but a second-declension neuter, an oblique case whose notional nominative would be **Meletium*. *Cunetione* of *AI* and *Cunetzone* of *Ravenna*, however, allow us to postulate **Cunetio* as the nominative. The various places called in our sources *Derventione* (accusative or ablative: see below) probably had a nominative *Derventio*; but this may not have had any real currency, and *Ravenna*'s *Dorvantium* is more likely to be a deformation of another **Dervention(e)* than it is to represent a nominative **Derventio*.

Sometimes names may have been current in different declensional forms at different periods. *Camboglanna* (three sources), at first sight is a feminine singular, but forms on the Rudge Cup and Amiens *patera* show final *-s*, presumably for *-is*, locative; hence the name was neuter plural when recorded as *-a* (*Ravenna* and *ND*), but neuter plural in the locative – like a number of other British names – when recorded in the second century on the vessels. *Maia/Maio*, which also shows *Mais*, may be a similar case. One could also argue that it is the official form of these names that shows *-a*, but the form current colloquially among soldiers (for whom the vessels may have been made) that shows *-is*, a difference of class usage rather than of period.

We know of changes of declension in some ethnic names, and list these under *Atrebates* in the Alphabetic List.

At this point one realises that the above analysis may be an attempt to restore linguistic logic and neatness to a mass of material in which none really existed. It is true that for a few well-documented names we can confidently say that a full declension existed and was used in writing and (to the limited extent to which declensional forms were current in spoken Latin) in speech also. This was true of *Eburacum*, *Londinium*, *Ratae* (above) and perhaps a few others. In most other instances we acquire the suspicion that place-names were indeclinable, or that even if they were declined in literary prose such as that of Caesar, Tacitus and Ammianus, they ceased to be so or never were so in common usage both spoken and written. One guesses that this was so after a time, perhaps always, with the numerous masculine and neuter names that end in *-o* in all our records. This may apply also to a name such as *Noviomagus* whose nominative is known to us but which also appears with *-o*. It has to be recalled that in Vulgar Latin accusative *-ŭm* was pronounced *-ŭ* and eventually this > *ŏ*, which coincided with *-ō* ablative in the general reduction of case-endings (as notions of distinctions of quantity were lost) and assisted their demise. The point seems to be proved by certain Continental names (to which Miller, 1916, drew attention) in which we find *Ad* agglutinated to the name proper, this turning out to be not the expected accusative but something else: *Ad Octavo*, *Ad Quintodecimo*. This could be thought an ablative, but is more properly an oblique case, the whole being no longer declinable.

In itineraries such as *AI*, and in part *Ravenna* where it depends on a road-map, the matter is even more indeterminate. Strict classical usage – so many miles from a place (*a*+ablative) to another place (*ad*+accusative) – hardly applied. In the *AI*'s British itineraries we find only two first-declension feminines with accusative *-am*: *Isuriam* 468_3 (an error), *Devam* 482_5; no masculines with nominative *-us* except *Traiectus* 486_2 (this perhaps because it was well-known as a common noun); and only five names in *-um*, presumably neuters, *Corstopitum* (?) 464_3, *Isurium* 465_3, *Eburacum* 466_1 and 468_4, *Clausentum* 478_1, *Galacum* 481_4. The generality of names in *AI* has *-a* for feminines, *-o* for masculines and neuters (leaving aside for the moment the few third-declension names, and allowing that *Ad Ansam* 480_3 and *Ad Pontem* 477_7 are handled correctly); and it appears that this *-a -o* represents a hardly declinable oblique case. In plural names there are only two with accusative *-as*, *Durobrivas* 475_1 and *Ratas* 477_4, none with nominative *-ae*, and no masculines at all with *-i* or *-os* (except the special instance *Icinos* 474_6, a rare tribal designation); but there are no fewer than sixteen names in *-is*, an ablative-locative plural. In one or two examples we know that this *-is* is the ablative or locative plural of a name which really did decline, as did *Ratis* 479_3; but in most, it is likely that this ablative-locative plural was the fossilised form which had become the sole oblique case of now indeclinable names. Thus it is with *Dubris* 473_2, which is supported by all records of this name, and the place is best quoted as *Dubris* and not as an entirely inexistent nominative **Dubrae* (especially as the *-s* is represented in Anglo-Saxon *Dofras*, about 700, and in French *Douvres*). In the same situation are *Lemanis*, the two *Magnis*, *Verteris*, and others, all with consistent support for *-is* in our texts. The same is nearly true for *Ritupis* of *AI* 466_5 and 472_6 (for *Rutupis*), in which four other records have *-is* and only Ptolemy breaks the pattern with *Rutupiae*; this could be either a learned restoration of an assumed nominative, or a sign that in the first century the name really was declined; the declined form *ad Rutupias* of Ammianus is to be expected in his literary usage, but may have had no currency. These plural ablative-locatives are paralleled by a few locative singulars of the second declension, notably *Vindomi* of *AI* 483_1 and 486_{10}, but it is clear that *Sorbiodoni* of *AI* 486_{13} is a truly declined form (that is, not a fossilised one) because the second element is the well-known *-dunum*. *TP* has a high proportion of such locatives in its surviving British section, seven out of sixteen names.

When *AI* duplicated a name in two itinera in different cases we can see how unsystematic the listing process was. There is *Ratas* 477_4 beside *Ratis* 479_3, *Durobrivis*[1] 472_3 and 473_8 beside *Durobrivas*[2] 475_1. Moreover in the short sentences which head sections the text sometimes offers a grammatical structure, such as *Item a Segontio Devam* 482_5, but in several others it offers, for example, *Item a Londinio Lindo* 476_7 (instead of *Lindum*). A few names were indeclinable from the first because of their form, for example *Condate* 469_1 and 482_3, which in this invariable form figures also in *Ravenna*; this is true also of the numerous records of this name in Gaul.

In the matter of third-declension names, *Derventione* of *AI* 466_2 and others may not be the ablative-locatives they seem, but rather accusatives in *-em* whose final consonant (long lost even in the pronunciation of classical Latin) was silent and in consequence often omitted in writing. One notes here the beginnings of the process by which many place-names assumed a single, oblique case, in the main that of the accusative without *-m*. This is amply documented in the Romance languages: Spanish *Ilice(m)* > Elche, *Legione(m)* > León, *Thermas* > Tiermas, *Viminarias* > Mimbreras, etc. For completeness we must add to this the ablative-locative plurals, noted above, which represent a different sort of oblique case. It is noteworthy that many French towns, especially old tribal capitals, derive their names from ablative-locative plurals in *-is*, which eventually subsumed *-ibus* also: *Pictavis* > Poitiers, *Cadurcis* > Cahors, *Remis* > Reims, etc.[1]

That the confusion of cases and the tendency towards a single oblique case was not of the copyists' making is shown by the four similar *Vases Apollinaires*.[2] Among the names on these are the following:

I	II
IN PYRAENEVM	IN PYRENEO
RVSCINONEM	RVSCINNE
SEXTANTIONEM	SEXTANTIO
CLANVM	CLANVM
CATVRRIGOMAGVM	CATVRRIGOMAGI

III	IV
IN PYRENAEO	SVMMOPYRENAE
RVSCINONE	RVSCINONE
SEXTANTIONE	SEXTANTIONE
CLANV	GLANO
CATVRIGOMAG	CATVRIGOMAGO

Many of the confusions, errors, variants, adaptations and oddities which we have discussed could be illustrated from the *Vases*. Their texts are the more extraordinary for being written within the Latin-speaking Imperial period, and at an early stage of it when there was no question of linguistic or cultural decline. The *Vases* show how free-and-easy was ancient practice in matters of spelling, case-usage, abbreviation, etc., and they illustrate on identical objects of slightly differing dates a range of usages

[1] W. D. Elcock, *The Romance Languages* (London, 1974), 193–94, has further examples and discussion. A. Vincent (1937), 114, concludes that 'Beaucoup de noms de lieux de la France datant de l'époque romaine proviennent d'un ablatif-locatif. . . Au Ve siècle, c'est la seule forme casuelle qui paraisse subsister dans les noms de lieux.'

[2] A most valuable study of case-usage in the itineraries (including some very early texts) is that of J. Heurgon, 'La Fixation des noms de lieux en latin d'après les itinéraires routiers', in *Revue de Philologie*, XXVI (1952), 169–78. He includes in his texts those of the *Vases Apollinaires*, and our names are taken from this source. The *Vases* (found in the nineteenth century at Vicarello on the shores of Lake Bracciano) bear the stations of the journey from Cadiz in Spain to Rome. Their dates (studied by Heurgon in *REA*, LIV (1952), 39–50) differ somewhat: *Vases* I, II and III were made early in the reign of Augustus, IV late in that reign or under Tiberius. There is a discussion of the forms of names in the itineraries by K. Miller in his *Itineraria Romana* (1916), xlvii–viii.

from more or less classically correct forms (Vase I) to the wilder but evidently still acceptable versions of less cultured craftsmen. With such texts before us, we may feel less indignant about the corruptions induced into texts by medieval copyists. More interesting is Heurgon's conclusion that the single 'oblique' (often ablative-locative) form of a name had often become standard at an early time, and did not simply result from some later decadence of classical norms: 'Ainsi, dès le début de notre ère, la fixation des noms de lieux à des cas de lieux, surtout à l'ablatif, était déjà passée dans l'usage courant. L'orthographe grammaticale n'était qu'une restitution artificielle, pratiquée par les écrivains comme Pomponius Mela et Pline l'ancien, et par les lapicides, lorsqu'ils gravaient sur le marbre une inscription faite pour l'éternité.'[1] It is not then a matter for surprise that the oblique cases of popular usage should appear so abundantly in a document like *AI* of official character; the surprise is to be reserved for the rare intrusions of classical 'correctness', such as the two feminine accusatives in *-am*.

The existence of two names for a place, or the change of name by a place, can naturally make for difficulty in our sources. In Gaul the 'proper' name of a city was often displaced in late Imperial times by a formation based on an oblique (ablative-locative) case of the ethnic name, and it is the latter which has evolved into the modern name: thus older *Samarobriva* was replaced by *Ambianis* > Amiens, and *Augustoritum* by *Lemovicis* > Limoges. There are two examples of this in Britain recorded in *AI*: *Icinos* 474_6 replacing *Venta Icenorum*, and *Regno* probably for **Regnis* 477_{10}, for *Noviomagus*. However, Britain differed notably from Gaul in that in no instance in the former does a modern name of an ancient cantonal capital derive from such an 'ethnic' form: Winchester, for example, preserves part of the 'proper' name, *Venta*, and does not derive from **Belgis*. Other examples of name-changes are rare in Britain. The fourth-century title of London, *Augusta*, was an honorific of no real currency. Ptolemy's καινὸς λιμήν 'Novus Portus' probably refers to a development at Dover, otherwise always known as *Dubris*, and did not gain currency; as a descriptive designation for a place with an established British name, it could hardly be expected to do so. As for *Petrianis* and *Uxelodunum* of *ND*, both apparently referring to Stanwix on Hadrian's Wall, the first is probably a ghost-name and the entries are to be emended (see p. 221). There may be other cases of double naming or changes of name, but if so, they lie well concealed in our texts. Examples of alternative names for the legionary centres, Caerleon and Chester, are given under *Deva*[1] and *Isca*[2] in the Alphabetic List; they reflect what must have been established spoken usage in British in post-Imperial times, but may also be earlier, and might echo a colloquial **Castra Legionis* of Roman times. For a possible alternative military designation for York, see p. 219, note.

[1] Heurgon, 'La Fixation...', 175–76.

CHAPTER TWO

THE LITERARY AUTHORITIES

1. THE NATURE OF THE LITERARY EVIDENCE

This chapter is concerned with those writers of the ancient world whose works are not treated under their particular headings in the rest of the book. It therefore excludes Ptolemy, the Itineraries, the *Notitia Dignitatum* and the *Ravenna Cosmography*, but includes not only the great historians such as Caesar, Tacitus and Cassius Dio, but also the geographers, ranging from Strabo to the repetitive lists of the later Empire, together with poets, grammarians, Christian Fathers and even the Law Codes. For many of these the adjective 'literary' is something of a euphemism, but they are best dealt with together since it is only through them that changes in terminology and spelling can be detected, and for the same reason Gildas and Bede, though they lie outside the main classical tradition, are also included. Because precise dates are sometimes difficult to establish, the texts which are appended are arranged in alphabetical order of their authors and references to them are indicated here by the use of capital letters.

Although Britain or the Britons are mentioned by more than a hundred such authors, the contribution which these references make to our study is small indeed, for several reasons. In the first place, most of the works of the earlier Greek writers have perished – notably those of Ephorus (*c.* 405–330 B.C.), Pytheas (ff. 330–310 B.C.), Timaeus (*c.* 356–260 B.C.), Eratosthenes (*c.* 275–194 B.C.), Hipparchus (*c.* 190–120 B.C.) and Poseidonius (135–50 B.C.)[1] – and we have to rely on chance allusions to them by later writers. But secondly, as the fragments of them preserved by STRABO and PLINY indicate, their main concern was not to record the names of individual places (what Ptolemy would have called 'chorography'), but rather to position the British Isles correctly on the globe and especially to establish the highest latitude at which human habitation was possible. So far as we know, the information they recorded was usually confined to the names of the major units, such as Britain and Ireland, sometimes with those of the headlands which defined their extent.

Unfortunately the writers of the Roman imperial period serve us little better. Most of the literary works of the ancients were designed in the first instance to be read aloud to an audience and in such circumstances barbarous names would be

[1] To these may be added the specifically geographical Book 34 of Polybius, on which see F. W. Walbank, *Polybius* (Berkeley, 1972), 122 ff.

meaningless, if not actually unpronounceable. The typical Roman attitude is well summed up by Pliny the Elder in writing of the Spanish province of Tarraconensis:

> The *conventus* of Lucus (Lugo) includes 15 peoples who, apart from the Celtici and Lemavi, are unimportant (*ignobilium*), but number some 166,000 free persons. In the same way the 24 *civitates* of Bracara (Braga) include 285,000 persons; of these, besides the Bracari themselves, the Biballi, Coelerni, Callaeci, Equaesi, Limici and Querquerni may be named without distaste (*citra fastidium*).[1]

Pliny was a glutton for facts, but enough is enough. It is, therefore, not surprising that the supreme stylist, TACITUS, who should have had access to a wealth of information on names in Britain, disdains to produce it.

Such detailed knowledge, however, was exceptional. Although Britain was very important militarily, at times tying down more than a tenth of the entire Roman army, it was also one of the most remote provinces and it played little part in Roman history; indeed in the later period, as we know from AMMIANUS and SULPICIUS SEVERUS, its remoteness was such as to make it a suitable place of exile. Some of its earlier governors, like Julius FRONTINUS, did publish books, but those that survive include only one mention of Britain, and in fact of all the classical authors here represented only three are known actually to have visited it: CAESAR, FRONTINUS himself, and SUETONIUS (who, according to the HISTORIA AUGUSTA, was in Britain when he was dismissed from his post of imperial secretary by Hadrian). Official records, such as those reflected in Ptolemy and the Itineraries, did of course exist and were available as sources, but in general the ancient writers were only too ready to repeat uncritically what they found in the works of their predecessors: as Pliny the Younger commented when he was considering writing history:

> If the period is an old one and others have written about it, the research has been done and the labour will consist simply in collating it.[2]

There are many cases of such mechanical repetition in our texts, and the most disappointing is that of PLINY the Elder, who is so informative on some other parts of the Empire but in Britain falls back on outdated sources like Timaeus.

Our two native authors, GILDAS and BEDE, differ both from the classical writers and between themselves. GILDAS was much better acquainted with the Bible than with the pagan classics and his turgidly written history of Britain before his own age is thoroughly confused, but his very ignorance makes him a useful guide to what forms of the few names which he mentions were acceptable in the fifth and sixth centuries. BEDE, on the other hand, whose lucid Latin rivals that of the best classical authors, was a critical scholar of the first rank and he compiled his *Ecclesiastical History of the English People* 'from knowledge gained either from the writings of the ancients or from what was handed down by our ancestors or from my own knowledge'.[3] Among the 'writings of the ancients' he draws freely on PLINY, SOLINUS, EUTROPIUS and especially OROSIUS, on GILDAS, and on various ecclesiastical documents. Most useful

[1] *NH* III, 28.
[2] *Epp.* V, 8, 12: *Vetera et scripta aliis? Parata inquisitio, sed onerosa collatio.*
[3] *Hist. Eccl.* V. 24.

of all for our purpose, however, is the care with which 'from his own knowledge' he often relates a Latin name to its Anglo-Saxon equivalent.

2. NAMES FOR BRITAIN

Paradoxically the earliest mention of Britain is to be found in a late work, the *Ora Maritima* of AVIENIUS. Though written in the fourth century A.D., this poem was ultimately based on a *periplus* composed by an anonymous citizen of Massalia (Marseille) in the sixth century B.C. This has generally been taken to reflect Greek knowledge of the British Isles at that date, but a recent study of Professor C. F. C. Hawkes[1] has suggested that the matter is more complicated than that – in fact that the 'British' passage referred originally to the coast of Iberia south of the Tagus (where there were both *Albiones* and a 'Sacred Cape') and that it was only after Britain had been discovered in the fourth century that it was transferred further north, perhaps by Ephorus. In either case the version used by AVIENIUS, who presents Britain as *insula Albionum*, 'the island of the *Albiones*', will have antedated the voyage of Pytheas. And though Pytheas himself seems not to have used it, the name *Albion* persists sporadically throughout antiquity (in PSEUDO-ARISTOTLE, PSEUDO-AGATHEMERUS, MARCIAN, STEPHANUS and EUSTATHIUS) and it re-emerges later in Irish sources,[2] but to judge from the reference by PLINY (*Albion ipsi nomen fuit*, in the past tense) it was regarded as an anachronism and was replaced in normal usage by Βρεττανία in Greek and *Britannia* in Latin.

There is little doubt that when the Greeks first picked up the name it was spelt Πρεττανία (*Prettania*), with an initial Π, not B. That this was the older form is specifically stated by EUSTATHIUS, in his commentary on DIONYSIUS PERIEGETES (cf. also the remark of STEPHANUS), though in the texts as they have come down to us it appears regularly only in DIODORUS SICULUS, MARCIAN and Ptolemy. A peculiar case is that of STRABO: in Book I of his *Geography* the name is spelt with a B-, and it is only in Book II that the Π- form begins to appear – as though the scribe of an early manuscript had automatically corrected it to current usage until he realised that Π- really was intended. The possibility of this kind of 'correction' must always be borne in mind, as also must the fact that the spelling might be varied to suit the metre of a poem: EUNAPIUS, again, notes a case of this in DIONYSIUS, and there is another in OPPIAN. In general, however, the regular Greek forms became Βρεττανία (*Brettania*) for Britain, with ἡ Βρεττανικὸς νῆσος, ἡ Βρεττανική and ἡ Βρεττανίς (the *Brettanic* island, *Brettanike*, *Brettanis*) as occasional variants; Βρεττανός (*Brettanos*) for a Briton; and Βρεττανικός (*Brettanikos*), or occasionally Βρεττανός for the adjective British – and they remained so throughout antiquity. A strange divergence from this spelling by PAUSANIAS is discussed below (p. 00), while the fantastic Βριττία (*Brittia*) of PROCOPIUS coexists in his work with the normal Βρεττανία. The plural αἱ Βρεττανικαὶ νῆσοι (the *Brettanic* islands) normally means Britain and Ireland.

[1] C. F. C. Hawkes, *Pytheas: Europe and the Greek Explorers* (the 8th J. L. Myres Memorial Lecture, Oxford, 1977), 17–25. The 'Sacred Cape' is Cape Sagres; for the *Albiones*, Pliny, *NH* IV, 111 (where they are concealed, through textual corruption, in *Navialbione*).

[2] Watson *CPNS* 10–11.

Britain does not appear in Latin literature until about the time of Caesar's campaigns, though at least one of the earliest references may actually antedate his expeditions to the island: LUCRETIUS, perhaps for reasons of metre, has *Brittanni*, while CATULLUS has both *Britannia* and *Britanni*, and from CAESAR onwards these are the normal classical forms. A Briton is *Britannus* and the adjective is *Britannicus* (which, in TACITUS at least, always means 'of Britain', never 'of the Britons'), though, again for reasons of metre, *Britannus* is also used as an adjective by the poets GRATTIUS FALISCUS, PROPERTIUS, STATIUS, JUVENAL, NAMATIAN and VENANTIUS (and once in prose, by QUINTILIAN). These Latin forms, however, did not remain unchanged. The word *Britto*, for a Briton, first appears in MARTIAL (at about the time when it is first found in inscriptions) and is used thereafter by JUVENAL, AUSONIUS (with one *-t-*), PROSPER TIRO, GENNADIUS and JORDANES, to emerge in BEDE, in the form *Bretto*, as the normal term. More interestingly, perhaps under the influence of the Greek spelling, *Brittania* and *Britannus* tend to replace *Britannia* and *Britannus*: they first appear in SOLINUS and by the fifth century are almost as common as the classical forms. The plural *Britanniae* normally means the British Provinces (after subdivision) rather than the British Isles.

3. NAMES FOR IRELAND

Ireland appears in AVIENIUS as the 'sacred island' (*insula sacra*), owing to a confusion of its name with the Greek adjective ἱερός (*hieros*); it is inhabited by *Hierni*. In DIODORUS SICULUS it is Ἶρις (*Iris*), but its usual name in Greek is Ἰέρνη (*Ierne*, so STRABO, PSEUDO-ARISTOTLE, STEPHANUS) or Ἰουερνία (*Ivernia*, PSEUDO-AGATHEMERUS, MARCIAN, STEPHANUS, EUSTATHIUS, with Ἰβερνία (*Ibernia*) as a variant form). In Latin it is *Hibernia* (CAESAR, PLINY, TACITUS, SOLINUS, a PANEGYRIST, OROSIUS, ISIDORE and BEDE), though MELA, JUVENAL and perhaps the HISTORIA AUGUSTA have *Iuverna*, while CLAUDIAN has *Hiverne* and JULIUS HONORIUS *Hibero*.

4. THE ORKNEYS, HEBRIDES AND OTHER ISLANDS

The Orkneys first appear in MELA (who says that they are 30 in number) as *Orcades*, and this name remains standard in PLINY (40 in number), JUVENAL, TACITUS, EUTROPIUS, OROSIUS (20 uninhabited, 13 inhabited), JULIUS HONORIUS, JORDANES (33, not all inhabited) and BEDE. In Greek, in PAEANIUS, they are Ὀρχάδες (as *Orchades* in EUTROPIUS) and the -χ- may possibly account for the Latin *Orchades* in the texts of JEROME and ISIDORE. The statement of TACITUS that they were conquered by Agricola's fleet is modified in EUTROPIUS, OROSIUS, JEROME, JORDANES and BEDE, all of whom say that they were added to the Empire by Claudius.

The Hebrides appear as *Hebudes* in PLINY (who says that there are 30 of them) and as Αἰβοῦδαι in STEPHANUS (who repeats Ptolemy's number of 5). The *Riginia* of PLINY may possibly represent Rathlin, which is listed among the Hebrides by Ptolemy as Ῥικίνα (Ricina) but might reasonably be detached from the rest because of its proximity to Ireland. Skye is not named in the literary sources, but PLINY has *Dumna* which is either Lewis and Harris or the whole of the Long Island, as in Ptolemy.

The Isle of Wight is *Vectis* in PLINY and SUETONIUS, *Vecta* in a PANEGYRIST, EUTROPIUS and BEDE, and Βέκτη in PAEANIUS. The names Ἴκτις in DIODORUS SICULUS and *Ictis* in PLINY (assuming that his *insulam Mictim* results from dittography) probably belong here too. The accounts of *Ictis*, originating with Pytheas, were evidently misunderstood by later writers, but, as Professor Hawkes has pointed out, T. C. Lethbridge's interpretation of its location by Timaeus (quoted in PLINY), *a Britannia introrsum sex dierum navigatione* as 'six days' sailing up-Channel from the west' must be correct, and this agrees well with the position of Wight; on this argument, DIODORUS (or his source) must have confused the original shipment of tin from Cornwall to Wight with its shipment from Wight to Gaul.[1]

The Isle of Thanet is *Tanatus* in SOLINUS (who picks it out for its freedom from snakes), *Thanatos* in ISIDORE (who takes it as the Greek Θάνατος and relates it to the *death* of snakes) and *Tanatos* in BEDE.

Anglesey and Man present a peculiar problem. CAESAR has *Mona* midway (*in medio cursu*) between Britain and Ireland, and this has sometimes been taken as a reference to Man. But Ptolemy's Μόνα is also (like most of his islands) situated much too far from the coast and there is little doubt that this, like the *Mona* of PLINY and TACITUS and the Μῶννα of XIPHILINUS, refers to Anglesey, while PLINY's *Monapia* must be Man. In later authors, however, the situation is confused. OROSIUS does not mention *Mona*, nor do JULIUS HONORIUS and JORDANES, but all three have *Mevania* and the plural of this, *Mevaniae*, is used by BEDE for Man and Anglesey together.

Still more difficult are the remaining islands. The seven *Haemodae* and the seven *Acmodae* of PLINY must refer to the same group, probably the Shetlands before they were misidentified with *Thule*. PLINY has also *Silumnus* and *Andros* 'between Britain and Ireland' (though he says the same of *Vectis*, Wight), and *Sambis* and *Axanthos* (Ouessant) 'below'. *Silumnus* is probably to be related with the *Sylinancis* (or *Sylina*) of SULPICIUS SEVERUS which, as a place of exile beyond Britain, almost certainly means the Scillies, and *Silura*, which SOLINUS relates to the *Dumnonii*, may well belong here too; or, if a genuine link with the *Silures* is to be supposed, either Steep Holm or Flat Holm is more suitably situated than Lundy. *Andros* must be equated with the Ἄδρου of Ptolemy and probably represents the Isle of Howth, while *Sambis* may be a garbled version of *Sena insula* (Ile de Sein), which is otherwise missing in PLINY. PLINY's *Glaesariae* (called *Electridae* by the Greeks, and so a source of amber) must lie towards the Baltic and his *Bergi* and *Berrice* ('from which one may sail to *Thule*') may be Scandinavian too, though Professor Hawkes argues for their location in the Outer Hebrides.[2]

[1] Hawkes, *op. cit.*, 29–31; T. C. Lethbridge, *Boats and Boatmen* (London, 1952), 127; for a survey of all the locations suggested for *Ictis*, J. S. Maxwell, 'The Location of Ictis', *Journal of the Royal Institution of Cornwall*, v (1972), 293–319. The interpretation adopted here does not, of course, imply that there was a causeway between Wight and the mainland of Hampshire.

[2] Hawkes, *op. cit.*, 33–34, relating the forms *Vergos* and *Ver(i)gon* to Ptolemy's *Oceanus Vergionius*, to Mela's *Bergae* and (with less geographical probability) to Ptolemy's *Rerigonius Sinus*; but if, as he argues, *Berrice* is North Uist, it is hard to see why Pliny should call it 'largest of all' (*maximamque omnium Berricen*), since the islands with which he is comparing it include *Scandia* and *Dumna*.

5. ISLANDS DESCRIBED BUT NOT NAMED

STRABO says that Poseidonius mentioned an island near Britain 'where rites are performed like those in Samothrace concerned with Demeter and Kore'. Kore is Persephone and the rites are presumably those of the Cabiri, for which Samothrace was famous and with which Demeter was sometimes associated, but is is impossible to tell from the brief reference what aspects of them Poseidonius claimed to recognise, so that no connection can be established with Celtic mythology or names. This could, perhaps, be Anglesey, but despite the early date it is tempting to believe that one of the Western Isles of Scotland is meant, since PLUTARCH records the statement of Demetrius of Tarsus that some of these were named after *daemones* and heroes. The specific island which he describes 'in which Cronos was held asleep under guard of Briareus' might be Jura. Briareus (or Aegaeon) was one of the Uranids, monsters with 100 arms and 50 heads, who aided Zeus against Cronos and the other Titans. He is often regarded as a sea god and might be seen as a Kraken-like creature inhabiting the notorious whirlpool of Corryvrechan, between Jura and Scarba; certainly the profile of the Paps of Jura would well suit the figure of a recumbent giant. Jura seems to be the *Hinba* of Adomnan, but this cannot be equated with any of the names given in the ancient authorities.[1]

6. THULE AND THE CASSITERIDES

These names demand a brief discussion here because they are often mentioned in connection with Britain and, according to STRABO, Pytheas actually classed *Thule* as a British island. Θούλη (Latin *Thule*, or more often *Thyle*),[2] was discovered by Pytheas towards the end of the fourth century B.C., but the evidence suggests that no one from the ancient world ever found it again – a circumstance which may be reflected in the fact that its name was never fully Latinised but continued to be declined as a Greek word by poets and prose writers alike. From VIRGIL onwards *ultima Thule* became a proverbial expression for the furthest place on earth and most of the references to it are in this sense. That TACITUS should apply it to Shetland (as also does Ptolemy) is thus not evidence that Shetland ever really bore the name: any hitherto unknown land beyond the Orkneys would naturally be so identified. A limited number of authors do, however, give us some idea of what Pytheas wrote about it. STRABO, who seems to be unique in quoting him at first hand, regards him as an utter liar but admits that his description would fit a country in the far north. MELA, who refers to *Thyle* as 'famous in the poems of Greek and Roman writers', says it was opposite the country of the *Belgae* (or *Bergae*?) and PLINY, who puts it 'six days' sailing northwards from Britain', says that a further day's sailing beyond it brings one to the frozen *Sea of Cronos*; and SOLINUS likewise says that the sea beyond it is sluggish and frozen. PLINY adds the information that one can sail to it from *Berrice*, which might point in the direction of Scandinavia. OROSIUS and ISIDORE, however, put it north-west of Britain, and JORDANES in the furthest west, which would favour

[1] On Hinba, Watson *CPNS* 81–84; on Demetrius, Ogilvie and Richmond, 32–35.

[2] Θούλη in five instances, *Thule* in 7, *Thyle* or *Tyle* in 13.

Iceland, and Professor Hawkes has produced strong arguments in favour of this.[1] The detailed description which PROCOPIUS gives in his account of the migration of the Heruli seems at first sight to fix it firmly in Scandinavia – but then it turns out that he is really guessing, since in a later passage he refers to the far northern location of *Thule* 'so far as men know'. The confusion arises from the fact that all these authors had nothing to go on but the account of Pytheas, usually received at second or third hand, and all that can be said with certainty is that *Thule*, wherever it was,[2] was not one of the British Isles.

The case of the *Cassiterides* is somewhat different. These islands are first mentioned by HERODOTUS, who disclaims all knowledge of them. DIODORUS SICULUS has them near Spain and STRABO, who mentions them several times, always does so in a Spanish context, placing them north of the Artabri of north-west Spain. In view of this it is easiest to believe that his account of the visit to them by Publius Crassus refers not to Caesar's *legatus* but to his grandfather, also Publius Crassus, who celebrated a triumph over the Lusitani in 93 B.C. MELA puts them vaguely 'in the Celtic regions' (but before, and so apparently south of, *Sena* or the Ile de Sein) and PLINY and SOLINUS opposite Celtiberia (Spain). Ptolemy, too, puts them off north-west Spain. DIONYSIUS PEREIEGETES actually identifies them with the Hesperides, and the single island of Κασσίτερα, which STEPHANUS places in the Indian Ocean, while perhaps interesting for its hint of Indonesian tin, is clearly irrelevant to our inquiry. There is a degree of vagueness in all the accounts and the reason for it is not hard to discover. *Cassiterides* is not a proper name but a descriptive one (derived from the Greek word Κασσίτερος, tin) and it appears to mean simply the area from which tin came, which might be north-west Spain or Brittany or Cornwall at any particular time.[3] Crassus's journey involved the crossing of a sea wider than the English Channel (which again should rule out his grandson) and the inhabitants of the *Cassiterides* were friendly, which echoes the account of *Belerium* given by DIODORUS SICULUS, but the other things which STRABO says about the inhabitants recall in part the account of the Oestrymnides in AVIENIUS and in part that of Sena in MELA. As with *Thule*, there is no reason for supposing that this was ever the proper name of any part of the British Isles.

[1] Hawkes, *op. cit.*, 33–39, with the persuasive argument that Pytheas was following the migration route of the whooper swans, which would certainly have indicated that there was land to the north-west. But this makes it all the more surprising that the journey seems never to have been recorded again in Roman times. For the only Roman finds in Iceland (three coins, of Aurelian, Probus and Diocletian), H. Shetelig, *Antiquity*, XXIII (1949), 161–63.

[2] The name has now reached its truly ultimate application in a settlement in north-west Greenland, founded by Knud Rasmussen in 1910 but moved 70 miles still further north after the construction of an American Air Force base in 1950–52.

[3] For a discussion, with a useful map showing the distribution of cassiterite deposits in western Europe, Hawkes, *op. cit.*, 22–32.

7. SEAS AROUND BRITAIN

To a large extent the application of sea names which occur in the literary sources can be controlled by reference to Ptolemy. The North Sea (Ὠκεανὸς Γερμανικὸς in Ptolemy) is *Mare Germanicum* in PLINY, while MARCIAN, as usual, repeats Ptolemy. The Straits of Dover (unnamed in Ptolemy) are *Fretum Gallicum* in SOLINUS and ISIDORE. The English Channel is *Oceanus Britannicus* in MELA, PLINY, the DIMENSURATIO and VIBIUS SEQUESTER, Ὠκεανὸς Βρεττανικός in PSEUDO-AGATHEMERUS and Ὠκεανὸς Πρεττανικός (as in Ptolemy) in MARCIAN; JULIUS HONORIUS calls it *Mare Britannicum*, SOZOMEN Βρεττανὸς Θάλασσα and STRABO Πρεττανικὸς Πορθμός (which, though it means '*Prettanic* Strait', must refer to the whole Channel because it washes the whole of the northern side of Gaul). Ptolemy's Ὠκεανὸς Οὐεργιονίος (the Western Approaches), Ὠκεανὸς Ἰουερνικός (the Irish Sea) and Ὠκεανὸς Δυτικός (west of Ireland) are repeated only by MARCIAN, but the Atlantic (not named by Ptolemy) appears as *Mare Atlanticum* in PLINY and *Oceanus Atlanticus* in MELA and the DIMENSURATIO. In the north, Ptolemy's Ὠκεανὸς Ὑπερβορείος and Ὠκεανὸς Δουηκαληδονίος again appear only in MARCIAN, but PLINY has both an *Oceanus Septentrionalis* and a *Mare Cronium* (Κρόνιον in PSEUDO-AGATHEMERUS), while JULIUS HONORIUS has a curious *Mare Orcades* and a *Mare Thule*. *Mare Gallicum* is used by TACITUS in a generalised sense, to mean the seas around Gaul, but although STRABO applies the name Γαλατικὸς Κόλπος also to the Bay of Biscay, *Sinus Gallicus* and *Mare Gallicum* alike usually (as in Livy and Pliny) mean the Golfe du Lion.

8. CAPES AND PROMONTORIES

Three names of promontories may ultimately be derived from the account of Pytheas – Ὄρκας, which appears in DIODORUS SICULUS and (after Ptolemy) in MARCIAN, Βελέριον in DIODORUS SICULUS, and Καντίον, in DIODORUS SICULUS and STRABO – and it is likely that these defined the extent of Britain as it was known in pre-Roman times; but for Caesar *Cantium* is a district rather than a cape. Apart from these, the only promontories which occur in the literary sources are those copied by MARCIAN, sometimes inaccurately, from Ptolemy.

9. FORESTS AND MOUNTAINS

Forests and fens (the alliteration is present also in the Greek phrase ὕλαι καί ἕλη) figure in the accounts of almost all battles of Romans against barbarians, but even when they are not merely rhetorical colouring they are seldom given names. The one exception in Britain is the Caledonian Forest, which Ptolemy seems to locate in the Great Glen. PLINY regards the *Silva Calidonia* as marking the limit of Roman knowledge of Britain in his day, SILIUS ITALICUS has *Caledonii Luci*, STATIUS has *Caledonii Campi*, and FLORUS, in his epitome of Livy, has an extraordinary story of Caesar pursuing the defeated enemy to the *Caledoniae Silvae* (elsewhere he has also *Saltus Caledonius*).

Apart from the strange *Vallum Britanniae* of JULIUS HONORIUS (presumably

Hadrian's Wall, unless the variant readings *balum* and *ballum* conceal an otherwise unknown name), the only mountain mentioned in the sources is the *Mons Graupius* of TACITUS. Many suggestions have been put forward for the location of this,[1] but the most plausible is that of Professor J. K. St Joseph[2] following his discovery at Durno of a Roman camp whose size indicates the concentration of two Flavian forces. *Mons Graupius* itself would then be Bennachie which, though the hill-fort which crowns it is relatively small, commands an unrivalled view of the surrounding countryside.

10. RIVERS

The only British river which obtains widespread mention is the Thames. This is *Tamesis* (with accusative *Tamesim*) in CAESAR, *Tamesa* in TACITUS, Ταμέσα (but still masculine) in CASSIUS DIO and XIPHILINUS and *Tamensis* in OROSIUS – whence it is also *Tamensis* in BEDE and perhaps in GILDAS (though there the better texts have *Tamesis*). For the rest the sole authority is TACITUS, sometimes backed up by GILDAS and BEDE. Thus we have *Bodotria* for the Forth, *Clota* for the Clyde (*Cluit* in BEDE), *Sabrina* for the Severn (so also GILDAS and BEDE). Besides these TACITUS has also *Taus*, apparently for the Tay (though the variant reading *Tanaus* has sometimes raised doubts)[3] and *Trisantona* for the Trent. This last depends on the acceptance of Bradley's amendment to *Annals* XII, 31, where the manuscript text reads *cunctaque castris antonam et sabrinam fluvios cohibere parat*. The substitution of *cis trisantonam* for *castris antonam* rationalises the passage (for *fluvios* is a perplexing object for *cohibere*), eliminates the otherwise unknown name *Antona* and makes excellent geographical sense; beyond this, *Trisantona* certainly was the name of the rivers called Trent and Tarrant, including the Arun, to which Ptolemy applies it.[4] On the other hand we do not accept the amendments to the text of *Agricola* 24 suggested by Postgate and Richmond, which would supply either *Ituna* (the Eden) or *Anava* (the Annan).[5]

Though they do not appear in the earlier writers, BEDE adds *Derventio* for both the Yorkshire and the Cumbrian Derwent, and *Tinus* for the Northumberland Tyne.

[1] Among the more recent, Raedykes, O. G. S. Crawford, *The Topography of Roman Scotland North of the Antonine Wall* (Cambridge, 1949), 130–32; 'somewhere in the pass between Auchinhove and Keith', Ogilvie and Richmond, 65; the Pass of Grange, with Knock Hill as the *mons*, A. R. Burn and T. A. Dorey (ed.), *Tacitus* (London, 1969), 56; Duncrub, Perthshire, R. W. Feachem, *Antiquity*, XLIV (1970), 120–24.

[2] *JRS*, LXVII (1977), 141–45; for the hill-fort (the Mither Tap of Bennachie), R. W. Feachem, *A Guide to Prehistoric Scotland* (London, 1963), 104–105.

[3] For a discussion, Ogilvie and Richmond, 57 and n. 2.

[4] H. Bradley, *Academy*, 28 April and 19 May, 1883. This is by far the neatest solution of the problem (though whether *castris* should remain, with the implication of haplography, must be doubtful); the older suggestions listed by H. Furneaux, *The Annals of Tacitus* II (2nd edition, revised by H. F. Pelham and C. D. Fisher, Oxford, 1907), 97–98, may safely be disregarded.

[5] The text reads: *Quinto expeditionum anno nave prima transgressus ignotas ad id tempus gentes crebris simul ac prosperis proeliis domuit*. For discussions, Ogilvie and Richmond, 235, and N. Reed, *Britannia*, II (1971), 143–47.

11. NAMES OF ROMAN PROVINCES

HERODIAN (III, 8) states that Severus divided Britain into two provinces, and whatever the precise date of the division [1] their names, *Britannia Superior* (administered from London) and *Britannia Inferior* (administered from York) are given by CASSIUS DIO (LV, 23, 2) and confirmed by inscriptions. The later Diocletianic division into four provinces – *Britannia Prima* (with capital at Cirencester), *Britannia Secunda* (York? or Lincoln?), *Maxima Caesariensis* (London) and *Flavia Caesariensis* (Lincoln? or York?)[2] – is first reflected in the Verona List (NOMINA PROVINCIARUM OMNIUM) of A.D. 312–14, and the names are repeated in the *Breviarium* of FESTUS. The naming of the fifth province, *Valentia*, is recorded by AMMIANUS as occurring after Theodosius's campaign of A.D. 368, and the name recurs in the *Notitia Dignitatum* and, as *Valentiniana*, in POLEMIUS SILVIUS. The most widely held view is that it was formed by a further subdivision of the most northerly province (*Britannia Secunda* or *Flavia*) and was administered from Carlisle; or that the governor of *Valentia*, as a *consularis*, ruled from York and Carlisle became the capital of a reduced province of *Flavia* or *Secunda*.[3]

12. PEOPLES, TRIBES AND DISTRICTS

The names most often referred to here are, not surprisingly, those for Scotland and its inhabitants as a whole. The forms *Caledonia* and *Caledonii*, with *Caledonius* as the adjective, are used by LUCAN, SILIUS ITALICUS, TACITUS (who, however, always uses a periphrasis for the inhabitants, never *Caledonii*), MARTIAL, VALERIUS FLACCUS, STATIUS, FLORUS, AUSONIUS, CLAUDIAN and SIDONIUS; CASSIUS DIO and XIPHILINUS similarly use Καληδονία and Καληδόνιοι, but the variant spelling *Calidonia*, *Calidonius*, appears in PLINY, SOLINUS and a PANEGYRIC (as *Calidones*), while JORDANES has *Calydonia*, *Calydonii*. The *Picti* appear first in a PANEGYRIC of A.D. 297–98 and thereafter in AMMIANUS, CLAUDIAN, SIDONIUS, a GALLIC CHRONICLE and BEDE, while the *Maeatae*, apparently located by Dumyat, near Bridge of Allan, are found only in excerpts from CASSIUS DIO (Μαιάται in XIPHILINUS, Meatae in JORDANES). The *Attacotti* of AMMIANUS are unlocated, but JEROME, who also mentions them (as *Atticotti*), calls them a *gens Britannica*. The *Scotti*, who achieve numerous mentions in the later period, were, of course, still in Ireland: they appear first in the same PANEGYRIC as do the *Picti*, and the name *Scotia* does not supplant *Hibernia* until the fifth century.

Of the more specific names, those of the tribes which caused most trouble to the Romans are the most common. Thus the *Brigantes* appear in SENECA, JUVENAL and TACITUS and, as Βρίγαντες, in PAUSANIAS (but see below) and STEPHANUS, while

[1] On the Severan division, A. J. Graham, *JRS*, LVI (1966), 92–107; J. C. Mann and M. G. Jarrett, *JRS*, LVII (1967), 61–64; and S. S. Frere, *Britannia* (2nd edn., London, 1974), 203–205, with notes.

[2] On these provinces, J. C. Mann, *Antiquity*, XXV (1961), 316–20; also M. Hassall in R. Goodburn and P. Bartholomew (edd.), *Aspects of the Notitia Dignitatum* (Oxford, 1976), 109.

[3] Mann, *ibid.*; Frere, *op. cit.*, 242–43; Hassall, *ibid.*

the *Silures* are found in PLINY, TACITUS and (as *Silores*) STEPHANUS, and the *Trinobantes* in CAESAR, TACITUS, OROSIUS and BEDE (who spells them *Trinovantes*, with a *-v-*, for the first time). The *Dumnonii* appear in SOLINUS and, by inference from τὸ Δάμνιον ἄκρον, in MARCIAN; GILDAS has them as *Damnonii*. The *Cenimagni* of CAESAR may stand for *Iceni Magni* and should therefore be connected with the *Iceni* of TACITUS. Of the rest, CAESAR is the sole source for the *Ancalites*, *Bibroci*, *Cassi* and *Segontiaci* (all unlocated), TACITUS for the *Boresti* (in Scotland, but not related to Forres[1]), *Decangi* (on the Welsh borders) and *Ordovices* (in north Wales), CASSIUS DIO for the *Catuvellauni* (but as Κατουελλανοί) and *Dobunni* (corrupted to Βοδούννοι[2]) and AMMIANUS for the *Dicalydones* (unlocated) and *Verturiones* (around Fortrenn). The *Novantae* are implied by the Νεουάντων Χερσόνησος in MARCIAN. As noted above, *Cantium* is a district name in CAESAR, like BEDE's *Cantia*, and the tribal name *Cantii* is never found.

There remains the vexed question of the 'Genunian Region', which PAUSANIAS says was attacked by the *Brigantes* in the reign of Antoninus Pius.[3] There were several people called *Brigantes* in the Celtic world, not only in Britain and (according to Ptolemy) in Ireland, but also in Hispania Tarraconensis (around *Flavium Brigantium* /Coruña) and in Raetia (around *Brigantium*/Bregenz). Immediately to the east of the Raetian *Brigantes* lived the *Genauni* and one would automatically assume that this was the scene of the trouble but for two circumstances: first, PAUSANIAS specifically places it in Britain, and second, as Professor E. Birley has pointed out,[4] he is listing the only deviations from peace which occurred in Pius's reign and could hardly omit the one campaign, that of Lollius Urbicus, for which he was saluted as *imperator*. There is good reason, however, to suspect that the text has been tampered with. Elsewhere PAUSANIAS uses the normal Greek spelling Βρεττανοί, but here 'in Britain' appears as ἐν Βριττανίᾳ – that is, with an iota instead of an epsilon, in all the manuscripts, – for which the only Greek analogy is to be found in THEOPHILUS of ANTIOCH, but which reproduces the late Latin spelling *Brittania*. It seems possible, then, that PAUSANIAS originally cited three wars – one with the Moors, one in Britain and one in Raetia – and that at some time in late antiquity the scribe of the archetype, faced with a defective manuscript, reconstructed it incorrectly. Certainly no one has ever located a Genunian Region in Britain.

[1] As claimed by J. Clarke in Richmond, *RNNB*, 52; but Watson *CPNS* 23 does not, as Clarke states, link them with Forres, and the latter name is derived from *Farais*, a Gaelic loan-word from French (Ogilvie and Richmond, 282).

[2] On the equation Βοδούννοι = *Dobunni*, C. F. C. Hawkes in E. M. Clifford (ed.), *Bagendon: a Belgic Oppidum* (Cambridge, 1961), 62–65.

[3] For a recent discussion of this passage, reaching a somewhat similar conclusion, J. G. F. Hind, *Britannia*, VIII (1977), 229–34.

[4] E. Birley, *Roman Britain and the Roman Army* (Kendal, 1953), 32 (= *Dumfries and Galloway Trans.*, XXIX, 3 (1952), 47).

13. TOWNS AND FORTS

London is mentioned by only six of our authors, appearing as *Londinium* in TACITUS and, in the adjectival form *Londiniensis*, in a PANEGYRIC of A.D. 397–98 and the ACTA of the Council of Arles, *Lundinium* in AMMIANUS and Λινδόνιον in STEPHANUS, to emerge as *Lundonia* in BEDE. The form *Augusta* does not appear before AMMIANUS (who says that it has replaced the ancient name), but is implied also in the *Notitia Dignitatum*. York, which was celebrated for the deaths there of both Severus and Constantius Chlorus, does rather better, appearing as *Eboracum* in EUTROPIUS (so Ἐβοράκον in PAEANIUS), AURELIUS VICTOR, the HISTORIA AUGUSTA, the EXCERPTA VALESIANA, JEROME, OROSIUS, PROSPER TIRO, CASSIODORUS, the CODEX IUSTINIANUS and (with bizarre variants) in the Arles Council ACTA; but it has become *Eburacum* or *Eburaca* in BEDE. Richborough has a peculiar status, both as the landing-place of the Claudian expedition and thereafter, it would seem, as the official port of entry to Britain.[1] Accordingly it sometimes stands for Britain as a whole in the poets, and the adjective *Rutupinus* occurs in LUCAN, JUVENAL and AUSONIUS. In AMMIANUS the name is *Rutupiae*, in OROSIUS *Rutupi Portus* (with variants *Ruthubi*, *Rutubi*), and *Rutubi Portus* in BEDE. Its role in the invasion followed by the foundation of the *colonia* and its destruction in the Boudiccan Revolt lead to the mention of *Camulodunum* by TACITUS and CASSIUS DIO, and PLINY also has it (as *Camalodunum*), but it does not appear in later writers, unless it is concealed in the garbled list of signatories to the ACTA of the Council of Arles. Richmond followed Haddan and Stubbs, Haverfield and Miller in believing that the mysterious *Colonia Londinensium* of the third line represented *Colonia Camulodunensium*; but Dr Mann's argument that the place should be Lincoln and that Sacerdos and Arminius represented a fourth place (presumably Cirencester, which, as the capital of *Britannia Prima*, would complete the tally of four provinces) seems more convincing.[2]

Verulamium is mentioned by TACITUS for its destruction in A.D. 60 and by GILDAS and BEDE for its association with St Alban. BEDE adds *Calcaria* for Tadcaster, *Campodonum* for the elusive *Cambodunum* of the Antonine Itinerary (see p. 159), *Cataracta* or *Cataracto* for Catterick, *Doruvernis* or *Doruvernensis Civitas* for Canterbury, *Dorubrevi* for Rochester, *Lugubalia* for Carlisle, the anglicised *Ythancaestir* for *Othona*, or Bradwell, and *Venta* for Winchester. He calls Caerleon *Legionum Urbs* (so also GILDAS) and Chester *Civitas Legionum*. Other Romano-British names may also be concealed in his reference to Dorchester-on-Thames as *Dorcic* and in his mention of a place called *Ad Lapidem*, on the mainland opposite the Isle of Wight; he does not give an Anglo-Saxon equivalent for this, as he usually does, but it has been identified with Stoneham. The *fontes calidi* dedicated to Minerva which SOLINUS describes (with an interesting reference to the use of Somerset coal) represent *Aquae Sulis*, or Bath, since Sulis is identified with Minerva in inscriptions.

The only specific place mentioned by TACITUS apart from London, Colchester and

[1] Protocol required that an incoming governor should always arrive at the customary port of entry 'for the provincials think the maintenance of customs and privileges of this kind very important': *Digest* I, 16, 4, 3–5.

[2] Richmond, *Arch. J.*, CIII (1946), 64; Mann, *Antiquity*, XXXIV (1961), 316–20.

St Albans is *Portus Trucculensis*. Some scholars have suggested that this is a garbled form of *Rutupensis* and so refers to the permanent base at Richborough[1] but, as A. R. Burn has pointed out,[2] the expression *unde...redierat* (in the pluperfect) suggests not that the fleet now returned to it but rather that they had sailed to and from it on a previous occasion and by reaching it now (from the opposite direction) completed the circumnavigation referred to in *Agricola* 10 in two parts. In this case a site in north-west Scotland is to be sought and Burn suggests an inlet associated with a stream called Twrch ('boar') – a name which, as Watson remarks,[3] is often given to Welsh rivers which form deep channels or disappear underground. If this is a correct interpretation, a possible site might be Sandwood Loch (Sutherland), once a sea-loch but now cut off from the sea by a wide sand bar. Whether *Trucculensis* is to be equated with the *Ugrulentum*[4] of the Ravenna Cosmography is another matter.

It remains to dispose of one false attribution of a name to Britain. AURELIUS VICTOR says that Severus Alexander died at a *vicus* of Britain called *Sicilia* and his account is copied by the author of the HISTORIA AUGUSTA. But the context of the story demands a place in Gaul and that Alexander did die in Gaul, not far from Mainz, is reliably stated by Herodian (VI, 7–9, confirmed by Eusebius, Jerome and others). No *vicus* called *Sicilia* has been identified there, but the explanation probably is that a nearby fort was garrisoned by a British auxiliary unit. The possibility remains, however, that the confusion arose because VICTOR's source knew of a place so named in Britain.

14. THE TEXTS

These are arranged in alphabetical order of authors or, in the case of anonymous works, of title. Each entry includes an indication of the date of composition; a translation of any passages which are relevant to the identification of place-names, with the names themselves in their original form (with variants); a note of other chance references to place-names; and a statement of the edition used. In making the translations the aim has been to produce literal rather than literary renderings and especially to reveal possible ambiguities of meaning.

ACTA CONCILII ARELATENSIS (A.D. 314)

Signatories include:

Eborius episcopus de civitate Eboricensi provincia Britania.
Restitutus episcopus de civitate Londenensi provincia qua supra.

[1] So Ogilvie and Richmond, 282–83, following Lipsius, though accepting *Trucculensem* as the better reading.

[2] In T. A. Dorey, *op. cit.*, 59. This has the additional advantage that it explains why Tacitus, who is usually so reticent, actually names it: it was the furthest known place on the mainland. Against this, J. G. F. Hind in *Britannia*, V (1974), 285–88, favouring an identification with *Tunnocelum* on the Cumberland coast.

[3] Watson *CPNS* 232.

[4] So N. Reed, *Britannia*, II (1971), 147–48, accepting Burn's arguments but following E. Hübner, *Hermes*, XVI (1881), 545, in this equation; against, J. G. F. Hind, *op. cit.*

Adelfius episcopus de civitate Colonia Londenensium, exinde Sacerdus presbyter, Arminius diaconus.

(Paris. Bibl. Nat., Cod. Lat. 12097, fol. 7, 6th–7th cent.)

Variants:

Ex provincia Britannia civitas Tobracentium Aeburius episcopus.
Civitas Londinientium Restitutus episcopus.
Civitas Londinientium Adelfius.
(Köln. Bibl. Capitularis, Cod. 212, fol. 30v, 6th–7th cent.)

Ex provincia Britannia Tububiacensium Eburius episcopus.
Ex civitate Londiniensium Restitutus episcopus.
Ex civitate Colonia Londiniensis Adelfius episcopus Sacerdos episcopus et Menius diaconus.
(Paris. Bibl. Nat., Cod. Lat. 1452, fol. 153, 10th cent.)

Ex provincia Britania civitas Tuburiacensium Eburius episcopus.
Civitas Londinensium Restitutus episcopus.
Colonia... Adelfius episcopus Sacer episcopus Arminius diaconus.
(Toulouse. Bibl. Munic., Cod. 364, fol. 24, 7th cent.)

Ex provincia Brittinia civitas Tubiricensium Evortius episcopus.
Civitas Coloniae Londininsium Adelfus episcopus.
(Paris. Bibl. Nat., Cod. Lat. 3846, fol. 138v, 9th cent., and Munich. Staatsbibl. Cod. Lat. 5508, fol. 16v, 8th cent.)

Text: C. Munier (ed.): *Concilia Galliae* (*Corpus Christianorum, Series Latina* CXLVIII), Turnhout, 1963.

AELIANUS, Claudius (*c.* A.D. 170–235)

Reference:

Βρεττανικός: *De Natura Animalium* XV, 8 (bis) (referring to pearls).

Text: ed. A. F. Scholfield, London and Cambridge, Mass., 1959.

'AELIUS LAMPRIDIUS': see HISTORIA AUGUSTA

'AELIUS SPARTIANUS': see HISTORIA AUGUSTA

PSEUDO-AGATHEMERUS (uncertain, but after 2nd cent. A.D.)

1. *Geographia Compendiaria* IV (13) (Europe)
Islands of this continent worthy of note in the outer sea are the two *Bretanikai* (Βρετανικαί), *Ivernia* ('Ιουερνία) and *Alvion* ('Αλουίων). *Ivernia*, lying further west, extends some way towards Spain; *Alvion*, in which forts are situated, is the greatest and most extensive; for beginning in the north it stretches to the west as far as the middle of Tarraconensis, to the east almost to the middle of Germany. Also noteworthy would be Thule (Θούλη) and Great Skandia.

2. *Geographia Compendiaria* VIII (27) (Largest Islands)
Among the greatest islands the first of all in the inhabited world is Salike (Ceylon), the second *Alvion*, the third would be *Ivernia*.

3. *Geographia Compendiaria* XIV (45) (Seas)
The great sea flowing round the whole inhabited world is called by the general name of Ocean, but it has different names according to latitude. For the whole of it lying in arctic latitudes is called Arktikos and Boreios, and of it the more easterly part is called Skythikos and the more westerly *Germanikos* and *Brettanikos* (Βρεττανικός); but the whole of this is also called the *Kronion* (Κρόνιον) and the *Pepegos* (Πεπηγώς, i.e. 'frozen') and *Nekros* (Νεκρός, i.e. 'dead') sea.

Text: *Geographi Graeci Minores*, ed. K. Müller, Paris, 1861, repr. Hildesheim, 1965.

AMBROSIUS (*c.* A.D. 339–397)

Reference:
Britanniae: Hexaemeron III, 3, 15 (39).

Text: *Migne*, Ser. Lat. XIV, Paris, 1844, repr. Turnhout, 1969.

AMMIANUS MARCELLINUS (*c.* A.D. 330–395)

1. *Res Gestae* XXVII, 8, 4
And since in describing the deeds of the Emperor Constans (i.e. in a passage now lost) I explained, so far as my powers allowed, the ebbing and flowing of the ocean and the situation of *Britannia*, I have thought it superfluous to repeat what has already been dealt with once, as Homer's Ulysses among the Phaeacians shrinks from repetition because of the excessive difficulty. But this it will suffice to say, that at that time the *Picti*, divided into two nations, the *Dicalydones* (*Dicalydonas*, acc.) and the *Verturiones* (acc., variant *Vecturiones*), and likewise the *Attacotti*, a warlike tribe of men, and the *Scotti*, ranging widely, were causing great devastation.

2. *Res Gestae* XXVII, 8, 7
When the Batavi who followed him had arrived, and the Heruli and the Iovii and the Victores, units confident in their strength, he set out and, making for *Lundinium*, an ancient town which posterity has called *Augusta*, he divided his troops into several parts and attacked the wandering bands of the enemy, laden with booty.

3. *Res Gestae* XXVIII, 3, 1
But Theodosius, that leader of famous name and spirit full of vigour, setting out from *Augusta*, which the ancients called *Lundinium*, with soldiers assembled with energy and skill, brought much help to the troubled fortunes of the *Britanni*.

4. *Res Gestae* XXVIII, 3, 7
And having recovered the province which had fallen under the rule of the enemy, he had so far restored it to its ancient condition that, by the same token, it both had a legitimate governor and was thenceforward called *Valentia* by the decision of the Emperor who was, as it were, celebrating an ovation.

Other references:
Attacotti: *Res Gestae* XXVI, 4, 5.
Britanni: XX, 9, 9; XXII, 3, 3; XXVI, 4, 5; XXVIII, 1, 21; XXX, 7, 9.
Britannia: XIV, 5, 6; XVIII, 2, 3 (plur.); XX, 1, 1 (plur.); 4, 3, (plur.); XXIII, 1, 2 (plur.); XXVII, 8, 1 (plur.); 8, 10 (plur.); 9, 1 (plur.); XXIX, 1, 44 (plur.); 4, 7 (plur.: text *Brittanas*).

Britannicus: XXIII, 6, 88 (*mare*); XXX, 7, 3 (text, *Britannum exercitum*); XXX, 9, 1 (*strepitus*).
Lundinium; XX, 1, 3.
Picti: XX, 1, 1; XXVI, 4, 5.
Rutupiae: XX, 1, 3; XXVII, 8, 6 (both *Rutupias*, acc.).
Scotti: XX, 1, 1; XXVI, 4, 5.

Text: ed. C. U. Clark, Berlin, 1910–15, repr. 1963.

AMPELIUS, L. (2nd–3rd cent. A.D.)

References:

Brittannia: *Liber Memorialis* 6, 12; 18, 20; 47, 6 (variant *Brittania*).
Thyle: 6, 12 (variant *Tile*).

Text: ed. E. Assmann, Leipzig, 1935.

ANTHOLOGIA LATINA (various)

Britanni: 424, 3; 425, 6 (prob. 1st cent. A.D.)
Britannia: 422, 1; 426, 1 (prob. 1st cent. A.D.)

Text: ed. A. Riese, Leipzig, 1868.

APOLLINARIS SIDONIUS, C. Sollius (*c.* A.D. 430–479)

References:

Britanni: *Carmina* vii, 89 (N.B. Sidonius also regularly uses this word for Bretons, in Armorica).
Caledonii: vii, 89 (acc., variants *Calidonias*, *Calidonios*).
Pictus (coll.): vii, 90.
Scotus (coll.): vii, 90 (acc., variants *Scottum*, *Schotum*, *Schottum*).

Text: *MGH* (*AA*) VIII, ed. C. Luetjohann, Berlin, 1887, repr. 1961.

APOLLONIUS (uncertain)

Reference:

τὴν Βρεττανικὴν νῆσον: *Historiae Mirabiles*, 15.

Text: *Rerum Naturalium Scriptores Graeci Minores* I, ed. O. Keller, Leipzig, 1877.

APONIUS (5th–6th cent. A.D.)

Explanationis in Canticum Canticorum Libri XII, XII, 237.
At the time of the appearance of Christ, which is called the Epiphany, Caesar Augustus, as Livy narrates, on coming back from the island of *Britannia*, demonstrated to the Roman people by shows that the whole world was subjected, whether by war or by alliance, to Roman rule, with peace abounding.

Text: edd. H. Bottino and J. Martini, Rome, 1843.

APPIANUS (*c.* A.D. 90–160)

References:

Βρεττανίς νῆσος: *Historia Romana, praef.* 5; IV (*Historia Gallica*), i, 5 (epitome).

Βρεττανοί: *Historia Romana, praef,* 1; IV (*Historia Gallica*), xix (from Suidas); VI (*Bella Hispanica*), i, 1; *Bella Civilia* II, 17; 150 (bis).

Text: edd. H. White, J. D. Denniston and E. I. Robson, London and Cambridge, Mass., 1912–13, revised 1932–33.

PSEUDO-ARISTOTLE (? 1st cent. A.D.)

De Mundo iii (393b)

Then a little above the Scythians and the land of the Celts it (sc. the ocean) binds together the inhabited world, towards the Gallic gulf and the Pillars of Hercules mentioned before, outside which the Ocean flows round the world. In it there are very large islands, two in number, called the Brettanic Islands (νῆσοι Βρεταννικαί), *Albion* (Ἄλβιων) and *Ierne* (Ἰέρνη), larger than those already mentioned and lying above the Celts...There are not a few small islands around the *Bretannic* islands and Iberia, wreathing the inhabited world, which, as we have said, is itself an island, in a ring.

Text: ed. D. J. Furley, London and Cambridge, Mass., 1955.

ATHANASIUS (*c.* A.D. 295–373)

References:

Βρεττανία: *Apologia contra Arianos* I (p. 98; plur.); *Historia Arianorum ad Monachos* 2 (p. 285); *Epistola ad Iovianum* 2 (p. 623; MSS Βρετανία).

Text: *Migne*, Ser. Graec. XXV and XXVI, Paris, n.d., repr. Turnhout n.d.

ATHENAEUS (*fl.* A.D. 200)

Reference:

Βρεττανίδες νήσοι: *Deipnosophistae* VI (273b).

Text: ed. C. B. Gulick, London and New York, 1929.

AURELIUS VICTOR, Sex. (*fl.* A.D. 360–390) (including the anonymous *Epitome de Caesaribus*)

Liber de Caesaribus 24, 2–4

(Alexander) hurried to Gaul, which was being troubled by German raids. There he firmly disbanded several of the legions which were mutinying; but this, though immediately to his credit, soon led to his destruction. For the soldiers were appalled by the strength of his severity (for which he had acquired the cognomen Severus) and when he happened to be operating with a few men in a *vicus* of *Britannia* which was called *Sicilia*, they slew him.[1]

[1] Cf. *Historia Augusta*: *Severus Alexander* 59, 6, probably derived from this passage; for a discussion, p. 49, above.

Other references:
Britanni: *Lib. de. Caes.* 20, 9.
Britannia: *Lib. de Caes.* 4, 2; 20, 18; 20, 27; 39, 21; 40, 2; *Epitome* 20, 4; 41, 2; 47, 7.
Britannicus: *Epitome* 4, 7 (*triumphum Britannicum*).
Eboracum: *Lib. de Caes.* 20, 27 (*in Britanniae municipio, cui Eboraci nomen*).

Text: ed. P. Pichlmayr, rev. R. Gruendel, Leipzig, 1966.

AUSONIUS, D. Magnus (*c.* A.D. 310–395)

Epigrammata cvii–cxii
cvii. That Silvius Bonus who attacks our verses has the more deserved a couplet, being a *bonus Brito*.
cviii. This is Silvius Bonus. Who is Silvius? He is a *Britannus*. Either this Silvius is not a *Brito* or he is bad.
cix. Silvius is called Bonus and also called a *Britannus*. Who would believe a *bonus* citizen had sunk so low?
cx. No *bonus* man is a *Brito*. If he should begin to be plain Silvius, let the plain man cease to be *bonus*.
cxi. This is Silvius Bonus, but this same man is a *Brito*. A simpler thing, believe me, is a bad *Brito*.
cxii. You, Silvius, are Bonus, a *Brito*, though you are said not to be a *bonus* man and no *Brito* can link himself with Bonus.

Other references:
Britanni: *Mosella* 68; 407.
Caledonius (adj.): *Mosella* 68 (*Britanni*); *Eclogae* vii (vi), 32 (*aestus*); *Technopaegnion* 94 (= x, 26: *nurus*); *Epistulae* v, 37 (*aestus*, or *Caledonii*, noun).
Rutupinus (adj.): *Parentalia* vii, 2 (*tellus*); xviii, 8 (*ager*); *Ordo Nobilium Urbium* 72 (= x (Aquileia)., 9: *latro*, i.e. Magnus Maximus).

Text: ed. R. Peiper, Leipzig, 1886.

AVIENIUS, Postumius Rufius Festus (4th cent. A.D.)

1. *Ora Maritima*, 94–134
Beneath the height of this promontory there opens out for the inhabitants the *Sinus Oestrymnicus*, in which appear the *Oestrymnides* islands, widely spaced and rich in the metal of tin and lead. Great is the strength of this race, proud their spirit, skilful their art, constant the care of all of them for business, and in their woven boats they ply the rough sea far and wide and the abyss of Ocean, full of monsters. For these men know not to build their barks of pine and maple and do not shape their skiffs in fir, as the custom is, but, for a marvel, they fit out their boats with hides joined together and often traverse the wide sea on skins. But from here it is two days' journey by ship to the sacred island (*sacram insulam*), as the ancients called it. This spreads its broad fields among the waves and far and wide the race of the *Hierni* inhabit it. Near it again lies the island of the *Albiones* (*insula Albionum*). The Tartessians were wont to

trade as far as the bounds of the *Oestrymnides*, and the colonists of Carthage and the people dwelling near the Pillars of Hercules went to these seas. And Himilco the Carthaginian says that they can scarcely be crossed in four months, as he says he had proved by voyaging there himself: such lack of breeze is there to drive on the boat, so sluggish is the water of the sticky sea. He adds this too, that there is much weed in the turbulent waters and often it holds back the ship like a thicket. He says nevertheless that the mantle of the sea is not deep and the land is covered by but a little water. He says that ever here and there sea beasts come to meet you and monsters swim between the slow and gently moving boats. If anyone dare from the Oestrymnic isles (*ab insulis Oestrymnicis*) to urge his craft into those waters where the air freezes beneath the turning of the Bear, he comes on a land of the *Ligures* void of inhabitants. For the fields have been made empty by the hand of the *Celtae* and by many battles.

2. *Ora Maritima* 259–261
Thence (i.e. west of Tartessos, in southern Spain) there swells the mountain *Cassius*; and it is from this that the Greek tongue first called tin *cassiteros*.

Other references:
Britanni: *Descriptio Orbis Terrae* 118, 749.

Texts: ed. A. Schulten, Barcelona and Berlin, 1922.
Geographi Graeci Minores, ed. K. Müller, 1861; repr. Hildesheim, 1965.

BASIL OF CAESAREA (*c.* A.D. 330–379)

Reference:

ἡ Βρεττανικὴ νῆσος: *Homilia IV in Hexaemeron* 4 (p. 36).

Text: *Migne*, Ser. Graec. XXIX, Paris, n.d., repr. Turnhout, n.d.

BEDA (A.D. 672–735)

1. *Historia Ecclesiastica Gentis Anglorum* I, 1
Britannia, an island of the ocean whose name was once *Albion*, is located between the north and the west, opposite, at a great distance, Germany, Gaul and Spain, the greatest part of Europe. It is 800 miles long towards the north and has a breadth of 200 miles, excluding some further extensions of various promontories, as a result of which its circuit is 4,875 miles. It has Gallia Belgica on the south and access for people crossing to its nearest shore is provided by a city called *Rutubi Portus*, now corruptly called Reptacaestir by the people of the Angli. With sea interposed the crossing from Gessoriacum on the nearest shore of the people of the Moryni is 50 miles or, as some writers have it, 450 stades. At its back, where it faces an unbounded ocean, it has the *Orcades* islands.

2. *Historia Ecclesiastica* I, 3
He (Claudius) also added the *Orcades* islands, situated in the ocean beyond *Brittania*, to the Roman Empire... By the same Claudius Vespasian, who became emperor after Nero, was sent to *Britannia* and subjected the island of *Vecta*, near Brittania on

the south, to Roman rule: from east to west it is about 30 miles long, from south to north twelve, and it is separated from the south coast of *Brittania* by six miles of sea in its eastern part, by three in the west.

3. *Historia Ecclesiastica* I, 7
The blessed Alban suffered on June 22nd near the city of *Verolamium*, which now is called Verlamacaestir or Vaeclingacaestir by the people of the Angli... At that time suffered Aaron and Julius, citizens of *Legionum Urbs*...

4. *Historia Ecclesiastica* I, 25
On the eastern shore of *Cantia* is the island of *Tanatos*, of some size, that is, by the English manner of reckoning, of 600 families. The river Uantsumu divides it from the mainland, about three stades wide, and it is crossable in two places only; for at each end it joins the sea.

5. *Historia Ecclesiastica* I, 29
We grant you the use of the pallium only for the performance of the solemn rites of the mass, so that you may ordain twelve bishops in separate places, who shall be subject to your jurisdiction, provided only that the bishop of the city of *Lundonia* (*civitatis Lundoniensis*, gen.) ought always hereafter to be consecrated by his own synod and receive the honour of the pallium from this holy and apostolic see which I, by God's authority, serve. We wish you to send a bishop to the city of *Eburaca* (*Eburacam civitatem*, acc.), whom you shall have decided to ordain, but only if the same city, together with the neighbouring parts, should receive the word of God; he himself is also to ordain twelve bishops and to enjoy the honour of a metropolitan, for on him too, if we live, we intend, with God's favour, to bestow the pallium. However we wish him to be subject to your control, brother; but after your death he may preside over the bishops whom he shall have ordained in such a way that he shall in no way be subject to the bishop of *Lundonia* (*Lundoniensis*, adj.). But between the bishops of *Lundonia* and *Eburaca* (*Lundoniae et Eburacae civitatis*, gen.) there should in the future be this distinction of honour, that he should be held senior who is first consecrated.

6. *Historia Ecclesiastica* II, 2
After the events of which we have spoken that very powerful king of the Angli, Aedilfrid, having collected a great army against the *Civitas Legionum*, which is called Legacaestir by the people of the Angli, but by the *Brettones* more correctly Carlegion, made a great slaughter of that perfidious people.

7. *Historia Ecclesiastica* II, 5
The fifth was Aeduini, king of the people of the Nordanhymbri, that is of those who dwell on the north shore of the river Humbra, who with greater power than all those who inhabit *Brittania*, ruled over the peoples, except only the *Cantuarii*, and even brought under the rule of the Angli the *Mevaniae* (*Mevanias*, acc.), islands of the *Brettones* which are situated between *Hibernia* and *Brittania*.

8. *Historia Ecclesiastica* II, 9
He (Edwin) even subjected the *Mevaniae* islands to the rule of the Angli, as we have said above. The former of these, which is to the south, is larger in size and more

favoured in the growth of crops and fertility, containing 960 families according to the reckoning of the Angli, while the latter has space for 300 and more.

9. *Historia Ecclesiastica* II, 14

But also in the province of the Deiri, where he used to stay very often with the king, he (Paulinus) baptised in the river Suala (Swale) which flows past the town of *Cataracta* (*vicum Cataractam*, acc.); for they could not yet build oratories or baptistries there at the beginning of the birth of the church. Nevertheless in *Campodonum* (*Campodono*, abl.), where there was then a royal dwelling, he built a basilica, which some time afterwards the pagans, by whom king Edwin was killed, burnt, together with the whole dwelling. In its place later kings built a dwelling for themselves in the region which is called Loidis (Leeds). But the actual altar, which was of stone, escaped the fire and it is preserved to this day in the monastery of the most reverend abbot and priest Thrythwulf, which is in the forest of Elmet.

10. *Historia Ecclesiastica* IV, 16 (14)

I think I should not pass over in silence the fact that among the first fruits of those who from the same island (Wight) were saved by believing were two royal children, brothers in fact of Arvald the king of the island, who were crowned with the special grace of God. When the enemy were threatening the island they escaped by flight and, having crossed from the island to the neighbouring province of the Iuti, when they had been brought to the place which is called *Ad Lapidem*, where they thought they could conceal themselves from the face of the victorious king, they were betrayed and ordered to be killed.

Forms of Romano-British names preserved in the *Ecclesiastical History*:
Albion: *Hist. Eccl.* I, I
Brettones: I, I etc. (normal form)
Brittanni: I, 2 etc. (when quoting ancient authorities)
Brittania: I, I etc.
Calcaria: IV, 23 (= Tadcaster)
Campodonum: II, 14 (= ?)
Cantia: I, 15 etc. (= Kent)
Cantuarii: Praef. etc. (= people of Kent)
Cataracta: II, 14 or *Cataracto*: III, 14 (= Catterick)
Derventio: IV, 29 (= R. Derwent, Cumbria)
Derventio: II, 9 (= R. Derwent, Yorks)
Dorcic: III, 7 etc. (= Dorchester-on-Thames)
Dorubrevi: II, 3 (= Rochester)
Dorvernensis civitas: I, 25 etc.; *Doruvernis civitas* V, 23 (= Canterbury)
Eburacum: II, 13 etc. or *Eburaca*: I, 29 etc. (= York), but *Eboracensis*: IV, 3
Hibernia: I, I etc. (= Ireland)
Lugubalia: IV, 29 (= Carlisle)
Lundonia: I, 29 etc. (= London)
Mevaniae Insulae: II, 5 and 9 (= Anglesey and Man)
Orcades: I, I etc. (= Orkneys)
Picti: I, I etc.

Rutubi Portus: I, I (= Richborough)
Sabrina: V, 23 (= R. Severn)
Scotti: I, I etc.
Tamensis: II, 3 etc. (= R. Thames)
Tanatos: I, 25 (= Thanet)
Tini (gen.): V, 6 (= R. Tyne, Northumbd)
Trinovantes: I, 2
Vecta: Praef. etc. (= Isle of Wight)
Venta: III, 7 etc. (= Winchester), with adjective
Ventanus: V, 23
Verolamium: I, 7 (St Albans)

Text: ed. B. Colgrave & R. A. B. Mynors, Oxford, 1969.

Other reference:
Thule (variant *Thyle*): *Quaestiones in Lib. Sam. et Reg.* XXX, 25B (on II Kings XX, 9).

Text: *Migne*, Ser. Lat. XCI, p. 372; *Corpus Christianorum* CXIX, 732.

CAESAR, C. Iulius (100–44 B.C.)

1. *De Bello Gallico* V, 11, 8–14, 4

When he arrived there, greater forces of *Britanni* had assembled at that place from all sides, the chief command and direction of the war having, by common consent, been entrusted to Cassivellaunus, whose territory a river called *Tamesis* (nom.) separates from the maritime states, at about 80 miles from the sea. At an earlier time there had been continual warfare between him and the other states, but the *Britanni*, alarmed by our arrival, had put him in charge of the war and its conduct.

The interior part of *Britannia* is inhabited by those of whom it is handed down by tradition that they were born in the island, the maritime part by those who had crossed from Belgium for plunder and making war, almost all of whose tribal names are those of the states from which they were sprung, and having made war they have remained there and begun to cultivate the fields. There is an infinite number of men, very numerous buildings, more or less like those of Gaul, and very numerous herds. They use either bronze or gold money or iron bars of fixed weight in place of money. Tin is produced in the inland regions (*nascitur ibi plumbum album in mediterraneis regionibus*), iron in the maritime regions, but there is very little quantity of it; they use imported bronze. There is timber of every kind as in Gaul, except beech and fir. They do not think it right to eat the hare, the cock and the goose, but they rear them for amusement and pleasure. The climate is more temperate than in Gaul, with the cold less severe.

The island is triangular in shape, with one side opposite Gaul. One angle of this side, which is at *Cantium* (*ad Cantium*), which is where almost all ships from Gaul land, looks towards the rising sun; the lower looks to the south. This side extends about 500 miles. Another side faces Spain and the setting sun. In this area is *Hibernia*, smaller by a half, it is thought, than *Britannia*, but the passage is the same distance as that from Gaul to *Britannia*. In the middle of this crossing (*in hoc medio cursu*) is an island which is called *Mona*. There are also thought to be several smaller islands nearby, about which islands some have written that in winter there is night for 30 continuous days. We ourselves by enquiry discovered nothing about that, except that by accurate measurements by water (i.e. the water clock) we saw that the nights were shorter than on the continent. The length of this side, as their opinion states, is 700 miles. The third side is towards the north and there is no land opposite this part, but an angle of this side looks mainly towards Germany. This is thought to be 800 miles in length. So the whole island is 2,000 miles in circumference.

Of all the people by far the most civilised are those who inhabit *Cantium* (*qui Cantium incolunt*), which is a wholly (or, the whole) maritime region (*quae regio est maritima omnis*). Most of the people of the interior do not sow crops, but live on milk and meat and are clothed in skins. But all the *Britanni* paint themselves with woad, which produces a blue colour, and they are thereby more terrifying of aspect in a fight. They wear their hair long and shave every part of the body except their head and their upper lip. Ten or twelve of them have wives in common, especially brothers with brothers and parents with children; but those born from them are considered to be the children of the man by whom the woman was first bedded.

2. *De Bello Gallico* v, 21, 1–3

The *Trinobantes* having been defended and protected from any violence of the soldiers, the *Cenimagni*, *Segontiaci*, *Ancalites*, *Bibroci* and *Cassi*, having sent embassies, surrender themselves to Caesar. From them he learns that the *oppidum* of Cassivellaunus is not far from that place, defended by woods and marshes, and that a considerable number of men and herds have assembled there. The *Britanni* call it an *oppidum* when they have fortified dense woods with a rampart and ditch, where they are accustomed to assemble to avoid the assault of enemies.

3. *De Bello Gallico* v, 22, 1

While these things are going on in these parts, Cassivellaunus sends messengers to *Cantium*, which we have said above is on the sea and over which there were four kings, Cingetorix, Carvilius, Taximagulus and Segovax.

Other references:

Britanni: *De Bello Gallico* IV, 21, 5.

Britannia: *De Bello Civili* I, 54, 1; *De Bello Gallico* II, 4, 7; 14, 3; III, 8, 1; 9, 9; IV, 20, 1; 21, 3; 22, 5; 23, 2; 27, 2; 28, 1, 2; 30, 1, 2; 37, 1; 38, 1, 4; V, 2, 3; 6, 5; 8, 2; 22, 4; VI, 13, 11; VII, 76, 1.

Tamesis: *De Bello Gallico* V, 18, 1 (*Tamesim*, acc.).

Trinobantes: *De Bello Gallico* V, 20, 1.

Text: ed. R. du Pontet, Oxford, 1900 & 1901.

CASSIODORUS, Flavius Magnus Aurelianus (*fl.* A.D. 519)

References:

Brittanni: *Chronica* A.U.C. 654 (A.D. 44) (variant *Prittannis*); A.U.C. 886 (A.D. 207).

Brittannia: A.U.C. 893 (A.D. 211) (variant *Brittania*).

Eboracum: A.U.C. 893 (A.D. 211).

Orcades: A.U.C. 654 (A.D. 44) (*Orcadas*, acc., added to the Roman Empire by Claudius).

Text: *MGH* (*AA*) XI, ed. Th. Mommsen, Berlin, 1894, repr. 1961.

CASSIUS DIO COCCEIANUS (*c.* A.D. 160–230)

(see also XIPHILINUS)

1. *Historiae Romanae* LX, 20, 1–2

Plautius then had great trouble in seeking them out, but when he found them (for they were not autonomous but subject to other kings), he defeated first Caratacus and then Togodumnus, the sons of Cunobellinus; for he himself had died. When they had fled, a section of the *Bodunni* (μέρος τι τῶν Βοδούννων), over whom they, being *Catuellani* (Κατουελλανοί), ruled, made peace; and thereupon leaving a garrison he marched forward. So they came to a certain river, which the barbarians did not think the Romans would be able to cross without a bridge...

2. *Historiae Romanae* LX, 21, 3–4

Having crossed to *Brettania* he (sc. Claudius) joined the forces which were waiting for him at the *Tamesa* (πρὸς τῷ Ταμέσᾳ, masc. dat.). Taking over command, he crossed it and coming to grips with the forces assembled to oppose him he defeated them and captured *Camulodunum* (Καμουλόδουνον, acc.), the royal seat of Cunobellinus.

Other references:

Βρεττανία: XXXIX, 1, 2; 50, 1; 53, 1; XL, 1, 2; 4, 2; XLI, 30, 2; XLIV, 42, 3; 43, 1; 49, 1; XLIX, 38, 2; L, 24, 4; LIII, 22, 5; 25, 2; LV, 23, 2, 3 and 6; LIX, 21, 3; 25, 1; LX, 19, 1; 22, 1; 23, 1 (bis).

Βρεττανικός: LIII, 12, 6 (ὠκεανός); LX, 23, 6 (τα βρεττανικὰ).

Βρεττανοί: XXXIX, 51, 1; XLI, 32, 2; 34, 3; LIII, 7, 1; LX, 19, 5; 20, 5; 21, 1.

Ταμέσα (masc.): XL, 31 (Ταμέσαν, acc.); LX, 2, 5 (Ταμέσαν, acc.).

Text: ed. U. P. Boissevain, Berlin, 1895–1931, repr. 1955.

CATULLUS, C. Valerius (84–54 B.C.)

References:

Britanni: *Carm.* xi, 12 (*ultimosque Britannos*).

Britannia (sing.): *Carm.* xxix, 4 (*ultima Britannia*).

Britanniae (plur.): *Carm.* xxix, 20, xlv, 22.

Text: ed. R. A. B. Mynors, Oxford, 1958.

CHRONICA GALLICA of A.D. 452 and 511

References:

Britannia/Brittania: A. 452, *pars posterior*, 6 (*Brittania*, variants *Britania*, *Britannia*); A. 511, 62 (*Britanniae*, plur., variants *Brittaniae*, *Britaniae*); 126 (*Brittanniae*, plur., variants *Britanniae*, *Brittaniae*).

Picti: A. 452, *pars posterior*, 7.

Scotti: A. 452, *pars posterior*, 7.

Text: *MGH* (*AA*) IX, ed. Th. Mommsen, Berlin, 1892, repr. 1961.

CICERO, M. Tullius (106–43 B.C.)

References:

Britannia: *Ad Fam.* VII, vi, 2; vii, 1, 2; x, 1; xiv, 1; xvi, 1; xvii, 3; *Ad Att.* IV, xv, 10; xviii, 5; *Ad Q. Frat.* II, xiv, 2; xvi, 4; III, i, 4; *De Nat. Deor.* II, 34 (88).
Britannicus: *Ad Fam.* VII, viii, 2; xi, 2; *Ad Att.* IV, xvi, 7; *Ad Q. Frat.* III, i, 3, 7; *De Nat. Deor.* III, 10 (24).

Texts: *Ad Fam.* ed. L. C. Purser, Oxford, 1952.
Ad Att. ed. W. S. Watt, Oxford, 1965.
Ad Q. Frat. ed. W. S. Watt, Oxford, 1958.
De Nat. Deor. ed. A. S. Pease, Cambridge, Mass., 1955.

CLAUDIANUS, Claudius (d. *c.* A.D. 404)

References:

Britanni: *Carmina* V, 149; XV, 19; XXIV, 149; XXVI, 416.
Britannia: III, 131, XVIII, 393; VIII, 73; XVII, 51; XXII, 247; XXVI, 568.
Britannus (adj.); VIII, 28 (*litus*); XXIV, 301 (*canes*); *Carmina Minora* XXX, 40 (*oceanus*).
Caledonius (adj.): *Carmina* VIII, 26 (*pruinae*); XXII, 247 (*monstrum*); *Carmina Minora* XXX, 45 (*exuviae*).
Hiverne (variant *Ierne*): *Carmina* VIII, 33; XXII, 251.
Picti: XVIII, 393 (sing.); VII, 54; VIII, 32; XXII, 254 (sing.); XXVI, 418 (sing.).
Scotti (variant *Scoti*): VII, 55 (sing.); VIII, 33; XXII, 251 (sing.); XXVI, 417 (sing.); *Carmina Minora* XXV, 90 (sing.).
Scotticus (variant *Scoticus*): *Carmina* XXII, 254 (*tela*).
Thyle (variant *Thule*): V, 240 (*Thylen*, acc.); VII, 53; VIII, 32; XXIV, 156 (*Thylen*, acc.); XXVI, 204 (*Thylen*, acc.).

Texts: ed. J. Koch, Leipzig, 1893 and V. Crépin, Paris, 1933.

CODEX IUSTINIANUS (A.D. 534)

Reference:

Eboracum: III, 32, 1 (*Eboraci*, loc.).

Text: ed. P. Krueger, Berlin, 1895.

CODEX THEODOSIANUS (A.D. 438)

Reference:

Britanniae: XI, 7, 2.

Text: edd. Th. Mommsen and P. Krueger, Berlin, 1904.

DIGESTA (A.D. 533)

References:

Britannia: XXVIII, 6, 2.
Britannicus (adj.): XXXVI, 1, 48 (46) (*classis*).

Text: ed. Th. Mommsen, Berlin, 1902.

DIMENSURATIO PROVINCIARUM (=EPITOME TOTIUS ORBIS) (*c.* A.D. 400)

Chap. 30.
Britannia (variant *Rittania*) is bounded on the east (and the west) by the ocean, on the south by the *Oceanus Atlanticus*, on the north by the *Oceanus Britannicus* (variant *Brittannicus*). In length it extends 800 (variant 700) miles, in breadth 300 miles.

Text: *Geographi Latini Minores*, ed. A. Riese, Berlin, 1878, rep. Hildesheim, 1964.

DIODORUS SICULUS (*fl.* 30 B.C.)

1. *History* v, 21–22
Opposite maritime Gaul and across from the forests called Hercynian, which we are told are the largest in Europe, there are many islands in the ocean, of which the largest is that called *Prettanike* (Πρεττανική, variant Βρεττανική). Anciently this was unvisited by foreign forces, for we are told that neither Dionysus nor Heracles nor any of the other heroes made an expedition to it; but in our time Gaius Caesar, who was called a god because of his deeds, became the first of those recorded to have conquered the island, and after subduing the *Prettanoi* (Πρεττανούς, variant Βρεττανούς, acc.) he forced them to pay a fixed tribute. But we shall write of the events of this in detail at their proper time; now, we shall discuss the island and the tin which is found in it.

The island itself is triangular in shape, very like Sicily, but its sides are not equal. It stretches obliquely along the side of Europe and the point which is least distance from the continent is the promontory (ἀκρωτήριον) which they call *Kantion* (Κάντιον) and say it is about 100 stades from the land, where the sea makes its outlet; another promontory, called *Belerion* (Βελέριον), is said to be distant four days' sailing from the continent; the last, they say, extends into the sea and is called *Orkas* (Ὄρκαν, acc.). It is said that of its sides the shortest, lying beside Europe, is 7,500 stades, the second, from the strait to the pointed top, is 15,000 stades, and the other is 20,000 stades, so that the whole perimeter of the island is 42,500 stades. They say that *Prettanike* is inhabited by autochthonous tribes and that they maintain in their dealings the ancient way of life. For they use chariots in war, just as the ancient heroes of the Greeks are said to have done in the Trojan War, and they have simple houses, mostly built of reeds and logs. They gather their grain crops by cutting off only the ears and store them in roofed (var. underground) dwellings; from these they pick out the old ears daily and grind them for food. They are simple in their habits and far removed from the cunning and vice of modern men. Their way of life is modest and they are free of the luxury which is begotten of wealth. The island is thickly populated and the climate is very cold, as it would be for a region lying under the Bear itself. Many kings and rulers hold it, and for the most part they live at peace with one another.

But we shall give an account of the customs of the island and its other peculiarities when we come to the expedition of Caesar to *Brettania* (Βρεττανίαν, acc., with initial B in all MSS; the passage referred to does not survive); here we shall discuss the tin which is produced in it. The inhabitants of *Prettanike* who dwell near the promontory called *Belerion* (κατὰ τὸ ἀκρωτήριον τὸ καλούμενον Βελέριον) are especially friendly to strangers and, because of their intercourse with foreign merchants, civilised in their dealings. These people prepare the tin, treating the earth which bears it skilfully. This, while rocky, has earthy layers in which they work the ore and purify it by smelting. Then they hammer it into the form of astragali and convey it to an island lying near *Prettanike* called *Iktis* (Ἶκτιν, acc.); for the area between being dry at ebb tide, they convey the tin in large quantities to it in wagons. And a peculiar thing happens concerning the neighbouring islands lying between Europe and *Prettanike*: for at flood tide the passage between them is full and they appear as islands, but at ebb tide, when the sea flows back and leaves a large area dry, they are seen as peninsulas. From there the merchants buy the tin from the natives and carry it across to Gaul. Finally, travelling on foot across Gaul for about 30 days, they bring their load on horseback to the mouth of the Rhône.

2. *History* V, 32, 3

And they say that some of them (sc. the Gauls of the north east) eat men, just as those of the *Prettanoi* (Πρεττανῶν, gen.) do who inhabit the (island) called *Iris* (Ἶριν, acc.).

3. *History*, V, 38, 4–5

For above the country of the Lusitani there are many mines of tin, and on the islets which lie near Iberia in the ocean, and because of this are named *Cattiterides* (Καττιτερίδας, acc.). Much tin is also conveyed from the *Prettanic* island to Gaul, lying opposite, and is brought on horses by merchants through the interior of Gaul both to the Massaliotes and to the city named Narbo.

Texts: ed. C. H. Oldfather, London and Cambridge, Mass., 1939.
ed. F. Vogel, Leipzig, 1890 (repr. Stuttgart, 1964).

DIONYSIUS PERIEGETES (*c.* A.D. 125)

(with Commentary by EUSTATHIUS, 12th cent. A.D.)

1. *Orbis Descriptio*, 283–85

Where in the north the cold stream of ocean flows, there dwell the *Bretanoi* (Βρετανοί) and the fair tribes of the fierce Germans. (*Eustathius*: *Brettanoi* (Βρεττανοί) is usually spelt with a double -t-, but in this place he drops one t for the sake of the metre).

2. *Orbis Descriptio*, 561–69

Beneath the Sacred Promontory, which they call the head of Europe, the wealthy sons of the noble Iberians inhabit the Hesperides islands, from which comes tin. But by the northern shores of Ocean are two other islands, the *Bretanides* (Βρετανίδες), opposite the Rhine, for there it pours its final flood into the sea. Great is their size, nor does any of the islands equal the *Bretanides* in extent. (*Eustathius*: 561. At the Sacred Promontory...are ten Cassiterides (Κασσιτερίδες) islands, near to each other and lying towards the north, which Dionysius calls Hesperides, because of their position; for they are in the west. 566. To the north where the Rhine pours its final flood into the ocean, are the two *Bretanides* islands, *Ivernia* ('Ιουερνία) and *Alvion* ('Αλουίων), or *Ibernia* ('Ιβερνία) and *Albion* ('Αλβίων); *Bretanides* is written with one -t- by this poet. 568. Not only Dionysius stresses the size of the *Brettanides* islands, which others, as has been said, call *Prettanides* (Πρεττανίδας, acc.) with a P, but also Ptolemy in his Geography (the reference back here is to his comment on Ambracia in line 492: 'But there are some who, following the older usage, write Ambrax with a p and call the region Ampracia; similarly they write the *Brettanic* islands as *Prettanic* (Πρεττανικάς, acc.); but the spelling with B is more common').

3. *Orbis Descriptio*, 580–83

But cutting a way much further through the Ocean you would come in your well-built ship to the island of Thule (Θούλην, acc.), where when the sun enters the region of the bears its fire is always visible day and night alike.

Text: *Geographi Graeci Minores*, ed. K. Müller, Paris, 1861, repr. Hildesheim, 1965.

DIOSCORIDES PEDANIUS (1st cent. A.D.)

References:

Βρεττανία: *Materia Medica* II, lxxxviii.
Βρεττανική: *Materia Medica* IV, ii, 1.

Text: ed. M. Wellmann, 1907–14, repr. Berlin, 1958.

DIVISIO ORBIS TERRARUM (*c.* A.D. 400)

Reference:

Insulae Britannicae (variant *Britanicae*): 7.

Text: *Geographi Latini Minores*, ed. A. Riese, Berlin, 1878, repr. Hildesheim 1964.

EUMENIUS (*fl.* A.D. 297): see PANEGYRICI LATINI

EUNAPIUS SARDIANUS (*c.* A.D. 345–420)

Reference:

ἡ Βρεττανικὴ νῆσος: *Historia*, frag. 12.

Text: *Fragmenta Historicorum Graecorum* IV, ed. C. Müller, Paris, 1928.

EUSEBIUS CAESARIENSIS (*c.* A.D. 260–340)

References:

Βρεττανία: *De Vita Constantini* III, 19.
Βρεττανοί: I, 8; 25; IV, 50.
Text: ed. I. A. Heikel, Leipzig, 1902.

EUSTATHIUS (12th cent. A.D.): see DIONYSIUS PERIEGETES

EUTROPIUS (*fl.* A.D. 365)

(with Greek paraphrase by PAEANIUS, late 4th cent. A.D.)
Breviarium ab Urbe Condita VII, 13, 3.

He (Claudius) added to the Roman Empire certain islands situated in the ocean beyond the *Britanniae* (*Britannias*, acc., variant *Brittanniam*: Greek Βρεττανούς, acc.) which are called *Orchades* (Greek 'Ορχάδες).

Other references:

Βέκτη (= Isle of Wight): *Breviarium* VII, 19, 1 (Βέκτην, acc.).
Βρεττανία: X, 2, 2.
Βρεττανικός: VII, 14, 4 (πόλεις); 19, 1 (νῆσοι); IX, 21, 1 (πόλεις); 22, 2 (abs.); X, 1, 3 (πόλις).
Βρεττανοί: VI, 17, 4; VII, 13, 2; 19, 1; VIII, 19, 1; IX, 22, 2.
Βρεττανός (adj.): VI, 17, 2 (νῆσοι).
Britanni/Brittani: VI, 17, 4 (*Brittani*); VII, 13, 2 (*Britanni*).
Britannia: VII, 13, 3 (plur. variant *Brittania*); 14, 4; 19, 1 (bis); VIII, 19, 1; IX, 21, 1; 22, 1 (plur.); 22, 2 (plur. bis); X, 1, 3 (variant *Brittani*); 2, 2.
Brittanicus (adj.): VI, 17, 2 (*oceanus*).
Eboracum: VIII, 19, 1 (*Eboraci*, loc., variants *Euoraci*, *Aeuoraci*, *Etuoraci*, *Teuoraci*); X, 1, 3 (*Eboraci*, loc., variant *Euoraci*).
'Εβοράκον: VIII, 19 1 ('Εβοράκῳ, dat.); X, 1, 3 ('Εβοράκῳ, dat., variant Κορακίῳ).

Text: *MGH* (*AA*) IV, ed. H. Droysen, Berlin, 1879, repr. 1961.

EXPOSITIO TOTIUS MUNDI ET GENTIUM (*c.* A.D. 350)

68 (the last entry): Then there is another island which is called *Britannia*, indeed the greatest, as those who have been there tell, and outstanding among them all.

Text: *Geographi Latini Minores*, ed. A. Riese, Berlin, 1878, repr. Hildesheim, 1964.

EXCERPTA VALESIANA (*c.* A.D. 390)

References:

Britannia: I (= *Origo Constantini Imperatoris*), 3, 6.
Eboracum: I, 2, 4 (*Eboraci*, loc.).

Text: *MGH* (*AA*) IX, ed. Th. Mommsen, Berlin, 1892, repr. 1961.

FESTUS, Rufius (*fl.* A.D. 365)

Breviarium, 6.

There are in Gaul with Aquitania and the *Britanniae* (variants *Britaniae*, *Brittanniae*, *Pritanniae*) 18 provinces...in *Britannia* are *Maxima Caesariensis*, *Flavia*, *Britannia Prima*, *Britannia Secunda*.

Other references:

Britannia (variants *Britania*, *Pritannia*): *Breviarium*, 3 (plural); 6 (bis, singular and plural).

Text: ed. J. W. Eadie, London, 1967.

FIRMICUS MATERNUS, Julius (*fl.* A.D. 335–350)

Reference:

Britannus (coll.): *De Errore Profanarum Religionum*, 29.

Text: ed. K. Ziegler, Stuttgart, 1953.

'FLAVIUS VOPISCUS': see HISTORIA AUGUSTA

FLORUS, L. Annaeus (*fl.* A.D. 120)

Epitomae de Tito Livio I, 45 (III, 10, 18)

So having returned to Gaul, he (sc. Julius Caesar) crossed the same ocean and attacked the same *Britanni* with a larger fleet and increased forces. Having pursued them to the *Caledonian* woods (*Caledonias in silvas*) he also took captive one of their kings, Cassuellaunus.

Other references:

Britanni: *Epit. de T. Livio* I, 45 (III, 10, 2: *toto orbe divisi Britanni*); I, 47 (III, 12, 4); *Poemata* i, 2.

Caledonius (adj.): *Epit. de T. Livo* I, 12 (I, 17, 3: *saltus Caledonius*).

Text: ed. H. Malcovati, Rome, 1972.

FRONTO, M. Cornelius (*fl.* A.D. 100–106)

Reference:

Britanni: *De Bello Parthico* 2 (A. 235).

Text: ed. M. P. J. van der Hout, Leiden, 1954.

GENNADIUS (5th cent. A.D.)

References:

Britanni: *De Scriptoribus Ecclesiasticis* 56 (Fastidius as *Britannorum episcopus*: Corbie MS has *Britto*).

Britto: *De Scriptoribus Ecclesiasticis* (of Pelagius, Corbie MS only).

Text: *Migne*, Ser. Lat. LVIII, Paris, 1844, repr. Turnhout 1967.

GILDAS SAPIENS (*c.* A.D. 540)

1. *De Excidio et Conquestu Britanniae*, 3

Brittannia is an island situated in almost the furthest bound of the world towards the west-north-west and west, poised, as is said, in the divine balance which holds the whole earth, stretched out from the south-west towards the north pole. It is 800 miles long, 200 broad, leaving out the more extended tracts of various promontories which are encompassed by the bowed gulfs of the sea. It is protected on all sides by the wide and, so to say, impassable circle of the sea, and by the strait of the southern shore over which men sail to Gallia Belgica, and improved, as it were with arms, by the mouths of two noble rivers, *Tamesis* (gen., variant *Tamensis*) and *Sabrina* (*Sabrinae*, gen.), up which foreign luxuries were long ago brought to it in ships, and of other smaller rivers. It is adorned by twice ten and twice four cities (*civitatibus*) and some forts (*castellis*), with great works, well-built, of walls, serrated towers, gates and houses, whose roofs, stretching up with threatening height, were firmly fixed in strong building...

2. *De Excidio et Conquestu Britanniae*, 10–11
God, therefore, wishing that all men should be saved and calling sinners no less than those who think themselves righteous, magnified his mercy with us and of His free gift, at the time above mentioned (sc. of Diocletian), as we conjecture, lest *Britannia* should be utterly enveloped in the thick fog of black night, He lit for us the most bright lamps of holy martyrs, the graves of whose bodies and the places of whose passion, if they had not been taken from the citizens through the sad division of the barbarians because of our many crimes, would now greatly inspire the minds of those who gazed on them with the ardour of divine grace. I speak of Alban of *Verolamium* (*Verolamiensem*, acc., variants *Verolamensem*, *Verulamiensem*, *Urelamensem*, *Vellamiensem*, *Vellomiensem*, *Vellovensis*, *Verolamius*), Aaron and Iulius, citizens of *Urbs Legionum* and others of both sexes who stood firm with the greatest nobility in the battle-line of Christ. The former of these when he had, for love – in this imitating Christ who laid down His life for his sheep – concealed in his home a confessor who was pursued by his persecutors and on the point of being captured and then having changed clothes with him he freely surrendered himself to be persecuted in the clothes of the above-mentioned brother. So between his holy confession and his execution among the impious men who bore the Roman standards with horrible thoughts he was pleasing to God and marvellously adorned with miracles, so that by fervent prayer he opened an unknown way across the bed of the noble river *Tamesis*, like the dry and ill-trodden way of the Israelites, when for long the ark of the covenant stood on the gravel in the midst of Jordan...

Other references:
Britanni: *De Excidio*, 6; 20.
Britannia: 1; 4; 7; 14; 21; 27; 35; 66.
Brittannia: 33; 37.
Damnonia: 28 (*Damnoniae*, gen., variants *Damnone*, *Dannoniae*, *Domnanie*).
Demetae: 31 (*Demetarum*, gen.).
Hiberni: 21 (variant *Hyberni*).
Picti: 14; 19; 21.
Scoti: 14, 19 (variant *Scotti*).

Text: *MGH* (*AA*) XIII, ed. Th. Mommsen, Berlin, 1898, reprinted 1961.

GRATTIUS 'FALISCUS' (late 1st cent. B.C.)

References:

Britanni: *Cynegetica*, 175.
Britannus (adj.): *Cynegetica*, 178 (*catulis Britannis*).

Text: *Minor Latin Poets*, edd. J. W. and A. M. Duff, London and Cambridge, Mass., 1935.

HEGESIPPUS (attrib.) (? 5th cent. A.D.)

References:

Brittania (variants, *Brittannia, Britania, Britthania, Britannia*): *Historiae* II, 9, 1 (bis): III, 1, 2; II, 29, 2 (plur.); V, 15, 1 (plur.); V, 46, 1 (bis, sing. and plur.).
Brittani (variants *Brittanni, Britthani*): II, 9, 1.
Scothia (variants *Scotia, Scotthia*): V, 15, 1.

Text: ed. V. Usani, Vienna and Leipzig, 1932.

HERODIANUS (*fl.* A.D. 235)

References:

Βρεττανία: II, 15, 1; 15, 5; III, 7, 1; 8, 2; 14, 1; 14, 2.
Βρεττανοί: III, 7, 2; 7, 3; 14, 2; 14, 3; 14, 4; 14, 5; 14, 6.

Texts: ed. C. Stavenhagen, Leipzig, 1922; ed. C. R. Whittaker, London and Cambridge, Mass., 1969–1970.

HERODOTUS (*c.* 485–420 B.C.)

Historiae III, 115

For I do not accept that there is a river called Eridanos by the barbarians which flows into the sea towards the north wind, from which they say amber comes, nor do I know that there are *Cassiterides* (Κασσιτερίδας, acc.) islands from which tin comes to us. For it is clear that the name Eridanos is Greek, not barbarian, invented by some poet, and although I have studied the matter I have never been able to hear from an eye-witness that there is a sea on that side of Europe; but tin and amber do come to us from the furthest parts.

Text: ed. C. Hude, Oxford, 1927.

HIERONYMUS, Eusebius (St Jerome) (*c.* A.D. 348–420)

References:

Atticotti: *Epistolae* 69 (= 82, p. 415); *Adversus Iovinianum* II (p. 335: gens *Britannica*, variant *Scoti*).
Britanni: *Comm. in Jeremiah* III, prolog. (p. 924); *Interpretatio Chronicae Eusebii*, A.D. 46; A.D. 207.
Britannia: *Epistolae* 60 (= 35, p. 333); 133 (= 43, p. 1038); 58 (= 49, p. 321); 77 (= 84, p. 466); 146 (= 101, p. 1082, plur.); *Interpretatio Chronicae Eusebii*, A.D. 212; A.D. 291 (plur.); A.D. 300 (plur.); A.D. 309; A.D. 375, '*Homilia IV Origen in Ezechielem* (p. 917).
Britannus (coll.): *Epistolae* 46 (= 44, p. 206: *divisus ab orbe nostro*).
Eboracum: *Interpretatio Chronicae Eusebii*, A.D. 212; A.D. 309. (*Eboraci*, loc.)
Orchades: *Interpretatio Chronicae Eusebii*, A.D. 46 (*Orchadas*, acc., added to Roman Empire by Claudius).

Scoti (variant *Scotti*): *Epistolae* 69 (= 82, p. 415); *Adversus Iovinianum* II (p. 335); *Comm. in Jeremiah* I, prolog. (p. 835).
Scoticus (adj.): *Epistolae* 133 (= 43, para. 1038: *gentes*); *Comm. in Jeremiah* III, Prolog. (p. 924, *gens*).

Texts: *Migne*, Ser. Lat. XXII, XXIII, XXV, XXIX, XXVII, Paris, 1845, repr. Turnhout 1969.

HISTORIA AUGUSTA (late 4th cent.)

1. *Severus Alexander*, 59, 6

Then when he was operating with a few men in *Brittannia*, or as others have it in Gaul, in a *vicus* called *Sicilia*. . . some soldiers killed him.[1]

2. *Tacitus*, 15, 2. (= *Florian*, 2, 2)

Then a reply was given by the soothsayers that at some time there would be a Roman emperor from their family, whether by female or male descent, who would give judges to the Parthians and Persians, control the Franks and Alamanni under Roman laws, not leave one barbarian in Africa, impose a governor on Ceylon, send a proconsul to the island of *Iuverna*,[2] judge all the Sarmatians, conquer all peoples and make the whole world which is surrounded by Ocean his own.

Other references:[3]
Brittanni: *Hadrian* 5, 16; *Pius* 5; *Marcus* 8; *Commodus* 8; *Severus* 23; *Gordiani* 3; *Firmus, Saturninus, Proculus & Bonosus* 14.
Brittania: *Hadrian* 11; 12; *Commodus* 13; *Pertinax* 2; *Albinus* 13 (plur.).
Brittannia:[4] *Pertinax* 3 (bis); *Severus* 6 (plur.); 18; 19 (bis); 22; 24; *Probus* 18 (plur., bis); *Carus, Carinus & Numerian* 16 (plur.).
Brittanicus: *Marcus* 8 (*bellum*); 22 (*bellum*).
Brittannicus: *Commodus* 6 (*bellum*); 8 (title); *Didius Julianus* 5 (*exercitus*); *Severus* 18 (title); *Albinus* 13 (*exercitus*).
Eboracum: *Severus* 19 (*Eboraci*, loc.).

Text: ed. E. Hohl, Leipzig, 1965.

HORATIUS FLACCUS, Q. (65–8 B.C.)

References:

Britanni: *Carm.* I, xxi, 15; xxxv, 30 (*in ultimos orbis Britannos*); III, iv, 33; v, 3 (*adiectis Britannis*); IV, xiv, 48.

[1] Cf. Aurelius Victor, *Liber de Caesaribus* 24, 4, which is probably the source of this passage.

[2] The text reads *ad Romanam insulam*, which is plainly wrong. *Iuvernam* is the conjecture of L. C. Purser, accepted by Hohl and others.

[3] We do not accept H. Peter's amendment of *Severus* 22, 4 (*Post murum apud Luguvallum visum* for the text's *Post Maurum apud vallum missum*).

[4] The variation in spelling (*Brittania, Brittannia; Brittanicus, Brittannicus*) is curious and, if not due to careless copying, may represent a deliberate attempt at archaism. The distribution of the different forms corresponds neither with the date of the subject matter nor with the alleged division of the lives between different authors.

Britannus (coll.): *Epod.* vii, 7 (*Britannus catenatus*).

Text: edd. E. C. Wickham and H. W. Garrod, Oxford, 1912.

ISIDORUS HISPALENSIS (*fl.* A.D. 620)

1. *Etymologiae* IX, 2, 102 (414)

Some suppose that the *Britones* are so called because they are brutes (*bruti*) – a people situated in the ocean, with sea between, as it were outside the world, of whom Virgil wrote 'the *Britanni* a world apart.'

2. *Etymologiae* XIV, 6, 2–6 (170–171)

Britannia, an island of the ocean, separated from the whole world by the sea between, is so called from the name of its people. It lies on the further side of Gaul, looking toward Spain. Its circuit is 4,875 miles. There are many great rivers in it, hot springs, and a large and varied quantity of metals. Jet especially occurs there, and pearls.

Thanatos, an island of the ocean in the *Fretum Gallicum*, separated from *Britannia* by a narrow estuary, has corn-growing plains and a rich soil. It is called *Thanatos* from the death (Greek *thanatos*) of serpents; for while it has none of its own, soil taken from it to any place whatsoever kills snakes there.

Thyle is the furthest island of the ocean beyond the shore of *Britannia* to the north west. It takes its name from the sun (*a sole*), because in it the sun makes its summer solstice and beyond it there is no day, whence it happens that its sea is sluggish and hard.

The *Orchades*, islands of the ocean, are placed beyond *Britannia*, 33 in number, of which 20 are unoccupied and 13 inhabited.

Scotia is the same as *Hibernia*, an island next to *Britannia*, smaller than it in size but more fertile in its situation. It stretches from south west to north and its nearer parts look towards Iberia and the Cantabric Ocean, whence it is called *Hibernia*...

Text: *Migne*, Ser. Lat. LXXXII, Paris, 1844, repr. Turnhout, 1969.

JOHANNES CHRYSOSTOMUS (*c.* A.D. 354–407)

References:

Βρετανοί: *In Pentecosten Sermo* I (LI, p. 808: wrongly attributed).

αἱ νῆσοι Βρεττανικαί: *De Incomprehensibili Natura Dei* II, 4 (XLVII, p. 714); *Contra Iudaeos* 12 (XLVII, p. 380).

Text: *Migne*, Ser. Graec. XLVII and LI, Paris, 1862–63.

JORDANES (*fl*, A.D. 550)

Getica I, 8–II, 15

But it (the ocean) contains other islands in its inner stream which are called the Baleares, and it contains also another, *Mevania* (variant *Evania*), and too the *Orcades* (*Orcadas*, acc.), 33 in number though not all inhabited, and it contains at the furthest part of the western shore another island, *Thyle* by name, of which the Mantuan wrote

'May furthest *Thyle* be your servant.' That immense sea also contains in its arctic, that is its northern, part a large island called *Scandza*, where, with God's help, our story will begin, since the race whose origin you seek came from the bosom of this island, like a swarm of bees spreading over the land of Europe; but how and in what manner we have, God willing, set out in what follows. But now I will, so far as I can, dispose in a few words of the island of *Brittania*, which lies in a gulf of the ocean between the Spains, the Gauls and Germany. Regarding its size no one in olden times, as Livy tells us, sailed round it, but different opinions were voiced by many in speaking of it. . . (He then explains how Julius Caesar opened it up and quotes Strabo and Mela on its size and shape, Tacitus on the *Silures* (here *Silores*) and the inhabitants of *Caledonia* (here *Calydonia*) and Cassius Dio on the *Maeatae* (here *Meatae*) and *Caledonii* (here *Calydonii*)) . . . Let it suffice to have said these few words about the nature of the island of *Brittania*.

Other references:
Brittania: *Romana*, 260 (bis); 297 (plur.); 308.
Brittanicus (adj.): *Romana*, 276 (*bellum*).
Brittones: *Romana*, 249 (variant *Britiones*, referring to Britons): *Getica*, XLV, 237 (referring to Bretons of Armorica).
Orcades: *Romana*, 260 (as added to the Roman Empire by Claudius).

Text: *MGH* (*AA*) V, ed. Th. Mommsen, Berlin, 1882, repr. 1961.

JOSEPHUS, Flavius (A.D. 37–*c.* 100)

References:

Βρεττανία: *De Bello. Iud.* III, 4; VII, 82.
Βρεττανοί: *De Bello Iud.* II, 363, 378; VI, 331.

Text: ed. B. Niese, Berlin, 1889.

JULIANUS, Flavius Claudius (Augustus A.D. 360–63)

Epistolae 7 (403 C–D)
To Alypius: It happened that I had already recovered from my illness when you sent the geography (γεωγραφίαν); none the less I was glad to receive the map (πινάκιον) sent by you. For not only does it include drawings (διαγράμματα) better than any hitherto, but you have also embellished it by adding iambic verses not, like the poet of Cyrene, to sing the war of Bupalus, but such as fair Sappho likes to fashion for her thoughts.[1]

Other references:
ἡ Βρεττανίς (variant Βρετανίς): *Epistola ad. S.P.Q.Atheniensium*, 279D.
αἱ Βρεττανίαι: 283A.

[1] This may refer to a map of Britain. Alypius of Antioch was at one time *Vicarius Britanniarum* (Ammianus XXIII, 1, 3, and XXIX, 1, 44) and in the latter part of the letter Julian congratulates him on his good administration, but in the preceding letter he had summoned him to Gaul. He later put him in charge of the projected restoration of the Temple at Jerusalem.

Texts: ed. F. C. Hertlein, Leipzig, 1875, and ed. W. C. Wright, London and New York, 1923.

'JULIUS CAPITOLINUS': see HISTORIA AUGUSTA

JULIUS HONORIUS (?5th cent. A.D.)

Cosmographia 15–18

The western ocean contains these seas. The sea of the strait of Gades, the sea which they call *Orcades*, the *Mare...mades*, the *Mare Thyle*, the sea which they call the Columns of Hercules, the Tyrrhenian Sea, the *Mare Britannicum*, the Adriatic Sea.

What islands there are in the western ocean and how many.

Hibero island, *Mevania* (variants *Mebania*, *Meubania*) island. *Britannia* (variants *Brittania*, *Bruttania*, *Brutannia*) island, *Ebusos* (variants *Ebuso*, *Ebusis*) island, Balearis Major island, Balearis Minor island, Corsica island, *Orcades* islands. They are nine.

Mountains which the western ocean contains. The Pyrenean mountain, the mountain of the Alps, *Montes II*, the *vallum* (variants *balum*, *ballum*) of *Britannia*, Haemus mountain, Rhodope mountain. (Note: Possibly mountain, but at 42 he has '*mons Pyramides*' in Egypt!).

Provinces which the western ocean contains...*Britannia*...

Text: *Geographi Latini Minores*, ed. A. Riese, Berlin, 1878, repr. Hildesheim, 1964.

JUVENALIS, D. Junius (*fl.* A.D. 105)

Brigantes: *Sat.* XIV, 196 (*castella Brigantum*).
Britanni: II, 161; XV, 111.
Britannicus: X, 14 (*ballaena Britannica*).
Britannus (adj.): IV, 126.
Brittones: XV, 124.
Iuverna: II, 160.
Orcades: II, 161.
Rutupinus: IV, 141 (*Rutupino edita fundo ostrea*).
Thyle: XV, 112.

Text: ed. W. V. Clausen, Oxford, 1959.

LIBANIUS (A.D. 314–*c.* 393)

References:

Βρεττανία: *Laudatio Constantini et Constantis*, 135; 141.

Text: ed. R. Foerster, Leipzig, 1908, repr. Hildesheim, 1963.

LUCANUS, M. Annaeus (A.D. 39–65)

References:

Britanni: *Pharsalia* II, 572; III, 78; VI, 68.
Britannus (coll.): IV, 134.

Caledonii: VI, 68.
Rutupinus: VI, 67 (*Rutupina litora*).

Text: ed. A. E. Housman, Oxford, 1927.

LUCRETIUS CARUS, T. (94–55 B.C.)

Reference:

Brittanni: *De Rer. Nat.* VI, 1106.

Text: ed. C. Bailey, Oxford, 1922.

MARCIANUS HERACLEENSIS (? *c.* A.D. 400)

1. *Periplus Maris Exteri* I, 8

Of the largest islands and peninsulas, of the first order, the first is the island of Trapobane (i.e. Ceylon), formerly called Palaesimundu but now Salike; the second is *Albion* of the *Brettanic* Islands (τῶν Βρεττανικῶν ἡ 'Αλβίων), the third is the Golden Chersonese, the fourth *Ivernia* of the *Brettanic* Islands (τῶν Βρεττανικῶν ἡ 'Ιουερνία), the fifth the Peloponnese... (for the spelling of *Brettanic* with initial B. see note below).

2. *Periplus Maris Exteri* II, 41–45

Concerning the *Pretannic* (Πρεττανικῶν, gen.) *Islands.*

The Prettanic Islands are two, the one called *Albion*, the other *Ivernia. Albion* is much the greater: it lies opposite Gaul, beside Lugdunensis and Belgica, stretching as far as Great Germany. For it is not compact, as other islands are, but as it were disjointed and distended and stretches through the greatest part of the northern (ἀρκτῴου, gen.) ocean, having two very long isthmuses, like a sort of feet. Of these the larger stretches to [the Cimbric Chersonese?], the smaller to Aquitania. The other island, *Ivernia*, lies above it, further to the west; it is smaller in size and has the same situation as the aforesaid. Of this, then, we shall first describe the periplus and then go on to the larger island.

Periplus of the Prettanic Island Ivernia

The *Prettanic* island of *Ivernia* is bounded on the north by the Ocean which is called *Hyperboreus* ('Υπερβορείῳ, dat.); on the east by that called *Ivernicus* ('Ιουερνικῷ, dat.); on the west by the Western (Δυτικῷ, dat.); and on the south by the Ocean called *Veguius* (Οὐεγουίῳ, dat. MSS: ?recte Οὐεργιουίῳ, *Vergivius*). And the whole arrangement of the island is like this...[lacuna, presumably including the *Aebudae* quoted from Marcian by Stephanus, q.v.]. The greatest length of the *Prettanic* island *Ivernia*, beginning from *Notium* Promontory (τοῦ Νοτίου ἀκρωτηρίου, gen.) and ending at *Rhobondium* Cape (τὸ 'Ροβόνδιον ἄκρον, MSS: ?recte 'Ροβόγδιον, *Rhobogdium*), to give the length of the island, is <3,> 170 stades. Its breadth begins at the Sacred Cape (τοῦ 'Ιεροῦ ἄκρου, gen.) and stretches to *Rhobogdium* Cape, so that the breadth of the island is 1,834 stades. Its capes are distant from the boundaries as follows: its northern cape is distant from the arctic circle 14,250 stades, its western cape...[lacuna]...from the equator 38,317 stades, its eastern 40,317 from the east. It has 16 peoples, 11 notable cities, 15 notable rivers, 5 notable promontories. The total length of the whole circuit of *Ivernia* is not more than 9,085 stades, not less than 6,845.

Periplus of the Prettanic Island Albion

Following on from this we shall now describe the periplus of the island of *Albion*. The *Prettanic* island of *Albion* is bounded on the north by the Ocean called *Duecolidonius* (Δουηκολιδονίῳ, dat., MSS: ? recte Δουηκαληδονιῷ, *Duecaledonius*); on the east by the *Oceanus Germanicus* (Γερμανικῷ, dat.); on the west by the *Oceanus Ivernicus* ('Ιουερνικῷ, dat.), beyond which is the island *Ivernia*, but also the *Oceanus Vergivius* (Οὐεργιουίῳ, dat.); and on the south by the *Oceanus Prettanicus* and the aforementioned regions and peoples of Gaul. And the description of the whole island is like this... [lacuna, presumably including '*Lindonion*' quoted from Marcian by Stephanus, q.v.]... The length of the *Prettanic* island *Albion*, beginning from the western boundary at *Damnium* cape (τὸ Δάμνιον ἄκρον) which is also called *Okrium* (τὸ καὶ Ὄκριον καλούενον) and finishing at *Taroaedunum* (Ταροαιδούνου, gen., MSS: ? recte Ταρουεδούνου) headland, which is also called *Orkas* (τῆς καὶ 'Ορκάδος καλουμένης ἄκρας), the greatest length is 5,225 stades. Its breadth begins at *Damnium* cape, which is also called *Okrium* and stretches to the peninsula of the *Nevantes* (τὴν τῶν Νεουάντων Χερσόνησον) and the promontory of the same name, so that its breadth along the longest line is 3,083 stades. It has 33 peoples, 59 notable cities, 40 notable rivers, 14 notable promontories, one notable peninsula, 5 notable gulfs, 3 notable harbours. The total length of the whole circuit of *Albion* is not more than 28,604 stades, not less than 20,526.

Other references:

'Αλβίων: *Periplus Maris Exteri* II, I.
Βρεττανικός[1]: *Periplus Maris Exteri, Prooem.*
'Ιουερνία: *Periplus Maris Exteri* II, I.
Πρετανία: *Periplus Maris Exteri* II, 27.
Πρεττανικός: *Periplus Maris Exteri* II, I (νῆσοι); II, 24 (ὠκεανός); II, 46 (νῆσοι).

Text: *Geographi Graeci Minores*, ed. K. Müller, Paris, 1861, repr. Hildesheim, 1965.

MARTIALIS, M. Valerius (*c.* A.D. 40–104)

References:

Britanni: *Epig.* X, xliv, I; XI, liii, I; XII, viii, 9; XIV, xcix, I.
Britannia: X, iii, 5.
Britto: XI, xxi, 9.
Caledonii: X, xliv, I.
Caledonius (adj.): *De Spectaculis*, vii, 3 (*Caledonio urso*).

Text: ed. W. M. Lindsay, Oxford, 1929.

MARTIANUS MINNEUS FELIX CAPELLA (*fl.* A.D. 410–439)

References:

Brittania (variants *Britannia, Bryttania, Brytthania*): VI, 594 (193G), 666 (215G); VIII, 876 (296G).

[1] This spelling is repeated in the MSS at I, 8, but see the comment on Marcian's usage by Stephanus, s.v.

Calidonia silva (variants *Calydonia, Colidonia*): VI, 666 (215G).
Orcades: VI, 666 (215G).
Tyle (variants *Tilae, Tile*): VI, 666 (215G).

Text: ed. A. Dick (rev. J. Préaux), Stuttgart, 1969.

MELA, Pomponius (*fl.* A.D. 40)

1. *De Chorographia* I, 3 (15)
Europe has as its boundaries on the east the Tanais (Don), the Maeotis (Sea of Azov) and the Pontus (Black Sea), on the south the rest of our sea (the Mediterranean), on the West the *Oceanus Atlanticus* and on the north the *Oceanus Britannicus*.

2. *De Chorographia* II, 6 (85)
From here the Pyrenees first of all run down to the *Oceanus Britannicus*.

3. In the Celtic regions there are several islands which, since they are rich in tin (*plumbo*, presumably for *plumbo albo*), are all called by the one name of the *Cassiterides*. *Sena* (Sein, off Brittany), in the *Mare Britannicum* opposite the Ossismican shores, is notable for the oracle of a Gaulish divinity whose priestesses, sanctified by perpetual virginity, are said to be nine in number. They call them Gallizenae and think that they are endowed with special abilities to rouse the seas and winds with their songs, to turn themselves into whatever animals they wish, to cure things which for others are incurable and to know and predict the future, though they only do this for people who sail there for the specific purpose of consulting them. What *Britannia* is like and what sort of people it produces we shall soon know more certainly and in greater detail, for behold, the greatest of emperors is now revealing this land so long hidden and, victor over races not merely unconquered but even unknown before him, having established the credibility of his own deeds in war, is soon to carry it in triumph. But so far as we know at present, it stretches between the north and the west and with a wide angle looks towards the mouths of the Rhine, then draws its sides back obliquely, with one facing Gaul, with the other Germany; then again with a continuous boundary of straight shore it is drawn back behind and with its different angles forms itself into a wedge (*se cuneat*), three-cornered and very like Sicily, huge with plains that are fertile, though with things that benefit herds rather than men. It has woods and groves and very large rivers which with alternate motion flow now towards the sea, now backwards from it, and some of them produce gems and pearls. It has peoples and kings of peoples, but they are all uncivilised and the further they are from the continent the less they know of other kinds of wealth, being rich only in herds and lands; whether for appearance or for some other reason, they paint their bodies with woad. Nevertheless they find occasions for wars and do fight them and often attack each other, mostly from a wish for domination and a desire to carry off what they possess. They fight not only on horseback and on foot but also from vehicles and chariots equipped in the Gaulish fashion: they call *covinni* those in which they use scythed axles. Above *Britannia* is *Iuverna*, nearly equal to it in extent but oblong, with equal sides to each of its shores, and with a climate unfavourable to the ripening of crops, but so rich in grass which is not only plentiful but sweet that the herds satisfy themselves in a very small part of a day, and unless they were kept off the pastures

they would feed too long and burst. Its farmers are uncouth and more ignorant of all virtues than other races, and almost entirely lacking in piety. There are 30 *Orcades*, separated from one another by narrow spaces, and seven *Haemodae*, located towards Germany... *Thyle*, famous in the poems of the Greeks and our own writers, is situated opposite the shores of the *Belgae* (*sic*; ? *Belcarum* ? or ? *Bergarum* ?). In it, because there the sun rises far from its setting, the nights are short; in winter they are dark as elsewhere, but light in summer, because at that time the sun raises itself higher and although it is not seen itself, yet it lights up the parts nearest to it with its neighbouring glow; but at the solstice there are no nights, because then it reveals not merely a glow but even the most part of itself.

Text: ed. G. Ranstrand, Göteborg, 1971.

MINUCIUS FELIX (*fl.* A.D. 200–240)

Reference:

Octavius: 18, 3.
Britannia (var. *Bryttania*) lacks sun, but is restored by the warmth of the sea flowing round it.

Text: ed. J. Beaujeu, Paris, 1964.

NAMATIANUS, Rutilius Claudius (*fl.* A.D. 416)

References:

Britannus (coll.): *De Reditu Suo*, I, 500.
Thule: *De Reditu Suo* I, 499.

Text: ed. E. Castorina, Florence, 1967.

NEMESIANUS, M. Aurelius Olympius (late 3rd cent. A.D.)

Reference:

Britannia: *Cynegetica*, 225 (*divisa Britannia*).

Text: *Minor Latin Poets*, edd. J. W. and A. M. Duff, London and Cambridge, Mass., 1935.

NOMINA PROVINCIARUM OMNIUM (LATERCULUS VERONENSIS) (A.D. 312–314)

Chap. 7

The diocese of the *Britanniae* (variant *Brittaniae*) includes provinces to the number of six: *Prima, Secunda, Maxima Caesariensis, Flavia Caesariensis*.

Chap. 13

Barbarian nations which have emerged under the emperors: *Scoti, Picti, Caledonii* (variant *Calidoni*).

Text: *Geographi Latini Minores*, ed. A. Riese, Berlin, 1878, repr. Hildesheim, 1964.

OLYMPIODORUS THEBAEUS (*c*. A.D. 380–425+)

References:

Βρεττανίαι: Frag. 12 (from Photius) (ter.).

Text: *Fragmenta Historicorum Graecorum* IV, ed. C. Müller, Paris, 1928.

OPPIANUS of Cilicia (*fl*. late 2nd cent. A.D.)

Reference:

Βρετανοί: *Cynegetica* I, 470 (Βρετανῶν, gen.).

Text: ed. A. W. Mair, London and New York, 1928.

ORIGEN (A.D. 185–255)

(see also Hieronymus for Latin translation)

Reference:

Βρεττανία: *Comm. on St. Matthew* X, 7 (bis).

Text: ed. R. Girod, Paris, 1970.

OROSIUS, Paulus (*fl*. A.D. 415)

1. *Historiae adversum Paganos* I, 2, 75–82

And since the ocean contains the islands which they call *Britannia* (variants *Brittania, Britania*) and *Hibernia* (variant *Ivernia*) and which are situated on the far side of the Gauls looking towards Spain, they shall be briefly described. *Britannia*, an island of the ocean, extends in length towards the north; on the south it has the Gauls. Access for people crossing to its nearest shore is provided by a city called *Rutupi Portus* (variants *Ruthubi, Rutubi*); from here it faces the Menapi and the Batavi, not far from the Morini. The length of this island is 800 miles, its breadth 200 miles. At its back, where it faces an unbounded ocean, it has the *Orcades* (*Orcadas*, acc.) islands, of which 20 are uninhabited, 13 inhabited. Then there is the island of *Thyle* (variants *Tyle, Tylae, Thulae, Thola, Tholae*), which is separated from the rest by an infinite distance, lying in the middle of the ocean towards the west-north-west; it is held to be scarcely known to few people. The island of *Hibernia* stretches between *Britannia* and Spain, with its greatest length from south-west to north. Its nearest parts, stretching in the Cantabric ocean, look towards the city of Brigantia (i.e. Coruña) in Gallaecia which faces them at some considerable distance, especially from the promontory where the river *Scena* (i.e. Shannon) has its mouth and where the *Velabri* and the *Luceni* dwell. This island is nearer to *Britannia*, smaller than it in extent but better favoured in the temperance of its soil and climate; it is inhabited by the peoples of the *Scotti*. Also very near this is the island of *Mevania*, itself not small in extent and with favourable soil. This too is inhabited by the peoples of the *Scotti*.

2. *Historiae adversum Paganos* VII, 6, 10

He (sc. Claudius) crossed to the island, which no one had dared to approach either before Julius Caesar or after him, and there, to quote the words of Suetonius Tranquillus, 'without any battle or bloodshed within a very few days he received the surrender of the greatest part of the island'. He also added to the Roman Empire the *Orcades* (*Orcadas*, acc.) islands, which lie in the ocean beyond *Britannia*, and returned to Rome in the sixth month after he had set out.

Other references:

Britanni (variant *Brittani*): *Historiae adversum Paganos* V, 22, 7; VI, 9, 5; 10, 1.
Britannia (variant *Brittania*): VI, 8, 9; 9, 2 (bis); 9, 4; VII, 5, 5; 6, 9; 17, 7 (plur.); 25, 3 (plur.); 25, 6 (bis); 25, 16; 28, 1 (plur.); 34, 9; 40, 4 (plur.).
Britannicus (variant *Brittanicus*): VII, 7, 11 (*clades*); *Liber Apologeticus* 12, 3 (referring to Pelagius).
Eboracum: *Historiae adversum Paganos* VII, 17, 8.
Tamensis: VI, 9, 6 (*Tamensem*, acc., variants *Tamensim*, *Thamesim*).
Trinobantes: VI, 9, 8 (*Trinobantum*, gen., variant *Trinovantum*).

Text: ed. C. Zangemeister, Leipzig, 1889, repr. Hildesheim, 1967.

ORPHICA (of unknown date, but derived from Apollonius Rhodius, so later than 3rd cent. B.C.)

Argonautica 1170–71

(The ship Argo speaks)

For now by sad and bitter suffering shall I be held, if I come nearer to the *Iernian* islands (νήσοισιν 'Ιερνίσιν, dat.).

Text: ed. E. Abel, Leipzig and Prague, 1885.

OVIDIUS NASO, P. (43 B.C.–A.D. 17)

Reference:

Britanni: *Amores* II, xvi (xvii), 39; *Metam.* XV, 752.

Texts: *Amores* ed. E. J. Kenney, Oxford, 1961.
Metamorphoses ed. G. Lafaye, Paris, 1957.

PACATIUS DREPANUS (*fl.* A.D. 389): *see* PANEGYRICI LATINI

PAEANIUS (late 4th cent. A.D.): see EUTROPIUS

PANEGYRICI LATINI (A.D. 289–389)

References:

Britanni: II(XII), 28, 4; VIII(V), 11, 4; 19, 1.
Britannia: II(XII), 5, 2; 38, 2; VI(VII), 5, 3; 5, 4; 7, 5; 9, 1; VII(VI), 4, 3 (plur.); VIII(V), 3, 3; 9, 5; 11, 1; 11, 3; 14, 2; 15, 2; 17, 2 (plur.); 18, 1; 18, 4; 18, 7; 20, 3; IX(IV), 18, 3; 21, 2; XII(IX), 25, 2.
Britannicus: VI(VII), 7, 1 (*tropaea*); VIII(V), 21, 2 (*victoria*).
Calidones: VI(VII), 7, 2.
Hiberni: VIII(V), 11, 4.
Hibernia: VI(VII), 7, 2.

Londiniensis: VIII(V), 17, 1 (*oppidum Londiniense*).
Picti: VI(VII), 7, 2; VIII(V), 11, 4.
Scotus (coll.): II(XII), 5, 2.
Thyle: VI(VII), 7, 2 (*Thylen ultimam*, acc.).
Vecta: VIII(V), 15, 1 (*Vectam insulam*, acc.).
Note: II(XII) = Pacati Drepani, Theodosio (A.D. 389, Rome)
VI(VII) = Anon., Constantino Augusto (A.D. 310, Trier)
VII(VI) = Anon., Maximiano et Constantino (A.D. 307, ?Trier)
VIII(V) = Anon., Constantio Caesari (A.D. 297–8, ?Trier)
IX(IV) = Eumenii, Pro Instaurandis Scholis (A.D. 297–8, Autun)
XII(IX) = Anon., Constantino Augusto (A.D. 313, Trier)

Text: ed. R. A. B. Mynors, Oxford, 1964.

PAUSANIAS (*fl.* A.D. 160)

Descriptio Graeciae VIII, 43
Antoninus...never willingly involved the Romans in war. But when the Moors began a war...he compelled them to flee from the whole country to the furthest parts of Libya...to the Atlas Mountain and to the people who dwell on Atlas. He sequestered a large part of the territory of the *Brigantes* in *Brittania* (τῶν ἐν Βριττανίᾳ Βριγάντων; variants Βριττανέα, Βριτογανέα) because they too began to invade with arms the *Genunian* region (τὴν Γενουνίαν μοῖραν) the inhabitants of which were subjects of the Romans.

Other reference:
Βρεττανοί: *Descr. Graec.* I, 33.

Text: ed. F. Spiro, Leipzig, 1903.

PLINIUS SECUNDUS, C. (the Elder, A.D. 23–79)

1. *Natural History* II, 186–87
Thus it happens that, through the varied lengthening of daylight, in Meroe the longest day embraces 12 8/9 equinoctial hours, but at Alexandria 14 hours, 15 in Italy, 17 in *Britannia*, where in summer the light nights confirm, what reason forces us to believe, that as the sun on summer days approaches the top of the world, with a narrow circuit of light the underlying parts of the earth have continuous days for six months, and continuous nights when the sun is withdrawn in the opposite direction towards winter. Pytheas of Massilia writes that this happens in the island of *Thyle*, which lies six days' sailing northwards from Britain, and some state that it happens also in *Mona*, which is about 200 miles distant from *Camalodunum*, a town of *Britannia*.

2. *Natural History* IV, 102–04
Opposite this area (*sc.* the mouths of the Rhine), between the north and the west, lies the island of *Britannia*, famous in Greek records and our own, opposite, at a great distance, Germany, Gaul and Spain – much the greatest part of Europe. Its own name was *Albion* when all the islands about which we are just going to speak briefly were

called the *Britanniae*. By the nearest crossing it is distant 50 miles from *Gesoriacum* (Boulogne) on the shore of the tribe of the Morini. Pytheas and Isidorus say that it extends 4,875 miles in circumference and in nearly thirty years now Roman arms have extended our knowledge of it, not beyond the neighbourhood of the *Silva Calidonia*. Agrippa believes its length to be 800 miles and its breadth 300 miles, and the breadth of *Hibernia* to be the same, but the length 200 miles less. This lies above it, 30 miles from the tribe of the *Silures* by the shortest crossing. Of the other islands none is said to be more than 125 miles in circumference. But there are 40 *Orcades*, separated from one another by moderate distances, seven *Acmodae*, 30 *Hebudes*, and between *Hibernia* and *Britannia* are *Mona*, *Monapia*, *Riginia*, *Vectis*, *Silumnus*, *Andros*, and, below, *Sambis* and *Axanthos*, and on the opposite side, scattered on the *Germanicum Mare*, the *Glaesariae*, which the more recent Greek authors have called *Electridae*, because amber (*electrum*) is produced there. The furthest of all to be recorded is *Thyle* in which, as we have mentioned, there are no nights in summer, when the sun is passing through the sign of Cancer, and conversely no days in winter; some think that this happens for six continuous months. The historian Timaeus says that six days' sailing inwards (*sic*) from *Britannia* is the island of *Mictis* (*insulam Mictim*) in which tin is produced, and that the *Britanni* sail to it in boats made of skins sewn round wickerwork. There are some who mention other islands too, the *Scandiae*, *Dumna*, the *Bergi* and, largest of all, *Berrice*, from which one may sail to *Thyle*. One day's sailing from *Thyle* is a frozen sea which some call *Mare Cronium*.

3. *Natural History* IV, 109

The seas around the shores (*sc*. of Gaul) are: at the Rhine the *Oceanus Septentrionalis*, between the Rhine and the Seine the *Oceanus Britannicus*, and between it and the Pyrenees the *Oceanus Gallicus*.

4. *Natural History* IV, 119

Opposite Celtiberia are several islands called the *Cassiterides* by the Greeks because of their richness in tin.

5. *Natural History* VII, 197

Midacritus was the first to bring tin from the island (sing.) of *Cassiteris*.

6. *Natural History* XXXIV, 156

This very precious metal (tin) is called *cassiterus* by the Greeks and according to fable was said to be sought in islands of the *Mare Atlanticum* and to be conveyed in boats made of skins sewn round wickerwork. Now it is known for certain that it is produced in Lusitania and Gallaecia.

Other references:

Britanni: XXII, 2.

Britannia: II, 217; III, 119; IX, 116; X, 56; XIV, 102; XVII, 42, 43, 45; XXV, 21; XXX, 13; XXXIII, 24, 54; XXXIV, 164; XXXVII, 35.

Britannicus (adj): IX, 169; XXV, 20, 99; XXVII, 2; XXXII, 62.

Text: edd. J. Beaujeu, A. Ernout, J. André et al., Paris, 1947–74.

PLUTARCHUS, L. Mestrius (*c*. A.D. 50–120)

De Defectu Oraculorum 18 (419e–420a)

Demetrius said that there were many desert islands scattered around *Brettania*, (Βρεττανία), some of which were named from spirits (δαιμόνων) and heroes. He said that he himself, having been sent by the Emperor to enquire into and inspect them, had sailed to the island nearest to the desert ones; it did not have many inhabitants, but they were all held sacred and inviolate by the *Brettanoi* (Βρεττανοί). Soon after he arrived, there occurred a great turbulence in the air and many portents, with rushing winds and raging thunderstorms. When these ceased, the islanders said that the passing of one of the great ones had taken place: for just as a lamp when it is lit shines without evil effect, but when it is extinguished is troublesome to many, so great souls (ψυχαί) are benign and mild, but their extinction and destruction often, as now, produce great winds and storms and often infect the air with pestilent effects. And there was one island there in which Cronos was held asleep under guard of Briareus; for that sleep had been contrived as his bonds and around him were many spirits (δαίμονες), his attendants and servants.

Other references:

Βρεττανία: *Caesar* 16, 5 (715b); *Crassus* 37, 2 (204b); *De Defect. Orac.*, 2 (410a); *Plac. Philos.* V, 30 (911b).

Βρεττανοί: *Caesar* 23, 2 (719b); *Cato Minor* 51, 4 (784b); *Pompeius* 51, 1 (646b).

Texts: *Vitae*, ed. C. Lindscog and K. Ziegler, Leipzig, 1964–73.
Moralia, ed. J. Mau, Leipzig, 1971.

POLEMIUS SILVIUS (*c*. A.D. 385)

1. *Nomina Omnium Provinciarum* 2, 9

Belgica Secunda, from which the crossing is made to *Brittania* (variant *Brittannia*, or transitus *Brittanorum, Britannorum, Britanorum*).

2. *Nomina Omnium Provinciarum* 11, 1–6

In *Brittania*, five: *Brittania Prima, Brittania Secunda, Flavia, Maxima, Valentiniana* (variants *Valentiana, Valenciana, Valentina*) (some MSS add *Orcades*).

Text: *MGH* (*AA*) IX, ed. Th. Mommsen, Berlin, 1892, repr. 1961.

POLYAENUS of Macedon (2nd cent. A.D.)

References:

Βρεττανία: *Strategemata* VIII, 23, 5.

Βρεττανοί: VIII, 3, 5 (quater).

Text: edd. E. Woelfflin and J. Melber, Leipzig, 1887, repr. Stuttgart, 1970.

POLYBIUS (*c.* 200–118+ B.C.)

Histories III, 57, 2–3
Some people will ask why, in writing a work largely concerning places in Libya and Iberia, we have not said more about the strait at the Pillars of Hercules, or about the outer sea and its peculiarities, or about the *Bretannic Islands* (περὶ τῶν Βρεταννικῶν νήσων) and the production of tin, or yet of the silver and gold mines in Iberia itself, over which the historians, disputing among themselves, spend much time. (Polybius explains that he has not done this so as not to make his history indigestible.)

Text: ed. J. de Foucault, Paris, 1971.

PRISCIANUS (early 6th cent. A.D.)

References:

Britanni: *Periegesis e Dionysio*, 274 (285).
Britannides: *Periegesis*, 578 (566).
Thule: Periegesis, 589 (582) (*Thulen*, acc.).

Text: *Geographi Graeci Minores*, ed. K. Müller, Paris, 1861, repr. Hildesheim, 1965.

PROCOPIUS (*c.* A.D. 500–565)

1. *De Bellis* VI (= *De Bello Gothico* II), 15, 1–26
When the Eruli, having been defeated in battle by the Langobardi (*c.* A.D. 512), left their ancestral homes, some of them, as I have explained, settled in places among the Illyrians, but the rest were reluctant to cross the river Danube and established themselves at the very limits of the inhabited world. At least, led by many of the royal blood, they passed through all the nations of the Slavs one after the other and then, having crossed a large barren area, they came to the people called Varni. After them they passed through the nations of the Dani, without the barbarians doing them any violence. Then arriving at the ocean they took ship and having come to the island of *Thule* (Θούλῃ, dat.) they settled there. *Thule* is exceedingly large, for it is more than ten times greater than *Brettania* (Βρεττανίας, gen., variant Βριτανίας) and it lies a long way from it toward the north wind. On this island the land is mostly barren, but in the inhabited area there dwell thirteen very numerous nations, with a king over each nation. There a thing most wonderful occurs, for around the summer solstice the sun never sets for 40 days, but throughout this time appears above the earth. But no less than six months later, about the time of the winter solstice, the sun never appears in this island for 40 days, but perpetual night envelops it; and as a result dejection overcomes the men there for the whole of this time, since they can by no means hold intercourse with one another. Although I desired to go to this island and become an eye-witness of what I have described, there was never any opportunity for me. But I did enquire of those who came to us from there how it was that they could reckon the length of days when the sun never rises nor sets there at fixed times, and they gave me a true and reliable account...Of the inhabitants of *Thule* there is one nation, called the Scrithiphini, who live like beasts...But practically all the other *Thulitae* (Θουλῖται) do not differ much from other men...and one of the most numerous nations is the Gaulti, beside whom the Eruli settled.

2. *De Bellis* VIII (= *De Bello Gothico* IV), 20, 1–10

At this time war and fighting broke out between the nation of the Varni and the islander soldiers who dwell in the island called *Brittia* (Βριττίᾳ, dat., variant Βρυτίᾳ)...The island of *Brittia* lies in the ocean not far from the coast, but about 200 stades off and about opposite the mouths of the Rhine, and it is between *Brettania* and the island of *Thule*. While *Brettania* lies toward the setting sun opposite the farthest point of the land of the Spaniards, distant not less than 400 stades from the continent, *Brittia* is towards the back parts of Gaul, those which are turned towards the ocean, that is to the north of Spain and *Brettania*; and *Thule*, so far as men know, lies in the farthest parts of the ocean towards the north. But matters concerning *Brettania* and *Thule* have been described by me above (note: he has *not* described *Brettania*). Three very numerous nations inhabit the island of *Brittia*, each having a king over it; and the names of these nations are the Angili and the Phrissones and the *Brittones* (Βρίττωνες), who have the same name as the island...Such are the facts concerning the island of *Brittia*.

3. *De Bellis* VIII (= *De Bello Gothico* IV), 20, 42–55

In this island of *Brittia* the men of old built a long wall, cutting off a large part of it, and the air and the soil and everything else is different on the two sides of it. For to the east of the wall there is healthy air, changing with the seasons, moderately warm in summer and cold in winter, and many men dwell there, living in the same way as other men, and the trees are rich in fruit which ripens at the appropriate season and the crops flourish as well as any others and the land seems to boast of its abundance of waters. But on the other side everything is the opposite of this, so that it is impossible for a man to live there for half an hour, but the viper and innumerable snakes and all kinds of other wild beasts occupy the place as their own; and, strangest of all, the natives say that if a man crosses the wall and goes to the other side, he forthwith dies, unable to bear the pestilential nature of the air there, and likewise death meets and overtakes wild beasts that go there. Now since I have reached this point in my account, I must relate a rather fabulous story, which did not seem at all trustworthy to me...(here follows an account of how the souls of the dead were ferried to *Brittia* from villages on the coast of Europe).

Other references:

Βρεττανία: III (= *De Bello Vandalico* I), 1, 17 (variant Βρετανία); 2, 31; 2, 38; VI (= *De Bello Gothico* II), 6, 28.

Βρεττανοί: V (= *De Bello Gothico* I), 24, 36 (variant Βριττανοί).

Text: edd. J. Haury and G. Wirth, Leipzig, 1914, repr. 1962–3.

PROPERTIUS, Sex. Aurelius (*c.* 50–3 B.C.)

Britanni: *Eleg.* II, xviii, 23; xxvii, 5.

Britannia: *Eleg.* IV, iii, 9.

Britannus (adj.): *Eleg.* II, i, 76 (*esseda Britanna*).

Text: ed. E. A. Barber, Oxford, 1960.

PROSPER TIRO (*c.* A.D. 390–455)

References:

Brittani/Britanni: *Epitoma Chronicon* 763 (*Brittanos*, variants *Brittannos*, *Brittandos*); 1301 (*Britannos*, variant *Brittanos*).

Brittania: 764 (plur.); 976; 1183; 1232; 1301.

Britto: 1252 (ref. to Pelagius, variants *Brito*, *Bruto*).

Eboracum/Eburacum: 764 (*Eburaci*, loc., variants *Eboraci*, *Euoraci*); 976 (*Eboraci*, loc., variant *Euoraci*).

Scotti: 1307.

Text: *MGH* (*AA*) IX, ed. Th. Mommsen, Berlin, 1892, repr. 1961.

QUINTILIANUS, M. Fabius (*c.* A.D. 32–100)

References:

Britannia: *Inst. Orat.* VII, iv, 2 (bis).

Britannus (adj.): VIII, iii, 28.

Text: ed. M. Winterbottom, Oxford, 1970.

SENECA, L. Annaeus, the Younger (*c.* 2 B.C.–A.D. 65)

References:

Brigantes: *Apocol.* xii, 3.

Britanni: *Apocol.* iii, 3; xii, 3; *Octavia* (falsely attributed) i, 28, 41.

Britannia: *Apocol.* viii, 3; *De Consol. ad Marciam* xiv, 3; *De Consol. ad Polybium* xiii, 2.

Texts: *Apocolocyntosis* ed. R. Walz, Paris, 1934.
De Consolatione ed. R. Walz, Paris, 1942.
Octavia ed. F. Leo, 1879, repr. Berlin, 1963.

SIBYLLINE ORACLE (3rd cent. A.D.?)

Reference:

Βρεττανοί: XII, 181; XIV, 175.

Text: ed. J. Geffcken, Leipzig, 1902.

SILIUS ITALICUS, Ti. Catius Asconius (A.D. 26–101)

References:

Caledonius (adj.); *Punica* iii, 598 (*Caledonios lucos*).

Thyle: iii. 597; xvii, 416 (*Thyles*, gen.).

Text: ed. L. Bauer, Leipzig, 1890–92.

SOCRATES SCHOLASTICUS (*c.* A.D. 380–450)

References:

Βρεττανία: *Historia Ecclesiastica* I, 2; V, 11.
αἱ Βρεττανικαὶ νῆσοι: VII, 12.

Text: ed. W. Bright, Oxford, 1878.

SOLINUS, C. Iulius (*fl.* A.D. 200+)

1. *Collectanea Rerum Memorabilium* 22, 1–12

The shores of the coast of Gaul were the end of the world but that the island *Brittania*, of not inconsiderable size, might deserve the name of another world; for it stretches 800 and more miles, if we measure to the angle of *Calidonia* (*in Calidonicum usque angulum*). In this fastness an altar inscribed with Greek letters proves that Ulysses was driven to *Calidonia*. It is surrounded by many not insignificant islands, of which *Hibernia* approaches it in size, inhuman in the savage practices of its inhabitants but otherwise so rich in fodder that if they were not kept off the pastures the herds would gorge themselves to the point of danger. There are no snakes there, few birds, and people who are unfriendly and warlike. When they have drained the blood of the slain the victors smear their faces with it. They make no distinction between right and wrong. There are no bees, and if anyone sprinkles dust or pebbles from there among the hives, the swarms will leave the honeycombs...The sea which flows between this island and *Brittania* is rough and stormy all the year, except for a few days when it is navigable, and those who have investigated the matter estimate that it is 120 miles wide. A rough strait also separates the island of *Silura* from the shore which the British (*Brittana*) tribe of the *Dumnonii* occupy. The inhabitants of this island preserve the ancient customs: they refuse money, give and accept things, obtain their necessities by exchange rather than by purchase, are zealous in their worship of the gods, and both men and women display a knowledge of the future. The island of *Tanatus* is washed by the *Fretum Gallicum* and is separated from the mainland of *Brittania* by a narrow estuary. It rejoices in fertile plains and a rich soil which is beneficial not only to itself but to other places too: for whereas it is crawled over by no snakes, earth brought from it to any other place kills snakes. There are many other islands around *Brittania*, of which the most distant is *Thyle*, where at the summer solstice, when the sun is passing through the sign of Cancer, there is no night, and likewise at the winter solstice no day. We hear that beyond *Thyle* the sea is sluggish and frozen. The circumference of *Brittania* is 4,875 miles, within which there are many great rivers and hot springs (*fontes calidi*) richly adorned for the use of men. Over these springs the divinity of Minerva presides and in her temple the perpetual fires never whiten into ash, but when the flame declines it turns into rocky lumps. Further, to pass over in silence the large and varied wealth of mines with rich veins in which the land of *Brittania* abounds, there is especially the stone jet (*gagates*): if you ask its appearance, it is like a black gem (*nigrogemmeus*), if its properties, it burns with water and is quenched with oil, if its powers, when it is warmed by rubbing it attracts things set by it, like amber. The region is partly occupied by barbarians who, even from boyhood, have pictures representing various animals put on their bodies by tattoo artists, and the marks grow on their flesh thus inscribed as they grow up.

2. *Collectanea Rerum Memorabilium* 23, 10
The *Cassiterides* look towards the side of Celtiberia, being rich in lead (*sic*, *plumbi*, but presumably meaning *plumbi albi*, tin).

Text: ed. Th. Mommsen, Berlin, 1895.

SOZOMENUS (d. *c.* A.D. 450)

References:

Βρεττανία: *Historia Ecclesiastica* VII, 13, 1; IX, 11, 2 (variant Βρετανία); 11, 3.
Βρεττανοί: I, 5, 3; 6, 3.
Βρεττανός (adj.): I, 7, 2 (θάλασσα); VII, 13, 10 (ἄνδρες).

Text: edd. J. Bidez and G. C. Hansen, Berlin, 1960.

STATIUS, P. PAPINIUS (*c.* A.D. 45–96)

References:

Britannus (adj.): V, ii, 149.
Caledonius (adj.): V, ii, 142 (*Caledonios campos*).
Thule: III, v, 20 (*Thules*, gen.); IV, iv, 62 (*Thules*, gen.); V, I, 91; V, ii, 55 (*Thulen*, acc.).

Text: ed. J. S. Phillimore, Oxford, 1918.

STEPHANUS of Byzantium (6th cent. A.D.)

Aebudae (Αἰβοῦδαι), five islands of *Pretannike* (τῆς Πρεταννικῆς) as Marcian states in his Periplus. The ethnic is *Aebudaeus* (Αἰβουδαῖος).

Albion (Ἀλβίων), a *Prettanic* (Πρεττανική) island, Marcian in his Periplus of it. The ethnic is *Albionius* (Ἀλβιώνιος).

Brettia, an island in the Adriatic, containing the river *Brettion*. The Greeks call it *Elaphoussa*, but some call it *Brettanis* (Βρεττανίδα, acc.). The ethnic is *Brettianus*... There are also *Brettanides* (Βρεττανίδες) islands in the ocean, whose ethnic is *Brettani* (Βρεττανοί). Dionysius (Periegetes) omits one -t- when he says 'the cold flood of ocean flows where dwell the *Bretani* (Βρετανοί)'. And others spell them with a P-, *Pretanides* (Πρετανίδες) islands, as Marcian and Ptolemy.

Briges (Βρίγες), a Thracian people. Herodotus in his seventh book says 'The Phrygians, as the Macedonians say, are called Briges'. And Trojan *Brigia*, that is *Phrygia*, is from *Brigos*, dwelling in Macedonia. Herodian (*sc.* the grammarian, not the historian) in his first book on the declension of nouns says they are *Brigantes* (Βρίγαντας, acc.), 'for nouns terminating in -gas decline isosyllabically only when they are proper names (i.e. not ethnic): I say this of the name *Brigas* (Βρίγας). There is a *Brettanic* (Βρεττανικόν) people, the ....' [lacuna].

Thule (Θούλη), a large island in the ocean towards the Hyperborean regions, where the sun makes the summer day 20 equinoctial hours long, the night four, and the opposite in winter. The ethnic is *Thulaeus* (Θουλαῖος), or equally *Thulites* (Θουλίτης).

Ierne ('Ἰέρνη), an island on the edge of the world towards the west. The ethnic is *Iernaeus* ('Ἰερναῖος), like Lernaeus.

Ivernia ('Ἰουερνία), a *Pretanic* (Πρετανική) island, the lesser of the two. The ethnic is *Iverniates* ('Ἰουερνιάτης).

Kassitera (Κασσίτερα), an island in the ocean, near India, as Dionysius in his Bassarica; from which comes tin (κασσίτερος).

Lindonion (Λινδόνιον), a city of *Brettania* (τῆς Βρεττανίας): Marcian in his Periplus. The ethnic is *Lindoninus* (Λινδονίνος).

Pretanike (Πρετανική), an island like a continent, next to Gaul. The inhabitants are called *Pretani* (Πρετανοί).

Text: ed. A. Meineke, Berlin, 1849, repr. Graz, 1958.

STRABO (64 B.C.–A.D. 21+)

1. *Geography* 1, 4, 2–5 (C. 62–64)

Next, in defining the breadth (or latitude) of the inhabited world, he (Eratosthenes) says that from Meroe, on the meridian that runs through it, to Alexandria is 10,000 stades, from there to the Hellespont about 8,100, then to the Borysthenes (Dnieper) 5,000, and then to the meridian which runs through *Thule* (Θούλης, gen.), which Pytheas says is distant six days' sailing from *Brettanike* (τῆς Βρεττανικῆς, gen.) and is near the frozen sea, about 11,500. If then we add a further 3,400 beyond Meroe, to include the Island of the Egyptians and the Cinnamon-bearing Land and Taprobane (Ceylon), there will be a total of 38,000 stades.

We will allow him his other distances, for they are well enough agreed, but what man in his senses would grant him that from the Borysthenes to the meridian of *Thule*? For not only has Pytheas, who tells of *Thule*, been proved an utter liar, but those who have seen *Brettanike* and *Ierne* ('Ἰέρνην, acc.) say nothing about *Thule* while they do speak of other small islands around *Brettanike*. The length (or longitude) of *Brettanike* is about the same as that of Gaul (τῇ Κελτικῇ) and lies alongside it, not more than 5,000 stades, being defined by the extremities (ἄκροις) lying opposite. For the eastern extremity of the one lies opposite the eastern extremity of the other, and the western opposite the western; and the eastern ones are near enough to each other to be visible, that is, *Kantion* (τὸ Κάντιον) and the mouths of the Rhine. But he (*sc.* Pytheas) declares that the length of the island is more than 2,000 stades and says that *Kantion* is some days' sailing from Gaul; and concerning the Ostimii and places beyond the Rhine as far as the Scythians he has told a pack of lies. So a man who has told such lies about known places could hardly be telling the truth about those which are unknown to all.

But Hipparchus and others conjecture that the meridian through the Borysthenes is the same as that through *Brettanike* from the fact that the meridian of Byzantium is the same as that of Massalia – the degree of shadow which he (Pytheas) states for Massalia being the same as Hipparchus says he found in Byzantium at a similar time.

But from Massalia to the middle of *Brettanike* is not more than 5,000 stades. Moreover if you advanced not more than 4,000 stades from the centre of *Brettanike* you would find a place barely habitable – this would be about *Ierne* – so that the further regions, where he places *Thule*, would be no longer habitable. By what guesswork he (Eratosthenes) could say that the distance from the meridian of *Thule* to that of the Borysthenes is 11,500 stades I do not see.

Being mistaken about the breadth of the world, he was also wrong about its length. For both the more recent and the most accurate of the older writers agree that the known length is more than double the known breadth: I mean the distance from the extremities of India to the extremities of Iberia, double that from the Ethiopians to the meridian of *Ierne*. Having defined the breadth as stated, from the furthest Ethiopians to the meridian of *Thule*, he extends the length more than is correct, to make it more than double the stated breadth.

2. *Geography* II, 1, 13 (C. 72)
But it is now said that the furthest voyage from Gaul to the north is that to *Ierne*, which lies beyond *Brettanike* and on account of the cold is barely habitable – and they say that *Ierne* is not more than 5,000 stades from Gaul.

3. *Geography* II, 1, 18 (C. 75)
But Hipparchus says that at the Borysthenes and in Gaul during the whole summer nights the light of the sun shines dimly, moving round from the setting to the rising, but at the winter solstice the sun does not rise more than nine cubits above the horizon; but among those who live 6,300 stades from Massalia (whom he takes to be still Gauls (Κελτούς), but I think they are *Brettanoi* (Βρεττανούς, acc.), being 2,500 stades north of Gaul) this is still more marked; and on winter days the sun rises only six cubits, and only four cubits among those who live 9,100 stades from Massalia, and less than three cubits among those who live beyond that (who according to our reckoning would be much further north than *Ierne*). But he, trusting in Pytheas, places this inhabited country further south than *Brettanike* and says that the longest day there has 19 equinoctial hours, but 18 hours when the sun rises only four cubits; and he says that these people are 9,100 stades from Massalia, so that the most southerly of the *Brettanoi* are further to the north than them. So they are either on the same meridian as the Bactrians who live near the Caucasus or on some meridian near it; for I have said that according to the school of Deimachus the Bactrians near the Caucasus are 3,800 stades further north than *Ierne*, and if these are added to the distance from Massalia to *Ierne* the result is 12,500 stades.

4. *Geography* II, 4, 1–2 (C. 104)
In his chorography of Europe Polybius says that he passes over the ancient writers but examines those who have criticised them, namely Dicaearchus, Eratosthenes, who had written the most recent work on geography, and Pytheas, by whom many have been misled when he says that he travelled over the whole of the accessible part of *Brettanike*, reported that the perimeter of the island was more than 40,000 stades and added things about *Thule* and those places in which there was neither sea nor air, but a substance composed of these resembling sea-lung, in which he says that earth and sea and all things are suspended and this is the bond of all things which could

not be walked on or sailed on; he says he saw this thing like sea-lung himself, but that he took the rest from hearsay. So much for the statement of Pytheas, and he adds that after returning from there he visited the whole coastline of Europe from Gades to the Tanais (Don).

Polybius then says that it is incredible that a private individual, and a poor one, could have made such land and sea journeys; and that although Eratosthenes was at a loss whether he should believe these things, nevertheless he did believe him about *Brettanike* and the region of Gades and Iberia. But he says it would be better to trust the Messenian (i.e. Euhemerus) than him: he only says that he sailed to one country, Panchaea (i.e. a mythical land in the Indian Ocean), while Pytheas claims to have visited the whole of northern Europe as far as the boundaries of the world – which no one would believe if Hermes himself claimed it! And he says that Eratosthenes calls Euhemerus a Bergean (i.e. a romancer, like Antiphanes of Berge), yet trusts Pytheas, though not even Dicaearchus believed him.

5. *Geography* II, 5, 7–8 (C. 114–116)
Above the Borysthenes dwell the Roxolani, the most remote of the known Scythians, though they are further south than the furthest known people above *Brettanike*; the regions beyond are already uninhabitable, because of the cold. Further south are the Sauromatae who live above the Maeotis (the Sea of Azov) and also the Scythians as far as the Eastern Scythians.

Pytheas the Massaliote says that the furthest regions are those around *Thule*, the most northerly of the *Brettanides* (τῶν Βρεττανίδων, gen., variant Πρεττανίδων), where the summer tropic is the same as the arctic circle. But I learn nothing from other writers, neither if there really is an island of *Thule* nor if there is habitation up to the point where the summer tropic becomes the arctic circle. But I think that the northern boundary of the inhabited world is much further south. For now historians have nothing to say of any place further than *Ierne*, which lies near *Prettanike* (Πρεττανικῆς, gen., variant Βρεττανικῆς) towards the north, a place of wild men who barely exist because of the cold, so I think that the boundary must be placed there. But if the meridian of Byzantium is about the same as that through Massalia, as Hipparchus says, relying on Pytheas – for he says that in Byzantium the relation of the gnomon to the shadow is what Pytheas said it was in Massalia – and if the meridian of the Borysthenes is about 3,800 stades distant from this, then because of the distance from Massalia to *Prettanike* the meridian of the Borysthenes should fall somewhere there. But Pytheas, who misleads people everywhere else, is thoroughly wrong here too...The distance from there (i.e. Massalia) to *Prettanike* may agree with that from Byzantium to the Borysthenes, but for the distance from there to *Ierne* it is no longer known what figure should be given, nor is it known whether there are habitable areas beyond. And we need not consider it, if we pay attention to what has been said. For it will suffice science to assume that just as it was appropriate for the southern parts to fix a limit of habitation by going 3,000 stades south of Meroe – not as a completely accurate limit, but as an approximation to accuracy – so here we should not set it more than 3,000 stades above *Prettanike*, or only a little more – say 4,000. For imperial purposes it would be no advantage to know such places and their inhabitants, especially if they lived in islands which could neither harm nor benefit us because of their inaccessibility. For although able to hold *Prettanike* the Romans scorned to do so, seeing that there was nothing at all to fear from them – for they are not sufficiently strong to cross over against us – nor would there be any corresponding advantage if they did control it. For it seems that at present more is produced from duties than tribute could bring in, if we deduct the cost of a garrison army and of tribute collection; and it would be even more unprofitable for the other islands round about it.

6. *Geography* II, 5, 15 (C. 120)
But for those sailing in the opposite direction from the Sacred Cape (τὸ Ἱερὸν Ἀκρωτήριον, here Cape St Vincent) to the people called Artabri (i.e. the north west corner of Spain) the journey is to the north, keeping Lusitania on the right. Thereafter the rest of the journey is eastward, making an obtuse angle, until the headlands of the Pyrenees, which abut on the ocean. The western parts of *Prettanike* (variant *Brettanike*) lie opposite these to the north and likewise the islands called *Cattiterides* (Καττιτερίδες) lie in the open sea (πελάγιαι) opposite the Artabri, set approximately in the *Brettanic* latitude (κατὰ τὸ Βρεττανικόν πως κλίμα).

7. *Geography* II, 5, 28 (C. 128)
After this (i.e. Iberia) Gaul extends as far as the river Rhine, with its northern side washed by the whole *Prettanic Strait* (τῷ Πρεττανικῷ Πορθμῷ, dat., variant Βρεττανικῷ).

8. *Geography* II, 5, 30 (C. 129)
Off Europe lie the islands which we have mentioned, outside the Pillars Gades and the *Cattiterides* and the *Brettanic Islands*, inside the Pillars the Gymnesiae...

9. *Geography* III, 2, 9 (C. 147)
Poseidonius says that tin...is produced among the barbarians who live above the Lusitani and in the *Cattiterides Islands* and that it is brought from the *Prettanic* (variant *Brettanic*) *Islands* to Massalia, but that among the Artabri, who are the furthest north-western people of Lusitania, the soil flowers with silver, tin and white gold (for it is mixed with silver).

10. *Geography* III, 5, 11 (C. 175–76)
The *Cattiterides* are ten in number and they lie close to one another in the open sea to the north of the harbour of the Artabri. One of them is uninhabited, but the rest are occupied by people in black cloaks, who are clad in tunics reaching to their feet, wear belts round their breasts and walk about with canes, like the Poenae in tragedies. They live off their herds, pastorally (νομαδικῶς) for the most part. Having mines of tin and lead, they exchange these and hides with merchants for pottery, salt and bronze vessels. In former times only the Phoenicians carried on this trade, from Gades, concealing the route from everyone else. Once when the Romans were following a certain shipmaster so that they too could discover the markets, out of spite the shipmaster deliberately drove his vessel on to a shoal, bringing his pursuers to the same disaster and, having escaped on a piece of wreckage, he recovered from the state the value of the cargo which he had lost. But by trying many times the Romans learned all about the route, and when Publius Crassus had crossed over to them and had learnt that the metals were being dug from only a shallow depth, and that the

people were peaceful, he provided plentiful information to those who wished to trade over this sea, although it is wider than that which separates *Prettanike* (variant *Brettanike*). So much for Iberia and the islands lying near it.

11. *Geography* IV, 1, 14 (C. 189)
Then (*sc.* along the Seine) traffic is conveyed to the ocean and to the Lexobii and the Caleti; from these it is less than a day's run to *Prettanike* (variant *Brettanike*).

12. *Geography* IV, 2, 1 (C. 190)
The Liger (Loire) flows out between the Pictones and the Namnites. Formerly there was a market on this river, Corbilo, concerning which Polybius, recalling the mythical tales of Pytheas, said that none of the Massaliotes who associated with Scipio had anything worth mentioning to say about *Prettanike* (variant *Brettanike*), nor had any of the people from Narbo, nor any of those from Corbilo, although these are the best cities of that country; yet Pytheas dared to tell such lies.

13. *Geography* IV, 3, 3 (C. 193)
Both rivers (*sc.* the Rhine and the Seine) flow northwards from the southern parts. *Prettanike* (variant *Brettanike*) lies opposite them, near enough to the Rhine for *Kantion*, which is the eastern extremity of the island, to be visible from it, but a little further from the Seine. Here too the deified Caesar set up his dockyard when he sailed to *Prettanike* (variant *Brettanike*).

14. *Geography* IV, 3, 4 (C. 193–94)
The crossing to *Prettanike* (variant *Brettanike*) from the rivers of Gaul is 320 stades. People setting sail on the ebb tide in the evening land on the island about the eighth hour on the following day.

15. *Geography* IV, 4, 1 (C. 194)
After the tribes mentioned, the rest are tribes of Belgae who live on the coast of the ocean. Of these, there are the Veneti, who fought a sea battle against Caesar, for they were prepared to hinder his voyage to *Prettanike* (variant *Brettanike*), since they were using the market.

16. *Geography* IV, 4, 6 (C. 198)
This story is rather fanciful, but what he (*sc.* Poseidonius) says about Demeter and Kore (i.e. Persephone) is more credible: he says that there is an island near *Prettanike* (variant *Brettanike*) where rites are performed like those in Samothrace concerned with Demeter and Kore.

17. *Geography* IV, 5, 1–5 (C. 199–201)
Prettanike (variant *Brettanike*) is triangular in shape and its longest side stretches beside Gaul, neither exceeding nor falling short of it in length; for each of the lengths is 4,300 or 4,400 stades, that of Gaul from the mouths of the Rhine to the northern ends of the Pyrenees which are near Aquitania and the length from *Kantion*, opposite the mouths of the Rhine, which is the most easterly point of *Prettanike* (variant *Brettanike*) to the western extremity (ἄκρον) of the island, which lies opposite Aquitania and the Pyrenees... There are four crossings which men customarily use from the continent to the island, from the Rhine, from the Seine, from the Loire and from the Garonne, but for those making the passage from places near the Rhine

the point of sailing is not from the mouths themselves but from the Morini, who border on the Menapii, where also is *Ition*, which the deified Caesar used as a naval base when he crossed to the island...[here follows a general account of Britain and of Caesar's expeditions]...There are other small islands around *Prettanike* (variant *Brettanike*), but *Ierne* is large and lies alongside it to the north, with its breadth (latitude) greater than its length (longitude)...[here follow notes on the savage customs of the Irish].

...Concerning *Thule* our information is still more uncertain, because of its remoteness, for they place this the furthest north of all named islands. But that the things which Pytheas said about this and other places there were fabricated is clear from the places that are known for, as we said before, he told mostly lies about them, so that he is clearly lying still more about remote places. Yet so far as astronomical and mathematical observation is concerned, he might seem to have made adequate use of the facts as regards those who are close to the frozen zone, when he says that there is a lack of some of our crops and animals and a shortage of others, and that they live on millet and other vegetables and fruits and roots; and those who have grain and honey get a drink also from them. Since they have no pure sunshine, they pound the corn in large houses, having gathered the ears together there, for threshing floors become useless because of the lack of sun and the rain.

Other references:
Ἰέρνη: II, 1, 17 (*bis*, C. 74 and 75); II, 5, 14 (C. 119).
τὰ Βρεττανικά: II, 1, 41 (C. 93).
οἱ Πρεττανοί (variant Βρεττανοί): II, 5, 12 (C. 117).

Texts: ed. A. Meinecke, Leipzig, 1852.
ed. H. Leonard Jones, London and New York, 1917–22.
ed. G. Aujac, Paris, 1969.

SUETONIUS TRANQUILLUS, C. (*fl.* A.D. 120)

Divus Vespasianus 4

Having been transferred from there (*sc.* Germany) to *Britannia* he fought 30 times with the enemy. He reduced to subjection two most powerful tribes and more than 20 *oppida* and the island of *Vectis* (*Vectem*, acc.) very near to *Britannia*, under the leadership partly of the consular legate Aulus Plautius, partly of Claudius himself.

Other references:

Britanni: *Julius*, 25; *Gaius*, 44.

Britannia: *Julius* 25; 47; 58; *Gaius*, 19; *Claudius*, 17; 21; *Nero*, 18; 40; *Titus*, 4; *Domitian*, 10.

Britannicus (adj.): *Claudius*, 28 (*triumphus*); Nero, 39 (*clades*); *Galba*, 7 (*expeditio*); *Vitellius*, 2 (*expeditio*).

Text: ed. M. Ihm, Leipzig, 1908.

SULPICIUS SEVERUS (*c.* A.D. 360–420)

Chronica II, 51, 3–4

Instantius who, as we have said above, was condemned by the bishops, was deported to the island of *Sylinancis* (*Sylinancim*, acc., variant *Sylinam*), which is situated beyond the *Britanniae* (*Britannias*, acc. plur., variant *Britanniam*, acc. sing.). Proceedings were then taken against the rest, with the following sentences: Asarivus and Aurelius the deacon were condemned to death, Tiberianus was deprived of his property and sent to the island of *Sylinancis*.

Other references:
Britanni: *Chronica* II, 41, 3 (bishops at Council of Ariminum).
Britannia: II, 41, 3; 49, 5.

Text: ed. C. Halm, Vienna, 1866, repr. 1966.

SYMMACHUS, Q. Aurelius (*c.* A.D. 340–402)

References:

Britannicus: *Epistolae* X, 9 (= 22 or 29), 4 (Theodosius as *Africanus quondam et Britannicus dux*); X, 43 (= 57 or 64), 2 (*bellum*).
Scotticus: II, 77 (= 76) (*canes*).

Text: *MGH* (*AA*) VI (i), ed. O. Seeck, Berlin, 1883, repr. 1961.

TACITUS, Cornelius (*c.* A.D. 56–115+)

1. *Agricola* 10–13

Though the position of *Britannia* and its peoples have been recorded by many authors, I shall describe it again – not to rival them in industry and ability, but because it was only then that it was completely conquered; so that where my predecessors spoke eloquently of matters not yet fully investigated, I shall offer hard facts. As regards extent and situation, *Britannia*, which is the largest of the islands embraced by Roman knowledge, faces Germany to the east, Spain in the west and is actually within sight of the Gauls to the south; its northern shores, with no lands opposite, are beaten by a huge open sea. Livy, the finest of the ancient authors, and Fabius Rusticus, the finest of the moderns, have likened the shape of the whole of *Britannia* to an oblong *scutula* or a *bipennis*.[1] That is its shape this side of *Caledonia*, which has resulted in its being applied to the whole, but when you go further there is a huge and shapeless tract of land running out to the furthest shore, where it narrows into a kind of wedge. Then for the first time a Roman fleet sailed round this shore to the furthest sea and proved *Britannia* to be an island, and at the same time discovered and conquered (*domuit*) the hitherto unknown islands which they call the *Orcades* (*Orcadas*, var. *Orchadas*, acc.). *Thule* (var. *Thyle*) too was sighted, but that was as far as their orders took them and winter was coming on. But they reported that the sea was sluggish and heavy to the rowers and is not raised up as much as other seas by the winds.

[1] For discussions of the meaning of these terms, Ogilvie and Richmond, 168–70 (with the suggestion of *scapulae* for *scutulae*), and N. Reed, *Latomus*, XXXII (1973), 766–68.

I believe this is because there are fewer lands and mountains, which are the efficient and material causes of storms, and the great body of unbroken sea is harder to set in motion. It is not the purpose of this work to investigate the nature of the ocean and the tides, and many writers have dealt with it. I would add one thing, that nowhere is the sea more widely master, with many currents set in different directions, and its ebb and flow does not stop at the coast but it penetrates far inland and winds about, making its way among ridges and mountains as though in its own domain.

Who the first inhabitants of *Britannia* were, whether aborigines or immigrants, is little known, as is usual with barbarians. Their bodily appearance varies, and that is suggestive. For the red hair and large limbs of the inhabitants of *Caledonia* proclaim a German origin; the swarthy faces of the *Silures* and their mostly curly hair, and the fact that Spain lies opposite, make one believe that Iberians (*Hiberos*, acc.) anciently migrated and settled there. Those nearest to the Gauls are also like them, whether because the effect of their origin persists or because the climate has produced this physical type in lands converging together. To form a general judgment, it is likely that Gauls settled in the neighbouring island. You may find the same rites and religious beliefs, the language is not much different, and there is the same rashness in inviting danger, the same fear in facing it when it comes. However, the *Britanni* display more fierceness, seeing that they have not been softened by protracted peace. For we know that the Gauls were once distinguished in warfare, but later sloth came in with ease and valour was lost with liberty. The same thing has happened to those *Britanni* who were conquered early; the rest remain what the Gauls once were.

Their strength is in their infantry, but some tribes also fight with chariots: the nobleman is the charioteer, his clients fight for him. Once they paid obedience to kings, now they are divided by warring factions among their leading men. Nothing has been more helpful to us in dealing with these powerful tribes than the fact that they do not cooperate. Seldom is there a combination of two or three states to repel a common danger; so, fighting separately, all are defeated. The climate is gloomy, with much rain and cloud, but there is no extreme cold. The length of the days is greater than in our part of the world: the night is light and in the furthest part of *Britannia* short, so that you may hardly distinguish between evening and morning twilight. They say that if no clouds hide it the glow of the sun is seen throughout the night and it does not set and rise but simply passes by. In fact the flat extremities of the land, with a low shadow, do not raise the darkness and so the night falls below the level of the heavens and the stars. The soil permits the growth of crops, except the olive and vine and others which usually grow in warmer lands, and is rich in cattle. The crops are slow to ripen, but spring up quickly. The same cause accounts for both, the great moistness of the land and the atmosphere. *Britannia* yields gold and silver and other metals, the reward of victory. The ocean too produces pearls, but they are dusky and blueish. Some think that the men who gather them lack skill, for in the Indian Ocean they (*sc.* oysters, or mussels?) are plucked alive and breathing from the rocks, while in *Britannia* they are collected as they are thrown up. I prefer to believe that nature rather than a lack of greed in men is responsible. The *Britanni* themselves readily submit to the military levy and tribute and the requirements imposed by government, so long as there is no abuse; this they object to, since they are tamed to obedience, not yet to slavery...

2. *Agricola* 22, 1
The third year of campaigning opened up new races, and tribes were ravaged as far as the *Taus* (*usque ad Taum*, var. *Tanaum*, acc.), which is the name of an estuary (*aestuarium*).

3. *Agricola* 23–26
The fourth summer was taken up with securing the areas which he (Agricola) had overrun, and if the valour of the army and the glory of Rome allowed it a boundary could be found in *Britannia*. For *Clota* and *Bodotria*, carried far inland by the tides of opposite seas, are only divided by a narrow strip of land. This was now strengthened with garrisons (*praesidiis*) and the whole sweep of country (*sinus*) on this side was held, with the enemy removed as it were to another island.

In the fifth year of campaigning, having crossed in the first ship (*nave prima transgressus*),[1] he defeated tribes hitherto unknown in many successful battles; and he lined that part of *Britannia* which faces *Hibernia* with troops, with an eye to the future rather than through fear, seeing that *Hibernia*, lying in the middle between *Britannia* and Spain and also convenient to the *Mare Gallicum*, would unite a very strong part of the empire, with great mutual advantages. If it is compared with *Britannia*, its extent is smaller, but it is still larger than the islands in our sea. Its soil and climate and the character and culture of its inhabitants are not much different from those of *Britannia*; the approaches and ports are known through merchants and trade. Agricola had received one of the chieftains of these people who had been driven out by a local rebellion and was detaining him, in the guise of friendship, with a view to the future. I have often heard him say that *Hibernia* could be conquered and held by one legion and a few auxiliaries, and that it would be useful for *Britannia* if Roman arms were everywhere and freedom were, so to say, removed from its sight.

In the summer in which his sixth year of office began he enveloped states situated beyond *Bodotria* and, because there were fears of a rising of all the more distant tribes and of harassment of his columns by hostile forces, he explored the ports with his fleet. The fleet was thus first taken up by Agricola to form part of his force and it continued as such with excellent effect, as the campaign was pressed forward simultaneously by land and sea; and often the infantry, cavalry and marines shared their rations and relaxation in the same camp (*castris*), each extolling their achievements and adventures, now in the depths of forests and mountains, now in the perils of storms and seas, the ones the defeat of enemies on land, the others of the ocean, boasting as soldiers will. Moreover, as was learnt from prisoners, the sight of the fleet dismayed the *Britanni*, as it laid bare the secret places of their sea and deprived the defeated of their last refuge. The inhabitants of *Caledonia* turned to armed resistance with a great force of men, began to attack forts (*castella*) and by taking the offensive added to the fear; and some cowards, in the guise of prudence, were recommending that it would be better to withdraw to this side of *Bodotria* than to be driven there, when he learned

[1] Following the MS text rather than the amendments of Richmond (*Anavam*) and Postgate (*Itunam*): see p. 45 and note 5.

that the enemy were on the point of attacking with several columns. So that he should not be bested by their superior numbers and knowledge of the country, he too divided his army into three parts and marched forward.

When the enemy learned this, they changed their plans and made a united attack by night on the Ninth Legion, as being the weakest, and having killed the sentries struck panic into the sleeping lines. Fighting was going on in the camp (*castris*) itself when Agricola, having learnt of the enemy's movement from his scouts and following their tracks, ordered the swiftest of his cavalry and infantry to attack in the rear and then all to raise a shout. As day broke the standards gleamed close at hand, so that the *Britanni* faced a double terror while the men of the Ninth recovered their spirits and, sure now of their lives, fought for honour rather than safety. They even made a sally on their own account and a savage battle developed in the narrow gates until the enemy were driven off, with one force striving to show that they had brought relief, the other to prove that they did not need it. If marshes and forests had not protected the defeated, that victory would have been the end of the war.

4. *Agricola* 29–35

At the beginning of the summer Agricola suffered a personal blow in the death of a son born the previous year. . . The prosecution of the war was one distraction from grief. So, having sent the fleet in advance to spread uncertainty and terror by plundering in several places, he moved the army forward in light order – now reinforced with the bravest of the *Britanni* of whom he was sure because of their long submission – and came to *Mons Graupius* (*montem Graupium*, acc.), where the enemy had already installed themselves. For the *Britanni* were not at all daunted by the outcome of the previous battle and, having at last learnt that a common danger must be met by united action, by embassies and treaties they had rallied the strength of all their states. So a force of more than 30,000 men were to be seen. . . [Here follow the speeches of Calgacus and Agricola]. . . The ardour of the troops was showing itself while Agricola was still speaking, and the end of his speech was greeted with great enthusiasm and they at once ran to take up arms. Inspired and eager to charge, he disposed them in such a way that the auxiliary infantry, of whom there were 8,000, held the centre, while 3,000 cavalry were spread out on the flanks. The legions took their stand in front of the rampart (*pro vallo*), for victory would be more glorious if no Roman blood were spilt and they would be a reserve in case of reverse. To create an impression and inspire terror, the battle order of the *Britanni* was established on the higher places (*editioribus locis*), in such a way that their front line was on level ground (*in aequo*) while the rest rose, packed together, up the side of the ridge (*per adclive iugum*); the charioteers filled the middle parts of the plain (*media campi*) with their noisy movement.

5. *Agricola* 38

(After the battle of *Mons Graupius*). The next day revealed the scale of the victory more clearly. Everywhere there was a desolate silence, houses smoked in the distance and the scouts encountered no one. They were sent out in all directions and found possible signs of flight but nowhere any indication of the enemy massing, and since the summer was now spent and the war could not be extended more widely he led the army into the territory of the *Boresti* (*Borestorum*, gen.). There he received hostages and ordered the commander of the fleet to sail round *Britannia*; he assigned troops for the purpose and terror had already preceded it. He himself, moving slowly so that the spirit of fresh tribes should be cowed by the deliberateness of his actions, placed his infantry and cavalry in winter quarters. At the same time the fleet, with a favourable wind and great success, reached *Portus Trucculensis* (*Trucculensem portum*, var. *Trutulensem portum*, acc.) whence, having sailed along the nearest side of *Britannia*, it had all returned (*unde proximo Britanniae latere praelecto omnis redierat*).

6. *Annals* XII, 31–33
Well aware that first impressions produce alarm or confidence, he (*sc.* Ostorius Scapula) quickly moved his light cohorts and having cut down those who opposed him and pursued those who fled, so that they should not reform and lest an uncertain peace should allow no rest to the general or his army, he prepared to contain everything this side of the rivers *Trisantona* and *Sabrina*.[1] The first to resist were the *Iceni*, a powerful people not yet broken in battle. . . The defeat of the *Iceni* quietened those who were hesitating between war and peace, and the army was led against the *Decangi* (*in Decangos*, acc.). Their lands were ravaged and booty was extensively taken, with the enemy not daring to offer a pitched battle or, if they tried to ambush the column, their deceit was punished. Now they had arrived not far from the sea which faces the island of *Hibernia*, when disputes among the *Brigantes* called the general back, determined as he was not to undertake new enterprises unless the earlier ones had been consolidated. In fact the *Brigantes* subsided, with the few who were beginning hostilities killed and the rest pardoned. But the people of the *Silures* were not restrained by savagery or leniency from carrying on war and had to be checked by legionary camps. To enable this to be done more quickly the strong veteran *colonia* of *Camulodunum* was founded on conquered territory as a defence against rebels and to imbue the allies with a respect for law. They then marched against the *Silures* (*Siluras*, acc.) a naturally fierce people, now even more confident in the might of Caratacus, whose experience of many an indecisive and many a victorious battle had raised him above the other chiefs of the *Britanni*. He, though inferior in strength, was superior in stratagem because of his knowledge of the country and transferred the war to the *Ordovices* (*Ordovicas*, acc.) . . . (Here follows the account of the last campaign of Caratacus, in which no place-names are mentioned).

7. *Annals* XIV, 29
At that time Paulinus Suetonius was beginning to govern the *Britanni*, a man who, in military skill and popular repute – which allows no one to be without competitors – was the rival of Corbulo and aspired by the defeat of his enemies to equal the glory of the recovery of Armenia. So he prepared to attack the island of *Mona*, whose inhabitants were powerful and which was a refuge for fugitives, and built flat-bottomed ships to contend with the shifting shallows. This was how the infantry crossed; the cavalry followed by fording or, where the water was deep, went over swimming beside their horses.

[1] Accepting Bradley's amendment to *cis Trisantonam et Sabrinam*: see the discussion on p. 45 and note 4.

8. *Annals* XIV, 32
Meanwhile for no obvious reason the statue of Victory at *Camulodunum* fell down and turned its back, as though yielding to the enemy. Women roused to frenzy chanted that doom was at hand, that barbarous raving had been heard in the senate house, that the theatre had resounded with wailings and that in the estuary of the *Tamesa* (*in aestuario Tamesae*) an image had been seen of the *colonia* turned upside down. Now the ocean had a bloody hue and as the tide ebbed the likenesses of human corpses were left on the shore, which led the *Britanni* to hope, the veterans to fear.

9. *Annals* XIV, 33
But Suetonius, with marvellous resolution, marched through the midst of the enemy to *Londinium*, a place not indeed dignified with the title of *colonia* but full of merchants and merchandise. There he debated whether to choose it as the point for a stand, but considering the smallness of his force and how clearly the rashness of Petilius had been punished, he determined to save everything by the loss of one town. Unmoved by the tears and weeping of people who begged his help, he gave the signal for departure, taking into his column those who wished to join him; those who were held there by the weakness of their sex or the weariness of age or love of the place were slain by the enemy. The same fate overtook the *municipium* of *Verulamium* (*Verulamio*, dat.), since the barbarians, delighting in booty, passed by forts and military garrisons and concentrated on the places that were ripest for plunder and insecure for defence. It is established that some 70,000 citizens and allies perished in the places I have mentioned... (Here follows the account of the suppression of the revolt, in which no place-names are mentioned).

Other references:
Brigantes: *Agricola* 17, 2; 31, 5; *Annals* XII, 36; 40; *Histories* III, 45 (bis).
Britanni: *Agr.* 15, 1, 4, 6; 21, 2; 23, 2; 28, 2; 32, 1, 3; 34, 1, 2; 36, 1 (bis); 37, 1, 2; 38, 1; *Ann.* XII, 35; XIV, 34; 35; 37; *Hist.* I. 70; III, 45; IV, 74.
Britannia: *Agr.* 5, 1, 3; 8, 1, 2; 9, 6, 7; 13, 2 (bis); 14, 1; 16, 2, 6; 17, 1; 18, 1, 4; 20, 3; 27, 1; 28, 1, 3; 30, 1, 3; 31, 2; 33, 2, 3; 40, 2; *Ann* II, 24; XI, 3; XII, 31; 36; XIV, 29, 39; XVI, 15; *Dialogus* 17, 4 (bis); *Hist.* I, 2; 6; 52; 59; II, 11; 27; 65; 66 (bis); 86; 97; III, 2; 15; 35; 44; 70; IV, 12; 25; 54; 68; 76; V, 16.
Britannicus (adj.): *Germania* 45, 2; *Hist.* I, 9; 43; 61; II, 32; 37; 57; 100; III, 1; 22; 41; IV, 15; 46; 79.
Caledonia: *Agr.* 27, 1; 31, 4.
Camulodunum: *Ann.* XIV, 31.
Iceni: *Ann.* XIV, 31 (bis).
Mona: *Agr.* 14, 4; 18, 4.
Ordovices: *Agr.* 18, 2, 3.
Silures: *Agr.* 17, 3; *Ann.* XII, 38, 39 (bis); 40; XIV, 29.
Trinobantes: *Ann.* XIV, 31.

Texts: *Agricola* edd. R. M. Ogilvie & I. A. Richmond, Oxford, 1967.
Annals ed. C. D. Fisher, Oxford, 1906.
Dialogus & *Germania* edd. M. Winterbottom, Oxford, 1975.
Histories ed. C. D. Fisher, Oxford, 1911.

TERTULLIAN (*c.* A.D. 160–240)

References:

Britanni: *Adversus Iudaeos*, 7 (bis).
Britannicus (adj.): *De Cultu Feminarum* i, 6 (*mare*).

Text: *Migne*, Ser. Lat. I and II, Paris, 1844, repr. Turnhout, 1956.

THEODORETUS CYRI (*c.* A.D. 393–466)

Reference:

Βρεττανούς: *Therapeutica* IX (*Leges*), 15.

Text: ed. P. Carnivet, Paris, 1958.

THEOPHILUS of Antioch (*fl.* A.D. 180)

Reference:

Βριττανοί: *Ad Autolycum*, II, 32.

Text: ed. R. M. Grant, Oxford, 1970.

TIBULLUS, Albius (*c.* 50–19 B.C.)

Reference:

Britannus (coll.): *Carm.* III, vii (*Pan. Messallae*, falsely attributed), 149.

Text: ed. J. P. Postgate, Oxford, 1915.

VALERIUS FLACCUS, C. (*fl.* A.D. 80)

Reference:

Caledonius (adj.): *Argonautica* i. 8 (*Caledonius oceanus*).

Text: ed. O. Kramer, Leipzig, 1913.

VALERIUS MAXIMUS (*fl.* A.D. 32)

Reference:

Britannicus: *Facta et Dicta Memorabilia* III, ii, 23 (bis, *Britannicae insulae* and *Britannicis oculis*).

Text: ed. C. Kempf, 1888, repr. Stuttgart, 1966.

VEGETIUS RENATUS, Flavius (*fl.* A.D. 390)

Reference:

Britanni (var. *Brittanni*, *Britani*, *Brittani*, *Britanii*): *Epitoma Rei Militaris* IV, xxxvii.

Text: ed. C. Lang, 1885, repr. Stuttgart, 1968.

VELLEIUS PATERCULUS (*c.* 19 B.C.–A.D. 30+)

References:

Britannia: *Hist. Rom.* II, xlvi, 1; xlvii, 1.

Text: ed. S. de Pritzwald, Leipzig, 1933.

VENANTIUS HONORIUS CLEMENTIANUS FORTUNATUS (*c.* A.D. 540–600)

References:

Britanni: *Vita S. Martini* III, 26.
Britannia: *Carmina* VIII, 3, 155 (variants *Britinia, Brittannia, Brittania*).
Britannus (coll.): *Carmina* VI, 5, 219 (variants *Britanus, Brittanus*); VIII, 1, 18 (variant *Brittannus*); X, 7, 8 (variants *Brittanus, Brittannus*); *Vita S. Martini* III, 494 (variants *Brittanus, Brittannus*).
Britannus (adj.): *Carmina* VII, 8, 64 (*crotta*; variant *Brittanna*).
Thyle: *Vita S. Martini* III, 394 (variants *Tyle, Thile*).

Text: *MGH* (*AA*) IV, ed. F. Leo, Berlin, 1881, repr. 1961.

VERGILIUS MARO, P. (70–19 B.C.)

References:

Britanni: *Ecl.* i, 66 (*penitus toto divisos orbe Britannos*); *Georg.* III, 25.
Thule: *Georg.* I, 30.

Text: ed. R. A. B. Mynors, Oxford, 1969.

VERONA LIST: see NOMINA PROVINCIARUM OMNIUM

VIBIUS SEQUESTER (?5th cent. A.D.)

Flumina, 98

The river Liger (Loire) which separates the Aquitani and the Celtae flows into the *Occeanum Brittannicum.*[1]

Text: ed. R. Gelsomino, Leipzig, 1967.

XIPHILINUS (11th cent. A.D.)

1. *Epitome Dionis Nicaeensis* 212 (= Cassius Dio LXVI, 20)

At this time, war having broken out again in *Brettania* (τῇ Βρεττανίᾳ, dat.), Gnaeus Julius Agricola both overran all the territory of the enemy and became the first of the Romans of whom we know to discover that *Brettania* is surrounded by water. For certain soldiers, having mutinied and murdered a centurion and a tribune, took refuge in ships and having put to sea sailed round the western part of it, just as the

[1] This passage does not appear in MSS before the 12th century and is almost certainly a late interpolation.

waves and the wind carried them, and without realising it, coming from the other side, put in at camps which were on this side. Thereafter Agricola sent others to attempt the circumnavigation and learned from them that it is an island. Such were the events in *Brettania*.

2. *Epitome Dionis Nicaeensis* 321–322 (= Cassius Dio LXXVI, 12)
There are two very great races of *Brettani* (Βρεττανῶν, gen.), the *Caledonii* (Καληδόνιοι) and *Maeatae* (Μαιάται) and the names of the others have, so to say, been merged in them. The *Maeatae* dwell near the cross-wall which cuts the island in two, the *Caledonii* beyond them, and both inhabit wild and waterless mountains and desolate and marshy plains, having no walls nor cities nor tilled land, but living off flocks and wild animals and some fruits; for they do not eat the fish which exist in huge and inexhaustible quantities. They live in tents, naked and unshod, holding their women in common and rearing all their offspring together. They are organised democratically for the most part and they delight in plundering. They go to war in chariots, using small and swift horses, and also on foot. They are very fast in running and very firm in standing their ground. Their arms are a shield and a short spear with a bronze apple on the end of the shaft, so that when it is shaken it clashes, to the dismay of the enemy; they also have daggers. They can bear hunger and cold and all kinds of hardship; for having plunged into the marshes they endure many days with only their head out of the water, and in the woods they live on bark and roots; and for all circumstances they prepare a food of which if they eat a piece the size of a bean they neither hunger nor thirst. Such is the island of *Brettania* and such are its inhabitants, at least of the hostile part of it. For it is an island and this, as I said, was clearly proved at this time. Its length is 7,132 stades, its greatest breadth 2,310 and its least 300. Of these lands we hold not much less than a half.

Other references (figures in brackets refer to the reconstructed text of Dio, as arranged by Boissevain):

Βρεττανία: 142 (LX, 30); 158 (LXII, 1); 159 (LXII, 32); 162 (LXII, 7); 164 (bis, LXII, 11); 196 (LXV, 8); 249 (LXIX, 13); 272 (LXXII, 9); 321 (bis, LXXVI, 10 and 11); 323 (LXXVI, 13).

Βρεττανικός: 142 (LX, 30: πόλεμος); 163 (LXII, 8: σύμφορα); 165 (LXII, 13: τὰ Βρεττανικά): 271 (LXXIII, 8: πόλεμος).

Βρεττανίς (adj.): 159 (LXII, 2: γυνή); 325 (LXXVI, 17: γυνή).

Βρεττανοί: 162 (LXII, 6).

Καληδονία: 322 (LXXVI, 13).

Καληδονίοι: 324 (LXXVI, 15); 325 (LXXVI, 16: sing.).

Μῶννα: 162 (LXII, 7: Μῶνναν, acc.); 163 (bis, LXII, 8: Μώνναν, acc. and Μώννης, gen.).

Ταμέσα (masc.): 159 (LXII, 2: Ταμέσᾳ, dat.).

Text: ed. U. P. Boissevain, Berlin, 1900, repr. 1945.

ZOSIMUS (*fl.* A.D. 500)

1. *Historia Nova* VI, 5, 2–6, 1

The barbarians beyond the Rhine, attacking everything they could, drove both the inhabitants of the *Brettanic* island (τὴν Βρεττανικὴν νῆσον, acc.) and some of the peoples of the Gauls to the necessity of defecting from the rule of the Romans and living in their own way, no longer subject to their laws. So those from *Brettania*, taking up arms and risking themselves, freed the cities from the barbarians who were threatening them, and the whole of Armorica and other provinces of the Gauls, imitating the *Brettani*, freed themselves in their turn, ejected the magistrates of the Romans and, so far as they could, set up their own government. And the defection of *Brettania* and of the Gaulish peoples took place during the usurpation of Constantine, the barbarians having attacked through the laxity of his rule.

2. *Historia Nova* VI, 10

He (*sc.* Alaric) brought over all the cities (*sc.* of Aemilia) with no difficulty, except Bononia, which withstood a siege for several days and which he could not take, and then went on to the Ligurians, compelling them to accept Attalus as Emperor. But Honorius having issued a rescript by letter to the cities in *Brettania* that they should protect themselves, and having rewarded the soldiers by gifts out of the supplies sent by Heraclianus, Honorius gained complete relief, having altogether won the goodwill of the troops. [1]

Other references:

Βρεττανία: *Historia Nova* I, 66, 2 (bis); 68, 3; II, 8, 2; 15, 1; III, 5, 2; IV, 35, 3; VI, 2, 1; 2, 2; 2, 4; 3, 1 (plur.).

ἡ Βρεττανικὴ νῆσος: I, 64, 1; II, 33, 2; III, 5, 2; IV, 3, 1; 12, 2; 19, 2; 35, 3 (plur.); V, 27, 2; VI, 1, 2.

Text: ed. L. Mendelssohn, Leipzig, 1887, repr. Hildesheim, 1963.

[1] The relevance of this much-quoted passage to Britain is very doubtful. The rest of the chapter deals entirely with Italy and it was to Italy from Africa that Heraclianus had sent supplies. The text certainly reads ἐν Βρεττανίᾳ, but Βρεττία is the Greek for Bruttium, in southern Italy (cf. Stephanus, s.v.).

CHAPTER THREE

PTOLEMY'S GEOGRAPHY

I. PTOLEMY'S AIMS

Claudius Ptolemaeus was a mathematician and astronomer who worked in Alexandria in the second quarter of the second century of our era. His *nomen* suggests that an ancestor had been granted Roman citizenship by one of the Claudian emperors and his *cognomen* attests his Macedonian descent, but most of what is known about him depends on internal evidence from his works. The most important of these, the Μαθηματική Σύνταξις, usually called the *Almagest*[1] from the Arabicised form of ἡ Μεγίστη ('The Greatest'), includes observations made up to A.D. 141, and since at the end of its second book he promises a fuller work on geography, the *Geography*[2] itself may confidently be dated to A.D. 140–150 – though, as we shall see, much of the material is derived from earlier writers. The work is divided into eight books. The first is an introduction, discussing general principles, criticising Marinus (who was his chief source of information) and explaining the theory of map projections; Books II to VII contain lists of latitudes and longitudes, taking the known world country by country, and further remarks on projections; and Book VIII is essentially a summary, listing the more important places in each of the sections into which he has divided the world. The full description of the British Isles is contained in Book II.

Ptolemy's aims in writing the *Geography* can best be understood by considering his own introductory words:

> Geography is the graphic representation of the known world as a whole, including the things that relate to it as a whole. It differs from chorography in that chorography takes single regions separately and deals with them individually, embracing every smallest detail, such as creeks, hamlets, villages, the reaches of rivers and such things; while the function of geography is to display the known world as a coherent unity, dealing with the nature and location only of such things as are suitable to a general and universal description, such as gulfs, great

[1] References to the *Almagest* here are to the edition of J. L. Heiberg (Leipzig, 1898–1903).

[2] References to the *Geography* are to the edition of C. Müller and C. T. Fischer (Paris, 1883–1901) for Books I–V, and to that of C. F. Nobbe (Leipzig, 1843–45, reprinted Hildesheim, 1966) for Books VI–VIII.

cities and nations, the more notable rivers and similar outstanding things in each category.

The aim of chorography is to concentrate on a part, as one might draw a single ear or a single eye, while that of geography is to look at the subject as a whole, as one would do when drawing the whole head.

For just as when a picture is planned the salient features must of necessity be deliberately drawn in proportion and, whether the whole or the part is being painted, the size of the canvas to receive the picture must be adapted to the distance from which the eye can comfortably take it in, so it is reasonable and useful that chorography should show the smallest details, geography the actual countries and their general features; because in the inhabited world the salient points and those which can be shown all together at a convenient scale are the locations of places, but included within those places there are still distinctive features.

For the most part chorography regards its subjects qualitatively, for it is not even concerned with their relative positions; while the approach of geography is quantitative rather than qualitative, in that in every case it is concerned with the relations of places in space and with qualitative relationships only insofar as they apply to the salient features and the general outlines.

Hence chorography demands skill in topography, and no one would undertake it unless he were a good draughtsman (γραφικὸς ἀνήρ), but geography does not, because it relies on bare lines (ψίλαι γράμμαι) and annotation to show positions and general shapes. Thus chorography has no use for mathematical method, but in geography it plays a major part.

For geography has to consider the shape and size of the whole earth and its relationship to the heavens, to determine the character and extent of the known part of it, and also beneath which of the celestial spheres the various places in it fall; whence we may discern the lengths of days and which of the fixed stars are in the zenith, both those above the earth and those which are at any time below the horizon, and all the other things which we are wont to consider in describing the inhabited world.

And this is the subject of the fairest and most sublime contemplation, to reveal to human perception, by mathematics, the nature of the heavens themselves, because they can be observed revolving about us, and of the earth by a figure, because the real earth, being very large and not, like the heavens, encompassing us, cannot be traversed either as a whole or as to all its parts by one and the same man.

Geography I, I

This passage gives a clear indication of what we may, and what we may not, expect from the work, and several points in it are worthy of note. First, Ptolemy, still the astronomer and mathematician, approaches the subject as a 'pure' scientist and while his work may prove to be of practical use, this is a secondary consideration; in this we may observe a marked difference from the highly practical Roman itineraries which are dealt with in the next chapter. Secondly, the geographer, as defined by Ptolemy, is concerned primarily with outlines, not with pettifogging points of detail, and this is reflected in the work in several ways. He does not even profess to locate anything more accurately than to $\frac{1}{12}$ of a degree of latitude (which, given the size of globe he was using, means $5\frac{1}{2}$ Roman miles) and, as Professor Tierney has pointed out, inspection suggests that in reality he does not aspire to anything better than a quarter of a degree ($16\frac{1}{2}$ Roman miles).[1] Again, while the mouths of rivers, even in Britain, are distinguished as gulfs (κόλποι), estuaries (εἰσχύσεις) or simply outflows (ἐκβολαί), it is only in the case of really large rivers, like the Rhône, that he gives coordinates for confluences or major changes of course. So far as places are concerned, since he is concerned with 'quantity', not 'quality', he lumps them all together as πόλεις, or 'cities', even in areas like northern Britain or free Germany, where no recognisable cities can have existed: in fact in Ptolemy the word πόλις means no more than 'place', or perhaps 'place-with-a-name', so that it is legitimate to seek his πόλεις not only in towns but also in forts or even camps. Thirdly, the Ptolemaic geographer is forced to be selective and will not be able to use all the material at his disposal, while what he does select will be determined not by the intrinsic importance of places, and certainly not by concern for posterity, but by his overall purpose, which is the mapping of the inhabited world as a whole. It follows that the omission of a town or fort or river does not necessarily mean that Ptolemy was unaware of its existence, but rather that he did not consider its inclusion necessary for his particular purpose; and conversely, in outlying areas like northern Britain, he might include places like *Tuesis* and *Pinnata Castra* which elsewhere would be squeezed out by more important entries – a practice preferable, at least, to 'placing elephants for lack of towns'.

2. PTOLEMY'S METHODS

After the passage quoted above, Ptolemy continues as follows:

> This must suffice as a summary account of the aims of the geographer and the way in which he differs from the chorographer.
>
> But since our present task is to draw our inhabited world as accurately as possible, we must first understand that accounts of travel (ἱστορία περιοδική) are of primary importance, in such an enquiry, because they preserve the fullest knowledge obtained from the reports of careful observers who have traversed the various countries; and that their observations and accounts fall into two classes, terrestrial and celestial, the terrestrial setting out the relative positions of places by simple measurement of the distances between them, the celestial by observations made with the astrolabe (ἀστρόλαβος) and the gnomon (σκιοθήρον) – the latter method being independent and more reliable, the former more general and dependent on the other.
>
> For first, if we have, by either of these methods, to establish to what part of the world the line between two places inclines (note that we do not simply want to know the distance between them but also the bearing, whether to the north, for example, or to the east, or to points between these) such a thing cannot be accurately determined except by the use of the instruments I have mentioned,

[1] J. J. Tierney, *JHS*, LXXIX (1959), 148.

with which at any place or time the position of the meridian can be observed and, with the help of this, the bearing of the distant point.

Further, even given this, a measurement of the mileage does not yield us secure knowledge of the truth, because our journeys are seldom completely straight and there are many deviations both in roads and in ships' courses, and because in journeys on land to find the length of the straight route one must subtract from the total mileage according to the nature and number of the deviations, while in sea voyages account must be taken of variations in the strength of the winds, which are rarely constant; and even if the distance between two places be accurately fixed, this does not tell us the relationship of that distance to the total circumference of the earth nor to the equator nor the poles.

But observation of the celestial bodies gives each of these accurately.

Geography I, 2

Here we may again note the stress on pure scientific methods, especially those of astronomy, but also the fact that Ptolemy makes no mention of the use of triangulation in relating one place to others; where astronomical observation is lacking, what are to be used are distance and bearing, and this, as we shall see, seems to be the method employed in Britain.

Ptolemy lays great stress on the need to use the most up to date information. 'In our enquiry', he says (*Geography* I, 6), 'it is necessary to pay attention to the latest accounts of our own time and, both in setting out what is now reported and in judging what had been reported previously, to decide what is worthy of belief and what is not.' In most respects, however, he seems to have felt that this requirement was met by taking the work of Marinus of Tyre and merely correcting it where necessary and improving its presentation. Our knowledge of Marinus[1] is derived exclusively from the references to him by Ptolemy, but from these it can be deduced that he did map the whole of the known world, from Britain to the Malay Peninsula, and that he flourished about the turn of the first and second centuries. The one reference to his work on Britain is discussed below and his date is of great significance for an understanding of the British section.

While his work undoubtedly represents the highest achievement of ancient geography, Ptolemy erred in one important respect. About the beginning of the 2nd century B.C. Eratosthenes,[2] by relating the distance between Aswan and Alexandria to the angle made by the sun's rays at the latter, had calculated the circumference of the Earth as 252,000 stades (44,775 km), and while it was based on three false assumptions (that Aswan was actually on the Tropic of Cancer, that the two places were on the same meridian, and that the measurement between them was accurate), this is only some 11 per cent in excess of the true figure (40,067 km). About a hundred years later Poseidonius,[3] using inaccurate observations of the star Canopus from Rhodes and Alexandria, had reduced the estimate to 180,000 stades, or more than

[1] On Marinus, see J. Honigmann, *P.–W.* XL (1930), 1767–96.

[2] The fragments relating to this are collected and discussed in H. Berger, *Die Geographischen Fragmente des Eratosthenes* (Leipzig, 1869, reprinted Amsterdam, 1964), 99–142.

[3] L. Edelstein and I. G. Kidd, *Posidonius I – the Fragments* (Cambridge, 1972), 181–83.

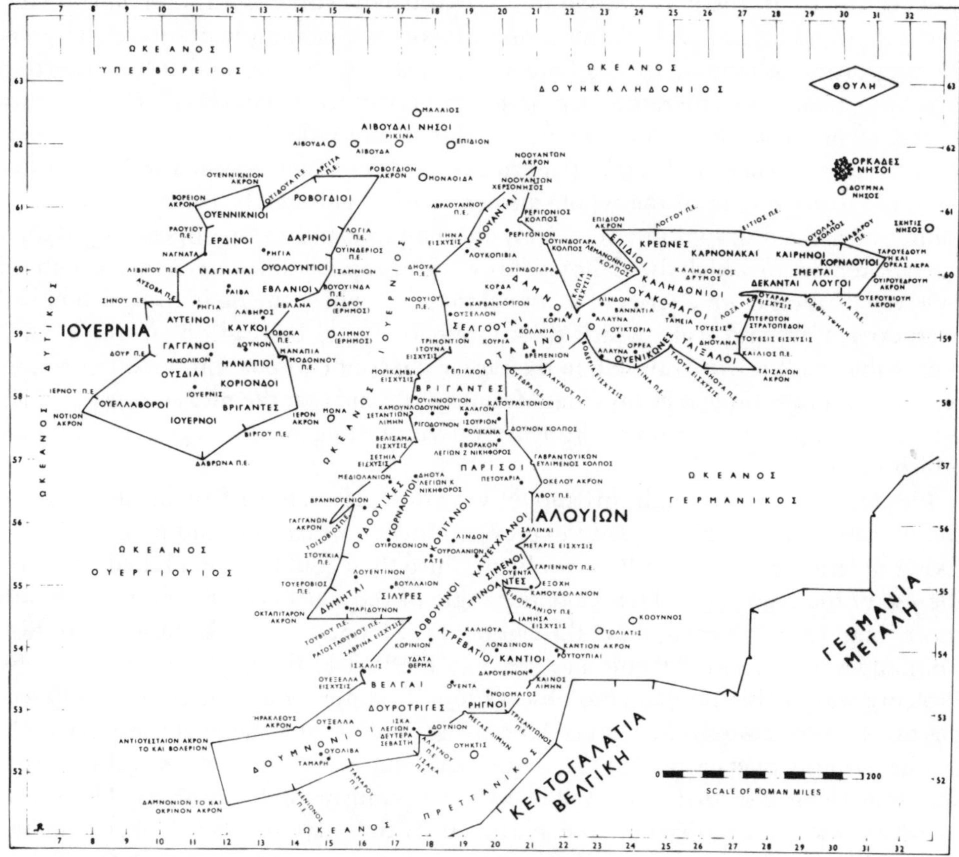

Fig. 1. Ptolemy's map of the British Isles.

16 per cent too little. Simply by implication, and with no more comment than that 'this accords with generally agreed measurements' (*Geography* I, 11), Ptolemy accepted the lower figure. This had disastrous effects on his world map (and led ultimately to the 15th-century discovery of America) but for our purposes the importance of the figure is that it gives us the scale of his maps: if 180,000 stades is taken to be the circumference of the earth, then one degree of latitude must represent 500 stades, or 62½ Roman miles.

Ptolemy does not tell us how he, or Marinus before him, reduced the mass of data which he received, from travellers' reports and other sources, to the orderly list of latitudes and longitudes which forms the main part of the work. As we have already remarked, he devotes a good deal of attention to map projections and in fact offers three possibilities, the first a simple conic one, the second (which is reproduced in Nobbe's edition) much more refined, with meridians, as well as parallels, curved, and the third, more complicated still, a plane within an armillary sphere.[1] All these,

[1] *Geography* I, 21–24; VII, 6.

however, relate to the presentation of the world as a whole and for sectional maps, like that of the British Isles, he authorises the use of a rectilinear graticule and gives the proportion of latitude to longitude to be used in each case, so that the distortion is not too great.[1] It is, therefore, legitimate to present the detail of so limited an area in this form, as we have done in fig. 1. But if one reflects on the sheer physical difficulty of working on sheets of papyrus, or even on a whitewashed wall, one must conclude that the map of the whole known world, with nearly 10,000 names on it, cannot have been drawn out accurately in one piece and in one operation. Rather the world map, to which the elaborate projections applied, must have been produced by generalisation from a series of sectional maps on which the basic compilation had been carried out and from which the coordinates could be read off. If this is so, it is probable that Ptolemy himself, in the earlier stages of compilation, used this simple rectangular projection (as he says that Marinus did)[2] and that the measurements which we can make from it represent Ptolemy's own plotting to the degree of accuracy which he claims.

Ideally, of course (though this applies very little, if at all, to Britain) the material should have come to him already expressed in terms of latitude and longitude. The fixing of latitudes presented little problem, since they could be established either by the use of the gnomon, which gave the angle of the sun's rays, or, more easily but more roughly, by observation of the length of the longest day at the summer solstice. Longitudes were more difficult and the only method of fixing them recognised by Ptolemy was by the simultaneous observation of eclipses of the moon from different places[3] – a very complicated procedure in the absence of reliable chronometers. In fact he seriously over-estimated the west to east length of the known world (and that was something else that contributed to the optimism of Columbus). His prime meridian was drawn through the Fortunate Islands (approximately Ferro in the Canary Islands) because this was the most westerly place known to him, but it is clear that this was merely the 'false origin' of his grid and its 'true origin',[4] as reflected in the tables in Book VIII of the *Geography*, was Alexandria.

3. EARLIER STUDIES OF PTOLEMY'S BRITAIN

Ptolemy's account of Britain had, of course, attracted the attention of British antiquaries from Camden onwards, but the modern study of it may fairly be said to begin with a scholarly and sensible paper which Henry Bradley read to the Society of Antiquaries in 1883.[5] Castigating alike the fanciful theories of amateur etymologists and what he called 'desultory attempts at textual criticism', Bradley drew his own map, from Nobbe's text of 1843–45, and interpreted it in the light of sound common

[1] *Geography* VIII, 1–2, with proportions for the British Isles in 3.

[2] *Geography* I, 20.

[3] *Geography* I, 4.

[4] Just as the true origin of the British National Grid is at 49° N 2° W, SSW of Jersey, but the false origin, from which Grid References are calculated, is for convenience set at a point W by S of the Scilly Isles.

[5] H. Bradley, 'Ptolemy's Geography of the British Isles', *Archaeologia*, XLVIII (1885), 379–96.

sense. Since Romano-British archaeology was then in its infancy, many of his locations of place-names were tentative, but most of the identifications in the coastal list which are now accepted as beyond question may be found in his paper. On the vexed question of the distortion of Scotland the hypothesis which he offered was that Ptolemy, or one of his predecessors, presented with three maps which covered the areas corresponding with Ireland, Scotland, and England and Wales, had fitted them together incorrectly.

A more ambitious approach was that of Thomas Glazebrook Rylands,[1] who in 1893 attempted to 'correct' Ptolemy's presentation mathematically and tried to distinguish errors of measurement and scale, errors of observation, and errors dependent upon projection. Despite its ingenuity, and although it included a few valuable insights, Rylands' work suffered from several shortcomings. He did not understand textual criticism and treated editions, and even maps, without regard to their relationship to the manuscripts, dismissing Müller's edition (which appeared while his own work was in progress) in a caustic footnote; he presupposed a much greater degree of accuracy in both observation and measurement than can possibly have obtained; and his methods led him to claim as proven some identifications which were geographically and onomastically absurd.[2]

This work seems to have been unknown to Sir William Flinders-Petrie, whose paper 'Ptolemy's Geography of Albion', published in 1917,[3] concentrates on distances but assumes and produces some strange identifications, but in 1921 it was taken up by Sir Ian Richmond,[4] when he made a fresh attempt at solving the problems of Ptolemy's Scotland. Following Rylands, Richmond argued that the distortion was due to the observation of a lunar eclipse in Scotland giving a longitude which conflicted with that already accepted by Ptolemy for London. This, coupled with faulty gnomonic observations and the small size of Ptolemy's globe, would have compelled the turning of Scotland, and Richmond set out to reverse the process. Having rotated the country north of the river *Vedra* (Wear) through 90° and then, as a corollary, converted latitude to longitude, with the implied reversal of ratio, he replotted the πόλεις and attempted to make identifications. South of the Forth–Clyde isthmus the results were fairly satisfactory, but further north the picture was little improved. So, following Rylands' theory that the variant readings in the manuscripts represented two original editions of the *Geography*, Richmond argued that the 'change' in the distance between *Orrea* (which he took to be Carpow) and *Bannatia* (which he took as Dalginross) justified a reduction of 3:1 in the distances between the other πόλεις. This produced a plausible picture and led him to suggest a number of identifications, notably that of Πτερωτὸν Στρατόπεδον (which Müller had already equated with the *Pinnatis* of the *Ravenna Cosmography* and so translated as *Pinnata Castra*) with the legionary fortress at Inchtuthil.

Thirty-seven years later Richmond[5] still maintained some of this argument, though

[1] T. Glazebrook Rylands, *The Geography of Ptolemy Elucidated* (Dublin, 1893).

[2] E.g. in placing *Novantarum Promontorium* at the Point of Aird, in Skye.

[3] W. M. Flinders-Petrie, 'Ptolemy's Geography of Albion', *PSAS*, LII (1917–18), 12–26.

[4] I. A. Richmond, 'Ptolemaic Scotland', *PSAS*, LVI (1921–22), 288–301.

[5] Richmond, *RNNB* (1958).

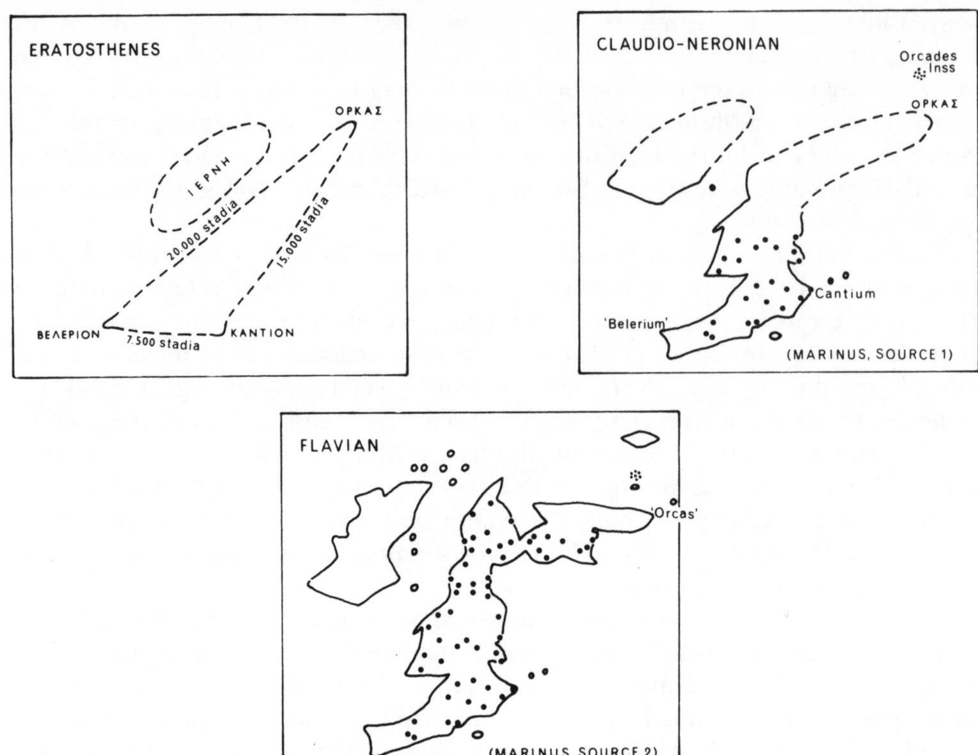

Fig. 2. The possible evolution of the map of the British Isles (after Tierney).

with the qualification that 'the result is neither Ptolemy nor any version of his work that ever in fact saw the light of day'; and in the last work in which he collaborated, the edition of the *Agricola*,[1] the astronomical aspect of the theory is relegated to a footnote, although some of the identifications (notably those of *Orrea* with Carpow and of *Pinnata Castra* with Inchtuthil) are still retained. The reason for this more cautious attitude may be found in the appearance in 1959 of an important paper of Professor J. J. Tierney.[2] Reviewing all the evidence, and especially that relating to earlier accounts of Britain, Tierney argued forcefully, first, that Ptolemy had no astronomical data for the British Isles at all, but that their position was established by a series of measurements from the accepted latitude of Marseille; and second, that the overall shape of Britain, including the apparent 'turning' of Scotland, was dictated by the tradition of an obtuse-angled triangle, reflected in the length of the three sides given in Diodorus Siculus v, 21 (p. 62) and derived from Eratosthenes (fig. 2). Tierney concluded: 'I hope I have shown, for those who undertake the task (*sc.* of the identification of places in Ptolemy), their scope and freedom of speculation need not be hampered by the *damnosa hereditas* of a list of apparently astronomical data which in fact never really existed.'

[1] Ogilvie and Richmond (1967), 36–46.
[2] J. J. Tierney, 'Ptolemy's Map of Scotland', *JHS*, LXXIX (1959), 132–48.

4. THE 'TURNING' OF SCOTLAND

Professor Tierney's conclusion is confirmed by the references made to Britain in the *Almagest*, which was written before the *Geography* and, because geography forms only a minor element in it, mirrors accepted opinion more uncritically than does the later work. Here Ptolemy is listing parallels of latitude at regular intervals of a quarter of an hour in the length of their longest day:

19. The 19th parallel, at which the longest day would be one of $16\frac{1}{2}$ equinoctial hours. It is at $51\frac{2}{3}$ degrees from the equator and is drawn through southern *Brettania.* With a gnomon of 60 units a shadow is cast of $31\frac{5}{12}$ units at the summer solstice, of $75\frac{5}{12}$ at the equinox, and of $229\frac{1}{3}$ at the winter solstice.
20. The 20th parallel, at which the longest day would be one of $16\frac{3}{4}$ equinoctial hours. It is at $52\frac{5}{6}$ degrees from the equator and is drawn through the mouths of the Rhine. With a gnomon of 60 units a shadow is cast of $33\frac{1}{3}$ units at the summer solstice, of $79\frac{1}{12}$ at the equinox, and of $253\frac{1}{4}$ at the winter solstice.
21. The 21st parallel, at which the longest day would be one of 17 equinoctial hours. It is at $54\frac{1}{2}$ degrees from the equator and is drawn through the mouths of the Don. With a gnomon of 60 units a shadow is cast of $34\frac{11}{12}$ units at the summer solstice, of $82\frac{7}{12}$ at the equinox, and of $278\frac{3}{4}$ at the winter solstice.
22. The 22nd parallel, at which the longest day would be one of $17\frac{1}{4}$ equinoctial hours. It is at 55 degrees from the equator and is drawn through *Brigantium* (Βριγαντίου, gen.) of *Magna Brettania* (Μέγαλη Βρεττανία). With a gnomon of 60 units a shadow is cast of $36\frac{1}{4}$ units at the summer solstice, of $85\frac{2}{3}$ at the equinox, and of $304\frac{1}{2}$ at the winter solstice.
23. The 23rd parallel, at which the longest day would be one of $17\frac{1}{2}$ equinoctial hours. It is at 56 degrees from the equator and is drawn through the middle of *Magna Brettania.* With a gnomon of 60 units a shadow is cast of $37\frac{2}{3}$ units at the summer solstice, of $88\frac{5}{6}$ at the equinox, and of $335\frac{1}{4}$ at the winter solstice.
24. The 24th parallel, at which the longest day would be one of $17\frac{3}{4}$ equinoctial hours. It is at 57 degrees from the equator and is drawn through *Caturactonium* (Κατουρακτονίου, gen.) of *Brettania.* with a gnomon of 60 units a shadow is cast of $39\frac{1}{3}$ units at the summer solstice, of $92\frac{5}{12}$ at the equinox, and of $372\frac{1}{12}$ at the winter solstice.
25. The 25th parallel, at which the longest day would be one of 18 hours. It is at 58 degrees from the equator and is drawn through the southern parts of *Parva Brettania* (Μικρὰ Βρεττανία). With a gnomon of 60 units a shadow is cast of $40\frac{2}{3}$ units at the summer solstice, of 96 at the equinox, and of $419\frac{1}{12}$ at the winter solstice.
26. The 26th parallel, at which the longest day would be one of $18\frac{1}{4}$ hours. It is at $59\frac{1}{2}$ degrees from the equator and is drawn through the middle of *Parva Brettania.*

Hereafter we have not used the increase of a quarter of an hour because the parallels are too close together, with the difference in the height of the pole less than a whole degree, and because we do not need the same exactness for the more northern parts. This is why we have thought it superfluous to give the relationship of shadows to the gnomon.

27. So where the longest day is one of 19 equinoctial hours, the parallel is 61 degrees from the equator and is drawn through the northern parts of *Parva Brettania*.
28. Where the longest day is one of 19½ equinoctial hours, the parallel is 62 degrees from the equator and is drawn through the islands called *Ebudae* (᾿Εβούδων, gen.).
29. Where the longest day is one of 20 equinoctial hours, the parallel is 63 degrees from the equator and is drawn through the island of *Thule* (Θούλης, gen.).
30. Where the longest day is one of 21 equinoctial hours, the parallel is 64 degrees from the equator and is drawn through unknown peoples of the Scythians.

Almagest II, 6

A number of points may be noted in this passage. First, at this stage Ptolemy is not interested in the precise details of the northern regions and there is no indication that he has yet done any serious work on them. Secondly, the nomenclature is different from that in the *Geography*: here Britain is Μέγαλη Βρεττανία (that is, 'Great Britain') and Ireland is Μικρὰ Βρεττανία ('Little Britain'), as opposed to *Alvion* and *Hivernia* in the *Geography*. Yet thirdly, the overall picture is very similar to that given in the later work. Ireland is already placed rather far north in relation to Britain, extending from 58° to 61° (as compared with 57° to 61°30′ in the *Geography*) and while the northern extremity of Britain is not separately stated, it works out at 60°20′ (as compared with 61°40′). Of the places mentioned, *Brigantium* (which does not appear elsewhere and must be a false deduction from the tribal name) is placed some 3° south of the location later given to the *Brigantes*, and *Caturactonium* is 1° south of the position it assumes in the *Geography* (where it is attributed to the *Brigantes*), but both the *Ebudae* and *Thule* are at the same latitude as later – although the selection of places is quite different from that in Book VIII of the *Geography*, and the two lists have only *Thule* and *Caturactonium* in common. All this tends to support the belief that, although several refinements have been introduced, the general shape of Britain in the *Geography* is traditional.

Nevertheless, the fitting into this shape of the new knowledge which was acquired in the course of the Roman conquest of Britain must have presented difficult problems. No competent sea captain can ever have claimed that the general trend of Scotland was from west to east, rather than from south to north, nor can his account have omitted Cape Wrath, whose modern name is in fact derived from the Old Norse *hvarf*, meaning 'turning point'.[1] If we wish to recover what the sea captains and others actually reported, before it was trimmed to fit the procrustean bed of Eratosthenes, we must first alter the alignment of Scotland in relation to southern Britain.

Richmond's solution was to rotate it through a right angle, using the mouth of the *Vedra* (Wear) as a pivot, but his justification for this was his belief that Ptolemy was, even at the preparatory stage, using latitudes and longitudes; and this, as we have seen, is highly improbable. There is, however, another way of attacking the

[1] We are grateful to Mr Ian Fraser of the School of Scottish Studies, Edinburgh, for information on this.

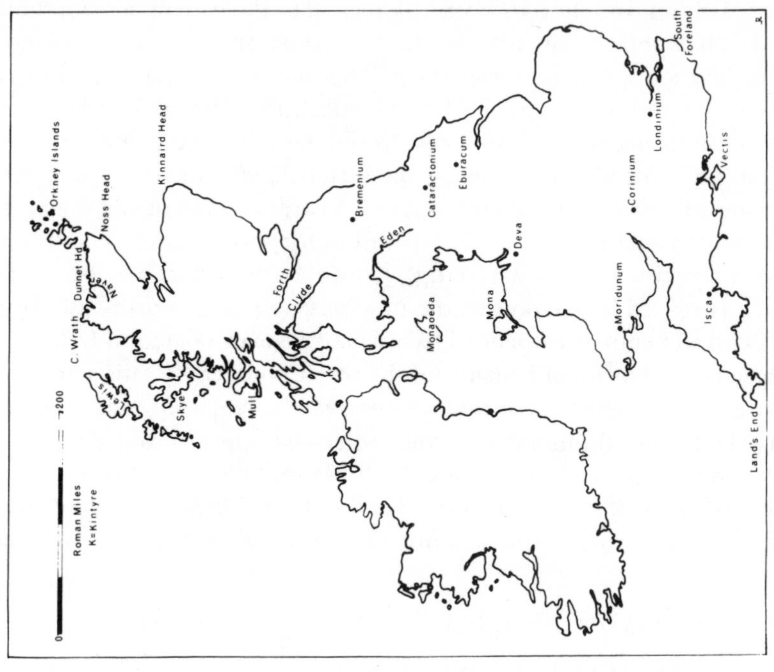

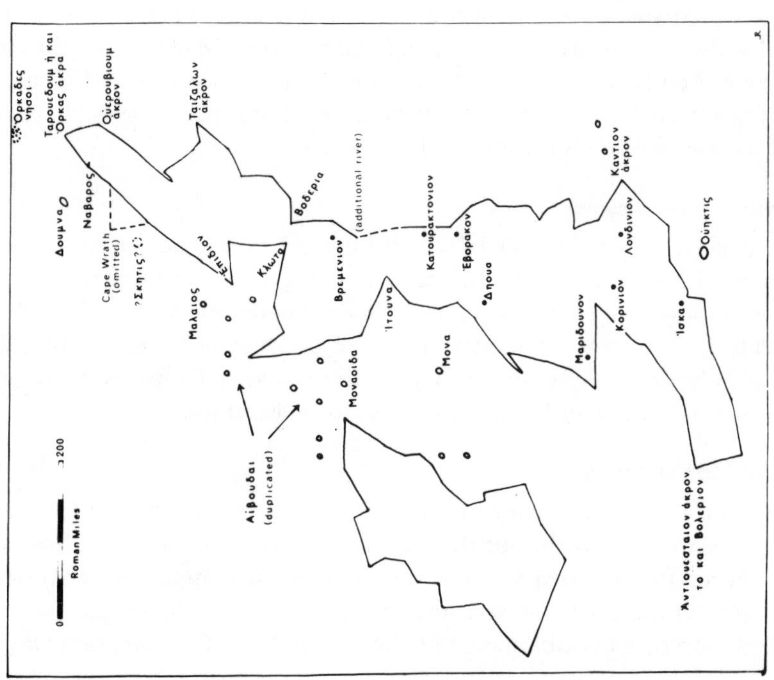

Fig. 3. Scotland turned to bring *Epidium Promontorium* and *Epidium Insula* into coincidence.

problem. The group of five *Aebudae*, or Inner Hebrides, are listed by Ptolemy under Ireland, not under Britain, and they are correctly related to the Irish mainland, though not to Scotland. They include an island called *Epidium*, and on the mainland of Scotland we also find an *Epidium Promontorium*. The two must surely be connected and they may even, as Bradley suggested,[1] be identical, for *Epidium Promontorium* is Kintyre which, though actually a peninsula, could be taken (and indeed has on occasion been taken) as an island. To bring these two *Epidia* into coincidence, we need to take the mouth of the *Ituna* (Eden), not the Wear, as the pivot and then rotate Scotland not through a quarter of a circle but through approximately one seventh. The result of this operation is shown at fig. 3. Some adjustment has been made to Ireland, which is resited in relation to the new position of its north-east corner, and we are left with the embarrassment of two sets of *Ebudae*, related to Ireland and to Scotland respectively, but for the mainland the result is generally satisfactory, and there are several good side-effects. On the east coast we have space for an additional river, which may be the Northumberland Tyne (otherwise missing), and in the north-west *Dumna* (which is certainly Lewis or the Long Island) falls into its correct place; even the position of *Scetis* (Skye), which is related only to *Dumna*, needs relatively little adjustment. The Orkneys, of course, must stay due north of *Orcas Promontorium*.

5. THE SOURCES OF PTOLEMY'S BRITAIN

In considering the sources of Ptolemy's map, one must always remember, first, that most of them were mediated through Marinus and that it is seldom possible to identify a contribution by Ptolemy himself; and second, that neither Marinus nor Ptolemy can actually have visited Britain, so that all their information was received at second or third hand. On internal evidence it is possible to distinguish four groups of data for Britain. In reverse chronological order these are:

(a) *The Positioning of the Legions*

The replacement of IX *Hispana* by VI *Victrix* did not take place before the reign of Hadrian, probably in A.D. 122, and the allocation of XX *Valeria Victrix* to *Deva*, of VI *Victrix* to *Eboracum* and of II *Augusta* to *Isca* may therefore be taken as an amendment made by Ptolemy. The attribution of II *Augusta* to the wrong *Isca* (Exeter instead of Caerleon) must simply reflect the fact that Exeter was the only *Isca* which appeared on the map he had inherited from Marinus.

(b) *The Northern Part of Britain*

Despite the modernity of the legionary list, there is no trace on the map of Hadrian's Wall, let alone the Antonine Wall, but the inclusion of so many names in Scotland shows that the source for this area was not earlier than the campaigns of Agricola in A.D 80–84. The mapping of this area may therefore be attributed to Marinus, relying on information recently obtained, whether or not Ptolemy made some minor alterations to it.

[1] H. Bradley, *op. cit.*

(c) *The Southern Part of Britain*

The main source for this, at least so far as the πόλεις are concerned, is clearly earlier than that for the northern part. Beside the omission of Caerleon, where the legionary base was established in the governorship of Frontinus, probably in A.D. 74–75,[1] there are other indications of an early date. Among the *Silures* not only *Isca* is missing but also *Venta* (Caerwent) and the only place attributed to them is *Bullaeum* (Usk) which seems, under Nero, to have preceded Caerleon as a legionary base.[2] Elsewhere *Durnovaria* (Dorchester, Dorset), also a Flavian foundation, is absent, its place being taken by *Dunium*. Most of the evidence for southern Britain, then, seems to date from Claudio-Neronian or at latest early Flavian times, but whether it was received directly by Marinus or through the medium of another geographer is questionable. Marinus certainly had some very precise information on *Noviomagus* (Chichester), which is cited below (p. 117), but it may be that it was the application of this to an older map that led him to make the error of which Ptolemy complains. The coastline of the southern part may also include some more recent material, and this too is discussed later (pp. 116–7).

(d) *Archaic Names*

We have seen that in the *Almagest* Ptolemy, presumably following current practice, had referred to Britain as Μεγάλη Βρεττανία or Great Britain, but in the *Geography*, having gone into the matter more thoroughly, he calls it *Alvion*. This name, as the reference in Pliny, *Natural History* IV, 102 (p. 79) clearly implies, was already an archaism in the first century, and it does not stand alone. It is notable that in three places Ptolemy gives alternative names to capes, *Damnonium* or *Ocrinum*, *Antivestaeum* or *Bolerium*, and *Tarvedum* or *Orcas*, and two of these are immediately recognisable as points of the Eratosthenean triangle *Belerium–Orcas–Cantium*. The third point, *Cantium*, would have presented no difficulty, since it had kept the same name, but it seems likely that the others had gone out of use well before the time of Ptolemy and were applied by him, for pedantic completeness, to the most likely features, which had in the meantime acquired new names. It is true that *Ocrinum* does not appear elsewhere in the literature (except in Marcian, who was copying Ptolemy), but since it must be related to the Greek word ὄκρις, meaning a point or prominence, it is highly likely that it represents the same tradition. Such considerations must lead us to question the reliability, and the application, of these names. The name *Albion* has already been discussed on page 39. *Bolerium* must, from Diodorus's reference to tin (p. 63), be situated in Cornwall, but it does not follow that Ptolemy is correct in making it Land's End rather than the Lizard, since the absence of references to *Ocrinum* may mean that it was a relatively unimportant cape. *Orcas* is thoroughly suspect as a promontory name and may originally have been adopted as a term of convenience to describe that part of Britain nearest to the *Orcades* islands.

[1] While an earlier auxiliary fort may have existed on the site, the legionary fortress is almost certainly of this date. See G. C. Boon in V. E. Nash-Williams, *The Roman Frontier in Wales* (2nd edn, revised by M. G. Jarrett, Cardiff, 1969), 29.

[2] *Britannia*, V (1974), 401.

Apart from these archaic names, which represent the received geographical tradition, there is no reason to doubt that the main sources of information were official Roman ones. Given the existence of administrative records and, presumably, of such documents as military maps and the movement orders of troops (like those which are incorporated in the Itineraries discussed in the next chapter), there was no need for Ptolemy or Marinus to trust the unreliable accounts of merchants (as was necessary, for example, in Ireland). This conclusion is confirmed by the fact that detailed mapping ceases just at the point which we know to have been reached by Agricola's forces and there are no πόλεις beyond the Moray Firth. We may, therefore, assume that the places named are most likely to be 'Roman' – that is, places which were, or had been, occupied by the Roman army. There is no evidence that Ptolemy names a purely 'native' settlement anywhere in Britain.

With these considerations in mind we may, before proceeding to a detailed examination of the text, note some of the characteristics and peculiarities of each of its component parts.

6. THE COASTLINE

It has long been realised that Ptolemy's coastline of Britain, in the south as well as in the north, sits somewhat awkwardly on the material which it encloses, especially in the relation of several πόλεις, like *Isca*, to their eponymous rivers and of *Londinium* to the river Thames. Several explanations have been offered for this, some of them depending on alleged astronomical observations, but the key to it may lie rather in two peculiarities of the list itself. In the first place, this list is almost unique in the whole *Geography* in being exclusively geographical, without any mention of coastal peoples or πόλεις. In Ireland πόλεις are sandwiched between natural features and the account of each coast is followed immediately by a list of the peoples along it, and similarly in Spain and Gaul peoples and πόλεις and natural features are freely interspersed. In Britain, on the other hand, even *Rutupiae* (Richborough), the chief port of entry, is not included in the coastal list but appears much later, among the πόλεις which are attributed to the *Cantii*.

Secondly, the coastal list, while omitting proper names of places, does include four descriptive names of harbours, which are not called πόλεις nor attributed to the peoples which are listed later. These are Σεταντίων λιμήν (*Setantiorum portus*, 'the harbour of the Setantii'), Γαβραντουίκων εὐλίμενος κόλπος (*Gabrantuicorum portuosus sinus*, 'the gulf of the Gabrantuici suitable for a harbour'), Μέγας λιμήν (*Magnus portus*, 'the great harbour') and Καινὸς λιμήν (*Novus portus*, 'the new harbour'). These names strongly suggest an official survey, and while neither of the first two is securely located, *magnus portus* is a suitable description of the whole sheltered area between the Isle of Wight and the mainland, and *novus portus* could well be Dover, later known as *Portus Dubris* and in the early second century developed as an alternative port to Richborough.[1]

[1] B. J. Philp in D. E. Johnston (ed.); *The Saxon Shore* (CBA Research Report 18, London, 1977), dating the Classis Britannica fort to this period. The importance attached to Dover for communications is underlined by the existence of a pair of Roman lighthouses, though the literary references show that Richborough always remained the official port of entry (p. 48).

The question remains whether we are dealing with one official survey or with two. There can be no doubt that the account of the northern coasts was derived from the activities of Agricola's fleet, as recorded by Tacitus (p. 95), but if the identification of *novus portus* with Dover is accepted, the southern part should be no earlier, and this would go far to explain the lack of congruity between the coastline and the inland detail.

7. THE SMALLER ISLANDS

All over his map of the world, Ptolemy's islands tend to drift out rather far from their parent shores. Notable examples elsewhere include *Menuthias* (Zanzibar or Pemba) and *Iabadiu* (Java),[1] and in the case of Britain we find *Vectis*, which is certainly the Isle of Wight, in the middle of the English Channel. This may, perhaps, be explained by his uncertainty as to its size: with the sole exception of *Thule* (which he, like Tacitus, identifies with Shetland), none of the islands around the coast is given dimensions, as opposed to a simple position. Thus the placing of *Mona* (Anglesey), though it is too near to Ireland (under which it is listed) and too far from Wales, is not entirely without analogy, but it must be remembered that Caesar (p. 58) had placed it *in medio cursu* between *Britannia* and *Hibernia* and we may suspect that an early source is here implied.

8. THE INTERIOR OF THE SOUTHERN PART OF BRITAIN

As we have seen (p. 106), Ptolemy's method of plotting the location of one place in relation to another was to use the bearing and the distance between the two, and the application of this to southern Britain seems to be demonstrated in two ways. First, in criticising Marinus, Ptolemy remarks:

> And having said that *Noviomagus* is 59 miles further south than *Londinium*, he then shows it as further north in latitude. *Geography* I, 15, 7

Ptolemy accordingly corrects the bearing, but for some unknown reason reduces the distance.

In fact it is the distance which gives us a clue to the accuracy of the information which was sometimes available to Marinus. The figure of 59 Roman miles is precise and it is the actual distance from London to Chichester, not along Stane Street but as the crow flies. As is well known, the northern stretch of this road (Margary 15), from London Bridge as far as Ewell, is aligned very accurately on Chichester and although the southern part of it deviates from it to take account of the terrain, it is clear that a through alignment was measured or computed. Nor is this long-distance alignment unique, and although most of the other examples in Britain link places which are not listed by Ptolemy, one of them supplies a useful parallel. This is the so-called 'Gartree Road' (Margary 57a), which runs south-east out of Leicester and is aligned on Colchester. The whole course of the road between the two places has not been found, and it is not even certain that it was ever completed, but the distance between *Ratae* and *Camulodunum*, as scaled off Ptolemy's map, gives the correct figure of 108 Roman miles. Both these roads are shown on fig. 4.

[1] Menuthias, *Geography* IV, 8, 2; Iabadiu, VII, 2, 29.

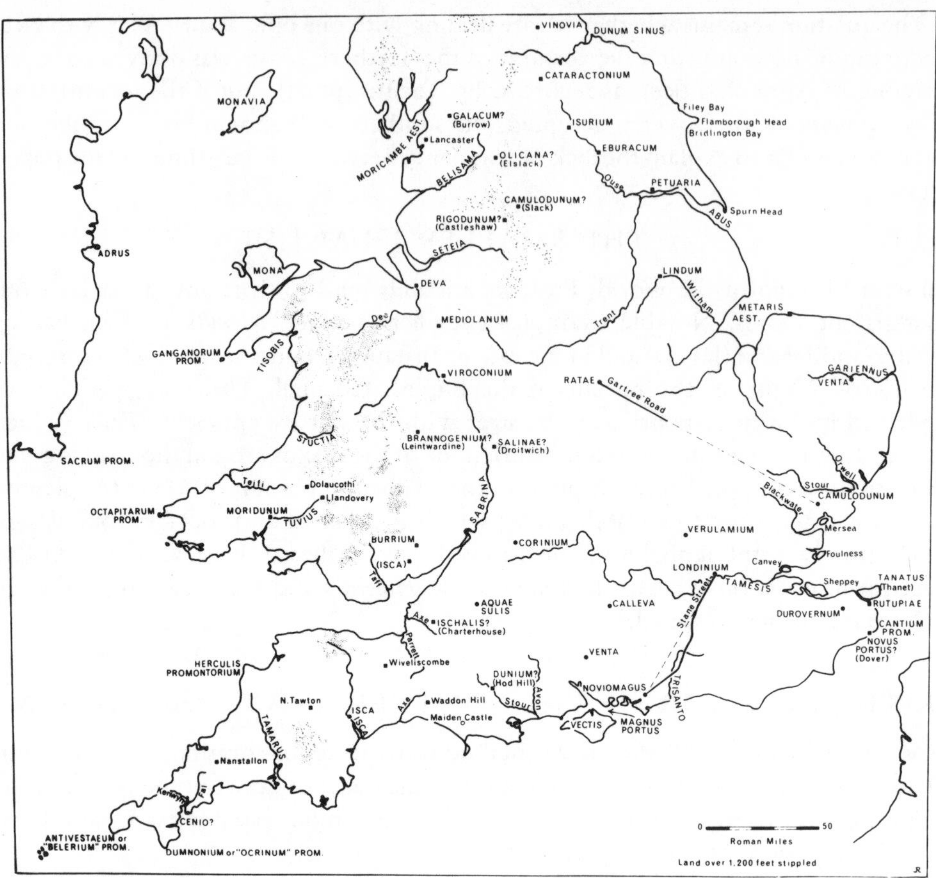

Fig. 4. Southern Britain, showing places listed by Ptolemy and the long road alignments referred to in the text; the forts in the south-west are included merely to demonstrate the military occupation of this area.

Analysis of the map, however, suggests that such cross-country measurements were the exception rather than the rule. While Ptolemy's distance from *Ratae* to *Corinium* (Leicester to Cirencester) is reasonably correct (82 Roman miles for 78), his distances from *Ratae* to *Verulamium*, *Lindum*, *Venta Icenorum* and *Burrium* are wildly wrong. Similarly, while his distance from *Verulamium* to *Camulodunum* is acceptable (65 Roman miles for 60), the distances from *Verulamium* to *Ratae*, *Corinium* and *Burrium* are excessive. *Camulodunum*, again, is acceptably related only to *Ratae* and *Verulamium* and even the distance to *Venta Icenorum* is nearly halved. All this leads to the suspicion that in most cases Ptolemy has used only one distance and bearing.

The town most likely to have been used as a datum point is London, which was already the administrative capital of Britain by the time of the Boudiccan revolt of A.D. 60, and that this was the case seems to be confirmed by the degree of correlation in Table 1.

On grounds of both dating and distance some of the more northerly places in this

Table 1. *Distances from London (to the nearest 5 Roman miles)*

Name in Ptolemy	Identification	Distance in Ptolemy	True distance
Aquae Calidae	Bath	**95**	**105**
Brannogenium	Leintwardine?	195	155
Bullaeum	Usk	**125**	**130**
Calagum	Burrow-in-Lonsdale?	**235**	**240**
Caleva	Silchester	**40**	**45**
Camudolanum	Colchester	70	55
Camunlodunum	Slack?	245	180
Caturactonium	Catterick	250	225
Corinium	Cirencester	70	90
Darvernum	Canterbury	40	60
Deva	Chester	**190**	**180**
Dunium	Hod Hill?	**105**	**110**
Eboracum	York	210	190
Epiacum	Whitley Castle?	**280**	**275**
Isca	Exeter	115	170
Ischalis	Charterhouse?	**140**	**125**
Isurium	Aldborough	230	200
Lindum	Lincoln	**120**	**130**
Luentinum	Dolaucothi?	**165**	**180**
Maridunum	Carmarthen	160	195
Mediolanium	Whitchurch	200	160
Noviomagus	Chichester	40	60
Olicana	Elslack?	**220**	**205**
Petuaria	Brough-on-Humber	**170**	**170**
Rate	Leicester	115	95
Rigodunum	Castleshaw?	230	175
Rutupiae	Richborough	**60**	**70**
Salinae	Droitwich?	**120**	**110**
Tamara	(on R. Tamar)	**200**	**210**
Urolanium	St Albans	95	20
Uxella	(in south-west)	190	—
Venta	Winchester	**55**	**65**
Venta	Caistor St Edmund	**85**	**100**
Vinnovium	Binchester	**265**	**250**
Viroconium	Wroxeter	**155**	**145**
Voliba	(in south-west)	210	—

Figures which agree within 15 Roman miles are shown in heavy type.

list may belong more properly with the northern than with the southern part of the map, but they are included here to demonstrate two points of plotting. Ptolemy's *Vinnovium* must surely be equated with the *Vinovia* of the *Antonine Itinerary*, the modern Binchester, yet it is placed far to the west, 85 Roman miles from Catterick. The actual distance from Catterick to Binchester is some 22 Roman miles, and this

Table 2. *Distances from Chester (to the nearest 5 Roman miles)*

Name in Ptolemy	Identification	Distance in Ptolemy	True distance
Brannogenium	Leintwardine?	**60**	**65**
Calagum	Burrow-in-Lonsdale?	**80**	**75**
Camunlodunum	Slack?	**65**	**60**
Eboracum	York	**90**	**100**
Mediolanium	Whitchurch	**25**	**20**
Olicana	Elslack?	**70**	**65**
Rigodunum	Castleshaw?	**50**	**50**
Viroconium	Wroxeter	70	40

Figures which agree within 10 Roman miles are shown in heavy type.

Table 3. *Distances from York (to the nearest 5 Roman miles)*

Name in Ptolemy	Identification	Distance in Ptolemy	True distance
Caturactonium	Catterick	**45**	**40**
Deva	Chester	**90**	**100**
Epiacum	Whitley Castle?	**85**	**90**
Isurium	Aldborough	**20**	**15**
Lindum	Lincoln	105	60
Olicana	Elslack?	**35**	**45**
Petuaria	Brough-on-Humber	45	30
Rigodunum	Burrow-in-Lonsdale or Low Borrow Bridge?	**70**	**70** **75**
Vinnovium	Binchester	95	60

Figures which agree within 10 Roman miles are shown in heavy type.

is not unreasonably represented by the difference of 15 Roman miles in Ptolemy's distances from London. This shows that Catterick was not, as has sometimes been claimed, the base for measurements in the north,[1] and that Ptolemy's bearings could be seriously wrong.

But secondly, it is only because, as Ptolemy himself notes, the *Brigantes* stretched from sea to sea, that *Vinnovium* remains attributed to them, and this raises doubts as to some of his tribal attributions, in particular that of *Salinae*, which he places near the Wash and attributes to the '*Catyeuchlani*'. Salt was extracted in this area in Roman times, but it is doubtful whether the industry had developed so early, and *Salinae* is at about the right distance (though again on the wrong bearing) to be Droitwich,

[1] E.g. Rylands, *op. cit.*, apparently followed by Richmond, *PSAS*, LVI (1921–22), 295.

Fig. 5. The Flavian occupation of Scotland, showing forts certainly occupied (black squares), forts probably occupied (open squares) and temporary camps north of the Tay attributed to the period (open rectangles).

which appears under that name in the *Ravenna Cosmography*. Similarly it is natural to equate Ptolemy's *Mediolanium* with the *Mediolanum* of the Itinerary, that is Whitchurch, in which case it should be attributed to the *Cornovii* rather than the *Ordovices*. In fact it seems likely that Ptolemy located the tribes merely by reference to their administrative centres (whether in the military or in the succeeding civilian phase) and that the tribal names, when written on the original map, attracted to themselves all the places in their areas when the coordinates were read off. If this is so, it has interesting implications, most notably in respect of Bath which, to judge by the distribution of the pre-Roman coinage,[1] should belong to the *Dobunni* rather than to the *Belgae*.

[1] For the coin distribution up to 1960, *O.S. Map of Southern Britain in the Iron Age* (Chessington, 1962), Introduction, p. 30 (Map 6).

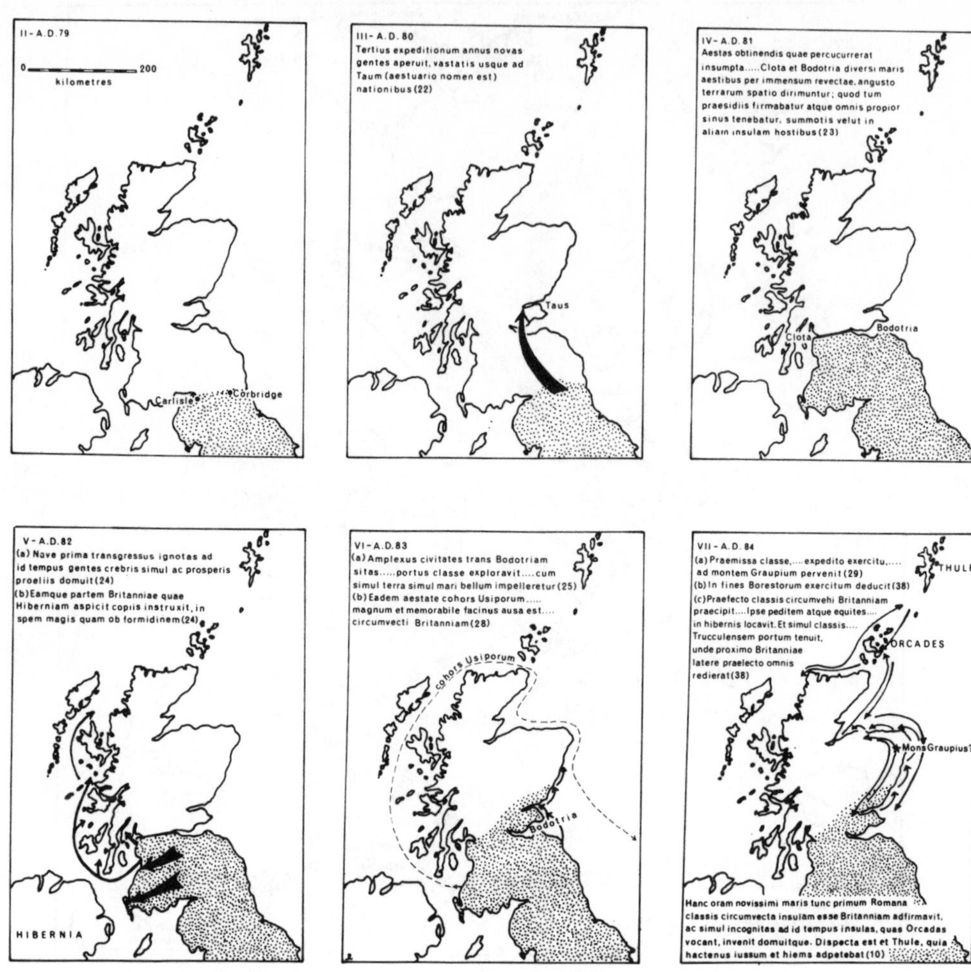

Fig. 6. Agricola's campaigns in Scotland.

After London, the most likely bases for calculation would be legionary fortresses. As already noted, Ptolemy confuses *Isca* (Exeter) with *Isca* (Caerleon), presumably because only the former appeared on his map, and this may account for the fact that it is dragged too far east, away from its eponymous river: the difference in the distances from London of the two places is 37 Roman miles and if, as a compromise between two sources, Ptolemy had made a 'correction' of half this figure, *Isca* would originally have been plotted 18½ Roman miles further west, on the river Exe. This operation, and the confusion which necessitated it, would have destroyed any correlation with other places, but the two northern legionary fortresses, Chester and York, yield satisfactory results. Not only are they well related to each other, but the distances of some other places from them, though not always the bearings, are remarkably accurate, as in Tables 2 and 3. In Table 2 it will be noticed that *Viroconium*, having already been well located in relation to London, is here placed much too far from Chester, while in Table 3 it is *Lindum* and *Vinnovium* whose relationship to London has been preferred to the distances from York.

It seems, then, that in the southern part of Britain the plotting of the πόλεις is the result of a compromise between distances measured from three (and possibly more) different places. While a location in Ptolemy can never on its own establish an identity, especially in view of the unreliability of his bearings, measurements made in this way can at least suggest probabilities.

9. THE INTERIOR OF THE NORTHERN PART OF BRITAIN

The case of the northern part of Britain, the area, that is to say, north of the Tyne-Solway isthmus, is somewhat different, since here there are no obvious points of reference and only the location of *Bremenium* is controlled by the *Antonine Itinerary*. There are, however, some compensatory advantages. First, for the reasons discussed above (p. 114), we can confine our attention to places which were occupied in the Flavian period (fig. 5) and some indication of likely troop movements can be derived from the account of the campaigns given by Tacitus in the *Agricola* (fig. 6). Secondly, the *Ravenna Cosmography* is more helpful here than in the south, since it lists ten places on the Forth-Clyde Isthmus and so splits its names in Scotland into three sections: on this basis Ptolemy's *Carbantorigum, Uxellum, Corda, Trimontium, Lindum, Bremenium* and perhaps the second *Alauna, Lucopibia* (? = *Lucotion*) and *Coria* (? = *Coritiotar*) should all lie south of the isthmus, *Colanica* and perhaps *Curia* (? = *Cibra*) should lie on the isthmus, and *Victoria, Pinnata Castra, Tuesis, Orrea* (= *Poreoclassis*), *Devana* (= *Devoni*) and perhaps *Tameia* (? = *Tagea*) should lie north of the isthmus. Thirdly, while Ptolemy includes only two places (*Bremenium* and *Trimontium*) whose precise identity is assured by other sources, there are two others whose approximate location can be inferred from his coastal list: *Rerigonium*, which must be on or very near his *Rerigonius* gulf (Loch Ryan), and *Vindogara*, which must be on or very near his *Vindogara* gulf (Irvine Bay). And finally, as Mr R. J. Wyatt has pointed out,[1] there are several instances where three places have been plotted in a straight line and it is reasonable to suppose that all three appeared in the same movement order or itinerary; these lines are shown on the maps at figs. 7 and 8.

It is simplest to take the southern part of Scotland first (up to and including the Forth–Clyde isthmus) and here we may begin by considering the distances between the four known places. As will be seen from the figures in Table 4, the worst-related of them is *Bremenium*, which seems to stand apart from the rest but which is well related to the legionary fortresses further south (95 Roman miles from York, as compared with 115 in fact, and 170 from Chester, as compared with 160 in fact). The best-related, on the other hand, is *Rerigonium* (taken as Stranraer), a fact which suggests that the movement orders involved in the concentration of troops on the coast facing Ireland (*Agricola* 24) supplied some of the evidence; and if this is so, the distances of other places from *Rerigonium* are likely to be the most reliable. Bearing this in mind, together with the need to place *Colania* on the isthmus and the fact that

[1] R. J. Wyatt, 'An Assessment of the Value of Some Literary Sources for Roman Britain', an unpublished thesis submitted for the degree of M.Phil., University of Southampton, 1974.

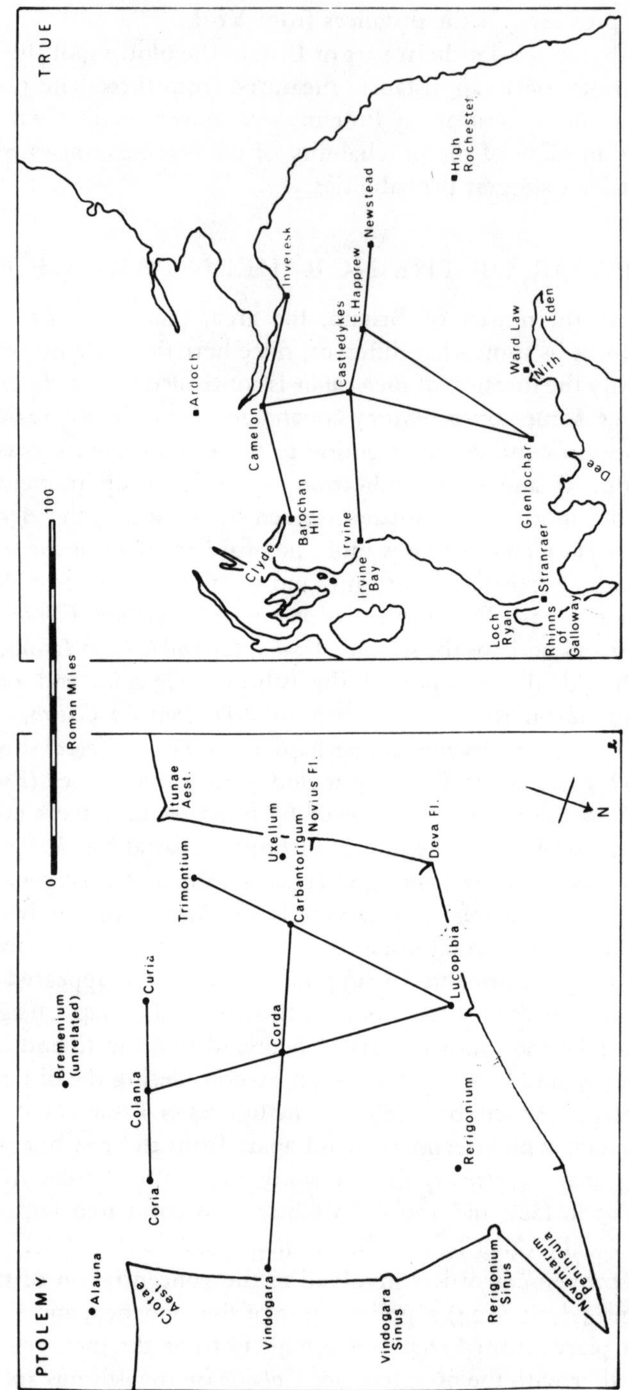

Fig. 7. An interpretation of Ptolemy's map of southern Scotland.

Table 4. *Distances between places in southern Scotland, to the nearest 5 Roman miles*

UXELLUM	TRIMONTIUM	RERIGONIUM	LUCOPIBIA	CURIA	CORIA	CORDA	COLANIA	CARBANTORIGUM	BREMENIUM	ALAUNA		Ardoch	High Rochester	Easter Happrew	Camelon	Castledykes	Barochan Hill	Inveresk	Glenlochar	Stranraer	Newstead	Ward Law
											ALAUNA = Ardoch											
										70	BREMENIUM = High Rochester	100										
									135	130	CARBANTORIGUM = Easter Happrew	50	50									
								65	25	70	COLANIA = Camelon	20	85	35								
							40	35	**70**	100	CORDA = Castledykes	45	**70**	20	25							
						55	**25**	85	40	**40**	CORIA = Barochan Hill	**40**	110	55	**30**	**55**§						
					50	**40**	**25**	50	35	90	CURIA = Inveresk	40	60	25	**30**	**35**	**60**					
				90	105	**50**	95	**50**	120	140	LUCOPIBIA = Glenlochar	95	75	**60**	80	**55**	75	**80**				
			45	**105**	95	65	**95**	**85**	**120**	**120**	RERIGONIUM = Stranraer	**110**	**120**	**90**	**100**	80	80	**115**	**45**			
		115	**85***	**40**	**90**	**55**	**60**	**30**	70	130	TRIMONTIUM = Newstead	70	30	**25**	**55**	**45**	**80**	**30**	**85**†	**110**		
	25	100	65	60	100	**55**	**75**	20	95	145	UXELLUM = Ward Law	95	60	50	**75**	**50**	80	75	20	65	60	
115	110	**65**	**90**	80	40	60	**60**	95	80	**55**	VINDOGARA = Irvine	**60**	105	65‡	**70**‡	45	20	70	**100**‡	**55**	90†‡	70

* Via Carbantorigum
† via Easter Happrew
‡ via Castledykes
§ via Camelon
Figures which agree to within 10 Roman miles are shown in heavy type.
The *Alauna* included in this table is that situated inland.

Table 5. *Distances between places in northern Scotland, to the nearest 5 Roman miles*

ALAUNA (on coast) = ? in E. Fife
ALAUNA (inland) = Ardoch
BANNATIA = Dalginross
COLANIA = Camelon
CORIA = Barochan Hill
DEVANA = Kintore
LINDUM = Drumquhassle
ORREA = ? Monifieth
PINNATA CASTRA = ?
TAMEIA = Cardean
TUESIS = Bellie
VICTORIA = Inchtuthil

	TUESIS	TAMEIA	PINNATA CASTRA	ORREA	LINDUM	DEVANA	CORIA	COLANIA	BANNATIA	ALAUNA (inland)	ALAUNA (on coast)
ALAUNA (on coast)											
ALAUNA (inland)											40
BANNATIA										45	60
COLANIA									115	70	80
CORIA								**25**	85	**40**	65
DEVANA							165	190	**85**	120	115
LINDUM						**115**	50	80	**35**	15	55
ORREA					60	80	**95**	95	**45**	**60**	35
PINNATA CASTRA				115	145	40	195	220	110	155	150
TAMEIA			75	50	**70**	**45**	120	195	**35**	80	80
TUESIS		60	20	**95**	190	20	180	205	**95**	135	130
VICTORIA	110	55	130	**25**	35	95	**70**	95	**35**	**35**	25

	? in E. Fife	Ardoch	Dalginross	Camelon	Barochan Hill	Kintore	Drumquhassle	Monifieth	?	Cardean	Bellie
? in E. Fife											
Ardoch	?										
Dalginross	?	10									
Camelon	?	20	30								
Barochan Hill	?	**40**	45	**35**							
Kintore	?	95	**90**	110	135						
Drumquhassle	?	30	**30**	30	15	**125**					
? Monifieth	?	**50**	**50**	55	**85**	60	75				
?	?	?	?	?	?	?	?	?			
Cardean	?	40	**40**	55	80	**55**	**70**	15	?		
Bellie	?	110	**105**	125	145	45	135	**90**	?	80	
Inchtuthil	?	**30**	**25**	45	**65**	70	55	**25**	?	10	85

Figures which agree to within 10 Roman miles are shown in heavy type.

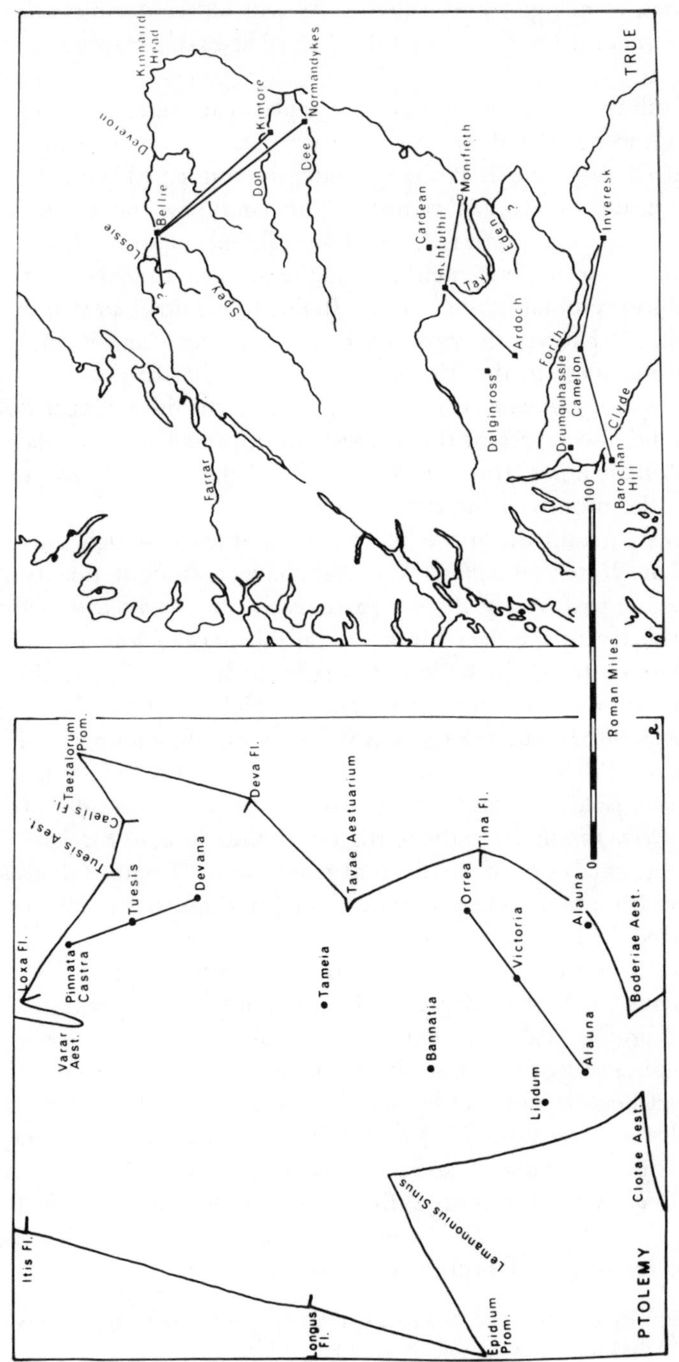

Fig. 8. An interpretation of Ptolemy's map of northern Scotland.

Corda, where two straight lines intersect, should be at a crossroads, we can establish some probabilities, as in fig. 7 and Table 4. As will be seen, some names, notably that of *Carbantorigum* for the crossing of the Tweed at Easter Happrew, fit their sites very well.

North of the isthmus there are two groups of places arranged in straight lines, and in each case they can be related, at least tentatively, to a probable base. In the more northerly group *Devana*, which Ptolemy evidently connected with the river *Deva* (Dee) should indicate the Roman camp at Normandykes, though if the *Ravenna Cosmography* form *Devoni* is preferred, the *Devona* (Don) is indicated, when the camp at Kintore would be meant; but in either case the distance to *Tuesis*, which must be on the Spey and so presumably the camp at Bellie, is too little, so that the scale here is seriously wrong. Whatever the reason for this, however – and it might be due to the omission of one stage in the itinerary – it is clear that to get to *Pinnata Castra* one went across the Spey. *Pinnata Castra*, then, which is the most distant πόλις plotted by Ptolemy, should also represent the furthest encampment of Agricola's army: the distance of 20 Roman miles from *Tuesis* suggests (if the scale is now correct) a site somewhere near the mouth of the river Findhorn.

For the southern group the most likely base is *Alauna*, which suits the fort at Ardoch, on Allan Water (*Alaunus*). We then have a straight line from Ardoch through *Victoria* to *Orrea* which, if it is equated with the *Poreoclassis* of *Ravenna* and so means 'the granary of the fleet', must be on the coast. *Victoria* is at the correct distance from Ardoch to be the legionary fortress at Inchtuthil, and this suggests a satisfactory explanation of this remarkable name (which is not translated by Ptolemy but merely transliterated): the reference is not to a specific victory, still less to one by the IX Legion,[1] but rather to the XX Legion Victrix which was its garrison. If this identification is correct, and if to get from *Alauna* to *Orrea* one went by way of *Victoria*, then *Orrea* should lie to the north, not to the south, of the Tay. This makes better sense of Agricola's use of the fleet, as recorded by Tacitus (*Agricola* 25), and a site in the area of Monifieth, where supplies from Strathmore could be concentrated, would best suit the distance.

As in southern Scotland, the identification of the remaining places must, to be satisfactory, provide the highest degree of compatibility and a suggested solution is shown on fig. 8 and in Table 5. The coastal *Alauna* defies location and, if it is not merely a duplication of the other by Ptolemy, it may represent a base in Fife which has not yet been found, but elsewhere two pieces of confirmatory evidence may be adduced. First, the name *Lindum* suits perfectly the fort at Drumquhassle, at the southern end of Loch Lomond; and secondly, *Victoria*, as Inchtuthil, is remarkably well related to *Deva* (Chester), with a distance of 245 Roman miles in Ptolemy, as compared with 250 in fact – and it is precisely to Chester that the XX Legion was posted when the fortress at Inchtuthil was evacuated.[2]

[1] So Ogilvie and Richmond (1967), 243–44, relating the name to the events recorded in *Agricola* 26, and (p. 43) identifying it as Strageath.

[2] For the argument that it did not return to Wroxeter before going to Chester, G. Webster, *The Cornovii* (London, 1975), 27.

10. TEXTUAL QUESTIONS

Though none is earlier than the 11th century, the manuscripts of the *Geography* are exceptionally numerous, not only in Greek but also in Latin translations. The reason for this is not hard to discern, for it contained solid information of a kind hitherto unknown in western Europe where Latin, not Greek, was the normal language of scholarship; in fact the earliest printed version, published by Angelus Vadius and Barnabas Picardus in 1475, used the first Latin translation, which had been made by Jacobus Angelus in 1409. It is generally agreed that the existing manuscripts are derived from two different ancient recensions, both of them incorporating amendments to Ptolemy's original text, the one being represented most faithfully by the late thirteenth-century Codex Vaticanus Graecus 191 (X), the other by the four distinct families of manuscripts into which it split in Constantinople in the 6th century; one of the latter includes the early fourteenth-century Codex Vaticanus Urbinas Graecus 82 (U), which was unknown to Müller but was claimed by J. Fischer to be the most reliable of all. There are also, however, several manuscripts, both Greek and Latin, which incorporate elements from both recensions and there is still no general agreement on the 'correct' text.

A further complication arises from the fact that 14 of the Greek and 38 of the Latin manuscripts have maps attached to them, and the origin of these has been much debated.[1] There can be no doubt that Ptolemy drew maps, and read his coordinates off them, but whether maps were issued with the text is another question. Professor Thomson has justly remarked that 'it seems likely that he would expect few readers with such bowels of brass that they would sit down to make their own atlas',[2] but it must be remembered that Ptolemy's main interest was in pure science and he does give instructions for drawing maps. Three manuscripts have a general map and 26 sectional maps, based on Ptolemy's main divisions of the world, while others have a general map and 64 others, based on his subdivisions; and some have a note at the end stating that 'from the eight books of Ptolemy's Geography Agathodaemon, an Alexandrian craftsman (μηχανικός), drew the whole inhabited world'. Neither his date nor anything else is known about Agathodaemon, nor is it clear whether he was claiming to have drawn the sectional maps or merely the generalised map of 'the whole inhabited world'. In any case, the significance of the maps is limited to the possibility that they may sometimes reflect more accurate coordinates, taken from earlier manuscripts which are now lost: details of the coastline between coordinates, or of the courses of rivers, can only have been imaginative or conventional, since neither Ptolemy nor any successor in the ancient world can have had access to a survey sufficiently refined to supply such information. This point also needs to be borne in mind when one is looking at the maps in the numerous editions printed in the fifteenth and sixteenth centuries: though they look more convincing than maps drawn by the modern convention of linking the coordinates with straight lines, they have no real validity.

[1] For a discussion of the maps, L. O. Th. Tudeer, 'On the Origin of the Maps attached to Ptolemy's Geography', *JHS*, XXXVII (1917), 62–76.

[2] J. O. Thomson, *History of Ancient Geography* (Cambridge, 1948), 346.

The first edition of the *Geography*, the *editio princeps*, was made by Erasmus in 1533 and there have been many others since,[1] but some of them deal only with areas other than Britain and for practical purposes we may confine our attention to four. The first is that of C. F. A. Nobbe, first published in 1843–45 and reprinted in 1966. The text of this is not always reliable and it lacks an *apparatus criticus*, but, as A. Diller remarks in his useful critical introduction to the reprint, it has the virtue of being complete, it has an index and it is the most convenient edition for rapid reference. The second is that of C. Müller, published in 1883 (Books I–III) and 1901 (Books IV–V, completed by C. T. Fischer), with a volume of maps. This is the most satisfactory edition to date, with variant readings and plentiful annotation, and it is also the one most widely to be found in libraries, but it suffers from two major defects: first, as already noted, Müller did not have access to manuscript U (nor, indeed, to the comparable manuscript K – the thirteenth-century Codex Seragliensis 57) and secondly, because of Müller's death, only the first five books were dealt with. The third is the sumptuous edition of Codex Urbinas Graecus 82 (U), with facsimiles of the text and maps, produced by Father Joseph Fischer in 1932. The fourth is the edition of P. Schnabel (1938), which is especially valuable for its discussion of the manuscripts. The text printed here is mainly that of Müller, with his conjectures eliminated, and with the more important variants, especially those from MS U, given below each section.

It remains to note the possible ways in which corruptions may have arisen in transmission. Since Ptolemy wrote in Greek, it follows that many amendments which suggest themselves in the latinised forms of names may be disregarded – except, of course, where it may be supposed that Ptolemy (or Marinus before him) misread some information which had come to him in a Latin form. The earliest copies of the text would have been written in uncials (effectively, small capitals) and the groups of letters most liable to confusion in this script are: *alpha*, *delta* and *lambda* (Α, Δ, Λ); *epsilon*, *theta*, *omicron* and *sigma* (Є, Θ, Ο, C); *iota* and *sigma* (Ι, C); and *gamma* and *tau* (Γ, Τ). Beyond this, some of the more extended letters might be broken down into two (as, for example, where TONATIC seems to have become TOΛΙΑΤΙC) and vice versa.

There are further complications in the case of the coordinates. These were expressed not in Arabic or Roman numerals but in the Greek 'Milesian' numeration. This used the letters of the Ionian alphabet accented, with the addition of *wau* (a variant form of the *digamma*) for 6, *koppa* for 90 and *sampi* for 900. So the numbers which concern us appear as follows:

1 = α′	6 = ς′
2 = β′	7 = ζ′
3 = γ′	8 = η′
4 = δ′	9 = θ′
5 = ε′	10 = ι′

[1] For an interesting list see J. Windsor, *A Bibliography of Ptolemy's Geography* (Library of Harvard University Bibliographical Contribution No. 18, Cambridge, Mass., 1884). Nine editions were published in the 15th century and 50 in the 16th, usually with additions, as of America, to bring the maps up to date. Up to 1605 the *Geography* was still considered the

20 = κ′   60 = ξ′
30 = λ′   70 = ο′
40 = μ′   80 = π′
50 = ν′   90 = ϙ′

Degrees of latitude and longitude are, of course, shown by simple figures, but what appear in Latin and English versions as minutes are, in the original, expressed as fractions of a degree. In the system used by Ptolemy there was a special sign for a half (ι″) and in other cases a simple fraction was expressed by the denominator with the addition of a double accent: so γ″ = $\frac{1}{3}$ (= 20′), δ″ = $\frac{1}{4}$ (= 15′) and ιβ″ = $\frac{1}{12}$ (= 5′). γο″ = $\frac{2}{3}$ (= 40′), but in other cases the numerator is not varied and more complex fractions are expressed cumulatively: thus $\frac{3}{4}$ appears as ι″δ″, that is, $\frac{1}{2}+\frac{1}{4}$ (= 45′). Within this system of numerals the letters most likely to be confused are the same as those noted above, with the addition of *koppa* to the second group. There are, in fact, many variations in the figures between the manuscripts, some of them probably due to attempts to collate manuscripts and maps, but since most of them involve only a fraction of a degree and hardly affect the identification of names they are listed here only in exceptional cases.

II. THE TEXT

The text given here follows Ptolemy's own order and three aspects of it need to be noted. First, the Inner Hebrides and the islands in the Irish Sea are listed not under Britain but under Ireland. Secondly, the account of the coasts of Britain precedes the description of the interior and is quite distinct from it. Thirdly, in dealing with the interior Ptolemy generally works from west to east, so that, with Scotland turned, his account of the southern peoples of Scotland precedes that of the northern peoples.

Islands near Ireland (*Geography* II, 2, 10)

Ὑπέρκεινται δὲ νῆσοι τῆς Ἰουερνίας αἵ τε καλούμεναι Αἰβοῦδαι πέντε τὸν ἀριθμόν, ὧν ἡ μὲν δυτικωτέρα καλεῖται			Above *Ivernia* lie islands which are called *Aebudae*, five in number, of which the most westerly is called		
Αἰβοῦδα	ιε′	ξβ′	*Aebuda*	15°	62°
ἡ δ᾽ἐφεξῆς αὐτῆς πρὸς ἀνατολὰς ὁμοίως			the next towards the east likewise		
Ἀιβοῦδα	ιε′γο″	ξβ′	*Aebuda*	15°40′	62°
εἶτα Ῥικίνα	ιζ′	ξβ′	then *Ricina*	17°	62°
εἶτα Μαλαῖος	ιζ′ι″	ξβ′ι″	then *Malaeus*	17°30′	62°30′
εἶτα Ἐπίδιον	ιη′ι″	ξβ′	then *Epidium*	18°30′	62°
καὶ ἀπ᾽ἀνατολῶν τῆς Ιουερνίας εἰσὶν αἵδε νῆσοι·			And to the east of *Ivernia* are these islands:		
Μονάοιδα	ιζ′γο″	ξα′ι″	*Monaoeda*	17°40′	61°30′
Μόνα νῆσος	ιε′	νζ′γο″	*Mona* island	15°	57°40′
Ἄδρου ἔρημος	ιε′	νθ′ι″	*Adru*, uninhabited	15°	59°30′
Λίμνου ἔρημος	ιε′	νθ′	*Limnu*, uninhabited	15°	59°

best basis for a world map and Ptolemy's name continued to be applied to atlases until 1695.

Variants

῎Εβουδαι, ῎Εβουδα (U).
Μαλεός (U).
Μοναρίνα.
῎Εδρου (U).

Comment

Of the *Aebudae* (apparently the Inner Hebrides, excluding Skye) *Malaeus* is certainly Mull and *Ricina* is probably Rathlin (*Ricina* in Pliny, *Regaina* in *Ravenna*, *Rechru* in Adomnan); on the possible equation of *Epidium* with *Epidium* promontory (Kintyre) see above, p. 114.

Monaoeda appears to be a garbled form of *Monavia*, the Isle of Man, and *Mona* is Anglesey; on its position see above, p. 117. *Adru* is probably the Isle of Howth and *Limnu* may be Lambay.

The northern (and north-western) coast of Britain (*Geography* II, 3, 1)

᾿Αλουίωνος νήσου Πρεττανικῆς Θέσις.			Setting out of the *Prettanic* island of *Alvion*.		
᾿Αρκτικῆς πλευρᾶς περιγραφή, ἧς ὑπέρκειται ᾿Ωκεανὸς καλούμενος Δουηκαληδόνιος·			Description of the northern side, above which lies the ocean called *Duecaledonius*,		
Νοουαντῶν Χερσόνησος καὶ ὁμώνυμον ἄκρον	κα′	ξα′γο″	Peninsula of the *Novantae* and cape of the same name	21°	61°40′
῾Ρεριγόνιος κόλπος	κ′ʟ″	ξ′ʟ″γ″	*Rerigonius* gulf	20°30′	60°50′
Οὐινδόγαρα κόλπος	κα′γ″	ξ′ʟ″	*Vindogara* gulf	21°20′	60°30′
Κλώτα εἴσχυσις	κβ′δ″	νθ′γ″	*Clota* estuary	22°15′	59°20′
Λεμαννόνιος κόλπος	κδ′	ξ′	*Lemannonius* gulf	24°	60°
᾿Επίδιον ἄκρον	κγ′	ξ′γο″	*Epidium* promontory	23°	60°40′
Λόγγου ποταμοῦ ἐκβολαί	κδ′ʟ″	ξ′γο″	Mouth of river *Longus*	24°30′	60°40′
Εἴτιος ποταμοῦ ἐκβολαί	κζ′	ξ′γο″	Mouth of river *Eitis*	27°	60°40′
Οὐόλας κόλπος	κθ′	ξ′ʟ″	*Volas* gulf	29°	60°30′
Ναβάρου ποταμοῦ ἐκβολαί	λ′	ξ′ʟ″	Mouth of river *Nabarus*	30°	60°30′
Ταρουεδούμ ἡ καὶ ᾿Ορκὰς ἄκρα	λα′γ″	ξ′δ″	*Tarvedum* or *Orcas* promontory	31°20′	60°15′

Variants

Δουηκαλληδόνιος, Δουηκαλλιδόνιος.
῾Ρερηγόνιος (U).
Νουάντων.
Οὐιδόγαρα (U), Οὐιδόταρα, Οὐινδόχαρα.
Λελααν όνιος, Λεμααν όνιος, Λελμααν όνιος.
᾿Ιτήου, ῎Ιτυος (Müller's ῎Ιτιος is a conjecture).

Οὐόλσας (U).
Ναβαίου, Ναυαίου.
Ταρουηδούμη, Ταρουιδούμ, Ταρουέδα.

Comment

The peninsula of the *Novantae* is the Rhinns of Galloway, with the Mull of Galloway as the promontory, and *Rerigonius* gulf, by both name and position, is Loch Ryan. As the only notable inlet between here and the *Clota* (Clyde), *Vindogara* gulf is presumably Irvine Bay. Since *Epidium* promontory is clearly the Mull of Kintyre (occupied by the *Epidii*, on whom see below), *Lemmanonius* gulf should be either Loch Long or Loch Fyne, and Watson favoured the former on the grounds that it adjoins Lennox (Gaelic *na Leamhnaich*); an identification with Loch Linnhe, suggested by Richmond (*RNNB*), would imply that Ptolemy had his points out of order. The same objection applies to the attempts to identify *Longus* with Loch Long, discussed at length by Watson: from its position it should be Loch Linnhe, and it may be that the name is a purely Latin one, conferred by the Roman fleet, with no native base. As Watson pointed out, *Eitis* cannot be related to Loch Etive linguistically, though it corresponds with its position reasonably well. *Nabarus* is certainly the river Naver (Gaelic *Nabhar*), so *Volas* (or *Volsas*) should lie to the west of this and since, as noted above (p. 112), Cape Wrath has been omitted, it could be on either the north or the west coast of Scotland. Macbain favoured Loch Alsh (but, as Watson showed, on unsatisfactory grounds) and Richmond Loch Broom. If, however, as seems likely, the inlets named represent points at which the fleet put in for supplies, the distribution of population and cultivation, as indicated by brochs, might suggest rather the Kyle of Tongue or Loch Eriboll or the Kyle of Durness: of these Loch Eriboll is the most notable. The spelling of Ταρουεδούμ, with the termination -ουμ rather than the more usual Greek form -ον, is interesting and may be compared with that of Οὐιρουεδρούμ and Οὐερουβίουμ (below). None of the manuscripts has the form Ταρουεδοῦνον (*Tarvedunum*) which appears in Marcian, but Watson and Richmond are no doubt right to take it as Dunnet Head, with associations with the 'Bull's Water' of Thurso Bay.

It may be noted that in the earlier part of this list Ptolemy completely disregards the important islands of Arran and Bute.

The western coast of Britain (*Geography* II, 3, 2)

Δυσμικῆς πλευρᾶς περιγραφή, ᾗ παράκειται ὅ τε Ἰουερνικὸς Ὠκεανὸς καὶ ὁ Οὐεργιόυιος· Μετὰ τὴν τῶν Νοουαντῶν χερσόνησον			Description of the western side, beside which lie the *Ivernicus* and *Vergiovian* oceans: After the peninsula of the *Novantae*		
Ἀβραουάννου ποταμοῦ ἐκβολαί	ιθ′γ″	ξα′	Mouth of river *Abravannus*	19°20′	61°
Ἰηνᾶ εἴσχυσις	ιθ′	ξ′ι″	*Iena* estuary	19°	60°30′
Δηούα ποταμοῦ ἐκβολαί	ιη′	ξ′	Mouth of river *Deva*	18°	60°
Νοουίου ποταμοῦ ἐκβολαί	ιη′γ″	νθ′ι″	Mouth of river *Novius*	18°20′	59°30′

Ἰτούνα εἴσχυσις	ιη′ι″	νη′ι″δ″	*Ituna* estuary	18°30′	58°45′
Μορικάμβη εἴσχυσις	ιζ′ι″	νη′γ″	*Moricambe* estuary	17°30′	58°20′
Σεταντίων λιμήν	ιζ′γ″	νζ′ι″δ″	Harbour of the *Setantii*	17°20′	57°45′
Βελισάμα εἴσχυσις	ιζ′ι″	νζ′γ″	*Belisama* estuary	17°30′	57°20′
Σετηία εἴσχυσις	ιζ′	νζ′	*Seteia* estuary	17°	57°
Γαγγανῶν ἄκρον	ιε′	νϛ′	Promontory of the *Gangani*	15°	56°
Τοισόβιος ποταμοῦ ἐκβολαί	ιε′γο″	νϛ′γ″	Mouth of river *Toesobis*	15°40′	56°20′
Στουκκία ποταμοῦ ἐκβολαί	ιε′γ″	νε′ι″	Mouth of river *Stuccia*	15°20′	55°30′
Τουερόβιος ποταμοῦ ἐκβολαί	ιε′	νε′	Mouth of river *Tuerobis*	15°	55°
Ὀκταπίταρον ἄκρον	ιδ′γ″	νδ′ι″	*Octapitarum* promontory	14°20′	54°30′
Τουβίου ποταμοῦ ἐκβολαί	ιε′ι″	νδ′ι″	Mouth of river *Tubius*	15°30′	54°30′
Ῥατοσταθυβίου ποταμοῦ ἐκβολαί	ιϛ′ι″	νδ′ι″	Mouth of river *Ratostathybius*	16°30′	54°30′
Σαβρίνα εἴσχυσις	ιζ′γ″	νδ′ι″	*Sabrina* estuary	17°20′	54°30′
Οὐεξάλλα εἴσξυσις	ιϛ′	νγ′ι″	*Vexalla* estuary	16°	53°30′
Ἡρακλέους ἄκρον	ιδ′	νβ′ι″δ″	Promontory of *Heracles*	14°	52°45′
Ἀντιουέσταιον ἄκρον τὸ καὶ Βολέριον	ια′ι″	νβ′ι″	*Antivestaeum* promontory which is also *Bolerium*	11°30′	52°30′
Δαμνόνιον τὸ καὶ Ὄκρινον ἄκρον	ιβ′	να′ι″	*Damnonium* which is also *Ocrinum* promontory	12°	51°30′

Variants

Ἀβραουάνου, Αὐραουάννου, Αὐραουάνου, Ἀβρανάνου.

Ἰκῶα, Ἰκόη.

Σεγαντίων, Γεσαντίων.

Σεγηία.

Καιαγκάνων, Ἰαγγάνων. Müller's Καιαγγανῶν is a conjecture; we follow U (and many other (MSS).

Τισοβίου.

Στουκία, Σουκκία, Τουκκία, Στουλκία.

Ὀκταποταρον.

Τοβίου (U and favoured by Müller), Τοιβίου, Τουβούα.

Ῥατοσταβίου (favoured by Müller); we follow U and most other MSS.

Οὐξέλλα (favoured by Müller), Οὐζέλλα; we follow U and most MSS.

Ἀντιουέστεον.

Βολαίριον.

Ὄκριον (favoured by Müller); we found U and most MSS.

Comment

Deva is certainly the Dee, so that *Abravannus* and *Iena* should represent Luce Bay (? and the Water of Luce) and Wigtown Bay (presumably the river Cree, whose modern name means simply 'boundary') respectively. *Novius* is the Nith and *Ituna* the Eden. *Moricambe* estuary fits Morecambe Bay well (though the modern name is not a survival but was reapplied to what had been Poulton Bay in 1771), but what river is meant is difficult to determine. The Kent, the most obvious candidate, should have been *Cunetio* and according to Ekwall *ERN* the names of the Lune, the Keer, the Crake and the Leven are all of Celtic derivation. This leaves only the little Winster, whose present name is Norse, and it may be that the name, meaning something like 'bend in the sea', really belonged to the bay or gulf (κόλπος) rather than to an estuary (εἴσχυσις). On the port of the *Setantii* see above, p. 116: it should be near Fleetwood. *Belisama* best suits the Ribble, in which case *Seteia* should be the Mersey; it is curious that Ptolemy omits the Dee, though later he names Chester (Δήουα). The promontory of the *Gangani* must be Braich-y-Pwll, but the name arouses suspicions, because there are *Gangani*, as a tribe, in the corresponding part of Ireland. *Toesobis* should be one of the streams flowing into Traeth Bach, Afon Glaslyn and Afon Dwyryd, but the names do not fit, neither does that of Afon Mawddach a little further south, and here again a bay rather than a river may be meant. *Stuccia* is the Ystwyth and *Tuerobis* should be the Teifi, though the name is difficult. *Octapitarum* promontory is St David's Head: the -ον termination shows that Ptolemy, at least, took it as a nominative and not as the genitive of a tribal name. *Tubius* is the Tywi, *Ratostathybius* should be the Taff, and *Sabrina* is the Severn. *Vexalla* should be either the Somerset Axe or the Parrett and although both have modern names of Celtic origin a case can be made for the former (see p. 21). The promontory of *Heracles* should probably be Hartland Point, as the most notable feature on this coast, but any of the headlands between Porlock and Braunton (Foreland Point, Highveer Point, Bull Point, Morte Point, Baggy Point) is a possibility: unless the cape was simply christened by sailors from the sea, the discovery of a shrine might settle the question. *Antivestaeum* is Land's End and *Damnonium* the Lizard: on the duplication of names see above, p. 115.

The southern coast of Britain (*Geography* II, 3, 3)

Τῆς ἐφεξῆς μεσημβρινῆς πλευρᾶς περιγραφή, ᾗ ὑπόκειται Πρεττανικὸς Ὠκεανός·			Next a description of the southern side, below which lies the *Prettanicus* Ocean		
μετὰ τὸ Ὄκρινον ἄκρον			After *Ocrinum* promontory		
Κενίωνος ποταμοῦ ἐκβολαί	ιδ′	να′ι″δ″	Mouth of river *Cenio*	14°	51°45′
Ταμάρου ποταμοῦ ἐκβολαί	ιε′γο″	νβ′ς″	Mouth of river *Tamarus*	15°40′	52°10′
Ἴσκα ποταμοῦ ἐκβολαί	ιζ′γο″	νβ′γ″	Mouth of river *Isca*	17°40′	52°20′
Αλαύνου ποταμοῦ ἐκβολαί	ιζ′γο″	νβ′γο″	Mouth of river *Alaunus*	17°40′	52°40′

Μέγας Λιμήν	ιθ'	νγ'	*Great Harbour*	19°	53°
Τρισάντωνος ποταμοῦ ἐκβολαί	κ'γ''	νγ'	Mouth of river *Trisanto*	20°20'	53°
Καινὸς Λιμήν	κα'	νγ'ʟ''	*New Harbour*	21°	53°30'
Κάντιον ἄκρον	κβ'	νδ'	*Cantium* promontory	22°	54°

Variants

Κεννίωνος.
Ἴσακα (U).

Comment

Cenio suits the position of the Kenwyn, a tributary of the Fal, and there are no other obvious candidates, but the modern river name is almost certainly a back-formation and so unacceptable. *Tamarus* is the Tamar and *Isca* the Exe, or just possibly, in this case, the Axe, which should also have been called *Isca* and for that reason can only be identified with *Alaunus* if one assumes that the Anglo-Saxons picked up only the generic and not the proper name (see p. 21); otherwise the fact that both the Stour and the Hampshire Avon have tributaries called Allen might suggest that *Alaunus* was once the name of their common estuary in Christchurch Harbour. On the significance of *Great Harbour* and *New Harbour* see above, p. 116: they are probably not proper names of places but descriptive names for the Solent and Dover respectively. *Trisanto* is the Arun (formerly Tarrant) and *Cantium* is the South Foreland (not the North Foreland because that is on the island of Thanet).

The eastern coast of Britain (*Geography* II, 3, 4)

Τῶν ἐφεξῆς πρὸς ἕω καὶ μεσημβρίαν πλευρῶν περιγραφή, αἷς παράκειται Γερμανικὸς Ὠκεανός. Μετὰ τὸ Ταρουεδοὺμ ἄκρον ἢ τὴν Ὀρκάδα, ὅπερ εἴρηται,

Next a description of the sides on the east and south, next which lies the *Germanicus* ocean. After *Tarvedum* or *Orcas* promontory, above mentioned,

Οὐιρουεδρούμ ἄκρον	λα'	ξ'	*Virvedrum* promontory	31°	60°
Οὐερουβίουμ ἄκρον	λ'ʟ''	νθ'γο''	*Verubium* promontory	30°30'	59°40'
Ἴλα ποταμοῦ ἐκβολαί	λ'	νθ'γο''	Mouth of river *Ila*	30°	59°40'
Ὄχθη ὑψηλή	κθ'	νθ'γο''	*High Bank*	29°	59°40'
Οὐάραρ εἴσχυσις	κζ'	νθ'γο''	*Varar* estuary	27°	59°40'
Λόξα ποταμοῦ ἐκβολαί	κζ'ʟ''	νθ'γο''	Mouth of river *Loxa*	27°30'	59°40'
Τούεσις εἴσχυσις	κζ'	νθ'	*Tuesis* estuary	27°	59°
Καίλιος ποταμοῦ ἐκβολαί	κζ'	νη'ʟ''δ''	Mouth of river *Caelis*	27°	58°45'
Ταιζάλων ἄκρον	κζ'ʟ''	νη'ʟ''	Promontory of the *Taezali*	27°30'	58°30'
Δηούα ποταμοῦ ἐκβολαί	κς'	νη'ʟ''	Mouth of river *Deva*	26°	58°30'
Ταούα εἴσχυσις	κε'	νη'ʟ''γ''	*Tava* estuary	25°	58°50'
Τίνα ποταμοῦ ἐκβολαί	κδ'	νη'ʟ''	Mouth of river *Tina*	24°	58°30'

Βοδερία εἴσχυσις	κβ′L″	νθ′	*Boderia* estuary	22°30′	59°
Ἀλαύνου ποταμοῦ ἐκβολαί	κα′γ″	νη′L″	Mouth of river *Alaunus*	21°20′	58°30′
Οὐέδρα ποταμοῦ ἐκβολαί	κ′ς″	νη′L″	Mouth of river *Vedra*	20°10′	58°30′
Δοῦνον κόλπος	κ′δ″	νζ′L″	*Dunum* gulf	20°15′	57°30′
Γαβραντουίκων εὐλίμενος κόλπος	κα′	νζ′	Gulf of the *Gabrantovices* suitable for a harbour	21°	57°
Ὀκέλου ἄκρον	κα′δ″	νς′γο″	Promontory of *Ocelus*	21°15′	56°40′
Ἄβου ποταμοῦ ἐκβολαί	κα′	νς′L″	Mouth of river *Abus*	21°	56°30′
Μεταρὶς εἴσχυσις	κ′L″	νε′γο″	*Metaris* estuary	20°30′	55°40′
Γαριέννου ποταμοῦ ἐκβολαί	κ′L″γ″	νε′γ″	Mouth of river *Gariennus*	20°50′	55°20′
Ἐξοχή	κα′δ″	νε′ιβ″	A *Projection*	21°15′	55°5′
Εἰδουμάνιος ποταμοῦ ἐκβολαί	κ′ς′	νε′	Mouth of river *Eidumanis*	20°10′	55°
Ἰαμησα εἴσχυσις	κ′L″	νδ′L″	*Iamesa* estuary	20°30′	54°30′
μεθ᾽ ἣν Κάντιον ἄκρον	κβ′	νδ′	After which *Cantium* promontory	22°	54°

Variants

Βερουβίουμ.
Ἴλλα.
Ὄχθη ὑψηλή κθ′ νθ′γο″ (U).
Λόξα ποταμοῦ εκβολαί κη′ς″ νθ′γο″ (U).
Οὐάραρ εἴσχυσις κη′ς″ νζ′γο″ (U).
(that is, U places *Loxa* to the east, or north, of *Varar*)
Τούαισις (U).
Κελνίου (U), Καιλνίου.
Διούα.
Τίννα.
Ὀκέλλου ἄκρον.
Μεγαρίς.
Γαρυέννου, Γαρυένου, Γαρρυένου.
Σιδουμάνιος (favoured by Müller; we follow U and many other MSS).
Ἰάμισσα.
(Müller's conjecture Ταμήσα, though obviously correct, lacks MS support).

Comment

If *Tarvedum* is Dunnet Head, then *Virvedrum* and *Verubium* (both, like *Tarvedum*, with the -ουμ termination) are presumably Duncansby Head and Noss Head respectively; the close grouping of headlands here may reflect the fact that, according to Tacitus (*Agricola* 10) the fleet visited the Orkneys, and also the difficulties of navigation in the Pentland Firth. *Ila* is the river Helmsdale (flowing through Strath Ullie which, like Strathnaver, was well populated and so able to provide supplies) and the *High Bank* is presumably Tarbat Ness. *Varar* estuary is certainly Beauly Firth, since the upper reaches of the Beauly are still called Farrar, but *Loxa* presents a problem. The equation with Lossie seems probable, though some have felt that it is rather far east and too near the Spey, and for this reason some have suggested the Findhorn, whose present name (meaning 'White Ireland') was acquired later. If, however, the text of U is correct, *Loxa* might even suit the Cromarty Firth. *Tuesis* is almost certainly the Spey, as the only river on this coast large enough to justify the term estuary, but there is no etymological connection. *Caelis* (or *Celnis*) is presumably the Deveron (again a later name) and the promontory of the *Taezali* is either Kinnairds Head or Rattray Head; it may be noted that here all the manuscripts spell the tribal name with a *-z-*, not an *-x-*. *Deva* is the Dee, *Tava* is the Tay and *Boderia* is the Forth. Some have suggested that *Tina* represents either the Northumberland Tyne or the Tyne of East Lothian, but all manuscripts place it north of the Forth and there is no reason why Ptolemy, who omits Hadrian's Wall, should have singled out the former for special mention. As Bradley pointed out, it exactly fits the Fife Eden in position, and it is likely enough that the name *Ituna* lost its initial letter in transmission to Ptolemy. *Alaunus* is the Aln and *Vedra* the Wear. *Dunum* gulf must be Tees Bay and the Gulf of the *Gabrantovices* either Filey Bay or Bridlington Bay. If it is the former, then the promontory of *Ocelus* is Flamborough Head, but if the latter, Spurn Head. This last identification affects the meaning to be given to *Abus* (or *Abu*). In a general sense the Humber estuary is clearly meant, but whether the Humber itself (which should surely have been listed as an estuary) or the Ouse, which gave access to the legionary fortress at York, is not so certain, and if Spurn Head is taken as the promontory the Ouse is the more probable. *Metaris* estuary clearly represents the Wash, but here again the identity of the actual river is in question. The most likely would be the Witham, leading to Lincoln, or perhaps the Nene, though Ekwall regards both these names as of Celtic origin; it may be that Ptolemy's name is really that of a bay rather than of a river. *Gariennus* is the Yare, but the projection to the south of it cannot be identified, because of the erosion to which this coast has been subject. *Eidumanis* (or *Sidumanis*) was identified by Ekwall with the Lincolnshire Witham, but with special pleading which involved the supposition that Ptolemy, or his copiers, had the points seriously out of order. As Bradley remarked, in position it suits the Blackwater, on which is the town of Witham, although it once had the Celtic name of *Penta* (see Alphabetic List). The form *Iamesa* for the Thames, without any I-forms in the manuscripts, demonstrates well how medieval scribes might fail to recognise even the name of London's river.

Peoples and Places in southern Scotland (*Geography* II, 3, 5–7)

Οἰκοῦσι δὲ τὰ μὲν παρὰ τὴν ἀρκτικὴν πλευρὰν ὑπὸ μὲν τὴν ὁμώνυμον χερσόνησον Νοουάνται, παρ' οἷς εἰσι καὶ πόλεις αἵδε·

There dwell on the northern side, below the peninsula of the same name, the *Novantae*, among whom are these cities:

Λουκοπιβία	ιθ′	ξ′γ″	*Lucopibia*	19°	60°20′
ʽΡεριγόνιον	κ′ς′	ξ′γο″	*Rerigonium*	20°10′	60°40′

ὑφ' οὓς Σελγοοῦαι, παρ' οἷς πόλεις αἵδε·			beneath whom are the *Selgovae*, among whom are these cities:		
Καρβαντόριγον	ιθ'	νθ'ι''	*Carbantorigum*	19°	59°30'
Οὔξελλον	ιη'ι''	νθ'γ''	*Uxellum*	18°30'	59°20'
Κόρδα	κ'	νθ'γο''	*Corda*	20°	59°40'
Τριμόντιον	ιθ'	νθ'	*Trimontium*	19°	59°
Τούτων δὲ πρὸς ἀνατολὰς Δαμνόνιοι μὲν ἀρκτικώτεροι, ἐν οἷς πόλεις αἵδε·			To the east of these are the more northern *Damnonii*, in whom are these cities:		
Κολανία	κ'ι''δ''	νθ'ς''	*Colania*	20°45'	59°10'
Οὐινδόγαρα	κα'γ''	ξ'	*Vindogara*	21°20'	60°
Κόρια	κα'ι''	νθ'γ''	*Coria*	21°30'	59°20'
'Αλαῦνα	κβ'ι''δ''	νθ'ι''γ''	*Alauna*	22°45'	59°50'
Λίνδον	κγ'	νθ'ι''	*Lindum*	23°	59°30'
Οὐικτωρία	κγ'ι''	νθ'	*Victoria*	23°30'	59°
'Ωταδινοὶ δὲ μεσημβρινώτεροι, ἐν οἷς πόλεις αἵδε·			The *Otadini* are more to the south, in whom are these cities:		
Κούρια	κ'ς''	νθ'	*Curia*	20°10'	59°
'Αλαῦνα	κγ'	νη'γο''	*Alauna*	23°	58°40'
Βρεμένιον	κα'	νη'ι''δ''	*Bremenium*	21°	58°45'

Variants

Νουάνται.
Λουκοπιβιάβια.
'Ρετιγόνιον (U and some other MSS).
Σελγοῦαι, Λελγοῦαι, 'Ελγοοῦαι.
Καρβαντόριδον.
Οὔζελλον, Οὔξελον.
Δάμνιοι (U and some other MSS).
Κολάνικα (favoured by Müller); we follow U and most MSS.
Οὐανδόγαρα (favoured by Müller), Οὐανδούαρα (U); but Οὐινδόγαρα seems required by analogy with Οὐινδόγαρα κόλπος in II, 3, 1.
Οὐικτορία.
Γαδινοί (U text), 'Ωταδηνοί (U map), 'Ωταλινοί (favoured by Müller), Ταδινοί; many MSS have ὑφ'οὓς Γαδινοὶ ἀρκτικώτεροι, 'Ωταδινοὶ δὲ μεσημβρινώτεροι.
Κορία (favoured by Müller); we follow U and most MSS.
U and many other MSS omit the second 'Αλαῦνα.

Comment

The certain names in this section are *Trimontium* (Newstead) and *Bremenium* (High Rochester); the reasons for the identifications suggested for the other πόλεις have been discussed above (pp. 123–128). *Rerigonium* (?Stranraer) must be near Loch Ryan and if *Lucopibia* is Glenlochar the *Novantae* should occupy Wigtownshire and the Stewartry of Kirkcudbright. *Carbantorigum* (for *Carbantoritum*, the 'wagon-ford' or 'chariot-ford') suits the crossing of the Tweed at Easter Happrew (later replaced by the fort at Lyne) and, with *Trimontium*, places the *Selgovae* in the Tweed basin; *Corda*

(?Castledykes) would stretch them a little far west and *Uxellum* (?Ward Law) seems too far south but, as we have seen, Ptolemy's tribal attributions are not always reliable. *Colania* (?Camelon), *Vindogara* (?Irvine), *Coria* (?Barochan Hill), *Alauna* (Ardoch), *Lindum* (almost certainly Drumquhassle) and *Victoria* (?Inchtuthil) make a coherent group and show the *Damnonii* stretching from Ayrshire and Renfrewshire across the Forth-Clyde isthmus into Stirlingshire and southern Perthshire. *Bremenium* and *Curia* (?Inveresk) place the *Otadini* (presumably for *Votadini*) along the east coast from Northumberland to the Lothians. It is tempting to identify the second *Alauna* with the fort at Learchild, on the Aln, but Ptolemy's siting of it does not support this and since it is omitted by many of the manuscripts it may be no more than a misplaced duplication of the first *Alauna*.

Peoples and Places in northern Scotland (*Geography* II, 3, 8–9)

Μετὰ δὲ τοὺς Δαμνονίους, πρὸς ἀνατολὰς ἀρκτικώτεροι μὲν, ἀπό τοῦ 'Επιδίου ἄκρου ὡς πρὸς ἀνατολὰς 'Επίδιοι, μεθ' οὓς
Κρέωνες, εἶτα
Καρνονάκαι, εἶτα Καιρηνοὶ καὶ ἀνατολικώτατοι καὶ τελευταῖοι Κορναούιοι· ἀπὸ δὲ τοῦ Λεμαννονίου κόλπου μέχρι τῆς Οὐάραρ εἰσχύσεως Καληδόνιοι καὶ ὑπὲρ αὐτοὺς ὁ Καληδόνιος δρυμὸς, ὧν ἀνατολικώτεροι Δεκάνται, μεθ' οὓς Λοῦγοι συνάπτοντες τοῖς Κορναουίοις, καὶ ὑπὲρ τοὺς Λούγους Σμέρται. ὑπὸ δὲ τοὺς Καληδονίους Οὐακομάγοι, παρ' οἷς πόλεις αἵδε·

After the *Damnonii*, towards the east but more northerly, from *Epidium* promontory eastwards are the *Epidii*, after whom further east are the *Creones*; then the *Carnonacae*; then the *Caereni*; and furthest east and last the *Cornavii*; from *Lemannonius* gulf to *Varar* estuary are the *Caledonii*, and above them the *Caledonius* forest, and east of them the *Decantae*, after whom are the *Lugi* adjoining the *Cornavii*, and above the *Lugi*, the *Smertae*. Below the *Caledonii* are the *Vacomagi*, among whom are these cities:

Βαννατία	κδ'	νθ'L''	*Bannatia*	24°	59°30'
Ταμεία	κε'	νθ'γ''	*Tameia*	25°	59°20'
Πτερωτὸν στρατόπεδον	κζ'δ''	νθ'γ''	*Pinnata Castra*	27°15'	59°20'
Τούεσις	κϛ'Lδ''	νθ'ϛ''	*Tuesis*	26°45'	59°10'

Ὑπὸ δὲ τούτους δυσμικώτεροι μὲν Οὐενίκωνες, ἐν οἷς πόλις ἥδε·

Below these towards the west are the *Venicones*, in whom is this city:

Ὄρρεα	κδ'	νη'L''δ''	*Orrea*	24°	58°45'

'Ανατολικώτεροι δὲ Ταίξαλοι καὶ πόλις ἥδε·

More toward the east are the *Taexali* and this city:

Δηουάνα	κϛ''	νθ'	*Devana*	26°	59°

Variants

Δαμνίους.

Many MSS have μεθ'οὓς Κέρωνες εἶτα ἀνατολικώτεροι Κρέωνες; Müller, probably rightly, brackets Κέρωνες εἶτα ἀνατολικώτεροι; U has simply Κερώνες.

Κάρνονες.

Καρινοί (U and many other MSS), Καρηνοί, Καιρινοί.
Κουρναούιοι, Κορνάβιοι.
Λεμανονίου, Λελαννονίου, Λαιλαννονίου.
Λεκάνται: Δεκάνται is inferred from δὲ Κάντεαι.
Λόγοι.
Μέρται.
Βανατία.
Ταμία.
The medieval Latin MSS translate Πτερωτὸν στρατόπεδον as *Alata Castra*; Müller first suggested *Pinnata Castra*.
Τούαισις (U and many other MSS).
Οὐενίκωμες, Οὐεννίκωνες, Οὐενίκονες, Οὐεννίκονες, Οὐενίκοντες (3 MSS only).
Ταίζαλοι (favoured by Müller), Ταξάλοι, Τεξάλοι; we follow U and most MSS, despite conflict with Ταιζάλων ἄκρον in II, 3, 4, above.

Comment

The *Epidii* are tied to Kintyre (the home, as Watson pointed out, of the MacEacherns) and the *Cornavii* evidently occupied Caithness, but there is insufficient evidence to place the intervening tribes of the western highlands, whether or not the *Creones* and the *Cerones* are to be taken as two distinct peoples. The *Caledonii* appear to stretch from the Beauly Firth (which is certainly *Varar* estuary) to Loch Long, but Loch Linnhe, which would place them neatly in the Great Glen, seems more likely and Ptolemy may have been confused by two sources; the Caledonian forest probably refers to a vague area and is not to be precisely located (cf. the references to it in the literary sources, p. 44 above). The *Decantae* should lie in eastern Ross and Cromarty, the *Lugi* in eastern Sutherland and the *Smertae* in central Sutherland. All this information must have been derived from intelligence reports, but with the *Vacomagi* we return to country actually invaded by Agricola's army. As explained above (p. 128). *Tuesis* should be on the Spey, probably the Roman camp at Bellie, and *Pinnata Castra* should be to the west of it, but *Bannatia* (?Dalginross) and *Tameia* (?Cardean) must be much further south and it is impossible to reconcile these locations with Ptolemy's tribal attributions: the *Vacomagi* evidently occupied either the area of Moray and Banffshire or that of eastern Perthshire and Angus, but they can hardly have occupied both. If, as we have suggested, *Orrea* lay north of the Tay (?near Monifieth), the *Venicones* are more likely to have held the latter. The *Taexali* (or *Taezali*) are tied to Aberdeenshire by *Taezalorum* promontory. So far as their πόλις is concerned, all the manuscripts spell *Devana* with an *-a-*, not an *-o-*, so that whether or not the *Devoni* of the *Ravenna Cosmography* refers to the Don, Ptolemy, or his copiers, clearly thought that the place was related to the river *Deva*, or Dee; see above, p. 128.

Peoples and Places in northern England (*Geography* II, 3, 10)

Πάλιν δ'ὑπὸ μὲν τοὺς Σελγοούας καὶ τοὺς 'Ωταδινούς, διήκοντες ἐφ'ἑκάτερα τὰ πελάγη, Βρίγαντες, ἐν οἷς πόλεις αἵδε·

Again below the *Selgovae* and the *Otadini*, stretching from sea to sea, are the *Brigantes*, in whom are these cities:

Ἐπίακον	ιη′ʟ″	νη′ʟ″	*Epiacum*	18°30′	58°30′
Οὐιννοούιον	ιζ′ʟ″γ″	νη′	*Vinnovium*	17°50′	58°
Κατουρακτόνιον	κ′	νη′	*Caturactonium*	20°	58°
Κάλαγον	ιθ′	νζ′ʟ″δ″	*Calagum*	19°	57°45′
Ἰσούριον	κ′	νζ′γο″	*Isurium*	20°	57°40′
Ῥιγόδουνον	ιη′	νζ′ʟ″	*Rigodunum*	18°	57°30′
Ὀλίκανα	ιθ′	νζ′ʟ″	*Olicana*	19°	57°30′
Ἐβόρακον, Λεγίων ϛ′ Νικηφόρος			*Eboracum*, Legio VI Victrix		
	κ′	νζ′γ″		20°	57°20′
Καμουνλόδουνον	ιη′	νζ′ʟ″δ″	*Camunlodunum*	18°	57°45′
Πρὸς οἷς παρὰ τὸν εὐλίμενον κόλπον Πάρισοι, καὶ πόλις			Next to whom, beside the gulf suitable for a harbour, are the *Parisi* and the city		
Πετουαρία	κ′γο″	νϛ′γο″	*Petuaria*	20°40′	56°40′

Variants

Ὠταλινούς, Ὠταδηνούς (U).
Ἐπείακον (U and most MSS).
Οὐινοούιον (favoured by Müller); we follow U and most MSS.
Κατουρρακτόνιον, Τατουρακτόνιον, Τακτουρακτόνιον.
Κάλατον (most MSS, but not U).
Ὀλόκανα.
Καμουλόδουνον (U); most MSS have Καμουνλόδουνον.
Παρείσοι.
Πετοναρία, Πετούαρα.

Comment

The certain identifications here are those of *Vinnovium* (Binchester), *Caturactonium* (Catterick), *Isurium* (Aldborough), *Eboracum* (York) and *Petuaria* (Brough-on-Humber). The suggested identifications of *Calagum* with either Lancaster or Burrow-in-Lonsdale and of *Camunlodunum* with Slack depend not only on Ptolemy but also on the appearance of these places in the *Antonine Itinerary* (below, pp. 172 and 158). The possible identifications of *Epiacum* with Whitley Castle, of *Rigodunum* with Castleshaw and of *Olicana* with Elslack (not Ilkley, for that appears to be *Verbeia*) depend entirely on the evidence of Ptolemy, specifically on their distances from London and from the two legionary fortresses of Chester and York (see Tables 1–3, pp. 119 and 120).

Peoples and places in northern Wales and midland England (*Geography* II, 3, 11)

Ὑπὸ δὲ τούτους καὶ τοὺς Βρίγαντας οἰκοῦσι δυσμικώτατοι μὲν Ὀρδοούικες, ἐν οἷς πόλεις·			Below these and the *Brigantes* there dwell furthest to the west the *Ordovices*, in whom are the cities:		
Μεδιολάνιον	ιϛ′ʟ″δ″	νϛ′γο″	*Mediolanium*	16°45′	56°40′
Βραννογένιον	ιϛ′ʟ″δ″	νϛ′δ″	*Brannogenium*	16°45′	56°15′
Τούτων δ᾽ἀνατολικώτεροι Κορναούιοι, ἐν οἷς πόλεις αἵδε·			Further east than these are the *Cornavii*, in whom are these cities:		

Δηοῦα, Λεγίων κ' Νικηφόρος	ιζ'L''	νς'L''δ''	*Deva*, Legio XX Victrix	17°30'	56°45'
Οὐιροκόνιον	ις'L''δ''	νε'L''δ''	*Viroconium*	16°45'	55°45'
μεθ'οὓς Κοριτανοὶ, ἐν οἷς πολεις·			after whom are the *Coritani*, in whom are the cities:		
Λίνδον	ιη'γο''	νς'L''	*Lindum*	18°40'	56°30'
'Ράτε	ιη'	νε'L''	*Rate*	18°	55°30'
Εἶτα Κατυευχλανοὶ, ἐν οἷς πόλεις·			Then the *Catyeuchlani*, in whom are the cities:		
Σαλῖναι	κ'L''δ''	νε'L''γ''	*Salinae*	20°45'	55°50'
Οὐρολάνιον	ιθ'γ''	νε'L''	*Urolanium*	19°20'	55°30'
μεθ' οὓς Σιμενοῖ, παρ'οἷς πόλις·			after whom are the *Simeni*, among whom is the city:		
Οὐέντα	κ'L''	νε'γ''	*Venta*	20°30'	55°20'
καὶ ἀνατολικώτεροι παρὰ τὴν 'Ιαμήσα εἴσχυσιν Τρινόαντες, ἐν οἷς πόλις·			and more to the east, beside *Iamesa* estuary, the *Trinoantes*, in whom is the city:		
Καμουδόλανον	κα'	νε'	*Camudolanum*	21°	55°

Variants

'Ορδούικες.

Βρανογένιον, Βρανογένειον.

Κορνάβιοι.

Δηούανα (U and some other MSS).

Κοριταυοί.

'Ράχε (U), 'Ραγε; Müller's 'Ράται is conjectural.

Κατυαιχλανοί (U), Κατυεύκλανοι, Κατευχανοί, Καπεχλανοί, Καπελάνοι; Müller's Κατουελλανοί is conjectural; we follow most MSS.

Σαλῆναι (U and most MSS).

'Ιμενοί; Müller's 'Ικενοί is conjectural; we follow U and most MSS.

'Ιμήσα, 'Ιμήνσα; Müller's Ταμήσα is conjectural; we follow U and most MSS.

Τρινοούαντες (one inferior MS); we follow U and all other MSS.

Καμρυδόλανον, Καμβρυδόλανον, Καμουδολάν; Müller's Καμουλόδουνον is conjectural; we follow U and most MSS.

Comment

This section is chiefly notable for the extraordinary degree of corruption of what must, in the earlier period, have been some of the best-known names in Roman Britain – the *Catuvellauni*, the *Iceni*, *Verulamium* and *Camulodunum* – and the extent of it must surely suggest garbling in an early source. It is, therefore, the more tempting to relate *Mediolanium* to the *Mediolanum* (Whitchurch) and *Brannogenium* to the *Bravonium* (Leintwardine) of the *Antonine Itinerary*. Apart from these, the only problem concerns *Salinae* and, as suggested above (p. 120), despite the location and tribal attribution given by Ptolemy, its distance from London supports its identification not with a site on the Wash but with Droitwich.

Peoples and Places in southern Wales and southern England (*Geography* II, 3, 12–13)

Πάλιν δὲ ὑπὸ τὰ εἰρημένα ἔθνη δυσμικώτατοι μὲν Δημῆται, ἐν οἷς πόλεις αἵδε·			Again below the above-named peoples, furthest to the west are the *Demetae*, in whom are these cities:		
Λουέντινον	ιε′L″δ″	νε′ς″	*Luentinum*	15°45′	55°10′
Μαρίδουνον	ιε′L″	νδ′γο″	*Maridunum*	15°30′	54°40′
Τούτων δ᾽ἀνατολικώτεροι Σίλυρες, ἐν οἷς πόλις·			More to the east than these are the *Silures*, in whom is the city:		
Βούλλαιον	ις′L″γ″	νε′	*Bullaeum*	16°50′	55°
μεθ᾽οὓς Δοβοῦνοι καὶ πόλις·			after whom are the *Dobuni* and the city:		
Κορίνιον	ιη′	νδ′ς″	*Corinium*	18°	54°10′
εἶτα ᾽Ατρεβάτιοι καὶ πόλις·			then the *Atrebatii* and the city:		
Καληοῦα	ιθ′	νδ′δ″	*Caleva*	19°	54°15′
μεθ᾽οὓς ἀνατολικώτατοι Κάντιοι, ἐν οἷς πόλεις·			after whom furthest to the east are the *Cantii*, in whom are the cities:		
Λονδίνιον	κ′	νδ′	*Londinium*	20°	54°
Δαρούερνον	κα′	νγ′γο″	*Darvernum*	21°	53°40′
῾Ρουτουπίαι	κα′L″δ″	νδ′	*Rutupiae*	21°45′	54°
Πάλιν τοῖς μὲν ᾽Ατρεβατίοις καὶ τοῖς Καντίοις ὑπόκεινται ῾Ρῆγνοι καὶ πόλις·			Again there lie below the *Atrebatii* and the *Cantii* the *Regni* and the city:		
Νοιόμαγος	ιθ′L″δ″	νγ′γ″ιβ″	*Noeomagus*	19°45′	53°25′
Τοῖς δὲ Δοβουννοῖς Βέλγαι καὶ πόλεις·			Below the *Dobunni* lie the *Belgae* and the cities:		
Ἴσχαλις	ις′	νγ′γο″	*Ischalis*	16°	53°40′
Ὕδατα Θερμα	ιζ′γ″	νγ′γο″	*Aquae Calidae*	17°20′	53°40′
Οὐέντα	ιη′γο″	νγ′L″	*Venta*	18°40′	53°30′
Τούτων δ᾽ἀπὸ δυσμῶν καὶ μεσημβρίας Δουρότριγες, ἐν οἷς πόλις·			West and south from these are the *Durotriges*, in whom is the city:		
Δούνιον	ιη′	νβ′γο″	*Dunium*	18°	52°40′
μεθ᾽ οὓς δυσμικώτατοι Δουμνόνιοι, ἐν οἷς πόλεις·			after whom, furthest to the west, are the *Dumnonii*, in whom are the cities:		
Οὐολίβα	ιδ′L″δ″	νβ′	*Voliba*	14°45′	52°
Οὔξελλα	ιε′	νβ′L″δ″	*Uxella*	15°	52°45′
Ταμάρη	ιε′	νβ′δ″	*Tamara*	15°	52°15′
Ἴσκα, λεγίων δευτέρα Σεβαστὴ	ιζ′L″	νβ′L″δ″	*Isca*, Legio II Augusta	17°30′	52°45′

Variants

Δημηκῆται.

Λουέντιον.

Μορίδουνον (one inferior MS only).

Σύληρες.

Βούλλεον, Βούλαιον.

Λοβοῦνοι.

Κορίννιον, Κορόνιον.

Καλίουα, Καλκούα, Ναλκούα.
Καντικοί (3 MSS).
Ἀουδίνιον.
Δαρούενον.
Καντικοῖς (same 3 MSS).
Ῥίγνοι, Ῥηγινοί (one inferior MS only).
Müller resites *Noeomagus* to 53°, without MS authority, to make it 59 Roman miles from *Londinium*.
Δοβουνοῖς, Λογούννοις.
Ἴσκαλις (favoured by Müller); we follow U and most MSS.
Δαμνόνιοι.
Οὐζέλα, Οὐεζέλα.

Comment

Most of the names here are readily identifiable. Of those which are not, *Bullaeum* is the *Burrium* of the *Antonine Itinerary* and so Usk. *Luentinum* and *Ischalis* may form a pair: on grounds both of position and of meaning (p. 400) it is tempting to identify *Luentinum* with the fort and gold-mining settlement at Dolaucothi, and if this is correct it strengthens the argument for attaching the name *Ischalis* to the lead and silver mines at Charterhouse on Mendip, near the Somerset Axe (**Isca*). For *Dunium* Maiden Castle has been suggested, but the distance from London suits even better Hod Hill where, uniquely, a Roman fort was inserted inside a pre-Roman hill-fort, which would explain the name. *Tamara* must be a fort, as yet unlocated, on the river Tamar, and while *Voliba* and *Uxella* are at present unidentifiable, the recent increase in our knowledge of the early Roman military occupation of the south-west offers hope for the future.

Islands off the coast of Britain (*Geography* II, 3, 14)

Νῆσοι δὲ παράκεινται τῇ Ἀλουίωνος·			Islands lie near that of *Alvion*:		
κατὰ μὲν τὴν Ὀρκάδα ἄκραν,			near *Orcas* promontory,		
Σκητὶς νῆσος	λβ′γο″	ξ′∟″δ″	*Scetis* island	32°40′	60°45′
Δοῦμνα νῆσος	λ′	ξα′γ″	*Dumna* island	30°	61°20′
ὑπὲρ ἣν αἱ Ὀρκάδες νῆσοι περὶ τριάκοντα τὸν ἀριθμόν, ὧν τὸ μεταξὺ ἐπέχει μοίρας	λ′	ξα′γο″	above which are the *Orcades* islands, about 30 in number, of which the middle point is	30°	61°40′
καὶ ἔτι ὑπὲρ αὐτὰς ἡ Θούλη νῆσος, ἧς τὰ μὲν δυσμικωτατα ἐπέχει μοίρας	κθ′	ξγ′	and yet above them is *Thule* island of which the western point is	29°	63°
τὰ δὲ ἀνατολικώτατα	λα′γο″	ξγ′	the eastern point	31°40′	63°
τὰ δὲ ἀρκτικώτατα	λ′γ″	ξγ′δ″	the northern point	30°20′	63°15′
τὰ δὲ νοτιώτατα	λ′γ″	ξβ′γο″	the southern point	30°20′	62°40′
τὰ δὲ μέσα	λ′γ″	ξγ′	the middle	30°20′	63°
Κατὰ δὲ τοὺς Τρινόαντας νῆσοι εἰσιν δύο αἵδε·			Near the *Trinoantes* are these two islands:		
Τολιάτις νῆσος	κγ′	νδ′γ″	*Toliatis* island	23°	54°20′

Κώουννος νῆσος	κδ′	νδ′ι″	*Counnus* island	24°	54°30′

Ὑπὸ δὲ τὸν Μέγαν Λιμένα νῆσος Οὐηκτὶς, ἧς τὸ μέσον ἐπέχει μοίρας ιθ′γ″ νβ′γ″ — Below the *Great Harbour* is the island *Vectis*, of which the mid-point is at 19°20′ 52°20′

Variants

Σκιτίς, Ὄκιτις (U and most MSS).
Τρινώαντας; Müller's Τρινοούαντας has no MS support.
Τολιάπις (U and most MSS).
Κώουνος (favoured by Müller), Κωούεννος, Κοούηννος; we follow U and most MSS.
Οὐικτίς.

Comment

Dumna is certainly Lewis (or, more properly, the whole of the 'Long Island') and *Scetis*, as Skye, is well related to it (though not at all to the mainland nor to the rest of the Inner Hebrides). The number of the *Orcades* (Orkneys) is the same as that recorded in the first century by Mela (p. 76, above), which suggests that Agricola's fleet brought back no new information on this matter. *Thule* is here, as in Tacitus, *Agricola* 10, equated with Shetland, and the dimensions given are presumably based on an estimate made by the fleet but, as noted above (p. 42), this need not mean that it ever really bore the name. The fact that Ptolemy relates the two south-eastern islands to the *Trinovantes* may not be significant, and it has always to be remembered that his islands are usually sited too far from the mainland. As Müller pointed out, ΤΟΛΙΑΤΙC could easily be a corrupt rendering of ΤΟΝΑΤΙC and if this is so Thanet (*Tanatus*) is presumably meant, and is more likely because it appears also in Solinus and Isidore. The traditional identification of *Counnus* with Canvey is based on no more than a superficial resemblance. The modern name is almost certainly of Germanic (post-Roman) origin, as also are the names of the other islands in the Thames estuary – Sheppey, Foulness and Mersea – and any of them might be intended: perhaps Mersea, which is near Colchester and was densely occupied in the Roman period, is the most likely.

From the Summary (*Geography* VIII, 3, 1–11, in Nobbe's numeration)

1. The first map includes the *Prettanic* islands, with the islands around them. At its centre the ratio of longitude to latitude is 11 to 20.
2. The map is bounded on all sides by oceans, on the east by the *Germanicus*, on the south by the *Prettanicus* and that called *Vergiovius*, on the west by the *Western* (Δυτικός), on the north by the *Hyperboreus* and that called *Duecaledonius*.
3. *Thule* has a longest day of 20 equinoctial hours and is 2 equinoctial hours west of Alexandria.
4. Notable cities of *Ivernia*: *Ivernis* has a longest day of 18 equinoctial hours and is $3\frac{1}{4}$ hours west of Alexandria.
5. *Rhaeba* has a longest day of $18\frac{7}{12}$ hours and is $3\frac{1}{5}$ hours west of Alexandria.
6. Of the island of *Alvion*: *Londinium* has a longest day of 17 hours and is 2 hours west of Alexandria.

7. *Eboracum* has a longest day of $17\frac{5}{6}$ hours and is $2\frac{1}{3}$ hours west of Alexandria.
8. *Caturactonium* has a longest day of 18 hours and is $2\frac{1}{3}$ hours west of Alexandria.
9. *Pinnata Castra* has a longest day of $18\frac{1}{2}$ hours and is $2\frac{1}{6}$ hours west of Alexandria.
10. The island of *Dumna* has a longest day of 19 hours and is 2 hours west of Alexandria.
11. The island of *Vectis* has a longest day of $16\frac{1}{3}$ hours and is $2\frac{1}{3}$ hours west of Alexandria.

Variants

Nobbe's text gives *Londinium* a longest day of 18 hours and puts it $2\frac{2}{3}$ hours west of Alexandria; we follow U.

Comment

Comparison with the map (p. 107) suggests that the selection of places for inclusion in this list was determined not by their intrinsic importance nor by the fact that accurate observations had been made at them, but simply by a desire to provide a representative sample. Thus Ireland is defined by *Rhaeba* to the north and *Ivernis* to the south, both of them placed near the middle of the island, and Scotland by the most remote πόλις, *Pinnata Castra.* So far as England is concerned, *Caturactonium* is no doubt included because it was already well embedded in the scientific literature (cf. *Almagest* II, 6, 24, p. 111 above) and on the map it is on the same meridian of 20° as *Londinium* and *Eboracum* – though here, probably through textual corruption, *Londinium* has slipped off it.

CHAPTER FOUR

ITINERARIES: THE PEUTINGER TABLE AND THE ANTONINE ITINERARY

1. THE NATURE OF ROMAN ITINERARIES

While Ptolemy's *Geography* illustrates the mainly theoretical attitude of the Greeks, itineraries represent the more practical approach of the Romans. This is well shown by the only ancient description of them which survives, that of Flavius Vegetius Renatus, who compiled his *Epitoma Rei Militaris* in the late fourth century:

> Those who have thoroughly studied military affairs maintain that more dangers are likely to arise on the march than on the actual field of battle. For in the battle everyone is armed and sees the enemy face to face, and comes to the fight with his mind prepared; on the march the soldier is less well armed and less alert, and is quickly thrown into confusion by a sudden attack or ambush. So a general ought to give every care and attention to seeing that he is not attacked on the march or that he can repel any attack easily and without loss. First of all, he should have itineraries of all those regions in which the war is being fought very fully set out, so that he may become fully acquainted with the distances between places in terms not only of mileage but also of the quality of the roads, and may have at his disposal reliable accounts of the short cuts, alternative routes, mountains and rivers: indeed the more able generals are said to have had not only annotated but pictorial itineraries of the provinces in which they were operating, so that they could decide which way to take not merely by mental calculation but by visual inspection too.[1]

No specifically military examples of the kind described by Vegetius have come down to us, and none of the itineraries which we have is as detailed as he demands. The Bordeaux Itinerary (fourth century)[2] does include some geographical, historical and religious annotation, but only in respect of Palestine; the Peutinger Table is indeed pictorial, but it is not drawn to scale, so that it is the mileage figures which are written

[1] *Epitoma Rei Militaris* (ed. C. Lang, 2nd edn., Leipzig, 1885, repr. Stuttgart, 1967), III, 6. On itineraries in general see W. Kubitschek, 'Itinerarien', *P.-W.* IX (1916), 2308–63, and the extensive bibliography in R. Chevallier, *Roman Roads* (London, 1976), 230–34.

[2] O. Cuntz, *Itineraria Romana*, I (Leipzig, 1929), 549_1–617_9; for annotation in Palestine, 587_1–599_9.

on it which are significant, not the graphic representation of distances, while for the relative positions of places it is thoroughly misleading; in the Antonine Itinerary annotation is confined to the occasional mention of an alternative route. Nevertheless it is reasonable to suppose that both the Antonine Itinerary and the Peutinger Table (which are the itineraries that extend to Britain) were distilled from documents of a more detailed character.

2. THE PEUTINGER TABLE[1]

The *Tabula Peutingeriana* derives its name from the fact that it was acquired by Konrad Peutinger in 1508. Now in the Hofbibliothek at Vienna, it consists of eleven parchment sheets joined together to make a roll 6·82 m. long and 34 cm. wide. Into this narrow strip is compressed a map covering the known world from Britain and Germany in the north to Africa in the south, and from Gaul in the west to India and Ceylon in the east. Seas, islands, lakes, rivers, mountains and forests are all shown and named, and some towns are represented by pictorial symbols. These symbols are of seven basic types, ranging from 'double towers' (much the most numerous class, with 429 examples) to the elaborate vignettes which distinguish Rome, Constantinople and Antioch. All these towns, and many others whose names are merely attached to kinks in roads, are linked by lines representing roads and figures are inserted to give the length of each stage.

The precise date and purpose of the map have been much debated, but a recent detailed study[2] suggests that the basis of it is the routes of the Roman *Cursus Publicus* (with the addition of those parts of the Persian imperial equivalent which might be of interest to official Roman travellers); that the different symbols represent not the intrinsic importance of places but the sort of facilities to be expected at them; and that the map was originally compiled in the third century, was revised in the eastern Empire under Theodosius II (A.D. 408–450) and assumed its present form in the thirteenth century.

Its use for Britain is restricted by the fact that at some stage before the existing copy was made the westernmost part of it (which would have included most of Britain, almost all of Spain and much of North Africa) had been lost. As a result, only the southern and part of the eastern coasts of the island are shown and a number of names which must have straddled the join appear in truncated form. Fortunately they can all be equated with names in the Antonine Itinerary, and so can be restored with some confidence, and the Table thus gives us the following 16 names:

[1] The most convenient edition is K. Miller, *Die Peutingersche Tafel* (Stuttgart, 1916, repr. 1962), but the coloured map included in it is not an exact facsimile. For a discussion, with photographs of varying quality of the whole map, see A. and M. Levi, *Itineraria Picta* (Rome, 1967). The best photograph of the western portion remains that published by O. G. S. Crawford in the *Illustrated London News* for 29 November 1924, but see now the full facsimile produced by E. Weber (Graz, 1977).

[2] Levi, *op. cit.* The authors disagree with the view of Miller (*op. cit.*, 1) that the map we have is that made by a monk of Colmar in 1265.

Name	Equivalent	Identification	Symbol
ISCA DUMNONIORUM	*Isca Dumnoniorum*	Exeter	Double towers
(Mo)*RIDUMO*	*Moridunum*	Sidford?	—
LEMAVIO	*Portus Lemanis*	Lympne	Double towers
DUROAVERUS	*Durovernum*	Canterbury	Double towers
DUBRIS	*Portus Dubris*	Dover	Double towers
RATUPIS	*Rutupiae*	Richborough	Double towers
DUROLEVO	*Durolevum*	nr Sittingbourne?	—
(Du)*RORIBIS*	*Durobrivae*	Rochester	—
(Novio)*MADUS*	*Noviomagus*	Crayford	—
(Ce)*BAROMACI*	*Caesaromagus*	Chelmsford	—
CAUNONIO	*Canonium*	Kelvedon	—
CAMULODUNO	*Camulodunum*	Colchester	—
AD ANSAM	*Ad Ansam*	Higham?	—
CONVETONI	*Combretovium*	Coddenham	—
SINOMAGI	*Sitomagus*	nr Yoxford?	Double towers
AD(Ven)*TA*(m) (Icinor)*UM*	*Venta Icinorum*	Caistor St Edmund	—

The map (Pl. I) also includes an island of some size between Britain and Gaul, but whether this represents Wight or Thanet is uncertain.

Many of the names have obviously been corrupted in transmission and it is curious that no symbol is used for Colchester, but the fact that the truncated names have clearly been repositioned shows that little attempt was made to produce an exact copy and for the same reason the symbol placed near *Sinomagi* may belong more properly to Caistor St Edmund or even to a missing town further west. Discrepancies in distances between the Table (fig. 9 and Pl. I) and the Antonine Itinerary are discussed below under the appropriate sections of the Itinerary.

3. THE ANTONINE ITINERARY[1]

The *Itinerarium Provinciarum Antonini Augusti* (fig. 10) is a collection of some 225 routes along the roads of the Roman Empire. In each case the beginning and end of a route are given, together with the total mileage, and there then follows a list of stopping-places on it with a statement of the number of miles (or, in Gaul, of *leugae*)[2] between each. The Itinerary begins in Mauretania, at Tingis, and then goes on to cover most, but not quite all, of the Empire in a somewhat random fashion. While six routes are given in Sardinia and one even in Corsica, there is none in Crete or Cyprus – in contrast to the Peutinger Table, which includes routes in Cyprus and

[1] This section is a revised version of A. L. F. Rivet, 'The British Section of the Antonine Itinerary', *Britannia*, I (1970), 34–68, where some other aspects of the Itinerary are discussed. It has benefited greatly from criticisms of that paper, especially those contained in W. Rodwell, 'Milestones, Civic Territories and the Antonine Itinerary', *Britannia*, VI (1975), 76–101.

[2] The Roman mile, consisting of 1,000 *passus* of five Roman *pedes* each, measured 1,480 metres (1,618 yards). The Gaulish *leuga* was equal to $1\frac{1}{2}$ Roman miles.

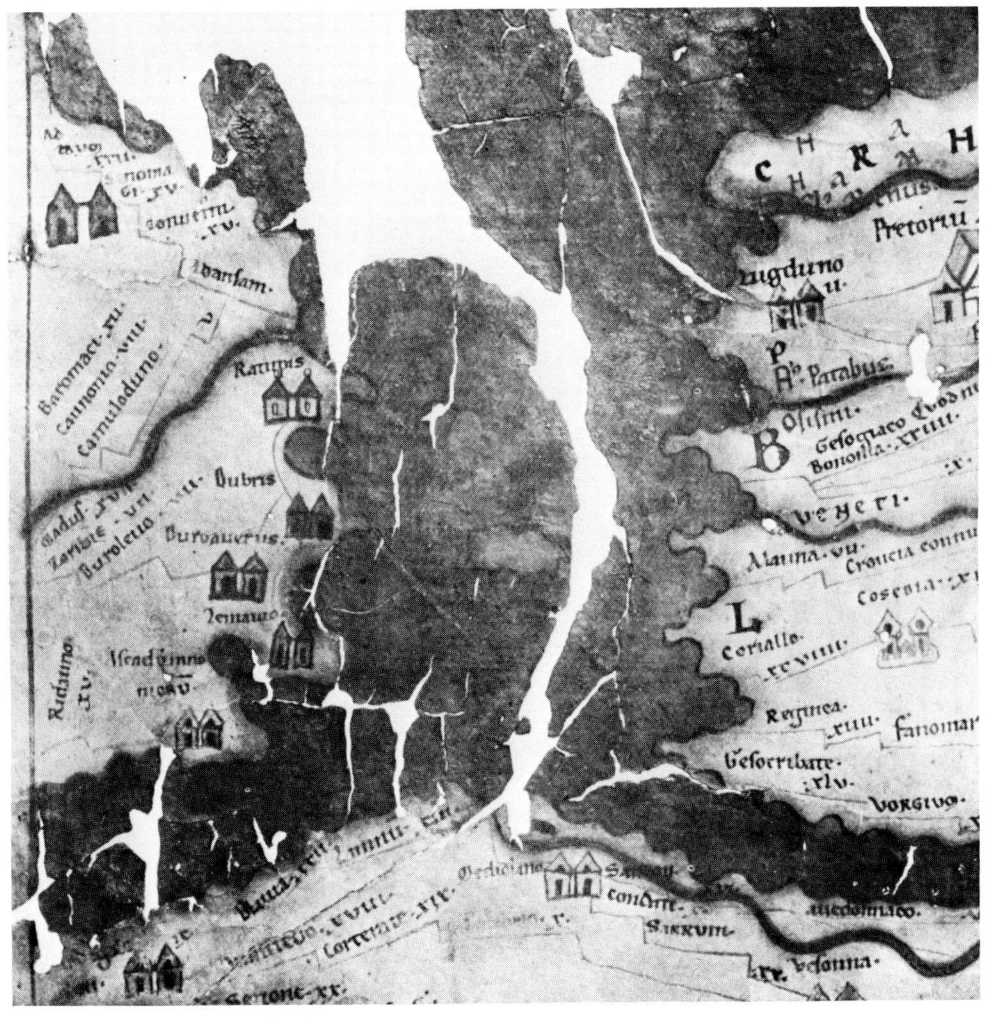

Plate I. The part of the Peutinger Table showing Britain (after *Antiquity*, I (1927), plate facing page 189).

Plate II. Manuscripts of the *Ravenna Cosmography*. (Reproduced by permission of the Society of Antiquaries, from *Archaeologia* XCIII (1949)).

perimus. In qua britania
plurimas fuisse ciuitates le
gimus. ex quib; aliquātas
designare uolumus. Jtē. Gia
no eltabo. Elconio. nemeto
tatio. Tamaris. puro coro
nauis. pilais. uernalis. Ar
dua rauenatone. deuonis
so. Stadio deuentia streno.
Durnarno. uxelis. uertevia.
Melamoni. Scaduna mor.
Termonin. Mestevia. Milu
dunum. Apaunaris. Maso
na. Alouerguim. Jterū iux
suprascriptam ciuitatem sta
tonior ē ciuitas que dicit
Moriduno. Alauna silua.
Omire tedertis. Lindinis.
Canza. Dolocindo. Clau
ino. Moionio. Bolueliaunio.
Alauna. Coloneas. Aranus.
Anicetis. Melezo. Jterno.
Bindogladia. nouio mag
no. Onna. uenta uelgar
om. Armis. Ardaoneon.
nauimagoie gentiū. leu
cu magna. Cunetzone. I
punctuobice. uentaslurū.
Iupania. Metambala. Albi

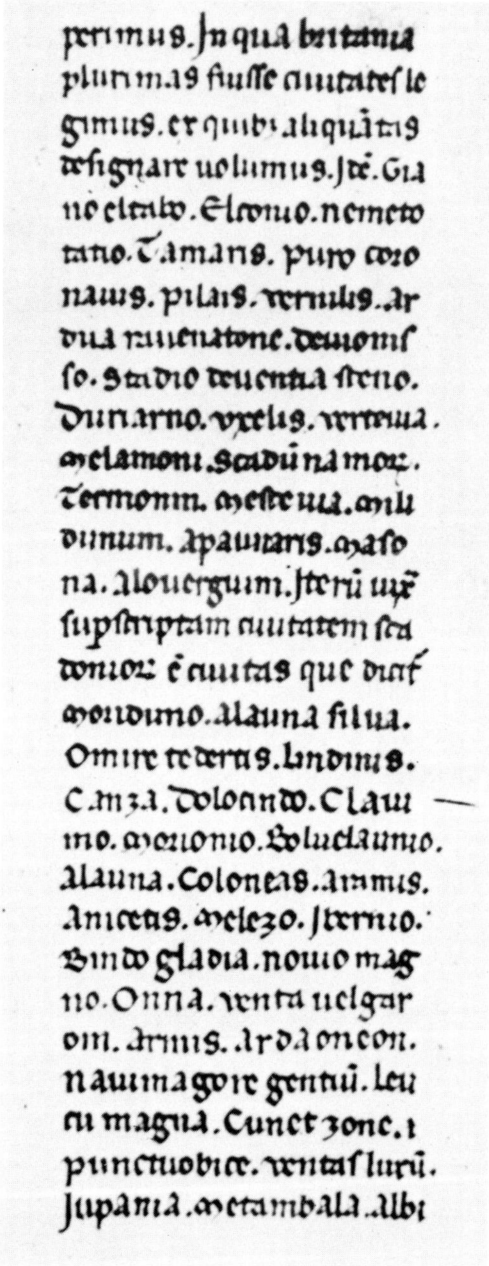

Cod. Vatican. Urb. Lat. 961, fol. 45*v*. The Vatican Library (= Schnetz MS 'A').

Cod. Paris. Lat. 4794, fol. 29*v*. Bibliothèque Nationale (= Schnetz MS 'B').

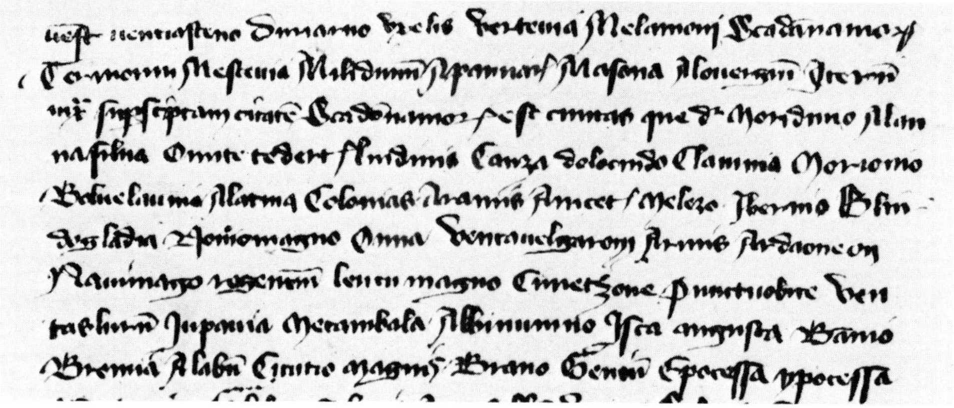

Cod. Basil. F.V. 6, fol. 107*v*. Basle University Library (= Schnetz MS 'C').

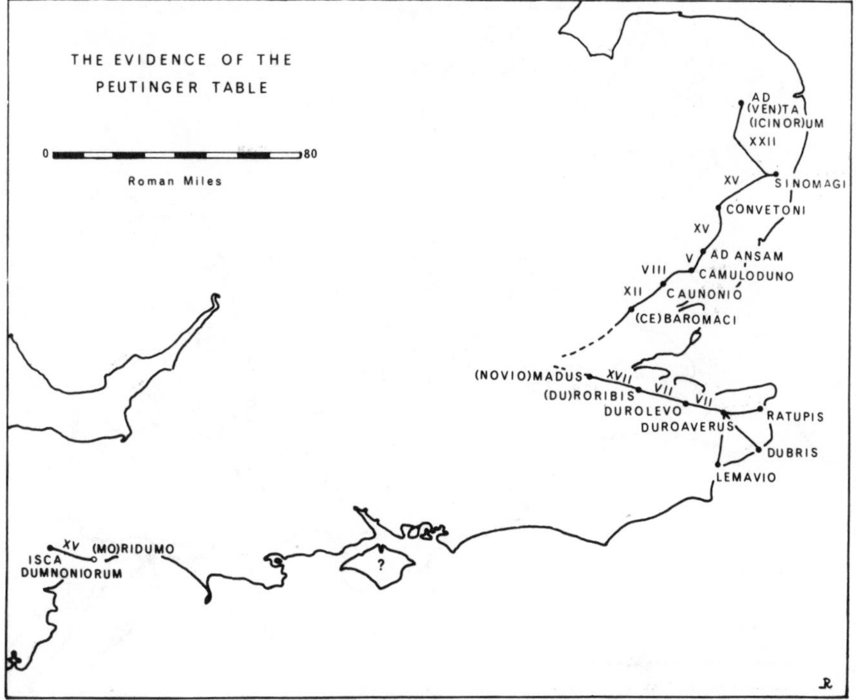

Fig. 9. The evidence of the Peutinger Table laid down on a modern map (cf. Plate I).

Crete but not in Corsica or Sardinia. On the mainland large areas in Gaul, the Balkans and Asia Minor are omitted (again in contrast to the Peutinger Table) and while Spain is well served it is not dealt with as a distinct entity, since some of its routes spill over into Gaul. A consideration of this and similar cases shows that the coherence of the British section is fortuitous and derives from the fact that Britain is an island.

At the end of the land itinerary there is added a Maritime Itinerary, headed *Imperatoris Antonini Augusti Itinerarium Maritimum*, which gives a few sea routes (usually measured in *stadia*,[1] but occasionally in miles) and a list of small islands. This list, which appears right at the end of the work, may well be an addition from another source, but there are no good grounds for dissociating the Maritime Itinerary proper from the land routes. The British section occurs at the end of the land itinerary, immediately before the maritime section.

As with the Peutinger Table, the origins and date of the Itinerary have been the subject of much discussion. While the roads and stopping-places listed must have been used by the *Cursus Publicus*, the view that it represents the actual *Cursus* network cannot be sustained, both because of the omissions and because of the random order of the work: indeed its chaotic nature has led some to suppose that despite its official title it cannot be an official document at all. But the title is not lightly to be brushed

[1] The *stadium* (Greek στάδιον) was equal to one-eighth of a Roman mile (i.e. 185 metres or 202¼ yards).

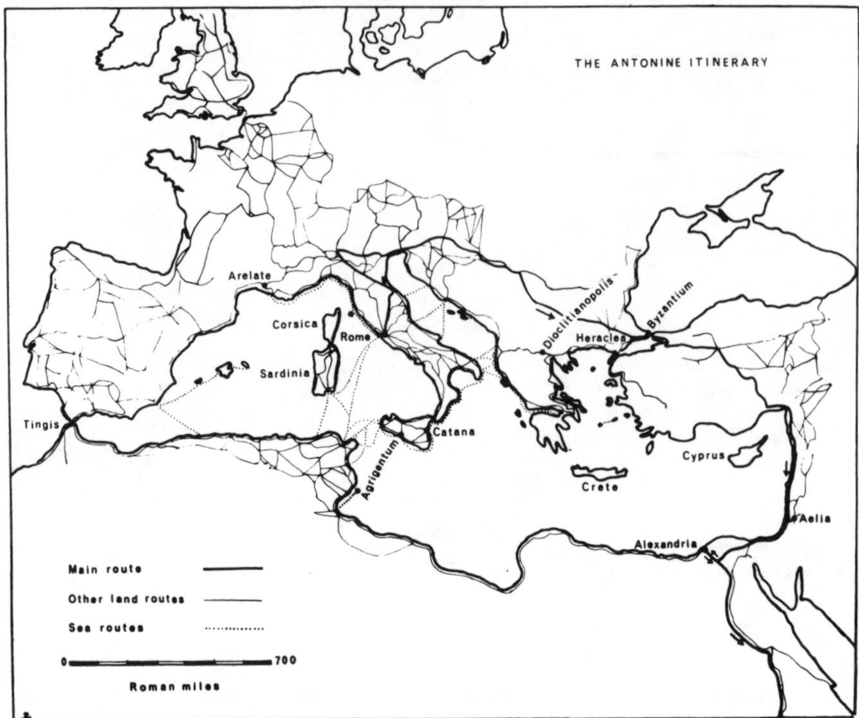

Fig. 10. The extent of the Antonine Itinerary (after Cuntz); the 'Main Route' is that identified by van Berchem.

aside, and the most convincing theory is that of Professor D. van Berchem.[1] Van Berchem argues that the Antoninus of the title is Caracalla; that the longest route of all, that from Rome to Egypt, represents the plan for his progress to the east in A.D. 214–15, giving the points at which supplies for it had to be collected; and that the other routes represent similar progresses or troop movements, or the plans for them. These other routes, however, need not refer to the time of Caracalla, for there are clear indications that the Itinerary is not all of one date. Even in Britain Colchester appears as *Colonia* in one route and as *Camulodunum* in another, and in Sicily, where alternative routes are offered for the journey from *Catana* to *Agrigentum*,[2] the second is headed *mansionibus nunc institutis* and is evidently intended to replace the first. In fact the earliest route of all, that from Rome to Arles in the Maritime Itinerary, must be earlier than A.D. 107, since *Centumcellae*,[3] where Trajan built a port in that year, is listed merely as an anchorage; while the latest date is provided by the appearance of *Diocletianopolis* (not *Pella*) and *Heraclea* (not *Perinthus*), though *Byzantium* appears

[1] D. van Berchem, 'L'annone militaire dans l'empire romain au IIIe siècle', *Mémoires de la Société Nationale des Antiquaires de France*, XXIV (= 8th series, X), 117–202, especially 166–81.

[2] 87_4–88_4 and 94_2–95_1.

[3] 498_4; cf. Pliny, *Epp.* VI, 31. For a discussion of this sea route, R. Lugand, 'Note sur l'Itinéraire Maritime de Rome à Arles', *Mélanges de l'Ecole Française à Rome*, XLIII (1926), 124–39.

as such (and not as *Constantinopolis*) and Jerusalem retains its pagan name of *Aelia.*[1] There are, therefore, no grounds for assuming that all the routes in Britain are of one and the same date and they could be distributed in time between the reign of Trajan and that of Diocletian, when the collection presumably acquired its final form.

Van Berchem's explanation also disposes of the idea, which has sometimes been put forward, that the Itinerary was derived from an amended copy of the map of Agrippa.[2] It is more probable that the reverse process operated and that map makers, including both Agrippa and Ptolemy, used itineraries as one of their main sources of information. Itineraries were no new thing, and the raw material for them was ready to hand as soon as the milestone survey of any road had been made; and Goodchild, in dealing with the coast road of Phoenicia,[3] demonstrated conclusively that there at least both the Antonine and the Bordeaux Itineraries are based directly on it. This is not surprising, since once a road had been officially measured it would not be sensible to measure it again, but the recognition of the connection has important implications when we come to consider the question of errors in mileage figures in the Itinerary.

Logically the errors may be of two kinds, errors in the original and errors of transmission, and we may consider the former class first. We have over 100 Roman milestones from Britain[4] and although few of them carry a mileage figure, those which do indicate that measurements were usually made either from a fort or from the capital city of a *civitas*, with a change from one series of milestones to another at the *civitas* boundary; occasionally, as in the case of *Durobrivae*[5] (Water Newton) measurements seem to have been made even from a subordinate town or *vicus*. In these circumstances confusion could easily arise because two converging series of milestones failed to agree, and this may account for the high incidence of errors of one mile either way. The distribution of errors, however, is weighted heavily on the minus side, and for this another factor is probably responsible. Apart from the doubtful case of the *colonia* of *Lindum* (Lincoln), where the stone found near the city centre may have been imported for re-use as building material,[6] we have no direct evidence as to where the distance was measured from – whether the city centre or the city boundary (or, in the case of a fort, from the boundary of the land sequestered for military use). When the latter was the case, the figure given by the Itinerary would obviously be less than that obtained by measuring from the city centre and this might account for errors of up to three miles, notably those which occur consistently in routes which include the large city of London. Dr Warwick Rodwell[7] has pursued

[1] *Diocletianopolis*, 330_6; *Heraclea* 333_3; *Byzantium, passim* (glossed '*qui et Constantinopoli*' once only, at 138_5).

[2] On this map, J. J. Tierney, 'The Map of Agrippa', *Proceedings of the Royal Irish Academy*, LXIII (1963), 151–66.

[3] R. G. Goodchild, 'The Coast Road of Phoenicia and its Roman Milestones', *Berytus*, IX (1949), 91–128.

[4] J. P. Sedgley, *The Roman Milestones of Britain* (B.A.R. 18, Oxford, 1975), listing 110, including a few of doubtful identification.

[5] *RIB* 2235 = Sedgley No. 25.

[6] *RIB* 2241 = Sedgley No. 29; Rodwell, *op. cit.*, pp. 86–87.

[7] Rodwell, *op. cit.*

this possibility further and used it to define 'town zones', which would include the cemeteries and other features surrounding towns.

Apparent errors of this magnitude, therefore, can be accepted with equanimity, but for errors greater than these an explanation must be sought in faulty transmission. There are many manuscripts of the Antonine Itinerary. For their edition of 1848 Parthey and Pinder used 21 and listed a further 17 which they recognised as derivative, but further work since then, mainly by Kubitschek and Cuntz,[1] has eliminated others and Cuntz's edition is based on seven, ranging in date from the seventh to the twelfth century, though only five of them include the British section, the oldest of these being Vindobonensis 181 (eighth century, with corrections by two ninth-century hands who were evidently using a different original). Several stages of copying probably intervened between the original document and our earliest version, and inspection of the errors enables us to define at least three stages of corruption: first, the introduction of a number of individual errors; second, at least in some manuscripts, the recalculation of the totals for some itineraries to accommodate these errors; and third, the further corruption of some itinera to produce totals which are wrong by the evidence of the individual stage lengths.

In dealing with errors of transmission the normal rules of textual criticism must be applied, though for the correct form of place-names some guidance may be obtained from our knowledge of Celtic and Latin usage: this aspect of the matter is best reserved for the final list (pp. 235–509), where all the comparative material is assembled. But since the Antonine Itinerary is the most precise and accurate document which we have, especial importance attaches to the accuracy or otherwise of the mileage figures. Here dittography and haplography both have to be considered, but particular attention needs to be paid to the corruptions to which Roman numerals are peculiarly liable, specifically the confusion of *ii* with *v* and of *v* with *x*.

In the texts which follow the edition of Otto Cuntz (1929)[2] has been used, with the few significant variants noted below. In accordance with international usage the figures in the left-hand column reflect the pagination and lineation of Wesseling's edition of 1735, but for convenience of reference the itinera are also numbered I to XV – an exclusively British system of numbering which has been in use since the eighteenth century. Figures for 'true' mileages are given to the nearest Roman mile of 1480 metres and measured from the centre of a town or fort: as noted above, an apparent shortfall in the itinerary mileage is often to be expected.

4. THE CROSSING FROM GAUL TO BRITAIN

The British section begins thus:

463.3	ITER BRITANNIARUM	
4	A Gessoriaco de Gallis	From Boulogne, from the Gauls,
	Ritupis in portu Brit-	to Richborough of the
5	anniarum	Britains
	stadia numero ccccl	450 stades

[1] W. Kubitschek, *Wiener Studien*, XIII (1891), 177–209; O. Cuntz, *ibid.*, XV (1893), 260–98; summary in preface to Cuntz's edition.

[2] O. Cuntz, *Itineraria Romana*, I (Leipzig, 1929).

Comment

It is notable that *Britanniarum* is plural, indicating a date after the Severan division of Britain into two provinces. The distance by the most direct route in some 350 stades, but the figure of 450 is not unreasonable, given the hazards of navigation, and it was evidently the generally accepted estimate, since it is also quoted by Bede (p. 55).

5. ITER I (fig. 11)

	Text		True mileage	Identification
464.1	A limite id est a vallo Praetorio			
2	m.p. clvi			
3	a Bremenio			High Rochester
	Corstopitum	m.p. xx	25	Corbridge
4	Vindomora	m.p. viiii	10	Ebchester
465.1	Vinovia	m.p. xviiii	20	Binchester
2	Cataractoni	m.p. xxii	22	Catterick
3	Isurium	m.p. xxiiii	25	Aldborough
446.1	Eburacum			
	leug. VI Victrix	m.p. xvii	18	York
2	Derventione	m.p. vii	20	Malton
3	Delgovicia	m.p. xiii	13	Wetwang?
4	Praetorio	m.p. xxv	22	Brough?

Variants

464.1 Pretorio.
3 Bremaenio; Corstopilum, Cor stopitu.
466.3 Delgovitia.

Comment

The figures given do add up to 156, but there are certainly some errors in them and since this Iter, like Iter II, states that it begins at the Wall but in fact starts north of it there is a possibility that here, as there, the first stage should be excluded from the total. It is in any case incorrect: *Bremenium* is nearly 25 Roman miles north of Corbridge, which is itself some three miles south of the Wall, but since its identity with the fort at High Rochester is attested by two inscriptions this question need not detain us. It may be noted, however, that the fact that High Rochester was not occupied in the Hadrianic period gives some clue to the date of the Iter.

It is not until the stages after York that serious problems arise. *Derventio* is almost certainly Malton, on the river Derwent, for a fort of this name is listed in the *Notitia Dignitatum* as garrisoned by a *Numerus Supervenientium Petueriensium*. *Delgovicia* appears, in the form *Devovicia*, in the *Ravenna Cosmography* next to *Decuaria*, which must be equated with the *Petuaria* of Ptolemy and *RIB* 707 – that is, Brough-on-Humber. *Praetorium* is a descriptive, not a proper, name and means an official residence: there was, of course, a *praetorium* in York (attested by *RIB* 662), but there is no reason why there should not have been others elsewhere (including, as Mr

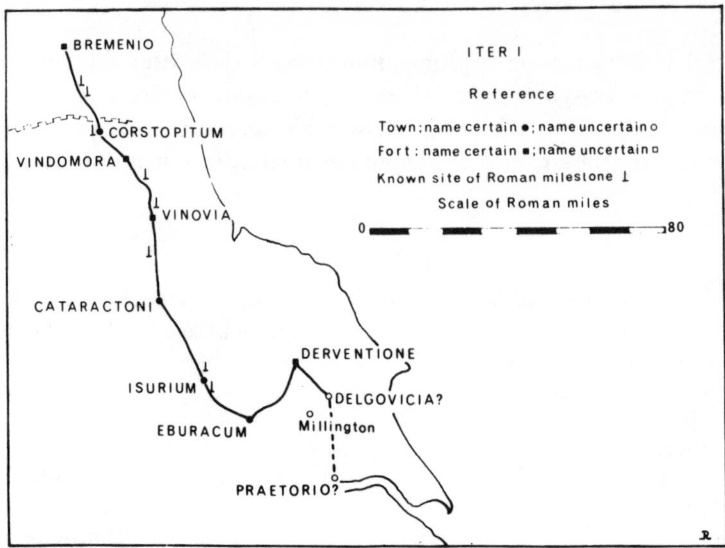

Fig. 11. The course of Iter I.

Wacher has suggested,[1] one at Brough), since *praetorium* appears as a staging-point in other provinces in the Itinerary (in Cappadocia, Cilicia, Pannonia, Dalmatia and Tarraconensis) at places which were neither legionary fortresses nor provincial capitals.[2] Nevertheless, the names and the mileages together raise several difficulties.

Several solutions have been proposed. First, as suggested by Margary,[3] we could simply add a *x* at 466_2, subtract a *x* at 466_4, and identify *Derventio* as Malton, *Delgovicia* as Millington and *Praetorio* (as a corruption of *Petuaria*) with Brough. The objections to this are that there are no significant Roman remains at Millington, that the final stage is too short (*xv* miles as against an actual 21) and that it does not explain how *Petuaria* came to be corrupted both in the heading and in the text. Secondly, in 1970 the present writer[4] suggested that perhaps we had here, as in Iter XII, a conflation of two routes, one of which originally terminated at the *praetorium* in York, and that after the two had been united a linking *vii* was introduced by dittography from the *xvii* which preceded it and the final name of the second route was changed from *Petuaria* (which the scribe had never heard of) to *Praetorio*, to agree with the heading. This explained the corruption of the name, but the explanation of the link was somewhat specious and the same objection still applied to Millington. Thirdly, Dr Rodwell[5] has suggested that a *x* has indeed to be added at 466_2, but that after visiting *Derventio* (Malton) and *Delgovicia* (Millington or possibly Wetwang), the traveller returned to the *praetorium* at York. The objection to this is that a route

[1] J. S. Wacher, *Excavations at Brough-on-Humber 1958–1961* (Society of Antiquaries Research Report xxv, London, 1969), 26; see also his suggestion, in *The Towns of Roman Britain* (London, 1974), 393–97, that in view of the apparently exclusively military nature of Roman Brough the *vicus Petuariensis* might be located at North Ferriby.

[2] 177_3, 212_2; 259_{13}; 260_6; 272_5; 398_3.

[3] Margary, 527.

[4] Rivet, *op. cit.* p. 41.

[5] Rodwell, *op. cit.* pp. 84–86.

turning back to a place which had already been passed would be unique in the whole Itinerary.

The introduction of the possibility that *Delgovicia* is not Millington but Wetwang, however, is important, and since Dr Rodwell wrote there have been significant improvements in our knowledge of this place, notably the identification of a five-mile-long aqueduct leading to it. Given this, and the discovery of a new Roman road leading north from Brough,[1] it seems best to adopt the following interpretation:

466.2	Derventione	xvii (for vii)	Malton
3	Delgovicia	xiii (as in text)	Wetwang
4	Praetorio	xxii (for xxv)	Brough

It may be noted, however, that none of the explanations offered gives a correct total, whether or not the first stage is included.

6. ITER II (fig. 12)

	Text		True mileage	Identification
466.5	Item a vallo ad portum Ritu-			
6	pis m.p. cccclxxxi sic			
467.1	a Blatobulgio Castra			Birrens
	Exploratorum	m.p. xii	14	Netherby
2	Luguvallo	m.p. xii	11	Carlisle
3	Voreda	m.p. xiii	14	Old Penrith
4	Brovonacis	m.p. xiii	14	Kirkby Thore
5	Verteris	m.p. xiii	13	Brough
468.1	Lavatris	m.p. xiiii	14	Bowes
2	Cataractone	m.p. xvi	21	Catterick
3	Isuriam	m.p. xxiiii	25	Aldborough
4	Eburacum	m.p. xvii	17	York
5	Calcaria	m.p. viiii	10	Tadcaster
6	Camboduno	m.p. xx	14	Leeds?
〈	Camuloduno	—	20	Slack 〉
7	Mamucio	m.p. xviii	23	Manchester
469.1	Condate	m.p. xviii	20	Northwich
2	Deva leg. XX Vici	m.p. xx	20	Chester
3	Bovio	m.p. x	10	Holt?
4	Medialano	m.p. xx	15	Whitchurch
5	Rutunio	m.p. xii	12	Harcourt Mill
6	Urioconio	m.p. xi	11	Wroxeter
7	Uxacona	m.p. xi	11	Red Hill
470.1	Pennocrucio	m.p. xii	12	Water Eaton
2	Etoceto	m.p. xii	14	Wall
3	Manduesedo	m.p. xvi	16	Mancetter
4	Venonis	m.p. xii	11	High Cross
5	Bannaventa	m.p. xvii	19	Whilton Lodge

[1] We are indebted to Mr H. G. Ramm for information on both the aqueduct and the road.

	Text		True mileage	Identification
6	Lactodoro	m.p. xii	12	Towcester
471 . 1	Magiovinto	m.p. xvii	16	Dropshort
2	Durocobrivis	m.p. xii	12	Dunstable
3	Verolamio	m.p. xii	13	St. Albans
4	Sulloniacis	m.p. viiii	9	Brockley Hill
5	Londinio	m.p. xii	13	London
472 . 1	Noviomago	m.p. x	13	Crayford
2	Vagniacis	m.p. xviiii	8	Springhead
3	Durobrovis	m.p. viiii	9	Rochester
4	Durolevo	m.p. xiii	?	Nr. Sittingbourne
5	Duroruerno	m.p. xii	?	Canterbury
6	ad portum Ritupis	m.p. xii	13	Richborough

Variants

466 . 6 The discrepancy is noted in two MSS
468 . 6 Campoduno
469 . 6 Urioconio
470 . 2 One MS has a letter erased before Etoceto
3 Manduessedo
5 Bennaventa
472 . 2 xviii
3 Duroprovis
5 Durorrerno

Comment

This Iter, like the first, claims that it is measured from the Wall but in fact begins at a place to the north of it. The stages add up to 502 miles, as against the stated total of 481 and, especially since amendment can only reduce the figure of the total, the discrepancy has to be explained. Certainly some reductions suggest themselves – at 469_4 (for *xx* read *xv*), at 471_1 (for *xvii* read *xvi*, to agree with Iter VI and, by inference, with Iter VIII) and at 472_2 (for *xviiii* read *viiii*, to put *Vagniacis* on the direct road; see discussion in next section) – but these only subtract 16 miles and some additions are also necessary. The figure at 468_2 must read *xxi*, not *xvi*, and there is clearly a whole stage missing between Tadcaster and Manchester, since the distance between them is some 55 Roman miles as the crow flies, as against the 38 allowed here. A substantial reduction can only be obtained by disregarding the 24 miles north of the Wall, which reduces the total to 467 and so leaves 14 miles for allocation to the missing stage, or 52 for distribution between Tadcaster and Manchester.

As Richmond and Crawford argued in their discussion of the entry *Pampocalia* in the *Ravenna Cosmography*, the missing station must be *Camulodunum*, which is placed in these parts by Ptolemy and whose name could easily be taken by a scribe as a duplication of *Cambodunum*. Working back from Manchester, the known Roman sites on the road are the fort at Castleshaw (at 15 Roman miles from Manchester) and the fort at Slack (at 23 miles). Neither of these suits the figure at 468_7, but if we make the simple amendment of *xviii* to *xxiii* we have the correct distance to Slack, leaving

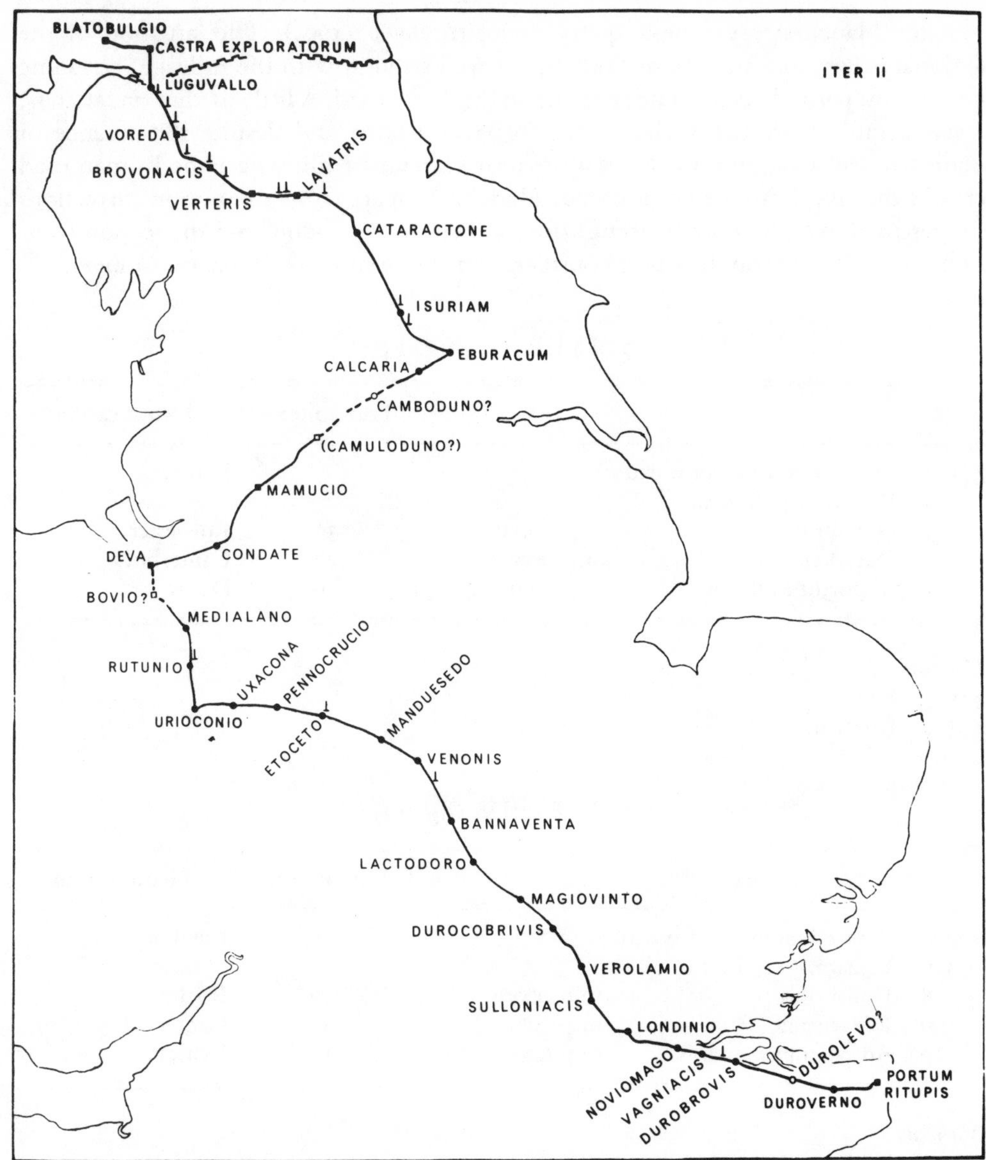

Fig. 12. The course of Iter II; for scale and reference see figure 11.

29 miles for the other two stages, with the high probability that one of the distances is the *xx* given in the text. Twenty Roman miles from Slack brings us to the conurbation of Leeds. The addition of *xiiii* for the 14-mile stage to Tadcaster gives us a total of 486, leaving only five miles to be lost, presumably by single figure deductions, elsewhere in the Iter. *Cambodunum* could, then, be found in Leeds, which agrees well with Bede's reference (*HE* II, 14) *in Campodono in regione quae vocatur Loidis*, and the name suggests that it was situated on a notable bend on the river Aire.[1]

[1] It is possible that the obliterated earthwork recorded by Thoresby and Carroll (*Gentleman's Magazine*, 1862(i), 607–14) at Wall Flat (SE 309337) was a Roman fort, but on

After Manchester the next query concerns *Bovio* (469_3). The situation of the legionary tilery and pottery at Holt agrees well enough with the mileage, but some doubt must persist because it does not lie on the direct road. A little further on, at 469_5, *Rutunio* must represent a place near the river Roden and despite the absence of definitive archaeological evidence a site near Harcourt Mill, where the Roman road crosses the river, cannot be doubted. Elsewhere, apart from the minor corrections suggested above, the route is straightforward as far as London, and the section from London to Richborough is best considered in the light of the next two itinera.

7. ITER III (fig. 13)

	Text		True mileage	Identification
473 . 1	Item a Londinio ad portum			London
2	Dubris m.p. lxvi sic			
3	Dubobrius	m.p. xxvii	30	Rochester
4	Durarveno	m.p. xxv	27	Canterbury
5	ad portum Dubris	m.p. xiiii	16	Dover

Variants

473 . 3 xvii

4 Duraruenno

8. ITER IV (fig. 13)

	Text		True mileage	Identification
473 . 6	Item a Londinio ad portum			London
7	Lemanis m.p. lxviii			
8	Durobrivis	m.p. xxvii	30	Rochester
9	Duraruenno	m.p. xxv	27	Canterbury
10	Ad portum Lemanis	m.p. xvi	16	Lympne

Variant

473 . 7 lxiiii

Comment

Iter II, Iter III, Iter IV and the Peutinger Table (fig. 13) together give us a full coverage of the route from London to the ports of the Kentish coast and only three names are of questionable application – *Noviomagus*, *Vagniacis* and *Durolevum*.

---

tactical grounds one would have expected a site slightly south-west of this, actually in the confluence of Sheepscar Beck (now conduited) and the Aire. We are grateful to Miss Margaret Faull for information on this matter in advance of the publication of her chapter in S. A. Moorhouse (ed.), *A Survey of the Archaeology of West Yorkshire* (Wakefield, forthcoming, 1979).

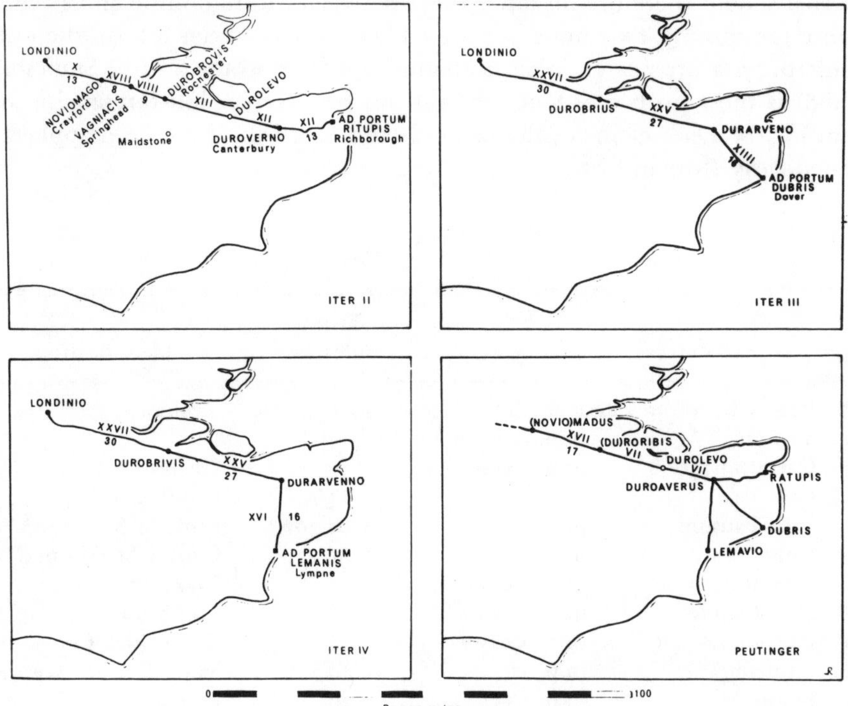

Fig. 13. The area of Kent as treated in Itinera II, III and IV and the Peutinger Table

Itinera II and IV both give the distance from London to *Durobrivae* (Rochester) at 27 miles, which is three miles short of the truth. *Noviomagus* is given as 10 miles from London in Iter II and 17 miles from *Durobrivae* on the Peutinger Table, which again makes the total 27 and so fixes the place firmly on the direct route. Since the missing three miles are almost certainly accounted for by the 'town zone' of London, *Noviomagus* should be located at Crayford (notable later as the place where the Britons made a stand against Hengest and Aesc in A.D. 457).

The name of *Vagniacis* occurs only in Iter II. If the direct route is still being followed, the stage length at 472_2 should presumably be emended from *xviiii* to *viiii*, in which case the name applies to the well-known settlement at Springhead. There is just a chance that a deviation has been made along an unidentified road to Maidstone, which is 21 Roman miles as the crow flies from Crayford and 9 (along a known road) to Rochester, but since the mileage for this Iter needs to be reduced to agree with the stated total, Springhead is almost certainly correct.

Durolevum appears in Iter II and in the Peutinger Table. The total distance from Rochester to *Durovernum* (Canterbury) is consistently given in all three of the Antonine itinera as 25 miles (two miles short of the truth), so that the Peutinger Table's total of 14 must be corrupt; this is presumably due to the common confusion of *x* with *v* and both its mileages should be read as *xii* (or perhaps in one case as *xiii*).

Durolevum should therefore lie somewhere between Sittingbourne and Faversham, and since the missing two miles are most likely to have been lost on the outskirts of Canterbury, a site nearer to Sittingbourne (perhaps in the area of Snipeshill and Bapchild) is most probable. Since there is no pre-Roman hill-fort in this area to account for the *Duro*-element, the name should originally have been applied to an unlocated early Roman fort.

9. ITER V (fig. 14)

	Text		True mileage	Identification
474.1	Item a Londinio Luguvalio ad			London
2	Vallum	m.p. ccccxlii		
3	Caesaromago	m.p. xxviii	30	Chelmsford
4	Colonia	m.p. xxiiii	24	Colchester
5	Villa Faustini	m.p. xxxv	41 or 36	Scole or Stoke Ash
6	Icinos	m.p. xviii	18 or 23	Caistor St Edmund
7	Camborico	m.p. xxxv	37	Lackford?
8	Duroliponte	m.p. xxv	25	Cambridge
475.1	Durobrivas	m.p. xxxv	36	Water Newton
2	Causennis	m.p. xxx	30	Saltersford or Sapperton
3	Lindo	m.p. xxvi	26	Lincoln
4	Segeloci	m.p. xiiii	15	Littleborough
5	Dano	m.p. xxi	23	Doncaster
6	Legeolio	m.p. xvi	18	Castleford
7	Eburaco	m.p. xxi	23	York
476.1	Isubrigantum	m.p. xvii	17	Aldborough
2	Cataractoni	m.p. xxiiii	25	Catterick
3	Levatris	m.p. xviii	21	Bowes
4	Verteris	m.p. xiiii	14	Brough
5	Brocavo	m.p. xx	20	Brougham
6	Luguvalio	m.p. xxi	21	Carlisle

Variants

474.2 ccccxliii
6 Icianos
476.6 xxii, xxv

Comment

This is one of two itinera which include East Anglia, and the first point to note is a difference in nomenclature: In Iter IX Colchester is *Camulodunum* and Caistor St Edmund is *Venta Icinorum*, but here they appear as *Colonia* and *Icinos*, in the latter case exemplifying the practice, common in Gaul but rare in Britain, of substituting the tribal name for the individual name of the city. This variation clearly indicates different sources, and presumably different dates, for the two routes.

Secondly, while the stages do add up to the stated total, the mileage allowed between Colchester and Caistor is inadequate. Both these places, as cities, might be

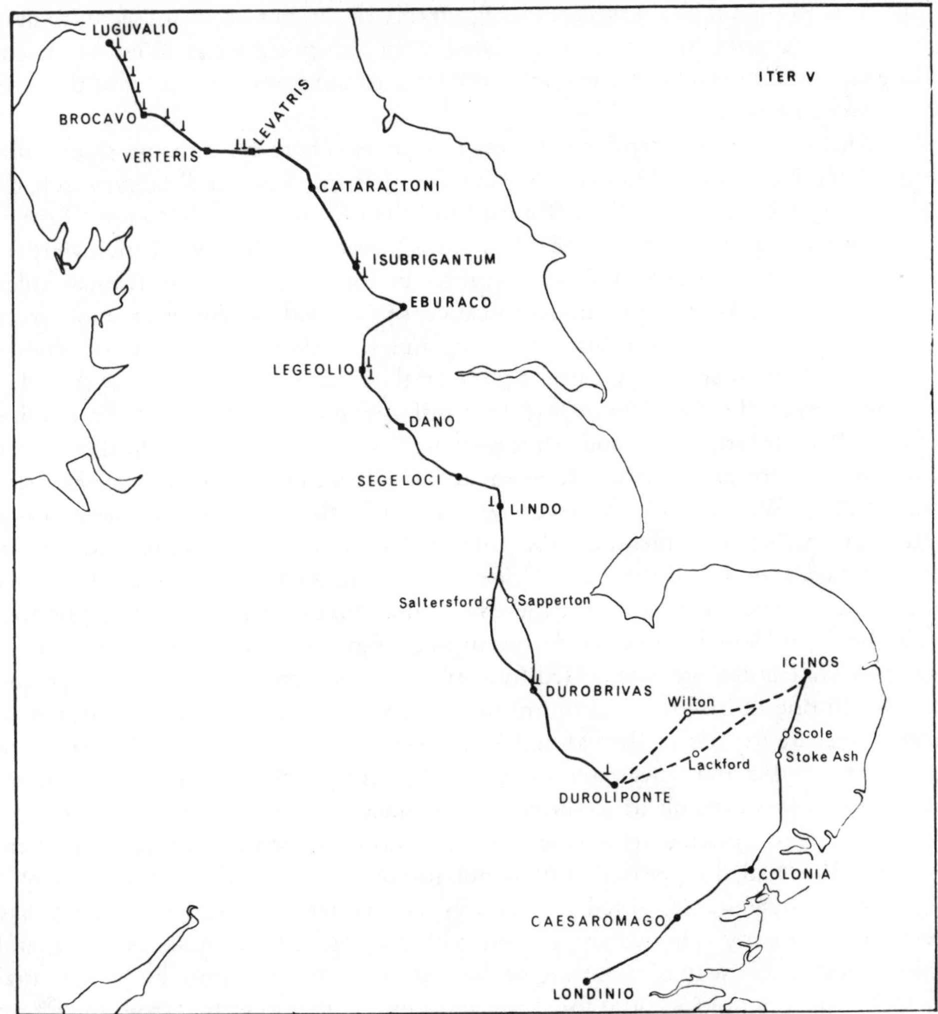

Fig. 14. The course of Iter v; for scale and reference see figure 11.

expected to have town zones, but the discrepancy of seven miles is unduly high and any alteration affects the identification of *Villa Faustini*. If we amend the figure of *xxxv* at 474_5 to *xxxx* it falls at Scole, but if we change the xviii at 474_6 to *xxiii* it becomes Stoke Ash. The appearance of a villa-name in the Itinerary need not surprise us, since one is listed in Italy and no less than seven in Africa,[1] but it does not necessarily imply the central building of an estate and could well refer simply to a road-station dependent on it. Since minor Roman settlements are known at both Stoke Ash and Scole (and no recognisable villa has so far been found near to either), the question must remain open.

The next problem concerns the identity of *Camboricum*. The name, presumably for *Camboritum*, indicates a site at a river crossing and two such places fit the distances reasonably well, Wilton on the Little Ouse and Lackford on the Lark. Our knowledge

[1] 124_8 in Italy and 42_6, 59_3, 60_3, 61_2, 62_1, 62_3 and 63_1 in Africa.

of east-west Roman roads in this area is regrettably slight, but Lackford seems to have been the more important place (associated with the potteries at West Stow and Icklingham) and the Celtic name could well refer to the age-old crossing of the river by the Icknield Way.

A further question of identity concerns *Causennis.* There are three possible routes from Water Newton to Lincoln, the first along Ermine Street (Margary 2c), the second along King Street as far as Bourne and then by Margary 26 to joint Ermine Street south of Ancaster, and the third by King Street and Mareham Lane (Margary 260), and each of them gives a distance near to the Itinerary total of 56 Roman miles. It seems clear that the traditional identification of *Causennis* as Ancaster is incorrect, since the distances specified place it seven miles further south, and no Roman settlement is known at the appropriate place on the third route, but both of the other two offer possibilities. On Ermine Street the mileages indicate a site at the intersection of Salters Way (Margary 58) and while nothing is known actually on the direct road there was an important Roman Settlement at Saltersford, 1½ Roman miles to the west, where Salters Way crosses the river Witham. On the other route, there was a somewhat smaller settlement on the road at Sapperton. It is difficult to choose between these two, but if the name *Causennis* contains an element relating to a river Saltersford is the better choice, since there is no more than a small stream at Sapperton.

The final problem is to reconcile the mileage figures for the iter as a whole. In locating *Villa Faustini* we have added five miles, which increases the total to 447, and there is still one more incorrect figure to be considered. The *xviii* given at 476_3 is hardly adequate for the 21 Roman miles between Catterick and Brough, neither of them a city, and in Iter II we have already had to correct the impossibly low figure of *xvi* to *xxi*. It is difficult to see how *xxi* (or indeed *xvi*) could be misread as *xviii* and one can only conclude that when this iter was compiled some milestones were overlooked or had disappeared: this is not impossible, since the substitution of a tribal for a proper name, noted above, was, at any rate in Gaul, a relatively late development. In any case, we are still left with a surplus of five miles or more, and the most reasonable way of disposing of them seems to be to amend the overall total to *ccccxlv*, which would account for three, and subtract the other two from the figure at 474_4 to allow a town zone to Colchester and to bring the distance into conformity with that given in Iter IX.

10. ITER VI (fig. 15)

	Text		True mileage	Identification
476.7	Item a Londinio Lindo	m.p. clvi sic		London
8	Verolami	m.p. xxi	22	St Albans
9	Durocobrius	m.p. xii	13	Dunstable
10	Magiovinio	m.p. xii	12	Dropshort
11	Lactodoro	m.p. xvi	16	Towcester
477.1	Isannavantia	m.p. xii	12	Whilton Lodge

	Text		True mileage	Identification
2	Tripontio	m.p. xii	11	Cave's Inn
3	Venonis	m.p. viii	8	High Cross
4	Ratas	m.p. xii	12	Leicester
5	Verometo	m.p. xiii	14	Willoughby
6	Margiduno	m.p. xii	12	Castle Hill
7	Ad Pontem	m.p. vii	7	East Stoke
8	Crococalana	m.p. vii	8	Brough
9	Lindo	m.p. xii	13	Lincoln

Variants

476.7 Lundinio
477.1 Isannavatia
6 Margeduno
8 Crocaocalana

Fig. 15. The course of Iter VI; for scale and reference see figure 11.

Comment

The total is correct and this iter presents no problems. The excess of a mile for the stage from Whilton Lodge to Cave's Inn suggests that a civitas boundary, where two sets of milestones met, may have lain here, presumably that between the Catuvellauni and the Coritani: unfortunately the milestone found at Cave's Inn in 1963[1] carries

[1] Sedgley No. 31; *JRS*, LIV (1964), 179.

no mileage figure. The corruption of *Bannaventa* into *Isannavantia* (clearly due to the breakdown of *B* into *IS*) is of some antiquarian interest, since it must be the origin of the invented name of *Isannavaria* in the spurious work of 'Richard of Cirencester' (see Appendix, p. 185).

11. ITER VII (fig. 16)

	Text		True mileage	Identification
477.10	Item a Regno Lundinio	m.p. xcvi sic		Chichester
478.1	Clausentum	m.p. xx	30 or 20	Bitterne or Wickham
2	Venta Belgarum	m.p. x	10 or 15	Winchester
3	Galleva Atrebatum	m.p. xxii	25	Silchester
4	Pontibus	m.p. xxii	27	Staines
5	Londinio	m.p. xxii	21	London

Variants
Nil

Comment
While the mileages do add up to the correct total, some of them are clearly wrong and some amendment is required, at the least to 478_4, but since the identities of *Venta*, *Calleva*, *Pontes* and *Londinium* are not in doubt this need not detain us.

More serious problems are raised by the first two names. *Regno* occurs only here and the nominative *Regnum*, which has often been inferred from it, is nowhere recorded. As we know from Ptolemy and the *Ravenna Cosmography*, the Roman name of Chichester was *Noviomagus* and it lay in the territory of the people referred to by Ptolemy as *Regni* and by the *Cosmography* as *Regentes* (the form *Regnenses*, which is widely cited, is no more than an inference by Haverfield).[1] If Ptolemy's form is nearer to the truth, any connection with the *regnum*, or kingdom, of Cogidubnus is out of the question, and on the analogy of *Icinos* in Iter v (474_6) it seems more likely that *Regno* is here corrupted from *Regnis*, with the tribal name supplanting the proper name of the city, as commonly occurs in Gaul.

The Iter, then, begins at Chichester, but the identity of *Clausentum* has still to be established. Since the eighteenth century this has been taken to be Bitterne, but there is no corroborative evidence for this, and while Bitterne is indeed approximately 10 Roman miles from Winchester it is approximately 30, not 20, from Chichester. A site which more nearly fits the first mileage is the settlement at the road junction of Wickham, which is just 20 Roman miles from Chichester, but 14¼ from Winchester. We therefore have the choice of amending the first figure from *xx* to *xxx* (leading to Bitterne), which would make the itinerary total wrong and also imply that Winchester had no town zone extending in this direction; or of taking the figures as they stand (leading to Wickham) and assuming a town zone for Winchester

[1] For a fuller discussion, Rivet, *op. cit.* p. 50, especially note 48.

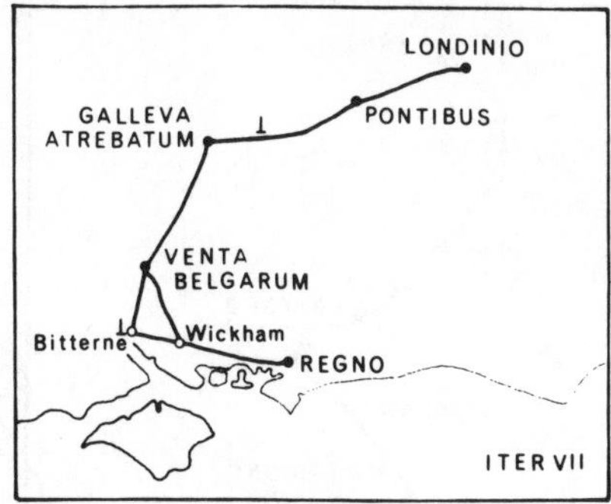

Fig. 16. The course of Iter VII; for scale and reference see figure 11.

extending some 4½ Roman miles, which seems excessive. In either case no provision is made for a town zone at Chichester, but a mile could have been cancelled out by a conflict between the milestones of the Belgae and those of the Regni.

12. ITER VIII (fig. 17)

	Text		True mileage	Identification
478.6	Item ab Eburaco Londinio	m.p. ccxxvii		York
7	Lagecio	m.p. xxi	23	Castleford
8	Dano	m.p. xvi	18	Doncaster
9	Ageloco	m.p. xxi	23	Littleborough
10	Lindo	m.p. xiiii	14	Lincoln
11	Crococalano	m.p. xiiii	13	Brough
479.1	Margiduno	m.p. xiiii	15	Castle Hill
2	Vernemeto	m.p. xii	12	Willoughby
3	Ratis	m.p. xii	14	Leicester
4	Vennonis	m.p. xii	12	High Cross
5	Bannavanto	m.p. xviiii	19	Whilton Lodge
6	Magiovinio	m.p. xxviii	28	Dropshort
7	Durocobrivis	m.p. xii	12	Dunstable
8	Verolamo	m.p. xii	13	St Albans
9	Londinio	m.p. xxi	22	London

Variants

478.7 Laiecio
8 Ano
11 Alano

Comment

The figures for the stages add up to 228, one mile in excess of the stated total. The figure at 478_{11} should presumably be reduced from *xiiii* to *xiii*, but even this is one mile more than the distance for this stage given in Iter VI, and this may indicate that the two itinera were independently compiled, one of them rather carelessly.

Fig. 17. The course of Iter VIII; for scale and reference see figure 11.

13. ITER IX (fig. 18)

	Text		True mileage	Identification
479.10	Item a Venta Icinorum			Caistor St Edmund
11	Lundinio	m.p. cxxvii sic		
480.1	Sitomago	m.p. xxxii	32	Nr Yoxford?
2	Conbretovio	m.p. xxii	23	Coddenham
3	Ad Ansam	m.p. xv	15	Higham
4	Camoloduno	m.p. vi	7	Colchester
5	Canonio	m.p. viiii	10	Kelvedon
6	Cesaromago	m.p. xii	13	Chelmsford
7	Durolito	m.p. xvi	16	Chigwell?
8	Lundinio	m.p. xv	16	London

Variants

480.2 Combretovio
6 Caesaromago
8 Lindinio, Londinio

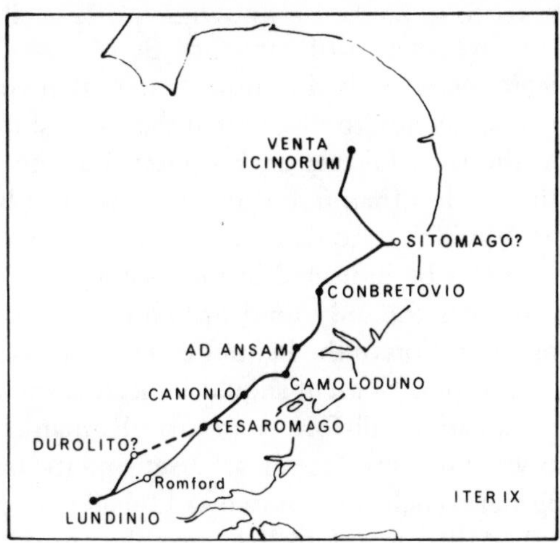

Fig. 18. The course of Iter IX; for scale and reference see figure 11.

Comment

This route covers some of the same ground as Iter v, with the interesting variations in nomenclature there noted, and it is also largely repeated in the Peutinger Table. While the Peutinger figures, like the names, have suffered through the truncation of the map, most of them confirm the Itinerary mileages. This can best be seen by tabulating them:

(Vent)ta (Icinor)um	
Sinomagi	xxii (?for (x)xxii)
Convetoni	xv (?for (x)xii)
Ad Ansam	xv
Camuloduno	v
Caunonio	viii
(Ce)baromaci	xii

This close correspondence limits the amendments that can reasonably be suggested to the Itinerary, and since the stages add up to 127, only one mile short of the stated total, it is likely to be free of major errors.

The first problem concerns the identity of the places between Caistor and Colchester. There is no doubt that *Ad Ansam* refers to a bend in the river Stour, but two northbound Roman roads from Colchester cross it, the one at Nayland (Margary 322) and the other not far from Stratford St Mary (Margary 3c). Either of these is at an appropriate distance, but though a Roman settlement is known at Nayland that road offers no probable identifications for the places further north. No settlement has been found at Stratford St Mary but, as Dr Rodwell has pointed out,[1] there was a settlement, also on a bend of the river, at Higham Hall, ¾ mile upstream, and this

[1] W. Rodwell, in correspondence with A.L.F.R., 18 August 1977, citing recent air photographs indicating settlement, partly plotted by I. McMaster in *Colchester Archaeological Group Bulletin*, XIV (1971), 14, fig. 15.

suits the course of the road, so far as it is known, equally well. The adoption of this solution (or indeed the acceptance of Stratford St Mary) leads inevitably to the identification of *Combretovium* with the important settlement at Baylham House, Coddenham. There is an objection to this, in that the name should mean 'confluence' and no tributary joins the river Gitting at this point, but the name might also have arisen from the fact that no less than five Roman roads meet here. For *Sitomagus* (or *Sinomagus*) there is no obvious candidate, but if we follow the courses of known Roman roads a site seems to be indicated in the vicinity of Yoxford.

In the later part of the iter the only unidentified place is *Durolitum*, and here we are deprived of the corroboration of the Peutinger Table. If, as seems likely, the name stands for *Duroritum* the second element should indicate a site on a ford and the first element suggests either a native hill-fort or an early Roman military post. The only Roman fort so far known in western Essex is at Orsett and the only earthwork situated near a river is the enigmatic enclosure known as Uphall Camp, and neither of these is on a suitable road. The distance of 16 Roman miles from Chelmsford along the direct road to London brings us to the eastern outskirts of Romford, in the area of Gidea Park, and this is approximately 15 Roman miles from London, but it is a mile too far east for the crossing of the river Rom (or Beam), it allows no town zone to London, and no Roman settlement, let alone an early fort, has been found there; and the only amendment likely is the addition, not the subtraction, of a mile. Dr Rodwell has suggested[1] that the direct road is not being followed and that *Durolitum* should be identified either with the Roman settlement at Little London, on the river Roding, north of Chigwell, or with Passinford Bridge, three miles further upstream. This suits the distances well enough, but while there is a Roman road from Chigwell to London, none is known from Chigwell to Chelmsford. Only further discoveries can solve the question.

14. ITER X (fig. 19)

	Text		True mileage	Identification
481.1	Item a Clanoventa Mediolano	m.p. cl sic		Ravenglass
2	Galava	m.p. xviii	20	Ambleside
3	Alone	m.p. xii	13	Watercrook?
4	Galacum	m.p. xviiii	13	Burrow-in-Lonsdale?
5	Bremetonnaci	m.p. xxvii	30	Ribchester
482.1	Coccio	m.p. xx	15	Nr Edgeworth?
2	Mamcunio	m.p. xvii	15	Manchester
3	Condate	m.p. xviii	20	Northwich
4	Mediolano	m.p. xviiii	24	Whitchurch

Variants

481.5 Bremetonaci

482.2 Mancunio

[1] Rodwell, *op. cit.* p. 93.

Fig. 19. The course of Iter x; for scale and reference see figure 11.

Comment

This is one of the most difficult routes to interpret. Although the figures add up to the stated total of 150 miles, there are serious problems of identification both north and south of *Bremetonnacum* (established as Ribchester by an inscription), which are made more difficult by the fact that the road system in Westmorland and Lancashire is imperfectly known (so that some of the 'true' distances may be slightly in error); and even further south there is clearly an amendment to be made at 482_4 (for *xviiii* read *xxiiii*) to bring the distance into accord.

Even the starting-point is uncorroborated, but Haverfield[1] made a strong case for Ravenglass as *Clanoventa* and no alternative seems possible. If this is correct, the case for Ambleside as *Galava* is equally strong, but the next station, *Alone*, poses a difficulty. Haverfield identified it with Watercrook, which fits the distance well enough, but the name (presumably a variant of *Alauna*) leads us to expect a site on a river with a name like Alne or Ellen. The river at Watercrook is the Kent (derived from the Celtic **Cunetịu*) and for this reason the present writer in 1970[2] suggested a possible identification with Low Borrow Bridge, where the current river name is a back-formation. Inspection of air photographs,[3] however, shows that a reasonably direct road linking the two places is out of the question, so it seems better to revert to Watercrook, acknowledging that here we may have a rare case of an *Alauna* which is not related to the name of a river.

This does not, however, help us very much with the identification of the next place, *Galacum* (which must presumably be equated with the Κάλαγον of Ptolemy II, 3,

[1] F. Haverfield, *Arch. J.*, LXXII (1915), 77–84; his argument was developed and modified by R. G. Collingwood, *Arch.*, LXXI (1920–21), 1–16.

[2] Rivet, *op. cit.* p. 54.

[3] Confirmed by Mr J. Fox, recently Archaeology Officer to the Ordnance Survey, to whom we are grateful for information.

10). The site chosen by Haverfield, Burrow-in-Lonsdale (sometimes referred to as Overborough), is 13 Roman miles from Watercrook (as against the *xviiii* of the text) and 30 from Ribchester (as against *xxvii* in the text). Another possibility, Lancaster, is some 20 Roman miles from Watercrook and 23 or more from Ribchester – the figures are speculative, because the Roman roads are inadequately known and measurements have to be made by the most direct modern route.

The final question concerns *Coccium*. There is a direct Roman road linking Ribchester and Manchester, but the distance along it is only some 30 Roman miles, and because the two stages add up to 37 Haverfield accepted a deviation to Wigan. This suits the figures (22 Roman miles against *xx* for the first stage, 18 against *xvii* for the second), but the route is curiously contorted, not all the roads are reliably authenticated and a Roman settlement at Wigan has still to be located. As we have already added five miles by our amendment at 482_4, perhaps we should bring the figures into line by subtracting five here. Since the *xvii* at 482_2 can only plausibly be amended by increasing it to *xxii*, a reduction of the *xx* at 482_1 to *xv* seems to be demanded, and this would indicate a site near Edgeworth. No such site has yet been identified, but some staging post on this long stretch is in any case to be expected and there is a notable change here in the alignment of the Roman road (Margary 7b).

It may be noted that all the solutions offered seem at some point or other to indicate an overstatement of the mileage rather than the normal understatement, but in hilly country a succession of minor bends could have confused measurement.

15. ITER XI (fig. 20)

	Text		True mileage	Identification
482.5	Item a Segontio Devam	m.p. lxxiiii sic		Caernarvon
6	Conovio	m.p. xxiii	24	Caerhun
7	Varis	m.p. xviii	18	St Asaph
8	Deva	m.p. xxxii	34	Chester

Variants

482.7 xviiii

Comment

The total is correct and the only question here concerns the identity of *Varis*. A fort at the crossing of the Clwyd is to be expected, but although Roman coins, and more recently pottery, have been found in St Asaph, it has so far escaped discovery: analogy with other forts in Wales suggests that it is more likely to be located on the west than on the east bank of the river. Neither the mileage nor the road pattern, as at present known, supports the alternative suggestion of Prestatyn.

Fig. 20. The course of Iter XI; for scale and reference see figure 11.

16. ITER XII (fig. 21)

	Text		True mileage	Identification
482.9	Item a Muridono Viroconi-			Carmarthen
10	orum	m.p. clxxxvi		
483.1	Vindomi	m.p. xv		
2	Venta Belgarum	m.p. xxi		
3	Brige	m.p. xi		
4	Sorvioduni	m.p. viii	Intrusive repetition	
5	Vindogladia	m.p. xii	of Iter XV	
6	Durnonovaria	m.p. viii		
7	Muriduno	m.p. xxxvi		
8	Sca Dumnoniorum	m.p. xv		
484.1	Leucaro	m.p. xv	19	Loughor?
2	Nido	m.p. xv	13	Neath
3	Bomio	m.p. xv	27	Cowbridge?
4	Iscae leg. II Augusta	m.p. xxvii	27	Caerleon
5	Burrio	m.p. viiii	8	Usk
6	Gobannio	m.p. xii	11	Abergavenny
7	Magnis	m.p. xxii	23	Kenchester
8	Bravonio	m.p. xxiiii	23	Leintwardine
9	Viriconio	m.p. xxvii	27	Wroxeter

Variants

483.4 viiii
6 Durnovaria
8 Dumnuntiorum, Dummuniorum, Dumnunniorum; xii, xvi
484.9 Viroconio

Comment

The first section of this iter, though it appears in all the manuscripts, is clearly intrusive, being merely a repetition of Iter XV, no doubt due to a confusion between the two places called *Moridunum*. But whether or not it is included, the total stated

Fig. 21. The course of Iter XII; for scale and reference see figure 11.

is wrong, since the stages add up to 292 or 146 miles. At least ten of the missing miles must obviously be added between *Nidum* and *Isca*, since Neath and Caerleon are 54 Roman miles apart along the Roman road, as against the 42 allowed here; but that would still leave a further 30 miles to be accounted for, and the most likely place to seek them is in the figures immediately following the intrusion – where also four successive *xv*'s arouse suspicion.

Muridunum is certainly Carmarthen and *Leucarum* should be the Roman fort at Loughor, but there are three difficulties here. First, though a supposed Roman road leaves Carmarthen on a south-easterly alignment (B. 4309), the most likely continuation of it (Margary 60d) swerves away to cross the river Loughor from Hendy to Pontardulais, some five miles above Loughor town. Secondly, even if a direct Roman road is assumed from Carmarthen to Loughor, the distance along it would be some 19 Roman miles, as against the *xv* in the text (and 16 to Hendy). Thirdly, such a direct road would involve a crossing of the river near its mouth, where it is fordable only at low tide (while Hendy, like most Roman coastal forts in Wales, stands above the head of tidal water). On the other hand, no Roman remains are recorded from Hendy or Pontardulais, and a possible solution to this problem might be that a whole stage has been omitted and that the text originally read:

Muridunum (Carmarthen)
Leuca (the river Loughor, at Hendy) *xv*
Leucarum (Loughor) *v* (or *x*, for the return journey)
Nidum (Neath) *xv*

Whether Hendy or Loughor is in question, the true distance onward to Neath is about 13 Roman miles, though in neither case is the precise course of the road established.

The insertion of an additional stage, with the implication that one of the *xv*'s originally read *v* or *x*, leaves us free to suppose that the distance from *Nidum* to *Bomium* has been lost, and if this is so it is most likely that it duplicated the next figure. In fact the only substantial Roman settlement known along this road (Margary 60c) is at Cowbridge and this is precisely 27 Roman miles from Neath in one direction and from Caerleon in the other.[1]

We have now added 17 or 22 miles to the total, bringing it up to 163 or 168, and since the remaining stages, though reasonably correct, tend towards overstatement of the distances, it is difficult to see where further additions can be made. The most likely explanation, therefore, though admittedly an unsatisfactory one, seems to be that the total must originally have read *clxviii*.

17. ITER XIII (fig. 22)

	Text		True mileage	Identification
484 . 10	Item ab Isca Calleva	m.p. cviiii sic		Caerleon
485 . 1	Burrio	m.p. viiii	8	Usk
2	Blestio	m.p. xi	13	Monmouth
3	Ariconio	m.p. xi	12	Weston under Penyard
4	Clevo	m.p. xv	15	Gloucester
⟨	Corinio	—	18	Cirencester ⟩
5	Durocornovio	m.p. xiiii	16	Wanborough
6	Spinis	m.p. xv	20	Woodspeen
7	Calleva	m.p. xv	16	Silchester

Variant

485 . 1 Bu.rio.

Comment

Iter XIII and Iter XIV give alternative routes between Caerleon and Silchester and each of them raises problems. In Iter XIII the mileages given add up to 90 as opposed to the stated total of 109, and it is in any case clear that a stage has been omitted, since the distance between Gloucester and Silchester is some 67 Roman miles as the crow flies, as against the 44 allowed here. It is equally clear that the missing stage must relate to *Corinium* (Cirencester), but it does not follow that all the miles to be added should go into the one stage. The final distance, from *Spinis* to *Calleva*, must stand, since it is repeated as *xv* in Iter XIV, but the distance of *xv* at 485_6 brings us to no known Roman site, whereas an amendment to *xx* fits well with Wanborough. We have, then, only 14 miles left to add, and since both Gloucester and Cirencester, the one as a *colonia* and the other as a tribal city, are likely to have had town zones, the *xiiii* should be the distance from *Glevum* to *Corinium*. This also helps to explain the omission: if the text originally read

[1] The suggestion made in 1970 (Rivet, *op. cit.* p. 57) that *Bomium* represents a lost Roman fort at the crossing of the river Ewenny is here abandoned, because intensive research by the Royal Commission on Ancient and Historical Monuments in Wales has failed to find any trace of it; we are grateful to Mr A. H. A. Hogg for this information.

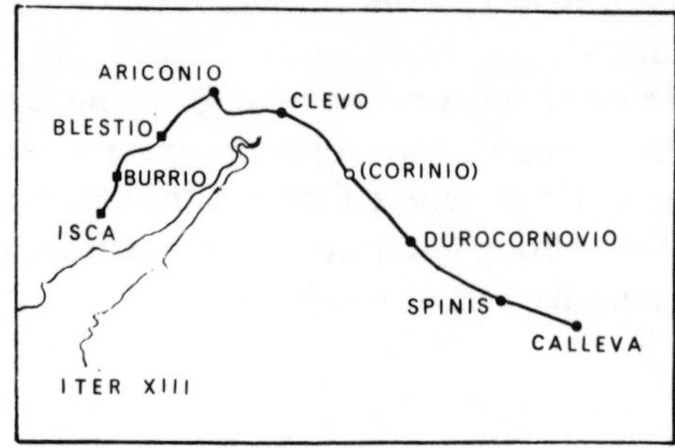

Fig. 22. The course of Iter XIII; for scale and reference see figure 11.

Corinio m.p. xiiii
Durocornovio m.p. xiiii

not only the identity of the mileage figures (as Dr Rodwell has pointed out)[1] but also the similarity of the names could have led the scribe to jump a line.

The location of *Spinis*, on which the identification of *Durocornovium* with Wanborough partly depends, is indicated by its distance from *Cunetio* in Iter XIV: it seems to lie west of the modern village of Speen, in the area with the suggestive name of Woodspeen.

18. ITER XIV (fig. 23)

	Text		True mileage	Identification
485.8	Item alio itinere ab Isca			Caerleon
	Calleva	m.p. ciii sic		
9	Venta Silurum	m.p. viiii	9	Caerwent
486.1	Abone	m.p. xiiii	?	Sea Mills
2	Traiectus	m.p. viii		(see below)
3	Aquis Sulis	m.p. vi		Bath
4	Verlucione	m.p. xv	15	Sandy Lane
5	Cunetione	m.p. xx	17	Mildenhall
6	Spinis	m.p. xv	15	Woodspeen
7	Calleva	m.p. xv	16	Silchester

Variants

486.1 viiii (with a note at 485_8 remarking on the discrepancy in the total)
3 Aquis Solis

[1] Rodwell, *op. cit.* p. 89. The distances suit Wanborough better than Popplechurch (which has sometimes been suggested) for *Durocornovium*, but the name is doubly perplexing: it suggests a settlement of Cornovii here, far from their otherwise-attested homelands, and the element *Duro-* should imply an early fortification, of which no trace has been found.

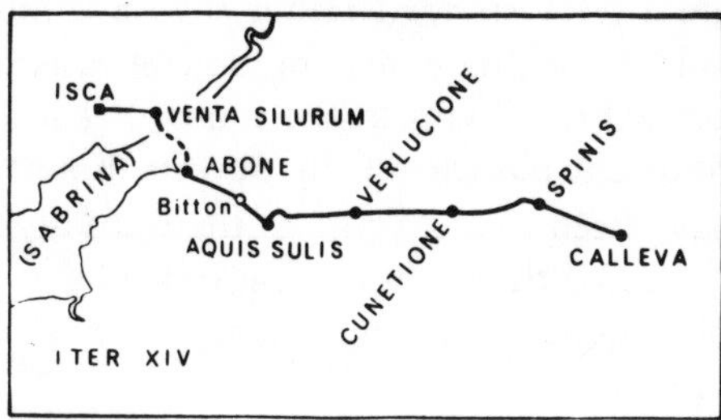

Fig. 23. The course of Iter XIV; for scale and reference see figure 11.

Comment

This alternative route involves a crossing (*traiectus*) of the Severn estuary and it is this which raises the greatest difficulty. Since the stages given add up to the correct total, however, and since one figure needs to be changed, it is best to deal with this first. There is no doubt about the identity of *Aquae Sulis* (Bath) and *Cunetio* (Mildenhall, on the river Kennet), but the distance between them, along a well-defined Roman road, is substantially less than that stated here; it seems that we must, therefore, amend the figure at 486_5 from *xx* to *xv* to produce a reasonable figure for the stage from Sandy Lane to Mildenhall. In considering the Severn crossing, then, we may have an additional five miles to allocate.

The ferry terminal on the west side of the river is not in question: one mile east of Caerwent, at Crick, a Roman road (Margary 60aa) branches off from the main road and leads to Sudbrook, and it was here or hereabout, according to the degree of erosion, that ferry passengers must have embarked. The eastern terminal, however, is far from certain. *Abone* must represent the river Avon, and the name has reasonably been applied to the Roman settlement at Sea Mills, but this lies some four miles up the river and a direct water passage to it is unlikely. A crossing to Aust (the eastern end of the 'old passage') or perhaps to Redwick (by the 'new passage') is much more likely, with the journey to Sea Mills being completed either by Cribb's Causeway (Margary 541) or by a coastal road which has now been washed away. *Traiectus* should, to judge by the distances, fall near Bitton, but the name is not obviously appropriate.

In the Itinerary the word *traiectus* is used in three slightly different senses. First, and most frequently, it is used in the maritime itinerary for a long sea-crossing, and in such cases the distance is expressed in stades.[1] Second, in the land itinerary it is used for a short sea-crossing which either forms part of a long iter, like the crossing of the Bosporus, or links two routes or groups of routes, like the crossing of the Dardanelles;[2] in the former case the distance is given in miles, in the latter in stades. Third, it is used in the land itinerary as the name of a place where a river is crossed, whether or not the route followed actually required the crossing to be made;[3] in such

[1] E.g. 493_{12-13}, from *Portus Augusti* to *Carthago*.

[2] E.g. 139_{1-2}; 333_{9-10} (cf. 463_{3-5}, cited above, p. 154).

[3] E.g. 461_9 and 369_2 (Utrecht, where the route does not cross the river).

cases it seems to indicate a ferry or ford rather than a bridge. It is, therefore, just possible that Bitton could bear this name, because it was there that a road (not followed by this Iter) crossed the Avon to the south. What is highly improbable is that the much more important *traiectus* of the Severn should escape notice.

Several conjectures have been made, some of them involving the transposition of names, but Haverfield[1] rejected these, suggesting instead that the word *Traiectus* had fallen a line and that the original text might have read:

Venta Silurum m.p. viiii
Abone Traiectus m.p. xiiii
(missing name) m.p. viiii

The objection to this is that it is the Severn, not the Avon, which is crossed, and bearing in mind that we have five miles in hand it seems more likely that a whole stage has been lost. We might, therefore, restore the text as:

Venta Silurum m.p. viiii
Sabrinae Traiectus m.p. v (inserted)
Abone m.p. xiiii
Traiectus m.p. viiii

The similarity of the names *Abon*(a)*e* and *Sabrin*(a)*e* could well explain the confusion and it may even be that the name of Bitton was not actually *Traiectus* but merely a name which resembled it.

19. ITER XV (fig. 24)

	Text		True mileage	Identification
486.8	Item a Calleva Isca Dumnonio-			Silchester
9	rum	m.p. cxxxvi sic		
10	Vindomi	m.p. xv	12	Wheatsheaf Inn
11	Venta Velgarum	m.p. xxi	12	Winchester
12	Brige	m.p. xi	6	Ashley
13	Sorbiodoni	m.p. viii	18	Old Sarum
14	Vindocladia	m.p. xii	23	Badbury
15	Durnonovaria	m.p. viii	20	Dorchester
16	Moriduno	m.p. xxxvi	42	Sidford
17	Isca Dumnoniorum	m.p. xv	15	Exeter

Variants

486.8 Dumnomiorum, Dumnuniorum, Dummuniorum, Dumnunniorum.
9 Shortfall of 10 miles noted in margin.
11 Vellgarum.
17 Dumnuviorum, Dummuniorum, Dumnunniorum.

Comment

This route forms the very last entry in the Land Itinerary, and since the final sheet of a manuscript would be subject to the most rubbing it is perhaps not surprising

[1] *VCH Somerset*, i (1906), 347–48.

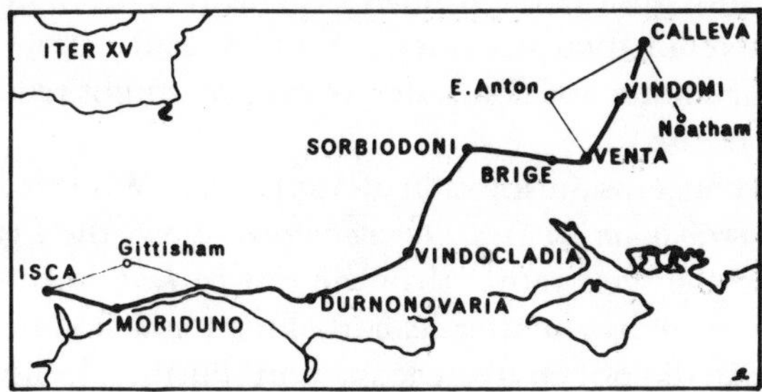

Fig. 24. The course of Iter xv; for scale and reference see figure 11.

that it has suffered the most corruption. The length of the last stage is confirmed as *xv* by the Peutinger Table, but all the other figures seem to require amendment.

To begin with, the stage lengths add up to 126 miles, as against the 136 given as the total. Secondly, the stages at 486_{14} and 486_{15} obviously need to be increased by 10 miles each, while the stages at 486_{12} and 486_{13} also need to be increased, since together they make up only 19 miles as against the 24 Roman miles along the direct route from Winchester to Old Sarum. An amendment at 486_{13} from *viii* to *xiii* (as suggested in 1970)[1] would restore the true distance and place *Brige* near Broughton, but since this area has been thoroughly combed archaeologically without any trace of a Roman posting station being found this solution is not satisfactory. As an alternative, we might suppose that the lacuna which obliterated the *x*'s in the next two stages extended to 486_{13}, and if we read

Brige vi (instead of xi)
Sorbiodoni xviii (instead of viii)

this still gives the correct total of 24 and *Brige* falls not at Broughton but at the polygonal enclosure 1½ miles south-east of Ashley, where a Roman settlement is known.

Even after these amendments, however, our overall total is still incorrect, having now risen to 151 (or 15 miles too much), and this casts doubt on the other stages, including the first two. There is a direct Roman road from Silchester to Winchester, but the distance along it is only some 24½ Roman miles, not 36. Earlier commentators, including Haverfield,[2] suggested a deviation to the west, by way of the well-known Roman crossroads at East Anton. This gave a satisfactory combined distance of 35 Roman miles, but the missing station of *Vindomis*, which should have lain north-west of St Mary Bourne, could not be located. The discovery of the Roman road from Silchester to Chichester, with an important settlement on it at Neatham, just 15 Roman miles from Silchester, raised the possibility that *Vindomis* should be situated here, and this was the solution adopted in 1970.[3] The necessary road linking Neatham with Winchester, however, has still not been found, and in view of the discrepancy in the total it may be the figures that are at fault. If we amend them to

Vindomi xii (instead of xv)
Venta Velgarum xi (instead of xxi)

[1] Rivet, *op. cit.* p. 61.
[2] *VCH Hants*, I (1900), 323.
[3] Rivet, *op. cit.* p. 61.

Vindomis falls neatly into place as the Roman settlement at the Wheatsheaf Inn, North Waltham, and the overall total becomes 138 miles. Since Iter VII gives the direct distance between Winchester and Silchester as *xxii*, we might reduce this still further by reading *xi* in each case.

The final problem concerns the location of *Moridunum*. While it confirms the length of the stage from *Moridunum* to *Isca Dumnoniorum* as *xv*, the Peutinger Table also appears to place it to the west rather than the east of *Isca*, but we must remember that the Table has been redrawn after its curtailment and the most that can be said is that the draughtsman did not envisage it as a port. Further, its listing in the *Ravenna Cosmography* seems to indicate that *Moridunum* should lie in some sense between Exeter and *Lindinis* (Ilchester). All this would seem to point to an inland location and it was on these grounds that in 1970[1] a site near Gittisham, on the most obvious Roman road out of Exeter, was suggested. The name, however, which must mean 'sea fort', clearly indicates somewhere not too far from the coast. Suggestions such as High Peak and Seaton may be ruled out, since neither of them is on a Roman road and *Moridunum* is listed as a road-station in two independent documents. If we follow the ill-defined southern road from Dorchester to Exeter (Margary 49), a possibility suggests itself at Sidford. This is about 15 Roman miles from Exeter, on a river crossing which might be expected to attract a road-station, and not too far from the sea to bear the name (which might indeed have been inherited from the hill-fort of Sidbury Castle); and the route from Exeter to Ilchester, which the *Cosmography* seems to imply, might lead either by way of Axminster and the Fosse Way or perhaps along the the modern A. 375 up the Sid valley. The main objections are that no Roman settlement had been found here (though it has not seriously been looked for) and that the distance from Dorchester is some 42 Roman miles, but whichever Roman road is followed the 51 miles allowed by the Itinerary from Dorchester to Exeter are too few. It seems therefore that here too we must make an amendment, from *xxxvi* to *xxxxi* – and this carries with it the need to amend the overall total from *cxxxvi* to *cxxxxi*, leaving only one mile to be deducted from one or other of the stages.

It is interesting to note that all the corruptions here postulated must have occurred before the stage of transmission at which this iter was erroneously incorporated in Iter XII, since there is no variation between the two sets of figures.

20. THE MARITIME ITINERARY (fig. 25)

The Maritime Itinerary proper concludes (497_9–508_2) with a voyage from Rome along the Italian and Gaulish coasts and up the Rhône to Arles. There then follows:

508.3 Item in mari oceano quod Gallias et
4 Britannias interluit
5 insule Orcades numero iii
509.1 insula Clota in Hiverione

[1] Rivet, *ibid.* pp. 61–62.

2 Vecta Riduna Sarmia Caesarea Barsa Silia
3 Andium Sicdelis Uxantis Ina
510.1 Vindilis Siata Iga.

Variants

509.1 Glota. Inverione.
2 Cesaria. Lisia.
3 Adium. Uxanis Ina, Uxantisma.
510.1 Vindelis.

Comment

This section, placing the Orkneys in 'the sea which flows between the Gauls and the Britains' can hardly be from an official source, and the number of the Orkneys should presumably be emended either to *xxx* (to agree with Mela and Ptolemy), or, more easily, to *xiii* (to agree with the number of inhabited islands in the group given by Orosius and Isidore). *Vecta* is the Isle of Wight (with the form of the name agreeing with that given in the Panegyric of A.D. 297–98, in Eutropius and in Bede). *Uxantis* is Ouessant (Ushant), *Sina* (having lost its initial *S-* by haplography) is the Ile de Sein (*Sena* in Mela), and *Vindilis* is Belle-Ile (formerly Guedel). It seems, therefore, that the list is taken from a map and runs from north to south, or perhaps (in view of the shape of Ptolemy's map) from north-east to south-west. If this is so, *Siata* (possibly Ile de'Houat) and *Iga* should be islands off the Atlantic coast of Gaul and do not here concern us.

Insula Clota in Hiverione is strange. *Hiverione* looks like a variation on *Hivernia* (Ireland) and *Clota* seems improbable as an island-name; it is likely that on the map the name of the Scottish river *Clota* (Clyde) was written in the sea and taken to refer to an island. See our entry in the Alphabetic List.

All the rest should lie between Wight and Ouessant and the names may thus apply to the Channel Islands – Jersey, Guernsey, Alderney, Sark, Herm, Jethou, les Minquiers (which, with a lower sea-level, would then have been one island) and the Iles Chausey; or the small islands along the northern Breton coast – Ile de Brehat, Ile St-Gildas, les Sept Iles and Ile de Batz. The identification of *Caesarea* with Jersey, traditional since Camden, has little etymological justification (the early forms Geresy, Gerese, Gersea are probably from the Norse, 'Geirr's Island') and that of *Sarmia* (often misquoted as *Sarnia*) still less, though Alderney (Aurigny) may well be *Riduna*, both because of its position in the list and because the earlier forms were *Adreni*, *Arenon*. There is, however, some evidence in the seventh-century life of St Sampson of Dol[1] that in the post-Roman (and pre-Norse) period Jersey was called *Angia* (= our *Andium*) and Guernsey *Lesia* (= our *Silia* or *Lisia*), and the same passage refers to *Sargia* and *Besargia*, possibly Sark and Little Sark and so to be equated with our *Sarmia*. This leaves out of account *Barsa*, which might be Herm (though there is no direct evidence to support it), and, above all, *Caesarea*. The suggestion of Poingdestre[2] that

[1] For a discussion, T. D. Kendrick, *The Archaeology of the Channel Isles*, I (London, 1928), 16; J. J. Hawkes, *ibid.* II (Jersey, 1937), 18.

[2] J. Poingdestre, *Caesarea, or A Discourse on the Island of Jersey* (1682; 10th edn., ed. W. Nicolle, St Helier, 1889), pp. 79–82.

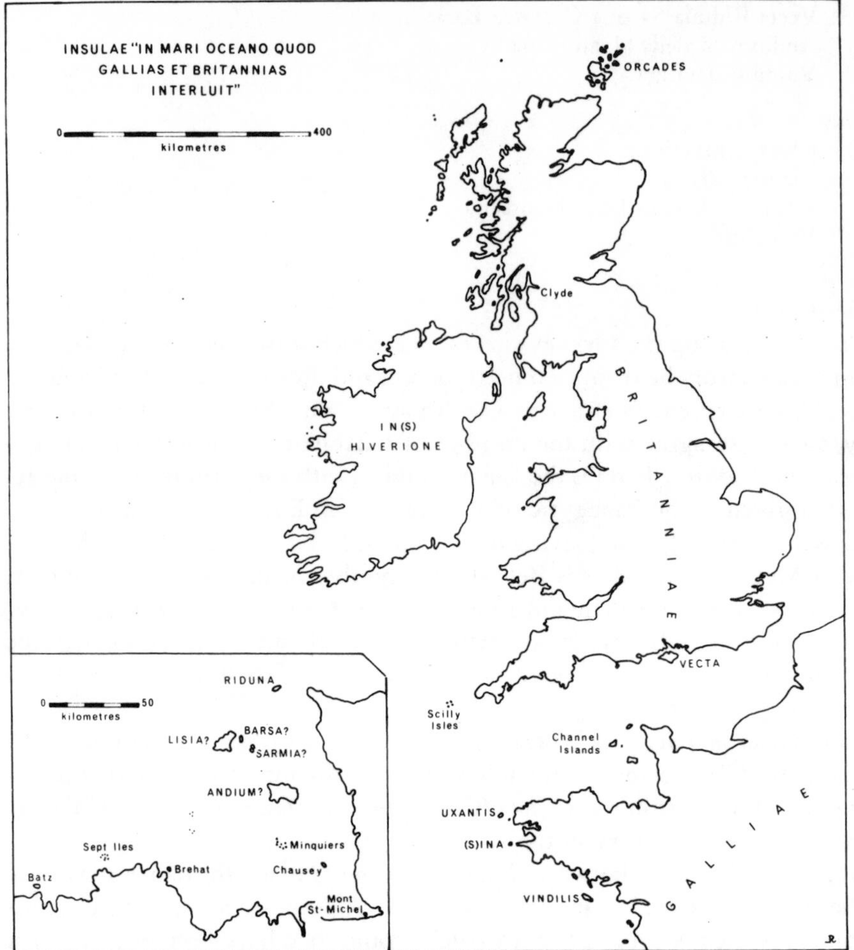

Fig. 25. Islands near Britain listed in the Maritime Itinerary.

Andium was the native name of Jersey and *Caesarea* a Roman addition is unconvincing, especially since the two names are separated in the list, and the logical corollary of the suggestions made here would seem to be Dr Kellett-Smith's conclusion[1] that *Caesarea* applied to a large island now represented only by les Minquiers.

21. APPENDIX: THE SPURIOUS *DE SITU BRITANNIAE* OF 'RICHARD OF CIRENCESTER'

On 11 June 1747 the celebrated English antiquary William Stukeley received a letter from Charles Julius Bertram, a teacher of English in the Marine Academy in Copenhagen. Though Bertram was previously unknown to Stukeley, his respecta-

[1] S. K. Kellett-Smith, 'The Old Names of the Channel Islands', *Société Guernésiaise Report and Transactions*, XVII (1962), 352–87.

bility seemed to be confirmed by the patronage of Gramm, the Danish royal librarian, and a correspondence developed between them. In the course of this Bertram mentioned that a friend of his had in his possession a manuscript 'of Richard of Westminster, being a history of Roman Britain, which he thought a great curiosity; and an antient map of the island annex'd'. Stukeley expressed interest and in due course obtained a specimen of the writing, which he 'showed to my late friend Mr Casley, keeper in the Cotton library, who immediately pronounced it to be 400 years old', and later a copy of the complete text and the map. On the basis of these he read a paper to the Society of Antiquaries on 18 March 1756, which was published in 1757 as *An Account of Richard of Cirencester*, with a copy of the map appended. In the following year Bertram himself produced another edition, combined with texts of Gildas and Nennius, also with a copy of the map, but one which differed somewhat from Stukeley's; and in his preface he said of the work that 'it is considered by Dr Stukeley, and those who have inspected it, as a jewel, and worthy to be rescued from destruction by the press. From respect for him I have caused it to be printed.'

With each editor citing the other as an authority, the work was thus well and truly launched, and it was to confuse the toponymy of Roman Britain for more than a century. Horsley's *Britannia Romana* had, of course, already been published, in 1732, but from Stukeley onwards almost every antiquary (notably Gough, Roy and Roach Smith) accepted it without question, and it is easy to understand why: it seemed to answer so many important questions. For example, it defines the boundaries of the fourth-century provinces of Britain (including a province called *Vespasiana* north of the Antonine Wall); it includes a list of 92 cities, 33 of them 'notable' (2 *municipia*, 9 *coloniae*, 10 with Latin rights, 12 *stipendiariae*); and its itinerary section fills many of the gaps left by the Antonine Itinerary (some of whose mileages are 'corrected', while some of its names are twisted or split into two). In fact it is an ingenious rehash of the ancient sources, mediated (as was later shown) by Gibson's Camden, Baxter and Horsley, with a few more or less plausible additions of its own – and it covers itself where its guesses are wildest: '"Where," you may ask, "are the remains of the cities you mention? There are none." You might as well ask where now are the Assyrians, the Parthians, the Sarmatians, the Celtiberians.' Finally, to add verisimilitude, the itinerary section in particular is liberally interrupted by *lacunae*.

A further warrant of authenticity seemed to be provided by the authorship. It will be noticed that Bertram originally referred only to Richard of Westminster and it was Stukeley who contributed the identification with Richard of Cirencester, because he knew, as Bertram probably did not, that a real monk of this name did belong to the abbey of Westminster in the fourteenth century. This genuine Ricardus de Cirencestria (never, incidentally, called Ricardus Corinensis, as Bertram made him) compiled the *Speculum Historiale*, together with other works which are now lost. So Gibbon who, though he cites it, does seem to have had some doubts about the *De Situ*, remarked that Richard 'shows a genuine knowledge of antiquity very extraordinary for a monk of the fourteenth century'.

In fact this 'very extraordinary knowledge' was one of the things which led to the exposure of the forgery, for nothing of the kind is displayed in the surviving work of the real Richard, nor does he ever refer to the *De Situ*. Needless to say, the original 'manuscript' has never been found, while the alleged fragment of the writing has been shown to represent no recognisable medieval script. The truth of the matter was finally revealed by Bernard Woodward (Librarian in Ordinary to Queen Victoria) in a series of communications to the *Gentleman's Magazine* from 1847 to 1867 and by J. E. B. Mayor in the Preface to his edition of the *Speculum Historiale* (Rolls Series, 1869). An entertaining further discussion, with some material unknown to Woodward and Mayor, may be found in H. J. Randall's article 'Splendide Mendax' in *Antiquity*, VII (1933), 49–60.

Unfortunately this was not the end of the matter. Growing doubts led Petrie and Sharpe to omit the *De Situ* from the *Monumenta Historica Britannica* in 1848, but it was included in Giles's *History of the Ancient Britons*, published in the same year, and it had become so embedded in received opinion that even after the publication of Randall's article it remained, in Collingwood's words, 'hard to disentangle Bertram's inventions from the body of credible knowledge'. Perhaps worst of all, Bertram's names and identifications had found their way on to the Ordnance Survey maps. From his appointment as Archaeology Officer in 1920 O. G. S. Crawford did his best to remove them, but so slow was the rate of map revision that some of them, like the grotesque '*Ptorotone*' applied to the native fort at Burghead in Morayshire, persisted on the 6-inch maps until after the second world war; indeed it was only with the production of the first metric series that the process could be completed.

CHAPTER FIVE

THE RAVENNA COSMOGRAPHY

1. GENERAL

Of all our sources, this is the most full (for Britain) but also the most baffling. It is also the latest in its date of compilation, though not with regard to the period to which its information refers. In view of the problems involved and in justice to the scholars who have laboured to solve those problems, some account of the textual tradition by which the *Cosmography* has reached us is necessary.

The text was compiled by an anonymous cleric of Ravenna for a brother cleric, Odo, at some date soon after A.D. 700.[1] There are no early MSS, but three survive from the later Middle Ages. These, with their designations in the editions of Schnetz and of Richmond and Crawford (R&C) are:

	Schnetz		*R&C*
Vatican, fourteenth century	A	=	V
Paris, thirteenth century	B	=	P
Basle, fourteenth/fifteenth century	C	=	B

According to Schnetz, his MSS A and B are much more trustworthy than C,[2] and he bases his 1940 edition on a collation of these two. The text was first printed in 1688 (Porcheron), then again in 1696 and 1722 (Gronovius). M. Pinder and G. Parthey produced their edition at Berlin in 1860, and this held the field as an

[1] R&C thought it of the late seventh century; Miller thought it of about A.D. 670; Schnetz placed it in the early decades of the eighth century, partly on the ground that a late date is needed by the mention of the *Francorum patria* attributed to Athanaridus (one of the alleged sources). The latest obviously datable reference in the text is to Isidore of Seville (5₂₅); he died in 636, was soon after regarded as a saint, and the Cosmographer refers to him as *sanctus*; but his work was hardly known outside Spain until churchmen fled from the Peninsula after the Moslem invasion of 711–13 bearing copies of Isidore's works, and diffused these from centres in France. There is no reference, however, to the Moslem invasion of Spain, and the Cosmographer was in the habit of adding such details where he knew them. Dillemann (p. 69) thinks the Cosmographer's phrase about Hadrian's Wall, *recto tramite*, may have echoed the same phrase in Bede's *Historia Ecclesiastica* I, 12, which is just possible, though it seems more likely that both Bede and the Cosmographer had a common source. Schnetz thinks late additions were made by copyists, perhaps into the ninth century for, for example, Venetia.

[2] The textual tradition and orthography of the MSS are studied by J. Schnetz, *Untersuchungen zum Geographen von Ravenna* (Munich, 1919).

authoritative work for many years. K. Miller in his *Itineraria Romana* (Stuttgart, 1916) has a good deal to say about *Ravenna*; some of his details and identifications are shaky, but his arguments about the nature of the British sections will be mentioned later, for they seem hardly to have been taken into account by British scholars. The latest edition of the complete text is that of J. Schnetz, *Ravennatis Anonymi Cosmographia*, vol. II of the *Itineraria Romana* (Leipzig, 1940), which we follow here and whose British section is reproduced at the end of this chapter, with a commentary. This is necessary for our purposes and may in any case be useful to scholars, because the date and place of publication have meant that Schnetz's admirable edition is a scarce item.

Study of the British section does not, however, end there. In 1949 there appeared the work of Richmond and Crawford.[1] Richmond explains the genesis of this in a note which makes it plain (though he refrains from excuses) how much the war interfered with scholarly tasks. He had written a paper on *Ravenna*, based on a study of the Vatican MS, in 1922. He then began collaboration with Crawford, and they worked from photographs of all three MSS, producing a joint paper which was read in January 1937. The 1949 study as printed has a three-page introduction, a detailed survey of each geographical region within the British section, each with a map and a comparison with the evidence from *AI* and other sources, followed by an edition of the text of the British section in which each name is numbered, with variants. Finally, with extensive additional notes by Professor Ifor Williams, there is a full 'Commentary upon individual names' – identification, mention of other sources, etymology, etc. It goes without saying that this study has been of great value to us, and reference to it will be constant in this chapter and in the Alphabetic List. But Richmond and Crawford were deprived by the war of the benefit of two important works of Schnetz: his 1940 edition, and his 1942 study of its sources.[2] Among other ill effects, this deprivation perhaps led them into a somewhat insular view of the British section; they tended to emphasise its uniqueness – erroneously – and failed to make textual and palaeographic comparisons with other parts of the text which would often have resolved problems for them. Moreover, R&C's version is on linguistic grounds in some respects a too correct and conflated one; they were also – perhaps an endearing fault – far too trusting in their approach to the text, believing both that it was palaeographically much more accurate than it is, and that it is logical in the order in which it lists names. Clearly a new start has to be made, and this can only be on the basis of the edition and studies of Schnetz; but since R&C's work is so widely known and used in Britain, their numeration of names is placed beside that of Schnetz, and due regard is had for their forms.

There is, finally, the study of M. Louis Dillemann, a very useful survey of the

[1] I. A. Richmond and O. G. S. Crawford, 'The British Section of the *Ravenna Cosmography*', *Archaeologia*, XCIII (1949), 1–50.

[2] 'Untersuchungen über die Quellen der *Kosmographie* des anonymen Geographen von Ravenna', in *Sitzungsberichte der Bayerischen Akademie der Wissenschaften*, VI (1942), 1–87. Schnetz also translated the *Cosmography*, with preface, notes, bibliography and further corrections of names, in *Nomina Germanica*, vol. X (Uppsala, 1951). An important and more recent study of the sources is that of U. Schillinger-Häfele, 'Beobachtungen zum Quellenprobleme der *Kosmographie* von Ravenna', *Bonner Jahrbücher*, CLXIII (1963), 238–51, whose chief conclusion is mentioned below.

problems raised by *Ravenna* in general and by its British section in particular.[1] Dillemann revises many of the forms and identifications proposed by R&C; many of his findings have been useful to us, but we are not always in agreement.

2. THE COSMOGRAPHER AND HIS AIMS

'Cosmography' is perhaps too dignified a name for the work of the Ravenna cleric, for in large part it consists of the merest listing in undifferentiated form of all the place-names in an area, this area itself being vaguely defined. The whole text contains some 5000 names. The compiler lists separately the *flumina* and *insule*, but all too often his lists of habitation-names introduced by the formula *Iterum sunt civitates*. . . include *coloniae*, cantonal capitals, small towns, forts, *mansiones* and the merest settlements without any distinction, except for an occasional defining term. Everything, grand or modest, is a *civitas*, a term equivalent in its looseness to Ptolemy's *polis*. There are moreover frequent confusions, towns being listed as rivers and vice versa, rivers as islands, etc.; and these confusions must go back to the compiler himself. The narrative passages which introduce sections betray a naive and credulous approach. Gibbon's notion of 'decline and fall' could be well illustrated by the contrast between the scientific method, breadth of information and scholarly inquisitiveness of 2nd-century Ptolemy and the strange standards and lack of perspective of the Ravenna writer, especially as Ravenna was one of the capitals of Christendom and (for its time) no more of a cultural backwater than Alexandria had been in the period of Ptolemy. The degree of inaccuracy of *Ravenna* is greater than that of *AI* and *TP*, transmitted to us in comparable ways, and although some of this is to be blamed on copyists, much must be imputed to the author. When we find in all three MSS (hence in the archetype, probably) *Staurinis* 66_{33} (also adjectival *Staurinensis* 67_{9}) for *Taurinis* (*AI*) – that is, a record of Turin, a place in the author's native north Italy – we naturally expect even wilder errors in the listing of places in remote Britain.

Ravenna begins with a long prefatory section about the geography of the world from India to Ireland, with much reference to scriptural authority and to Christian cosmology. The author confesses that he has not travelled himself but has derived his information from writers, *sicut in eorum libris sub multorum imperatorum temporibus mundus iste descriptus est* (1_{39}). His reliance on some of the *sancti patres* leads him at one point into a lengthy discussion of the whereabouts of Paradise, but for more mundane geographical notions he depends on older pagan writers whom he dignifies by the name *philosophi*. At times, however, these are described as *quasicosmographi* (7_{5}) and *fallaces pseudocosmographi* (7_{56}) when they contradict the Bible, as Dillemann notes. The work is organised on a basis which enables the Cosmographer to proceed from East to West; the British section is near the end (v. 31, with some elements in v. 30 and v. 32).

When this much has been said about the shortcomings of the author, R&C must be allowed a word in his defence. They refer sympathetically to the union of three cultures – Roman, Greek and Gothic – at Ravenna, and to the fact that

[1] 'Observations on Chapter v. 31, *Britannia*, in the *Ravenna Cosmography*', *Archaeologia*, CVI (1978), 61–73. We are most grateful to M. Dillemann for kindly allowing us access to his work before publication.

> The Cosmography takes it [the union] as established, looking upon the cosmos which it is describing as the formal continuation of the Roman world...This attitude is not to be dismissed as fanciful archaism, divorced from contemporary thought and facts, even if such criticism might indeed seem particularly invited by the inclusion of Roman Britain, then lost to the Empire beyond recall. For, whatever later events were to prove, it was not incorrect in the seventh century to assert that the framework of the Roman Empire, as described by pagan geographers and considered to be ordained by the Scriptures, still remained a reality in men's minds.

This is a noble effort on the Cosmographer's behalf, but as Dillemann points out, his inclusion of India and Ireland and other non-Roman countries does not fit a 'formal continuation of the Roman world', and the mention of Babylon and Ctesiphon as though they still existed does indeed show a lapse into 'fanciful archaism'. The essential would-be *romanitas* of the Cosmographer's mind and work is not in doubt; it is simply that their realization is sadly limited by his impoverished culture. The basis of his description may indeed be in large measure that of the late Empire, strong and intact, but later changes are sketched in, even though in such a way as to suggest that they are superficial or unlikely to be permanent. Thus there is mention of the Franks, Vandals, Goths, Saxons and Huns, of Bulgars between Thrace and Lower Moesia, etc. The mixture of ancient Celtic tribal names with Roman provincial designations and new Germanic states is sometimes disconcerting, e.g. *Item iuxta praelatam Galliam Belgicam Alobroges ponitur patria quae dicitur Burgundia, quam Burgundiam Secundam esse legimus Galliam* (62_{40}). In connection with the *romanitas*, it should be noted that the compiler uses for the most part the present tense, giving an air of actuality and some force to what R&C say about his attitude: *in ipsa Burgundia sunt civitates*...(64_{14}). But he occasionally distances himself in time – perhaps indicating a lack of real belief in a continuing *romanitas* – by using past tenses: *Item ad aliam partem in ipsa Burgundia regione fuerunt civitates, id est*...(63_{43}); *In qua Septimania plurimas fuisse civitates legimus* (64_{42}). The fact that the world of Rome is now largely Christian is constantly emphasised in the regular introductory formulae: *Christo domino adiuvante...designare cupimus* (104_{26}); *Christo nobis auxiliante volumus enarrare* (105_{17}).

3. SOURCES IN GENERAL

Ravenna's sources might hypothetically be of very diverse kinds: literary-descriptive, geographical (like Ptolemy), military (like *ND*), maps (like *TP* or of other kinds), road-books (like *AI*), etc. We know from the total lack of correspondences that the Cosmographer did not know *ND* or *AI*. About other sources, the Cosmographer himself is loquacious beyond the point of carrying conviction. A few literary writers that he mentions are respectable enough, such as Orosius and Jordanes,[1] but there has been much disagreement about the numerous other writers he mentions who cannot be shown (from any independent source) to have existed: Livianus, Lollianus,

[1] J. Schnetz, 'Jordanes bei Geographen von Ravenna', *Philologus*, LXXXI (1926), 86–100.

etc., and the Goths Athanaridus, Anaridus, Eldebaldus, and so on. Schnetz in his 1942 study (pp. 50 ff.) argues that the Cosmographer is telling the truth when he says that for different regions he used the descriptions of all these writers. In a few cases his proofs are textual and therefore worth considering, e.g. that a number of entries for North Africa show traces of being taken from a source in a language such as Berber, that a Greek source containing the error *Damiupolis* for *Lamiupolis* betrays a Δ confused with Λ, that a German source gave the compiler the adjective *Rinensis* (three times), with Germanic *-i-* against the original Gallic *Rēnos*; but this hardly proves the real existence of the authors named by the Cosmographer in all cases, and even the 'proofs' cited may have other explanations. Schnetz thinks in any case that it was not the Cosmographer's habit to follow a single source for a single region, but rather that he adapted and married together a diversity of sources much of the time. This, as will be shown, is certainly what he did for Britain. British scholars have shown themselves very unwilling to believe in the many dubious *philosophi* cited in *Ravenna*, regarding them as mere names made up by the Cosmographer in order to dignify his work in accordance with rhetorical practice and to conceal the fact that his sources, though abundant, were often anonymous.

As for maps, Schnetz judges from an allusion of the author that for his opening general description of the world he had before him a round (circular or elliptical) map, a *Weltkarte*, upon which he imposed a division of the horizon into the hours of the day and night and proceeded with his description from East to West. For the detailed information about the regions which follow, Miller (1916)[1] and Schnetz hold that the source was in large part that 'Castorius' to whom the author repeatedly refers, and whom the German scholars credit with the production of the *TP*: 'Es steht bekanntlich seit langem fest, dass der *Ravenna* in grossern Umfang die *Tabula* als Quelle benützt hat' (Schnetz, 1942, p. 20); that is, it was an *Itinerärkarte*. Their case is strengthened by what the Cosmographer says about his potential capacity: *Potuissemus etenim Christo nobis iuvante subtilius dicere totius mundi portus et promuntoria atque inter ipsas urbes miliaria* (15_{15}), which makes it seem that he had before him a map giving distances between places in miles (as *TP* does); however, *Ravenna* does not in fact go on to give such mileages, and – wishing to abbreviate, *polylogiam fugientes* – the Cosmographer does not often mention *promuntoria* either. Schnetz adds that although there is often close agreement between *TP* and *Ravenna*, there are important differences too, and that since the latter drew upon other sources in addition, the fuller *Ravenna* text cannot be used to expand or restore the surviving *TP* (as was attempted by Miller). For some Continental and other regions, there may indeed by these partial correspondences between *TP* and *Ravenna*, as Schnetz says; but, as will be shown below, the correspondences in Britain are slight. We certainly need the notion of a map as a source, and it was probably of the *TP* type, but for Britain at least we can assert that it was larger and very much more detailed.

It seems that the Cosmographer knew the classical geographers, Pliny and Ptolemy,

[1] In fairness to him, Miller's long discussion of *Ravenna*'s sources and accuracy, and of its dependence upon the work of 'Castorius', should be studied in his *Itineraria Romana* (Stuttgart, 1916), pp. xxvii–xxix. An independent authority, J. O. Thomson in his *History of Ancient Geography* (Cambridge, 1948), dismisses Castorius out of hand (p. 379).

but probably only in confused excerpts of which he made rather ignorant use. Dillemann notes (p. 62) that

> Extracts from Ptolemy show up clearly in comparison with *TP* in several countries of Asia, in the islands, perhaps in Carniola (IV. 21),[1] since they are in a form which betrays their origin... Anonymous, fragmentary, often disfigured, they have been inserted into the text in distinct or dislocated groups, without regard to geography, to the extent that they are sometimes repeated in different provinces with a different spelling.

Whether these disjointed excerpts were known in book form is unsure; they could have been entered (as were phrases from Jordanes and others) as legends on the map. In the case of Britain in particular we shall need very firmly the idea of a map as a major source. Dillemann (p. 71) thinks that the Cosmographer had recourse to Pliny – again in garbled form – for what he says about certain islands in the Mediterranean and off northern Britain; again, perhaps, via excerpts entered as legends on a map.

4. NATURE AND SOURCES OF THE BRITISH SECTION

The number of names in the British section was reckoned by R&C as 306; it is really somewhat lower, as there are many more duplications than R&C allowed, but the total approaches 300. It is surprising to find that this is a much greater quantity than that which *Ravenna* gives for Gaul. In part the difference is accounted for by the large number of names given for minor places in two regions: the little-romanised south-west, and the unromanised north of Britain. While one naturally assumes that for Britain the same sources were used as for the rest of the world, it is obvious that for these two regions one must postulate sources of information additonal to those used for the adjacent Continental provinces. Taken together these sources all dated from Imperial times; except for the narrative mention of the *adventus Saxonum*, which does not affect the lists of names, R&C (following Haverfield) emphasise that the British section shows no trace of post-Imperial additions, influence or contamination; further,

> As Haverfield long ago stressed, the list contains features which are quite without significance when divorced from the Roman province. These are, firstly, the definition of *coloniae* by their official titles, and the distinction of cantonal capitals by their tribal suffixes; secondly, the honorific attributes of London and the legionary fortresses; thirdly, Roman administrative terms, such as *statio* and *praesidium*...

Let us first consider the nature of the *Itinerärkarte* or road-map whose British sheet was a principal source for the Cosmographer in composing his section on Britain. R&C refer (p. 3) to the fact that 'Unless a given section can be shown to embody post-Roman material, it may be taken to rest upon Roman road-books in list or map form resembling, in other words, either the *Antonine Itinerary* or the *Peutinger*

[1] See Dillemann on 'Carneola patria', *Philologus*, CXVI (1972), 319–22.

Map', and say elsewhere (p. 4) that 'The [*Antonine*] *Itinerary* or *Peutinger Map* are not the only documents to be cited'. However, this is too limiting. There is no evidence that the Cosmographer knew the *AI* for any part of his work, nor that he was working from a list of that type. It can readily be shown from his narrative remarks thoughout his text that he was reading a good deal from a map, for he constantly describes it as ocular evidence. In the British section, for example, the two Walls are seen crossing the country *recto tramite* (107_{20}, 107_{49}), and the Antonine Wall is *ubi et ipsa Britania plus angustissima de oceano in oceano esse dinoscitur* (107_{49}), a visual impression. One place is *iuxta* another (106_{6}) as observed on a map. The phrase *Item ad aliam partem* (109_{17}) occurs many times in the Cosmography and is similarly visual; and there is conclusive proof in the closing description of the position of Britain (108_{43}) with adjacent lands *seen* in relation to it. But this map was not *TP*, nor did it closely resemble it. The proof of this is the lack of correspondence between the small surviving portion of *TP* for south-east England and the relevant parts of *Ravenna*. *TP* has 16 names, of which *Ravenna* has only 11, and equally, *Ravenna* has a number of names which 'ought' to appear on the surviving part of *TP* but which do not, for the good reason that *TP* was much smaller and less detailed than the map *Ravenna* used as a source. The eleven names given in common by *Ravenna* and *TP* are in some cases stated very divergently (*Manulodulo Colonia* – *Camuloduno; Cesaromago* – [*Ces*]*aromaci*, etc.). Among *TP*'s 16 names, no fewer than 7 are locatives, a far higher proportion than that anywhere in *Ravenna*.[1]

We can, perhaps, say something more about this fundamental map. It may have resembled *TP* in some external ways – perhaps the British sheet was first or last on a long series of sewn-together sections which between them took in the whole of the Empire; probably the island of Britain was represented only in schematic fashion, as countries are on *TP*, with considerable distortions and much north–south compression. This would not have mattered greatly in a map which was chiefly designed to show the road-system for the practical purposes of road-users, but it may have seriously misled the Cosmographer when he tried to use it for the position of islands (both the preliminary set of four islands, and the western Scottish ones and others at the end). Its representation of rivers must have been often unclear, since the Cosmographer read several as though they were islands and others as though they were settlements, showing that they evidently had no distinctive script. It was a map on which the writing was very crowded, leading the Cosmographer into making several conflations, and it had abbreviations for *Flumen* and *Insula* which he often did not comprehend. It often separated elements of compound names, placing the second below the first, and the Cosmographer failed to reunite them; thus from

Glevum	Duro	Sorvio
Colonia	Bravis	Doni

he took respectively a second part as *Colonea*(*s*) 106_{14}, a second part (with correction wrongly incorporated) as *Brinavis* 106_{39}, and two separate elements which he attached

[1] There is however one curious agreement between *TP* and *Ravenna*. For Canterbury, *TP* has *Duroaverus*, *Ravenna Duro Averno Cantiacorum*, both with intrusive -*a*- (a strange -*a*- is found also in two itinera of *AI*, but it does not correspond precisely to that of *TP* and *Ravenna*).

to preceding and following names, *Alauna Silva* 106_9 and *Omi(re...)* 106_{10}. Yet the original map had virtues too. It was quite exceptionally full, containing much more information than *AI* or *TP* (if complete) did. It consistently gave the tribal designations of the cantonal capitals, attached *Colonia* where appropriate (but not to York), and gave details of military establishments. Where there are omissions in *Ravenna*, they can probably be attributed to the Cosmographer's carelessness (or perhaps to his desire to abbreviate, to list no more than *aliquantas* 105_{44}) rather than to any deficiency of the original map. This map must have served its primary purpose of guiding road-users, no doubt chiefly military and administrative officers, much better than *AI* or *TP* could have done, simply because it had many more names, and because unlike *AI* with its fifteen itinera, it included branch roads. Whatever its shape and degree of compression, this map must have been several times larger than that for Britain on *TP*. It might, indeed, have been not simply one sheet of a general map of the Empire (as was *TP*), but a special product whose size and quality explains the wealth of *Ravenna*'s information for Britain in comparison with that for Gaul; it might have been the 'geography' or 'map', with drawings and legends in verse, which Alypius sent to the Emperor Julian (A.D. 360–63) and which was possibly of or included Britain, of which Alypius had been *vicarius* (see JULIANUS in Chapter II). It is to be noted that such a date would account for the inclusion in the map – and thence in *Ravenna* – of the only piece of information which we know to be late, the naming of London by the honorific title *Augusta* (miscopied by the Cosmographer as *Augusti* and added to *Londinium* rather than replacing it, 106_{50}), which is thought to have been granted in the 4th century. If it was a mid-4th-century map, it probably represented Hadrian's Wall and its few outlying forts to the north, with the road-system up to those points (as in *AI*) in accordance with the Roman dispositions of the time; for northern Britain, *Ravenna* had a different source, discussed below.

R&C were certainly correct in insisting that *Ravenna* derived much of its material from a road-map, but (as in other respects) they were far too trusting, and were unable to grasp that an apparently intelligent man – the Cosmographer – could proceed in a way which is to our minds criminally nonchalant. R&C assumed that *Ravenna* was taking them on a logical journey along the Roman roads, was taking due account of crossroads and branches, was not repeating stations, and so on. Their trust in this enabled them to identify eleven diverse but not in all very extensive areas in which the Cosmographer does seem to have operated intelligently. In many parts – most of Roman Britain – such an analysis fails. Dillemann (p. 63) is much more severe in his assessment of the Cosmographer's lack of method. He notes (among other factors) that 'A place missed out on one road is taken up in the following one... Sometimes a part of a corrected name has been written in over the name and has then been taken to be a different name... Names at the end of a chapter may be additions having no bearing on the road network', and so on. In particular – a point which the too trusting R&C failed to appreciate, and which led them into avoidable errors – 'Two names having roughly the same form and adjacent are two forms of the same name, one correcting the other.' Dillemann is able amply to prove his points by comparison with better-documented areas of the Continental and other provinces. One could go still further and assert that for Britain the Cosmographer, although using the road-map, did not always even try to follow the lines of the roads, but simply copied out the names of a region, this region not necessarily being one which corresponded to a geographical area or bore any relation to a cantonal capital. It is as though the Cosmographer, in the early eighth century, did not appreciate the central importance of the roads in the whole Roman system, and did not realise that his map had been chiefly designed to show it.[1]

For northern Britain – above Hadrian's Wall – it is certain that a different map provided the Cosmographer with his source. Its basis was probably the official military map of Flavian times which was used by Marinus and, through him, by Ptolemy. Its northern British information was that gathered during Agricola's campaigns in Scotland, partly from direct observation, partly from military intelligence in respect of areas and peoples never actually reached during Agricola's campaigns. This map bore names of tribes, habitations (in this case, forts of the Roman army), rivers and islands; and possibly the capes also, though these were not copied by the Cosmographer, who had said in his prefatory remarks that *potuissemus... subtilius dicere...promuntoria* ('we could have listed...') and does not do so to any extent in any part of Britain or the other provinces. This dependence of *Ravenna* on a Flavian map of northern Britain can be demonstrated in several ways by using the evidence of Ptolemy who similarly depended on it. Nearly all Ptolemy's names of northern British tribes and *poleis* are taken up by *Ravenna*, and the military map must have been the only source for these in any quantity. This information was transmitted in map form, not as lists in a book, as can be shown by the fact that tribal names were misread by the Cosmographer (but not of course by Marinus or Ptolemy) as though they were place-names, and from the non-textual order in which the Cosmographer copies the names. This misreading of ethnic names as place-names seems not to have happened in any other part of *Ravenna*, a sign of the uniqueness of *Ravenna*'s map-source for northern Britain. If it be objected that *TP* gives many tribal names (e.g. for Gaul *Bituriges*, *Cadurci*, *Mediomatrici*), it can be answered that this is irrelevant, because it was – as shown above – not *TP* that was used by the Cosmographer for Britain, and because even if he had some knowledge of *TP*, the surviving portion of it for south-east Britain would not have given him any ethnic names, since there are none (in that portion one might have expected a mention of one or two out of *Iceni*, *Trinovantes*, *Cantiaci*, *Regini*, *Durotriges*). It is most noteworthy that the misreading of ethnic names as place-names in northern Britain is never

[1] Some of the Cosmographer's apparent lack of method may be explained if the conclusion of Ute Schillinger-Häfele, following study of several sections of the text (not Britain) is correct: 'Die angeführten Beispiele von Namensverwechslungen – die sich noch vermehren ließen – erweisen, wie gesagt, für die entsprechenden Partien mit größter Wahrscheinlichkeit eine Karte ohne Wegelinien als Quelle' (p. 251). This finding is adopted by Dillemann in 'La Carte routière de la *Cosmographie de Ravenna*', *Bonner Jahrbücher*, CLXXV (1975), 165–70: on the map, 'Les routes n'y étaient pas indiquées par un trait, mais seulement par l'alignement des noms d'étages'; hence, 'Le Cosmographe n'a pas rédigé un routier mais une géographie donnant pour chaque pays les villes, les rivières, parfois les provinces. Quand il a puisé ses informations sur une carte routière, il ne s'est pas cru obligé de la copier servilement' (p. 170).

paralleled in *Ravenna*'s sections on Britain south of Hadrian's Wall; the 'first map' (road-map) which was the source for southern Britain did not bear the ethnic names as separate items, though of course it had many as adjuncts to the cantonal capitals. Correspondences between the military map's ethnic names (as preserved by Ptolemy) and those of *Ravenna* (misread as place-names) are set out below, the forms being the notional Latin ones which can be assumed to have figured on the map.

(Ptolemy's sections)	Military map as known from Ptolemy	Ravenna
II, 3, 5	*Novante	—
II, 3, 6	*Selgoves	Segloes 108_{20}
II, 3, 7	*Damnoni	Daunoni 108_{20}
	*(V)otadini	Volitanio 107_{52} ?
II, 3, 8	*Epidi	Ebio 107_{40} ?
	*Creones	Credigone 107_{56}
	*Carnonace	—
	*Cerini	Cerma 108_{2}, Cermium 108_{11}
	*Cornavi	—
	*Caledones	Lodone 108_{6}
	*Decante	Decha 108_{8} ?
	*Lugi	—
	*Smerti	Smetri 107_{36}
	*Vacomagi	Maromago 107_{42} ?
II, 3, 9	*Venicones	Venutio 107_{43} ?
	*Texali	—

The tribes not copied into *Ravenna* among these sixteen names are minor ones to whom Ptolemy assigned no *polis* or only one *polis*: *Novantae*, *Carnonacae*, *Cornavii*, *Lugi*, *Taexali*, and may have been omitted for that reason from the map when it was revised (see below), or perhaps these tribes had been absorbed into larger units by the time the map was revised; certainly history heard no more of them, and none has left any trace of itself in later toponymy. For justification of the equations made, see the Alphabetic List. The initial *V-* of *Votadini*, omitted in all MSS of Ptolemy and therefore almost certainly omitted in his archetype, may have been left out by error of Marinus (see the Alphabetic List for a different reason suggested by Williams). It will also be noted that adjustments were made in the declensional forms of some of the tribal names when the map was revised: the original forms, as preserved by Marinus and Ptolemy, were *Selgovae*, *Caledonii* and *Smertae*, but *Ravenna*'s record shows that eventually the map set them down with changes as above. Such changes are paralleled in Britain and abroad; see ATREBATES in the Alphabetic List.

As for the *poleis*, the following close correspondences emerge between the military map (again known to us from Ptolemy) and *Ravenna*:

(Ptolemy's sections)	Military map as known from Ptolemy	Ravenna
II, 3, 5	*Novante*	—
	Lucopibia	Lucotion 107_{37} ?
	Rerigonium	Brigomono 107_{39} ?
II, 3, 6	*Selgoves*	*Segloes* 108_{20}
	Carbantorigum	Carbantium 107_{33}
	Uxellum	Uxela 107_{37}
	Corda	Corda 107_{38}
	Trimontium	Trimuntium 107_{44}
II, 3, 7	*Damnoni*	*Daunoni* 108_{20}
	Colania	Colanica 107_{54}
	Vindogara	Brocara 107_{30} ?
	Coria	Cibra 107_{56} ?
	Alauna	Litana 107_{55} ?
	Lindum	Clindum 107_{32}
	Victoria	Victorie 108_{11}
	Votadini	*Volitanio* 107_{52} ?
	Coria	Coritiotar 107_{41} ?
	Alauna	Alauna 107_{46}
	Bremenium	Bremenium 107_{45}
II, 3, 8	*Vacomagi*	*Maromago* 107_{42} ?
	Bannatia	—
	Tameia	Tagea 108_{12} ?
	Pinnata (Castra)	Pinnatis 108_{5}
	Tuesis	Tuessis 108_{5}
II, 3, 9	*Venicones*	*Venutio* 107_{43} ?
	Orrea	Poreo Classis 108_{10}
	Texali	—
	Devana	Devoni 108_{7}

Here one can see a certain logic in *Ravenna*'s order, but it amounts to logic within a region, not to a following of Ptolemy's textual order nor to a following of stations on roads, which of course were few in these parts. There is, however, one truly logical section, that in which *Ravenna* lists the *poleis* of the *Selgoves* in the same order as Ptolemy, no doubt because both were there following a stretch of road in the same direction as shown on a map; but *Ravenna* adds names, either later settlements which were not early forts, or places on branch roads, or a mixture of the two.

There is a further curious feature or set of features which shows *Ravenna* coinciding with Ptolemy in the use made of the military map: the errors they have in common. Both Ptolemy and *Ravenna* have *Corda*, which we think is a mistake for **Coria* (of the Selgovae). They coincide in having *Damnoni* – *Ravenna*'s *Daunoni* is from **Dannoni*, *Damnoni* – for correct *Dumnonii*. With *Ravenna*'s *Colanica* there coincides one branch of Ptolemy MSS which has Κολάνικα (= *Colanica*), for *Colania*.

It is clear that the 'second' map for northern Britain was basically Flavian but received important additions before it achieved final form (that in which it became known to the Cosmographer, much later). These were:

1. Tribal names in new declensions, as mentioned above.

2. One important new ethnic name, **Pecti*, if this is represented by *Pexa* 107_{53}; this – see below – might be the earliest record of this name.

3. The line of the Antonine Wall, *recto tramite*, with several forts named on it. However, the only name which we can be sure (from epigraphic evidence) applies to such a fort is *Velunia* (Carriden) which *Ravenna* places first in what purports to be a group of ten names (107_{52}); several of the others may be fort-names, but we cannot be sure, and several certainly are not (see our discussion of this section, below). *Velunia* is definitely an addition to the map, for the only occupation attested so far at Carriden is of the Antonine period. The Cosmographer misread some names as though they were forts of the Antonine Wall because they were written adjacent to it on the map.

4. Many place-names of Scotland both south and north of the Antonine Wall. These were not necessarily, as Ptolemy's names had been, those of first-century Roman forts; some may have been names of later forts (e.g. *Velunia*), but others are presumably native settlements. There is no evidence here or in the separate section of *diversa loca*, which was completely misinterpreted by R&C, about Roman organisation north of Hadrian's Wall in the fourth century.

This rich new information, the gathering of names for small places north of the Antonine Wall, and the preservation of it after this Wall was abandoned late in the second century, can hardly have responded to disinterested geographical inquiry, and we know of no successor to Ptolemy who could have undertaken it. The obvious motive is military need, and it may be suggested with some confidence that the old Flavian military map was modernised, enlarged and improved during the Scottish campaigns of Severus in A.D. 208–11. All the northern British information in *Ravenna* could have been gathered at that time, and none is obviously posterior to it. One notes that the names of northern rivers and islands are more numerous than those acquired by Ptolemy following the Agricolan naval expeditions, and must reflect a later and more consolidated body of knowledge obtained by the Roman fleet and perhaps by traders (though we do not know, of course, whether Ptolemy in fact used all the information available to him); again, the impetus to set this down on a map would have been present in the time of Severus.

Such is the degree of corruption of many North British names that we should not attribute all of it to the Cosmographer and his scribes. As can be seen from the above list of *poleis*, the map's assumed original names (as known to us from Ptolemy) were preserved quite well by the Cosmographer – who even copied with a correctness not habitual in him the map's four names in *-um*[1] – but the tribal names

[1] It may be that endings provide an important clue about the two sets of names (those of the original Flavian map, and those added to it at the Severan modernisation). Feminines are not capable of being differentiated, since *-a* served for both nominative and oblique case (*-am* is very rare in the Cosmography); but neuters and probably the few masculine names show both *-um* and *-o* in quantity. We know that Ptolemy always cites names in the

were probably already corrupt on the map, and the newly added place-names are sometimes impenetrably corrupt. Moreover, the Antonine Wall fort-names were so carelessly set down that the Cosmographer's eye confused adjacent names with them, and even then the map gave him only ten names for what were nineteen or twenty forts. The Severan map did not have, then, the clear qualities of the Flavian original. In any case, it is unlikely that the Cosmographer had before him an actual Severan map; he would have had a copy perhaps made much later, adding a further stage of corruption (perhaps, for example, *Decãte* in a script which abbreviated *n* in some situations, since this helps to explain *Ravenna*'s *Decha* 108_8).

At some stage – possibly when the Severan map was made, possibly much later as a copy of it was made (in Ravenna?), certain northern British information from Ptolemy was added to the map. Where this Greek information was properly latinised we cannot identify it, because it is inseparable from the existing Latin information. Where, however, it was carelessly and ignorantly latinised, we can identify it. One extraordinary instance is the entry *Eirimon* 109_{23} (= R&C 300), which originated in the Greek adjective which Ptolemy attached to mention of two islands at II, 2, 10, Ἄδρου (= *Adru*) and Λίμνου (= *Limnu*). The adjective ἔρημος means 'deserted, uninhabited', and was simply transposed into Latin letters without being translated as it should have been – presumably because the man who was copying and notionally improving the map did not recognise the Greek for what it was. Even more startling is the possibility that Ptolemy's Πτερωτὸν στρατόπεδον of II, 3, 8 was transcribed in the same way into Latin letters and entered on the North British map in a form which has come down to us – no doubt with further miscopying – as the *Stodoion Sinetriadum* of 107_{31-32}, producing a duplication of the original Flavian (and purely Latin) *Pinnata Castra* which the Severan map had as *Pinnata* and which the Cosmographer copied as *Pinnatis* at 108_5 (see, for our reasoning, *Pinnata Castra* in the Alphabetic List). Possibly other hitherto unidentified North British entries in *Ravenna* will respond to similar investigation; see further below, 'Linguistic Considerations', and the views of Dillemann.

For the opening section of twenty-four names in south-west Britain we must postulate a third source. Few of these can be identified with certainty, and with the exception of Exeter all the places must have been small, though the name of Bath probably lies concealed. The density of names known here to the Cosmographer is greater than in any other part of Britain. Since there were few Roman roads west

---

nominative, and we may take it that such was the practice of the classically-minded maker(s) of the first-century Flavian map of North Britain: hence it might be possible to argue that the North British names in *-um* (and *-on*, representing *-um*), which are numerous, are those of the forts and camps of the Agricolan campaign, whereas those in *-o* are of second-century and Severan origin and were entered on the map with the more colloquial oblique termination. However, it may be that the Cosmographer's system is not to be trusted to this extent, and in any case there is an exception, since (if we are right in the equation) Ptolemaic *Rerigonium* = *Ravenna*'s *Brigomono*. It is perhaps also significant that within the Roman province, the names of the cantonal capitals always have the tribal name correctly with genitive plural *-orum* or *-um*, never *-on* (except *Venta Velgarom*, which at least still has its *-m*); this might indicate an early source carefully preserved.

of Exeter, it is unlikely that these names were present on the 'first' map, which was based on the road-system. It is possible that they were derived from some list kept for administrative purposes, and R&C made out a case for the two *Statio* names being those of taxation offices. There are, however, two indications that after all a map was being used. *Vertevia* 106_1 and *Mestevia* 106_3 are miscopied versions of **(Anti)vesteum*, that is Ptolemy's *Antivestaeum* (Land's End); this strongly suggests a map, and a Ptolemaic one, in which **Anti* was written above the rest of the name (or on the sea) and then omitted by the Cosmographer. The other indication of a map is that this section figures first in the Cosmographer's survey of Britain because it was the lower corner of an island portrayed as a triangle and was the part most adjacent to the Continent, in a deformed representation, making an obvious starting-point.

These three sources, then, are the minimum that one needs to postulate. Their quality and dates are diverse, but the Cosmographer managed to impose a reasonable unity upon them. He might have been aided a little if he had had the use of *AI*, but some of the information which this gives was available to him in visual form on the fourth-century road-map. It is clear that he did not know *ND* – which originated in Ravenna or Rome – for he had no systematic knowledge of late Roman military dispositions in Britain; from *ND* he would have obtained a better listing of the forts of Hadrian's Wall, and a knowledge of the forts of the Saxon Shore (he names five of these out of the nine or ten which existed, but does not put them into a series, and his information could relate to early forts or habitation at these places). However, the relatively complete coverage which the Cosmographer gave Britain, and the relative wealth of his information (compared with Gaul), led Miller in 1916 (cols. 1–3) to think that for Britain *Ravenna* did not depend upon any itinerary but was undertaking 'einer systematischer Beschreibung des Landes', whose six sections corresponded to the five provinces (presumably of Theodosius's arrangement after A.D. 368) plus a sixth area of *Britannia barbara* north of the Antonine Wall. Miller confidently identifies the provinces: *Britannia Prima*, that is south-west Britain with Exeter as its capital; *Britannia Secunda*, that is Wales and the Marches with Caerleon and Wroxeter as capitals; and so on. But it is at once apparent that this is to use the six divisions of *Ravenna* in a thoroughly arbitrary way. We do not know what the boundaries of the late provinces were, nor, for certain, which were their capitals, nor where *Valentia* was. The only definite piece of evidence is the statue-base from Cirencester which shows that this was in *Britannia Prima* (*RIB* 103) – and, it is conjectured, its capital – whereas *Ravenna* places *Corinium* 106_{31} firmly in the middle of its second section, upsetting Miller's notion. There is probably nothing worth retaining in this idea, and we do not need to think that the Cosmographer was making any sort of 'systematic description' from sources unknown to us, except, naturally, that the road-map as principal source was superior to the *TP* 'of Castorius' in which Miller placed so much faith.

As for the use which the Cosmographer made of his sources, his omissions and duplications tell us a good deal. If we assume that any respectable road-map would have had routes equivalent to the important Itinera II, VI and VIII of *AI*, we find that *Ravenna* omits most of Iter II in its central and southern English portions, most of Iter VI and virtually all Iter VIII. There are omissions too from Iter XII (Carmarthen to Wroxeter) and from Itinera xiii and xiv (both Caerleon to Silchester), while the eastern counties (Itinera v and ix) are somewhat neglected also. It is true that often the Cosmographer says he is listing merely *aliquantas civitates*, but he lists the places of some districts – especially in the Midlands and north of England – with what must be near completeness (that is, with regard to his source) and is curiously inattentive at other times. If we look at the matter in another way, we find that *Ravenna* omits several places which figure in three Itinera of *AI* – ii, vi and viii – and which as road-junctions ought to have been prominent to his eye as he worked from his map: *Bannaventa*[1], *Durocobrivis*, *Magiovinium* and *Venonis*. It is possible that some of *Ravenna's* seeming omissions may not be omissions at all, the places concerned lying instead concealed in impenetrably corrupt forms; but in the above cases and in others it seems that the Cosmographer's haphazardly selective methods are to blame. He did not, after all, know Britain or most of the provinces he describes, and he was ignorant of much that seems obvious to us (e.g. in taking *Tamese* 106_{38} as a habitation-name). There are fewer omissions of river-names than R&C thought (pp. 15–16), since a number have now been found concealed (like *Tamese*) in the lists of places, and others are present in the lists of *diversa loca* and even of islands, so poor was the Cosmographer's comprehension of what he found on his maps.

Duplications are of two kinds. The first, recognised by R&C only in the case of *Epocessa–Ypocessa*, occurs when the compiler realised he had miscopied a name and wrote it again differently, immediately after (in one case next but one), failing each time to delete the former attempt. These are:

Epocessa 106_{28} – Ypocessa 106_{28}
Calunio 107_{1} – Gallunio 107_{1}
Leviodanum 108_{9} – Levioxaua 108_{10}
Intraum 108_{34} – Antrum 108_{34}

These seem to have no significance beyond showing us the compiler wrestling with a difficult script, or perhaps in *Ypo-* thinking that he recognised a Greek root. The second category is of greater interest:

Vertevia 106_{1} – Mestevia 106_{3}
Melamoni 106_{2} – Milidunum 106_{4} and
Moridunum 106_{9} – Morionio 106_{13}
Alauna 106_{9} – Alauna 106_{14}
Coloneas 106_{14} – Glebon Colonia 106_{29}
Noviomagno 106_{17} – Navimago Regentium 106_{20}
Aramis 106_{15} – Armis 106_{19}
Durobrabis 106_{37} – Brinavis 106_{39}
Landini 106_{38} – Londinium Augusti 106_{50}
Mediomano 106_{41} – Mediolano 106_{43}
Maio 107_{5} – Maia 107_{29} (also ? Maiona 109_{22})
Gabaglanda 107_{11} – Cambroianna 107_{36}
Coccime(da) 107_{45} – Coguve(usuron) 108_{38}
Cerma 108_{2} – Cermium 108_{11}
Leuca 108_{29} – Leugo(sena) 108_{30}
(Leugo)sena 108_{30} – Senua 108_{41}

These duplications affect all parts of the list (though rare in North Britain), and all kinds of names, including one cape, three rivers and one ethnic name. At times there is a curious rhythm: in the early part of the table above, the repetition occurs in eight instances two, three, four or five points after the first mention. This makes one think that the Cosmographer was fitting together two different sources in which names were listed in roughly the same order – perhaps he had not one but two versions of his road-map. It is just possible that he had only one map, and in tracing his way round it with a finger in no systematic way returned to a place and wrote it again; but it is hard to imagine anyone of the slightest intelligence not realising that he was doing so, and adjusting accordingly. Some of the pairs diverge so much in spelling that the notion of two sources seems to impose itself; they had scripts of different types and misled the Cosmographer in different ways. One source listed the compound names as one-line items (*Glebon Colonia*, *Durobrabis*), the other listed them with elements separated one above the other, leading the compiler to take only one part when he repeated the name. One source had simply *Londini* (*Landini*), the other *Londinium Augusta*. One spelled *Horrea* thus, the other without *H-* (these are names of distinct places). One had city-names only (like *TP*), *Noviomagno*; the other regularly gave the tribal name, *Navimago Regentium*. And so on: other features would emerge if other possible duplications, more tendentious than those listed above, were brought into play. Repetitions in the British section seem much to exceed those found in other sections, a sign that the Cosmographer had for Britain more diverse sources than he had for those other sections; but it is also possible that as he neared the end of his work, a certain tiredness and increased carelessness overcame him, leading to the otherwise wholly inexplicable fourfold mention of *Moridunum*[1]. A link in this instance with *TP* as a source should not be ruled out, for it is notable that on the small surviving part of Britain this place with Exeter alone figures among south-western names in what looks like an isolated depiction, and both may thus have assumed an unwarranted prominence in the Cosmographer's eyes.

5. LINGUISTIC CONSIDERATIONS

The Cosmographer wrote a rather pedestrian Latin, not without an occasional indulgence in elaboration and rhetorical flourish derived from his ecclesiastical training. Schnetz (1942, pp. 24–29) is firm in asserting that his work as it has come down to us is not a Latin translation of a text originally composed in Greek, an opinion current in Mommsen's day and in part adopted for the British Section by R&C in 1949. They claimed that the British list had some connection with a Greek source during its transmission to *Ravenna*, since 'No fewer than 25 names from all parts of the [British] list still retain a Greek inflexion or case-ending.' This illustrates the danger of considering the British section as something apart from the rest of the Cosmography, for vaguely Greek-seeming forms occur sporadically throughout it. The only place in which Schnetz allows a Greek source is (naturally enough) for that part of *Ravenna* which describes Greek-speaking areas, in which such miscopyings as that of Λ for Δ could arise, as mentioned above. No such miscopying in Greek letters needs to be assumed for any British name (see e.g. *Itunocelum*). There was, however, according to Dillemann (p. 64) occasionally an 'insertion – often ancient – of Greek materials into Latin sources', and we have discussed two instances of this above. Dillemann's further opinion that names with *okelon* are using a Greek element 'and probably came from Greek seafarers at an unknown time' (p. 65) is unwarranted, since **ocelo-* is a British word known also in other Celtic regions of the Continent.[1] The erroneous opinion about a fully Greek original of the Cosmography arose because of the presence of numerous names in all its parts which end in *-on*, and was by no means illogical when the text had been composed in a city subject to strong Greek influence from A.D. 568, and when such graecisms as *chersonesum* and *(he)micosmin* regularly appear in it. Schnetz's explanation of this *-on*, which affects both masculine accusative and neuter names of the second declension, and which to some extent alternates with other instances of the same names in *-o* and *-um* when these are repeated, is based on the evolution of sounds in late Latin. Final *-m* of accusatives had long been silent, and in the Romance speech of the compiler it was probably already represented in monosyllables by *-n* (CŬM > *con*, SŬM > *son* in Old Italian), a change already noted by a grammarian of Trajan's time. The development of *ŭ* > *o* was also ancient, with isolated examples from as early as the second century B.C. The resulting uncertainties of both vowel and consonant aided the fusion of neuter with masculine words within the second declension (e.g. PRATUM > masculine *il prato*, *el prado*, *le pré*). Schnetz concludes that the Cosmographer in many cases allowed the writing of his work to be influenced by the Romance speech-habits of his region as they were about A.D. 700. He adopted Vulgar Latin *-o* and made a half-gesture towards proper latinity by often using the final *-n* which was still heard in monosyllables, producing the Greek-seeming *-on*, but he did neither consistently, since forms in *-o* and also *-um* abound too. If it be pointed out that the *-on* forms appear only in the lists of names, never in the narrative prose, the reason is either that the Cosmographer wrote his connected Latin with more care, or that later in the Middle Ages scribes possessed of a purer latinity corrected all the writer's *-on* forms to *-um*, but were naturally unable to restore the classical forms of place-names because they did not know them.

The writing of *-um* as *-on* is not the sole indication of the ways in which the Cosmographer's Romance speech-habits affected his writing. Among other cases to which Schnetz draws attention are (pp. 29–32) *Artemida* 22_{13} for *Artemita* (*TP*), showing voicing of *t* > *d*; *Segutione* 66_{31} for *Segusione* (*TP*), a hypercorrection which acknowledges the assibilation of /*tj*/ in Vulgar Latin; and *Briptonum* 3_{58} beside *Britonum* 5_{21}, another hypercorrection which shows that already *pt* > *t* in Latin (e.g. SEPTEM > *sette*, *siete*). Beyond this, Schnetz affirms (pp. 33–34) that Vulgar Latin

[1] As noted earlier, Dillemann has good evidence for Carniola of the use of a Greek source at some stage, with miscopyings of Greek letters that explain some strange Latin forms. In other parts of his paper on Britain he hankers after Greek influence, partly in the source but also, it seems, in the naming process. In the name *Metambala* he wishes to see an involvement of Greek *metabolè* (p. 67); in *Pampocalia*, which we explain (with R&C) as a conflation, he thinks he sees Greek *calia* 'dwelling' (p. 69); and of *Abisson* and *Duabsisis* he observes that 'both derive just as well from the Greek *abyssos* as they do from a Celtic root' (p. 69). These suggestions are in our view completely erroneous, unless it is being suggested that compiler or scribe assimilated some British names to Greek elements, as is possible.

developments within *Ravenna*'s diverse sources can often be recognised. A clear case is the duplication of *Rubricatum* 79_8 with *Lubricatum* 87_{20}; the former, meaning 'red river' (strictly, 'reddened [river]'), is the original name, while the latter shows the dissimilation *r-r* > *l-r* which survives in the modern name of this river in Catalonia, Llobregat. This is not a scribal error nor a scribal metathesis, and is not a change caused by the Cosmographer's own speech, but could only have come from his Hispanic source. Schnetz happens to give no examples from the British section, but they are readily supplied. They embrace such typical Vulgar Latin changes as *e* for *ae* (*Cesaromago* 106_{51}), *-s* for *-x* (*Deva Victris* 106_{44}), and simplification of geminated consonants (*Avalana* 107_{29}) or variation in these (*Uxelis* 106_1, *Uxelludamo* 107_{28}). The fifth-century assibilation of *c* and *t* plus yod, /*kj*/ and /*tj*/, is documented by *Ravenna* in its form *Aquis Arnemeza* 106_{57} (for *-tiae*) and others gathered in this entry in the Alphabetic List, and there are Continental parallels (e.g. *Dizezeia* 62_{19} = *Decetia* of *AI* 367_1); but British forms showing this assibilation owe it to the writer's Romance speech and not to Vulgar Latin in Britain, which could hardly have shown this development before the end of Imperial rule. The same applies to the common *b*/*v* equivalences, since it seems that in the Latin of Britain the distinction between these was always maintained on the whole.

6. ERRORS OF COPYING

The above errors of forms which had evolved in Vulgar Latin are not to be confused with errors due to simple miscopying, whether by the Cosmographer or by his later scribes. These are extraordinarily numerous. Schnetz wrestles (pp. 37–49) with the kinds of error involved, and can often show how they arose in the copying process. He gives no British examples, but it is worth summarising typical features, partly as a guide for those who wish to undertake detective work among the remaining unresolved corruptions. What follows is built up exclusively on variations in the same names in the three extant MSS, and on forms which we know to be entirely sound; it would naturally be improper to argue on the basis of forms which are in themselves tendentious.

Consonants

b/*r* Cactabactonion 107_{14}
Birila = Ririla (MS C)
c/*g* Coganges 107_{17}
Bindogladia 106_{17}
(perhaps influenced by V.L. voicing of *c* > *g*)
cl/*d* Terdec 109_5 = Terclec (MS A)
Daroecla 109_{20} = Daroeda (MS A), Doroeda (MS C)
c/*t* Coantia 108_{30} = Coancia (MS C)
(perhaps influenced by V.L. assibilation of /kį/ and /tį/)
Decuaria 107_{15}
ch/*m* Manulodulo 106_{52}
ct/*t* Cactabactonion 107_{14} (via *-tt-* ?)
Lectoceto 106_{48}

d/t Statio 105_{51} = Stadio (MS A)
(cf. Evidensca 107_{47} for *(H)avitanco)
(perhaps influenced by V.L. voicing of *t* > *d*)
D-/P Decuaria 107_{15}
Purocoronavis 105_{48}
l/r Valteris 107_{9} (but perhaps a phonetic dissimilation *r-r* > *l-r*)
Melamoni 106_{2}, Milidunum 106_{4}
m/r Venta Cenomum 106_{54}
m/v Mestevia 106_{3}
n/v/u Nauione 106_{56} = Nanione (MS B)
Avalana 107_{29}
r/s Vertevia 106_{1}
r/t Lutudaron 106_{45} = Lutudaton (MS C)
Scoream 108_{48} (for Scotiam)

Consonants with vowels

inn/um Pinnatis 108_{5} = Pumatis (MS C)
ini/un Trimuntium 107_{44} = Triminitium (MS A)
ium/umi Lagubalumi 107_{10} = Lagubalium (MS C)
m/ni Clavinio 106_{12} = Clavimo (MS A)
Salinis 106_{31} = Salmis (MS A)
Venta Velgarom 106_{18} = Venta Velgaroni (MS B)
m/vi Durolavi 108_{37} = Durolam (MS A)
mi/nu Aramis 106_{15} = Aranus (MS B)
(or: virtually any combination of *m-n-i-u-v* was liable to be miscopied)

Consonants/vowels

l/i Melezo 106_{16} = Meiezo (MS B)
Iacio Dulma 106_{49}
t/i Iacio Dulma 106_{49}
-a/-is Uxelis 106_{1}

Vowels

a/e Vindolande 107_{12}
Victorie 108_{11}
a/i Vernalis 105_{49} = Vernilis (MSS A, C)
Cantiventi 107_{2} = Cantaventi (MS A)
a/o Mediolano 106_{43} = Mediolana (MS A)
Calunio 107_{1} = Colunio (MS C)
e/i Medibogdo 107_{2} = Medebogdo (MS C)
e/o Stene 105_{52} = Steno (MSS A, C)
Tinoa 108_{35} = Tinea (MS A)
i/u Lugunduno 107_{17} = Lugundino (MSS B, C)

Intrusion of letter

Litinomago 108_{6} = Lintinomago (MS C)
Bindogladia 106_{17} = Blindogladia (MS C)

Wrong division

Melamon(i) → Scadum namorum 106_2
Ventaslurum 106_{22} = uentas lurum (MS A)
Camulo dono 106_{59}
Glebon. colonia 106_{29}
Leugosena 108_{30}

Omission of initial letter(s)

Bannio 106_{25} for Gobannio
(cf. in Gaul, Arascone 63_{42} for Tarascone
Urdunno 64_{11} for Turdunno)

Omission of interior letter(s)

Fanocodi 107_{30} = Fanococidi (MSS A, C)
Bdora 108_{32}
Caleba Arbatium 106_{32}

Scribal metathesis

Cironium 106_{31} (= Corinium)
Termonin 106_3 (= Terminon, for Terminum)
Condecor 107_{24} (for Conderco)
Durbis 108_{38} = Dubris 106_{35}

7. THE TEXT

We reproduce the British sections from the edition of Schnetz (1940), dividing it in order to insert a commentary after each part. The main divisions number six, with four islands listed in a preliminary way and a concluding list of islands, presented in two groups, probably including non-British material. The text of the British section as printed by R&C in 1949 is, as noted earlier, too correct and thus misleading. Their division of it into neat small sections each with an editorial heading and with numeration (e.g. 'The West Country, to Exeter. 1–16'; 'Exeter to the North-East. 17–22') gives no idea of the relative lack of organisation in the text as conserved in the MSS and presented by Schnetz.

Variants are not entered here but are (where significant) given for each name in the Alphabetic List. The names offered in the second column are forms to be assumed in the source used by the Cosmographer; they are to some extent notional and do not always correspond to the original or classical forms under which the names are studied in the Alphabetic List. The intention is to show what may have been in the sources and what copying errors the Cosmographer (rather than later scribes of the MSS) may have been responsible for. Hence a good many vulgar forms, oblique cases and non-classical spellings (like those recorded by *AI*, *TP*, etc.) are used. In the third column are identifications, where possible. All textual material is printed in roman, non-textual material in italic (or enclosed within parentheses).

The numeration is that of Schnetz (who prints the names in pairs, and two columns to the page), with that of R&C added in parentheses.

v. 30 (*end*)

Iterum sunt in ipso oceano [insule] que dicuntur

105_{29} (303)	Vectis	**Vectis*	*Wight*
105_{29} (304)	Malaca	**Malaia* ?	*Mull*
105_{30} (305)	Insenos	**Ins. Senos*	*Ile de Sein* (*France*)
105_{30} (306)	Taniatide	**Tanatide*	*Thanet*

(The 'oceano' is defined a few lines earlier: 'in ipso oceano septentrionali'. It is hard to see what could have grouped these scattered islands in the Cosmographer's mind; on his map-source they were too vaguely positioned for him to relate three of them properly to Britain. None is repeated in the concluding lists of islands.)

v. 31

In oceano vero occidentale est insula quae dicitur Britania, ubi olim gens Saxonum veniens ab antiqua Saxonia cum principe suo Ansehis modo havitare videtur;[1] quamvis insulam, ut diximus, quidam Grecorum phylosophi quasi [i]micosmin appellaverunt; nam nos tam magnam insulam neque in supra scripto Mari Magno neque in praefato oceano dilatissimo neque in quo praediximus sino oceani legendam nullo modo reperimus.

In qua Britania plurimas fuisse legimus civitates [et castra], ex quibus aliquantas designare volumus, id est

105_{46} (1)	Giano	**Glano*	—
105_{46} (2)	Eltabo	**Fl Tavo*	*R. Taw* (*N. Devon*)
105_{47} (3)	Elconio	**Fl Cenio*	—
105_{47} (4)	Nemetotacio	**Nemeto Statio*	*North Tawton* (*Devon*)
105_{48} (5)	Tamaris	**Tamara*	—
105_{48} (6)	Purocoronavis	**Durocornovio*	—
105_{49} (7)	Pilais	?	—
105_{49} (8)	Vernalis	**Vernalis*	—
105_{50} (9)	Ardua }	**Fl Derventione* ?	*R. Dart* (*Devon*)
105_{50} (9)	Ravenatone }		
105_{51} (10)	Devionisso }	**Devionisso Statio*	—
105_{51} (10–11)	Statio }		
105_{51} (11)	Deventia }	**Derventio Statio*	—
105_{52} (11)	Stene }		
105_{52} (12)	Duriarno	**Durnovaria*	*Dorchester*
106_{1} (13)	Uxelis	**Uxela*	—
106_{1} (14)	Vertevia	*(*Anti*)*vesteum*	*Land's End*
106_{2} (15)	Melamoni	**Moriduno*	*Sidford* (*Devon*) ?
106_{2} (16)	Scadu namorum	**Isca Dumnoniorum*	*Exeter*
106_{3} (17)	Termonin	**Terminum*	—
106_{3} (18)	Mestevia	*(*Anti*)*vesteum*	*Land's End*

[1] No one seems to have drawn attention to this mention of Hengist. The only variant noted for the name by Schnetz is *ansehys*; R&C put *Anschis* in their text.

106_4	(19)	Milidunum	**Moridunum*	*Sidford* ?
106_4	(20)	Apaunaris	**Aque Sulis* ?	*Bath*
106_5	(21)	Masona	?	—
106_5	(22)	Alovergium	**Alobergium*	—

(This first group consists mainly of names in Devon and Cornwall. It could be said that the only utterly safe identification is that of Exeter, but other restorations and consequent identifications seem reasonable. The names of three rivers and one cape were misread from his map by the Cosmographer, all these presumably having their names written 'inland' and leading him to take them as places. *Fl Cenio* is probably duplicated by *Cunis* at 109_{11}; the version of *(*Anti*)*vesteum* is duplicated; and **Moriduno* or **Moridunum* appears four times in all, twice here and twice in the next group, the form with *-dunum* indicating use of a different source. The names of Dorchester and Bath, otherwise missing from *Ravenna*, were evidently written on the map in a way which took them far to the west, and the compiler took the names as applying to places at their western rather than eastern ends. For discussion of the special source which this group had, and the reason why the Cosmographer began here, see above (p. 197).)

Iterum iuxta super scriptam civitatem Scadoniorum est civitas quae dicitur

106_9	(23)	Moriduno	**Moriduno*	*Sidford* ?
106_9	(24)	Alauna silva	**Alauna*	—
106_{10}	(25)	Omire	**Sorvio doni* ?	*Old Sarum*
106_{10}	(25)	Tedertis	**Re...* ?	—
106_{11}	(26)	Lindinis	**Lindinis*	*Ilchester*
106_{11}	(27)	Canza	**Cantia*	—
106_{12}	(28)	Dolocindo	**Durocinto* ?	—
106_{12}	(29)	Clavinio	**Glevum* ?	*Gloucester*
106_{13}	(30)	Morionio	**Moriduno*	*Sidford* ?
106_{13}	(31)	Bolvelaunio	**Bolvelaunio*	—
106_{14}	(32)	Alauna	**Alauna*	—
106_{14}	(33)	Coloneas	**Colonia*	*Gloucester*
106_{15}	(34)	Aramis	**Armis*	*R. Erme*
106_{15}	(35)	Anicetis	**Anicetis*	—
106_{16}	(36)	Melezo	**Meletio*	—
106_{16}	(37)	Ibernio	**Ivernio*	—
106_{17}	(38)	Bindogladia	**Vindocladia*	*Badbury*
106_{17}	(39)	Noviomagno	**Noviomago*	*Chichester*
106_{18}	(40)	Onna	**Onna*	—
106_{18}	(41)	Venta Velgarom	**Venta Belgarum*	*Winchester*
106_{19}	(42)	Armis	**Armis*	*R. Erme*
106_{19}	(43)	Ardaoneon	**Ardaonium* ?	*Portchester*
106_{20}	(44)	Navimago	**Noviomago*	*Chichester*
106_{20}	(44)	Regentium	*Reginorum*	
106_{21}	(45)	Leuco magno	**Leucomago*	*East Anton* ?
106_{21}	(46)	Cunetzone	**Cunetione*	*Mildenhall*
106_{22}	(47)	Punctuobice	**Portu Abone*	*Sea Mills*
106_{22}	(48)	Ventaslurum	**Venta Silurum*	*Caerwent*
106_{23}	(49)	Iupania	**Lupania* ?	

106_{23} (50)	Metambala	**Nemetobala* ?	*Lydney* ?
106_{24} (51)	Albinumno	**Albiniano*	—
106_{24} (52)	Isca Augusta	**Isca Augusta*	Caerleon
106_{25} (53)	Bannio	**Gobannio*	*Abergavenny*
106_{25} (54)	Bremia	**Bremia*	*Llanio*
106_{26} (55)	Alabum	**Alabum*	*Llandovery* ?
106_{26} (56)	Cicutio	**Cicucio*	*Brecon Gaer* ?
106_{27} (57)	Magnis	**Magnis*	*Kenchester*
106_{27} (58)	Brano. Genium.	**Branogenium*	*Leintwardine*
106_{28} (59)	Epocessa	**Eposessa*	—
106_{28} (60)	Ypocessa	**Eposessa*	—
106_{29} (61)	Macatonion	**Magalonium* ?	—
106_{29} (62)	Glebon. colonia	**Glevum colonia*	*Gloucester*
106_{30} (63)	Argistillum	**Argistillum*	—
106_{30} (64)	Vertis	?	*Worcester*
106_{31} (65)	Salinis	**Salinis*	*Droitwich*
106_{31} (66)	Cironium Dobunorum	**Corinium Dobunnorum*	*Cirencester*
106_{32} (67)	Caleba. Arbatium	**Calleva Atrebatum*	*Silchester*
106_{33} (68)	Anderelio	**Anderito*	*Pevensey*
106_{34} (68)	Nuba	**Nova*	*R. Adur* ?
106_{34} (69)	Mutuantonis	**Fl Trisantona*	*R. Arun*
106_{35} (70)	Lemanis	**Lemanis*	*Lympne*
106_{35} (71)	Dubris	**Dubris*	*Dover*
106_{36} (72)	Duro averno Cantiacorum	**Duroverno Cantiacorum*	*Canterbury*
106_{36} (73)	Rutupis	**Rutupis*	*Richborough*
106_{37} (74)	Durobrabis	**Durobrivis*	*Rochester*
106_{38} (75)	Landini	**Londini*	*London*
106_{38} (76)	Tamese	**Tamese*	*R. Thames*
106_{39} (77)	Brinavis	**(Duro)brivis*	*Rochester*
106_{39} (78)	Alauna	**Alauna*	*Alcester* (*Warwicks*) ?
106_{40} (79)	Utriconion Cornoviorum	**Viriconium Cornoviorum*	*Wroxeter*
106_{40} (80)	Lavobrinta	**Lavobrinta*	—
106_{41} (81)	Mediomano	**Mediolano*	*Whitchurch*
106_{42} (82)	Seguntio	**Segontio*	*Caernarvon*
106_{43} (83)	Canubio	**Canovio*	*Caerhun*
106_{43} (84)	Mediolano	**Mediolano*	*Whitchurch*
106_{44} (85)	Saudonio	[**Santonum*]	—
106_{44} (86)	Deva victris	*Deva Vitrix*	*Chester*
106_{45} (87)	Veratino	**Vernemeto*	*Willoughby*
106_{45} (88)	Lutudaron	**Lutudarum*	*Chesterfield* ?
106_{46} (89)	Derbentione	**Derventione*	*Littlechester*
106_{46} (90)	Salinis	**Salinis*	*Middlewich*
106_{47} (91)	Condate	**Condate*	*Northwich*
106_{47} (92)	Rate Corion	**Rate Coritanorum*	*Leicester*
106_{48} (93)	Eltauori	**Fl Tamum*	*R. Tame* (*Leics.*)
106_{48} (94)	Lectoceto	**Letoceto*	*Wall*
106_{49} (95)	Iacio Dulma	**Lactodoro*	*Towcester*
106_{50} (96)	Virolanium	**Verulamium*	*St Albans*

106_{50} (97)	Londinium Augusti	**Londinium Augusta*	*London*
106_{51} (98)	Cesaromago	**Cesaromago*	*Chelmsford*
106_{52} (99)	Manulodulo. colonia	**Camuloduno colonia*	*Colchester*
106_{52} (100)	Durcinate	**Durolipōte* ?	*Cambridge*
106_{53} (101)	Duro viguto	**Duro-* ?	*Godmanchester*
106_{54} (102)	Durobrisin	**Durobrivis*	*Water Newton*
106_{54} (103)	Venta Cenomum	**Venta Icenorum*	*Caistor St Edmund*
106_{55} (104)	Lindum colonia	**Lindum colonia*	*Lincoln*
106_{55} (105)	Bannovallum	**Bannovallum*	*Horncastle* ?
106_{56} (106)	Nauione	**Navione*	*Brough-on-Noe*
106_{57} (107)	Aquis Arnemeza	**Aquis Arnemetie*	*Buxton*
106_{58} (108)	Zerdotalia	**Ardotalia*	*Melandra Castle* ?
106_{58} (109)	Mantio	**Mamucio*	*Manchester*
106_{59} (110)	Alūna	**Alauna*	*Watercrook*
106_{59} (111)	Camulo dono	**Camuloduno*	*Slack* ?
107_{1} (112)	Calunio	**Galava*	*Ambleside*
107_{1} (113)	Gallunio	(*as above*)	(*as above*)
107_{2} (114)	Medibogdo	**Mediobogdo*	*Hardknott*
107_{2} (115)	Cantiventi	**Glannoventa*	*Ravenglass*
107_{3} (116)	Iuliocenon	**Itunocelum*	—
107_{3} (117)	Gabrocentio	**Gabrosento*	*Moresby* ?
107_{4} (118)	Alauna	**Alauna*	*Maryport*
107_{4} (119)	Bribra	**Bibra*	*Beckfoot* ?
107_{5} (120)	Maio	**Maio*	*Bowness*
107_{5} (121)	Olerica	**Olenaco*	*Elslack?*
107_{6} (122)	Derventione	**Derventione*	*Papcastle*
107_{6} (123)	Ravonia	**Bravoniaco*	*Kirkby Thore*
107_{7} (124)	Bresnetenaci Veteranorum	**Bremmetenaci Veteranorum*	*Ribchester*
107_{7} (125)	Pampocalia	**Campo(dunum)+ Calcaria*	*Leeds+Tadcaster*
107_{8} (126)	Lagentium	**Lagentium*	*Castleford*
107_{9} (127)	Valteris	**Verteris*	*Brough*
107_{10} (128)	Bereda	**Voreda*	*Old Penrith*
107_{10} (129)	Lagubalumi	**Luguvalium*	*Carlisle*
107_{11} (130)	Magnis	**Magnis*	*Carvoran*
107_{11} (131)	Gabaglanda	**Camboglanna*	*Castlesteads*
107_{12} (132)	Vindolande	**Vindolanda*	*Chesterholm*
107_{12} (133)	Lineoiugla	**Longovicio*	*Lanchester*
107_{13} (134)	Vinovia	**Vinovia*	*Binchester*
107_{13} (135)	Lavaris	**Lavatris*	*Bowes*
107_{14} (136)	Cactabactonion	**Cataractonium*	*Catterick*
107_{14} (137)	Eburacum	**Eburacum*	*York*
107_{15} (138)	Decuaria	**Petuaria*	*Brough-on-Humber*
107_{16} (139)	Devovicia	**Delgovicia*	*Wetwang* ?
107_{16} (140)	Dixio	**Dicto*	*Wearmouth* ?
107_{17} (140)	Lugunduno	**Luguduno*	—
107_{17} (141)	Coganges	**Concangis*	*Chester-le-Street*
107_{18} (142)	Corie Lopocarium	**Coriosopitum* ?	*Corbridge*

(This section is nearly the longest in the whole of the Cosmography, and it is clear that the source-map (of all the country up to Hadrian's Wall) gave the compiler no hint about how he might divide it – e.g. by provincial boundaries. Some eight subdivisions can be made out, but within each there is little logic and roads are hardly followed consistently. (1) A continued perambulation round the south-west from Exeter to Salisbury, with a return to *Moridunum* and a fairly straight progress through Dorset to Winchester, Chichester (twice) and then by leaps to South Wales, back to Kenchester and thence via Gloucester (again) to Silchester; (2) a surprising new beginning at Pevensey, perhaps because it was isolated and prominent on the source-map, then to Kent and London; (3) a new start at Wroxeter, a tour of North Wales, and a return via Cheshire and Derbyshire to London; (4) two Essex names and the London to Lincoln route, with a detour to Caistor St Edmund (again presumably a name which was written on the map so that its start at the western end made it seem that it belonged to a station on the London–Lincoln route); (5) the northern counties, Derbyshire, Manchester to Cumbria; (6) a new start from Manchester – not named again – over into the West Riding, then back to Carlisle, with three forts of Hadrian's Wall; (7) south from Durham to York and into the East Riding; (8) a few names from the area south of Hadrian's Wall. Serious confusions by the compiler are shown in the eight duplications which occur within this second group, and a further three names in it are duplicated in the third group. Three rivers are misread as though they were places, again because their names were written along their inland courses on the map-source. These factors show how perilous it is to assume any logic in the Cosmographer's following of the road-system, and to use *Ravenna* (as R&C tried to do) in order to assign its many unidentified names to places on the roads in logical sequence, especially when some names turn out not to be those of settlements at all.)

Iterum sunt civitates in ipsa Britania que recto tramite de una parte in alia, id est de oceano in oceano esistunt, hac dividunt in tercia porcione ipsam Britaniam, id est

107_{24} (143)	Serduno	**Segeduno*	*Wallsend*
107_{24} (144)	Condecor	**Conderco*	*Benwell*
107_{25} (145)	Vindovala	**Vindobala*	*Rudchester*
107_{25} (146)	Onno	**Onno*	*Halton Chesters*
107_{26} (147)	Celūno	**Cilurno*	*Chesters*
107_{26} (148)	Brocoliti	**Brocolitia*	*Carrawburgh*
107_{27} (149)	Velurtion	**Vercovicium*	*Housesteads*
107_{27} (150)	Esica	**Esica*	*Great Chesters*
107_{28} (151)	Banna	**Banna*	*Birdoswald*
107_{28} (152)	Uxelludamo	**Uxelloduno*	*Stanwix*
107_{29} (153)	Avalana	**Aballava*	*Burgh-by-Sands*
107_{29} (154)	Maia	**Maio*	*Bowness*
107_{30} (155)	Fanocodi	**Fano Cocidi*	*Bewcastle*
107_{30} (156)	Brocara	**Vindogara* ?	*near Irvine*
107_{31} (157)	Croucingo	**Croucinco*	—
107_{31} (158)	Stodoion	**Pteroton*	—
107_{32} (159)	Sinetriadum	**Stratopedum*	
107_{32} (160)	Clindum	**Lindum*	*Drumquhassle* ?

107_{33} (161)	Carbantium	**Carbantoritum*	*Easter Happrew* ?
107_{33} (162)	Tadoriton	**Tadoritum*	—
107_{34} (163)	Maporiton	**Maporitum*	—
107_{34} (164)	Alitacenon	**Alaunocelum* ?	—
107_{35} (165)	Loxa	**Loxa*	*R. Lossie*
107_{35} (166)	Locatreve	**Locatrebe*	—
107_{36} (167)	Cambroianna	**Camboglanna*	*Castlesteads*
107_{36} (168)	Smetri	**Smerti*	*Smerti (tribe)*
107_{37} (169)	Uxela	**Uxela*	*Ward Law* ?
107_{37} (170)	Lucotion	**Lucovium*	*Glenlochar* ?
107_{38} (171)	Corda	**Corda*	*Castledykes* ?
107_{38} (172)	Camulosessa	**Camulosessa*	—
107_{39} (173)	Presidium	**Presidium*	—
107_{39} (174)	Brigomono	**Rerigonio*	*Stranraer* ?
107_{40} (175)	Abisson	?	—
107_{40} (176)	Ebio	**Epidii* ?	*Epidii (tribe)*
107_{41} (177)	Coritiotar	**Coria Votad.*	—
107_{41} (178)	Celovion	**Gelovium* ?	—
107_{42} (179)	Itucodon	**Itunodunum* ?	—
107_{42} (180)	Maromago	**Vacomagi* ?	*Vacomagi (tribe)*
107_{43} (181)	Duabsisis	**Dubabissum* ?	—
107_{43} (182)	Venutio	**Venicones* ?	*Venicones (tribe)*
107_{44} (183)	Trimuntium	**Trimontium*	*Newstead*
107_{44} (184)	Eburo caslum	**Eburo castellum*	—
107_{45} (185)	Bremenium	**Bremenium*	*High Rochester*
107_{45} (186)	Coccimeda	**Coccuveda*	*R. Coquet*
107_{46} (187)	Alauna	**Alauna*	*R. Aln*
107_{46} (188)	Oleiclavis	**Orea clasis*	—
107_{47} (189)	Evidensca	**Avitanco*	*Risingham*
107_{47} (190)	Rumabo	**Flum Abo*	*R. Ouse (Yorks.)*

(This third group announces itself as listing the forts of Hadrian's Wall, perceived *recto tramite* on a map; but the compiler sees them merely as *civitates* curiously arranged, and has no idea that they form a defensive system. He lists twelve forts, not repeating three listed earlier (*Magnis*, *Gabaglanda*, *Vindolande*); presumably these twelve names were written north of the Wall on his map, the earlier three to the south. It seems certain, as Dillemann (p. 63) notes, that after *Maia* at 107_{29} a narrative phrase has dropped out, perhaps **Iterum sunt civitates*; such a phrase occurs after the listing of what the Cosmographer thinks are forts of the Antonine Wall. The forts of Hadrian's Wall are followed by places mainly in the Scottish Lowlands, all unidentified. In its sequence of four names from *Carbantium* to *Trimuntium*, the Cosmographer does seem to be following the line of a road, because (as noted earlier) the same sequence occurs in Ptolemy; these must be names of early forts. In the rest there is some confusion. The *Loxa* > Lossie is a river of Moray, well to the north of the Antonine Wall; the *Smerti* (*Smertae*) also lived well to the north. We seem to return southward with the gravely anomalous mention of *Cambroianna* on Hadrian's Wall. *Coritiotar* seems to be an abbreviated name of a tribal centre, misread, and *Venutio* may conceal another tribal name. The group ends in total illogicality as we return to parts of Northumberland north of Hadrian's Wall and then to the

Yorkshire Ouse, **Flum Abo*, far to the south of it; presumably the Cosmographer realised he had omitted it earlier (though he did not recognise it as a river) and simply tacked it on here. It is again in many instances hopeless to use the order of *Ravenna* for the attempted location of unknown places.)

Iterum sunt civitates in ipsa Britania recto tramite una alteri conexa, ubi et ipsa Britania plus angustissima de oceano in oceano esse dinoscitur, id est

107_{52} (191)	Velunia	**Velunia*	*Carriden*
107_{52} (192)	Volitanio	**Votadini* ?	*Votadini (tribe)*
107_{53} (193)	Pexa	**Pecti* ?	*Picts (people)*
107_{53} (194)	Begesse	?	—
107_{54} (195)	Colanica	**Colania*	*Camelon* ?
107_{54} (196)	Medio Nemeton	**Medio Nemetum*	*Arthur's O'on* ?
107_{55} (197)	Subdobiadon	?	—
107_{55} (198)	Litana	**Alauna* ?	*Ardoch* ?
107_{56} (199)	Cibra	**Coria* ?	*Barochan Hill* ?
107_{56} (200)	Credigone	**Creones*	*Creones (tribe)*

(In this fourth group the only certain name belonging to an Antonine Wall fort is the first, *Velunia*, confirmed by an inscription from its *vicus*. Among the others not more than four names, two much corrupted, could belong to further forts. The tribal names must have been written on the source-map so that at one end they abutted on to the line of Wall. The **Coria* in question (*Cibra*) is that which Ptolemy at II, 3, 7 assigns to the Dumnonii, and must have been their centre. The Creones dwelled on the west coast above the Antonine Wall, and the Picts, of course, much to the north of it, so this group of names is again seriously confused.)

Iterum est civitas quae dicitur

107_{58} (201)	Iano	**Lano*	—
107_{58} (202)	Maulion	**Matovium* ?	—
108_{1} (203)	Demerosesa	**Demerosessa*	—
108_{1} (204)	Cindocellum	**Cintocellum*	—
108_{2} (205)	Cerma	**Cerini*	*Caereni (tribe)*
108_{2} (206)	Veromo	?	—
108_{3} (207)	Matovion	**Matovium*	—
108_{3} (208)	Ugrulentum	?	—
108_{4} (209)	Ravatonium	?	—
108_{4} (210)	Iberran	**Ibernia* ?	*Ireland*
108_{5} (211)	Pinnatis	**Pinnata*	—
108_{5} (212)	Tuessis	**Tuessis*	*Bellie* ?
108_{6} (213)	Lodone	**Caledones*	*Caledones (tribe)*
108_{6} (214)	Litinomago	**Litanomago*	—
108_{7} (215)	Devoni	**Devona*	*Kintore*
108_{7} (216)	Memanturum	**Novantarum (Pen.)* ?	*Rhinns of Galloway*
108_{8} (217)	Decha	**Decante* ?	*Decantae (tribe)*
108_{8} (218)	Bograndium	**Bocrandium*	—
108_{9} (219)	Ugueste	?	—

108_9 (220)	Leuiodanum	**Leviodunum*	—
108_{10} (221)	Poreo classis	**Horea classis*	—
108_{10} (222)	Levioxaua	**Levioduno*	—
108_{11} (223)	Cermium	**Cerini*	*Caereni (tribe)*
108_{11} (224)	Victorie	**Victoria*	*Inchtuthil ?*
108_{12} (225)	Marcotaxon	**Marcotaxum*	—
108_{12} (226)	Tagea	**Tameia ?*	*Cardean ?*
108_{13} (227)	Voran	**Varar*	*R. Farrar*

(In this fifth group most of the names seem to relate to places north of the Antonine Wall. Here no particular order could be expected, since there was no road-system. Places which do not belong here, if our restorations are right, are *Iberran* for **Ibernia* (written across a much-narrowed sea between Ireland and Scotland), and *Memanturum* if this represents the *Novantae* people far to the south-west. *Poreo classis* 108_{10} is distinct from *Oleiclavis* 107_{46}. On *Devoni*, see p. 128 and the Alphabetic List. For the special source of this group and its date, see p. 196).

Sunt autem in ipsa Britania diversa loca, ex quibus aliquanta nominare volumus, id est

108_{17} (228)	Maponi	**(Locus) Maponi*	—
108_{17} (229)	Mixa	?	—
108_{18} (230)	Panovius	**Fl Novius*	*R. Nith*
108_{18} (231)	Minox	?	—
108_{19} (232)	Taba	**Tava*	*R. Tay*
108_{19} (233)	Manavi	**Manavia*	*Isle of Man*
108_{20} (224)	Segloes	**Selgoves*	*Selgovae (tribe)*
108_{20} (225)	Daunoni	**Damnoni*	*Dumnonii (tribe)*

(This sixth and last group seriously misled R&C, who thought *loca* was here being used in a technical sense to mean 'tribal meeting-places' in the organisation of the region north of the Roman frontier. Their argument about this is detailed but unsound. The group is really no group at all, but a collection of 'odd places' (*diversa loca*) which the Cosmographer had omitted to mention earlier. He may have been misled himself by **Locus Maponi*, taking *Locus* to be a common noun; but he then unpardonably rounded up two rivers, a major island (its name written on the map towards the Scottish mainland, and taken to be a name pertaining to this), and two Scottish tribal names. See also Dillemann (pp. 70–71).)

Currunt autem per ipsam Britaniam plurima flumina, ex quibus aliquanta nominare volumus, id est

108_{24} (236)	Traxula	**Traxula*	*R. Test ?*
108_{24} (237)	Axium	**Axium*	—
108_{25} (238)	Maina	**Moina*	*R. Meon*
108_{25} (239)	Sarva	**Sabrina ?*	*R. Severn*
108_{26} (240)	Tamaris	**Tamarus*	*R. Tamar*
108_{26} (241)	Naurum	?	—
108_{27} (242)	Abona	**Abona*	*R. Avon*

108_{27} (243)	Isca	*Isca		R. Usk	
108_{28} (244)	Tamion	*Tamium		R. Taff ?	
108_{28} (245)	Aventio	*Aventio		R. Ewenny	
108_{29} (246)	Leuca	*Leuca		R. Loughor	
108_{29} (247)	Iuctius	*Stuctius		R. Ystwyth	
108_{30} (248)	Leugosena	{ *Leuca *Sena		R. Loughor 	 —
108_{30} (249)	Coantia	*Cenio ?			—
108_{31} (250)	Dorvantium	*Derventio		R. Derwent	
108_{31} (251)	Anava	*Anava		R. Annan	
108_{32} (252)	Bdora	*Boderia ?		R. Forth	
108_{32} (253)	Novitia	*Novius		R. Nith	
108_{33} (254)	Adron	*Vedra		R. Wear	
108_{33} (225)	Certisnassa	{ *Certis *Nassa		 R. Ness	—
108_{34} (256)	Intraum		?		—
108_{34} (257)	Antrum		?		—
108_{35} (258)	Tinoa	*Tinea		R. Tyne	
108_{35} (259)	Liar		?		—
108_{36} (260)	Lenda	*Linda			—
108_{36} (261)	Vividin		?		—
108_{37} (262)	Durolavi	*Durolevi			—
108_{37} (263)	Alauna	*Alauna		R. Aln	
108_{38} (264)	Coguveusuron	{ *Coccuveda *Isurum		R. Coquet R. Ure	
108_{38} (265)	Durbis	*Dubris		R. Dour	
108_{39} (266)	Lemana	*Lemana		R. Lympne	
108_{39} (267)	Novia	*Novia		R. Adur ?	
108_{40} (268)	Raxtomessa		?		—
108_{40} (269)	Senua	*Senna			—
108_{41} (270)	Cunia	*Cenio			—
108_{42} (271)	Velox		?		—

(This river-list does on the whole contain rivers, but to it must be added a number in previous sections, and several in sections that follow, which were mistakenly thought by the Cosmographer to be places or islands. The group starts apparently in Hampshire and goes clockwise round Britain, mentioning only rivers that flow into the sea (inland ones having been mistaken for places in several instances); it ends in Kent or perhaps Sussex. There are three conflations arising from misreading a map; this evidence, together with the inclusion of *Durolevi* (the name of an early fort in Kent) and other less certain features (e.g. if *Vividin* is for *Virvedrum*, a cape) leads us to think that all river-names were written on the map-source on their inland courses or near their mouths, but not at their mouths or 'in the sea'; the earlier presence of *Tamese* and other names among habitation-names shows this too. The duplications may help in identification: e.g. *Sena* conflated with *Leuca* has *Coantia* after it, and when *Sena* appears later as *Senua* it is again followed by *Cunia*.)

Finitur autem ipsa Britania a facie orientis habens insulam Thile vel insulas Dorcadas, a facie occidentis ex parte provinciam Galliam et promuntorium Pyrenei, a facie septentrionalis insula Scotia, a facie meridiana Germania Antiqua.

v. 32 Iterum in eodem oceano occidentali, post ipsam magnam Britaniam, simulque et amplius longius, ut diximus, quam omnes insule a terra magna finita [ex] parte septentrionali, magis ex ipsa occidentali, est insula maxima quae dicitur Ibernia, que, ut dictum est, et Scotia appellatur. cuius post terga, ut iam praemisimus, nullo modo apud homines terra invenitur.

Per quam Scotiam transeunt plurima flumina inter cetera quae dicuntur, id est

109_{4}	(272)	Etsodisinam	?	—
109_{4}	(273)	Cled	**Clota*	*R. Clyde*
109_{5}	(274)	Terdec	?	—

(The interest of this small group is that *Cled* could represent the Clyde, otherwise omitted from *Ravenna*. The name would have been written across a very narrow Irish Sea on the source-map. Since there is no evidence that the Cosmographer had any information at all for Ireland, it is possible that the other two names also refer to western British rivers. See ETSODISINAM in the Alphabetic List.)

Iterum in ipso oceano occidentali ponuntur diverse insule, ex quibus aliquantas nominare volumus, id est

109_{9}	(275)	Corsula	**Insula* ?	—
109_{9}	(276)	Mona	**Mona*	*Anglesey*
109_{10}	(277)	Regaina	**Ricina*	*Rathlin* ? (*Irish*)
109_{10}	(278)	Minerve	**Minerve*	(*attribute of Aquae Sulis* ?)
109_{11}	(279)	Cunis	**Cenio*	—
109_{11}	(280)	Manna	**Monna* ?	*Anglesey*
109_{12}	(281)	Botis	**Botis*	*Bute*
109_{12}	(282)	Vinion	?	—
109_{13}	(283)	Saponis	**Saponis* ?	—
109_{13}	(284)	Susura	**Susurra*	—
109_{14}	(285)	Birila	?	—
109_{14}	(286)	Elaviana	**Fl Avona* ?	*R. Avon* (*Bristol*)
109_{15}	(287)	Sobrica	**Sabrina* ?	*R. Severn*
109_{15}	(288)	Scetis	**Scetis*	*Skye*
109_{16}	(289)	Linnonsa	**Limnu Ins*[a]	*Lambay Island* ? (*Irish*)

Item ad aliam partem dicitur insula

109_{18}	(290)	Magantia	**Magantia* ?	—
109_{18}	(291)	Anas	**Anas*	—
109_{19}	(292)	Cana	**Cana*	*Canna*
109_{19}	(293)	Atina	?	—
109_{20}	(294)	Elete	**Fl Ete* ?	—
109_{20}	(295)	Daroecla	**Daruveda* ?	—
109_{21}	(296)	Esse	?	—
109_{21}	(297)	Gradena	**Grandina*	—
109_{22}	(298)	Maiona	**Maio* ?	*Bowness*
109_{22}	(299)	Longis	**Longus*	*Loch Linnhe*
109_{23}	(300)	Eirimon	**Eremon*	—
109_{24}	(301)	Exosades, ubi et gemme nascuntur, [sicut] legimus.		

Item in ipso oceano sunt numero insule triginta tres quae et Dorcades [109_{27} (302)] appellantur, que quamvis non existant omnes exculte, attamen nomina illarum volueramus Christo nobis iuvante designare; sed quia peccatis emergentibus suete a diversis gentibus ipsa dominatur patria et, ut barbarus mos est, varie vocationes easdem insulas appellant, ideo earum reliquimus nomina designandum.

(In this final gathering the Cosmographer lists islands. Most of them are unidentifiable western Scottish islands, but non-Scottish islands such as Anglesey and probably Man are included, together with Irish examples. The initial **Insula* probably went with *Mona*, but was misread from the map-source. The names of two rivers and one loch were (exceptionally) written 'in the sea', leading the Cosmographer to suppose them islands. For the curious *Eirimon*, see p. 197 and the Alphabetic List. The long note on the Orkneys (*Dorcades*) evidently refers to post-Celtic settlement there and to the disappearance of older names, though it seems unlikely that the Cosmographer can in fact have known these. There is a further mention of *Thyle*, unrelated to Britain, at 109_{47}.)

CHAPTER SIX

THE NOTITIA DIGNITATUM

The *Notitia Dignitatum* ('register of offices') has been the subject of such intense and also high-quality debate that it is perilous ground.[1] In this case the basis of the document rather than its text is in question. The text comes down to us in a good number of manuscripts, of which four were used by Seeck for his edition:[2] C = Oxford ('Canonicianus'), copied in A.D. 1436; P = Paris, fifteenth century; V = Vienna, fifteenth century; M = Munich, copied probably in A.D. 1542. These are humanist copies directly made from the MS called the Codex Spirensis (from the Cathedral Library 'of Speyer' in Germany), which contained in all twelve important works: in second place the *Antonine Itinerary*, in fifth place the *Notitia Galliarum* and *Laterculus Polemii Silvii*, and last the *Notitia Dignitatum*. The Codex was last heard of in 1566, and was probably dismembered and largely destroyed in the early years of the seventeenth century. From the kind of errors contained in the copies, the

[1] The basic bibliography for Britain includes: J. B. Bury, 'The *ND*', *JRS*, x (1920), 131–54; F. S. Salisbury, 'On the Date of the *ND*', *JRS*, XVII (1927), 102–106, with an addition in *JRS*, XXIII (1933), 217–20; E. Birley, 'The Beaumont Inscription, the *ND*, and the Garrison of Hadrian's Wall', *CW*², XXXIX (1939), 190–226; C. E. Stevens, 'The British Section of the *ND*', *Arch. J.* XCVII (1940), 125–54 (valuable partly because Stevens gives credit to early ideas of Camden and Horsley, and summarises and applies views of Polaschek in P.-W. XVII, cols. 1077–1116 [1936] and Nesselhauf [1938]); J. P. Gillam, 'Also, along the line of the Wall', *CW*², XLIX (1949), 38–58; D. A. White, *Litus Saxonicum* (Madison, 1961), especially Chapter III, with a summary of *ND* scholarship; A. H. M. Jones, in *The Later Roman Empire, 284–602* (Oxford, 1964), Appendix II in Vol. III, 347–80; S. S. Frere, *Britannia*, 2nd edition (London, 1974), pp. 260–68, 394–95, 404–405; J. H. Ward, 'The British Sections of the *ND*: An Alternative Interpretation', *Britannia*, IV (1973), 253–63; *Aspects of the ND* (Oxford, 1976; British Archaeology Reports, Supplementary Series, 15), the record of a 1974 conference, edited by R. Goodburn and P. Bartholomew; in this, most relevant to our interests are contributions by J. C. Mann, 'What was the *ND* for?' (1–9); J. J. G. Alexander, 'The Illustrated Manuscripts of the *ND*' (11–49, with plates); M. W. C. Hassall, 'Britain in the *Notitia*' (103–17); and C. E. Stevens, 'The *ND* in England' (211–24); D. J. Breeze and B. Dobson, *Hadrian's Wall* (London, 1976), with discussion of *ND* in Chapter VII and in an important Appendix IV; *The Saxon Shore* (London, 1977; CBA Research Report 18), edited by D. E. Johnston.

[2] O. Seeck, *Notitia Dignitatum*... (Berlin, 1876). All references are to this edition, and its essential sections are reproduced below. Seeck also wrote studies of the text, such as his *Quaestiones*... (1872).

orthography of the Spirensis was conjectured to have been of early tenth-century date; this is confirmed by a study of a surviving two-folio fragment of *AI*, found in 1906 and recognised in 1927 as having come from the Codex. The *ND* part of the Spirensis was itself probably copied from a Carolingian MS (about A.D. 825?), based in its turn on a fifth-century original. Agreement among the surviving MSS is reasonably close, and it could be said that few problems arise on this score. The *ND* was first printed in 1552 (Gelenius), again in 1593 (Pancirolus), and has been well known since. In recent important studies, I. G. Maier reviews the whole MS tradition, with many corrections to statements by Seeck, and promises a new edition; he shows that the four MSS used by Seeck may not be the only ones copied direct from the Spirensis, and that variants in others are signficant, but these seem not to affect the information in the British chapters.[1] On the illustrations in the MSS, and on the activities of the humanists in the Renaissance, a recent study by J. J. G. Alexander is of great interest.[2]

The *ND* is in two parts, the *Notitia Orientis* for the Eastern Empire and the *Notitia Occidentis* for the Western. It is helpful to consider the two parts as complementary though not exactly similar, and to view the British section of the *Occidentis* first (despite its special problems) in the context of what is said about the Western Empire as a whole, for here, as with our other texts, an insular approach could be a distortion. Both parts of *ND* were preserved together in the West, probably at Rome or Ravenna, in the office of the *primicerius notariorum* of the West. This functionary is defined by Bury (1920) as 'a high civil servant whose duty was to issue the *codicilli* (*tabulae honorum*) to every high official, on his appointment to his post'. He was one of the chiefs of the Imperial chancery as reorganised by Constantine, and a sort of Minister for War in that he kept the complete survey of the distribution of military forces in the provinces. It is assumed that the eastern *ND* was prepared in the East and sent to the western *primicerius*, with whom it remained as a clean copy from which some details were lacking because there was no impulse to keep it up to date; the western *ND* was prepared in the West and sent to the eastern *primicerius* (in a copy now lost), while the copy that remained in the West with the *primicerius* at Rome or Ravenna was to a limited extent revised as dispositions changed.

The *ND* is a register 'of all offices and ranks both civil and military' (XVI). It presents a survey of the administrative structure of the late Empire, in theory complete, and its special value is that it contains considerable detail about finance, mints, imperial industrial enterprises such as weaving-houses, and long lists of the military stations with the name of the unit which garrisoned each. An example of the last type of entry, that which will mainly concern us, is: *Sub dispositione uiri spectabilis comitis litoris Saxonici per Britanniam – Praepositus numeri Fortensium*, OTHONAE ('Under the command of the honourable Count of the Saxon Shore in Britain – the commander of the units of Fortensians, at OTHONA', XXVIII$_{12-13}$).

1 There is now much superior information available about the MS tradition. The studies of Maier are in *Latomus*, XXVII (1968), 96–141, and XXVIII (1969), 960–1035.

2 *Aspects* (1976). The contribution of Stevens to this shows (with much else of interest) that a MS of *ND* was in Britain, perhaps at Oxford, about 1200; there is a discussion of the statement by Gelenius (the 1552 editor) that a MS had come *ex ultimis Britannis*.

This much seems to be generally agreed, though Eric Birley (1939) objected to the standard view that the *ND* had governmental status and had emanated from the top of the Imperial bureaucracy. He says: 'The origin of the *ND*, I suggest, is to be sought not in the official activities of a public department, but in the private enterprise of an amateur of military matters...who had obtained possession of official documents of various kinds.' Only on such a view, Birley thought, can the shortcomings – indeed, the downright military inefficiency – of the *ND* be explained. Polaschek (1936) saw the problem and offered a sort of compromise: that the *ND* had been put together by some *notarius* perhaps in the Eastern bureau, who was acting unofficially for some purpose of his own but who had access to the official 'returns' (reports of troop dispositions, etc.) sent in by the commanders in the provinces, his information being partly current and partly obsolete. These ideas are supported by Maier after his detailed textual work: 'There is sufficient internal evidence to show that either the original compiler(s) or later copyists of our *ND* have transmitted the official documents at their disposal in such an incomplete, abbreviated and inaccurate manner, that no-one can seriously suggest that *our ND*, as it now exists, could ever have been *the* official or *working copy* of the primicerius.' [1]

The debate has centred also on the date to be assigned to *ND*. Much more is involved here for the history of Britain than for that of other provinces, since on the question of date turns the whole problem of the moment at which Roman forces finally left Britain, the period during which the Imperial adminstration still felt responsible (however remotely) for Britain, and similar issues; for it is the case that in the absence of other good information about these vital matters, *ND* itself is a prime source of knowledge. Again our judgement about dates cannot be restricted to that of the British section alone. The most comprehensive view of the problem, and one founded on a very detailed analysis of all the evidence, is that of Jones (1964). He says (III, 351); 'To sum up, the Eastern part of the *Notitia* must be earlier than 413...and need not be later than 395. Plausible dates for its transmission to the West would be either 395 or 408, when diplomatic relations were resumed after Stilicho's fall. The document was no doubt revised for the occasion, but not very thoroughly, and still contained many anomalies.' Jones concludes that 'prima facie one would expect that the Western section would have been revised for transmission to the East at the same time', that is, probably in 408; but he adds the essential proviso that corrections to the Western section were made later, down to 423, and gives details of them. As for the *distributio* (analytical index), Jones thought it was based on 'a working Army list of about 420' (III, 351 and 381). To this Mann (1976) adds a special emphasis. He notes that *ND* is 'much concerned with seniority and order of precedence', and thinks that the Western part was a document 'no longer controlled by the *primicerius* of the notaries' but was rather a version which had been acquired for use by the clerks responsible for recording information about infantry units of the field armies only. On dating, Mann thinks the document was 'collated after 395, and was then brought up to date, in a haphazard way, down to about 408'.

The British section of *ND* and its date cannot be discussed without a view of its text. What follows is extracted from Seeck's edition, only those portions relevant to

[1] Note 3 to p. 97 of Maier's first article. The italics are his.

place-names being reproduced (two references to British names in Chapter XI are not reproduced here: see AUGUSTA[1] and VENTA BELGARUM in the Alphabetic List). Seeck's numeration is retained as being essential for cross-referencing. The *picturae* (illustrations) of the MSS are represented as sketches by Seeck, but can be studied as full plates in the volume *Aspects* (1976); names given under the *picturae* of forts which represent British places are not reproduced below but are mentioned in the Alphabetic List, since occasionally they have variants of interest. Variants are similarly excluded here but are present in our Alphabetic List. Our material enclosed in parentheses gives the identification of each name, where known, together with a corrected Latin form when this is not obvious. Seeck's text is followed by our proposed emendations, the entries concerned in the main text being asterisked.

Text

XXIII Uicarius Britanniarum

3. Maxima Caesariensis
4. Ualentia
5. Britannia prima
6. Britannia secunda
7. Flauia Caesariensis

XXVIII Comes litoris Saxonici per Britanniam

12. Sub dispositione uiri spectabilis comitis litoris Saxonici per Britanniam:
13. Praepositus numeri Fortensium, Othonae (*Bradwell*)
14. Praepositus militum Tungrecanorum, Dubris (*Dover*)
15. Praepositus numeri Turnacensium, Lemannis (*Lympne*)
16 Praepositus equitum Dalmatarum Branodunensium, Branoduno (*Brancaster*)
17. Praepositus equitum stablesianorum Gariannonensium, Gariannonor (*Burgh Castle*)
18. Tribunus cohortis primae Baetasiorum, Regulbio (*Reculver*)
19. Praefectus legionis secundae Augustae, Rutupis (*Richborough*)
20. Praepositus numeri Abulcorum, Anderidos (*Pevensey*)
21. Praepositus numeri exploratorum, Portum Adurni (*Portchester*)

XL Dux Britanniarum

17. Sub dispositione uiri spectabilis ducis Britanniarum:
18. Praefectus legionis sextae (*York*)[1]

[1] To this Seeck adds editorially: '*adde* uictricis, *Eburaci*'. This may not be justified. The sketch of the corresponding fort has the caption *Sextae*, showing that there was no merely scribal omission in the archetype and that the illustrator took the reference in the list to be a place-name, no doubt interpreting the entry as meaning 'The commander of the legion, at *Sexta*.' Stevens (1940, p. 141) disregards Seeck's emendation: '*Legio sexta* is given no place of garrison, and this is likely to be no mere scribal error. . . This should mean that the compiler of the returns for the *dux Britanniarum* knew that the sixth legion was on the strength, but he did not know where it was or where it was likely to be. Yet it had been at York for two hundred years and more. The explanation can only be that the legion was on the move. Surely this must be the *legio praetenta Britannis* of Claudian (*Bell. Goth.*, 416) – the force which Stilicho

19. Praefectus equitum Dalmatarum, Praesidio (?)
20. Praefectus equitum Crispianorum, Dano (*Doncaster* ?; *Jarrow* ?)
21. Praefectus equitum catafractariorum, Morbio (?)
22. Praefectus numeri barcariorum Tigrisiensium, Arbeia (*South Shields*)
23. Praefectus numeri Neruiorum Dictensium, Dicti (*Wearmouth* ?)
24. Praefectus numeri uigilum, Concangios (*Chester-le-Street*)
25. Praefectus numeri exploratorum, Lauatres (*Bowes*)
26. Praefectus numeri directorum, Uerteris (*Brough*)
27. Praefectus numeri defensorum, Braboniaco (*Kirkby Thore*)
28. Praefectus numeri Solensium, Maglone (*Old Carlisle* ?)
29. Praefectus numeri Pacensium, Magis (*Burrow Walls* ?)
30. Praefectus numeri Longouicanorum, Longouicio (*Lanchester*)
31. Praefectus numeri superuenientium Petueriensium, Deruentione (*Malton*)
32. Item per lineam ualli:
33. Tribunus cohortis quartae Lingonum, Segeduno (*Wallsend*)
34. Tribunus cohortis primae Cornouiorum, Ponte Aeli (*Newcastle*)
35. Praefectus alae primae Asturum, Conderco (*Benwell*)
36. Tribunus cohortis primae Frixagorum, Uindobala (*Rudchester*)
37. Praefectus alae Sabinianae, Hunno (Onnum: *Halton Chesters*)
38. Praefectus alae secundae Asturum, Cilurno (*Chesters*)
39. Tribunus cohortis primae Batauorum, Procolitia (*Carrawburgh*)
40. Tribunus cohortis primae Tungrorum, Borcouicio (Vercovicium: *Housesteads*)
41. Tribunus cohortis quartae Gallorum, Uindolana (*Chesterholm*)

*42. Tribunus cohortis primae Asturum, Aesica (*Great Chesters*)

43. Tribunus cohortis secundae Dalmatarum, Magnis (*Carvoran*)

*44. Tribunus cohortis primae Aeliae Dacorum, Amboglanna (Camboglanna: *Castlesteads*)

*45. Praefectus alae Petrianae, Petrianis (*Stanwix*)

*46. . . .

47. Praefectus numeri Maurorum Aurelianorum, Aballaba (*Burgh-by-Sands*)
48. Tribunus cohortis secundae Lingonum, Congauata (*Drumburgh*)

*49. Tribunus cohortis primae Hispanorum, Axeloduno (– *see below* –)

50. Tribunus cohortis secundae Thracum, Gabrosenti (*Moresby*)
51. Tribunus cohortis primae Aeliae classicae, Tunnocelo (?)

---

borrowed for the campaign against Alaric. The expectation (not in fact realised) of its return is expressed in this curious entry. We are thus led to date Chapter XL of the *ND* to *c.* A.D. 402. . .' This is ingenious, and as Stevens goes on to say, it fits in with Nesselhauf's arguments and dating of the corresponding Gallic sections to A.D. 402; but it seems rather thin evidence on which to date a whole section of *ND*. The compiler and his illustrator were not necessarily wrong in taking *Sexta* as a kind of place-name, for this style is used in the 'Marble of Thorigny' text: *Ad Legionem Sext[am]* means 'at York'. It is also the case that in one of the Spanish itineraries of *AI* (395_4) the city which is now León (< *Legione*) is designated *Ad Leg. VII Geminam*, that Gildas and Bede call the old station of *Legio II* 'the city of the legions' (> Caerleon), and that Bede gives names for Chester in Latin, Anglo-Saxon and British which mean the same. It thus seems possible that the manner of listing York in *ND* neither needs Seeck's addition nor bears Stevens's interpretation.

52. Tribunus cohortis primae Morinorum, Glannibanta (*Ravenglass*)
53. Tribunus cohortis tertiae Neruiorum, Alione (*Maryport*)
54. Cuneus Sarmatarum, Bremetenraco (*Ribchester*)
55. Praefectus alae primae Herculeae, Olenaco (*Elslack*)
56. Tribunus cohortis sextae Neruiorum, Uirosido (*Brough by Bainbridge* ?)

Emendations

42. For *primae*, read *secundae*, as suggested by Seeck. The second cohort is recorded as the garrison at Great Chesters on *RIB* 1738 (A.D. 225). Seeck's suggestion is adopted by Breeze and Dobson (1976), pp. 245, 252 and 274. The error would have arisen in copying numerals, *I* being an error for *II*.

44. M. W. C. Hassall in *Aspects* (1976), 113, regards the text here as a conflation of two entries, the unit from one and the fort from the other. In view of *RIB* 1905 (see BANNA in the Alphabetic List) and the well-attested presence at Birdoswald of *cohors I Aelia Dacorum*, he supposes a lacuna in an early MS of *ND*, to be restored as follows:
XL$_{43a}$: Tribunus cohortis primae Aeliae Dacorum, [Banna
XL$_{44}$: Tribunus cohortis secundae Tungrorum], Camboglanna
This seems most acceptable; on all counts mention of *Banna* (Birdoswald) is to be expected in *ND*.

45. *Petrianis* is almost certainly a ghost-name, which probably arose because an early copyist found a gap after mention of the unit, the *ala Petriana*, and simply repeated its name as a locative in *-is*. *Petrianis* is not known as a fort-name from any other source, and is anomalous, since except for *Castra Exploratum* (not precisely analogous) we have no forts in Britain named from the units which garrisoned them. The correct entry should probably be:
XL$_{45}$: Praefectus alae Petrianae, Uxeloduno (*Stanwix*)
It should be noted that Hassall, and Breeze and Dobson (1976), 275, also think *Petrianis* a ghost, and replace it by *Uxel(l)oduno*. See also 49, below.

46. Seeck here inserts '. . . Luguuallii', with a long note in justification. But there is no expectation of a lacuna here (given the order which is being followed), and Carlisle was by then a town, not a fort.

49. After 48, *Congauata* (Drumburgh), one would expect a mention of Bowness, the next fort to the west and the last of Hadrian's Wall (it is the first, *Mais*, proceeding from the west, on the Rudge Cup and Amiens *patera*). Mention at 49 of *Axeloduno* (= *Uxeloduno*, Stanwix) is anomalous at this point and a clear error, though it is impossible to guess how it happened in the copying process. The garrison of Bowness is not known from any inscription. We therefore suggest that the entry should read:
XL$_{49}$: Tribunus cohortis primae Hispanorum, Mais (or Maio) (*Bowness*)
Breeze and Dobson (1976), 275, propose that *Axeloduno* is a separate name and assign it to Netherby; but for this, they have to argue that the name *Castra Exploratorum* was for some reason discarded, and assume (without argument) that *Axelo-* is a good Celtic form, which it is not. It seems an obvious duplication of *Uxeloduno*.

In the above, Chapter XXIII lists the five provinces as they were after the new division of A.D. 368; on these, see p. 46. Chapter XXVIII, the Saxon Shore, is notable for the odd way in which the first three forts are listed, but it is logical after that. It is assumed by some that a tenth coastal fort, Walton Castle (whose name is not known to us from other sources) was omitted; this may have been because it was already unusable (the site has now been completely eroded by the sea), but M. W. C. Hassall in *The Saxon Shore* (1977), pp. 7–10, suggests that the entry for it was written at the head of a page (the fort being 'paired' with *Othona*, which now comes first) and was omitted by a scribe, presumably at an early stage before the *picturae* were executed (since these are only nine in number). The presence of Legio II at Richborough, after centuries at Caerleon, shows that this part of the list is late, for the legion was evidently on the move in the disturbed conditions of the late fourth century. It is also probable that it was a late move which took the original Pevensey *classis Anderetianorum* to Paris (XLII$_{23}$), their replacement being the *numerus Abulcorum.*[1]

Chapter XL has in effect three divisions. In the first, the forts numbered from 17 to 31 are in north-east England, with two in eastern Cumbria. In the second, numbers 32 to 45, introduced by the heading *Item per lineam ualli*, are the forts of Hadrian's Wall, with serious copying confusions towards its western end which we think that the table of Emendations should have resolved.[2] Collingwood suggested that the third group, numbered from 47 to 56, should have had some such subheading as *Item per litus occidentale*, for these are the forts of the Cumbrian coast and others more southerly inland.[3] Apart from omissions mentioned above, it is possible that a short list of Welsh forts has been dropped from the end; but there is an alternative explanation for this, mentioned below.

The most recent full discussion of the complex problems posed by the northern part of *ND*'s British chapters is that of Frere in the second edition of his *Britannia* (1974), pp. 260–68, 394–95, 404–05, while the work of Breeze and Dobson (1976) on Hadrian's Wall, especially Chapter VII and Appendices 2 and 4 (the last on the names of the forts) is valuable also. Frere takes *ND*'s text as reasonably trustworthy and tries to square its data with the archaeological and other evidence. Noting that the section headed *per lineam ualli* consists (with two exceptions) of units which are old-style *alae* or cohorts and that many of these can be shown to have been present at their *ND* forts in the third century, Frere is inclined to date this information to the period A.D. 296–367: 'If we are to believe that the same units remained on after 367 in the Wall-forts, we must explain how, in the great disturbances of that and the following year,...so great a proportion of regiments should have emerged unscathed and allowed to continue unreformed' (p. 263). That the outpost forts to the north of the Wall are omitted from *ND* even though in some cases they were held down to 367 is no objection, since several other forts known to have been occupied in the same period are also omitted, such as Ambleside, Low Borrow Bridge,

[1] The names and identifications of Chapter XXVIII are naturally discussed by contributors to *The Saxon Shore* (1977), *passim*. The contributors take the same view of names and identifications as we do in this book. B. Cunliffe discusses the dating of *ND*'s Saxon Shore section (p. 3) and after discussion concludes, for example, that *Portus Adurni* is Portchester.

[2] A further word is necessary, perhaps, about *Congauata*. We are firm both about the form of the name, *Concavata*, and its application to Drumburgh. Breeze and Dobson (1976), pp. 255 and 275, express doubts about the nature of the fort (rightly) and consequently about its name, since this is omitted from all sources other than *ND*. Our explanation is given in Note[2] to this entry in the Alphabetic List. To this it may be added that the exceptional Latin name might have been a new fourth-century coining, the earlier Hadrianic fort having had a name based on Celtic elements like most others but this name having passed into oblivion because of the long gap in occupation of the site.

[3] In his paper 'The Roman Evacuation of Britain', *JRS*, XII (1922), 74–98, at 79.

Watercrook, Overborough (= Burrow-in-Lonsdale), probably Old Penrith (Frere, note 21 to p. 263). Even so, anomalies remain, as Frere recognises. As for the earlier list of forts in north-east England, the units known to have occupied them in the third century appear with quite different garrisons in *ND*: 'Virtually the only context for this would be the expedition of Magnus Maximus in 383, followed by the restoration by Stilicho about 396. But the distribution of the listed forts is not reasonable for a restoration... The best explanation... is that the first part of the Duke's list shows us what troops were left holding northern Britain after Maximus had withdrawn a large part of the available troops... It lists not an intentional deployment of forces but a remnant' (p. 266). Again, some forts survived for perhaps twenty years after 383, but we lack evidence to distinguish these; hence 'Until some of these forts can be positively proved to have been occupied after 383, the theory that they were among those evacuated by Maximus fits the available facts; this part of the Duke's list will then merely show us how much of the reorganisation of 369 survived the movements of 383, and indeed... those of 396' (p. 266). Frere continues that the Welsh forts were probably omitted from *ND* because they were evacuated by Maximus, and that Legio XX was taken also by him in 383 to the Continent as the nucleus of his force. On the other hand, the inclusion in *ND* of Lancaster (= *Olenacum*, in Frere's view), Ribchester and Bainbridge may mean that they were not evacuated by Maximus, but were abandoned by Stilicho. Frere's general view is thus that (p. 267) 'Our conclusion must be that the first part of the Duke's list reflects the position in Britain after 383, though the list as we have it is based on a later "return". Indeed, it is unlikely that returns were made to the Western *primicerius* from Britain during Maximus's supremacy.' Finally (p. 405) Frere, correcting what was almost an article of faith among older commentators, states that it can no longer be held that it was Magnus Maximus who finally evacuated the Wall in 383, since both coins (though scarce) and pottery prove continued occupation. Certainly archaeological information is now very much superior to that available in the 1920s and 1930s, but in fairness the scholars of those years can be allowed their opinions through their papers (see note to p. 216). On the mode by which *ND* was compiled, Frere himself had begun by quoting a variety of opinions, accepting that of Jones on dating but leaning towards that of Birley (1939) about composition by a private person.

A radical view published since Frere's first edition is that of J. H. Ward (1973), who in some respects revives the idea of Bury (1920) but without his extremely late dates.[1] Ward notes that *ND* was a document current in the 420s, and that since Britain is included in it, the Imperial writ still ran in Britain into that period. *ND* with its rather odd order represents the stages by which Roman commanders secured a limited reoccupation of south-east, east and north England, including the Wall, following an initial landing on the south-east coast; the north-west, Wales and the west were not recovered, but left in the charge of *protectores*. *ND* then represents a 'return' made

[1] Bury concluded that the *Notitia* of the West described real troop dispositions of A.D. 428–37 (except possibly for the Wall section), and that from this the Roman abandonment of Britain could be put as late as 442, as is implied by a Gallic chronicle. This view sems to have been generally rejected.

of units and stations in this situation. The date of this partial recovery was perhaps 416 or 417, but the process was halted by a policy decision a year or two later. The idea, we might say, is attractive, but without independent evidence of any kind.

One respects the efforts of scholars to interpret *ND*'s data in line with archaeological and historical evidence and to make it yield a picture of a historical situation, but feels that classical scholars, archaeologists and other notoriously methodical persons are in danger of taking *ND* as more perfect than it is. We know that it has copying errors, possibly errors of the compiler, in the western part of Hadrian's Wall, and a most unmilitary way of listing the Saxon Shore forts. Scribes may have been responsible for the loss of a heading which would have made more sense of the last part of Chapter XL. We are unsure of the identity of some eight forts in *ND*'s British sections, which increases the peril of arguing logically about the occupational evidence revealed by archaeology in this connection. Birley was surely right to remark that 'The information which it [*ND*] presents is nothing better than a patchwork, whose different pieces are joined together without any regard for their wide variation in accuracy at a time when the document assumed its present form' (leading to his conclusion about compilation by an amateur). It can hardly be doubted – unless we take Ward's view – that much of *ND*'s information about Britain was obsolete, not to say archaic. Even if the document had official status, by the 420s its contents for Britain represented something of a pious memory, or a statement of what Stevens called 'official optimism' about the eventual recovery of the province. This was Collingwood's opinion also: 'I see no difficulty in supposing that in 428, and after, he [the *primicerius notariorum*] still regarded the British provinces as theoretically part of the Empire, and transferred bodily into the new *Notitia* the British section of the old because it would at least keep the place warm.'[1] This is well put too by Hassall (1976): 'It is misleading to say that, at the date when the Western *Notitia* was compiled, certainly after 410, the inclusion of the British sections was anachronistic: for they were only "out-of-date" once the British diocese was officially renounced, and this probably never actually happened. If Britain had been recovered and new appointments made, the lists of troops under the relevant commanders would, of course, have had to be revised. While the diocese remained lost to Rome this could not be done, but it might still be useful to know what the old establishment had been for each command.' There is a similar observation in Hassall's 1977 paper. On the one hand, if the document had official status, the very disturbed conditions of the late fourth century and early fifth century must have meant a decline in the efficiency of the Roman chancery, and its officials had a good deal to worry about nearer home than the slim chance of recovering an increasingly remote Britain. On the other hand, those same officials can hardly be blamed for failing to see that the final collapse was imminent; not only had the Empire stood for centuries and become the only political structure known to men as a reality, but its recent christianisation had fitted it into the divinely ordained structure of the universe. Hence their inclusion of Britain in *ND* was in no way anachronistic or merely pious, for usurpers and barbarians had come and gone before, and there was good reason to hope, even to expect, in the 420s, that Roman rule would be re-established in Britain. From thoughts of this kind

[1] Collingwood, in his 1922 article, p. 84.

one can see why an exact time-scale, and total accuracy within a moment of time, were not necessarily important to the Empire's functionaries. Had the *primicerius* been the man whose job it was actually to move military units about, pay them, and ensure that their commanders had their promotion at the right moment, his records would have had to be exact; but clearly, *ND* was never intended to have that detailed character and practical function.

ND in its present state gives us in its British sections the names of the five provinces, the Saxon Shore and the Wall, and forty-six forts and stations. A few mentions of regiments by adjectival names derived from places give us further forms, as does the mention of the financial officer at London in XI_{37} (see AUGUSTA[1]); there is also mention of two British units serving at Continental stations (see ANDERITUM and SEGONTIUM in the Alphabetic List). The form in which the place-names are set down is that to be expected in late-fourth-century usage, notably the way of referring to London and York (the first a piece of officialese, the second an almost colloquial Army usage). It is noticeable that the names of the units are registered with much greater accuracy than those of the forts, presumably because they were more perfectly familiar to the *primicerius*. In the fort-names, there are the usual errors arising from either late Latin speech-habits (e.g. confusions of *b/v*) or from the sort of scribal mistakes met in our other texts (*c/g*, *c/t*, etc.). When dealing with other kinds of inaccuracy on which all four of the main MSS (those used by Seeck) agree, we do not know whether an error goes back beyond the common source in the Codex Spirensis to one of its predecessors or to the fifth-century archetype; but it seems possible that e.g. *Anderidos*, with its strange *-s*, goes back to the original. In a few cases *ND* preserves for us a truer form than that known from other texts, e.g. *Cilurno*. It should be noted that in some ways Seeck's is a compounded and corrected edition; he prints, for example, item XL_{23} as *Praefectus numeri Neruiorum Dictensium*, but his apparatus makes it clear that all four MSS have *Dictentium*, this *-ti-* being a hypercorrection resulting from the assumption that original *-si-* was a vulgar assibilation. The *ae* diphthong which regularly appears is a humanistic restoration of the classical norm, for it is certain that the original regularly had *e* (**Prefectus*, **Othone*, etc.; the only exceptions are *Maglone*, *Alione*, presumably because the humanist scribes allowed these to stand as putative third-declension forms).

The declensional forms in which *ND* lists its forts are of some interest. A few entries give the impression that classical locatives are being employed to express 'the unit of . . . s at *X*': thus *Othonae* XXVIII_{13}, *Dicti* XL_{23}, *Maglone* XL_{28}, *Gabrosenti* XL_{50}. Other locatives are of the fossilised kind in which some names had settled down in regular usage, such as *Dubris* XXVIII_{14} and *Uerteris* XL_{26}, as is shown by other records of these names. Most of the remainder have the oblique case by which most places were currently known, *-a* for feminine first declension, *-o* for masculine and neuter second, *-e* for third. On the whole the names in the *picturae* seem to be secondary, having been taken from the lists, but there are occasional forms of interest, such as *Dictim* in the *pictura* for *Dicti* in the text at XL_{23}; this is presumably guesswork by the illustrator as he re-established what he thought was a nominative against the locative given in the list. This illustrator was quite happy to take the textual *Sextae* of XL_{18} as a proper form, and indeed we have argued that it may have been.

CHAPTER SEVEN

INSCRIPTIONS

1. GENERAL

Epigraphic evidence – that provided by writings on stone, metal, pottery, etc. – is for place-names the most valuable kind there is; but inscriptions which mention place-names are unfortunately rare in Roman Britain. The evidence is valuable because it is contemporary with the event to which it relates, as on a tombstone which marks a burial, or a statue which honours an emperor, or a building-stone which records the completion of a task. Moreover, such items can often be dated. Formal inscriptions were cut by masons well acquainted with the name of the person or military unit or town they were recording, and – unlike the literary documents, itineraries, etc. – what the mason cut has not been subject to the corruptions of copyists over the centuries. Even so, mistakes did sometimes occur, either from ignorance or because the mason misread a draft written for him in a cursive hand, and there could be difference of opinion about the unstressed vowel in a name of Celtic origin; but such factors hardly affect our consideration of the scanty toponymic evidence. The more formal inscriptions are assumed to have been cut in a correct classical Latin, but such an assumption is perhaps too readily made for the less formal and later texts and may need qualification (see below); it remains true that only rarely is there intrusion from the spoken Latin of the community or of the mason (examples are given under BANNA and VINDOLANDA). The general reliability of epigraphic evidence is such that it is to be preferred to any other: thus the abbreviated name of the fort at Housesteads, VER in *RIB* 1594, enables one to confirm a suggestion of Mommsen's long ago, that the true form was *Vercovicium*, and to relegate as inferior the *Borcovicio* of *ND*. An altar inscription of *Vindolanda* serves to confirm a consonant group (*-nd-*) in the form given by *Ravenna*, against the slightly corrupt (or vulgar) form of *ND*.

The practice of the masons – inevitable when they had a long text to cut in handsome capitals on a stone of limited size – of considerably abbreviating not only the formulaic parts of their texts (such as D M, V S L M) but much of the rest also, is much to our disadvantage. A name may be so reduced that it is virtually useless to us as evidence, as on the milestone *RIB* 2241 whose inscription ends... A L S M P XIIII, almost certainly to be interpreted '*...a L(indo) S(egelocum) m(ilia) p(assuum) XIIII*, of which we could say that while we hardly need confirmation of the name of Lincoln, a full form of *Segelocum* in authentic local spelling would be valuable. The same applies to tile-stamps, lead sealings, etc., in which extreme brevity leads to the names of Britain, Chester, Gloucester and other places being reduced to one or two letters of small interest to us. The expansion of these abbreviations can lead to uncertainty. The Chester tile-stamps LEG XX VVDE are those of the 20th Legion *Valeria Victrix*, but the last letters may stand for *De(ciana)* 'of the Emperor Decius' rather than for *De(vensis)* or *De(vae)* 'of or at Chester', particularly in view of another inscription (*RIB* 449; see the discussion on p. 146 of *RIB*). Finally, the abbreviations seem always to be expanded by scholars in terms of pure classical Latin, and perhaps they have no alternative; but one's suspicion is that if the masons had given us fuller readings, many local and vulgar forms of interest would have been recorded, as they were for *Banna* and *Vindolanda*.[1]

2. FORMAL INSCRIPTIONS ON STONE

Inscriptions giving place-names are rare for a variety of reasons. Inscriptions of any kind are not common in many parts of southern and eastern Britain, mainly because the stone for them had been brought from a distance, remained a valuable commodity and was often re-used in later Roman building, in defences, in Saxon and medieval churches, etc., and was in the process often recut and its lettering removed or defaced. In this a comparison with Roman Gaul is interesting. One reason for the fact that we have so many more inscriptions from Gaul than from Britain lies in the different periods at which town walls were built: in Britain in the late second and early third centuries, before any barbarian raids, so that both public and private monuments were still intact and were not re-used as building stone, being hence left a prey to medieval builders; but in Gaul the walls were built in the late third and early fourth centuries, after barbarian raids had wrecked the monuments, so that their larger stones were re-dressed and used in the foundation courses of walls and so preserved for archaeologists to find them. Some control for this is provided by the inscriptions, mainly milestones, from Bitterne, whose walls were built late (in the fourth century; *RIB* records one formal inscription and seven milestones so used).

Frequently when a town site has continued in unbroken occupation, or has had substantial later occupation – as so many of our important settlements in lowland Roman Britain have had – the Roman levels lie not merely concealed but often deep, and more, are often inaccessible under modern buildings (not only department stores, which may be transient, but cathedrals). It is therefore only in patches and by good fortune, almost, that the archaeologist is able to investigate them in many cases. However, even sites which have lain more or less empty since Roman times, and which are known to have been important in those times, seem to produce disappointingly little in the way of inscriptions even when subject to archaeological examination. Twenty-two inscriptions is not a vast number for Silchester, a cantonal capital and busy road-junction, nor is seventeen from Wroxeter, to which the same

[1] For example, on the Lincoln milestone, *RIB* 2241, some vulgar form such as *SEG-ELOCO, *SECELOCO or *SEGILOCUM could readily by hypothesised, particularly as this is a secondary text cut rather roughly on an older stone, in A.D. 268–70.

description applies. These two figures are comparatively large for lowland settlements as a class. It is plain that conditions of life and community habits did not often require the naming of a place within the place itself, and we reflect that this is really the case today if we discount modern road-signs and railway-stations. Our library may well say 'Public Library' in stone over its door, and the only other epigraphic feature likely to endure is the plaque which records that the building was opened by Lord X (perhaps with a title confusingly taken from another part of the country, as with the Devonshires in Derbyshire) or by 'The Mayor of this Town', with the date and perhaps a Latin tag, but no place-name. This applies also to our town-halls, baths, local government offices, and so on; the relative absence of place-names from Romano-British formal stones should hardly surprise us. The Romano-British town perhaps had typically a statue of an emperor or a divinity, perhaps a few of local worthies and patrons (as at Caerwent, *RIB* 311), with an inscription, dedicatory slabs for the forum and baths, and not much else. Shops and industries did not name themselves on durable materials, there was no public advertising, and it seems that with one possible exception[1] the starting-points of roads within towns or at gates were either not indicated at all, or were not shown in any fashion that survives for us today. Along the major roads, and some lesser ones too, there were numerous milestones, but these often suffered the fate of being re-used in later masonry or as gateposts, etc. Of the ninety-six milestones recorded in *RIB*, only nine mention a place-name in even the most abbreviated form, and not many give a distance either, though all were apparently meaningful to road users (perhaps because of painted rather than inscribed texts). The relevant portions of the inscriptions of the nine are:

Canovium:. . .A KANOVIO M P VIII (*RIB* 2265)
Eburacum:. . .EB(ORACO) M P XXII (*RIB* 2274)
Lancaster:. . .L M P IIII
Lindum: two, very abbreviated (an initial letter only, in both cases: *RIB* 2240 and 2241)
Navio:. . .A NAVIONE M P XI (*RIB* 2243)
Ratae:. . .A RATIS M II (*RIB* 2244)
Segelocum: one, very abbreviated (an initial letter only: *RIB* 2241)
Trimontium:. . .[TRI]MONTI(O) M P [. . .]

The more personal inscriptions on tombstones and votive slabs are of course among the richest groups of epigraphic materials, but they mention place-names only incidentally – for example, when recording the city offices held by the deceased (*RIB* 674 and 678, respectively of a *decurio* and a *sevir* of York). Our greatest loss remains that of the official monumental texts from the centres of the larger towns of the lowlands, and from such structures as that at Richborough (which seems to have become ruinous through neglect and then been demolished). Though always few, for the reasons noted, their significance for us would have been enormous.[2]

[1] The exception is the same Lincoln milestone, *RIB* 2241, which was 'found in 1879 at the intersection of the main streets of the Roman city'. But a recent writer argues that the milestone did not originally stand in the city centre, but outside the north gate: W. Rodwell in *Britannia*, VI (1975), 86–87.

[2] For example, the 'Agricola' inscription at St Albans, which may or may not have mentioned *Verulamium*, as interpreted by Wright in *JRS*, XLVI (1956), 146–47. From the four

Military sites and the great civil *coloniae* which originated as military stations require a separate commentary. It can be no accident of archaeology that such a preponderance of texts on stone comes from the legionary fortresses (Caerleon, eighty; Chester, one hundred and twenty-nine; York, sixty-seven), from the *coloniae* originally established for legionary veterans at Colchester (twenty-two), Lincoln (twenty-eight) and Gloucester (only six),[1] from the forts, milecastles and quarries of Hadrian's Wall (791), and in smaller numbers from many other forts in northern England and Wales and southern Scotland. In all these places it was evidently the custom for soldiers, whether Roman citizens of the legions from Italy and from the continental provinces, or auxiliaries, to record durably on stone their dedication of an altar, the interment of a comrade with the record of his service, and other things. Presumably they had habits of literacy to a substantial degree, and appreciated such memorials. Often the military unit collectively dedicated an altar or recorded its building work, and often too, after soldiers were allowed to marry locally, their native-born wives (whether themselves literate or not) carried on the custom of recording burials on stone. The officer class had financial resources to set up not only impressive tombs and complete shrines, but to erect other fine monuments as dignified records of service, and even to commemorate success in hunting (*RIB* 1041, 1905). At military stations, or in the civilian *vici* often attached to them, there were masons regularly employed in the craft of lettering; and since so many of these sites are in the rockier parts of Britain, north and west, one could conjecture that the local supply of usable stone made the demand easier to satisfy than in many areas of the lowlands. Whatever the reasons, we are faced with such odd but undeniable facts as that about Exeter, a cantonal capital, which cannot show a single inscription from its own area,[2] whereas the fort at Tomen-y-Mur (Merionethshire) – whose Roman name we do not even know – has produced ten inscriptions, and that at Lancaster has produced nine. Some cantonal capitals and other major settlements have as yet shown very little, for one or other of the reasons mentioned above. A count of those known up to the time of *RIB* I shows Chichester with eight, Caistor St Edmund one, St Albans eight (despite extensive excavation), Leicester two, Canterbury five. *Durobrivae*², an industrial centre of note, has produced two milestones and one other inscription. The late military sites of the south and east, that is the Saxon Shore forts, have shown very little indeed.[3]

fragments of the text, dated to A.D. 79, it has been calculated that the whole was four metres long. Other examples are provided by the fragment of the very large civic inscription found at Winchester, whose *V* (said in the city's museum to be the tallest letter of any Roman inscription known in Britain) possibly comes from the Imperial name ANTONINVS, and by the fragments of the huge monumental text at Richborough, listed in *RIB* 46, and presumably in most of the following *RIB* items up to 65.

[1] Inscriptions for the York civil *colonia* are included in the total for the legionary base, since they are not easily differentiated.

[2] *RIB* p. 62 alludes only to a post-Roman tombstone. The building-stones which record repair-work on Hadrian's Wall by the *civitas Dumnoniorum* may refer to the tribal canton rather than to the city specifically (*RIB* 1843, 1844).

[3] There is one inscription from Lympne (*RIB* 66), a dedication to Neptune from the east gate of the early fort, about A.D. 135. The numerous Richborough fragments relate to inscriptions of the early military site and port, not to the Carausian fort. The text on the tile

There are a few special cases. London has forty stones recorded in *RIB* and would probably have more if more excavation were possible. From Bath no fewer than forty-one inscribed stones are known, the result in large part of the devotion professed by the infirm to the goddess Sulis and other divinities, and of their relative wealth. (But in contrast, the cult of Arnemetia at Buxton must have been for those who were poor or illiterate, or both, for not a single text is known from those other *Aquae*.) The total of inscriptions from Hadrian's Wall is to some degree swollen by what are in many cases very brief building-stones, technical jottings, and so on. The villas have in no case produced inscriptions bearing a place-name, and not many texts of any kind; the lettering set in tessellated pavements is of great interest, but none so far names a villa, though one (Thruxton, *VCH* Hants, I (1900), 299, now in the British Museum), may perhaps give us a name of an owner.

A few names comes to us from inscriptions abroad. See, for example, CAMULODUNUM, EBURACUM and especially TAMPIUM in the Alphabetic List.

3. *INSTRUMENTUM DOMESTICUM*, COINS, GRAFFITI, ETC.

A wide range of inscriptions (in many cases, more properly designated jottings and scrawls) on materials other than stone provides much epigraphic evidence, but here again it is rare for this to mention place-names. Much of it, as a glance at the annual record in *JRS* and (recently) *Britannia* shows, consists of numerals which mark a quantity or a linear measure, the personal names of owners scratched on pots, fragmentary numbers of military units, and the like. Longer texts of a personal nature, and of enormous linguistic and social interest, do sometimes appear – letters, a legal document, curses on lead, etc.; among these, place-names make an appearance in rare instances.

In point of time the very oldest of our place-name evidence occurs on the coins of certain tribes in southern Britain, in the period when a superficial romanisation was under way before the conquest of A.D. 43. Coins of the Atrebates bear the legend CALLEV or REX CALLE (in Roman times *Calleva Atrebatum*, Silchester); coins of the Catuvellauni show VER, VERL, VERLAMIO and other forms of the place we know in Latin as *Verulamium* (St Albans); the Iceni of East Anglia had coins which mention the tribal name in abbreviation; and coins also bear the name of Colchester, in forms ranging from CA to CAMVL-ODVNO.

On industrial artefacts, mention of a place-name is often now a guarantee of quality (e.g. 'Sheffield Steel' on knives), but in earlier times – in a world less commercially competitive but much given to thieving – such mention was also a way of asserting origin and preventing improper use. The products of the British mining industry, an imperial property which was exploited by private concessionaries, were presumably marked in the same way when gold or silver as are the surviving lead pigs. The latter

---

from Pevensey is now known to be a forgery. There is an important building inscription from Reculver, on which J. C. Mann in D. E. Johnston (ed.), *The Saxon Shore*, CBA Research Report 18 (1977), 15, remarks that it was set up at 'any time in the 3rd century after the reign of Severus, or less probably [in] the late 2nd century. We have no way of pinning down its date more closely.'

give the names of four of the British lead-producing areas, in adjectival form. Pigs found in Yorkshire carry the stamp BRIG, for *metallum Briganticum* (that is, produced in the tribal lands of the Brigantes); various pigs found in widely separated parts of Britain carry different stamps having in common LVT or a longer form, an adjectival reference to *Lutudarum*, the mining area of Derbyshire; VEB on pigs from the Mendips seems to be an abbreviation for the otherwise unknown name of the mining area or centre there; and finally, pigs from Flintshire bear an abbreviation for *metallum Deceanglicum*, an adjective for the uncertain name of the local tribe.

The stamping of tiles produced for official bodies, before firing, clearly had the purpose of preventing their diversion to private building. Both civil and military stamps are known, such as those of Gloucester *colonia* (R P G = *Rei publicae Glevensium*)[1] and London, and those from Binchester (N CON = *Numerus Concangiensium*, the unit stationed at Chester-le-Street, *Concangium*). There are also series of legionary stamps without place-names. Lead sealings used for official purposes carry abbreviations for the same reason; two types certainly identified refer to the Upper and Lower provinces of Britain: P BR S = *Provincia Britanniae Superioris* and P B I = *Provincia Britanniae Inferioris*.

Inscriptions denoting pride in a commercial product were by no means unknown in Roman Britain. There is a professional pride in the oculists' stamps, and an artistic claim is made by the potters' stamps. Place-names were, it seemed, unknown on Romano-British pottery until the discovery in 1937 of a large *mortarium* fragment at Water Newton bearing the name of the maker and his town (painted in slip): SENNIANVS DVROBRIVIS VRI[T] '(fired by) Sennianus at *Durobrivae*'. Another *mortarium* is stamped CVNOARVS VICO DVRO(BRIVAE). Rather different is the graffito LONDINI / AD FANVM ISIDIS = 'London: next door to the temple of Isis', on a jug; since this was scratched after the pot was fired, it has been thought to give the address of a wine-merchant rather than that of the manufacturer of the vessel. The purpose of two small bricks found on a villa site in Glamorgan in 1965 and inscribed BOV has not been determined, but the reference may be to the name of a settlement in the area (see BOVIUM[1] in the Alphabetic List).

Documents of a personal kind – letters and other individual records – rarely survive from Roman Britain, since most writing on papyrus, wax or wood has perished. Occasionally, however, the damp conditions of a former river-bed, well or ditch preserve wood. The traces of a remarkable letter (the stylus having scored not only the wax of the writing-tablet but also its wooden casing), found in the London Walbrook in 1927, form the name LONDINIO as the address in addition to parts of the text.[2] LONDINIO appears also within the text of another letter written on wood found in the capital in 1959; this seems to have been addressed from *Durobrivae*[1] (Rochester), though this has to be conjectured from a damaged line.[3] Official but also personal is the well-known bronze diploma granting citizenship to

[1] These are classified by E. M. Clifford, 'Stamped Tiles found in Gloucestershire', *JRS*, XLV (1955), 68–72.

[2] On this letter of Rufus Callusini to Epillicus, see *Ant. J.*, XXXIII (1953), 206, and Burn (1969), no. 49.

[3] See E. G. Turner and O. Skutsch in *JRS*, L (1960), 108–11.

the Briton Marcus Ulpius Novantico in A.D. 106, found at ancient Porolissum in Dacia: by origin he was 'from Leicester', RATIS. For the copy of a letter from a governor of Lower Britain which mentions an otherwise unknown British place, TAMPIUM, inscribed on the 'Marble of Thorigny', see the Alphabetic List.

4. THE RUDGE CUP AND AMIENS *PATERA*

These vessels, whose very purpose was to preserve place-names on souvenirs as a matter of pride and sentiment, differ so much in nature from other epigraphic evidence that they deserve separate treatment.

The definitive study of the Rudge Cup is that of Cowen and Richmond, that of the Amiens *patera* an article by Heurgon.[1] From these studies most of the following details are taken. The Rudge Cup was found in the filling of a well on a villa site at Rudge Coppice, near Froxfield, some six miles east of Marlborough (Wilts) in 1725. It was known to Horsley in 1732, and is now deposited at Alnwick Castle Museum (Northumberland), thus returning to the vicinity of the Wall which the Cup commemorates. Although the traditional name 'cup' is used here, the object is really a small bowl closely akin to the Amiens *patera*. It is of bronze, with a band of lettering below the lip, and a series of turrets or crenellations all round in bronze relief on an enamelled background, this being a stylised representation of the Wall. The band of lettering reads:

A.MAISABALLAVAVXELODVMCAMBOGLANSBANNA

to be divided A MAIS ABALLAVA VXELODVM CAMBOGLANS BANNA. Richmond thought that *A* is a preposition and that this, together with the order of the forts, shows that the inscription is derived from an itinerary source (since he observes that four out of the five forts are named in a group in *Ravenna*, though in reverse order; CAMBOGLANS is the fort omitted by *Ravenna*, at any rate in this sequence). The five forts are in the Cumbrian group at the western end of the Wall, coming inland from its western termination at MAIS (Bowness). The Cup presents some odd Latin forms, perhaps because of the ignorance or confusion of the craftsman, more likely because of his need to compress in order to fit the series into the space available. Thus MAIS is both *Maio* and *Maia* in different parts of Ravenna; VXELODVM is more properly VXELODVNVM; and CAMBOGLANS is a shortened form of *Camboglan(ni)s*, presumably a locative plural and a contrast to the forms preserved by *Ravenna* and *ND*.

The analogue to the Rudge Cup was found in 1949 at Amiens (N. France). It bears traces of damage by fire, but more of its three-colour enamel decoration survives. Its manner of decoration is a little different from that of the Rudge Cup, but the *patera* has the same stylised representation of the Wall. The inscription given by Heurgon is:

MAISABALLAVAVXELODVNVMCAMBOG...SBANNAESICA

[1] J. D. Cowen and I. A. Richmond, 'The Rudge Cup', *Arch. Ael.*[4], XII (1935), 310–42; J. Heurgon, 'The Amiens *patera*', *JRS*, XLI (1951), 22–24. The Amiens vessel has been described as a 'skillet', but this may be no more familiar to English readers of today than is the Latin *patera*.

that is, MAIS ABALLAVA VXELODVNVM CAMBOG...S BANNA ESICA. The suspension points indicate the place at which the rim is broken (where the handle – also found in Amiens – came off); Heurgon states that in the break the lower part of *L* and *A* can be clearly seen, and that there is space for four missing letters, so the fourth name can be restored as CAMBOG[LANI]S. He notes that the *patera* restores the full spelling of the third name, *Uxelodunum*. But the chief importance of the *patera* for our purposes is, as Heurgon clearly saw, that to the five names of the Rudge Cup it adds that of ESICA (Great Chesters), the ninth fort from the east on Hadrian's Wall and the one which precedes mention of *Banna* in *Ravenna*, thus providing further confirmation of the common derivation of Cup, *patera* and *Ravenna* from an itinerary source (with the further peculiarity, common to all three, that they omit *Magnis*[2], Carvoran fort, though *Ravenna* mentions this at an earlier stage; the reason being that it was not linked physically to the Wall).

The date of the Rudge Cup is put by Cowen at some time in the mid-second century. Heurgon does not discuss the date of the *patera*, but presumably does not dissent from this. The use and purpose of the *paterae* is not altogether clear. What is known as the Hildburgh Fragment came from a similar vessel (the surviving part without text, unfortunately) and was found in north-west Spain, between León and Zamora; Heurgon speculates that it could have belonged to an officer of the *Cohors I Asturum* who returned to his home in those parts after service on the Wall. Heurgon further recalls that Amiens was a town where a *primipilus* (senior centurion) of *Legio VI Victrix* – the legion long stationed at York, and which did much building work on the Wall – has his epitaph (*CIL* XIII. 3497). Heurgon's view of the origin of these vessels is thus that 'No doubt they were made for the Army on the Wall, and the soldiers were pleased to take them back in their baggage when they went home.' That is, they were akin to modern gift-shop souvenirs with lettering ('A present from Penarth'). But Cowen took a different view of the purpose of the Rudge Cup. He thought it one of a set used as a complete table-service, and pointed out that other examples of tableware were known with series of place-names, in particular a set of four silver vessels found in 1852 in a spring at Aquae Apollinaris, 34 miles from Rome, each bearing the stages of an itinerary from Cadiz to Rome (the 'Vases Apollinaires'). Richmond took this idea further by suggesting that the Rudge Cup 'may be regarded as the first member of a series, no doubt forming a table-service in the manner of small Samian cups, which contained the whole list of Wall-forts'. Nobody seems to doubt that all three *paterae* were of Romano-British manufacture. The Amiens discovery of 1949, and the belief of both Cowen and Richmond that a whole table-service with the complete list of Wall forts was involved, give a lively hope of further discoveries. (The remaining eight forts might divide into two groups for texts on similar vessels: continuing from west to east, a central group from *Vercovicium* to *Onnum*, and an eastern group from *Vindobala* to *Segedunum*. The central group would have some thirty-four letters, the eastern group about thirty-six – which neatly compares with the thirty-six letters of the Rudge Cup text.)

Our epigraphic evidence is thus, though scanty, of great diversity and interest. At present it gives us the names of some forty places. Its study is in a sense more forward-looking than that of other kinds of evidence, in that while there is no hope of new documentary or literary evidence appearing, archaeology year by year produces altogether unknown material from beneath the soil, not only of Britain but all over the vast extent of the Roman Empire. Nor is it only an empty expression of hope to say that evidence of wholly unknown place-names may come to light. For long it seemed that the only place-name known to us from an epigraphic source alone was that of *Habitancum* (Risingham), though this name also lies concealed, we now think, in a corrupt entry of *Ravenna*. However, others have emerged which, though offering some difficulty and unclear in their status, are important additions to our knowledge: possibly *Civitas Carvetiorum* (Carlisle – *RIB* 933, as interpreted by Stevens in 1937); *Curia Tectoverdorum*, perhaps a tribal centre at, or to be equated with, the civil *vicus* attached to *Vindolanda* fort (*RIB* 1695); and the recent possibility of nothing less than a new tribal centre and, indeed, a new tribe, glimpsed in the reference to a *Civitas Corielsoliliorum*.[1] Other discoveries may provide important indications of how a section of an itinerary or cosmography is to be read, as in the case of the *Velunia* text found in 1956, or may lead to necessary rethinking, as with the BOV name from Glamorgan.

[1] See *JRS*, LVI (1966), 223, and the Alphabetic List. For suggestions about three more possible 'new' names, see S. Applebaum in *JBAA*³, XVII (1954), 77–79, with criticism by A. L. F. Rivet in *Britannia*, I (1970), 61, note 87.

PART TWO

ALPHABETIC LIST OF NAMES

PREFATORY NOTE

The system followed should be self-explanatory. Cross-references are provided for names which have figured as proper forms but no longer seem so, notably those from the *Ravenna Cosmography* which were used by Richmond & Crawford in their 1949 edition, also for major variants which at times have had a certain currency as main forms; but it is not intended that all variants and deviant forms should be listed in this way. In general no attempt is made to follow an ancient name systematically through to its modern form, though there is usually some allusion to this, and where a modern derivative exists it is naturally an obvious point in the 'Identification' section of the entry. Readers wishing to trace the later evolution of a name and its modern form should consult the standard works of Ekwall, the county volumes of the *EPNS* series, and similar works.

The asterisk before a name or word means that this is a hypothetical or restored form not recorded as such in any source. The question-mark after a name means that an original form is reproduced without emendation, or with very little emendation, but does not seem satisfactory and cannot be trusted as a correct form. A combination of asterisk, and question-mark in a few cases means that we have restored a name to a more acceptable form but still do not find it fully satisfactory.

In most cases the heading of each entry states a nominative form, even though (as explained in Chapter 1 (3)) this may often be purely notional and may have had no real currency.

Under 'Identification' the type of place referred to is defined, whether civil or military, but in the case of towns the early Roman forts which usually preceded their development are not mentioned unless they help to explain the name, while the *vici* which normally grew up beside forts are also to be taken as understood. The location of modern places is defined by reference to the older counties, rather than to the administrative conveniences which have recently replaced them, and by four-figure National Grid References.

ABALLAVA

SOURCES

Rudge Cup and Amiens *patera*: ABALLAVA

Inscription: *RIB* 883, an altar found in 1886 built into Cockermouth Castle, which mentions the transfer of an officer IN C[U]NEUM FRISIONUM ABALLAVENSIUM 'to the formation of Frisians of Aballava', and is dated to A.D. 241–42 or 244–49.

Ravenna 107_{29} (= R&C 153); AVALANA. Schnetz notes no variants. In their text R&C read AVALAVA, also without variants. From the photographs in R&C's paper, it appears that MS A has *-ana*, B and C have *-aua*

ND XL_{47}: Praefectus numeri Maurorum Aurelianorum, ABALLABA

DERIVATION. The name is from Celtic **abállā-*; there is Gaulish *avallo* = 'poma' in the Vienna Glossary. The modern languages show Welsh *afall* 'apple-tree', Welsh *afal* 'apple' and Breton *aval*, Irish *ubhall*, *abhall*. Cognate Germanic words include English *apple* and others which go back to a common North European base **abl-*. Latin *nux avellana* 'hazel-nut' may involve a borrowing from Celtic, though there was possibly a native Italic representative of the group (see below).

Romano-British *Aballava* can hardly refer to a fruit or to a single distinguished tree, although it might (as with other tree-references in place-names) allude to a sacred tree. A more mundane explanation is that the name is a collective, 'orchard'; Irish *abhall* is used in this sense in some parts. The name is paralleled in Gaul: *Aballo TP* = *Aballone AI* 360_4 > Avallon (Yonne, France), and there are other places called Avalon in France. In Italic lands there was *Abella* (Campania), described as *malifera* 'rich in apples' in the *Aeneid* VII. 740.

The name has the derivational suffix *-ava* (British **-au̯ā*), as in *Galava*, *Manavia*, and abroad *Genava*, etc.; see Holder I. 305. It is now represented by Welsh *-au*, Breton *-aou -ou*.

IDENTIFICATION. The Roman fort at Burgh-by-Sands, Cumberland (NY 3259).

Note. Presumably the Avalon of Arthurian legend has a like origin. The name appears first in Geoffrey of Monmouth, and the equation with Glastonbury was made with the discovery of the pretended tomb of Arthur at the abbey in 1191: *Hic iacet sepultus inclitus rex Arturius in insula Avalonia*. This was adopted in Welsh as *Ynys Afallon* 'Isle of Apples', perhaps a Celtic version of the Greek *Hesperides*.

ABISSUM

SOURCE

Ravenna 107_{40} (= R&C 175): ABISSON

DERIVATION. The root is Celtic **ab-* 'river', as in *Abona*, *Abus*; Indo-European **ap-* **ab-* 'water', Sanskrit *apas*, Old Irish *ab* (also *aba*, *oub*, etc.), and probably Latin *amnis* (by assimilation of **ab-nis*, according to Ernout & Meillet). Williams, following Holder II. 80, notes that **-isso-* is a common suffix in Gaul, as in personal names *Dubnissus*, *Dumnissus*; in place-names its sense may be simply 'place where', as in *Epoissum* 'horse-place' of *AI* 366_1, > Yvois or Ivoy in French (Ardennes, France) = Ipsch in German, and a *Navissus* river. The suffix occurs also in British *Devionissum* and **Dubabissum*, the latter possibly paired with the present name. The sense may therefore be 'riverplace, place by a river', On this and other ⋆*ab-* 'river' names, see C. Watkins in *Ériu*, XXIV (1973), 80–89.

IDENTIFICATION. Unknown, but perhaps in south-west Scotland.

ABONA (river, Gloucestershire)

SOURCES
Ravenna 108_{27} (= R&C 242): ABONA
109_{14} (= R&C 286): ELAVIANA

Ravenna's first mention, in its river-list, is straightforward. The second, to be amended *Fl Aviana* (see ELAVIANA entry in this List), is in the section of *diverse insule*, but like other names in this group is really that of a river which – having been written 'in the sea' on a map – was taken by the Cosmographer to be an island. The name could be that of the *Anava* of Dumfries, but this is already in *Ravenna* at 108_{31}. It is hardly that of the Lanarkshire Avon Water, for this was an inland river. The best probability is that the entry is a garbled version of *Fl Avona*, well within *Ravenna*'s range of miscopying; and that since in the list it is immediately followed by *Sobrica* which we take to be *Sabrina* (the Severn), it is likely to be the Bristol Avon. That this is already present in the Cosmography as *Abona* is no objection; the compiler drew names for rivers from at least two maps, one of which gave the simple name, the other (or another) of which used *Fl* – for *flumen* – at least occasionally.

DERIVATION. For ⋆*ab-*, see ABISSUM. The name derives from British ⋆*abonā* 'river', to which correspond Welsh *afon*, Breton *aven*, Cornish *avon*; Old Irish *abann* and Irish *abhann*, *abhainn* ['owen].

Fig. 26. River-names derived from *Abona*: 1. Avon; 2. Avon Water; 3. Avon; 4. Little Avon; 5. Avon; 6. Avon; 7. Avon Water; 8. Avon. (*Abona*, whence Welsh Afon, means simply 'river' and it may be that some of these rivers had qualifying names which were not taken into English.)

All mean 'river'. The same Celtic bases underlie the common British river-name Avon (see the map), on which see Ekwall *ERN* s.v. and Jackson *LHEB* 272 & 558, and several Irish rivers called Avonmore, Owenmore (e.g. the Blackwater of Co. Cork, < *abhainn-mór* 'great river'). Both ⋆*Abona* and ⋆*Abono-* existed as river-names in Gaul, though little mentioned in the classical sources. The *Abona* of *Ravenna* 79_{35} in Portugal is more correctly *Aquabona* of *AI* 416_{5}.

The name has ⋆*-ona* suffix, as in British *Devona* and many Continental river-names; see C. Watkins in *Ériu*, XXIV (1973), 80–89.

IDENTIFICATION. The river Avon, Gloucestershire.

ABONA (settlement)

SOURCES

AI 486_1 (Iter XIV): ABONE

Ravenna 106_{22} (= R&C 47): PUNCTUOBICE

R&C think *Ravenna*'s form probably a scribal error for *Portu Abone*, more classically *Portum Abonae* 'port of (or at) Avon'. This correction is daring but acceptable. The compiler of *Ravenna* or an early copyist has made up two reinterpretations of a name that had become unintelligible, assimilating the first element to Latin *punctu* 'point' and the second perhaps to Latin *obice* (*obex*, *obicem*) 'bar, bolt; barricade'. *AI*'s form might represent a genitive with 'port' no longer expressed, or a locative in *-ae*.

DERIVATION. See the previous entry. Latin *portus* appears in several British names. As a common noun it passed from Vulgar Latin in Britain into Celtic speech (Welsh *porth*, Breton *porz*), and into Anglo-Saxon.

IDENTIFICATION. The Roman settlement at Sea Mills, Gloucestershire (ST 5575).

ABRAVANNUS

SOURCE

Ptolemy II, 3, 2: 'Αβραουάννου ποταμοῦ ἐκβολαι (= ABRAVANNI FLUVII OSTIA), vars. 'Αβραουάνου (= ABRAVANUS), Αὐραουάννου (= AVRAVANNUS), Αὐραουάνου (= AVRAVANUS), 'Αβρανάνου (= ABRANANUS).

DERIVATION. This is unknown. Bradley alludes hopefully to *aber-afon* 'river-mouth', and Müller in editing Ptolemy proposes a relation with the name of the *Abrincatui* people of Gaul, but these are thought by Holder I. 10 to be the *A-brinc-atui* with a name based on **ber-* 'to bring'. The name has nothing to do with Spanish *abra* 'inlet', which is from French *havre*.

IDENTIFICATION. A river of south-west Scotland, probably the Water of Luce.

ABUS

SOURCES

Ptolemy II, 3, 4: "Αβου ποταμοῦ ἐκβολαι (= ABI FLUVII OSTIA)

Ravenna 107_{47} (= R&C 190): RUMABO

Ravenna's form as it stands has no explanation in British, and as in other cases (see ELAVIANA) it seems probable that the compiler misread **Flum Abo* from a map-source as though it were a habitation-name, further misreading *Fl-* as *R-*. The name occurs in the list at the very end of a section; immediately before, the compiler has listed a group of names in what is now Northumbria just north of the eastern end of Hadrian's Wall (which was marked on his map). If he is in fact listing the *Abus* here, he has returned south of the Wall; but as Dillemann (p. 63) has shown, in many cases at the end of a section he gathers in names omitted earlier and having no necessary relation to the section.

DERIVATION. The name means simply 'river'; see ABISSUM. The root does not seem to be found abroad in this bare form.

IDENTIFICATION. The Yorkshire Ouse, with its estuary, the Humber.

ACMODAE of Pliny: see AEMODAE

AD ANSAM

SOURCES
AI 480_3 (Iter IX): AD ANSAM
TP: AD ANSAM

DERIVATION. Latin *ansa* (> French *anse*, Spanish *asa*) is 'handle, haft; loop (of a sandal)'; hence the name means 'at the bend (of the river)'. The name is paralleled by *Ansa Paulini* > Anse (near Lyon, Rhône, France). In Roman times scores of names were formed with *Ad* + noun, e.g. *Ad Aras*, *Ad Ensem*, *Ad Cisternas*; and in Britain, the next entry. The name presumably applies to a settlement where none existed before, at the point where the Roman road crossed the river.

IDENTIFICATION. The Roman settlement at Higham, Suffolk (TM 0334), near where the Roman road from Colchester crosses the river Stour.

AD PONTEM

SOURCE
AI 477_7 (Iter VI): AD PONTEM

DERIVATION. The name is Latin, 'at the bridge'. Among Continental *Ad Pontem* names are one in Spain (*AI* 409_2) and another (*TP*) near St Georgen or Pölshals in Austria. The name suggests a new Roman construction for which Celtic **briva* 'bridge' was deemed an inadequate designation.

IDENTIFICATION. The Roman settlement at East Stoke, Thorpe, Nottinghamshire (SK 7550).

ADRON of *Ravenna* 108_{33} (= R&C 254); see VEDRA

AEBUDAE INSULAE: see EBUDAE INSULAE

AEMODAE

SOURCES
Mela III, 6, 54: septem HAEMODAE contra Germaniam vectae
Pliny *NH* IV, 103: VII ACMODAE
Since both authors give the islands' number as seven, they are presumably distinct from the *Ebudae*; their position 'towards Germany' also argues this, as does the fact that the two sets of islands appear as separate items in Pliny. But the possibility that the *Acmodae* (Mela's *H-* is merely decorative) and *Ebudae* are really the same cannot be ruled out. Ptolemy has only the latter (as *Aebudae*); Holder regarded them as identical, though without arguing the point, and Burn in 1969 thinks the same. The problem of form is well illustrated in the text of Pliny; Detlefsen in printing this in 1904 notes as variants with *-c- Acmode* (A), *Accomode* (Par.), *Haec Modoe* (E^2), *Haec Modae* (E^1, D, R).

DERIVATION. This is unknown.

IDENTIFICATION. Probably the Shetland Islands, which were misidentified as *Thule* by Agricola's fleet.

AESICA

SOURCES

Amiens patera: ESICA

Ravenna 107_{27} (= R&C 150): ESICA

ND XL_{42}: Tribunus cohortis primae Asturum, AESICA

DERIVATION. The name is connected with that of the Celtic god *Esus* or *Hesus*, variously equated with Mars, Apollo and Mercury, and known to Latin authors. His name is interpreted as 'seigneur, maître' by Anne Ross, *EC*, IX (1961), 405; for other possible meanings and etymologies, see L. H. Gray in *EC*, VI (1953–54), 70. Here it has an adjectival termination which could be Latin or Celtic (represented now by Breton *-ek*, etc.; in Old Irish *-ech*, Holder I. 21), but we cannot guess what the unexpressed noun might have been. It is not known whether the god's name originally had *E-* or *Ae-* (British *ai*), since records show the same variation as does the British place-name. While *ai* > $\bar{ę}$ early in British, the *ae/e* uncertainty is common also in Vulgar Latin, as Jackson notes (*LHEB* 324). From a Celtic point of view the *-s-* is a fossil (*LHEB* 523), but if the name is considered as Latin, in the usage of a Latin-speaking garrison and army administration, this *-s-* of course continued unchanged. The name may have survived for a time: R&C observe that 'The *Vita S. Cuthberti* mentions *Ahse*, midway between Hexham and Carlisle, which Cadwallader Bates (*Hist. Northumb.*, 67) identified with *Aesica*. This may well be correct.' The name *Aes-* is found in toponymy abroad, but in areas where there is no obvious Celtic influence: the *Aesis* river > Esino (Piceno, Italy) had a settlement *Ad Aesim* upon it (*AI* 316_{4}), its ethnicon being *Aesinates*, and there was an *Aesius* river in Bithynia. The divine name or more probably a personal name derived from it is present on the coins of three British tribes: of the Dobunni (Mack Nos. 388–89), EISV; of the Iceni (Mack Nos. 432 and 434[a]), respectively AESV and ESICO; and of the Coritani (Mack. No. 456[b]), ESVP ASV.

IDENTIFICATION. The Roman fort at Great Chesters, Northumberland (NY 7066), whose third-century garrison was *Cohors I Asturum* (*RIB* 1738).

ALABUM

SOURCE

Ravenna 106_{26} (= R&C 55): ALABUM

DERIVATION. One cannot improve upon Williams: 'Presumably a latinised form of British **alabon*, neuter. Two Welsh words may be derived from such a form: (1) *alaf* "herd, cattle; wealth"; (2) *alafon*, in the context *alafon dwyfron*...probably the breastbone,...a possible root is **alebh*, **alobh*, seen in Greek λόφος "ridge, crest; cockscomb".' Williams goes on to prefer the second possibility; the name would be simply 'hill, crest'. One may compare Ptolemy's Ἀλαυῶνα (II, 6, 66) = *Allabone AI* 444_{1} (> Alagón, Zaragoza, Spain), a settlement of the Vascones, and Ptolemy's Ἀλάβα (II, 6, 57) with its *Alabanenses* people of Pliny *NH* III, 25, a settlement of the Celtiberi at an unknown place in Hispania Tarraconensis.

IDENTIFICATION. Probably the Roman fort at Llanfair-ar-bryn, Llandovery, Carmarthenshire (SN 7735).

ALAUNA[1]

SOURCES

Ravenna 106_9 (= R&C 24): ALAUNA SILVA

106_{14} (= R&C 32): ALAUNA, var. ALATINA

R&C take the first of these entries literally; it was early identified with the Blackmore Forest in Dorset. However, the Cosmography does not normally mention forests. We think *Silva* a corruption of another name: see SORVIODUNUM. As often in *Ravenna* a name is duplicated, either from careless use of one map or from use of two maps.

DERIVATION. This is a Celtic name of unusual diversity; a name not only of rivers (both *Alauna* and *Alaunus*) and settlements, those of the latter presumably taken from the former, but also of persons, a tribe and of divinities. In addition to the numerous British names there are many on the Continent: among settlements *Alaunium* (*Vases Apollinaires*, *AI* 343_1 and 388_3, *TP*) > Alaun (Basses-Alpes, France); *Alauna* (*AI* 386_6, *TP*) > Alleaume-les-Valognes (Manche, France); *Alaona*, *Aulauna* (*DAG* 595) > Allonnes (Sarthe, France). In Noricum lived the Ἀλαυνοὶ (*Alauni*) tribe (Ptolemy II, 13, 2). Among divine names are *Alaunius* (*CIL* XII. 1517) in Gallia Narbonensis, *Alauna* of the Treveri (*DAG* 756), and the *Alounae* goddesses of *CIL* III. 5572, etc. (see Holder I. 107). Ekwall relates to these the Welsh personal name *Alun* and Breton personal name *Alunoc* (*ERN* 6–8).

The etymology proposed by Watson (*CPNS* 32, 467–69) for the *Alauna* names of Scotland is attractive: British **al*- or **alo*- 'rock', with suffixes as in Gaulish **acaunos* **acounos*, hence 'rocky place' or

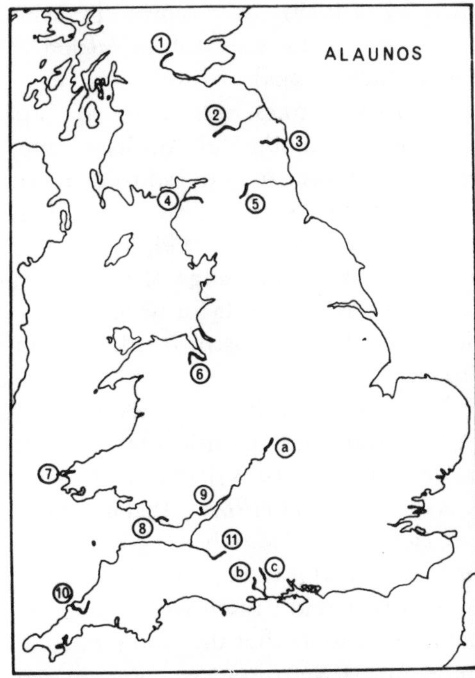

Fig. 27. River-names derived from *Alauna* or *Alaunos*: 1. Allan Water; 2. Ale Water; 3. Aln; 4. Ellen; 5. Ayle Burn; 6. Afon Alyn; 7. Alan; 8. Afon Alun; 9. Nant Alun (Eln Wall Reen); 10. Allen (Camel); 11. Alham. Possible examples: (*a*) Alne; (*b*) Allen; (*c*) Allen.

(for a river) 'rocky one'. But as Ekwall and others have noted, the name has such a wide application that it cannot be confined to such a sense. Since we find the name in both masculine and feminine forms, and applied in a range of references, the only reasonable assumption is that it is adjectival and broad in meaning. Ekwall *ERN* suggests that 'some meaning such as "holy" or "mighty" would give a suitable starting-point'. Dauzat *TF* 46 remarks of *Alauna* in Gaul that 'le radical doit être le même que celui du gaulois *(*vel*)-*launos*', and this seems reasonable, because it takes us towards the second element in the British name *Bolvelaunium*, where it probably means 'good'. The latest view is that of Pokorny 31, who relates the name to Gaulish **alausa* > French *alose*, a kind of fish, and gives to the *Alauna* names the sense of 'die glänzende' ('shining' or 'brilliant' one) relating this ultimately to Indo-European **albho*-'white' (Latin *albus*, etc.). This clearly has the necessary wide sense to be applicable in a wide range of references, and is especially suitable for water-names. See also W. Nicolaisen in *BZN*, VIII (1957), 227–28.

As to the form of the names, most of the British and Continental sources record the stressed syllable with *-au-*. Jackson shows in *LHEB* 313 that in British '*au*, *ou* and *eu* fell together in *ọ̄* in the late first century, at least in part'. Hence most of these names in Britain were taken into Latin usage soon after the Conquest, and in that usage were preserved with an *-au-* which must have appeared fossilised to Celtic speakers but was normal in Latin (*au* > *o* in major areas of Latin speech only very much later). For further discussion and for the implications of the *-o-* recorded in forms of ALAUNA[3], see pp. 25–26. A Continental name which offers a parallel is the Greek colony 'Αλωναί (= *Alonae*) of Ptolemy II, 6, 14, perhaps now Guadamar near Benidorm (Alicante, Spain), whose form shows the same *au* > *o* development as in British and probably at an earlier date, since by Ptolemy's day Celtic speech is thought to have been extinct for some time in Iberia.

IDENTIFICATION. Unknown, but from its position in the list evidently in south-west Britain and probably to be associated with Ptolemy's river ALAUNUS[1]. The suggestion of S. Applebaum in *JBAA*[3], XVII (1954), 77, that it is represented by the name Alcester in Shaftesbury, Dorset, must be dismissed, because this is related to land granted to the abbey of Alcester, Warwickshire, in A.D. 1307.

ALAUNA[2]

SOURCE

Ravenna 106_{39} (= R&C 78): ALAUNA

DERIVATION. See ALAUNA[1].

IDENTIFICATION. Probably the Roman town of Alcester, Warwickshire (SP 0858), on the river Alne. Ekwall *ERN* 8 interprets this river name differently, but the early forms he cites are equivocal.

ALAUNA[3]

SOURCE

AI 481_3 (Iter X): ALONE

DERIVATION. See ALAUNA[1]. The *-o-* of the present name is discussed there, and in more detail on pp. 25–26. Final *-e-* here is probably for classical *-ae*, locative, as in one record of ALAUNA[4] and in other names.

IDENTIFICATION. Probably the Roman fort at Watercrook, Westmorland (SD 5190). This is on the Kennet, so that the name here seems not to be derived from that of the river.

ALAUNA[4]

SOURCES

Ravenna 107_4 (= R&C 118): ALAUNA

ND XL_{53}: Tribunus cohortis tertiae Neruiorum, ALIONE.

DERIVATION. See ALAUNA[1]. The development of the vowel *au* > *o*, which may be an exceptional indication of the British sound-change, and its implications, are discussed there and also on pp. 25–26. *ND*'s form has what is probably locative *-e*, for classical *-ae*; its *-i-* is inexplicable except as the error of a scribe.

IDENTIFICATION. The Roman fort at Maryport, Cumberland (NY 0337), at the mouth of the river Ellen.

ALAUNA[5] (river)

SOURCE

Ravenna 108_{37} (= R&C 263): ALAUNA

DERIVATION: See ALAUNA[1]. This name figures in *Ravenna*'s list of rivers; it is presumably identical with that listed by Ptolemy, our ALAUNUS[2].

IDENTIFICATION. The river Aln, Northumberland.

ALAUNA[6] (settlement, fort)

SOURCES

Ptolemy II, 3, 7: 'Αλαῦνα (= ALAUNA), a *polis* of the (V)otadini

Ravenna 107_{46} (= R&C 187): ALAUNA

DERIVATION. We can be certain of this *Alauna* of *Ravenna* 107_{46} because it stands next-but-one to *Bremenium* at 107_{45}; both *Alauna* and *Bremenium* are given as *poleis* of the (V)otadini by Ptolemy II, 3, 7. For the name, see ALAUNA[1].

IDENTIFICATION. Probably the Roman fort at Low Learchild, Northumberland (NU 1011), near the river Aln. Ptolemy's name is omitted from many MSS and although his tribal attribution to the *Votadini* is correct, his misplacing of it suggests that it may be no more than a confused repetition of our ALAUNA[7] (Ardoch).

ALAUNA[7]

SOURCES

Ptolemy II, 3, 7: 'Αλαῦνα (= ALAUNA), a *polis* of the D(u)mnonii

Ravenna 107_{55} (= R&C 198): LITANA, var. LICANA

Ravenna's name has not previously been associated with Ptolemy's. R&C take it literally and give it an etymology, by no means unreasonably, based on British **litano-* 'broad'. It is also possible that the name is merely a part of *Litanomagus* (*Ravenna* 108_{6}), apparently north of the Antonine Wall; such fragmentation is not rare in this text. However, identity with Ptolemy's *Alauna* is nearly certain. The reason is partly textual, in that *Alauna*[1] in *Ravenna* 106_{14} has a variant *Alatina*, and that what we take to be **Alaunocelum* at 107_{34} is *Alitacenon* in the text; within this kind of miscopying emendation of *Litana* to *Alauna* is no problem. There is also a sound reason within the ordering of material by Ptolemy and the Cosmographer. Ptolemy lists as *poleis* of the D(u)mnonii in Scotland *Colania*, *Vindogara*, *Coria*, *Alauna*, *Lindum* and *Victoria*, and it can be shown that *Ravenna* (with adjustments) lists all of these, naturally enough, since both depended ultimately on the same map source. See Chapter V, p. 195.

DERIVATION. See ALAUNA[1].

IDENTIFICATION. The Roman fort at Ardoch, Perthshire (NN 8309), on the Allan Water.

ALAUNA[8] (?)

SOURCE

Ravenna 106_{59} (= R&C 110): ALŪNA, var. ALICINCA

This name is very uncertain. *Ravenna*'s main form is probably an abbreviation for **Alauna* (perhaps via a mistaken **Alanna*, with *n* for *u*, as often; the stroke over the preceding letter normally indicates omission of *n* or *m*), even though this name is not abbreviated elsewhere in the text. The *Alicinca* variant may have borrowed its last two letters from initial *Ca-* of the next name (also 106_{59}), *Camulo dono*: there are cases of this not uncommonly in the Cosmography. The variant just possibly might represent a form of Ptolemy's 'Ολίκανα (= *Olicana*). In the ordering of *Ravenna*'s list, the name occurs in a group of names in Derbyshire, Lancashire and the West Riding.

DERIVATION. See ALAUNA[1].

IDENTIFICATION. Unknown but, if not a misplaced repetition, apparently not far from Manchester.

*ALAUNOCELUM

SOURCE

Ravenna 107_{34} (= R&C 164): ALITACENON, var. ALITHACENON

Ravenna's forms must be corrupt, as they suggest no etyma Celtic or Latin. In favour of our emendation, it should be noted that *Ravenna* 106_{14}, *Alauna*, has a variant *Alatina*, a miscopying which illustrates how the present form could have arisen: see also *Alauna*[7] for *Litana* = *Alauna*. The second element as given by *Ravenna* almost certainly stands for *-celon*, that is *(o)celon*, *ocelum*; compare *Ravenna*'s *Iuliocenon* for **Itunocelum*.

DERIVATION. For the first element, see ALAUNA[1]. The second is British **ocĕlŏ* 'headland, promontory, spur'. It appears in British **Cintocelum*, *Itunocelum* and *Ocelum Promontorium*, and quite widely on the Continent. Ptolemy (II, 6, 22) gives Ὄκελον (= *Ocelum*), a *polis* of the Calliaci in Hispania Tarraconensis, now perhaps Navia near Bilbao; *Ocelodurum* was on a famous promontory overlooking the river Duero, now Zamora (Zamora, Spain); Strabo IV, 1, 3 and V, 1, 11 mentions another Ὤκελον > Ocello south of Susa (Torino, Italy). *Ocel(l)io* appears also as a personal name (Holder II. 826), and a divine name, of a god associated with Mars and others and known in inscriptions at Caerwent (*RIB* 309, 310) and Carlisle (*RIB* 949), also in Gallia Narbonensis and Germania Inferior (Whatmough *DAG* 836); presumably he is 'the first, chief'. The name seems to have had British *-l-* but often appears with *-ll-* in Latin sources. It may be ultimately related to Greek ὄκρις Latin *ocris* (also *medi-ocris*), Irish *och(a)ir*; see A. Tovar in *Homenaje al Profesor Alarcos* (Valladolid, 1966), 85, and Pokorny 21.

IDENTIFICATION. Unknown, but from its position in the list apparently in south-eastern Scotland and presumably sited on a spur or promontory.

ALAUNUS[1]

SOURCE

Ptolemy II, 3, 3: 'Αλαῦνου ποταμοῦ ἐκβολαί (= ALAUNI FLUVII OSTIA)

DERIVATION. See ALAUNA[1].

IDENTIFICATION. From its position in Ptolemy this should be the Axe which flows into the sea at Seaton, Devon, but this name ought to be derived from *Isca*. Two possible solutions suggest themselves, neither of them entirely satisfactory. First, both the Hampshire Avon and the Dorset Stour have tributaries called Allen, and although they are not attested in early sources (Ekwall, *ERN* 4) the common mouth of the two rivers at Christchurch might once have been called *Alaunus*. Second, the distribution of the river names derived from *Isca* (as also that of names derived from *Abona*–see maps) suggests that at some stage Anglo-Saxons misunderstood the names they were given and mistook the generic word 'water' (or 'river') for the proper name, which was thus lost; in that case *Alaunus* here could still represent the Axe.

ALAUNUS[2]

SOURCE

Ptolemy II, 3, 4: 'Αλαῦνου ποταμοῦ ἐκβολαί (= ALAUNI FLUVII OSTIA)

DERIVATION. See ALAUNA[1]. The name seems to be the same as that of ALAUNA[5] (river), the Northumbrian Aln. The river could well have been known in both forms (both *-a* and *-us* being recorded elsewhere as river-names), or a slight error could have occurred in Ptolemy's text or in *Ravenna*.

IDENTIFICATION. The river Aln, Northumberland.

*ALBINIANO

SOURCE

Ravenna 106_{24} (= R&C 51): ALBINUMNO

DERIVATION. The name in *Ravenna* is almost certainly corrupt, and its second element has no analogies. An attractive correction produces **Albiniano*, on the assumption that as often happened original *ni* was miscopied as *m*; there is a parallel for this, in that some modern editors have read *Albanianis* of *TP* (also *AI* 369_1 = Alphen, Holland) as *Albamanis*. *Albinianus* seems an acceptable Latin name, in which case we presumably have the name of a villa-owner. The name is perhaps a kind of locative (strictly *-i*) expressed by an ablative, signifying 'at Albinianus's'. The few other probable estate-names known in Britain are expressed in similar ways: *Anicetis* and *Sulloniacis*, probably locative (and plural in form, perhaps with reference to 'the family of' or 'the descendants of'); and *Villa Faustini*, in which *Villa* may originally have been an itinerary ablative rather than the nominative it seems.

IDENTIFICATION. Unknown, probably in Monmouthshire or Glamorgan.

ALBION

SOURCES

Pseudo-Aristotle III (393b): Ἄλβιων (= ALBION)

Pliny *NH* IV, 102: ALBION ipsi nomen fuit cum Britanniae vocarentur omnes

Ptolemy II (prologue) and II, 3 (heading of chapter): 'Αλουίωνος (= ALVIONOS gen.)

Pseudo-Agathemerus IV, 13: 'Αλουίων (= ALVION)

Marcian I, 8 (also II, 1 and II, 41 and 44): Ἄλβιων (= ALBION)

Avienius 112: INSULA ALBIONUM ('island of the Albiones')

Stephanus of Byzantium: 'Αλβίων (= ALBION) and ethnic 'Αλβιώνιος (= ALBIONIUS)

The name undoubtedly had *-b-*; on Greek ου for β, see Jackson *LHEB* 35.

DERIVATION. The older idea was that the name was based on a supposed Celtic word equivalent to Latin *albus* 'white', the sense being 'white land', that is with reference to the white cliffs of Kent as seen from the Continent. Holder I. 83 adopted this, but modern specialists think that no such word existed in Celtic. Williams in *BBCS*, VI (1931–33), 134, drew attention to medieval Welsh *elfydd* 'world, land', derived from a British stem **albio-*. A meaning 'the land, the country' given by its own inhabitants is perfectly acceptable. Dottin *LG* 95 mentions a Gaulish divinity *Mars Albiorix* 'king of the world'. Pliny (*NH* IV, 111) notes the tribe of the *Albiones*, a people of Hispania Tarraconensis in the area of the *Navia* river (Lugo and Oviedo, Spain); the existence of this tribe may have induced confusion into Avienius's reference to Britain as *insula Albionum*: see C. F. C. Hawkes, *Pytheas: Europe and the Greek Explorers* (Oxford, 1977), 17–22.

The name was recalled by Bede (I, 1): *Britannia Oceani insula, cui quondam Albion nomen fuit*, a reference evidently taken from Pliny, whose work he knew. The name was obsolete by Pliny's time, but such was its authority that it continued in the Greek tradition; Avienius's mention depends upon very ancient sources and not on any currency contemporary with his work. See further Chapter II, p. 39. The name continued strongly in Irish tradition: in Irish and in Gaelic up to the twelfth century, *Alba* (genitive *Albu*, *Albou*) was the regular name for the region of Scotland north of the Forth, and some Irish writers use the name for the whole of Britain (see Rhys (1904), 206, and Watson *CPNS* 11).

IDENTIFICATION. An ancient name for Britain.

ALIONE of *ND* XL_{53}: see ALAUNA[4]

ALOBERGIUM

SOURCE

Ravenna 106_5 (= R&C 22): ALOVERGIUM

DERIVATION. If we take it that *Ravenna*'s *-v-* is for *-b-*, as often, the name seems to have British **alo-* 'rock' and **berg-* 'hill, mountain; heap', with the common derivational suffix *-i̯o-*, giving a sense 'rocky hill', a very acceptable type. The first element is cognate with Gothic *hallus* 'rock' and Anglo-Saxon *heall* 'stone, rock' (rare except in personal names).

Other possibilities are less attractive but in view of uncertainties over *Ravenna*'s forms cannot be ruled out. If this text has reduced *-ll-* to *-l-*, the first element might be **allo-* 'other, second', as in the ethnicon *Allobroges* of Gaul. If *Ravenna*'s *-v-* is correct, there might be a relation with a word corresponding to Gaulish **u̯erco- u̯ergo-*, for which see VERCOVICIUM; but this would not make for an easy sense here. It may be relevant, in support of our original etymology, that Scandinavian *Bergos* is *Vergos* in one of the texts of Pliny.

Dillemann (p. 65) regards the name as a corruption, *Alovergium* involving an erroneous transliteration of Ptolemy's Οὐεργιόνιος, one of the two oceans that lie to the west of Britain, this name being misread from a map. However, the suggestion seems rather strained. Against it, we note that: (1) the name as it stands has a good British etymology; (2) at no other point has *Ravenna* included ocean names as though they were inland habitation-names (though the Cosmographer was not incapable of doing so, as shown by his misreading of the name of Land's End: see ANTIVESTAEUM); (3) if *Ravenna* is here following the course of a road from the Devon coast (*Moridunum*[1]) to Bath, we know of no named place along its considerable length, and this name could well apply to a station on it.

IDENTIFICATION. Unknown, but probably in Devon or Somerset.

ALONE of *AI* 481_3; see ALAUNA[3]

AMBOGLANNA of *ND* XL_{44}: see CAMBOGLANNA

ANAS

SOURCE
Ravenna 109_{18} (= R&C 291): ANAS

DERIVATION. If we take this at face value, it is the Latin word for 'duck' (*anas*, *anitis* or *anatis*; > Spanish *ánade*, etc.). Richmond in *Antiquity*, XIV (1940), 194, paired this name with *Atina* of *Ravenna* 109_{19} and thought the references might be to 'duck' and 'drake'; in their 1949 study R&C seem to have accidentally moved their note about *Anas* 'duck' to *Atina*, where it certainly does not belong. The name of the latter is of unknown meaning, and there is really no evidence for the pairing, especially since *Atina* in *Ravenna* is not next to *Anas* but next-but-one. If 'duck' is right for the present name it might be a picturesque, perhaps humorous creation, doubtless one made by the Roman fleet during its exploration of the Western Isles in Flavian times; this is the only explanation for the existence of the Latin names for wholly unromanised islands off W. Scotland – *Anas*, *Cana*, *Grandina*, *Susurra* and possibly *Sapónis*. These are not likely to be translations of native British names. It is unsure how much currency they had; *Cana* may survive, but the others do not (R&C note that the names of the Western Isles were so thoroughly changed by Norse settlers that the older names have almost completely disappeared. However, R&C draw attention to the possible survival of the present name for a time, as the unidentified *Inis Ane* in the Book of Leinster, 182a, 42, 183a 10.)

IDENTIFICATION. Unknown, but apparently an island off the west coast of Scotland.

ANAVA

SOURCES
Ravenna 108_{31} (= R&C 251): ANAVA
CIL XI. 5213, the tombstone from Fulginiae (now Foligno) of a man who among other offices had held that of CENSITO(RI) BRITTONUM ANAVION[EN(SIUM)]. He operated under Trajan, perhaps about A.D. 112, and it is likely that his sphere of duty lay in the region of the present *Anava*. For discussion, see Richmond in *Arch.* XLIII (1949), 42; Frere, *Britannia*[2] (1974), note to 230; Rivet's review of the first edition of this in *JRS*, LIX (1969), 248; and the note on p. 95 of *RIB*. The association by some of the present name with *Navio* in Derbyshire is erroneous, as they are distinct and of different origins.
(*Tacitus*: It was suggested by Richmond that this river, in its accusative form *Anavam*, should be read as an addition to *Agricola* 24, 1; but Ogilvie (p. 236 of the 1967 edition) does not support

this, and N. Reed agrees with the rejection in *Britannia*, II (1971), 144.

DERIVATION. R&C, following Watson *CPNS* 55, note that the modern name Annan is the genitive of *anau*, cognate with Welsh *anaw* 'riches' and Gaelic *anu*; and that *Anu* was an Irish goddess of prosperity. Their sense for *Anava*, 'rich river', seems fully acceptable. Holder III. 606 cites eight Continental rivers and settlements which seem to derive from *Anava*, none documented in ancient sources. Dottin *LG* 226 cites Gaulish **anau̯o-* as a 'thème de nom propre'.

IDENTIFICATION. The river Annan in south-west Scotland.

ANCALITES

SOURCE

Caesar *BG* V, 21, 1: ANCALITES

DERIVATION. Holder I. 137 analyses the name *An-calites*, with **an-* intensive prefix. For the base Watson (*CPNS* 21, writing of *Calidonia*) indicates **kal-* 'hard'; Holder I. 696 and Dottin *LG* 239 list **călĕt-* **călĕtŏ-* with senses 'hard; severe; austere; firm; tough, hardy'; cf. Old and Middle Irish *calath*, *calad*, Welsh *caled* 'hard', in Pokorny 524. For this tribal name a sense of 'very hard men, very tough men' seems appropriate. There was a Gaulish tribe of *Caleti* or *Caletes* in the region of modern Caux and Bray (Seine-Maritime, France); their name is usually spelled with *-e-*, but *Calitius*, *Calitix* are recorded as personal names (Holder I. 700), and it seems that in Gaulish these related names showed the same *e/i* variation as that to be noted in British *Calidonia*, *Calidonii*; see our entries for these.

IDENTIFICATION. A British tribe mentioned only by Caesar; presumably they were located in south-eastern Britain and were later absorbed by a larger confederation.

ANDERITUM

SOURCES

ND XXVIII_{10} (*pictura*): ANDERIDOS, var. ANDERITOS
XXVIII_{20} (text): Praepositus numeri Abulcorum, [ANDERITOS] (the name is missing from the text and is supplied by the editor)

Ravenna 106_{33} (= R&C 68): ANDERELIO
(The tile inscription HON AUG ANDRIA is now known to be spurious)

There are further probable records of this name. Stevens in *Arch. J.*, XCVII (1940), 136–37, drawing support from Jullian and Nesselhauf, studies mention in *ND* VII_{100} of the *Anderetiani*, a unit serving in Gaul. In the MSS they are the *Anderenitiani* (var. *Andereniciani*). In the same list, XLI_{17}, there is mentioned the *Praefectus militum Anderetianorum, Uico Iulio* [Germersheim] (vars.: *Anderecianorum*, *Andericianorum*); and at $\text{XLII}_{22,\ 23}$ we find *Praefectus classis Anderetianorum, Parisius* (with similar vars.). Stevens thought that these *Anderetiani*, both the *milites* and the sailors of the naval squadron, 'derive their name from a fort called something like *Anderetia*', originally Pevensey. This is indeed a likely solution. That proposed by Miller in 1916, that the *Anderetiani* in Gaul originated at *Anderitum Gaballorum* (*TP*, etc.), now Javols (Lozère, France) might suit the soldiers but could not apply to the sailors, for Javols is an entirely inland place. Moreover, on the analogy of other *civitates* in Gaul, one might expect people of this place to be known as *Gaballi* (> Javols), which further removes them from consideration here. The original garrison of the port at Pevensey, the *Anderetiani*, had evidently been moved to Gaul and replaced in Britain by the *numerus Abulcorum*.

DERIVATION. The first element is **ande-*, an intensive prefix conveying 'great, big', on which see Jackson in *JRS*, XXXVIII (1948), 54, with references to work of Dillon and criticisms of senses ascribed to **ande-* by Holder, Zachrisson and Ekwall; also *GPN* 136–41. The prefix occurs in a good many Continental place-names and some personal names. *Anderitum Gaballorum* (Javols, mentioned above) is recorded as 'Ανδέρηδον (= *Anderedum*) by Ptolemy II, 7, 11, *Andereton* in *Ravenna* 63_{25}, and *Anderitum* in *TP*. A Colchester dedication (*RIB* 193) is to *Mercurio Deo Andescocivouco*, thought by Jackson to mean 'the great activator'.

The second element is British **ritu-* 'ford', plural **rita* (Welsh *rhyd*, Cornish *rid*; Irish *rith*; cognate with Latin *portus*, English *ford*, Norwegian *fjord*, etc.). It is found in the British names *Camboritum*, *Carbantoritum*, *Durolitum* (earlier **Duroritum*), *Maporitum*, *Tadoritum*), and in many Continental names, of which the best-known is *Augustoritum* now Limoges (Haute-Vienne, France), but seems to be not known in N. Italy or Spain. These names all show **ritu-* singular; see Vincent 225 and 229, *GPN* 249–51. The same element is present in the modern English names Penrith (Cumbria), Ridware (Staffs.) and Rhydd (Worcs.). Hence, for the present name, a sense 'great ford(s)' is proper, presumably with reference to a crossing of an inlet at Pevensey; the coastline here has changed so much since Roman times that one cannot be specific.

The form in which the name should be cited is unsure. *Anderida* seems to be traditional, but is not likely to be right. Jackson observed that, with respect to a possible *-d-*, 'to the eye of the Celticist the correct form is obviously Romano-British *Anderitum* or plural *Anderita*'. The *-d-* in Ptolemy's form for the corresponding place in Gaul is likely to be casual, and that under *ND*'s *pictura* of the British name a scribal error. The most likely correction of *Ravenna's* form is **Andereto*. It is not likely that *ND*'s form reflects the Vulgar Latin development (voicing) of *t* > *d*, which hardly began in Gaul before A.D. 400, though it might echo the speech of a later copyist on the Continent; and *-t-* did not lenite in British until the later fifth century, when the name was taken over into Anglo-Saxon with *-d-* (*Andred-*: see below). *ND*'s *-s* is unexplained. As for the choice between singular **ritu-* and plural **rita*, it must be noted that all the British and Continental analogues show *-ritum*, singular, and that the two sources for the name of Pevensey fort show *-o-*, the usual oblique case for places whose nominative was in *-um*. Final *-a* really has no more authority than that engendered by the spurious title with its '*Andria*'; philology can discount the inscription just as thermoluminescence dated the material of the tile. On all grounds, then, the proper form for the name is *Anderitum*.

IDENTIFICATION. The Roman fort at Pevensey, Sussex (TQ 6404).

Note. The name *Anderitum* survived for a long time after being taken into Anglo-Saxon. The *Anglo-Saxon Chronicle* says under A.D. 477 that a Saxon expedition into Sussex slew many Britons 'and drove some to flight into the wood which is called *Andredesleag*'. This is taken to be the forest which covered the Sussex Weald. An entry in the Chronicle for 491 names the fort itself: 'In this year Aelle and Cissa besieged *Andredesceaster* and slew all the inhabitants; there was not even one Briton left there.' As a forest-name the usage continued much longer: *desertum Ondred* in the *Life of St Wilfred* (about 700); in *ASC* entries for 755 (*Andred*, the Hampshire end) and 893 (*Andred*), and in 1018 *Andredesweald*; finally, in the Hampshire Domesday, *Andret* was applied to part of the New Forest. That the name should have applied so far west is extraordinary, but is confirmed by the *ASC* for 893: '...the mouth of the Lympne...that estuary is in east Kent, at the east end of the great forest which we call *Andred*. This forest from east to west is 120 miles or longer, and 30 miles broad.' The extension of a fort-name in this way is extraordinary enough, and apparently a unique case; it testifies to the importance of the fort in its region in the third and fourth centuries, perhaps to its continued importance at the time of its final capture by the Saxons.

ANICETIS

SOURCE

Ravenna 106_{15} (= R&C 35): ANICETIS

DERIVATION. This is probably the designation of an estate, based on the Latin personal name *Anicetus*. Its plural form might indicate 'the family of' or 'the descendants of' Anicetus, as in the other British estate-name having plural form, *Sulloniacis*. Two N. African villa-names in *AI* show the same plural with perhaps the same implication: *Casas Villa Aniciorum* 61_2 and *Megradi Villa Aniciorum* 62_3. *Anicetis* then has locative plural case, for reasons suggested on pp. 34–35. In all, sixteen British names come to us exclusively in this form: *Anicetis, Causennis, Concangis, Dubris, Lavatris, Lemanis, Lindinis, Magis, Magnis*[1], *Magnis*[2], *Pontibus, Spinis, Vagniacis, Varis, Venonis, Verteris*, and others such as *Rutupis* show this usage nearly established as standard. There are also indications that a few names of singular number were also becoming established in this fossilised ablative-locative case.

There have been attempts to identify the *Anicetus* in question. R&C remind us that there was a famous Anicetus, freedman of Nero, 'who might well have acquired British estates'. S. Applebaum in *JBAA*[3], XVII (1954), 77–79, wonders whether Q. Pompeius Anicetus, a Roman citizen who dedicated an altar to Sulis at Bath (*RIB* 148) might be the man.

IDENTIFICATION. Unknown, but probably in southern Britain between Gloucester and Badbury.

ANTIVESTAEUM PROMONTORIUM

SOURCES

Ptolemy II, 3, 2: 'Αντιουέσταιον ἄκρον τὸ καί Βολέριον (= ANTIVESTAEUM SIVE BOLERIUM PROMONTORIUM), var. 'Αντιουέστεον (= ANTIVESTEUM)

Ravenna 106_1 (= R&C 14): VERTEVIA

106_3 (= R&C 18): MESTEVIA

The two forms of *Ravenna* (taken as separate Devonian names by R&C, who even provide an etymology for the latter) are rightly referred by Dillemann (p. 65) to Ptolemy's name. On the map(s) used by the Cosmographer, the first element *Anti-* must have been written 'in the sea', or separated by being placed above, and the remaining portion was understandably taken to refer to a settlement on land. That the Cosmographer also duplicates, with different mistakes each time, might show that he was using two maps which coincided in their manner of entering the name; and both seem to have written the ending of the name as *-eum* (Ptolemy's var.), then misread as *-evia*. There is no ready parallel for the miscopying of initial *V-* as *M-*, but probably the line of the coast on the map interfered with the letter. A further indication of the identity of *Ravenna*'s names with Ptolemy's entry comes in the order of their listing: Dillemann notes that *Ravenna* lists *Vertevia* immediately after *Uxelis*, just as Ptolemy does; also, *Ravenna*'s two forms both immediately precede listing of *Moridunum*[1] in mistakenly duplicated forms.

DERIVATION. As is plain from Ptolemy, *Antivestaeum* is an alternative name to *Belerium*, and we know the latter to be much the older. It is also Graeco-Latin whereas *Belerium* (**Beleri̯on*) is the native British name. *Antivestaeum* probably represents a coining by the Roman fleet; in the same region, 'Promontory of Hercules' is another. The name seems to be adjectival. The first element is Graeco-Latin *anti-* 'opposite', found in such names as *Antilibanus* 'mons celeber Syriae, ita dictus, quia Libano oppositus', *Antirrhium* . . . 'promontorium . . . ita dictum, quod sit adversus Rhion'. The second element is based on *Vesta*, not so much a divine name but one representing Greek Ἑστία. This equivalence is doubted by Ernout & Meillet, but Hamp in *Ériu*, xxv (1974), 258–61, links the Latin name with an earlier **u̯osta*, a 'personified noun of instrument', = 'thing to burn with', i.e. 'hearth', with the suggestion that in Latin *vesta* actually meant 'hearth'; the Indo-European root is **eus-* burn. This takes us towards a sense of 'ever-burning flame' or 'beacon', and implies that Latin *-vestaeum* is a translation of, or refers to the same feature as, earlier *Belerium*. The precise significance of the element *anti-* is uncertain. Possibly the tip of the promontory was, in the eyes of the fleet, opposite another on which a beacon stood. But perhaps, as Professor C. Thomas suggests to us, the reference is to the important shrine at Nor'nour in the north-eastern Scillies; and, as he points out, this possibility would be strengthened if the name of the Scillies (see SILINA) was ultimately connected with that of the goddess *Sulis*, of Bath, who, though equated by the Romans with Minerva rather than Vesta, was connected with an ever-burning flame (see Solinus, 22, 11, p. 00). This sacred site might then have been identified as an Ἑστιαῖον (latinised as *Vestaeum*).

IDENTIFICATION. Land's End, Cornwall.

ANTRUM (?)

SOURCE
Ravenna 108_{34} (= R&C 257): ANTRUM

DERIVATION. This name is problematical, and may be corrupt. It is in the river-list, but we know this to be untrustworthy in several instances. If it does represent a river, an equivalence to the *Vedra* (R. Wear) cannot entirely be ruled out, perhaps via a map in which an unintended mark over the first vowel was taken to represent the abbreviation of *n*, this *n* then being written out in full by the Cosmographer; but since the Wear already figures in his text (as ADRON), this seems unlikely. O'Rahilly in *EIHM* 14 notes that Ptolemy's Ἄδρου (gen.; *Adros*) is Pliny's *Andros*, perhaps a corruption of **Antro* = Irish *Étar*, the Hill of Howth (Ireland, mistaken for an island); but *Ravenna*'s *Antrum* can hardly represent this, as the name is grouped with others on the north-east British coast. An association with *Ravenna*'s preceding entry, *Intraum* at 108_{34}, is more likely; there are instances in which, in a pair of adjacent names, one represents a correction of the other. If this is right, neither form seems preferable by offering an obvious etymology. In any case, *-um* is not a proper termination for a river-name, and other instances of it (or of *-on*) in *Ravenna*'s river-list are known to be corrupt. There are three possible analogues abroad, also apparently of unknown meaning: an *Antro Vico* > Antre (Franche-Comté, France: see *DAG* 1087); *Antrum insula* > Indre (Loire-Inférieure, France), mentioned in late authors; and *Antros insula* in Aquitania (*DAG* 360).

IDENTIFICATION. Uknown.

APAUNARIS of *Ravenna* 106_4 (= R&C 20); see AQUAE CALIDAE, AQUAE SULIS

AQUAE ARNEMETIAE

SOURCE

Ravenna 106_{57} (= R&C 107): AQUIS ARNEMEZA, var. ARNEMEYA

DERIVATION. The name is Latin, 'waters of Arnemetia', here in the locative (as in one record of the next name). Many places having hot or medicinal springs were so designated; well-known Continental examples include *Aquae* > Aachen (Aix-la-Chapelle), *Aquae Sextae* > Aix en-Provence, *Aquae Terebellicae* now Dax.

In *Ravenna*'s form the genitive ending of the goddess's name should be *-e* (for *-ae*). The *-z-* shows assibilation of *c* and *t* plus yod, /kj/ and /tj/, in the Cosmographer's speech: the same is shown by his forms *Canza* 106_{11}, *Cunetzone* 106_{21} and *Melezo* 106_{16}, in all of which *-ti-* is to be re-established. *Arnemetia* contains the British elements **are-* **ar-* 'in front of' (*are-* = 'ante', Vienna Glossary) plus *nemet-* 'sacred grove'. The goddess herself is mentioned in *RIB* 281, an altar from the Roman fort at *Navio* (Brough-on-Noe, Derbyshire): *Deae Arnomecte*... (dative), where it is odd to find a doubly incorrect spelling in the latinised form of British *nemet-*, which must have been widely known. Another goddess *Nemetona* appears on an altar at Bath, *RIB* 140, and is known on the Continent also. *CIL* XII. 2820 records the *Arnemetici*.

Nemet-nemeton is a widespread and fundamental word of the early Celtic world. It designated natural sacred groves and artificial constructions also (in Ireland, *nemed* was glossed 'sacellum' = 'sanctuary'), and was well known to Latin speakers in Celtic areas, cf. 'de sacris silvarum quae *nimidas* vocant' cited by Holder from an *Indiculus superstitionum et paganiorum*. The word is based on an assumed **nem-os* 'heaven', cf. Sanskrit *nam* 'to worship' and Old Irish *nemhta* 'holy'; cognates in the sense 'grove' are Greek νέμος and Latin *nemus*. See Holder II, 712; Whatmough *DAG* 166–67; T. G. Powell, *The Celts* (1958), 138–40; A. Ross, *Pagan Celtic Britain* (1967), 36–37. Place-names with this element are frequent (Holder II. 708 ff.). Of interest are *Augustonemetum* now Clermont-Ferrand (Puy-de-Dôme, France), *Nemetacum Atrebatum* now Arras (Pas-de-Calais,

France), *Nemetodurum* > Nanterre (Seine, France), and *Nemetobriga* near modern Pueblo de Tribes (Orense, Spain). In Galatia the Celtic tribes had *Drunemeton* as their common sanctuary. In Britain the element is represented in *Medionemetum*, *Nemeto Statio and Vernemetum*. The Mole and Yeo rivers of Devon were known in older times as Nymet, Nemet (Ekwall *ERN* 304), a name which survives in that of three places in Devon (Ekwall *EPN*). There are finally two items of epigraphic evidence from Britain. In *JRS*, LII (1962), 192, there is recorded the finding at Nettleham (Lincs.) of a dedication slab to *Mars Rigonemetos* 'king of the sanctuary', a god known also abroad. In *JRS*, XLIV (1954), 110, a dish found in the City of London is published, having a graffito]*Nemet* on the base, presumably the name of the owner (possibly with a missing prefix).

IDENTIFICATION. The Roman spa at Buxton, Derbyshire (SK 0673).

AQUAE CALIDAE, AQUAE SULIS

SOURCES

Ptolemy II, 3, 13: Ὕδατα Θερμά (= AQUAE CALIDAE), a *polis* of the Belgae

AI 486_3 (Iter XIV): AQUIS SULIS, var. SOLIS

Ravenna 106_4 (= R&C 20): APAUNARIS, with
109_{10} (= R&C 278): MINERVE

Ravenna's form *Apaunaris* was taken by R&C to refer to a separate place 'somewhere N.E. of Exeter', but (*a*) its elements suggest no meaning in British or Latin, (*b*) the name of Bath is otherwise missing from *Ravenna* (which would be unexpected), (*c*) the placing of *Apaunaris* in the list could well be for Bath, though the Cosmographer in reading from his map-source possibly took the name as applying to a place at its western rather than eastern end, and thus grouped it with more south-westerly names, and (*d*) the corruption of **Aque Sulis* is well within the range of miscopying of this text (e.g. *Age* for *Aque*, *Aquae* at 65_{10} and 65_{14}). Dillemann explains *Apaunaris* as a corruption of **A Tamaris*, but there are no examples in the British section of such a use of *a*, and (a lesser objection) *Tamaris* is already present at 105_{48}. If our proposal here does not satisfy and another is sought, *Apauna-* in this entry might represent the *Alauna* of *Ravenna* 106_9 and 106_{14}, but this is unlikely because the name is already duplicated, and because it would leave the *-ris* unexplained.

Minerve (for *-ae*, genetive) has not previously been related to the name of Bath as it appears in our texts. R&C take the entry at face-value on its appearance in what purports to be a list of Scottish islands, explaining that it belongs with the group of these islands named in Latin by the Roman fleet, '(island) of Minerva'. However, the equation of the goddess *Sulis* with Minerva is well established (see e.g. *RIB* 146). We suggest that on a map – perhaps different from that which gave him *Apaunaris* – the Cosmographer found **Aquae Sulis Minervae*, neglected the first word, and carelessly took the second as a version of **insula*; he then reserved the name for mention in his list of islands, which is very confused in other respects too. Alternatively, *Minerve* might be a real island-name or attribute, if the ancient name of the Scillies is connected with that of *Sulis*: see our entry SILINA.

DERIVATION. Ptolemy's name *Aquae Calidae* 'hot springs' is presumably that by which the place was first known, and has numerous Continental parallels in the names of what are today e.g. Vichy (France), Banolas (Catalonia), Caldas de Reyes (N.W. Spain) and Dzamal near the Romanian coast. It is noteworthy that Solinus mentions the *fontes calidi* of what is evidently Bath, together with the cult of Minerva there (see p. 85).

The nominative form of the goddess's name is **Sulis* not *Sul* as used to be said (Jackson; see note on pp. 42–43 of *RIB*). Her name is cognate with Irish *súil* 'eye', but Jackson is doubtful whether there is also connection with Celtic words for 'sun' (Dottin *LG* 289 mentions Welsh *haul* and Breton *heol* 'sun'); *AI*'s variant *Solis* is best regarded as an inspired copying error rather than a meaningful assimilation to Latin *sol*, since the latter would suppose a knowledge of Celtic in the copyist. The name is probably to be associated with that of the *Suleviae* goddesses whose cult was widespread. Texts from Bath name the goddess in the genitive, *Sulis* (*RIB* 141d, 155), and dative, *Suli* (*RIB* 143, 144, 146–50). As a place-name apparently on its own is *Sulim* (accusative, for nominative **Sulis*) in *TP*, now Castel-Noëc (Morbihan, France). See also CORIA SOLILIORUM.

IDENTIFICATION. The Roman spa at Bath, Somerset (ST 7564). The attribution of the place to the Belgae depends entirely on Ptolemy and the distribution of pre-Roman coins of the Dobunni suggests that it may be incorrect (see p. 121).

ARAMIS of *Ravenna* 106_{15} (= R&C 34): see ARMIS

ARBEIA

SOURCE

ND XL$_7$ (*pictura*): ARBEIA
XL$_{22}$ (text): Praefectus numeri barcariorum Tigrisiensium, ARBEIA

DERIVATION. This is unknown. There are possible parallels in *Arba*, an island of Liburnia (Dalmatia) > Arbe, Pliny *NH* III, 140; *Arva* in S. Spain, now Peña de la Sal (Sevilla), Pliny *NH* III, 11; *Arviates*, a people of Pannonia, Pliny *NH* III, 148. The *-*e̯ia* suffix (Holder I. 1410) is found in British *Seteia*, *Tameia*, *Verbeia*, which are, or are built on, river-names, and abroad in *Mendiculeia* (*AI* 452_1), *Vindeleia* (*AI* 454_6) and *Beleia* (*AI* 454_8), all in Spain; also in personal names *Cobeia*, *Derceia* (Dottin *LG* 108). Holder thinks the suffix may be a substitute for -*acum*, as in *Anceium* for **Antiacus*, etc.; its force is unclear.

IDENTIFICATION. The Roman fort at South Shields, Durham (NZ 3667), since this is the only suitable base for a *Numerus Barcariorum*.

Note. *Arbeia* may have been the site of *Horrea Classis*^{2}, q.v.

ARDAONEON of *Ravenna* 106_{19} (= R&C 43): see PORTUS ARDAONI

*ARDOTALIA

SOURCE

Ravenna 106_{58} (= R&C 108): ZERDOTALIA

DERIVATION. Since *Zer*- is impossible in British and Latin, the name must be corrupt. R&C suggest a scribal contamination with the end of the previous name in *Ravenna*, *Aquis Arnemeza*, which at an earlier, more correct stage probably had *-ze* (a Vulgar Latin development of *-tie*, genitive); hence **Ardotalia* is a well-reasoned supposition. We follow R&C's suggestions about the two elements. The first is British **ardu-* 'high' or 'height', from which comes Welsh *ardd* 'height' (as in *Penn-ardd*), and with which Irish *ard* 'high' and Latin *arduus* are cognate. The second is the British word from which Welsh *tal* 'brow, edge, end' is derived; hence a meaning 'high brow' or 'brow-height' for the whole name. Parallels for the first element exist: possibly the next name, *Ardua*, if it really is an independent item; very probably *Portus Ardaoni*; perhaps the 'Αρδώτιον (= *Ardotium*) of Ptolemy II, 16, 6, in Illyricum; *Adrobriga* if for **Ardobriga* of Mela III, 1, 13 (N. Spain); and most notably *Arduenna*, *Ardenna* > Ardennes, in which the root seems to have evolved from 'height' > 'wooded height' > 'wood' (cf. Spanish *monte*). See Holder I. 186, Vincent 232.

IDENTIFICATION. The Roman fort of Melandra Castle, Glossop, Derbyshire (SK 0095); as R&C point out, this suits both the position of the name in the list and the description of the site 'on the edge of the brow'.

(ARDUA)

SOURCE

Ravenna 105_{50} (= R&C 9): ARDUA

R&C read this name jointly with the next in *Ravenna*'s list, *Ravenatone*. Schnetz in his edition prints them separately. If *Ardua* is taken separately, it is presumably a latinised form of British **ardu-*, for which see the previous entry, perhaps assimilated to Latin *ardua* 'high places'. However, this is very doubtful. We prefer to consider this jointly with *Ravenatone* as a garbled entry: see DERVENTIO[5].

ARGISTILLUM

SOURCE

Ravenna 106_{30} (= R&C 63): ARGISTILLUM

DERIVATION. Williams finds the origin of this name in a British word which has given Welsh *gwystl* (Irish *giall*) 'hostage', drawing attention to Holder I. 1993 (**geislos*, **geistlos*), and the modern Welsh place-name *Arwystli*; there is prefixed **are-* **ar-* 'in front of' (as in *Arnemetia* – see AQUAE ARNEMETIAE – and *Ariconium*). The meaning is thus perhaps 'at the hostage', 'with a folk-lore reference now lost'. This seems possible, and we have nothing better to offer, even though this makes difficult sense. It should not be forgotten that in a gravely miscopied text like *Ravenna* there are no certainties when this text alone gives us a name. The present entry could be a garbled version of *Ariconium*, on the ground that this stands next to Gloucester in Iter XIII of *AI*, just as in *Ravenna* *Argistillum* stands next to Gloucester at 106_{29}. It is also possible that a root in Celtic **arganto-* 'silver', which is common in place-names, is involved.

IDENTIFICATION. Unknown, probably near Gloucester.

ARICONIUM

SOURCE

AI 485_{3} (Iter XIII): ARICONIO

DERIVATION. The name is formed from British **are-* (**ari-*) 'in front of' and

**conio-*, of unknown meaning but perhaps the same as in *Viroconium*. Among names formed in this way (Holder I. 188) are possibly British *Argistillum* (and divine name *Arnemetia*), and abroad *Armorici* (*Aremorici*, the people 'in front of the sea'), *Arelaunum silva*, *Areduno vico* > Ardin (Deux-Sèvres, France); these do not help to guess a meaning for the present name, though Jackson observes that the prefix is 'usually used in place-names of regions *beside* some feature such as a forest, a marsh, the sea, etc.' (*Britannia*, I (1970), 68).

IDENTIFICATION. The Roman settlement at Weston under Penyard, Herefordshire (SO 6423).

Note. The name has interesting survivals. In *EPNS*, XL, 192, its first part, with Anglo-Saxon *-ingas* attached, is recorded as *Ircingafeld* in the *ASC* (918) and *Arcenfelde* in *DB*, modern Archenfield, a deanery of the diocese of Hereford. There is also *Ergyn(g)*, the Welsh name for a district in Herefordshire. Possibly the first element survives in a different form in the name Yartleton; the Roman site is some three miles to the north-west of this place.

ARMIS (?)

SOURCE

Ravenna 106_{15} (= R&C 34): ARAMIS, var. ARANUS
106_{19} (= R&C 42): ARMIS

DERIVATION. The entries make an obvious duplication, but it is hard to know which form is the better. It is likely that a river-name is in question, the Cosmographer as often having misread this from his map-source(s) as though it were a habitation-name. There are several possibilities:

(*a*) If *Armis* is approximately right, the name compares with *Armis(s)a*, earlier **Armīsā*, > Erms (a tributary of the Neckar, Germany), and with the *Arma* river of Piedmont (N. Italy), a tributary of the Stura, whose name survives in that of Botro dell'Arme near Siena. These names are ultimately related to **Arā*, commonly found in water-names (Indo-European **ora* 'to set in motion'), according to Nicolaisen in *BZN*, VIII (1957), 229. See also, for **ar(a)* as suffix or element, British LEUCARUM. If this is right, *Ravenna*'s *Armis* could be for **Armisa*, with *-s-* (in absolute internal position) still heard in British speech (before its loss in the second half of the first century: see *LHEB* 521–25). Equally, since final *-is* in *Ravenna* sometimes represents *-a*, the name could have been **Arma* like that of the Italian river. In either case, the river might be the modern Erme of S. Devon, or a place on it. Ekwall *ERN* 149–50 discusses this name and its possible but difficult English origin, leaving open the possibility that it might be British, as would be natural enough in Devon. For the vowel development, compare **Arno-* > Earn river of Somerset, and several in Scotland. The Erme seems to have sufficient size to warrant mention on a Romano-British map.

(*b*) *Armis* is readily adjusted to **Arnus*, and the var. *Aranus* may support this. If so, the name is the common **Arno-* river-name of Celtic (Holder I. 218), discussed by Ekwall *ERN* 139 as the origin of the Somerset Earn; but this is too small to have been mentioned on an early map, and the name might apply to another southern or south-western river.

(*c*) If the form *Aramis* is of any value, it might represent a British equivalent of Gaulish **aramon*, Indo-European **ar(ə)mo-*, Germanic *arm* (English *arm*) *aram-*, discussed by Whatmough *DAG* 1205; a metaphorical application as in 'arm of the sea, *brazo de mar*' would be possible.

IDENTIFICATION. Probably the river Erme, Devon.

ATEÇOTTI

SOURCES

Ammianus Marcellinus XXVI, 4, 5: ATTACOTTI (again XXVII, 8, 4)

St Jerome, *Epistolae* 69 (= 82, p. 415): ATTICOTORUM (gen. pl.); *Adversus Iovinianum* II (p. 335): ATTICOTOS (acc. pl.), gens Britannica (var.: Scoti)

ND Or. $IX_{8, 29}$: ATECOTTI (and several other references)

DERIVATION. The name is made up of Celtic **ate-*, an intensive prefix (as in *Atepomari*, etc.; cognate with Latin *et*, and as in *etiam*; *atavus, atnepos*), and **cotto-* 'old', found also in the personal names *Cottos, Cottius* (*Alpes Cottiae*), etc., whose derivatives include Cornish *coth* and Breton *coz* 'old'. Hence for the tribe, 'very old ones, oldest inhabitants'; for such a sense, one may compare Irish *Tuath Sen-Cheneóil* 'tribe of the old race' and *Tuath Sen-Érann* 'tribe of the old Hibernians' (Holder I. 254; Pokorny 70). For the expression of an older view, see Sir W. Ridgeway in *JRS*, XIV (1924), 135–36.

IDENTIFICATION. A tribe, or a confederation of tribes, of Scotland or possibly Ireland.

ATINA (?)

SOURCE

Ravenna 109_{19} (= R&C 293): ATINA

DERIVATION. None can be given; as it stands the name suggests no root Latin or Celtic, and is most likely corrupt like others in this part of *Ravenna*'s list; nor, despite its appearance in the list of islands, can there be any certainty that an island is in question. For further observations, see ANAS.

IDENTIFICATION. Unknown.

ATREBATES

SOURCES

Caesar *BG* II, 4, etc.: ATREBATES (of Gaul)

Ptolemy II, 3, 12: Ἀτρεβάτιοι (ATREBATII)

AI 478_3 (Iter VII): GALLEVA ATREBATUM

Ravenna 106_{32} (= R&C 67): CALEBA ARBATIUM

DERIVATION. Jackson in *Britannia*, I (1970), 70, analyses the name as a compound of **trebā-* 'to inhabit', from **trebo-* 'inhabitation, settlement', with prepositional prefix **ad-* 'to' and verbal-adjectival suffix **-tis*. He adds that the force of the preposition is unclear; early Irish *aittreb*, Welsh *athref* 'inhabitation, dwelling', from **ad-trebo-*, suggest that **ad-* had no special force in the compound. The meaning is 'settlers, inhabitants'. The main element appears in the place-name *Locatrebe* of Scotland, the name of the deity *Contrebis* known from altars at Lancaster and Overborough (*RIB* 600, 610), the place *Contrebia* of the Celtiberi in Spain (now Baños de Sacedón, Guadalajara) and the tribe *Arrotrebae* of N. Spain mentioned by Pliny. Further *treb-* names in Spain are listed by Tovar in *EC*, XI (1966–67), 246. Cognates include Latin *tribus*, Germanic *thorpa* (English *thorp*); modern Celtic derivatives are mentioned by Williams. In Gaul the name of the *Atrebates* survives in that of

Arras (Pas-de-Calais, France). On the suffix, stated by some as *-(*i*)*atis*, see Holder I. 253 and O'Rahilly *EIHM* 147; a study of it by G. Combarnous in *RIO*, 27 (1975), 17–35, is extremely unsound, as it confuses this suffix with others and with elements similar only in appearance.

Tribal names seem much given to variation of declension when taking Latin forms. The *Atrebates* are not only *Atrebatii*, as above, but their Gaulish part is also *Atrebatae* in Orosius. In Britain we find *Calidonii–Caledones*, *Novantae* beside *Trinovantes*, *Selgovae–*Selgoves* and *Smertae–*Smerti*. Such variations are found not uncommonly also in Gaul, Spain, etc.

IDENTIFICATION. A people of southern Britain with their capital at *Calleva*, Silchester, Hampshire.

AUGUSTA[1]

SOURCES

Ravenna 106_{50} (= R&C 97): LONDINIUM AUGUSTI

Ammianus Marcellinus XXVII, 8, 7: ad Lundinium, vetus oppidum quod AUGUSTAM posteritas appellavit (*concerning an event of A.D. 368*)

XXVIII, 3, 7: ab AUGUSTA profectus, quam veteres appellavere Lundinium (*concerning an event of A.D. 369*)

ND XI_{37}: Praepositus thesaurorum Augustensium [in Britannis]

Mint-mark on fourth-century coins of London: AVG

DERIVATION. Ammianus's form is the correct one; *Ravenna*'s a slight misunderstanding. This is an honorific Latin title awarded to London and evidently used in official parlance and as a by-name. *ND* has the adjectival form. The name was not remembered in post-Imperial times.

It is not known when the title was conferred. It has been suggested by Richmond (followed by Frere) that the city was known as *Caesarea* when made capital of the province of *Flavia Caesariensis* or that called *Maxima Caesariensis*, and then became *Augusta* on the occasion of the visit of Constantius in A.D. 306.

IDENTIFICATION. The Roman city of London (TQ 3281).

AUGUSTA[2] (?) – See the Appendix

AVENTIUS

SOURCE

Ravenna 108_{28} (= R&C 245): AVENTIO

It is likely that *Ravenna*'s form in *-o* represents the oblique case of a name whose nominative is in *-us*, second declension masculine, even though in the river-list of the Cosmography this is the sole name in *-o*; it is paralleled by the names of rivers mistakenly included in the lists of habitation-names, such as *Eltabo* 105_{46} (*Fl Tavus*) and *Rumabo* 107_{47} (*Flum Abus*). *Aventius* is the form demanded by the modern derivative (below). The name as given by *Ravenna* can hardly be a third-declension nominative, despite appearances; there are very few nominatives in this text. Dillemann's wish (p. 65) to correct *Aventio* or to make it a version of Ptolemy's Λουέντινον (= *Luentinum*) cannot be accepted; for this, he postulates a misreading of Greek initial Λ as A, but there is no evidence elsewhere of this kind of use of a Greek source for Britain.

DERIVATION. This is not really a difficult name as it has seemed to some. We are helped by the fact that it survives as the Welsh river-name *Ewenni* (var.: *Ewenydd*). Williams discusses and rejects several suggestions, including that of

Holder I. 312 of a root **au̯entos* 'just, right' (a possibility retained by Dottin for Gaulish **au̯ento-* perhaps with this sense). He did not favour a connection with the numerous Continental water-names assembled by Pokorny 78 and others (see e.g. Pokorny in *VR*, X (1948–49), 225–26; Nicolaisen in *BZN*, VIII (1957), 233), including *Avara*, *Avens*, *Aventia* > Avenza (Etruria, Italy), *Aventia* > Avance (four names in France and one in Switzerland), *Aventicum*, Avançon, etc., on the ground that *Aventia* would give Welsh **Eweint* or **Awenedd* but not the surviving *Ewenni*; this, with its *-i* or *-ydd*, demands original **-i̯os* (masculine) or **-i̯on* (neuter). As we have argued above, *Ravenna*'s *Aventio* does indeed stand for Romano-British *Aventius*, British **Au̯enti̯os*, so there is no problem of form. Williams concludes that *Aventia* is best related to the root of Latin *aveo*, Welsh *ewyll-ys* 'will, wish'. However, this is a most unlikely base for a river-name, and Pokorny's Continental names in their widespread and coherent group are surely not to be dismissed. Pokorny cites the root as **au̯(e)* **au̯ent-* with meanings 'benetzen, befeuchten, fließen', and gives ample cognates in languages other than Celtic which justify such meanings, suggesting that the basic *Aventia* was perhaps a spring goddess. As for the ending of the British name, Jackson *LHEB* 351 thinks it may originally have had an **-īson* suffix, giving **-īon* in British; Pokorny himself suggests original **Avantīsa* (> *Aventia*) > Welsh *Ewenni*, but this overlooks the problem to which Williams drew attention.

IDENTIFICATION. The river Ewenni, Glamorgan.

AXELODUNO of *ND* XL_{49}: see UXELODUNUM

AXIUM

SOURCE

Ravenna 108_{24} (= R&C 237): AXIUM

DERIVATION. This is unknown. The name has not produced that of the modern R. Axe (Somerset) as R&C think, improperly criticising Ekwall, since a modern Axe supposes (like Exe) an original *Isca*. There are parallels abroad: *Axima* > Ayme-en-Tarentaise (Tarentaise, France); *Axona* river with a settlement *Axona*, *Axuenna* upon it > R. Aisne (Aisne, France). *Axantia*, *Axanthos* (Ushant) has more properly *U-*. In Macedonia there was the *Axius* river (modern Vardari or Wardar), but this is in non-Celtic territory and can hardly be relevant. The British name is not certainly that of a river, since *-um* is not natural for a river-name, and a number of entries in this section of *Ravenna* turn out to be the names of forts or settlements.

IDENTIFICATION. Unknown, but probably in southern Britain.

BANNA

SOURCES

Rudge Cup and Amiens *patera*: BANNA

Ravenna 107_{28} (= R&C 151): BANNA

Inscription: *RIB* 1905, a dedication to the god Silvanus set up by the VENATORES BANNIESS(ES), found inside Birdoswald fort

ND: M. W. C. Hassall in *Aspects of the ND* (Oxford, 1976), 113, proposes, in view of *RIB* 1905 and the well-attested presence at Birdoswald of *cohors I Aelia Dacorum*, to suppose a lacuna in an early MS of *ND*, and to restore it as follows:

XL_{43a}: Tribunus cohortis primae Aeliae Dacorum, [BANNA

XL$_{44}$: Tribunus cohortis secundae Tungrorum], CAMBOGLANNA. This seems not only acceptable, but, once demonstrated, obvious.)

DERIVATION. The root is British **banno-* **banna* 'peak, horn', surviving in Welsh and Breton *ban*, and known in Old Irish as *benn*, all with the original senses. For Gaulish Dottin *LG* 85 and 231 identified **benno-* in the sense 'tongue, horn' applied to promontories. The word entered an area of Vulgar Latin and produced Old Provençal *ban*, *bana*, Catalan *banya* 'horn' (*ELH* I. 146). In toponymy the root is well known. In Britain were *Bannatia*, *Bannaventa*, *Bannovalium*; abroad **Banna* > Bannes (Marne, France: Holder III. 799), *Cantobenna* > Chantoin (Puy-de-Dôme, France) with adjectival *Canto-benn-icus* 'white-peaked' (Watson *CPNS* 31), *Brigobanne* (*TP*) now Hüfingen (Austria), **Bannobriga* > Bañobre (Coruña, Spain). There seems to have been a personal name also; a moulded text on a small pan probably from an apothecary's scales, found at Sea Mills, reads [B]ΛNNΛF 'Banna fecit' (*JRS*, LIV (1964), 179), a mark known also from several Continental places (Holder I. 341, III. 799). In place-names *Banna* clearly indicates a notable 'horn', 'spur' or promontory of rock. According to Rostaing *ETP* 86–87, **ban-* **ben-* is, beyond Celtic, a pre-Indo-European element whose sense evolved from 'hauteur' to 'pointe', which fits neatly with 'horn, peak'; his examples include a *Banata* in Mesopotamia, the *Banienses* people of Lusitania, *Bantia* in Apulia and the famous fountain *Bandusia* of Horace.

Adjectival *Banniess(es)* in the inscription shows Vulgar Latin assimilation of *-ns-* > *-ss-*; compare a similar adjective with assimilation under VINDOLANDA, and see p. 25.

IDENTIFICATION. The Roman fort at Birdoswald, Cumberland (NY 6166).

BANNATIA

SOURCE

Ptolemy II, 3, 8: Βαννατία (= BANNATIA), a *polis* of the Vacomagi; var. Βανατία (= BANATIA)

DERIVATION. See the previous entry: **Banna*, with a Latin suffix which might be a version of a different British one.

IDENTIFICATION. Probably the Roman fort at Dalginross, Perthshire (NN 7721).

BANNAVENTA[1]

SOURCES

AI 470$_5$ (Iter II): BANNAVENTA, var. BENNAUENTA
477$_1$ (Iter VI): ISANNAVANTIA
479$_5$ (Iter VIII): BANNAVANTO

The correct form is certainly *Bannaventa*. The form in Iter VI is much the same in all MSS and probably goes back to the archetype, but is none the less a misreading; perhaps compare the reverse, *B-* for *S-*, in *TP*'s *Baromaci* for [*Ce*]*saromaci*.

DERIVATION. For **Banna*, see BANNA. *Venta* is a well-known problem. It is found again as a second element in *Glannoventa*, and as an independent word in the city-names *Venta Belgarum*, *Venta Icenorum* and *Venta Silurum*. Neither Latinists nor Celticists wish to claim it. Those who have favoured a Latin origin have not considered their Du Cange carefully enough. They seek a Latin *venta* 'market' and find it ('Locus, ubi merces venum exponuntur') copiously documented as a medieval Latin legal word; they also find in Du Cange *venda*, *venta* in the sense 'toll on goods for sale'. But these are mere medieval relatinisations of vernacular French *vente* 'sale', etc. *Vente* itself proceeds from a late Latin *vendĭta* abstracted from *vendere*, this *vendĭta* replacing classical *venditio*. It is just possible in theory for *vendĭta* > *venta* by the time of Ptolemy, who records *Venta Belgarum* and *Venta Icenorum*, in spoken Latin; elision of both pre-tonic and post-tonic vowel is recorded in the graffiti of Pompeii, e.g. *oriclas* for *auriculas*, and was repeatedly censured by grammarians. This elision is abundantly registered in Latin texts of Britain; among the few datable examples are some from the second century, such as *Hercli* for *Herculi* (*RIB* 2177), *piissma* (*RIB* 369), perhaps *sanctissmo* (*RIB* 600). Yet it is almost inconceivable, for several reasons, that the British *Venta* names should really show a derivative of this Latin *vendĭta* 'market': (1) because these names are recorded for us in official, that is classical Latin forms; (2) because Ptolemy nowhere offers us a vulgar rather than a classical form; (3) because *vendĭta* itself is not registered as a Latin word until long after the period in question, and it is virtually impossible to suppose that a usage arose within the Latin of this province alone. Most telling of all is the fact that no Continental places have *Venta* as an independent element. Holder I. 174 mentions Ventadour < **Ventadornum* (Corrèze, France), but there are no ancient forms recorded for this and it may well be of different origin. Spanish *venta*, both 'sale' and 'inn, hostelry' has been temptingly mentioned in this connection but is not relevant; it is either a native word proceeding from *vendĭta*, or a later borrowing from French *vente*; the numerous place-names in Iberia having *venta*, the best-known of which is Venta de Baños (Palencia, Spain), are medieval names based on the sense 'inn', in no way Roman. Nor does an origin in *venio* and a sense of 'coming together, assembly' seem possible; from the supine *ventum* were formed *adventus*, *conventus*, but both in *-us* and both with prefix.

If on all these grounds the word cannot be Latin, it can hardly be other than Celtic. Certainly it is easier for a word to belong exclusively to Insular Celtic than for it to be uniquely British Latin. Williams discussed the problem under *Venta Belgarum* and less fully under *Glannoventa*. He noted that *venta* produced Welsh *gwent* (which does not of course prove that *venta* was originally Celtic, since many words were borrowed into British and preserved as this evolved into Welsh), and continued: 'I suggest that *gwent* in Welsh meant "field". *Cadwent* occurs for "battle", and since *cad-* itself means "battle" or "host", *-went* can mean "field". *Llinwent* in mid-Wales is *llin-* "flax", with an element *-went* which should mean "field". *Arddunwent*, in which *Arddun* is a woman's name, is naturally explained as "Arddun's field".' He concluded that *venta* was a Celtic word for 'field', perhaps with a secondary meaning 'market-place', comparing *magus* with similar sense-development. The meaning of *Bannaventa* is, then, 'prominent field', 'market on the spur', or the like, acceptably enough; a similar sense for this element suits *Glannoventa* and the *civitas*-names.

Jackson in *Britannia*, I (1970), 80, objects very properly to the proposed Latin origin of *venta* and observes that 'no convincing Celtic etymology has been proposed'; that is, no Indo-European roots are visible, no cognates known in Gaulish, etc., and no derivatives of supposed British **u̯enta* appear in Cornish or Breton. He also objects to Williams's reasoning out the sense 'field' and thinks his evidence 'slight', concluding 'One may well *guess* that it means something like "town", but this can be nothing but a speculation.' The problem, then, remains. It is diminished, but not solved, if we note that in both *Bannaventa* and *Glannoventa* the word is associated with impeccably Celtic elements, and that in the three *civitas*-names the *venta* element is distinctive, unusual in our toponymy – that it may have been brought in exceptionally to designate artificial tribal centres newly founded under Roman pacification of the Belgae, Iceni and Silures. We have seen that there are no names on the Continent having *Venta* as an independent element; but in form there is very close resemblance to such centres as *Forum Gallorum* (now Gurrea, Huesca, Spain), *Forum Gigurnium* (now La Rúa S. Esteban, Orense, Spain), and *Forum Segusiavorum* > Feurs (near Lyon, Rhône, France), the sense of *forum* in all being 'market (of the tribe)'. We lean, then, towards Williams's solution, while not denying that the problem remains.

A possible solution lies in Rostaing's identification of a pre-Indo-European **vin-* 'hill', which with the common infix *-t-* figures in such compounds as *Ventabren* (a mountain in Alpes-Maritimes, France) and *Ventabrun* (a mountain in Basses-Alpes, France), and in the names of a village and three other hills outside Provence: *ETP* 295–96. Possibly French *Ventadour*, noted earlier, belongs with these. Unfortunately there are only medieval, not ancient, records for Rostaing's examples. A sense-development 'hill > flat hill > flat place > field' would be by no means impossible; for the sense 'field > market' compare then *magus*. Rostaing *ETP* 86–87 has a further element from pre-Indo-European, **ban-* **ben-*, with the same meaning (see BANNA), citing among examples *Beneventum* of S. Italy and British '*Bennaventa*' (which is more properly *Bannaventa*). If we are right in following Rostaing (and recalling Gaulish **benno-* indicated by Dottin) we are in sight of a solution: *Bannaventa* is equivalent to *Beneventum*; both could mean 'spur-hill' or 'promontory-hill', but equally both have further sense-developments (especially **u̯enta* within Celtic) which carry the names some distance from that primitive meaning. There are also hints in Rostaing's work which explain the reluctance of Celticists to accept *venta* as Celtic. The word – like **banna*, probably – was indeed not Celtic originally, but was adopted by Celts in contact with pre-Celtic peoples presumably on the Mediterranean fringes, leading thereafter a somewhat tenuous existence (being little known in Gaulish) until emerging as an element with a very specific sense in Romano-British toponymy. It might also have some relation to *Vendum*, a place of the Japodes people (described by Strabo as a mixture of Celts and Illyrians) which J. G. von Hahn in *Albanesische Studien* (Jena, 1854, p. 243) identified as having a root meaning 'Ort, Land, Platz', a word related in turn by E. Çabej to *Venta* in the British names (*Studi Linguistici in onore di Vittore Pisani* (Brescia, 1969) I, 175–76), that is, another originally non-Celtic element absorbed into Celtic speech; see further Pokorny, *Zur Urgeschichte der Celten und Illyrier* (Halle, 1959), 136. On the whole, one feels that to follow Rostaing's trail produces better results, mainly because his examples are numerous and because some of them are in Gaul, providing a geographical link – though hardly a close one – with Britain.

In this context, a note by E. McClure (*Archaeologia Cambrensis*, 6th series, IX (1909), 239–40) has its importance. This note has been dismissed, rightly, because

McClure insisted on a Latin origin of *venta*, on very weak arguments. But he did have the merit of assembling relevant names. To S. Italian *Beneventum* he adds a *Mutatio Beneventum* (*Bordeaux Itinerary*, 558_{10}), between Brescia and Verona in N. Italy; three modern names from Spain – *Benaventa* south of Astorga (Zamora), *Benavent* north of Lérida (Lérida), *Benavente* near Oviedo (Oviedo) – and one from Portugal, *Benavente* near the mouth of the Tagus. There are several other such names in Iberia. McClure also adds all the recent Spanish *Venta* names, which, as noted above, are to be removed from the discussion. McClure's interpretation of the name was erroneous, naturally, since of the S. Italian *Beneventum* he observes that Pliny *NH* III, 11 took the name as an auspicious one, it formerly having been '*Maleventum*' – but this was mere amateur etymologising.

Even if further evidence should show that we are right in arguing the claims of one of the non-Celtic words taken into Celtic and known in British, and in the senses we have applied to it, it remains true that unlike *Bannaventa*, *Glannoventa*, which seem natural enough, the three *civitas*-names with *Venta* are a puzzling feature considered as an isolated and untypical naming act.

IDENTIFICATION. The Roman settlement at Whilton Lodge, Northamptonshire (SP 6164); the name was presumably transferred from the Iron Age hill-fort on Borough Hill, Daventry, two miles to the south-west.

BANNAVENTA[2] – See the Appendix

BANNOVALIUM

SOURCE

Ravenna 106_{55} (= R&C 105): BANNOVALLUM, vars. BANNOUALUM, BAUNOUALUM

DERIVATION. The first element is as in BANNA. The second is **u̯al*–, **u̯ali̯o*- 'strong', attested in Insular and Continental Celtic in such personal names as *Dumno-valos* 'strong one of the world' (or possibly 'deeply strong'; > Irish *Domnall*, English *Donald*), *Touto-valos* 'strong one of the tribe', *Cuno-valos* 'strong hound', and in toponymy British *Luguvalium* (Carlisle) and *Coriovalium* in Germania Inferior, now Heerlen (Holland). In Welsh there are *gwlad* 'country, realm' and *gwledig* 'lord, king', and personal names *Cadwaladr*, *Cynwal*, *Buddwal* (Williams), with elements derived from this root. The Celtic root is cognate with Latin *valeo*, *validus*, *valor*, and hence with *Valentia* in place-names. The present name seems to mean 'strong spur, prominent height'.

Ravenna's form with -*vallum* shows assimilation by Latin speakers to the common Latin noun *vallum* 'wall, rampart'. It is not an isolated scribal assimilation, in view of the same in *Luguvallo* of *AI* 476_2 and *Coriovallum* of *AI* 375_6, and other types of assimilation in other names (see p. 32).

IDENTIFICATION. The name could refer to either Caistor or Horncastle, Lincolnshire, both of which were small Roman towns. At Caistor there is a spur of the Wolds. At Horncastle the 'spur' could be that formed by the junction of two rivers, one of them the Bain (which might then have taken its name by back-formation from the town, though Ekwall derives the name of this and other rivers from Norse *beinn* 'straight'). It is also worth noting that this place, *Hornecastre* in *DB*, has in its first element an Anglo-Saxon translation of British **banno-* 'horn', or at least a coincidental reference to the same topographical feature. There seem to be no grounds on which to decide between these two identifications.

BDORA of *Ravenna* 108_{32} (= R&C 252); see BODOTRIA

BEGESSE (?)

SOURCE
Ravenna 107_{53} (= R&C 194): BEGESSE

DERIVATION. Williams identified this as derived from an Indo-European root **bheg-* 'bend, curve' (as in English *back*), adding that here it could signify 'ridge'. Holder I. 138 relates to this the river *Vegeria* > Vègre (Seine-et-Oise, France), the personal names *Vegeto(n)*, *Vegiso(n)* and *Vegisonius* (perhaps 'bent, hunch-backed' ?), and the place-names *Begosum* > Bégot (Hérault, France) and *Begonium* > Begon (Aveyron, France). Possibly related also is *Bigeste* of *Ravenna* 55_{30} and *TP*, in Dalmatia, modern Humac (Yugoslavia); cf. also *Begensis* in CIL VI. 37045. Possibly, then, having these analogues, the name seems less strange than it does at first glance, though its ending presents a problem (**-isso-*, miscopied ?). There might be a relation to *Ravenna*'s *Ugueste* 108_{9}, which we examine further in that entry.

IDENTIFICATION. Unknown, but evidently in Scotland.

BELERIUM

SOURCES
Diodorus Siculus V, 21: Βελέριον (= BELERIUM), two mentions
Ptolemy II, 3, 2: Βολέριον (= BOLERIUM), var. Βολαίριον (= BOLAERIUM).

DERIVATION. Ptolemy equates this with *Antivestaeum*, evidently citing *Belerium* as the native and perhaps obsolete name; it was certainly very ancient, and was long known to the Greeks in the tradition of Pytheas. Most seem to take *Bel-* as the better form, though without arguing the point; it is just possible that *Bol-* is a genuine alternative, as argued by O-Rahilly *EIHM* 54 in citing *Belgae–*Bolgi* (*Fir Bolg*), *Celtae–Galatae*, though these relate to peoples in very different regions, not to variations of the same name; *divertomu–divortomu* in the Coligny Calendar is perhaps more relevant. Watson *CPNS* 65 compared Irish *Dùn Bhalaire*, N. Irish *Carn Bhalair* < **Balarios*, and wondered whether present *Belerium*, *Bolerium* could derive in the same way from a personal name and mean 'place of **Boleros*', but it is difficult to attribute the naming of a great promontory to a personal possessor. The best etymology is that which associates this name with the divine name *Belenos*, *Belinos*, equated with Apollo, the *bel-* element here being 'bright, shining', as in *Belisama*. The Indo-European root is **bhele-* 'to shine' (Sanskrit *bhāla* 'shine, lustre'). Since the cliffs in these parts hardly shine, the reference is presumably to a beacon, and this is strongly supported by the equation with *Antivestaeum* and the meaning of this. The final part of the name is unexplained but is paralleled in the related items from Irish cited by Watson.

IDENTIFICATION. Land's End, Cornwall, and in Diodorus the Penwith peninsula.

BELGAE

SOURCES

Ptolemy II, 3, 13: Βέλγαι (= BELGAE)
See also VENTA BELGARUM (listed by *AI*, *Ravenna*)

DERIVATION. The name is based on Celtic **belg-* from **bhelgho-*'to swell', from which derived Old Irish *bolc bolg* 'sack' and *Fir-bolg* 'bag-men' (an etymology scornfully rejected by O'Rahilly *EIHM* 43–57), and the personal name Βόλγιος (= *Bolgios*), King of the Celts in Macedonia in 280 B.C. Latin *bŭlga* 'bag, knapsack' was a borrowing from Gaulish; cf. Middle High German *belgen* and English *bulge* (from French). The meaning of the ethnic name was presumably a figurative one, 'proud ones' or the like (Jackson), via a sense 'puffed up'. An individual of the people in Britain is recorded on the military diploma of *M. Ulpio Sacci F. Longino, Belgae* (dat.), *CIL* XVI. 163; see E. Birley, *Roman Britain and the Roman Army* (Kendal, 1953), 21. Compare the British name BLATOBULGIUM.

IDENTIFICATION. A people of southern Britain, with their capital at *Venta*, Winchester; Ptolemy also attributes to them *Ischalis* and *Aquae Calidae*, but on this see p. 121. The fact that in Gaul the name *Belgae* was applied to a collection of tribes, not an individual tribe, suggests that the British *Civitas Belgarum* was an artificial creation of the Roman government.

BELISAMA

SOURCE

Ptolemy II, 3, 2: Βελισάμα ἔισχυσις (= BELISAMAE AESTUARIUM) (see also 'ETSODISINAM').

DERIVATION. This river-name is that of a goddess widely worshipped in Gaul and there equated with Minerva (Vincent 261; M. Lejeune in *EC*, XII (1968–69), 43); shrines and dedications to her are known, including one important text from Roustang in Gaulish written in Greek script (Holder I. 386, III. 834). Dauzat *TF* 144–45 finds that among the numerous French place-names, in Auvergne and Nivernais the divine name had *-i-* preserved in Belime (Puy-de-Dôme) and Blisme (Nièvre), but elsewhere and more commonly *-ĭ-* or possibly *-ē-*, in view of Beleymas (Dordogne), Balesme (Corrèze) and others. There is another detailed study of these by C. J. Guyonvarc'h in *Ogam*, XIV (1962), 161–67; it cannot be determined in all cases whether the modern name represents a cult of the goddess or is derived from a personal name. For most authorities *Belisama* has the root **bel-* 'bright, shining' (see BELERIUM) with the Celtic superlative ending *isama*, of which Dauzat lists examples from the toponymy of Gaul at 145–49, and of which Hispanic *Bletisama* > Ledesma (Salamanca) and *Uxama* > Osma (Soria) are further instances. A meaning 'most shining one' is clearly appropriate for both divinities and rivers. However, Whatmough (*DAG* xi) proposes to see in the name the prefix **be-* (cognate with *bi- be-* in Germanic) and a stem **lĕs* > **lis*, with a termination *-āma* carrying the stress, the whole name *Belisama* meaning 'gatherer'. This seems perverse, and the stress is not that which could have given the medieval and modern names of France. Related to the present name are *Belisarium* of *Ravenna* 80_{60}, between modern Astorga and Palencia in Spain, the divinity *Deo Belisamaro* (dative) at Chalon-sur-Saône (Seine-et-Loire, France: *Revue Epigraphique*, I (1913), 95), and a large number of personal names in Gaul; in Britain there was the woman *Julia Belismicus* at Caerleon (*RIB* 318).

IDENTIFICATION. The river Ribble, Lancashire.

BIBRA

SOURCE
Ravenna 107_4 (= R&C 119): BRIBRA

DERIVATION. The first *r* in *Ravenna*'s form is intrusive (compare *Bribilia*, *Ravenna* 71_{40}). *Bibra* seems to be the feminine of the British word for 'beaver', strictly a river-name transferred (as often) to a settlement. The animal was **bebro-s* or **bibro-s* (Old Cornish *befer*) and in Gaulish **bebro-s* (recorded by two late Latin writers in latinised form as nom. *beber* and acc. *bebrum*), cognate with Latin *fiber*; there is also Gaelic *beabhar*. The Indo-European word is postulated as **brebhr* or **bhe-bhrú-s*, a reduplication of the word for 'brown'. As a river-name *Bibra* is 'the brown one', but a literal 'beaver-river' is by no means impossible; the animal existed in Britain into Anglo-Saxon times, and it may be significant that Tacitus (*Histories* II, 24) mentions another place *Bebriacum* as 'locus castorum'. The Celtic word for 'beaver' entered into a number of names, such as *Bibracte* > Mont Beuvray (Nièvre, France) and *Bibrax Remorum* now Vieux-Laon or Vieux-Reims (Aisne, France). Dottin *LG* 89 mentions the river *Bebronna* > Brevenne (Rhône, France) and the river **Bebris* > Bièvres (Aisne, France). Others are mentioned by Holder I. 362, I. 415 and III. 819. Compare BIBROCI (next entry). See R. Sindou, 'Noms de lieux qui rappellent celtique **bebros* "fiber"', *Actes et Mémoires du Ier Congrès International de langue et littérature du Midi de la France* (Avignon, 1957), 303–308.

IDENTIFICATION. Probably the Roman fort at Beckfoot, Cumberland (NY 0848), at the mouth of the little stream which issues from Wolsty Springs.

BIBROCI

SOURCE
Caesar *BG*, V, 21, I: BIBROCI

DERIVATION. This ethnic name is based on Celtic **bebro-s*, **bibro-s* 'beaver'; see the previous entry. The suffix is a rare one whose force is not clear. The tribe is thus 'beaver-men', but the name can hardly be meant literally (contrast *Epidii* 'horse-people'); possibly they had a beaver-emblem, or were dwellers on a now unknown **Bibra* river.

IDENTIFICATION. A British tribe mentioned only by Caesar; presumably they were located in south-eastern Britain and were later absorbed by a larger confederation.

BLATOBULGIUM

SOURCE
AI 467_1 (Iter II): BLATOBULGIO

DERIVATION. Jackson explains this in *Britannia*, I (1970), 69, with further details in a note in A. S. Robertson, *Birrens*

(_Blatobulgium_) (Edinburgh, 1975), 3–4. The British name was *_Blātobolgi̯on_. The first element was *_blāto-_ 'bloom, blossom' (Welsh _blawd_, Irish _bláth_; cognate with Latin _flos_, English _bloom_), or *_blāto-_ from earlier *_mlāto-_ 'flour' (Welsh _blawd_; cognate with Latin _molo_ and English _meal_). The second was *_bolgo-_ 'bag, bulge', etc., cf. Gaulish *_bulga_ (cognate with English _belly_), on which see further BELGAE. The sense of the name is thus 'flowery hillock' or 'flowery hollow'; but better, Jackson thinks, is 'flour-sack', given as a sort of nickname, for there were three large granaries at the fort; if this is right, it provides an admirable illustration of how archaeology gives precision to place-name studies. Among very few comparable names abroad is _Blatomagus_ 'flowery field' > Blond (Haute-Vienne, France), which is _Blatomago_ and _Blatomo_ on Merovingian coins: Dottin _LG_ 74. Rhys (1904), 283 draws attention to Blebo near St Andrews (Fife, Scotland), earlier _Blabo_ < _Blabolg_ < _Blathbolg_, identical with the present name.

IDENTIFICATION. The Roman fort at Birrens, Dumfriesshire (NY 2175).

BLESTIUM

SOURCE
_AI_ 485_2 (Iter XIII): BLESTIO

DERIVATION. Jackson in _Britannia_, I (1970), 69, indicates a probable origin in the personal name _Blestus_, known in Gaulish, which with *-_i̯o_-derivational suffix might indicate 'Blestus's place'; but he calls this 'highly speculative'. It may help to know that the personal name is recorded in Britain: _RIB_ 1254 is the tombstone of _Blescius Diovicus_ at Risingham. In _CIL_ II. 5087 there is mention of _T. Blestus_ (or _Blestius_) at León (León, Spain).

IDENTIFICATION. The Roman settlement or fort at Monmouth (SO 5012).

BOCRANDIUM

SOURCE
Ravenna 108_8 (= R&C 218): BOGRANDIUM

In view of the etymologies proposed below, the name needs _Boc-_; _c/g_ miscopyings are common in our texts.

DERIVATION. Of the two possibilities for *_bŏc-_ offered by Holder I. 454, Williams took the second: a root connected with Irish _boc_ 'soft' and which produced Breton _bouk_ 'soft, tender', in the plural _bocion_ glossed 'putres'; hence 'soft tract of land, moss'. Holder's first sense for *_bŏc-_, 'tumor', that is 'swelling', is more frequent in place-names, and there are Celtic derivatives which Holder lists. The second element of the name is the word which in Gaul was *_randa_ or *_rando-s_ 'parcelle, partie' (> Spanish _randa_, etc.), as in _Aequoranda_ and other names, perhaps here with the common *-_i̯o_- suffix. Hence 'hilly part', 'rising part', or (Williams) 'mossy part'.

IDENTIFICATION. Unknown, but apparently in Scotland.

BODOTRIA (?)

SOURCES
Tacitus _Agricola_ 23, 1; 25, 1; 25, 3: BODOTRIA
Ptolemy II, 3, 4: Βοδερία ἔισχυσις (= BODERIAE AESTUARIUM), var. Βογδερία (= BOGDERIA)
Ravenna 108_{32} (= R&C 252): BDORA

DERIVATION. Tacitus's three mentions command respect. Schnetz restores *Ravenna*'s version, presumably with an eye on Ptolemy, as *B[o]der[i]a*, following Pinder and Parthey. None the less there have been efforts to disregard all the ancient forms as suspect. In a long discussion R&C and Williams postulated firmly **Voritia*, which can be more or less explained in terms of Celtic elements; this, however, was because they were keen to derive the modern name Forth directly from the Romano-British names recorded above. O'Rahilly *EIHM* 529 thought (following Fraser) that both *Boderia* and *Bodotria* were corruptions of **Voretia* (see also BORESTI). It seems that Forth may well derive from **Voritia* (**vo*- 'somewhat' plus a root as in Irish *rith* 'act of running'), that is 'slow-running one', this **Voritia* being a later name or a by-name. But this cannot directly represent the forms in the ancient sources, which have in common B . . . D . . . R . A. It is hardly likely that in all cases there were scribes who consistently represented original *V*- by *B*-, and although in the period of the sources of Tacitus and Ptolemy (and probably, for north Britain, *Ravenna*) confusion of *b*/*v* was beginning in spoken Latin – it is recorded at Pompeii – it seems too early for this to have affected Britain; while in British, *b* and *v* remained distinct throughout. A better idea is that of F. G. Diack in *RC*, XLI (1924), 128–30, who equates *Bodotria* and *Boderia* as different forms of the same name, **Bodot(o)-eria* being the full stem and **Bod(o)-eria* the nominative stem, the stems being **bodos* with genitive **bodotos*.

The argument for retaining *Bod*- is strengthened by the fact that this figures commonly in toponymy and anthroponymy in Celtic lands. Holder I. 456–62 and Ellis Evans *GPN* 156–58 assemble many names, the latter noting that some have the root **boud*- 'victory, excellence' or the like, but that Gaulish names are probably of multiple origin even when ending up as *Bod*-. In Britain BODVOC (for *Boduocus*) is the name of a ruler on coins of the Dobunni about A.D. 43 (Mack Nos. 395, 396; see also D. F. Allen in E. M. Clifford, *Bagendon: A Belgic Oppidum* (Cambridge, 1961), 79 ff.), and *Boudica* is well known. Spanish personal names are assembled in *ELH* I. 354, all based on an assumed **boud*- 'victory, excellence', including *Bodecius* (*CIL* II. 2633), *Boderus* (*CIL* II. 5711), *Bodon* (*CIL* II. 2114), and an altar to *Deo Bodo Veicius* (*CIL* II. 5670) is known from north Spain, these showing a variety of suffixation. However, the sense in which these probable **boud*- names could be linked to that of the Forth is unclear, as Ellis Evans reminds us; 'victory' is hardly a possible name for a river, though notions of 'excellence' are fitting for great ones.

It is possible that there is a link with the older name of the north Italian Po (< *Padus*). Pliny (*NH* III, 122) deals with this at length, quoting Metrodurus of Skepsis to show that the name was earlier *Bodincus*, that this was Lingurian and in that language meant 'fundo carentem' ('bottomless'); he adds for good measure that there was a town near it called *Bodincomagum*. Whether Pliny was right about the sense we cannot tell; that the name was Ligurian and that it survived long enough for Celts to compound it with their **magos* element, there is no reason to doubt. Diack thinks *Bodincus* and *Bodotria* were formed from a root **bhudh*- 'bottom' (Latin *fundus*, English *bottom*, etc.), the sense being 'bottom river', not as Pliny has it but as the name of a part of the river only, that is 'the lower portion where the plain is markedly flat'; against this, however, is the fact that neither Walde nor Pokorny lists *Bod*-

forms as deriving from the **bhudh-* root (which seems to have been weakly represented in Celtic in any case), and neither associates *Bodincus* or *Bodotria* with it. This is not to deny necessarily that the names of these two major rivers are associated and derive from some pre-Celtic root now unknown to us; river-names are often very ancient and, moreover, survive well.

A possible etymology within Celtic was suggested by Watson *CPNS* 51–52, and should not be too hastily dismissed. He thought the name was properly **Bodortia*, involving a slight metathesis. He notes that Irish *bodhar* occurs freely in place-names with connotations of absence of sound, of stillness; *Bodar usce* in Old Irish is 'stagnant or sluggish water', and his **Bodortia* corresponds to Irish *bodartha* 'deafened, the deafened one'; or if **Boderia* or **Bodoria*, the sense would be 'the deaf one, silent one'.

Finally, within Celtic possibilities, one might retain Ptolemy's variant *Bogd-*; with the comment that to Roman ears the *-gd-* group would sound unnatural and might easily be represented as simple *-d-* on a map-source. **Bogdo-* is 'bend, curve', as in British MEDIOBOGDUM; such a name would well suit part of a river.

In the absence of firm forms, this variety of speculation is the best that can be offered.

IDENTIFICATION. The river Forth, Scotland.

BOLVELLAUNIUM

SOURCE

Ravenna 106_{13} (= R&C 31): BOLVELAUNIO

There is no reason to doubt this name, which is textually and etymologically sound, as does Dillemann (p. 66) when thinking it a corruption of SILVA (*Ravenna* 106_9, repeated), etc.

DERIVATION. Williams identifies the first element as British **bol-* **bul-* 'round, swelling', citing Welsh *ar-fwl* (name of a horse) and Irish *ad-bol* 'huge' as related words; in a noun function **bol-* was thus 'hill'. This enters into several names in Celtic lands: *Bolvinnus*, a by-name of Mars in two dedications of Gaul (*CIL* XIII. 2899, 2900; Nièvre, France); Βωλέντιον (= *Bolentium*) in Pannonia Superior (Ptolemy II, 14, 4); *Bolegasgus* in Galatia (Miller, 1916, col. 672). Rostaing *ETP* 82 identifies **bol-* as a common pre-Indo-European element meaning 'hauteur' of very wide use, citing *Bola*, city of Latium (*Aeneid* VI. 775); *Bolbulae*, an island near Cyprus (Pliny *NH* V, 137); Βολβίτινον (= *Bolbitinum*), one of the mouths of the Nile (Herodotus II, 17); also in Provence, Beuil (Alpes-Maritimes) < **Bolium*. This element passed into Celtic with the same meaning, or perhaps coincided with a native Celtic root.

The second element is British **u̯ellauno-* probably meaning 'good', a sense suggested by Holder III. 150 and widely, but not unanimously, adopted since. It is represented later by Welsh and Breton *guallaun* and Welsh *gwell* 'better'. Ellis Evans assembles examples in *GPN* 272–77 and concludes that the sense assigned to the word is possible though still uncertain. Barruol (1969), 373 thinks the name of the *Velaunii* people of the southern Alps (whose name appears in Greek on a bronze hand, traditional emblem of hospitality) meant 'bienveillant'. Latin and Greek records of the numerous names show *-l-* and *-ll-* in roughly equal quantity, but it seems more properly to have had *-ll-*. Holder's analysis of the word as **vell-avo-s* > **vellav-io* seems to leave the regularly present *-n-* without explanation. It may be better to follow the hint of Dauzat *TF* 46, supported by O'Rahilly *EIHM* 9 (note), that **vel-launos* resulted from the assimilation of the intensive prefix **ver-* to *(*a*)*launos*, with resulting elision of a syllable. This would strain somewhat the sense assigned to **alauno-* (see our ALAUNA[1]). In support are the forms of the name of the *Segovellauni* of Gallia Narbonensis, who are thus in Pliny *NH* III, 34, but with contraction the Σεγαλλαυνοὶ (= *Segallauni*) in Ptolemy II, 10, 7. Barruol compares *non volumus* > *nolumus*, **juvenior* > *junior* as contractions by Latin speakers, and it can probably be assumed that the same process sometimes occurred in Celtic. However, it may be preferable to follow the view of Pokorny 1137, who assigns the word to an Indo-European root **u̯el-* **u̯lei*, etc., with senses 'wollen, wählen'.

British examples cover a good range of the applications of **u̯ellauno-*. The earliest are king *Cassivellaunus* and the *Catuvellauni* people. King *Dubnovellaunos* is so spelled in full on coins of the Trinovantes (Mack No. 282) and is *Dubnovillaun* (No. 275) and in more abbreviated form on others; among the Coritani *Volisios Dumnovellaunos* is so spelled in full on one coin (Mack No. 466). *RIB* 369 is the second-century tombstone of a woman *Tadia Vallaun*[*i*]*us* at Caerwent. *RIB* 309 is a statue-base with a dedication of A.D. 152 to [*Deo*] *Marti Leno* [*s*]*ive Ocelo Vellaun*(*o*); Wright notes that *Vellaunus* – here presumably an adjective qualifying *Ocelus* – is a distinct god equated with Mercury in *CIL* XII. 2373 (Allobroges of Gaul). Numerous other applications of the word in names of every kind on the Continent may be studied in Holder, Ellis Evans, etc.

IDENTIFICATION. Unknown, but apparently in south-western Britain.

BORCOVICIO of *ND* XL$_{40}$: see VERCOVICIUM

BORESTI

SOURCE

Tacitus *Agricola* 38, 3: BORESTORUM (gen. pl.)

DERIVATION. None can be suggested. Holder I. 1490 suggests a connection with Graeco-Latin *boreas* and mentions the Hyperboreans. Rhys (1904) 283–84 thinks the name a British equivalent of late Latin *floresta* (presumably on the grounds of general resemblance and because Latin *f-* = British *b-*, as in *fiber*/**bebro-*). O'Rahilly *EIHM* 529 suggests that *Boresti* might be a corruption of **Voretii*, meaning 'dwellers by the Forth', the latter having had the ancient name **Voretia* (see BODOTRIA); this is perhaps just possible if one can assume a *V-* represented as *B-* in an early medieval MS of Tacitus, but the confusion is unlikely in the Latin of Tacitus's own time and is not possible in British. We have insufficient evidence on which to choose or reject these proposals. Holder and Rhys think the tribe the same as the *Verturiones* documented in the fourth century. The fact that Ptolemy does not mention it, when he ultimately drew his North British material from the very Flavian military map which had been composed in large part on the basis of Agricola's campaigns, might indicate that the tribe was a subdivision of one of the larger units that do in fact figure in

Ptolemy. As noted by Ogilvie and Richmond in their edition of the *Agricola* (1967), 282, the name has nothing to do with that of Forres, as was once proposed.

IDENTIFICATION. A people of north-east Scotland apparently located beyond *Mons Graupius* (q.v.) and so, as Ogilvie and Richmond suggest, on the Moray coast.

BOTIS

SOURCE
Ravenna 109_{12} (= R&C 281): BOTIS

DERIVATION. Williams's view cannot be improved upon: that the name is from a root which has given Welsh *bod*, Irish *both* 'dwelling', here in plural form (though hardly a locative plural as Williams suggests, for this was not on a road nor in romanised territory); hence 'the dwellings'. Williams notes that the island was well populated in early times. However, the plural appearance may be deceptive: one could well assume here **Bot īs.* (for *insula*), misread by the Cosmographer from a map, as elsewhere in this group of names. Modern Bute (called in Old Irish *Bot*, in Gaelic *Bod*) has kept the name. Holder I. 495 has Gaulish names which may be related: *Botanis*, *Botcalia*, *Boteria*.

IDENTIFICATION. The island of Bute, Scotland.

BOVIUM[1]

SOURCES
AI 484_{3} (Iter XII): BOMIO
Inscription: In *JRS*, LVI (1966), 220, there are published two moulded bricks with letters left in relief by a die reading BOV. They were found at Whitton Cross-roads, St Lythans, Glamorgan, on a site (eventually of a villa) whose occupation lasted from before the Conquest until late in the fourth century. The bricks may have served as tallies. 'BOV may indicate the name of the local settlement, for which *AI* gives the form BOMIVM, perhaps to be amended to BOVIVM.'

DERIVATION. *Bomium* can hardly be retained; Jackson in studying the names of *AI* simply puts a query against it. As is further noted in *JRS* (above), the emendation to *Bovio* is easy, and obvious in view of the British precedent *Bovium*[2] whose name is not in doubt. There may, however, have been some local variation whose reason escapes us but which is paralleled in the *m*/*v* alternation in the name of the Gaulish deity *Bormo* or *Borvo*, god of hot springs, best known from the site in Gallia Lugdunensis which shows both spellings on its inscriptions: *Borvoni et Damonae*/*Bormoni et Damonae* (dat.). The form with *b* or *v* eventually triumphed, > Bourbon-Lancy; see Whatmough *DAG* 598. This variation is not connected with genuine lenition of $m > \mu > v$ in Britain, which is dated by Jackson to the later part of the fifth century. The two Glamorgan bricks with BOV, and what is said about them in *JRS*, provide convincing arguments for a Glamorgan *Bovium*.

This, as Jackson says of *Bovium*[2] in discussing *AI*, looks like a derivative of British **bou-* 'cow', with the common **i̯o-* suffix; perhaps 'cow-place'. There are many *Bov-* names on the Continent, most no doubt from Latin *bos bovem*; Holder I. 499 has a few forms from Gaul which are probably of Celtic origin.

IDENTIFICATION. Probably the Roman settlement at Cowbridge, Glamorgan (SS

9974), $5\frac{1}{2}$ miles from the villa at Whitton Cross-roads (ST 081713).

BOVIUM[2]

SOURCE
AI 469_3 (Iter II): BOVIO

DERIVATION. See BOVIUM[1].

IDENTIFICATION. Probably the Roman legionary tile and pottery factory at Holt, Denbighshire (SJ 4054).

BRANODUNUM

SOURCE
ND XXVIII_6 (*pictura*): BRANODUNO, var. BRANADUNO
XXVIII_{16} (text): Praepositus equitum Dalmatarum Branodunensium (MSS: Branodun), BRANODUNO, var. BRANADUNO

DERIVATION. The first element is British **bran(n)o-*, in some parts (presumably here) 'crow', in others 'raven'; *bran* means this in Welsh, Breton and Irish, and there are personal names *Bran*, *Brandub(h)* < **brano-dubos* 'black raven', etc. The element was well known in Gaulish also; from it derive Braine (Aisne, France) and Braisnes (Oise, France; Vincent 234). The tribe *Aulerci Brannovices* took its name from a personal name **Branno-s*, and the *Brandobrici* of Gallia Narbonensis presumably show *-nd-* re-established as a hypercorrection for *-nn-*. In British *Branodunum* the reference could be either to the crow – in some cultures a bird of omen – or to a site owned by a person **Bran(n)os*.

Dūnum is one of the most important elements in Celto-Latin toponymy. Sixteen names in Britain, perhaps more, are formed of it or with it, and scores on the Continent. It appears uncompounded (British *Dunum*[1], *Dunum*[2], *Dunum Sinus*; there was a *Dunum* in Ireland, Ptolemy II, 2, 9; Vincent 209a has ten examples from Gaul), more commonly compounded and then always in second place. Its geographical range was immense: common throughout Britain and Gaul, it extended into north Italy, eastward as far as Belgrade (*Singidunum*), *Carrodunum* on the Oder (modern Krappitz) and *Noviodunum* now Isaccea near the mouth of the Danube; it is also known, though not commonly, in Iberia (five names in E. and N.E. Spain, two in the south). For a map of *dunum* names in Europe, see H. Rix in *Festschrift für Peter Goessler* (Stuttgart, 1954), 103, and S. Piggott, *Ancient Europe* (Edinburgh, 1965), 173.

The Celtic word was apparently **dūnŏs-*, a neuter with *-s* stem; as *dūnon* it was regularly represented in Latin as *dūnum*, neuter. In sense it seems to have developed from 'hill' (it is glossed 'montem' in the Vienna Glossary) to 'fort', perhaps strictly 'ville close' (Barruol); see P. Lebel in *RIO*, XIV (1962), 171. Derivatives include Welsh *din-as* 'fortress; town, city', pl. *dinion*, and Irish *dun* 'fortress'. Cognates include Germanic *tūna-*, whence Anglo-Saxon *tun* and English *town* (*-ton* in place-names), German *Zaun* 'fence'. Evidently *dunum* had an independent existence in Vulgar Latin as a borrowing from Celtic. While some uncompounded names were originally – if recorded in ancient sources – the creation of Celtic speakers, others not so recorded are probably of early medieval date and were created by Latin speakers, as shown by, for example, Thun (Berne, Switzerland), and in France Dun-le-Poelier (Indre), Châteaudun (Eure-et-Loire), Dun-sur-Meuse (Meuse) and Dun-sur-Auron (Cher). The word was taken into Latin as a common noun and survives in dialects of Cantal and Haute-Loire: *dun* 'colline', *dunet* 'petite colline' (Vincent). The free way in which the element was used by Latin speakers is shown by such creations as *Caesarodunum* (now Tours, Indre-et-Loire, France) and *Augustodunum* > Autun (Seine-et-Loire, France); these were not latinisations of older Celtic names. The present name *Branodunum* shows the same free use of the element, since it applies to a third-century construction and means 'fort (of any kind)', there being no hill on the site.

IDENTIFICATION. The Roman fort at Brancaster, Norfolk (TF 7844).

BRANOGENIUM

SOURCES

Ptolemy II, 3, 11: Βραννογένιον (= BRANNOGENIUM), a *polis* of the Ordovices: vars. Βρανογένιον (= BRANOGENIUM), Βρανογένειον (= BRANOGENEIUM)

AI 484_8 (Iter XII): BRAVONIO

Ravenna 106_{27} (= R&C 58): BRANO GENIUM

AI's form has not previously been associated with that in the other two sources; Jackson in *Britannia*, I (1970), 69, provides it with a good etymology. However, it seems likely that the above equation is proper. In *AI*, the form quoted is that present in all the MSS, and so presumably goes back to the archetype; in this, original *v* (*u*) represents *n*, as often, and the loss of a syllable might have resulted from an abbreviation in the source which was not understood. In support of our equation, note that in *AI* '*Bravonio*' stands next to *Magnis*, just as *Brano Genium* is next to *Magnis* in *Ravenna*.

DERIVATION. For the first element, see BRANODUNUM. The second, *gen-*, is documented by Holder I. 2002 and in *GPN* 59–60, 207, as a verb root, in Gaulish **cen-* **gen*(*n*)- or **geno-* 'to be born of, descend from'. Derivatives include Welsh *geni* 'to be born', and there is *gein* in Irish. Latin cognates include *gigno*, *indi-gena*. The element was much used in compounds after the name of a god (*Camulogenus*) or an animal (*Matucenos*, *Matugenus* 'born of the bear', etc.) to form personal names, on which Ellis Evans comments: 'Names such as these suggest that the Celts were fond of representing a child's father as a deified animal.' British **Brannogenos* comes into this category by form and meaning; with *-*i̯o-* suffix, the name indicates 'Brannogenos's place'. The second element is possibly that found in British *Cenio* (a river).

IDENTIFICATION. The Roman settlement at Leintwardine, Herefordshire (SO 4074). Ptolemy's attribution to the *Ordovices* may be an error (see pp. 120, 143).

BRAVONIACUM

SOURCES

Inscription: *CIL* VIII. 4800: the tombstone from *Gadiavfala* (now Ksar Sbai) in Numidia Proconsularis of a man who had served IN BRITANIA... MILITANS BRAVNIACO

AI 467_4 (Iter II): BROVONACIS

ND XL_{12} (*pictura*): BRABONIACO
XL_{27} (text): Praefectus numeri defensorum, BRABONIACO (var. BARBONIACO)

Ravenna 107_6 (= R&C 123): RAVONIA

ND has the best form, erring only in the common *b*/*v* confusion of Vulgar Latin. The African inscription has a vulgar form in which a typical Latin elision of the unstressed syllable has occurred: **Brāvŏn-* > **Braun-*, presumably with *u* eventually treated as a vowel and forming a diphthong *au*; whether this reflects the Latin of Britain or that of Africa is impossible to say (it can hardly represent syncope in British, which did not occur until much later). *Bro-* for *Bra-* in *AI*'s form is probably scribal only, perhaps an assimilation. The final *-is* of *AI*'s form is mystifying; it looks like a locative plural, and might be a genuine variant, perhaps influenced by the locative plural of other fort-names in its area (*Verteris*, *Lavatris*, which are recorded always with *-is*).

DERIVATION. Jackson in *Britannia*, I (1970), 69, identifies the British form of the name as **Brāu̯oni̯acon*, with a base in **brāu̯on-* 'quern' (Welsh *breuan*). This looks like a personal name **Brāu̯oni̯os* 'Quern man' plus the *-āco-* suffix in the special sense 'estate of'; but **Brāu̯on(i̯)ācon* could mean 'Querny place', i.e. either a quernstone quarry or perhaps a place full of quern-like rocks.

The Celto-Latin suffix *-āco-*, *-ācum* was widespread in Celtic lands (uncommon in N. Italy and Iberia) and was very greatly used in Vulgar and medieval Latin. A diversity of uses is illustrated by its appearance in British *Bremetenacum*, **Calacum*, *Eburacum*, *Epiacum*, *Sulloniacis*, *Uxacona*, *Vagniacis*, and in ethnic *Cantiaci*, *Segontiaci*; see our notes on certain of these names, e.g. *Eburacum*. In the present instance, possibly, and in *Epiacum*, *Sulloniacis*, the suffix is seen in its most typical function, signifying 'estate of', 'property of', so common in late Antiquity especially in Gaul; see the long analysis by Dauzat *TF* 239–307.

IDENTIFICATION. The Roman fort at Burwens, Kirby Thore, Westmorland (NY 6325).

BRAVONIUM of *AI* 484_8: see BRANOGENIUM

BREMENIUM

SOURCES

Ptolemy II, 3, 7: Βρεμένιον (= BREMENIUM), a *polis* of the (V)otadini

Inscriptions: *RIB* 1262, an altar found in the strong-room of High Rochester fort, to be dated A.D. 238–41: the dedicators (in the genetive) are the N(UMERI) EXPLORATOR(UM) BREM(ENIENSIUM)

RIB 1270, an undated altar-base from High Rochester which mentions the DUPL(ICARII) N(UMERI) EXPLOR(ATORUM) BREMEN(IENSIUM)

AI 464_3 (Iter I): BREMENIO, var. BREMAENIO

Ravenna 107_{45} (= R&C 185): BREMENIUM

DERIVATION. As explained by Jackson in *Britannia*, I (1970), 69, the name is based on British **brem-* 'to roar' (Welsh *brefu*; cognate with Latin *fremo* and Greek βρέμω). The name of the stream at High Rochester, now the Sills Burn, was presumably **Bremi̯ā* 'roaring stream' or the like, and the name of the fort was formed from this with suffixes **-en-* (see further CAERENI) and **-i̯o-*. Compare BREMETENACUM, BREMIA. There seems to be only one analogue abroad: **Brem(e)tonicum* now Brentonico in the Tyrol, for which there are medieval but not ancient sources (Holder III. 928).

IDENTIFICATION. The Roman fort at High Rochester, Northumberland (NY 8398).

Note. Jackson in *Antiquity*, XXIII (1949), 48–49, studies the possibility that this was the site of one of Arthur's battles: the name continuing for a time as *Bregion* (var. *Breuoin*) in Nennius and as Middle Welsh *Brewyn*.

BREMETENACUM VETERANORUM

SOURCES

Inscription: *RIB* 583, found at Ribchester, the shaft of the pedestal of a monument to Apollo Maponus dedicated for the welfare of the N(UMERI) EQ(UITUM) SAR[M(ATARUM)] BREMETENN(ACENSIUM): dated to A.D. 238–44, perhaps later

AI 481_5 (Iter x): BREMETONNACI, var. BREMETONACI

Ravenna 107_7 (= R&C 124): BRESNETENACI VETERANORUM, var. BRESNETENOTI

ND XL_{54}: Cuneus Sarmatarum, BREMETENRACO, vars. BREMETEMRACO, BREMETERACO

DERIVATION. Given the inscription, the correct form of the name is not in doubt, the slight variations in other texts being readily explicable as scribal errors; the *-nn-* in some forms has no authority. Jackson in *Britannia*, I (1970), 69, gives the British name as **Bremetonācon*, based as often on a river-name, **Bremetona* 'roaring river'; this in turn has a base **brem-* as in the previous entry, with suffixes **-et-* (perhaps as in *Carvetii*), **-on(o)-* (as in *Carnonacae*, *Creones*, *Dumnonii*, *Uxacona*, *Venonis*), and adjectival **-āco-* (see BRAVONIACUM), in this instance comparable with its use in **Calacum*. Forms other than those in *AI* show an assimilation (confirmed by the inscription) of *e-e-o* to *e-e-e*.

The Sarmatians, brought to Britain in A.D. 175, were subsequently settled in this area (Richmond, 'The Sarmatae, *Bremetennacum Veteranorum* and the *Regio Bremetennacensis*', *JRS*, XXXV (1945), 15 ff.) and this accounts for the name in *Ravenna*.

IDENTIFICATION. The Roman fort at Ribchester, Lancashire (SD 6535); the river Ribble, whose proper name seems to have been *Belisama* (q.v.), has swept away about a third of the fort.

BREMIA

SOURCE

Ravenna 106_{25} (= R&C 54): BREMIA

DERIVATION. See BREMENIUM; this is the simple form of the name, 'roaring river', transferred with Celto-Latin suffix *-ia* to a place on its banks. The name survived in Welsh and provides a clue to the identification, as R&C note: *Afon Brefi*, *Llandewi Brefi*, the latter mentioned as *civitate Brevi* in the medieval *Life* of St Cadoc, 10.

IDENTIFICATION. The Roman fort of Cae'r Castell, Llanio, Cardiganshire (SN 6456); the Afon Brefi joins the major river, Afon Teifi, one mile downstream (south) of the fort, and Llandewi Brefi lies 1½ miles to the south-east of it.

BRIGA

SOURCE

AI 486_{12} (Iter XV): BRIGE (and the same in Iter XII, 483_3, by error of the copyist)

DERIVATION. From Celto-Latin **brĭgā*. Jackson in *Britannia*, I (1970), 69, thinks *AI*'s form perhaps Latin nominative plural for British nom. pl. **Brigas*. However, the name is best taken as singular, since nominative forms are rare in our sources (other than Ptolemy), and as genitive-locative; compare *Abone*. Final *-e* for *-ae* is a common Vulgar Latin feature.

This is a very common Celtic place-name element, surprisingly rare (with this single instance) in Britain, at least in our ancient sources. **Brĭgā* means 'hill', often particularised as 'hill-fort'. It seems to belong to an early period of Celtic expansion, through Gaul into Iberia, and to represent an older stratum than *dūnum*; in contrast to the latter, on which see BRANODUNUM, it has been thought to apply to places generally remote from the main roads (Vincent 207). Its antiquity is held by Dauzat *TF* 198 to be indicated by the fact that it is an element in common between Ligurian and Celtic.

**Brĭgā* rarely appears uncompounded as in the present instance; Jackson expresses surprise that this one carries no suffix. Parallels are provided by Brie in France, certainly from **brĭgā* (Bede *HE* III, 8) but for which no ancient forms are known, and Briges (Lozère, France) < **brigia* (plural), on which see L.-F. Flutre in *RIO*, VIII (1956), 279–80, who also has a general discussion of these names. *Brica* is a woman's name in *RIB* 744 (Greta Bridge). The name is also rare as a first element in compounded forms, the only obvious example being *Brigobanne* (*TP*; now Hüfingen, Austria; British '*Brigomono*' of *Ravenna* 107_{39} = *Rerigonium*). On the Continent it appears with a variety of suffixes, e.g. *Brigetio* (Pannonia Superior, now Szöny), *Brigaecium* (Hispania Tarraconensis), and *Brigiosum* > Brioux (Vienne, France). It is most common as a second element, for example in Gaul *Eburobriga*, *Litanobriga*, and in Spain *Mirobriga*, *Nemetobriga*, *Segobriga*. Holder I. 533 ff. lists many names; for France, see Vincent 207; and in general, M. Richards in *EC*, XIII (1972), 366 ff. For map of *briga* names in Europe, see H. Rix in *Festschrift für Peter Goessler* (Stuttgart, 1954), 104, and S. Piggott, *Ancient Europe* (Edinburgh, 1965), 172.

**Brĭgā* is cognate with Germanic *berg*, hence also with Gothic *baurgs*, etc., all from an assumed Indo-European **brga*. Celtic adjective **brig-* 'high' is found in *Brigantes* and other names. There are derivatives in the modern Celtic languages: Welsh and Breton *bre* 'hill', Irish *bré*, while *brae* has entered English from Scots speech. Not all Continental names in *-briga* are necessarily of strict origin in Celtic times, for the word was well known in Latin. It was compounded with Latin names to give the high-sounding *Augustobriga* (two towns) and *Flaviobriga* in Spain, was often represented as *-brica* in Latin texts (with hypercorrect *-c-*) or reduced to *-bria* in accordance with Vulgar Latin usage, and as a common noun it survived in certain French Alpine dialects as *bric-* (which supposes an original **bricca*). In compounds the element was unstressed, the accent falling on the preceding vowel (*-óbrĭga*) in Latin, which explains the reduced form in which it survives in many instances. For the Indo-European ramifications, see A. Carnoy in *RIO*, VI (1954), 8–10.

IDENTIFICATION. Probably the Roman settlement south-east of Ashley, Hampshire (SU 4029), just north of Farley Mount.

BRIGANTES

SOURCES

Seneca *Apocol.* xii, 3: BRIGANTES
Juvenal *Sat.* xiv, 196: BRIGANTUM (gen. pl.)

Tacitus *Agricola* 17, 2 and 31, 5; *Annals* XII, 32 (twice) and 36, 40; *Histories* III, 45 (twice): BRIGANTES
Ptolemy II, 3, 10: Βρίγαντες (= BRIGANTES)
AI 476_1 (Iter v): ISUBRIGANTUM
Stephanus of Byzantium: Βρίγαντας (= BRIGANTAS, acc. pl.)

The tribal name is amply represented in adjectival and other forms. *CIL* VII. 1207 records two lead pigs from Hayshaw Moor (Yorks.), stamped BRIG and dated to A.D. 81 by a mention of Domitian; this is interpreted as an adjective *Brig(anticum)*, agreeing with an unexpressed *metallum*. A building-stone from the Wall, presumably of A.D. 369, now lost, has been read in part CIVITAT BRICIC, for which Stevens conjectured the expansion *Civitat(is) Brig(ant)ic(ae)*; see *RIB* 2022 and notes. Seven altars dedicated to the goddess *Brigantia* are known, e.g. *RIB* 630 (Adel, Yorks.); in some she is *Victoria Brigantia*, e.g. *RIB* 628 (Castleford, Yorks.). *RIB* 2091, a statuette of the goddess showing attributes which equate her with Minerva Victrix, has the same dedication to *Brigantia*; it was found at Birrens (Dumfries) and indicates the northward extension of the territory of this people. There was also a male deity: *RIB* 623 (Slack, Yorks.) is an altar to *Deo Breganti*. **Brigantia* was also a river-name, assumed origin of the Brent of Middlesex and the Braint of Anglesey; and a hill-name, assumed origin of various places called Brent in Devon and Somerset (Ekwall). There is no direct evidence for **Brigantia* as the name of the region occupied by the tribe, though it could well be assumed; it is not now possible (in view of Jackson *LHEB* Appendix) to hypothesise **Brigantia* as the origin of the later regional name *Bernicia*, as was long taken to be the case.

DERIVATION. Jackson in *Britannia*, I (1970), 75, explains *Brigantes* as a masculine participial formation (British **Brigants* in the singular) on the base **brig-* 'high', the sense of their name being 'high ones, mighty ones'. From the feminine **Briganti* the Romano-British name of the tribal goddess *Brigantia* was derived, as was the later Irish name *Brighid*. Welsh *brenin* 'king' is from the British derivative **brigantīnos*, although this special sense (in contrast to senses of derivatives in Cornish and Breton) seems to represent a dialectal development within a part of Brythonic: see the admirable survey of forms and senses of *Brigantes* and related words by T. M. Charles-Edwards in *Antiquitates Indogermanicae* (Innsbruck, 1974), 35–45. The name *Brigantia* was widely used abroad for places, e.g. with direct derivation > Bragança (Portugal), and *Brigantium* > Bregenz (Austria), etc. There were also *Brigantes* in Ireland (Ptolemy II, 2, 6). In view of this very widespread group of names the people can hardly have been one, and one doubts whether in all parts they could have been 'high ones, mighty ones', perhaps 'overlords'; a sense 'upland people' is more mundane but might be preferable. In his important paper mentioned above, Charles-Edwards argues convincingly for a sense 'freemen, free people', and for the same notion of 'free' as basic to other words and names in this group, without quite showing how this could be related to what we know of the root **brig-* in other formations; see further BRIGA.

IDENTIFICATION. A people of Britain, occupying what is now the northern part of England, with their capital at *Isurium*, Aldborough, Yorkshire. Ptolemy also attributes to them *Epiacum*, *Vinnovium*, *Cataractonium*, *Calagum*, *Rigodunum*, *Oli-*

cana, *Eburacum* and *Camulodunum* (qq.v.) and remarks that they extended from sea to sea, while Tacitus (*Agricola* 17, 2) states that they were said to be the most numerous people of the whole province. For the reference to *Brigantes* by Pausanias see pp. 47 and 79.

BRIGANTIUM

SOURCE
Ptolemy *Almagest* II, 6, 22: Βριγαντίου (gen.; = BRIGANTII)

DERIVATION. As noted above (p. 112), this name does not appear in any other source and must be a false deduction from the tribal name; it therefore counts as a 'ghost'.

BRIGOMONO of *Ravenna* 107_{39} (= R&C 174): see RERIGONIUM

BRINAVIS of *Ravenna* 106_{39} (= R&C 77): see DUROBRIVAE[1]

BRITANNI

SOURCES. As with *Britannia*, there is no point in listing all occurrences of this name and related forms. An outline is given in Chapter II, pp. 39–40. Good guides in following the origin and development of the name are Jackson in *PP* 158–60, with other details in *Scottish Historical Review*, XXXIII (1954), 16, and the extensive survey of O'Rahilly in *EIHM* 444–52.

The original Celtic name was **Pritani*, **Priteni*; the former, Jackson thinks, current in southern Britain, the latter in northern parts. The name would be that which the first speakers of *P*-Celtic in these islands gave themselves (but see below) and passed to Pytheas during his exploration, **Pritani* being represented in Greek as Πρεττανοί. The antiquity of the spelling with Π- is the subject of a comment by Eustathius, who, like Stephanus of Byzantium, draws attention to the -ττ-. Diodorus and Strabo (in part) preserve the Π, presumably following Pytheas, but eventually in Greek (doubtless influenced by the standard Latin form) the spelling with *B*- became common. In Latin usage from the first records *Britanni* was standard, with *-tt-* spelling also in the later Imperial period. The name is first found in Latin in Catullus and then Caesar; it can hardly have been learned by the Romans from Greek sources (since it would then have been **Prettani* from the start in Latin, presumably), but seems to have been picked up from the Celtic of Gaul. It may have been, however, that the equivalences of Greek Π and Latin *B*- had been noted; attention has been drawn, for example, to Πύρρος = *Burrus*, Πύξος = *buxus* 'box'. Another explanation is suggested by O'Rahilly *EIHM* 451–52: that within Gaulish the name heard as **Pritani* was assimilated to Gaulish words in **brit*-, of which there were a number, and that in this form the name passed to Latin speakers.

In the Celtic speech of these islands, beside official *Britanni* introduced by Latin speakers at the conquest of A.D. 43, older **Pritani* naturally survived, and from it came eventually Welsh *Prydain* 'Britain': the ethnic name became a name for the island. Moreover, the inhabitants of Roman Britain went on using the name **Priteni* as a designation for the unromanised peoples north of the Antonine Wall, since from this derived Welsh *Prydyn* with the sense 'Picts, Pictland'. This **Priteni* was the form known to the Irish, because of their close contacts with northern Britain; adapted to Q-Celtic phonetics, **Quriteni* **Quritenii* produced Old Irish *Cruithin*, *Cruithni* 'Picts'.

The Latin adjectival form was *Britannicus*, with a learned variant used for metrical reasons in verse, *Britannus*. The latter seems to have retained its learned quality, its more popular noun-form for the individual of the people being *Britto*, first recorded in Martial XI, xxi, 9, and well known in inscriptions; this was used as a personal name in the Continental provinces as *Britto*, *Brittus*, *Britta*, or perhaps coincided there with an older personal name of the same form. Ethnic *Brittŏnes*, first recorded in Juvenal XV, 124, is thus a full alternative to Britanni and was in fact adopted officially: auxiliary units – *alae*, *cohortes* and *numeri* – of *Brittones* are well attested in *diplomata* and in inscriptions on the Continent from the late first century onwards and in *ND* we have *Britones seniores* and *iuniores* (*Or.* IX_{22}, *Occ.* VII_{127}), *secundani Britones* (*Occ.* VII_{84}) and the *ala IV Britonum* (*Or.* XXXI_{45}), as well as the *cohors III Britt*(an)*orum* (*Occ.* XXXV_{25}). This *Britto*, *Brittones* might be of Celtic origin, but it could also be a hypercoristic form of *Britannus* (O'Rahilly, citing Morris Jones, notes that in shortened forms of names a consonant was often doubled). *Brittones* was at any rate taken into, or survived in Celtic usage, > Welsh *Brython*. It survived long also (*Britanni* being forgotten after the collapse of Roman rule) in learned usage, for Bede regularly uses *Bretto*, *Brettones* when referring to the Celtic inhabitants of the island in his day.

It cannot be regarded as wholly certain that original **Pritani* was the name which the *P*-Celts of the island gave themselves at a very early stage, although it is clear that at a later period this name became standard among them. To suppose such self-naming as Jackson does perhaps implies a higher degree of national consciousness and unity than is warranted by what we know of tribal divisions, successive migrations and (for example in the decades which immediately preceded the Roman Conquest) endemic warfare. In many cases a people does not *need* to name itself; a name is often given by outsiders, foreigners, and only taken to itself by a people at a later stage. An alternative hypothesis is, then, that the inhabitants of these islands were named **Pritani* by the Gauls, this name being passed to the Greeks of Massilia, to those interested in the tin trade, etc., at first in pure form with Π and, much later, to the Romans with *B*- (after the assimilation mentioned above had occurred). There may be a further argument in the fact that the name is descriptive (see below), that is, the sort of name given by one people to others; it is not heroic or divine or specially dignified.

DERIVATION. The accepted view is that the **Pretani* are 'figured folk, tattooed folk', from an Indo-European root **qrt*- 'to cut' (Latin *curtus*, Gaelic *cruth* 'form, shape'), with the **pr*- of *P*-Celtic. They are probably not the only people so named. In *RC*, LI (1934), 339, there is a summary of work of Hubschmid on the name Prätigau (Switzerland), in Rheto-Romance *Val Partêns*, *Purtêns* or *Portenz*, in older times *Portennis* or *Pertennis*, these probably deriving from ethnic **Pretani* or **Pretanni*; other names in the area, *Partnun* and *Partennen*, may derive from ethnic **Prettennones*. These would then be a people named in the same way as those of Britain. Pokorny in *VR*, X (1949), 232, sought a different root for both names, nothing less than Illyrian with a sense

'Kämpfer' ('warriors'), concluding that 'Die *Pritenni* in Graubünden sind dann auf ihrer Wanderung nach den Britischen Inseln dort sitzen gebleibene keltisierte Urnenfelderleute'. However, there seems no need to revise the traditionally accepted explanation of the name.

IDENTIFICATION. The inhabitants of Britain.

BRITANNIA

SOURCES. As in the previous case, it is pointless to list occurrences of this name. The main considerations have been outlined in Chapter II, pp. 39–40. The oldest name of the island known to us was *Albion*, and Avienius when citing it may well have drawn it from the most ancient source of all. It is likely that the name learned by Pytheas suggested the creation of Greek Πρεττανική (*Prettanike*) as we find it in Diodorus and Strabo (also with *B*-), alternatively τῶν αἱ Βρεταννικαὶ νῆσοι ('Brettanic Islands') in Polybius, who gives the earliest instance of the name which is textually known to us. In Latin *Britannia* was standard from before the Conquest (apparently first in Catullus, 84–54 B.C., and next in Caesar). The only two inscriptions published in *RIB* which give the name both show it with this spelling: *RIB* 643 (York) has *Britanniae* (dative) and *RIB* 1051 (found at Jarrow but belonging to a monument at the eastern end of Hadrian's Wall) has *Britannia* (ablative: reign of Hadrian, after A.D. 119). The spelling *Brittania* is first found in Solinus, and by the fifth century was nearly as frequent as the older form. The Welsh name *Prydain* (older *Prydein*) 'Britain' shows that speakers of British kept the older form of these names with *P*- and with one -*t*- (on these questions, see the previous entry); but *Bretagne* appears to demand derivation from a form with -*tt*-, although it is always possible that with such a name learned influence led to the retention of original single -*t*-.

Other usages of note are Ptolemy's references in the *Almagest* to Μέγαλη Βρεττανία 'Great Britain' and Μικρὰ Βρεττανία 'Little Britain', i.e. Ireland; early αἱ Βρεττανικαὶ νῆσοι 'British Isles' (Britain with Ireland); and the plural *Britanniae*, used for no very apparent reason by Catullus but standard in the third and fourth centuries when the country was divided into two, four and finally five provinces.

It is noteworthy that the earliest writers in Greek do not use the term Βρεττανία (*Brettania*) as such; this seems to have been adopted by later Greek writers following Latin usage.

DERIVATION. *Britannia* has no direct Celtic origin, but is almost certainly a Latin abstraction from earlier ethnic and adjectival forms. It may even have been at first a poetic creation (Catullus), and shortly after became established as a proper geographical term during Caesar's campaigns and in his writing. It must be remembered that the tribes of Britain before the conquest of A.D. 43 had no political unity and hence no need of a term with which to express their collectivity. The Latin formation of the word corresponds precisely to that of *Gallia*, *Hispania*, etc.

IDENTIFICATION. The island of Britain. For subdivisions of the Roman province, see Chapter II, p. 46.

BROCARA of *Ravenna* 107_{30} (= R&C 156): see VINDOGARA

BROCAVUM

SOURCE

AI 476_5 (Iter v): BROCAVO

DERIVATION. This must be taken together with the next name, *Brocolitia*, with *Brocomagus* (*AI*, Ammianus, *TP*, etc) > Brumath (Bas-Rhin, France), perhaps with *Brocaria* (later *Brogaria*) > Bruyères-le-Châtel (Seine-et-Oise, France), and the widespread personal names *Broccus*, *Brochus*, *Broccius*, *Brocina*, and *Brocomaglos*. For *Brocavum* of *AI* Jackson in *Britannia*, I (1970), 69, suggests an origin in British **brocco-* 'badger', **Broccāu̯on* being 'place of badgers'; and Williams favours the presence of badgers in *Brocolitia*. There is nothing impossible in this; **brocco-* has left derivatives in this sense in all the Celtic languages, e.g. Welsh and Cornish *broch*, Breton *broc'h*, Irish *broc*. The word passed into late Latin and has left various descendants; there is also English *brock*, either from Celtic or via Romance. However, 'badger-place' for *Brocavum* and '(place) infested by badgers' for *Brocolitia*, and other badger-associations for the Continental places and the personal names listed above, are not very logical. The animal is rarely present in numbers, and seems to have few folkloric associations; it is nocturnal by habit and hardly comes to notice. We seem to have no other British names which we can say with certainty are based on those of wild animals (*Bibra* comes closest). In all England Ekwall lists no *badger*-names, only two with *brock* (and two other probables), and such naming is rare abroad.

It is therefore best to regard the sense 'badger' as secondary and turn to the notion which underlies it. Latin has *broccus* 'pointed', used especially of the teeth, e.g. *dentes brocc[h]i* in Varro II, R. R. 7, 3, a word seemingly borrowed from Gaulish or cognate with a Celtic root (Pokorny 108, Whatmough *DAG* 444–45). The badger as **brocco-*, then, is 'he with the pointed teeth', and persons named *Broccus*, *Brochus*, etc., are 'toothy, having protruding teeth'. Dauzat *TF* 217 is of the same mind: of **brocco-*'badger' he says that 'le sens primitif paraît avoir été "pointe" (cf. français *broche*). Le sens topographique paraît être "éperon de montagne" (le mot a signifié "épine" au Moyen Age).' A sense for **broc-*, then, in the British and other place-names, of 'pointed rock, sharp peak' or the like, seems probable.

A further, more attractive possibility for the place-names (but not the personal names) is that which involves a British version of Celtic **u̯roicā* **u̯roico-*'heather' (Holder III. 454; Welsh *grug*, Cornish *grig*, Breton *brug*; Old Irish *fróech* glossed 'brucus'). In late Latin (from Gaulish) one finds *brūca brūcus*, the Romance *bruc-* (Old Provençal *bruc*, Catalan *bruch*, Spanish *broza* 'dead leaves, brushwood' and dialectal *bruza* 'heather'); with suffix, **brūc(g)āria* > French *bruyère*. See L.-F. Flutre in *RIO*, VIII (1956), 280–81; J. Hubschmid in *ELH* I. 142. P. Aebischer in *RC*, XLVIII (1931), 312–24, studied the name *Vroica*, a deity, on an inscription of Rognes (Bouches-du-Rhône, France), relating this to 'heather' and seeing it as the original name of two streams now called Broye in Vaud Canton (Switzerland). This, we can now see, is the first element in *Brocomagus*, the Latin version of **U̯roico-magos* 'heather-plain', with which O'Rahilly *EIHM* 534 equates Irish *Fraechmag*, while in Gaul *Brocaria* > *Brogaria* > *Bruyères*(-le-Châtel) is clearly another 'heather'-name also. Moreover, in one record, that of Ptolemy II, 9, 9,

Brocomagus is Βρευκόμαγος (= *Breucomagos*), a representation of an earlier stage of the vowel development; and in *CIL* XIII. 9097 the same name is *Vro(comagus)*. It was natural that the awkward group **u̯ro-* should be represented as *Bro-* in Latin, both in speech and in writing; however, one does exceptionally find a Latin initial *V-*, in *Vrocatae* (genitive or dative), a graffito on a cooking-pot of the early fourth century used as a cremation-urn at Beckfoot (*JRS*, XLIII (1953), 131), this of course being a **broc-* 'toothy' personal name. See also VIROCONIUM in part.

As for the vowels, original *-oi-* diphthong proceeded via *ō* to *ū* in the second and third centuries (while *-au-*, *-ou-* and *-eu-* became *-ō-* in the late first century 'at least in part' – Jackson *LHEB* 313–14, and this *-ō-* also > *-ū-* by the end of the third century); so there is no problem in regarding our two *Broc-* names as fairly representing, in Latin guise, original British **u̯roico-* 'heather'. The root has **-au̯o-* suffix (compare ABALLAVA) of derivation. The sense 'heathery place' cannot be absolutely affirmed, but seems natural, especially in view of the topography of the present place and of the next.

IDENTIFICATION. The Roman fort at Brougham, Westmorland (NY 5328).

Note. Although the stages are not clear, there is no reason why modern Brougham should not derive from *Brocavum*. There are early forms: *EPNS* XLIII, 128, gives the first recorded instance of the modern name as *Bruham* (1130), then *Bruham* (1228) and Burgham (1362), explaining this as probably a metathesised form of Anglo-Saxon *Burh-ham* 'homestead near the fortification'. For good measure there is appended the note: 'It may be added that the first element of *Brougham* cannot be derived from *Brocavum*, as with lenition that would have given *Brog-* for which Old English would have substituted *Broc-*.' No doubt this is so, but it takes no account of possible disturbances of the phonological rules by analogy, hypercorrection, assimilation to related words, and so on. In the absence of records over so many centuries one cannot guess at the process, but the fact remains that the *Bru-* forms of 1130 and 1228 very strongly recall Celto-Latin *Bro-*, and that *Burg-ham* of 1362 could be a mere Germanic rationalisation into commonly used elements, as often. It seems rash to dismiss the possibility that the old name survived.

BROCOLITIA

SOURCES

Ravenna 107_{26} (= R&C 148): BROCOLITI

ND XL_{39}: Tribunus cohortis primae Batauorum, PROCOLITIA

ND's form shows either hypercorrection (compare *Patavia* for *Batavia* in *TP*, Gaul) or a scribal assimilation to Latin *pro-* or possibly *procul*.

DERIVATION. For the first element, see the discussion under *Brocavum*. On the second element Williams is authoritative: *-lītu-* 'feast', represented in Irish by *líth* and in Breton by *lid* 'fête', and present in the Gaulish names *Litumaros*, *Litugenos*, *Lituviros*, etc. 'In modern and medieval Welsh adjectives formed by adding *lyt*, *llyd* to a noun correspond to English adjectives in *-y*, as *creu-lyd* "bloody", *tan-llyd* "fiery".' His sense for *Brocolitia* is consequently 'infested by badgers'; in view of the discussion under *Brocavum*, we suggest 'full of pointed rocks', or better 'heathery, covered with heather'.

IDENTIFICATION. The Roman fort at Carrawburgh, Northumberland (NY 8571).

BURRIUM

SOURCES

Ptolemy II, 3, 12: Βούλλαιον (= BULLAEUM), a *polis* of the Silures; vars. Βούλλεον (= BULLEUM), Βούλαιον (= BULAEUM)

AI 484_5 (Iter XII): BURRIO

485_1 (Iter XIII): BURRIO

DERIVATION. Jackson in *Britannia*, I (1970), 69, explains the name as a derivactive of **burro*- 'stout, study, big' (Welsh *bwr*), probably from a personal name **Burros*, which is known in Gaulish, with the common *-*įo*- derivational suffix. Hence 'place of **Burros*'. Compare nearby BLESTIUM formed in the same way. Holder I. 642 lists many *Burrus* and *Burra* names from many parts of the Continent. However, at I. 631 Holder refers British BURRIUM to *Bullaion*, that is, taking Ptolemy's form as the prime one, and indeed he lists many persons and small places with *-ll-* (*Bullius*, etc.). It may be that *-ll-* did exist as a spoken variant of *-rr-*; *r* and *l* are very liable to interchange in many languages, and in early Latin such a variation as that which produced *tellus/terra* is suggestive.

IDENTIFICATION. The Roman fort at Usk, Monmouthshire (SO 3700).

CABABUM (?)

SOURCE

A writing-tablet found in London in 1959 was published by E. G. Turner and O. Skutsch in *JRS*, L (1960), 108–11. The relevant part is:

scito me manẹṛẹ aput [Duro]ḅriụas et cabạḅi et...

DERIVATION. The writers comment that perhaps *C. Ababi(us)*, a personal name, is intended, 'or perhaps a place-name is in question (in the locative case?)'; possibly, then **Cababum* in the oblique case, though *aput* with a correct accusative followed by a sort of fossilised locative is very odd. If there is such a place-name, it should be sought in the area of Rochester, since the letter-writer says he is remaining 'at Durobrivae and...' *Cab-* is unpromising as a root; only *Cabellione* > Cavaillon (Vaucluse, France) and *Cabillionum* > Chalon-sur-Saône (Saône-et-Loire, France) offer remote parallels in Gaul, but there are not enough letters in the above text for a name related to these. If *C-* is for *G-* (as often, e.g. *Burdecala* for *Burdigala*, etc.) there might be other possibilities.

IDENTIFICATION. Unknown, but possibly in the area of Rochester, Kent.

CAELIS (?)

SOURCE

Ptolemy II, 3, 4: Καίλιος ποταμοῦ ἐκβολαί (= CAELIS FLUVII OSTIA), vars. Κέλιος (= CELIS), Καιλνίου (= CAELNIUS), Κελνίου (= CELNIUS; MS U)

DERIVATION. The form of this name is uncertain. In modern British works it has been variously presented as *Celnius* by Bradley in 1885, who thought it 'the stream which runs by the town of Cullen', as *Caelivs Fl.* on the O.S. map, as *Caelis* by Richmond in *Roman and Native in North Britain* (1958; p. 137), and as Κελνίος by Ogilvie and Richmond in their text of the *Agricola* (1967). The only reason for preferring Καίλιος (*Caelis*) with Müller is that it does have Continental analogues, none of them rivers: *Celio Monte AI* 250_7 in Raetia; an assumed **Caeliacum* (from **Caelius*) > Ciago (Trentino, Italy: Holder I. 675); Κοιλιόβριγα (= *Coeliobriga*: Ptolemy II, 6, 41) > Calabre (Lamas de Moledo near Viseo, Portugal). In some of these and in the British name there may have been assimilation to Latin *caelum*. The meaning of the root in Celtic is not known; Watson *CPNS* 49 discusses possibilities.

IDENTIFICATION. Probably the river Deveron, Banff.

Note. This river might be the same as that which *Ravenna* lists at 108_{33} as *Certis* (conflated with *Nassa*). If they are the same, Ptolemy's uncertain forms and the untrustworthy nature of *Ravenna* in general do not allow us to assert that one version is the better, though *Certis* has an analogue among rivers and a known etymology.

CAERENI

SOURCES

Ptolemy II, 3, 9: Καιρηνοί (= CAERENI), vars. Καιρινοί (= CAERINI), Καρηνοί (CARENI), etc.

Ravenna 108_2 (= R&C 205): CERMA
108_{11} (= R&C 223): CERMIUM

Ravenna's forms are corrupt. As in many other instances for Britain north of Hadrian's Wall, the Cosmographer in reading from his map did not realize that he was dealing with tribal names, and entered them in his lists as ordinary place-names. See the table of names and discussion in Chapter V, 194–96. Comparison with the much more accurate forms of Ptolemy, who drew indirectly on the same map, enables us to make a number of useful identifications among *Ravenna*'s corrupt forms, as here. In this text miscopying of *m* and *n*, especially when in association with *i*, was common, and both the above entries are readily amended to *Cerin-* (with *-e-* correct, as a normal Vulgar Latin rendering of classical *-ae-*). Dillemann (70) agrees with these corrections and identifications. There is a further curiosity here, in that the present pair of names represents the only duplication in *Ravenna's* N. British sections; the name seems to have been read twice from the single map-source.

DERIVATION. The base is British **caero-* 'sheep', especially 'ram, he-goat', now represented in Welsh *caer-iwrch* 'roebuck' (male kid); cognates (some based on **caerac-*) include Irish *caera*, gen. *caerach*, and Gaelic *caora* 'sheep'. The root existed in Gaulish also and is found in the Rhineland names *Caeracates* 'shepherds' (Tacitus *Histories* IV, 70) and *Caeroesi* (Caesar *BG* II, 4, who says they are 'Germani'). The sleeveless hooded cloak known as the *caracalla* in Latin was < **caeracalla*, presumably made originally from wool produced by one of these or a similarly-named people. The British name has a suffix seen also in *Bremenium* and in such Gaulish words as **ep-ēnos* 'knight' (based on **epos* 'horse'): see J. Hubschmid in *RIO*, VII (1955), 179. The tribal name is thought by Watson to be a literal one, 'sheep-men', and not to have any totemic significance; but see H. Birkhan in *Germanen und Kelten* (Vienna, 1970), 465, where the tribe is taken to be 'Schafverehrer' ('sheep-worshippers'), a view which C. Thomas in *Arch. J.*, CXVIII (1961), 40, would support (see EPIDII).

IDENTIFICATION. A people of northern Scotland, placed by Ptolemy next to the Cornovii and so presumably in Sutherland.

CAESAROMAGUS

SOURCES

AI 474_3 (Iter V): CAESAROMAGO
480_6 (Iter IX): CESAROMAGO
Ravenna 106_{51} (= R&C 98): CESAROMAGO
TP: BAROMACI

It was suggested by K. Miller (*Itineraria Romana*, 1916, note to p. xxvi) that *TP*'s locative form resulted from the name coming at a join in the sheets of the map, the first part *Ce-* being on the sheet now lost and the first letter of the remainder being misread as *B-* when the surviving copy was made. This explanation has been generally accepted. The parallel suggested by R&C with *Saragossa* (Zaragoza) in Spain is not relevant (this was *Caesaraugusta* with distortions resulting from Arabic). In *-maci* we find the *-c-* which often appears by hypercorrection or miscopying.

DERIVATION. The combination of Latin imperial name with Celtic element is unique in Britain. Presumably in each case there was artificial creation of a new settlement by administrative act, and a name of special dignity was hopefully assigned (for discussion of the present case, see C. E. Stevens in *EHR*, LII (1937), 198). On the Continent *Augusto- Claudio- Julio- Flavio-* are known as first elements in such names. *Caesarodunum* was the early name for what is now Tours (Indre-et-Loire, France), and *Caesarobriga* that of Talavera de la Reina (Toledo, Spain). The precise duplicate of the British name is *Caesaromagus Bellovacorum* in Gallia Belgica (*Bellovacis* > Beauvais, Oise, France).

Magus is a common element in British and Gaulish toponymy. It seems to belong to the later stages of Celtic settlement, when permanent habitation was possible in settled conditions and in undefended lowland sites, this being implied in the sense of the word (see below). It represents a later stratum than *briga* and *dunum*, and it is significant that it is unknown in Iberia. *Magus* names are listed by Holder II. 384, the Gaulish names by Vincent 222–27, and Scottish examples by Watson *CPNS* 377–78. There are seven names known in Britain in ancient sources in addition to the present one: *Leucomagus, Litanomagus,* two *Noviomagus, Sitomagus,* uncompounded *Magis* and the ethnic *Vacomagi.* For a map of the European names, see H. Rix in *Festschrift für Peter Goessler* (Stuttgart, 1954), 106, and S. Piggott, *Ancient Europe* (Edinburgh, 1965), 174.

The sense of original British **magos* was 'field, plain', then 'market'. The latter sense is preferred for the present name by P. J. Drury in W. Rodwell & T. Rowley (eds.), *The 'Small Towns' of Roman Britain* (British Arch. Reports 15, Oxford, 1975, p. 163). The use of *-magus* in Celto-Latin toponymy was equivalent to that of Latin *forum*; indeed *Juliomagus* = *Forum Julii.* Derivatives include Welsh *ma* 'place' (now only in composition and then in the mutated form *fa*), Breton *ma* 'field'; and there is Irish *mag(h)*, with *moy* 'plain' in place-names. See M. Richards in *EC*, XIII (1972), 366 ff. Although the compounds and formations like *Noviomagus* suggest long Latin familiarity with the word, it seems not to have passed (unlike *briga*, *dunum*) into Vulgar Latin as a common noun, and has left no Romance descendants. In compounds it was unstressed, the accent falling on the preceding vowel (*-ómăgus*). It does not appear as a first element, and is known in only one instance used alone, British *Magis*.

IDENTIFICATION. The Roman town at Chelmsford, Essex (TL 7006).

*CALACUM

SOURCES

Ptolemy II, 3, 10: Κάλαγον (= CALAGUM), a *polis* of the Brigantes; var. Κάλατον (= CALATUM)

AI 481_4 (Iter X): GALACUM

DERIVATION. The form must be the result of conjecture. To take Ptolemy's initial *C-* and *AI*'s medial *-c-* is not really arbitrary, given the frequency of *c/g* confusions in copying and the fact that there are good analogues for **Calacum*. Some confusion has been introduced by the fact that R&C call this place *Galacum* and add to their sources for it the *Calunio* of *Ravenna* 107_1 (112 in their numeration); we refer this to GALAVA.

The British form would have been **Calācon*. Jackson in *JRS*, XXXVIII (1948), 55, offers the root **cal-* 'to call', citing Irish *coileach*, Welsh *ceiliog* 'cock' from Celtic **caliācos*, literally 'the caller'; and in *Britannia*, I (1970), 74, preferring **cal-* to **gal-* after discussion, he further relates this **cal-* root to the second element in *Crococalana* (q.v.). British **Calacum* has a precise parallel in Gaulish *Calagum* of *TP* (again with *c/g* scribal confusion) > Chailly-en-Brie (Seine-et-Marne, France). Other names in France go back to **Caliacus*: Chaillac, Chaillé, Chailly, etc. (Holder I. 699). Birley in CW^2, XLVI (1946), 152, discusses the names and quotes Hübner on a stream called *Calacum* near Tarento (S. Italy). A sense 'noisy stream', literally '(loud-)calling one' is – following Jackson – very appropriate, the stream-name (or reach-name) being transferred to a settlement, as often. For the *-ācum* suffix, here adjectival, compare *Bravoniacum*.

Other names containing **cala* **gala* are listed by Holder I. 685 and discussed by Dauzat *TF* 98 ff. They include *Obucala*, *Burdigala* > Bordeaux, *Cala* > Chelles (Seine-et-Marne, France), and contain a pre-Indo-European root thought to be an early variant of **cara* 'stone', with sense-development 'rock > shelter > habitation > fortress' (*gala* 'fortress' in Lithuanian). These should not be confused with **cal-* in the present name, despite the association of pre-Indo-European **cala* with Celtic *dūnon* in *Caladuno AI* 422_5 (now Montealegre, León, Spain), and the same in a medieval record of *Caladunum* > Châlons (Mayenne, France). See further CROCOCALANA, VINDOGARA.

IDENTIFICATION. Probably the Roman fort at Burrow-in-Lonsdale (= Overborough), Lancashire (SD 6175); the reference is presumably to a reach of the river Lune.

CALCARIA

SOURCES

AI 468_5 (Iter II): CALCARIA

Ravenna 107_7 (= R&C 125): PAMPOCALIA

R&C note that *Ravenna*'s form is 'a

recognisable conflation of CAMBODUNUM and CALCARIA', adjacent names presumably misread from a map.

DERIVATION. The name is the Latin for 'lime-works', 'limestone quarries' (*calx* 'chalk, lime'). There was another *Calcaria* > Calas (Var, France), and another presumed in Germania Inferior (Whatmough *DAG* 922). The name survived for a time within the British Kingdom of Elmet, with Anglo-Saxon adjustments, as recorded by Bede IV, 23: *secessit ad civitatem Calcariam, quae a gente Anglorum Kaelcacaestir appellatur.*

IDENTIFICATION. The Roman settlement at Tadcaster, Yorkshire (SE 4843). Its position in *AI* rules out the suggestion of Ekwall (*EPN*, s.v. Kelk) that Kelk is meant, since this lies far away in the East Riding (TA 1058).

Note. For the importance of Bede's reference, see CAMBODUNUM.

CALIDONIA

SOURCES

Tacitus *Agricola* 10, 4, etc.: CALEDONIA (five mentions)

Xiphilinus 322 (= Cassius Dio LXXVI, 13): (= CALEDONIAM)

Solinus 22, 1: Καληδονίαν CALIDONIA

Jordanes 2, 13 (quoting Tacitus): CALYDONIA

(See also ethnic and personal names and adjectival forms in the next two entries)

DERIVATION. The *e/i* variation in recorded Latin forms is probably of little account: this applies not only to the present name of the region but also to the ethnic and personal names and the adjectival forms. It is noteworthy that whereas Pliny has *-i-* ('correctly', see below), the other mentions in the first century A.D. which have *-e-* are all from verse: it is likely that *Călēdŏnĭus* has *ē* in order to fit the hexameter, since *ĕ* or *ĭ* would not serve, and that such was the authority of verse that the name tended to settle down in Latin – but not exclusively – in this form. The same *e/i* variation is in any case recorded on the coins and in personal names mentioned in the next entries. Holder analyses the personal names in Latin form with vowels *Căl-ēdŭ*, *Căl-ēdŏn-es*. We are led back towards the original British form by the statement in Nennius 56 that Arthur's seventh battle was the *bellum in silva Calidonis* (var.: *Celidonis*), *id est Cat Coit Celidon*: this derives from an original *Calidon-* with *-ĭ-*; the modern Welsh would be *Coed Celyddon*. The name is represented also by the second element in Dunkeld (from *Dúnchailden* or *Dún Chailleann*), Schiehallion and Rohallion, all in Perthshire, these being Gaelic forms of names taken earlier from British; see Jackson in *Scottish Historical Review*, XXXIII (1954), 14–16; also, in general, Watson *CPNS* 21, and *LHEB* 607, 616. It seems, then, that *Calidonia* has the better authority.

For **cal-* **calet-*, the base of this name, see ANCALITES. To the base is added the **-on(o)-* suffix (see BREMETENACUM). The regional name is doubtless a Roman creation, following the example of *Hispania*, *Gallia*, *Britannia*, etc.; a sort of abstraction from the ethnic name *Calidonii*, who seem to be (like the *Ancalites*) 'hard men, tough men'. With this base and these analogues, it is not easy to understand Jackson's reservation about the name, as he expressed it in *PP* 135: 'it cannot be proved to be Celtic, and may therefore very possibly be pre-Celtic'.

IDENTIFICATION. A name applied generally to Scotland north of the Forth–Clyde isthmus and occasionally to the whole of northern Britain.

CALIDONIA SILVA

SOURCES

Pliny *NH* IV, 102: SILVAE CALIDONIAE (gen.)

Florus, *Epit. de T. Livio*, I, 12 (I, 17, 3): SALTUS CALEDONIUS

Ptolemy II, 3, 8: Καληδόνιος δρυμὸς (= CALEDONIUS SALTUS)

Martianus Capella VI, 666: CALIDONIA SILVA

There are two further mentions: Florus, *Epit. de T. Livio*, I, 45 (III, 10, 18) has CALEDONIAS...SILVAS (acc.); Silius Italicus, *Punica*, iii, 598, has CALEDONIOS LUCOS (acc. pl.). These in their different ways, but especially in their plural form, hardly seem to refer to a single (however extensive and ill-defined) place and are not real toponyms.

DERIVATION. See CALIDONIA. The forest is discussed, on the basis of Nennius's mention of Arthur's seventh battle (see previous entry), by O. G. S. Crawford in *Antiquity*, IX (1935), 286–87. There is much of interest about the sources and their implications, including medieval references, in B. Clark's 'Calidon and the Caledonian Forest', *BBCS*, XXIII (1969), 191–201.

IDENTIFICATION. The forest appears to be localised by Ptolemy in the region of the Great Glen, but in general classical usage the name seems to mean simply 'the wilds of Calidonia'.

CALIDONII

SOURCES

Lucan vi, 68: CALEDONII

Martial x, xliv, 1: CALEDONII

Ptolemy II, 3, 8: Καληδόνιοι (= CALEDONII)

Ravenna 108_6 (= R&C 213): LODONE, for *(Ca)ledone(s)* ?

Xiphilinus 321 (= Cassius Dio LXXVI, 12): Καληδονίοι (= CALEDONII, twice); also 324 (= LXXVI, 15) and 325 (= LXXVI, 16)

Panegyrici Latini VI (VII), 7, 2 (A.D. 310): CALIDONES

Nomina Provinciarum Omnium (Verona List): 13: CALEDONII (var. CALIDONI)

Apollinaris Sidonius vii, 89: CALEDONII (var. CALIDONII)

Jordanes 2, 14 (quoting Cassius Dio): CALYDONII

Ravenna's form has not hitherto been associated with these names. As argued in Chapter V (pp. 193–94), *Ravenna* took from the same map-source as that on which Ptolemy ultimately depended many tribal names, misreading them as place-names, and it is logical for **Caledonii* or **Caledones* to figure in *Ravenna* as it does in Ptolemy. The two letters at the start of the name may have been separated from the rest by a line of some sort on the map; *o* for *e* is a not uncommon error.

To these must be added a variety of other records. Ammianus mentions the *Dicalydones* (q.v.). *RIB* 191 (Colchester) is a votive tablet of *Lossio Veda...Nepos Vepogeni Caledo*, the last word designating 'the Caledonian'. *Caledu*, *Calidu* appear on coins of the Arverni and Caletes of Gaul (Dottin *LG* 43, Watson *CPNS* 21), and presumably the latter people, the Καλῆται (= *Caletae*) of Ptolemy, with their settlement *Juliobona Caletum* now Lillebonne (Seine-Maritime, France) were related at least in name to the Caledonii of Scotland. There is a range of personal names listed by Holder I. 691, Kajanto, etc.: *Calidius*, *Caleidius* (*CIL* VI. 33968), *Calezius* (*RIB* 764, Kirkby Thore; a *nomen* restored by Wright as *Caledius*, but a good vulgar form as it stands), *Callidianus*, etc. Two building-stones from the Wall, *RIB* 1679 and 1854, record work under the centurion *Caledonius Secundus*, whose name was thought by Birley in *Arch. Ael.*[4], XVI (1939), 234, to the Umbrian. It is probable that not all these widespread personal names are of the same Celtic origin. For the *e/i* variation, compare CALIDONIA. The third-declension form *Calidones* of the Panegyric and (?) *Ravenna* may not be erratic but a genuine variant; cf. *Attrebates*.

The adjective *Caledonius* (always with -*e*-) is used by Silius Italicus, *Punica* iii, 598; Valerius Flaccus, *Argonautica* i, 8; Statius v, ii, 142; Martial, *Epig.* vii, 3; Ausonius, *Mosella* 68, etc.; and Claudian, *Carmina* VIII, 26, etc. See also CALIDONIA SILVA. In Solinus 22, 1, the adjective is *Caledonicus*.

DERIVATION. See CALIDONIA. The ethnic name must have preceded the regional name.

IDENTIFICATION. Ptolemy locates a specific tribe of this name in the area of the Great Glen, but it may be significant that Tacitus never uses the tribal name as such but always a periphrasis (*habitantes Caledoniam*, etc.). In general classical usage the name came to be applied to all the inhabitants of Scotland north of the Forth–Clyde isthmus, but in the reference by Xiphilinus (= Cassius Dio) they are specifically a confederation of tribes occupying northern Scotland, as opposed to the *Maeatae* (q.v.) who occupied the south.

CALLEVA ATREBATUM

SOURCES

Belgic coins: on coins of Eppillus (fl. A.D. 10, son of Commius) there is the legend CALLEV or REX CALLE (*Archaeologia*, X (1944), 7–8; Mack Nos. 107, 108)

Inscriptions: *RIB* 70 found on the site of a temple at Silchester records an act A CON[LEGIO PERE]GR[I]NORUM [CONSISTENTI]UM CALLEVAE 'by the guild of *peregrini* dwelling at Calleva'. *RIB* 69 and 71 record acts by the same guild but the place-name is abbreviated to a simple C. The fragmentary inscription *RIB* 73 has been conjecturally restored in very diverse ways and may have mentioned *Calleva* or the *Civitas Atrebatum*, as may the fragment *RIB* 76.

Ptolemy II, 3, 12: Καληοῦα (= CALEVA), a *polis* of the Atrebatii

AI 478_3 (Iter VII): GALLEVA ATREBATUM
484_{10} and 485_7 (Iter XIII): CALLEVA
485_8 and 486_7 (Iter XIV): CALLEVA
486_8 (Iter XV): CALLEVA

Ravenna 106_{32} (= R&C 67): CALEBA ARBATIUM

DERIVATION. *Calleva* represents British **Callēu̯ā* (Jackson), probably '(town in the) woods'. Holder I. 701 (following Rhys) identifies a stem **calli-* (for **caldi-*) 'wood', which is represented by Welsh *celli*, Irish *coill*, *caill* 'wood'. Holder and Jackson *LHEB* 432 add that the -*ld*- of earlier **caldi-* is present in Gaulish *Caldis* and *Caldeniacum*, and in the cognate English *holt*. For the uncommon -*ēva* suffix, Holder compares *Luteva* in Gaul. See ATREBATES.

IDENTIFICATION. The Iron Age settlement, succeeded by the Roman city, at Silchester, Hampshire (SU 6462).

Note. The modern name Silchester possibly derives its first element from British-Latin *Cal-*. Ekwall, hostile to such notions in general, thinks the name may be a derivative of Anglo-Saxon *sealh* 'sallow', Anglo-Saxon **siele*, **sele* 'sallow-copse', but Crawford in *Archaeologia*, XCIII (1949), s.v., very properly draws attention to the fact that the earliest form *Silcestre* of Domesday Book is *Cil-* in other medieval documents 'and may represent a survival of the original name'. The absence of intermediate Anglo-Saxon records prevents certainty: if the site was abandoned for centuries, survival of the Romano-British name is less likely, despite the earlier importance of the town.

CALUNIO of *Ravenna* 107_1 (= R&C 112): see GALAVA

CAMBODUNUM

SOURCES

AI 468_6 (Iter II): CAMBODUNO, var. CAMPODUNO

Ravenna 107_7 (= R&C 125): PAMPOCALIA

For *Ravenna*'s conflation, see CALCARIA. The forms with *-mp-* indicate an assimilation of the first element to Latin *campus* 'field'; if we had only *AI*'s variant, we should think it a merely scribal assimilation, but the fact that *Ravenna* has it too, and that Bede in *HE* II, 14, shows the same (*in Campodono*) indicates that the assimilation took place among speakers of Latin, not of British, in the place concerned. See also p. 32. It is noteworthy that the exactly parallel *Cambodunum* (now Kempten, Austria) is recorded with original *-mb-* in Ptolemy, *ND* and *TP*, but with the same assimilation to Latin *campus* in *AI* 237_2, 250_8 and 258_{12}.

DERIVATION. **Cambo-* in Celtic is basically 'curved, crooked', now represented by Welsh *cam*, Breton and Irish *camm*. The root was taken into late Latin and produced a large word-family, including Italian *gamba* and French *jambe* 'leg' (the 'bent limb'), French dialectal *chambon* 'terrain fertile' via the sense 'partie concave d'un méandre étant formée d'alluvions riches' (Vincent 237), etc.; while from related **cumbo-* as a noun 'receptacle, trough' comes Welsh *cwmm* 'valley' and such Romance words as Spanish *comba* 'bend, bulge', Galician *comba* 'valley'. Germanic *Hamm* is cognate (hence Hamburg = *Cambodunum*). *Cambo*, a common personal name, perhaps indicated 'hunch-backed'. Other *Cambodunum* names are known: one > Chambezon (Haute-Loire, France), another > Chandon (Fribourg, Switzerland), another > Kempten (Zurich, Switzerland), in addition to that mentioned above; *RC* XLII (1925), 99, and XLIII (1926), 347. The element **cambo-* is present in the next two British names, and in many others abroad: *Cambate* > Gross-Kembs (Switzerland), *Cambaetum* > Cambezes (Orense, Spain), *Cambracum* > Cambarco (Santander, Spain), and others listed by Holder I. 710 and Ellis Evans *GPN* 322.

For *-dunum*, see BRANODUNUM. The sense of *Cambodunum* is 'fort at the bend' (of the river), less probably 'crooked fort'. P. Lebel in *RIO*, XIV (1962), 171, suggests that **cambo-* here and in *Camboritum* has a secondary sense, 'dangereux': '*Cambodunum* ne serait pas "la forteresse courbe" mais celle qui est dangereuse pour l'assiégeant: ce serait un nom de bon augure.' But there seems little need to depart from the literal sense as we have given it.

IDENTIFICATION. Probably an unlocated Roman fort at Leeds, Yorkshire, at the confluence of the Sheepscar Beck with the Aire (SE 3033).

Note. It is remarkable that this Romano-British name should have been known to Bede (*in Campoduno*, II, 14). *Calcaria* and *Cataracta/Cataractone*, together with the present name, do not figure in the classical sources which were known to Bede (Pliny, Solinus, Orosius, etc.) and from which he took other Romano-British names. *Calcaria*, *Cambodunum* are listed by *AI* and *Ravenna*, and *Cataractonium* by these and also by Ptolemy, but these texts were not known to Bede. He can have taken them only from the continuing Latin tradition of the British-speaking Kingdom of Elmet, which retained its independence into the seventh century (the reference in II, 14 is to Paulinus building his church *in Campoduno*, an event to be dated to soon after A.D. 627); but since the existence of the Kingdom did not extend to Bede's youth, he must have had a written source deriving from it and presumably preserved by the Church. The point is not without significance for Bede studies.

CAMBOGLANNA

SOURCES

Rudge Cup: CAMBOGLANS

Amiens *patera*: CAMBOG[LANI]S

Ravenna 107_{11} (= R&C 131): GABAGLANDA

107_{36} (= R&C 167): CAMBROIANNA

ND: In Seeck's edition the entry at XL_{44} reads:

Tribunus cohortis primae Aeliae Dacorum, AMBOGLANNA

M. W. C. Hassall in *Aspects of the ND* (Oxford, 1976), 113, supposes a lacuna in an early MS of *ND*, and restores it as follows:

XL_{43a}: Tribunus cohortis primae Aeliae Dacorum, [BANNA

XL_{44}: Tribunus cohortis secundae Tungrorum], CAMBOGLANNA

See further BANNA. The presence of *cohors II Tungrorum* at Castlesteads is attested on *RIB* 1981–83 and 1999.

The sources need some elucidation. On the restored form of the Amiens *patera*, see p. 230. The Rudge Cup and the *patera* tell us that a locative plural in *-is-* is being recorded (compare *Mais*, locative plural of *Maia*, on the same vessels); in the other texts *Camboglanna* is therefore a nominative or accusative neuter plural, not a feminine singular. *Ravenna*'s first form has initial *G* for *C*, a common scribal error, and has at some stage lost *-m-*, which was often abbreviated, like *-n-*, in medieval MSS. *Ravenna*'s second form has not previously been equated with *Camboglanna*. R&C indeed specifically deny the possibility; they emend the *Cambroianna* of the text to **Cambolanna*, by no means unreasonably, and find an etymology for its second element in British **landa*, **lanna* (see VINDOLANDA), placing this **Cambolanna* in S.W. Scotland. However, it should be noted that R&C's emendation leaves the original one letter short, whereas equation with *Camboglanna* does not; also, duplications in *Ravenna* are much more common than R&C allowed (see Chapter V). The wide separation of the two names in *Ravenna*'s list is no bar to uniting them;

compare the duplication of the name of another Wall-fort, *Maio-Maia*, again widely separated in the text. The Cosmographer was working here from two maps, whose differing scripts led him to duplicate in differing ways. See also Crawford's earlier study in *Antiquity*, IX (1935), where he had other arguments for maintaining the separateness of the two places and for locating **Cambolanna* well to the north of the Wall. Finally, *ND*'s omission of the initial *C-* may be merely a scribal accident or an assimilation to Latin *ambo-* 'both'.

DERIVATION. For **cambo-*, see the previous entry. British **glanno-* is now Welsh *glann* 'bank, shore', found also in British *Glanum* (if for **Glannum*) and *Glannoventa*. The present name is thus 'curved bank' or 'bank at the bend'.

IDENTIFICATION. The Roman fort at Castlesteads, Cumberland (NY 5163), beside the Cam Beck.

Note. Survival of the name for a time may be indicated if the *Camelon* of Harleian MS 3859, where Arthur fought two of his battles (one placed at A.D. 537), is really for *Camlann* or *Cambglan*. See discussion in *Antiquity*, IX (1935), 289–90, and *Modern Philology*, XLIII (1945), 56; also *LHEB* 437. Hassall notes, in support of the identification with Castlesteads, that the Cambeck, the river at the site, may preserve the first element of the old name.

CAMBORITUM

SOURCE

AI 474_7 (Iter V): CAMBORICO

DERIVATION. It is certain, in view of Continental examples, that we should read *-t-* for *-c-* in *AI*'s form; confusion of these two letters was common in medieval scripts. The name means 'the ford at the bend (of the river)', a more natural solution than the 'crooked ford' suggested by Jackson. For the first element, see CAMBODUNUM; for the second, ANDERITUM. The name is found in Gaul: *Camboritum* > Chambord (Loir-et-Cher, France), and there are three other instances. P. Lebel in *RIO*, XIV (1962), 171, suggests (in line with his remark about *Cambodunum*) that **cambo-* here has the secondary sense 'dangereux', the whole meaning 'le gué qui peut faire du tort', but this seems strained.

IDENTIFICATION. Probably the Roman settlement at Lackford, Suffolk (TL 7871), where the Icknield Way crosses the river Lark.

CAMULODUNUM[1]

SOURCES

Coins of Cunobelinus (who ruled at Colchester from about 5 B.C. till about A.D. 40) have the legends CA, CAM, CAMV, CAMVL and once CAMVLODVNO (Mack Nos. 186 and 201–60, passim; see also D. F. Allen in *Britannia*, VI (1975), 1–19)

Pliny *NH* II, 187: A CAMALODUNO Britanniae oppido (var. CAMALDUNO)

Tacitus *Annals* XII, 32: COLONIA CAMULODUNUM
XIV, 31: In COLONIAM CAMULODUNUM
XIV, 32: CAMULODUNI (loc.)

Ptolemy II, 3, 11: Καμουδόλανον (= CAMUDOLANUM, U and most MSS); vars. Καμρυδόλανον (= CAMRUDOLANUM), Καμβρυδόλανον

(= CAMBRUDOLANUM), Καμουδολάν (= CAMUDOLAN)

Cassius Dio LX, 21, 4: Καμουλόδουνον (= CAMULODUNUM)

Inscriptions: *CIL* III. 11233, a tombstone found near Petronell (Hundsheimer Krautäcker; ancient Pannonia Superior):

T STATIUS T CLA VITALIS CAMULODUNI STI III AN XXIII...

CIL XIV. 3955 (=Burn, 1969, No. 90, p. 71). A tombstone from near Nomentum (now La Mentana) in Latium, which records the career of an officer, Gn. Munatius Aurelius Bassus, who had served in Britain as *censitor civium Romanorum coloniae Victricensis quae est in Brittannia* CAMALODUNI

AI 480_4 (Iter IX): CAMOLODUNO

TP: CAMULODUNO

Ravenna 106_{52} (= R&C 99): MANULODULO COLONIA

(See also COLONIA[1])

The sources provide certainty about the form of the name, and also show how it declined. *Ravenna*'s extravagant form is easily restored; Schnetz thinks that initial *M-* proceeded via a *Ch-* spelling from original *C-*. *AI*'s form with *-olo-* perhaps shows the Vulgar Latin development *ŭ > o*.

DERIVATION. For *-dunum*, see BRANODUNUM. The first element is the name of the Celtic war-god *Camulos*, whose cult, perhaps brought to Britain by the Belgae, was widely extended (e.g. *RIB* 2166 from Bar Hill, Dunbarton, is an altar to *Deo Marti Camulo*). The name is very commonly compounded in proper names of Gaul, Iberia, Britain and Galatia, e.g. in personal names of Gaul *Camulogenus*, *Andecamulos*, and in the other British toponyms *Camulodunum*[2] and *Camulosessa* (see Holder I. 727, Ellis Evans *GPN* 160–61, Dottin *LG* 33 and 39). The name is also found uncompounded as a personal name in western Iberia (*ELH* I. 356), *Camalus* and *Camala*. Ellis Evans discusses but does not resolve the meaning of the name; Palomar Lapesa in *ELH* suggests a root **kem-* 'to tire, break, fight', known only in Greek and Celtic. The *a/u* variation in the second vowel (*-a-* in Pliny and in *CIL* XIV. 3955) may be no accident but a genuine variant, in view of the Iberian names.

The British name **Camulodunon* was 'fortress of Camulos'.

IDENTIFICATION. The Iron Age settlement, succeeded by the Roman *colonia*, at Colchester, Essex (TL 9925).

CAMULODUNUM[2]

SOURCES

Ptolemy II, 3, 10: Καμουνλόδουνον (= CAMUNLODUNUM), a *polis* of the Brigantes (most MSS); var. Καμουλόδουνον (MS U; = CAMULODUNUM)

Ravenna 106_{59} (= R&C 111): CAMULODONO

DERIVATION.

See CAMULODUNUM[1].

IDENTIFICATION. Probably the Roman fort at Slack, Yorkshire (SE 0817); presumably the name was transferred from a native hill-fort, either Almondbury (SE 152140) which, though large and impressive, is five miles away, or the smaller, but much nearer, work on Old Lindley Moor (SE 091182).

CAMULOSESSA PRAESIDIUM

SOURCE
Ravenna 107_{38-39} (= R&C 172–73): CAMULOSSESA PRESIDIUM

We have no means of knowing whether *Ravenna* is citing two distinct places, or a place-name to which *Praesidium* is in apposition. Both solutions can be justified from other texts: *ND* lists a *Praesidio*, alone, in north-east England, and other cases of this are known from the Continent; equally, two N. African places listed by *AI*, *Ballene Praesidio* 37_3 and *Tamariceto Praesidio* 38_8 show clear appositional use. Our slight preference for the latter in the present instance is based on the frequency with which *Ravenna* in its British section lists appositional adjuncts such as *Glebon Colonia*, **Eburo Castellum*.

DERIVATION. *Praesidium* is Latin, 'small fort, post'. For *Camulo-*, see CAMULODUNUM[1]. **Sessa* is 'seat' in British, from earlier **sed-ta*, whose root is represented in Latin by *sedeo* (supine *sessum*), *sessio*, etc. This element is found also in British *Demerosessa*, *Eposessa*, and a related one in *Manduessedum*. The name is thus 'small fort at the seat of Camulos'. R&C aptly note 'For this fashion in naming hills, cf. Arthur's Seat'.

IDENTIFICATION. Unknown, but apparently a Roman fort in southern Scotland.

CANA

SOURCE
Ravenna 109_{19} (= R&C 292): CANA

DERIVATION. R&C suggest that the name is the Latin adjective *cānus* 'white', here feminine to agree with an unexpressed *insula*, 'white one, white island'. For other Latin namings among the western isles, see ANAS. It is more doubtful whether the name has anything to do with 'reeds': 'reed' in British was **căno-* (as in the next names), in Latin *canna*, but one would expect at least a plural form and, if the name were originally British, a suffix too.

IDENTIFICATION. An equation with the island of Canna, off the west coast of Scotland, is usually rejected on the grounds that all the modern names of the western islands are of Scandinavian origin. But since the name appears in the list of islands and *Ravenna*'s spelling is unreliable in detail, the coincidence should not be rejected out of hand.

CANONIUM

SOURCES
AI 480_5 (Iter IX): CANONIO
TP: CAUNONIO

DERIVATION. Jackson explains the name in *Britannia*, I (1970), 70, as perhaps representing British **Cănoni̯on*. This could be formed from **Cănonā* with derivative suffix **-i̯o-*, this being in turn a river-name based on **căno-* 'reed' (Welsh *cawn*) plus the **-on(o)* suffix (see BREMETENACUM). Hence 'place on the reedy river'. The name thus has the set of suffixes **-on-i̯o-n* seen also in *Cataractonium*, *Lemannonius Sinus*, **Londoni̯on* (see LONDINIUM), *Ravatonium* (?) and possibly *Viroconium*. *Canovium*, with a different suffix, is comparable. Earlier in *JRS*, XXXVIII (1948), 55, Jackson had suggested that *TP*'s *Caunonio* 'might show an attempt to render what was possibly already the rather rounded pronunciation of British *-a-*; to emend to **Cannonio* would imply a latinising pronunciation of the name. But **Cannonium* might be merely a V.L. spelling for *Cānonium*'. It should indeed be argued that Latin *canna* 'reed' with *-nm-* has influenced the spelling, naturally enough if the word for 'reed' were understood – correctly – to be involved; a copyist then misrepresented the first *n* as *u*, of which there are many examples in our sources.

IDENTIFICATION. The Roman settlement at Kelvedon, Essex (TL 8517), beside the river Blackwater.

CANOVIUM

SOURCES

Inscription: *RIB* 2265 (= Burn, 1969, No. 45, p. 42); a milestone of the fifth year of Hadrian, A.D. 120–21: A KANOVIO M P VIII '8 miles from Kanovium'

AI 482_6 (Iter XI): CONOVIO

Ravenna 106_{43} (= R&C 83): CANUBIO

DERIVATION. The milestone gives certainty of the correct form. The first *o* of *AI*'s form is a scribal assimilation to the stressed *o*, while *Ravenna* misreads *o* as *u* and has the common Vulgar Latin confusion of *b/v*. Jackson in *LHEB* 38 and 379 seems disposed to take *AI*'s *Con-* form with some seriousness, perhaps in view of the development to Welsh *Conwy*, but rectifies this in his treatment of the name in *Britannia*, I (1970), 71: 'The Welsh *Conwy*, the river Conway on which Caerhun stands, must be from **Canou̯i̯o*, presumably from **cāno-* "reed" plus **-ou̯i̯o-* suffix.' Compare *Canonium*, and for this suffix, *Combretovium*, *Cornovii*, **Leucovia*, *Matovium*, *Vinovia*. As often, the name of a river is the basis of that of a settlement on its banks.

IDENTIFICATION. The Roman fort at Caerhun, Caernarvonshire (SH 7770), beside the river Conway.

*CANTIA

SOURCE

Ravenna 106_{11} (= R&C 27): CANZA

The proper form is established by comparison with other names in *Ravenna* in which the compiler represented original /*tj*/ when assibilated in Vulgar Latin as *z* (see AQUAE ARNEMETIAE). Dillemann (66) thinks that Kent is here referred to; he notes that the previous name in *Ravenna* is *Lindinis*, which he (like Pinder & Parthey) takes to be for *Londinis*, London, and thinks that *Canza* could have arisen from an over-zealous scribe who added to it the gloss *in Cantiū* 'in Kent'. But there is no reason to believe that in this section the Cosmographer has moved outside south-west England, and there is no trace of other interpolations or glosses of this kind elsewhere in the British section; moreover, *Lindinis* (q.v.) is a good distinct name, and in none of our numerous records of London does it figure in plural form.

DERIVATION. There are exact parallels to **Cantia* in the names of Gaulish rivers and others. **Cantia* (perhaps earlier **Quantia*) > Cance, a tributary of the Rhône; > Chanza, a tributary of the Guadiana (Spain); and > Kinz, near Aachen (*RIO* XXV (1973), 205). To these Ellis Evans (see below) adds other Canche, Cance rivers of France. In Britain *Cantium* belongs with these. Williams mentions *Ynys Gaint* near the Menai Bridge. It is not certain how many other Continental names are relevant here. One notes particularly *Cantilia* (*Ravenna* 77_{30}) > Chantelle (Allier, France), *Canta*

Insula in Illyria (*DAG* 143), and a *Cabricantium* on or near the Spanish coast (*Ravenna* 79_{43}) for which a sense 'goat-cliff' would be fitting (Spanish *acantilado* 'cliff'); possibly also *Cantabria* 'pays des falaises', though a variety of other suggestions are made about this. Many other names and nouns are assembled by Holder I. 737, Whatmough *DAG* 143 and Ellis Evans.

An admirable treatment of the etymological problem is that of Jackson in *JRS*, XXXVIII (1948), 55, in studying *Cantium*. He begins by dismissing a supposed Celtic **canto-* 'white', lovingly applied by older authorities (and some not so old) to the 'white land' of the Kentish cliffs. No such word existed. Jackson lists three possible roots:

(1) **canto-* 'rim, border, circumference, circle, tyre' (Pokorny 526: **kantho-*, with many derivatives).

(2) Middle Welsh *cant* 'host, party', probably to be seen also in Old Irish *céte* '(place of) assembly'; from **cantia*.

(3) **canto-* 'a hundred' (Welsh *cant*, Irish *cét*).

Hence, for *Cantium*, Jackson suggests a variety of possible meanings: 'encircled (seagirt) land'; 'land on the periphery', 'borderland'; or 'land of hosts'; or perhaps 'land of hundreds'. Of these, as we argue under *Cantium*, Jackson's first meaning, 'corner land, land on the edge', or similar, seems the most natural. Jackson, however, further thinks that in any case *Cantium* derives from an ethnic name (see CANTIACI), in which case his second sense 'armies, hosts' is the best. He cites the Penmachno tombstone of *Cantiorix* (about A.D. 500), for whose name a sense 'king of hosts' is obviously proper. However, against Jackson's view is the fact that '*Cantii*', though long accepted, is probably a ghost which has arisen from an erroneous form in Ptolemy; there may have been no unity among the peoples of Kent until the Romans formed them into a canton of the *Cantiaci*, and if this is so, *Cantium* is the prime form and is not (because so ancient) dependent upon any prior ethnic name.

Jackson's study is supplemented by D. Ellis Evans, 'Some Celtic Forms in *cant-*', *BBCS*, XXVII (1977), 235–45, which provides a great deal of information about Jackson's three main etyma and a good deal else besides. It was not, of course, Ellis Evans's intention to resolve the problem of the name of Kent as such, and he expresses no preference about this.

An important recent study by P. Quentel, 'Le nom celtique du canton en Gaule et en Grande-Bretagne', *RIO*, XXV (1973), 197–223, with further notes by G. Néel in *RIO*, XXVIII (1976), 118–25, helps to link several of the apparently disparate senses of names in *cant-*. Citing Gaulish **cant-*, Welsh *cant*, Breton *can*, *kant* (= Irish *cét*), Quentel identifies in widespread place-names the senses '100', 'circle' and 'edge', together with an adjective 'bright', and a pre-Indo-European base meaning 'stone'. Eventually discarding these last two as unrelated to the Celtic word in question, Quentel concludes (pp. 212 ff.) of the other senses that they can be seen as originating in a Celtic **kn-to* from Indo-European **km-to*. 'La notion de "cercle" est liée à celle de "territoire", car le territoire est conçu comme un "cercle" [Quental had discussed this earlier: cf. German *Kreis*, French *arrondissement*]...Ceci explique le sens général de *kant* "cercle", d'où dérive celui de "bornage", éventuellement de pierre.' Quentel goes on to explain as derived or related terms German *Kante* 'corner, edge', Dutch *Kant* 'edge',

English *cant*, Spanish *canto* 'edge; corner', also 'stone, pebble'. The sense '100' is part of this series, the numeral deriving from the custom of organising territories on the basis of 100 hearths and the soldiers these provided (Welsh *cant tref*). As for modern *canton*, it is Gaulish **cant-* with *-on* suffix, well-known in many names and words.

It is clear from the above that a sense 'corner land, land on the edge' still seems the likeliest for *Cantium*. For *Cantia* it is hard to make suggestions, especially if – as in the numerous Continental **Cantia* names – it is really a river-name which was adopted for a settlement, as often, or was a river-name misread from a map as though it referred to a settlement, as is also frequent in *Ravenna*. R&C concluded that 'corner stream' was intended; perhaps 'river at the edge' (of a tribal area?) is possible too, but there can be no certainty.

IDENTIFICATION. Unknown, but apparently in south-west Britain.

CANTIACI

SOURCES

Ptolemy II, 3, 12: Κάντιοι (= CANTII), with var. in three MSS Καντικοί (= CANTICI), etc.

II, 3, 13: Καντίοις (= CANTIIS, dat.), with var. in three MSS Καντικοῖς (= CANTICIS)

Ravenna 106_{36} (= R&C 72): DURO AVERNO CANTIACORUM

DERIVATION. See CANTIA, CANTIUM. It is hard to say which is the proper form of the ethnic name, but the variant in Ptolemy could be important in showing that *Ravenna*'s form for once deserves credence. R. Radford in 'The Tribes of Southern Britain', *Proceedings of the Prehistoric Society*, new series XX, (1954), 1–26, at 6–7, thinks that *Cantiaci* is more likely to represent the official name than *Cantii*, adding that there was no Belgic people of either name; the Roman organisation of this canton represented an artificial creation (it is noteworthy that Caesar avoids mentioning an ethnic name, describing the inhabitants by an apparent circumlocution, *qui Cantium incolunt*). The only other evidence is provided by *RIB* 192, a votive tablet of *Similis Atti f(ilius) ci(vis) Cant(ius)*, 'Similis...tribesman of the Cantii', as the editor interprets it, though the last Latin word could evidently be expanded *Cant(iacus)*. In support of this form of the name is the ethnicon *Segontiaci*. P. Quentel in *RIO*, XXV (1973), 220, cites *Cantiaci* as the proper form: '*Cantiaci* est la forme adjectivale correspondant à *Parisiaci*, etc. [these being also *Parisii*]. En anglo-saxon *Cantiaci* sera traduit *Cantware* "les hommes du Kent". Voilà qui est, dans ce domaine, un autre indice de continuité, à remarquer d'autant plus que les noms celtiques qui ont subsisté dans ce comté sont par ailleurs peu nombreux.' (The reference is to *Cantwara-burg* 'fort of the men of Kent' > Canterbury.)

IDENTIFICATION. A people of Britain inhabiting Kent and adjoining parts of Surrey and Sussex, with their capital at *Durovernum*, Canterbury. Ptolemy also attributes to them *Rutupiae* and *Londinium* (the latter evidently in error, since the Roman city of London lay north of the Thames). As noted above, the *civitas Cantiacorum* was an artificial creation of the Roman government.

CANTIUM

SOURCES

Caesar *BG* v, 13, 1 etc. (three mentions): CANTIUM

Strabo I, 4, 3 etc. (three mentions): Κάντιον (= CANTIUM)

DERIVATION. For discussion, see CANTIA. The name is very ancient, and was presumably known to Diodorus (next entry) and Strabo from Pytheas. One cannot dismiss Jackson's view (*JRS*, XXXVIII (1948), 55, and *LHEB* 39) that *Cantium* – British **Cantịon* – may derive from an ethnic name; but if we bear the early seafarers in mind and the geographers' efforts to define the shape of Britain, the sense for *Cantium* of 'corner land, land on the edge' seems preferable; indeed the terms in which Diodorus and Strabo mention it seem almost to impose this view. Perhaps to Pytheas, followed by the Greek geographers, the name applied especially to a promontory logically named **Cantịon*, this name being extended by Caesar to the hinterland and the whole region; the name is thus best expressed as **cant-* with the common *-*ịo*- derivational suffix.

Bede in *HE* has numerous references, his name always being *Cantia* (e.g. I, 25), meaning the whole kingdom of Kent of his day. This is evidently a relatinisation of ecclesiastical origin (compare his *Lundonia*).

IDENTIFICATION. The peninsula of Kent.

CANTIUM PROMONTORIUM

SOURCES

Diodorus Siculus v, 21: ἀκρωτήριον... Κάντιον (= PROMONTORIUM...CANTIUM)

Ptolemy II, 3, 3 and II, 3, 4: Κάντιον ἄκρον (= CANTIUM PROMONTORIUM)

DERIVATION. See CANTIA.

IDENTIFICATION. The South Foreland, Kent (not the North Foreland, since that is on Thanet, which was then a distinct island).

CANTIVENTI of *Ravenna* 107_2 (= R&C 115): see GLANNOVENTA

CARBANTORITUM

SOURCES

Ptolemy II, 3, 6: Καρβαντόριγον (= CARBANTORIGUM), a *polis* of the Selgovae; var. Καρβαντόριδον (= CARBANTORIDUM)

Ravenna 107_{33} (= R&C 161): CARBANTIUM

Ravenna's form is merely garbled. In Ptolemy's it seems likely that there has been a confusion of capitals, Γ for T (R&C); restoration to *Carbantoritum* gives a good form and the best sense. However, it should be noted that Ptolemy's -*rigon* has been taken by some at face-value, by Holder I. 782, by Ellis Evans *GPN* 248 (he places it among the **rig*- 'king' names), and also by Watson *CPNS* 35 (he cites Welsh *rhiw* 'slope', comparing *Fán na Carpat* 'slope of the chariots' at Tara in Ireland, which obviously makes very good sense).

DERIVATION. *Carbantoritum* is 'wagon-ford, chariot-ford'. For *-ritum*, see ANDERITUM. Continental analogues for the first element include *Carbantorate Meminorum* > Carpentras (Vaucluse, France) and *Carbantia AI* 340_4 now Balzola in N. Italy, which it has been suggested is properly **Carbantio-briga* 'fortress of Carbantios'. The base is British **carbanto-*'wagon, chariot', cognate with Irish *carpat*; the similar Gaulish word was taken into Latin as *carpentum*, its *p* for *b* (shown also in many records of Gaulish *Carbantorate*) being explained as due to the voiceless *-t-* of the next syllable.

IDENTIFICATION. Probably the Roman fort at Easter Happrew, Peeblesshire (NT 1940) on the Lyne Water, just above its confluence with the Tweed. It is possible that the name was transferred to the fort at Lyne (NT 1840) which replaced the fort at Easter Happrew in late Flavian and Antonine times.

CARNONACAE

SOURCE

Ptolemy II, 3, 8: Καρνονάκαι (= CARNONACAE), var. Κάρνονες (= CARNONES)

DERIVATION. Holder I. 794 offers two **carno-* words, one meaning 'horn, trumpet' (cf. Latin *cornu*), the other 'pile of stones' (cf. Welsh *carn*, *cairn*, and *cairn* as taken into English). The Gaulish *Carnutes* are usually taken to be 'trumpet-people', but Watson *CPNS* 19 thinks 'cairn-people' the more likely sense for the British tribe, *cairn* being taken not in its modern English meaning but rather as 'high rocky hill', appropriate to their area. The name has suffixes **-on(o)*, frequent in ethnic names (see BREMETENACUM) and **aco-* (see BRAVONIACUM).

IDENTIFICATION. A people of Britain located by Ptolemy between the *Creones* and the *Caereni* and so apparently dwelling in the western Highlands of Scotland.

CARVETII

SOURCES

Inscriptions: *JRS*, LV (1965), 224; a milestone of Postumus A.D. 258–68, set up by the C(IVITAS) CAR(VETIORUM); found at Brougham, 1964
RIB 933, a tombstone (Old Penrith) set up to a SEN(ATORI) IN C(IVITATE) CARVETIOR(UM)

On these, see the notes in *JRS* and *RIB*. Also possibly relevant is *RIB* 2283, a milestone found at Middleton which gives a distance M P LIII ('53 miles'), possibly measured from Carlisle (see C. E. Stevens in *EHR*, LII (1937), 200, and E. Birley in CW^2, XLVII (1947), 178) but probably before the recognition of the *civitas*. The Carvetii seem to have constituted a *civitas* in the third century, with its centre at Carlisle, and for some administrative purposes *Civitas Carvetiorum* may have been an alternative name to *Luguvalium*.

DERIVATION. The name seems to have as a root British **carvo-s* 'deer, stag' (Welsh *carw*, etc.), cognate with Latin *cervus*. Other names into which this enters are *Carvone* (*TP*) now Arnhem (Holland), *Carvancas* mountain of Ptolemy II, 13, 1 (Καρουάγκας), later *Cirvencus*. The British name has **-et-* suffix (see *Bremetenacum*, etc.), as in other ethnic names such as *Caletes*, *Namnetes* (Holder I. 1480). Williams in *Canu Aneirin* (Cardiff, 1938),

p. 136, associates with *Carvetii* the Welsh names *Carwed*, *Carwed(-fynydd)*; see also *GPN* 329 ff. The sense of the name is presumably, then, 'deer-men', with reference to an emblem of the tribe.

IDENTIFICATION. A people of Britain, probably originally part of the confederation of the *Brigantes*, later recognised as a separate *civitas*, with their capital at *Luguvalium*, Carlisle.

CASSI

SOURCE
Caesar *BG* v, 21, 1: CASSI

DERIVATION. The name is older Celtic **cad-ti* 'excelling, surpassing; fine, handsome' (Irish *cais* 'clean, smart', etc.); hence as a tribal name 'excellent ones, fine ones'. The root is found in many personal names such as *Cassius*, *Cassinus*, and compounded in *Cassivellaunus* ('surpassing good' or 'handsomely good'); also in ethnic names *Bodiocasses*, *Cassignates*, *Tricasses*, for which see *RC*, XL (1923), 172. There were also *dii Casses*, with a cult in the Rhineland. For the contrast in declension between British *Cassi* and Gaulish *-casses*, see *Atrebates*.

IDENTIFICATION. A British tribe mentioned only by Caesar; presumably they were located in south-eastern Britain and were later absorbed by a larger confederation. Attempts to relate them to the hundred of Cashio, Hertfordshire, are misguided (Ekwall, *EPN*, s.v. Cassiobury).

(CASSITERIDES)

See the discussion in Chapter II, p. 43.

CASTRA EXPLORATORUM

SOURCE
AI 467_1 (Iter II): CASTRA EXPLORATORUM

DERIVATION. The name is entirely Latin, 'camp or fort of the scouts'. This is the only instance of *castra* in British toponymy (there is however **Eburo Castellum*), but it was commonly used in place-names abroad. As a common noun *castra* passed into Anglo-Saxon (having possibly been learned by the Saxons in their Continental homeland before migration, or early picked up by Saxon mercenaries in late fourth-century Britain), and in a variety of forms, depending on dialect, came to designate either alone or compounded a great range of Roman towns, settlements, forts and sites (*Chester*, *Caster–Caistor*, *-cester*, *-xeter*, etc.).

IDENTIFICATION. The Roman fort at Netherby, Cumberland (NY 3971).

CATARACTONIUM

SOURCES
Ptolemy II, 3, 10 (also I, 24, 1 and VIII, 3, 8; and *Almagest* II, 6, 24): Κατουρακτόνιον (= CATURACTONIUM), a *polis* of the Brigantes, vars. Κατουρρακτόνιον (= CATURRACTONIUM), Τατουρακτόνιον (= TATURACTONIUM), Τακτουρακτόνιον (= TACTURACTONIUM)
AI 465_2 (Iter I). CATARACTONI
468_2 (Iter II): CATARACTONE
476_2 (Iter V): CATARACTONI
Ravenna 107_{14} (= R&C 136): CACTABACTONION

The forms in the sources require comment. Ptolemy's, with ου (*u*) in the second syllable in all MSS, seems to show an assimilation to British ★*catu-* 'battle' (but see below). *AI*'s two forms in *-i* are respectable enough as locatives, but the form in *-e* which gives the appearance of a third-declension oblique or ablative is erroneous and should be restored as *-i* again (compare, however, one of Bede's forms, mentioned below). *Ravenna*'s form involves a *-ct-* which mistakenly anticipates the *-ct-* later in the name, as also in one Ptolemy variant.

DERIVATION. Williams and Jackson (*Britannia*, I (1970), 70, and *LHEB* 409, note, etc.) agree with the traditional explanation of the name: < Latin *cataracta* 'waterfall, rapids', with British ★*-on(o)* suffix (see *Bremetenacum*). The rapids referred to are those on the Swale near Richmond, and it is likely that the Swale itself, or a reach of it, was called ★*Cataractōnā*, the name being transferred to the fort with derivational suffix ★*-i̯o*, giving British ★*Cataractōni̯on*, latinised as *Cataractonium*. Certainly the sources support, or are restored to support, this etymology. A few other names are based on *cataracta*: Catterick near Settle (Yorks), mentioned by Williams, and Catterick Moss (Co. Durham) thought to be named from the well-known Catterick; abroad, Chalette (Aube, France) was *Cataracta* in the ninth century, and Cadarache (Bouches-du-Rhône, France) was *apud Cateractam* in 976; there is also La Chorache (Drôme, France), and in Aragón (Spain) Cadereita and Caderechas; but there seem to be no fully ancient names other than the present one based on *cataracta*, or at least we know of none in our sources.

It is proper to feel some disquiet about the traditional etymology, despite the support it has from Williams and Jackson. In the first place, *cataracta* was not a native Latin word but a borrowing from Greek καταράκτα; it probably remained a literary word in Latin, and has left no popular (only learned) progeny in the Romance languages, except possibly in Italian *cateratta*. The Continental names noted above are probably early medieval creations by churchmen or lawyers, and are based on literary Latin. Whether the word would have been used by soldiers, settlers and officials in a new province is therefore doubtful. In the second place, it seems most unlikely that a major river like the Swale should not have had a native Celtic name, this being taken over in Latin form as were dozens of others in the country; and such new naming in Latin is rare in the Celtic regions of the Continent (in Britain, *Ravenna*'s *Velox* is almost certainly a corruption). Moreover, since *cataracta* was hardly a spoken Latin word, it is hard to see how speakers of British could have borrowed it at any early stage in order to form their supposed ★*Cataractōnā* name. In the third place, *Cataractonium* would be a unique case in which a Latin name (whether of river or habitation) appears with a Celtic suffix at an early date; *Caesaromagus* is not in this category. In the fourth place, it is hard to believe that in the short space of time between assumed Roman naming of these *cataracta* and the gathering of materials by Ptolemy's sources or informants, the folk-etymology inherent in *Catu-* for *Cata-* would have operated among speakers in the place, and *would then have gone unrecognised* for what it was – a folk-etymology – by those recording names in official forms on the map which was ultimately Ptolemy's source. That *Cataractonium* did eventually become the accepted form, and that it was taken to have a base *cataracta*, is undoubted, for *AI* and *Ravenna* show it; but that this was truly the original base must be extremely doubtful.

Our suggestion is that behind the name recorded in the Greek and Latin sources there lies a purely Celtic original, as logic demands. Ptolemy's form is vital here. Celtic **catu*- 'battle' occurs in very many personal and place-names, as first element. As a second element the best possibility is Celtic **ratis* 'rampart, fortification, fort' (see RATAE). For this, *-racte* sometimes appears as a variant (Dottin *LG* 280). In names this word can carry a suffix, as in *Ratiaria*, *Ratiaton* (*DAG* 153, 241). There is, then, no inherent difficulty in supposing that the present name was originally British **Catu-ra(c)t-ōn-i̯on*, with the sense '(place of the) battle-ramparts'; and given the numerous parallels provided by the *Duro-* names, this could well refer to a Roman fort, not to a native one. Ptolemy records this precisely in Latin form. Thereafter, at some time before *AI* was compiled, there occurred an assimilation by Latin speakers in the area to *Cataracta*, via a mistaken association with the rapids of the Swale. Some support for our supposed British form may be forthcoming from Middle Welsh *cadrawt* 'war-band, troop of soldiers', perhaps < British **catu-rāto-* or the like, on which see Williams in *BBCS*, I (1921–23), 21 ff., and in *Canu Aneirin* (Cardiff, 1938), 220 (note to *cadrawt*, line 604). It should also be noted that the change from *Catu-* to *Cata-* may have been assisted by uncertainty among British speakers (that is, in addition to the assimilation by Latin speakers), for there are many examples of *Cata-* for earlier *Catu-* in names registered by Ellis Evans in *GPN* 67. Something of our idea was already present in the mind of Sir John Morris Jones (as discussed in *EPNS*, V (1928: Yorks N.R.), 242–43): he supposed that the original British name had two forms, **Caturacto*, genitive **Caturactonos*, beside **Caturact-on*, genitive *-ion*; this being heard by the Romans as though it were their *cataracta*.

Bede used the name three times: in II, 14 and II, 20 it is *Cataractam* (acc.), but in III, 14 it is *Cataractone* (abl.). The difference is curious. Neither form is a relatinisation from the Celtic speech of Bede's day. The first might proceed from a written record of late Latin pronunciation preserved in the kingdom of Elmet (see *Cambodunum*); the second looks more like a form taken from an official record of the Imperial period, since it accords with those of *AI*, a point not without interest for Bede studies; but such a source is today unknown to us. Bede's first two references are ecclesiastical – to Paulinus baptising converts in the Swale, and to the story of James the Deacon; the third is secular, concerning the killing of King Oswine in A.D. 642.

For the development of the name via *Catraeth* (as recorded in Welsh) to Catterick, see especially Jackson *LHEB* 409 (note) and 564. The base supposed is simple *Cataracta* rather than any of the recorded Romano-British forms.

IDENTIFICATION. The Roman town at Catterick, Yorkshire (SE 2299). The name would have been applied in the first instance to the fort which preceded the town.

CATUVELLAUNI

SOURCES

Ptolemy II, 3, 11: Κατυευχλανοί (= CATYEUCHLANI), Κατυαιχλανοί (= KATYAECHLANI, MS U); etc. Müller's Κατουελλανοί (= CATUE LLANI) is conjectural only

Cassius Dio LX, 20, 2: Κατουελλανοί (= CATUELLANI)
Inscription: *RIB* 1962, a building-stone from the Wall (probably of A.D. 369): CIVITATE CATUVELLAUNORUM TOSS[O]DIO
There is no doubt about the correct form of the name, assured by the inscription. Ptolemy's forms show that the name was already corrupt in his source. Cassius Dio's has -ου- but ought to have -oου- (-*uv*-); for similar instances, see *LHEB* 34. In another inscription we have a further useful example of the tribal name: *RIB* 1065 (South Shields) is the tombstone of *Regina... Catvallauna*, in which it is likely that a Vulgar Latin pronunciation with loss of unstressed *ŭ* is recorded (though Jackson remarks that it may show a purely orthographic V for VV: *LHEB* 646 note).

DERIVATION. For the first element **cătŭ-* 'battle', see CATARACTONIUM and Holder I. 847 ff. (e.g. *Caturiges* 'battle-kings' of Gaul). For the second, British **u̯ellauno-*, see BOLVELLAUNIUM. The sense of the name is plainly 'men good in battle, battle-experts'.

IDENTIFICATION. A people of Britain centred on *Verulamium*, St Albans, which may however have been elevated to the rank of *municipium*. Besides '*Urolanium*' Ptolemy also attributes to them *Salinae*, but on this see p. 120.

Note. The name is not to be confused with that of the *Civitas Catalaunorum* who appear thus in the *Notitia Galliarum* VI$_3$, in Belgica Secunda. A variant of this text calls them the *Civitas Catuellaunorum*, but this can be no more than an accident or the act of some scribe acquainted with the name of the British tribe; in many other mentions (Holder has 38) the Gaulish people is regularly the *Catalauni*.

CAUSENNIS

SOURCE
AI 475$_2$ (Iter V): CAUSENNIS

DERIVATION. *Caus-* is known in Gaulish toponymy, but no meaning can be assigned to it: e.g. (Holder I. 870) *Causella* > Chuzelles (Isère, France), *Causila* > Choiselle, a tributary of the Loire (Indre-et-Loire, France), and *Causostis Castrum* > Chausot (Marne, France). There is also *CIIC* No. 417 (pp. 394–95), presumably a tombstone, inscribed]*Cavoseni Argii* (with a mark before the second name which may indicate *et*), at Llanfor in Merioneth, Wales; this – pointed out to us by Dr R. Coates – seems to have two personal names in the genitive, and it seems most improbable that the first could be connected in any way (except etymologically) with the place-name in eastern England. Holder lists the suffix *-*enna* (*-*innus*, *-*inna*) at I. 1439; well-known examples include *Arduenna*, *Ravenna*, *Vienna*, and there is British *Gariennus*. The present name is usually cited as having nominative *Causennae*; but it could equally well be *Causenna* or even *Causenni*. It is best to leave it as a fossilised locative in -*is*, in line with many other names (see ANICETIS).

IDENTIFICATION. Either the Roman settlement at Saltersford, Little Ponton, Lincolnshire (SK 9233) or that at Sapperton, Lincolnshire (TF 0132). The latter is actually on a Roman road, but if the name contains a river element the former, at the crossing of the Witham by the Salters Way, is to be preferred.

CELOVION of *Ravenna* 107$_{41}$ (= R&C 178): see *GELOVIUM

CENIMAGNI of Caesar *BG* v, 21, 1: see ICENI

CENIO

SOURCES

Ptolemy II, 3, 3: Κενίωνος ποταμοῦ ἐκβολαί (= CENIONIS FLUVII OSTIA), var. Κεννίωνος (= CENNIONIS)

Beyond this it is probable that four names from *Ravenna* are, with different types of corruption, versions of this name:

105_{47} (= R&C 3): ELCONIO

108_{30} (= R&C 249): COANTIA, var. COANCIA

108_{41} (= R&C 270): CUNIA

109_{11} (= R&C 279): CUNIS

It is apparent, first, from other examples, that *Elconio* is *Fl(umen) Conio*, misread from a map and then listed as though it were a habitation-name. *Coantia* and *Cunia* both figure properly in the river-list, but it is to be noted that each time the name is listed immediately after *Sena* (*Senua*), giving strong indication of being a repetition, and probably a clue to identification. *Cunis* figures in the island-list and might just possibly be an island (Ptolemy's Κώουννος ?), but this part of *Ravenna*'s list is so corrupt that this is not a strong argument. *Cunis* follows mention of *Minerve*, which we take to be an attribute of Sulis at Bath (see AQUAE SULIS), and it is very probable that *Cunis* is yet a further repetition of the same river-name. For the miscopyings involved, see p. 203. It seems *a priori* likely that Ptolemy, whose MSS agree on Κεν- (= *Cen-*), would have a more trustworthy form than any in *Ravenna*. As is their usual practice, R&C regard all the forms as distinct and try to provide each with an etymology and a location, but this is to place a naive trust in the textual source. Quadruplication in *Ravenna* has a precedent, in the four versions of the name of *Moridunum*[1]; moreover, the present name seems to be somewhere in the south-west, to judge by Ptolemy's position, by the citation of *Cunis* after *Minerve*, and by the listing of *Fl(umen) Conio* in a group of south-western names and after **Fl(umen) Tabo* (see TAVUS[2]) in N. Devon: it was precisely for south-west England that *Ravenna* employed an extra source, which enhanced the danger of repetition (see p. 197). Dillemann (65) thinks that at least *Ravenna*'s *Elconio* and *Cunia* = Ptolemy's *Cenio* and refer to the same river.

DERIVATION. This name can hardly have the Celtic root **cen-* **gen(n)-* 'to be born of, descend from', discussed under BRANOGENIUM, for although this is quite common in personal and place-names it is normally present in compounded forms only (for examples, see *GPN* 175–77). It is impossible to see how the sense of this could be present in uncompounded *Cen-* names or in simple forms with suffix, and it is still more difficult to see how such a sense could suit the present river-name (**Cen-* with **-i̯o-* suffix?), which is the only river-name listed under this head in *GPN*. Since, however, we know of such place-names as *Cenabum/Genabum* (now Orléans) and personal names *Cenia*, *Cennia*, *Cennius*, etc., it is likely that these and others are formed on an element **cen-* of unknown meaning, which was able to use a variety of suffixes in name-formation; the other **cen-* roots mentioned in *GPN* seem inapplicable here, for different reasons, and the name is best left unresolved.

IDENTIFICATION. Ptolemy's location suits the river Kenwyn, Cornwall, and the Fal estuary, by which it reaches the sea, would certainly have been noted in any coastal survey. But the modern river-name is almost certainly a back-formation from the village of Kenwyn, so the identification must remain uncertain.

CERMA of *Ravenna* 108_2 (= R&C 205) *and*
CERMIUM of *Ravenna* 108_{11} (= R&C 223): see CAERENI.

CERTIS

SOURCE
Ravenna 108_{33} (= R&C 255): CERTISNASSA

DERIVATION. *Ravenna*'s entry has the appearance of a conflation, and we have so treated it: see NASSA. R&C following Holder I. 995 suggest a root **s(q)err-* or **qert-* 'to turn, twist', and 'winding one' makes good sense here. Holder cites Livy XXVIII, 22, 1 for *Certis* (acc. *Certim*) as an alternative name for the Baetis of S. Spain. A place *Certis* in *TP* in Pannonia Inferior (now Diakovar) is *Cirtisa* in *AI* 260_9 and *Cirtisia* in *AI* 268_5, Κέρτισσα (= *Certissa*) in Ptolemy II, 15, 4, and may be comparable. See also, however, CAELIS.

IDENTIFICATION. A river which, from its position in *Ravenna*'s order, is probably in eastern Scotland or north-east England; or which may be identical with Ptolemy's *Caelis*.

CIBRA of *Ravenna* 107_{56} (= R&C 199): see CORIA[1]

CICUCIUM

SOURCE
Ravenna 106_{26} (= R&C 56): CICUTIO

DERIVATION. Williams identifies a root *cic-*, citing Irish *cich* 'pap, breast' and Welsh *cig* 'meat, flesh'; Spanish *chicha*, a child's word for 'meat', might also be relevant. R&C add that 'The site of Brecon Gaer...is a rounded spur which is strikingly like a female breast in contour and outline.' This is not far-fetched; one may compare *Mamucium* and other parallels cited under that heading. The suffix in both names is a latinised version of Celtic **-ŭ̈c-i̯o-*, present also in the personal name *Vindomorucius* and documented by Ekwall *ERN* lxxviii, with adjectival force. Copyings of *c* for *t* and vice versa are common in our sources (and /*kj*/ /*tj*/ were sounded alike, a sibilant, in Vulgar Latin).

IDENTIFICATION. Probably the Roman fort of Brecon Gaer, Fenni Fach, Breconshire (SO 0029).

CILURNUM

SOURCES
Ravenna 107_{26} (= R&C 147): CELUNNO, var. CELUMNO
ND XL_{38}: Praefectus alae secundae Asturum, CILURNO

DERIVATION. Williams explains the name by citing Irish *cilorn*, Old Welsh *cilurnn*, Welsh *celwrn* 'bucket, pail', in older usage more of a cauldron able to hold four gallons. See Holder I. 1015 and Pokorny 555; the British word was presumably **cilŭrno-*. The name seems to refer to a natural feature, a 'cauldron pool' of the North Tyne river or 'a large deep natural pool known as "The Inglepool"' (R&C) near the fort, this name having been transferred to the fort. It has been held that the name survives in nearby Chollerford, Chollerton, but there are no Anglo-Saxon forms to help us, and Ekwall has other explanations which seem more satisfactory.

IDENTIFICATION. The Roman fort at Chesters, Northumberland (NY 9170), beside the North Tyne, whose third-century garrison was the *Ala II Asturum* (*RIB* 1463-65, 1480).

*CINTOCELUM

SOURCE
Ravenna 108_1 (= R&C 204): CINDOCELLUM

DERIVATION. For **ocĕlŏ-* 'headland, promontory, spur', see *ALAUNOCELUM. *Cindo-* suggests no Celtic etymon. Rostaing *ETP* identifies a pre-Indo-European root **kend-* **kind-* 'mountain' (present e.g. in Mont Cénis), and a sense 'mountain-headland' might be proper for the British name; however, Rostaing's forms provide no real support for this. R&C suggest that the name might have *Vindo-*, but *Ravenna* seems to have no instance of *c* for *v*. They go on very reasonably to suggest that *Cindo-* is a slight corruption of *Cinto-*, whose base is the well-known **cĭnto-* 'first', represented by Welsh *cynt* 'first', Breton *cint* 'before', Irish *cét-* 'first', etc., and in many ancient names such as *Centus*, *Cintus*, *Cintugenus* ('first-born'), all of potters; see Dottin *LG* 246 and 356, Ellis Evans *GPN* 179, for numerous personal names. There seem to be no place-names with this root apart from the present one, but a sense 'chief headland, principal spur' is obviously acceptable.

IDENTIFICATION. Unknown, but apparently in Scotland.

CLANOVENTA of *AI* 481_1: see GLANNOVENTA

CLAUSENTUM

SOURCE
AI 478_1 (Iter VII): CLAUSENTUM

DERIVATION. This is a difficult name. There is no reason to doubt the accuracy of *AI*'s form; it may be associated with *Clausetia* in Aquitanica Prima and *Clausonna* > Clausonne (Alpes-Maritimes, France), to be analysed *Claus-etia* and *Claus-onna* (*onna* being a recognised Gaulish element). If this is right, we are not able to take the second element as British *-sentŏ-* (see below) and must conclude that the whole is of unknown meaning. Indeed Jackson in his study of *AI*'s names simply enters a query.

It may be, however, that *AI*'s form reflects a development of spoken Latin. If we consider it as a development from **Clavi-sentum* several possibilities emerge, together with further analogues such as *Clavenna* > Chiavenna to the north of Lake Como (N. Italy) and *Clavicum* in Spain (but not British '*Clavinium*', q.v.). **Clavisentum* as a restoration of a more classical form does not present too much difficulty. One might compare in Gaul *Lautro-* for earlier *Lavatro-*, and perhaps *Quadruis* (dat.) for *Quadrivis* (*JRS*, LIV (1964), 178), *Suleis* for *Sulevis* (dat.) in *RIB* 105 (Cirencester).

For *Clavi-* two roots are possible. Williams lists a root **kleu* 'to hear' (now Pokorny 605), in other forms 'what is heard, famous', and **cleu̯os* (with cognate Greek κλέος) which has produced Welsh *clyw*, Breton *clevet* with the sense of 'something heard, fame' (also Irish *clú* 'glory'), seen in the compound *Dumnoclevios*. The other root is suggested by

R&C (under their *Clavinium*): a British **clau̯o-s* 'nail' equivalent to the Latin root seen in *clāva* 'cudgel', *clāvis* 'key' and *clāvus* 'nail' (related to *claudo, claudĕre*: Pokorny 604, **klēu-* **klāu-*); they cite also Welsh *clo-yn, clo-en* from the root **kel-* **klā-* (now Pokorny 545) 'schlagen, hauen', and try to give the present name a meaning perhaps associated with 'log-built enclosures, as in English place-names from *stocc-*'. Evidently none of these possibilities impressed Jackson enough for him to mention them, but they seem reasonable. For the *-sentum* element, Celtic **sentŏ-* 'path', compare *Gabrosentum*. If *Clausentum* is a coastal site, and since concrete elements are commoner in toponymy than abstracts such as 'famous', we might take the second proposed root for *Clavi-* and speculate on an allusion to a 'nailed' or 'hewn' path, perhaps a causeway or a quay or similar construction.

IDENTIFICATION. Either the Roman town and naval base at Bitterne, Hampshire (SU 4313) or the settlement at Wickham, Hampshire (SU 5711); see the discussion on p. 166. The final suggestion above would favour the former, since Wickham lies inland.

CLAVINIUM (?)

SOURCE

Ravenna 106_{12} (= R&C 29): CLAVINIO, var. CLAVIMO

DERIVATION. This name if taken literally (as it is by R&C) could have any of the roots mentioned for the previous name; or it could perhaps be analysed *Clavinium*, with a second element as in *Magiovinium*, where it is unexplained. However, the form is most probably corrupt. Dillemann (p. 66) thinks it a conflation of parts of two other names, and has a detailed argument in support of this. We think it more likely that *Ravenna*'s form is simply a corruption of *Glevum*, misread from a map. It should be noted that there is a detached **Colonia* floating in the Cosmographer's list at 106_{14} (textually *Coloneas*), which is almost certainly an adjunct of the name of Gloucester, the only *colonia* in this region, so that the present *Clavinio* at 106_{12} could well represent *Glevum*, the two parts of the name having been written separately (one above the other, perhaps; see p. 191); the full name, taken by the Cosmographer from a different map, figures as *Glebon colonia* at 106_{29}. For miscopyings involving *-nio* or *-mo*, see p. 203.

IDENTIFICATION. Probably a duplication of *Glevum*, q.v.

CLED of *Ravenna* 109_4 (= R&C 273): see CLOTA

CLINDUM of *Ravenna* 107_{32} (= R&C 160): see LINDUM[2]

CLOTA

SOURCES

Tacitus *Agricola* 23, 3: CLOTA

Ptolemy II, 3, 1: Κλώτα εἴσχυσις (= CLOTA AESTUARIUM)

IM 509_1: INSULA CLOTA IN HIVERIONE, var. GLOTA

Ravenna 109_4 (= R&C 273): CLED

The forms of *IM* and *Ravenna* have not been previously associated with this name by others who have shown a perhaps unwarranted trust in the accuracy of the texts. See, on the *IM*, p. 181. The compiler of this Itinerary will have taken his information from a map, since he places this item among others *in mari oceano quod Gallias et Britannias interluit*, surely a visual impression. The name of the Clyde would have been written on the map against its mouth, in such a way that it stretched across a very much narrowed Irish Sea and was associated with Ireland (*in Hiverione*) and also mistaken for an island. *Ravenna* similarly used a map-source, perhaps even a version of that used for *IM*, for it commits the same mistake of thinking the river an Irish one (though not an island); final *-a* of the name on the map was presumably lost because written against a coastline or other feature and hence unclear. It should be noted that mention of the Clyde is otherwise omitted from *Ravenna*, and is certainly to be expected.

DERIVATION. *Clota* represents original British **Clouta*, according to Watson *CPNS* 44 and 71; the root is **clou-* 'to wash', cognate with Latin *cluo, cluĕre* 'wash, purify' and *cloaca* 'sewer'. Related names include an Italian river *Cluentus* and Gaulish river *Clutoida*, and Hispano-Latin personal names *Clouta, Cloutius*, etc. According to the *Life* of Gildas (quoted by Holder I. 189) the saint was a native of the *Arecluta* region, that 'before the Clyde'. Original British *ou* passed to *ō* in the late first century A.D., when the name was first set down in the Latin tradition, then to *ū* by the end of the third century; the Welsh name for the river is *Clut*, the older Gaelic (from British) *Cluad* and the modern *Cluaidh*. Watson thinks that 'Like many other river-names, *Clota* is really the name of the river-goddess, "the washer, the strongly-flowing one", or such'; this seems a necessary proposition particularly in view of the personal names, doubtless derived from the divine name rather than based directly on any root meaning 'to wash'.

IDENTIFICATION. The river Clyde, Scotland.

COANTIA of *Ravenna* 108_{30} (= R&C 249): see CENIO
(R&C are in error in seeking a possible relation with the name of *Coventina*, which has *-v-* in all the numerous records of this name as registered in *RIB*. There can be no connection either, as R&C wish, with the modern Kent of Cumbria, for this – like other *Kent* and *Kennet* names – derives from a British **Cunetio*.)

COCCIUM

SOURCE
AI 482_1 (Iter x): COCCIO

DERIVATION. Jackson in *Britannia*, I (1970), 71, explains that the British name was **Coccįon*, from **cocco-* 'red' (Welsh *coch*) with the **-įo-* derivative suffix. The adjective might refer to the town, or to its soil, or might be a river-name transferred to the settlement. Holder I. 1056 lists personal names *Coccus, Coccillus*; recorded in inscriptions are British *Cocceia Irene* (*RIB* 507), *Cocceianus* (*RIB* 902), *Cocceius* (*RIB* 932), perhaps originally 'red-headed'. Among place-names abroad, seemingly based on personal names, were *Coccacus* and *Cocciacus* (Holder) and a *Mutatio Cocconis* of the *Bordeaux Itinerary* 562_4. Compare also British *Coccuveda*.

IDENTIFICATION. Probably an unlocated Roman fort or settlement near Edgeworth, Lancashire (SD 7317), where the waters of the streams, especially when in spate, run red with iron.

COCCUVEDA

SOURCES

Ravenna 107_{45} (= R&C 186): COCCIMEDA, vars. COCUNEDA, COCENNEDA; but R&C read COCCUVEDA, vars. COCUNEDA, COCCIMEDA 108_{38} (= R&C 264: COGUVEUSURON)

These sources need discussion. In *Ravenna* 107_{45} R&C's decipherment of scripts seems preferable to that of Schnetz (which we normally follow); there is agreement about the first element, but Schnetz's main reading leaves us with *-meda* as second element, and this, though a well-known word in many languages (including Celtic, = 'mead', the drink), is an unlikely place-name element. *Ravenna*'s *Coguveusuron* is in the list of rivers; R&C rightly thought it looked like a conflation, but did not attempt to solve the riddle. The second part – say USURON – is probably for the town *Isurium*, for which see our entry. The first part, COGUVE, strongly suggests COCCUVEDA; we have to assume at some stage a reduction of *-cc-* to *-c-* (*Ravenna* is much given to simplifying geminated consonants), then *g* written for *c* (as is common), and omission of two final letters. The conflation would have arisen from misreading tightly-packed lettering on a map.

DERIVATION. *Ravenna* thus cites what appears to be a habitation-name at 107_{45} and a river at 108_{38}, both called *Coccuveda*. This is by no means impossible, but it seems likely that at 107_{45} the Cosmographer, reading from a map, mistook a river-name on his map for a habitation-name, as we can be certain he did elsewhere (the most glaring case is *Tamese* at 106_{38}); from another map he then again read the same name, this time correctly as a river, at 108_{38} (but conflating it with an adjacent name). It is best to conclude, then, that we are dealing with one river-name, *Coccuveda*. The point is important in determining the meaning. Williams, not thinking of a river, gave the root as **cocco-* 'red' (see the previous name) plus *-veda*, which represented a root as in Welsh *-wedd*, either 'slope' as in *llechwedd* or as in *cochwedd* 'red appearance'. For a river-name we can now affirm that only the second of these is applicable; indeed R&C observe of the Coquet that it is 'filled with red porphyritic detritus from the Cheviot' (in which case, compare Río Tinto and *Rubricatum* > Llobregat river of Catalonia, etc.).

IDENTIFICATION. The river Coquet, Northumberland.

COLANIA

SOURCES

Ptolemy II, 3, 7: Κολανία (= COLANIA), a *polis* of the D(u)mnonii; var. Κολάνικα (= COLANICA)

Ravenna 107_{54} (= R&C 195); COLANICA

There is little doubt that *Colania* is the proper form; in which case there must have been a common source in a map for Ptolemy's variant and for the *Ravenna* Cosmographer; this raises questions which cannot be followed up here.

DERIVATION. Jackson in *JRS*, XXXVIII (1948), 56, taking up a suggestion of Watson *CPNS* 32, indicates a connection with Welsh *celain* 'corpse', from British **colanio-* (see Holder I. 1064). He compares the unknown *Cair Celemion* of Nennius, a *civitas*, probably to be emended *Cair Celeinion* 'City of Celeinion', from British *Colanįon-, a tribal name from the same stem as *celain*. A tribal base for the present name would be easier than a sense 'corpse', though folkloric references of this kind do occur in toponymy.

IDENTIFICATION. Probably the Roman fort at Camelon, Stirlingshire (NS 8681).

COLONIA[1]

SOURCES

AI 474_4 (Iter v): COLONIA
See also Tacitus and *Ravenna* under CAMULODUNUM[1]

DERIVATION. This is Latin *colonia* (of Roman citizens), the legal definition of the city's status. It is notable that *AI* in Iter x calls it *Camuloduno*, an indication that different sources were used; it is clear that eventually *Colonia* and not *Camulodunum* was the name used in local parlance, since as we argue below, the modern name derives from this. The name had begun in official usage only. Under CAMULODUNUM[1] we quote *CIL* XIV. 3955, the tombstone of an officer who had been *censitor* of the *Colonia Victricensis*. This appears again on a London tombstone, published in *JRS*, LII (1962), 190–91, of G POMPONI G F VALENTIS VICTRICENS[IS], 'Gaius Pomponius Valens, son of Gaius of the Victricensian (*colonia*)'. The adjective may refer either to the victory of Claudius, or, more probably, to the suppression of the Boudiccan Revolt, after which the *colonia* was refounded.

IDENTIFICATION. The Roman *colonia* at *Camulodunum*, Colchester, Essex (TL 9925).

Note. Ekwall *EPN* says of modern Colchester that it is 'The Roman station on R. Colne', and of this river that its name 'is identical with *Colne* (Herts.) and with *Clun*. It is of British origin and had the form *Colun* originally, cf. Clun and early forms of Colchester. The etymology is obscure.' This is also the view of Reaney in *EPNS*, XII (1935: Essex), 368–69: 'There can be no doubt...that the first element [of Colchester] is the name of the river Colne...(the river-name cannot be a back-formation as there are on the river, some distance from Colchester, four parishes which are named *Colne*, a form which occurs twice in the tenth century. The *Cair Colun* of Nennius is an exact equivalent of the *Colne ceastre* of the Chronicle, and is paralleled by Geoffrey of Monmouth's *Kaerleir* or *Leircestre* for Leicester, "the camp on the Leire".' Reany specifically denies that 'modern *Colchester* is pleonastic, consisting of the addition of OE *ceaster* to a syncopated *colonia*'.

It is certain that the name of the various *Colne* rivers is of British origin; but to assume that the Essex Colne is one of them, *ab initio*, and that Colchester took its first element from that is perverse. Against the example of Leicester 'camp on the Leire' there are many examples of *-chester* attached to a surviving first part of the Romano-British town name: Binchester, Brancaster, Lanchester, Manchester, Rochester, Winchester, etc., none of which involves a river-name. That *Colonia* was a way of naming the town is shown by *AI*'s entry and by analogues abroad, most notably *Colonia* > Cologne, Köln (*Agrippensis civitas quae nunc Colonia dicitur*: Gregory of Tours). Above all there is the parallel of Lincoln < *Lindum Colonia*, whose *colonia* survived so 'naturally' in spoken usage that it was eventually not remembered as such (cf. Bede's erroneous association with *colina* when latinising the name). Neither Köln nor Lincoln has anything to do with a river Colne. Our suggestion about the Essex river is that it had originally a *Colne* name like others, from which the parishes were named, but this has nothing to do with the modern name of the town; or that the Essex river originally had a name resembling *Colne* which became assimilated to it, either under the influence of the town-name or because of the existence of other *Colne*-names in Britain; but even simple back-formation, as proposed by Zachrisson in 1927, from Anglo-Saxon *Colne-ceaster*, should not be ruled out as it is by Reandy.

The early forms are *Cair Colun* of Nennius (*c.* 800), *Colneceastre* in *ASC* (921) and *Colenceaster* in a charter of 931. In *Lincoln* and *Köln* it can be seen that Latin *colōnia* had undergone a shift of stress when taken into Germanic speech (with further complications in the case of the former). This is reflected in *colonia* > *Colchester*; perhaps in Nennius's Celtic form *Cair Colun* the stress was still on the *u*, but in the Anglo-Saxon forms with the extra *-ceaster* element one may assume erosion of the now unstressed syllable, *Cólenceaster* > Colchester, which is the pattern of all our *-chester* names.

COLONIA[2]

SOURCE

Ravenna 106_{14} (= R&C 33): COLONEAS

R&C take *Ravenna*'s form as a true one, think it from a personal name *Colonius*, and locate it in Dorset. But it is simplest to regard the name as properly *Colonia*. Schnetz in a note thinks the *-s* could belong to the start of the following name, *Aramis*, or it could have arisen accidentally from a mark on the map being followed by the Cosmographer. In Vulgar Latin, *-ĕa* for *-ĭa* is a typical confusion (*Appendix Probi* 55: '*vinea* non *vinia*'; *illeus* for *illius* in *RIB* 7, *palleum* for *pallium* in *RIB* 323, etc.). In *Ravenna* the present entry represents a duplication, as so often, arising from the use of two map sources; this entry is probably to be paired with *Clavinium* for **Glevum* (106_{12}), for which see CLAVINIUM. If however *Colonia* were used independently as a designation for Gloucester on a map, compare such usage for Colchester (COLONIA[1]).

DERIVATION. See COLONIA[1]. This *colonia* was in its full official form *Colonia Nervia* (or *Nerviana*) *Glevensium*, founded in A.D. 97.

IDENTIFICATION. The Roman *colonia* at Gloucester (SO 8318).

COMBRETOVIUM

SOURCES

AI 480_2 (Iter IX): CONBRETOVIO, var. COMBRETOVIO

TP: CONUETONI

DERIVATION. Jackson in *Britannia*, I (1970), 71, explains this as British **Combritou̯ion*, made up of **com* '(together) with', **brit-* a derivative of **ber-* 'carry', and the **-ou̯io-* suffix. The name is '(place on the) bearing-together', thus 'confluence', a very typical place-name; compare *Condate*. In *JRS*, XXXVIII (1948), 56, Jackson gives further details, citing Welsh *cymmer* and Old Irish *commar* 'confluence', and the Gaulish place-name *Comberane*. Dauzat *TF* 42 adds a mention of Gaulish **comboro-*, in toponymy *combre-* 'confluence', origin of Combleux near

Orléans (Loiret, France); in *RIO*, IX (1957), 31–32, there are details of Les Combres and Combret (Lozère, France) from the same root. *TP*'s form of the British name may have *n* miscopied for *v* in the termination, as is frequent, but Jackson points out that either suffix is possible in Celtic terms (**-onio-* or **-ouio-*; perhaps compare *Canonium/Canovium*). The 'confluence' in these names is usually that of waters, but here may have applied to a meeting of roads; see p. 170.

IDENTIFICATION. The Roman settlement at Baylham House, Coddenham, Suffolk (TM 1152).

CONCANGIS

SOURCES

Ravenna 107_{17} (= R&C 141): COGANGES, var. CEGANGES

ND XL_9 (*pictura*): CONCANGIOS, var. CONCAGIOS

XL_{24} (text): Praefectus numeri vigilum, CONCANGIOS

Inscription: *CIL* VII. 1234, a tile from Binchester inscribed N CON, which Richmond in *Arch.* XLIII (1949), 29, thought might well stand for N(UMERUS) CON(CANGIENSIUM)

The form of the name is unsure, but it certainly had *Con-Cang-*. *Ravenna*'s form, its variant and the variant of *ND* without *n* show that as often this letter was abbreviated by a tilde, this then being overlooked in a subsequent copy. In the ending there is no authority at all for the *-ium* which seems to be traditional. *Ravenna* and *ND* agree in showing a plural. *Ravenna* has no other form in *-es* among its British names, but it has many in fossilised locative form *-is* (see ANICETIS), including those of several forts in the north-east; it is therefore probably best to restore *Ravenna*'s name to *-is* (more classically *-iis*) and to regard *ND*'s also as a mistake for this or perhaps as a genuine accusative.

DERIVATION. This is a difficult name. It can have nothing to do with N. Welsh *Ceangi*, itself a dubious form, although Seeck associated them when editing *ND* and Holder I. 879 followed him. The ending *-ang-* might just possibly represent the *-anc-* suffix of *Habitancum*, but it is then hard to discern what the base might be. The best possibility is an association with forms studied by H. Birkhan in *Germanen und Kelten*... (Vienna, 1970), 426–31. Noting personal names such as *Congonnus, Congonius, Conconnetodubnus*, he identifies a Celtic root **konkos*, perhaps present in the name of the *Concani* people and their place *Concana* (Κογκάνα, Ptolemy II, 6, 50) in N. Spain, with 'horse' associations perhaps of a totemic kind (Horace *Odes* III, 4, 34); and a further Celtic **kankos* 'horse'. Birkhan does not bring the present name into the discussion, but it could well be relevant, even though isolated on the British map. Since the root cited seems to be well represented in Celtic personal names but has left (apparently) no descendants in the modern Celtic languages – they abound in Germanic, as listed by Birkhan – the association cannot be wholly affirmed; but it may be suggested that *Concangis* was originally an ethnic name, perhaps 'horse-people' either in a literal or totemic sense.

IDENTIFICATION. The Roman fort at Chester-le-Street, Durham (NZ 2750).

Note. The name survived for a long time. Ekwall in *EPN* (Chester-le-Street) notes that it was *Concecaestre* c. 1050; his suggestion that the first element is *Cunca-*, *Cunce-* and may represent a hill-name derived from British **cuno-* 'high' is not supported by the Romano-British name, and the existence of British **cuno-* has been challenged (see CUNETIO). The place is on the Cong Burn, which presumably still preserves part of the ancient name.

CONCAVATA

SOURCE

ND XL_{48}: Tribunus cohortis secundae Lingonum, CONGAVATA

DERIVATION. The name is properly *Concavata*, Latin for (presumably) 'hollowed out, scooped out', an adjective whose unexpressed noun we cannot guess; applied to the shape of a coastline or to some other natural feature. That the name is Latin – wholly exceptional among the forts which make up the defensive system in this region – may show that the fort was built in exceptional circumstances. In the source, *g* for *c* is a commonly recorded miscopying.

IDENTIFICATION. The Roman fort at Drumburgh, Cumberland (NY 2659).

Note 1. M. W. C. Hassall in *Aspects of the ND* (Oxford, 1976), note 49 to p. 113, suggests that 'In uncials *Congavata*, minus the first *a*, would look suspiciously like the *Torquata* title of the *ala Petriana* (cf. *ILS* 2778 and *RIB* 957)'. Against this, it should be noted that the *ala Petriana* at XL_{45} does not immediately precede the present name at XL_{48}, so it is hard to see how a copying error could have arisen. Moreover, the *ND* entry would have had the regiment's name in the genitive (**Praefectus alae Petrianae torquatae*), as in *RIB* 957, which gives an extra letter to be explained away in any miscopying. For these reasons the suggestion of Hassall, though ingenious, is probably not right.

Note 2. Archaeologically Drumburgh is the least well known fort on Hadrian's Wall. The existence of an earth fort attached to the Turf Wall seems to be established, but neither its earlier garrison nor the date at which it was rebuilt in stone is known. The hypothesis that a fort was included here in the original scheme but was then found to be superfluous until the changed conditions of the fourth century would explain both the absence of inscriptions (for the building stones *RIB* 2051–53 may, as is there noted, have come from the Wall itself rather than the fort) and the omission of *Concavata* from the Rudge Cup, the Amiens *patera* and the *Ravenna Cosmography*.

CONDATE

SOURCES

AI 469_1 (Iter II) and 482_3 (Iter X): CONDATE

Ravenna 106_{47} (= R&C 91): CONDATE

DERIVATION. Although Dauzat *TF* 42 thinks that the name 'ne s'explique pas par le celtique' and that it must have been borrowed into Gaulish from another language, Williams and Jackson (*Britannia*, I (1970), 71) agree on Celtic roots. The name is British **Condatis* or neuter **Condati*, from **com* 'with', *da-* a reduced grade of either Indo-European **do-* 'give' or **dhē-* 'put', and verbal-adjectival suffix **-ti(s)*; the whole having the sense of 'confluence'. Pokorny 175 prefers to relate the second element to the root **dā-* found in **danu-* 'river' (as in British *Danum*, etc.). In Latin the name is indeclinable and always appears as above. The distribution of the name is curious. It is found in many parts of Gaul, once in Britain, once in Wurtemburg (Vincent 238–41), but is unknown in Spain and N. Italy. Williams notes that in Wales and Brittany it was ousted (in expressing the notion of 'confluence') by Cymer, Quimper, etc., from **com-bher* (see *Combretovium*). In Iberia the idea was expressed by **com-plut*- 'flowing together', as in *Complutum* now Alcalá de Henares (Madrid, Spain) and *Complutica* > *Compludo* (León, Spain). Such names as Κομφλοέντα (= *Comfluenta*) in Ptolemy II, 6, 54 may be translations of older Celtic names of the **com-plut-* type, as also happened at Lyon (France), where the Gaulish settlement at the junction of the Rhône and Saône was *Condate* but later **Confluens*, *Ad Confluentem*. In Gaul *Condate* evolved differently depending on whether it was stressed in the Gaulish way, *Cóndate* > *Condes*, or in the Latin fashion, *Condáte* > Condat, Condé, etc. We have no means of knowing how the solitary British name was stressed.

Condatis was also a god 'of the waters-meet', associated with Mars. Altars to him are known at Bowes (*RIB* 731), Piercebridge (1024) and Chester-le-Street (1045).

IDENTIFICATION. The Roman settlement at Northwich, Cheshire (SJ 6673), at the confluence of the rivers Dane and Weaver.

CONDERCUM

SOURCES

Ravenna 107_{24} (= R&C 144): CONDECOR

ND XL_{35}: Praefectus alae primae Asturum, CONDERCO

ND's is the proper form, that of *Ravenna* having a scribal metathesis or perhaps an assimilation to Latin *decor*.

DERIVATION. The name is Celtic **com* 'with' plus a verb root which Holder I. 1266 gives as **derc-* **derco-* 'to see', in a long entry having many ramifications. Among these a form very close to *Condercum* is cited in Old Irish, *condercar* 'conspicitur', i.e. 'look round'. Dottin *LG* 251 cites **derco-* in Gaulish names, Irish *derc* 'eye' and Greek δέρκομαι as related. Among personal names are *Derco* and *Derceia*, and among place-names possibly a *Dercenna* river in Iberia, cited by Martial I, xlix, 17.

The sense of the name is thus something like '(place for) looking around', '(place with a) wide view'. R&C note that Benwell 'overlooks its neighbourhood for miles in every direction'. The sense 'place with a *fine* outlook' and discussion of the sense 'fine, noble' for the root by Williams seems slightly erroneous, in that this sense is a figurative extension of the basic one and is not warranted here.

IDENTIFICATION. The Roman fort at Benwell, Northumberland (NZ 2164), whose third-century garrison was the *Ala I Asturum* (*RIB* 1334, 1337).

CORDA (?)

SOURCES

Ptolemy II, 3, 6: Κόρδα (= CORDA), a *polis* of the Selgovae

Ravenna 107_{38} (= R&C 171): CORDA

DERIVATION. This name seems always to have been taken at face-value, perhaps rightly (but see below). Williams suggests a root **kerdho-* 'herd, host', perhaps connected with Irish *crod* 'cattle'; from this R&C concluded that the name referred to the 'hosting-place' or tribal centre. Rostaing *ETP* 149 identifies a pre-Indo-European root **kor-d-* **kor-*, a variant of **kar-* 'rock', which may be present in the name of a mountain in Provence, Cordes ('in Cordoa', 1221), from **kor-d-owa*; this is analogous to *Cordŭba* > Córdoba in Spain, a very ancient name usually held to be Iberian, that is non-Indo-European. There is also *Cordanum insula* > Cordouan (Gironde, France). However, we have no right to suppose derivation from a non-Celtic element until all else has failed.

It is possible that R&C were right, by accident, as it were, at least with regard to the sense of the name. It will be noted that in II, 3, 7 Ptolemy lists the *poleis* of the *D(u)mnonii* of Scotland, followed by those of the *(V)otadini*. Among these are a *Coria* for each people, our *Coria* (*Dumnoniorum*) and *Coria* (*Votadinorum*). In II, 3, 6, Ptolemy lists the *poleis* of the Selgovae; what more natural than that he should list a *Coria* (*Selgovarum*) for them also? Our present *Corda* could very well be for *Coria*. That the name occurs as *Corda* in *Ravenna* also is no guarantee of accuracy; as shown on p. 193, both Ptolemy and *Ravenna* depended ultimately on the Flavian military map of N. Britain, on which an unclear *-i-* could have been misread as a *-d-*. If this is right, the name is indeed 'hosting-place, tribal centre', and is in line with the other *Coria* names of N. Britain.

IDENTIFICATION. Probably the Roman fort at Castledykes, Lanarkshire (NS 9244), the name being transferred from a native meeting-place which it controlled.

CORIA[1] of the Dumnonii

SOURCES

Ptolemy II, 3, 7: Κόρια (= CORIA), a *polis* of the D(u)mnonii

Ravenna 107_{56} (= R&C 199): CIBRA

Ravenna's form has not been hitherto associated with Ptolemy's, but it seems likely that it is a corrupt form of the other. Of the six *poleis* assigned by Ptolemy to the *D(u)mnonii*, the rest were probably taken up by the Cosmographer from the same source as that ultimately available to Ptolemy, and it is logical that the present *Cibra* should represent the 'missing' *Coria*.

DERIVATION. Seven names need to be considered here collectively: *Coria* of the *Dumnonii*, (probably) of the *Selgovae*, and of the *Votadini*; *Coria Soliliorum*; *Coriototae*; **Coriosopitum*; and *Curia Tectoverdorum*. We are thus concerned with three items: *Coria*, used alone; *Corio-*, compounded in first place; and *Curia*, used as an independent word. Our study needs the support of Continental analogues. *Coria* is apparently not found there (but see below). For the rest we find, in ethnic and place-names:

Corio- in first place: ethnic *Coriosolites* > Corseul (Côtes du Nord, France), *Coriosedenses* of Gallia Narbonensis, perhaps *Coriolani* of Italy (Pliny *NH* III, 69). In place-names, *Coriallum* (for earlier **Coriovalium*, *Coriovallum*) > Cherbourg (Manche, France), *Coriovallum* (for **Coriovalium*: see C. J. Guyonvarc'h in *Ogam*, XVII (1965), 351–54, and in *Apulum*, VI (1967), 119–22, discussing a study by P. L. M. Tummers) now Heerlen (Holland; < **hariwalia*, a direct translation of **Coriovalium* into Germanic), Κοριδοργίς (= *Coridorgis*: Ptolemy II, 11, 15) in Germania Magna, *Cortoriacum* (for **Corio-*: Courtrai) in *ND* v_{96}.

Corio in second place: ethnic *Petrucorii* (> Périgueux), *Tricorii*, *Toloscorii*, *Vertamocorii*, etc.

Curia: *Curia Raetorum* > Chur (Switzerland), always so spelled (e.g. *AI* 277_6 and 278_4, *TP*), on which see Hubschmid in *Rätisches Namenbuch*, II (ed. A. Schorta, Berne, 1964), 107 and 658, and in *Romanica Helvetia*, XIV (1939), 111 ff.; a probable *Curia Grusduas*, name of a *pagus* at Cologne, and a probable *Cur(ia) Cassiciate*, a *pagus* of the Carnutes, in *CIL* XIII. 3071, on both of which see R. Demangel in *REA*, XXXVI (1934), 481.

(On *Corio* as a personal name, see references in CORINIUM DOBUNNORUM).

The words present in these names are:

**corio-* (British) 'host, army', represented by Welsh *cor* 'host, tribe'; in Old and Middle Irish *cuire* 'band, army' (Watson *CPNS* 32). Cognates include Germanic **harja*, Gothic *harjis* from a stem **hario-* (as in *Ario-vistus*), and the root is widespread in Indo-European (Holder I. 1126). The *Tricorii* are thus the '(people of the) three hosts', the *Petrucorii* '(people of the) four hosts', and so on. Some Continental scholars have preferred to follow Pokorny 615 in assigning a sense 'Stamm, Sippe' to the word, and Stevens in his chapter 'Roman Gaul' in J. M. Wallace-Hadrill (ed.), *France* (2nd ed, 1970), 22, has followed this, defining the *Petrucorii* as 'four kinship-groups'. Against this C. J. Guyonvarc'h in *Ogam*, XVI (1964), 429–31, argues for an Indo-European base **koro-s*, **korio-s* 'guerre, armée': 'Nous pensons devoir corriger ou biffer la possibilité des "trois tribus" pour ne conserver que celle des "trois troupes" dans le nom des *Tricorii*, allusion évidente aux facultés mobalisatrices des trois cantons d'une nation gauloise.' This is surely right.

**coria* (British), originally with the probable sense 'hosting-place' (Jackson in *JRS*, XXXVIII (1948), 56), thus 'tribal centre', this meaning being that of the three *Coria* names among the tribes of S. Scotland, later under Roman rule evidently 'centre of a *pagus*' (as in *Coria Soliliorum*, in the English Midlands). This word is a derivative of, or is derived from the same base as, **corio-*.

cūria (Latin), as in *Curia Tectoverdorum* and the three Continental names, has among its senses in administrative language 'court; ward; assembly', and in the case of the toponyms quoted is evidently 'centre of a *pagus*' in Britain and in Gaul.

As between *Coria*/*Curia*, then, the issue is unclear. Stevens in *Arch. Ael.*[4], XI (1934), 138–45, discussed the nature of the *Curia Tectoverdorum* in the Beltingham inscription, and possibly related items, taking the *Coria* names, *Curia Raetorum* and the Κούρια which appears in some MSS of Ptolemy (II, 3, 7), equating *Coria* with *Curia* as phonetic variants within Celtic and concluding that '. . .*curia* is a Celtic word meaning "army", which was used not only as a sub-division or *pagus* of the tribe, but as a place-name to describe the meeting-place of the *pagus*'. To the linguistic argument of this Jackson (op. cit.) objected:

'[Stevens] regards *Curia* and *Coria* as forms of the same name, in the belief that "the mutation of *o* and *u* is a very familiar phenomenon in Celtic phonetics." This is a misconception.

> British *Coria*, if from **corįo-* 'host', has original *-o-*, and a vowel-affection of *-o-* to *-u-* in words of this type happened only in Goidelic, not British or Gaulish, and that towards the end of the fifth century, certainly not earlier. It is very improbable therefore that Ptolemy's Κούρια is a spoken variant of *Coria*, and equally unlikely that the *curia* of the Beltingham inscription contains Celtic **corįo-* and means *pagus*... *Coria* presumably means "place of hosts", and Κούρια is a mere scribal corruption.'

This is obviously right so far as Celtic phonetics go. But the matter continues unresolved (after Jackson's correction of Stevens), because interference of one kind and another there certainly was. Ptolemy's ου could be a scribal error, as Jackson says, but it could well be a latinising interpretation, not by a scribe, but by Marinus or even by the man who drew up the map which Marinus used; that is, someone associated the Celtic name with Latin *curia*. It is not the only instance. The *Coriosolites* of Gaul are usually so spelled, but in Caesar *BG* are spelled *Curiosolites* no fewer than four times (II, 34; III, 7; III, 11; VII, 75). We further have the situation within Britain that, while the S. Scottish *Coria* places retain their Celtic purity, in romanised regions *Curia Tectoverdorum* is scarcely to be distinguished linguistically from *Coria Soliliorum*, both names being recorded in inscriptions and therefore unimpeachable. There is no way forward in arguing about Celtic phonetic developments, as Jackson showed, but it is worth noting that in spoken Latin, although the long *ū* of *cūria* remained unchanged, it was sometimes represented as *o*: a British instance is provided by *RIB* 1337, of A.D. 205–208, where we find *Asto(rum)* for *Astū(rum)*; hence *Coria Soliliorum*, in a text which has several vulgar features, could well be for **Curia*, which brings it into line with the Beltingham inscription.

Stevens was right, one suspects, in scenting some relationship between Celtic *coria* and Latin *curia*, though he did not argue it correctly. Hubschmid lists the Swiss *Curia* (*Raetorum*) as being originally a Celtic **corįa* name. The simplest solution is to propose – and this in no way infringes Jackson's definition of Celtic phonetics – that *all* the *Coria/Curia* names, in Britain and on the Continent, originally were Celtic **corįa* 'hosting-place, tribal centre'; that some in little-romanised regions (S. Scotland) naturally remained as *Coria*, as possibly *Coria Soliliorum* did too; but that as romanisation proceeded, there was inevitably some assimilation to Latin *cūria*. This is already shown in Caesar, is probably shown in Ptolemy's Κούρια, is certainly shown in *Curia Tectoverdorum* in the latinised military zone and in the three Continental *Curia* names. The assimilation might have been a written one only: in the mixed Latin-Celtic society of Vindolanda *vicus*, all may well have pronounced *coria*, but when an inscription was to be cut, a more dignified Latin-looking *curia* was adopted.

IDENTIFICATION. Probably the Roman fort at Barochan Hill, Renfrewshire (NS 412690), the name being transferred from a native meeting-place which it controlled.

*CORIA[2] of the Selgovae
On the possibility of this, see CORDA

CORIA[3] of the Votadini

SOURCES

Ptolemy II, 3, 7: Κούρια (= CURIA: MS U and most MSS), a *polis* of the (V)otadini; var. Κορια (= CORIA)

Ravenna 107_{41} (= R&C 177): CORITIOTAR

R&C thought that *Ravenna*'s corrupt form could conceal *Coria* plus the name of the *Votadini*. We agree, against Dillemann (p. 69) who associates the *Corie Lopocarium* of *Ravenna* with the present name (see our *CORIOSOPITUM). What *Ravenna*'s form was originally it is hard to say. The *-a* of *Coria* was evidently omitted, and *-ti-* must represent the initial *V-* of *Votadini*; the ending was presumably abbreviated *Votād* on the map-source, miscopied as **Votar* in the first instance.

DERIVATION. See CORIA[1].

IDENTIFICATION. Probably the Roman fort at Inveresk, Midlothian (NT 3472), the name being transferred from a native meeting-place which it controlled (in this case perhaps Arthur's Seat, 4 miles to the west).

CORIA SOLILIORUM

SOURCE

An inscription, published in *JRS*, LVI (1966), 223. It was found in 1965 in the remains of a Roman building on the west side of Watling Street near Caves Inn (*Tripontium*), Warwicks. It consists of four lines cut before firing on a *tegula* (now in two portions):

> [CIV]ITATISCORIELSOLILIO-
> ROM[. . . /
> / . . .]NIOM/
> . . . .]M/
> . . . .]CESOM

'*Corielsoliliorom* seems to indicate the genitive plural of a tribal name and perhaps adds a new *civitas* in Britain.'

DERIVATION. If we construe '(property of) the *civitas* of *Coria Soliliorum*', as seems natural, we can isolate *Corie* of the text as a Vulgar Latin genitive singular (*e* for classical *ae*, as is normal). The *-l-* seems meaningless in Celtic or Latin, and must be intrusive; perhaps the man who cut the text from a handwritten draft was confusedly anticipating the two *l*s which follow. The text has further Vulgar Latin features which mark it as careless and probably late: not only the genitive plural in the first line, *-orom* for classical *-orum*, but in lines 2 and 4 further genitive plurals of the third declension (or less probably second-declension masculine accusatives or neuters), which show the same *o* for *ŭ*.

The ethnicon is presumably in the nominative *Sōlilii*, or possibly *Soliliores*. This is unrecorded elsewhere. There are several personal names in *Soli-*, notably *Solimarus* and related forms, also the place-name *Curio-soli-magus* (Holder II. 1602) and the *Coriosolites* of Gaul, whose name is clearly an important parallel for the British ethnicon. The group is studied by K. H. Schmidt in *ZCP*, XXVI (1957), 270–71, with the suggestion that *Soli-* in these names is connected with the divine name *Sulis* (see AQUAE SULIS), Irish *súil* 'eye', etc.; a problem remains in that *Soli-* with *-o-* does not have the expected *-u-*, but Schmidt cites *Solinus* as a latinised version of Celtic *Sulinus* and is inclined to think that Celtic names with *-o-* have been influenced by Latin *sol* 'sun' (which may indeed ultimately be related). The sense of the present name as a whole is still not easy to analyse. For *Coria*, see CORIA[1].

IDENTIFICATION. Unknown, but apparently in the Midlands of England.

CORINIUM DOBUNNORUM

SOURCES

Ptolemy II, 3, 12: Κορίνιον (= CORINIUM), the *polis* of the Dobunni; vars. Κορίννιον (= CORINNIUM), Κορόνιον (= CORONIUM)

Ravenna 106_{31} (= R&C 66): CIRONIUM DOBUNORUM

Ptolemy's main form is undoubtedly correct (in view of the analogue mentioned below, and the modern derivative); that of *Ravenna* shows a scribal metathesis of vowels.

DERIVATION. This is unresolved. A precise parallel is *Corinium* in Illyricum (Liburnia), mentioned by Ptolemy (Κορίνιον, II, 16, 2) and by Pliny III, 140, > Karin in Yugoslavia. Williams suggests a relation with *Ceri*, a district in mid-Wales, Welsh *ceri* 'medlar-tree', also 'kernels, seeds'; the present place is indeed the *Cair Ceri* of Nennius. A name referring to a botanical feature is acceptable (cf. *Aballava*, *Blatobulgium* (?), and names involving trees and perhaps tree-divinities), but the absence of early forms and comparable names makes certainty impossible. The suggestion is made by O'Rahilly in *EIHM* 33 that *Corinium* perhaps represents British **Corin(n)ion* (cf. Ptolemy's var.), and that behind the Irish mythical name *Cuirenn* might lie a **Corio(nos)* or **Corin(n)nos*; moreover, that the Κοριόνδοι (= *Coriondi*) people of Ireland (Ptolemy, II, 2, 8) might more properly be the **Corioni*, slightly miscopied; but these Irish names seem to be better referred to a base **corįo-* with **-no-* suffix (see *Corionototae*), a base found in many names. The most one can say, then, is that the present name has *Corin-* or *Corinn-* with the common derivational suffix **-įo-*. The name may have been newly given to the Roman fort at Cirencester, or it may have been originally that of the Belgic *oppidum* at Bagendon three miles to the north.

Wacher in *TRB* 293 suggests that the name might contain *Corio-*, not only because this occurs in place-names in Gaul and Britain, but also because coins of the Dobunni have the legend CORIO, a ruler at the time of the Roman invasion. This seems very unlikely. In the first place, the toponym does not show **Corio-* in any of its forms, and there is the Illyrian *Corinium* in support of it. In the second place, toponyms seem to appear on British coins only when the ruler's name appears also; when a name appears alone, it seems in all other cases that can be checked from other evidence to be the name of a ruler. In the third place, although this *Corio* on the coins might (as often) be a shortened form, it is also known – even though not in Britain – as a personal name *Corio*, *Corius*, *Coria* (Holder I. 1126). It is further the case that the Dobunnic coins with this legend are distributed (that is, by find-spots) in a way which does not suggest a particular relation with Bagendon. See further the chapter on coinage by D. F. Allen in E. M. Clifford (ed.), *Bagendon: A Belgic Oppidum* (Cambridge, 1961), especially 79 ff.; it was Allen who first suggested the possibility of an association *Corio-Corinium*, also expressing several reservations (see esp. p. 92).

IDENTIFICATION. The Roman city of Cirencester, Gloucestershire (SP 0201), on the river Churn.

Note 1. On the omission of the name from *AI*, see pp. 175–76.

Note 2. The modern name derives from the ancient. Jackson *LHEB* 665, note, indicates *Corinium* > Primitive Welsh **Corin* > Primitive Anglo-Saxon **Curin* > **Cyren* > *Ciren*(-cester). Intermediate forms are recorded by Nennius (*Cair Ceri*) and Asser ('*Cirrenceastre* qui Britannice *Cair Ceri* nominatur'). The river-name Churn is from *Corinium* also, via an Anglo-Saxon development from the old name, though it might also be by back-formation from the town name (*Chirenchestre* in Layamon: Zachrisson, 1927, p. 78). Ekwall in *EPN* has an erroneous entry because he associates *Corinium* with the *Durocornovio* of *AI*.

CORIONOTOTAE

SOURCE
An inscription, *RIB* 1142 (Hexham Abbey, but thought to have been brought from Corbridge); an officer sets up an altar *caesa Corionototarum manu* 'after slaughtering a band of Corionototae'

DERIVATION. We follow the admirable analysis of this name by T. M. Charles-Edwards in 'Native Political Organisation in Roman Britain', *Antiquitates Indogermanicae* (Innsbruck, 1974), 35–45, at 38. The first element is British **cori̯o-* (see CORIA[1]) with *-*no-* suffix (cognate with the suffix in Latin *tribus-tribunus, domus-dominus*), 'used to form words for leaders or representatives of a group'. The second element is British **tōtā*, earlier **teu̯tā*, **tou̯tā* 'people, state', represented by Welsh *tud* (Latin cognate *tōtus* < **tōutos* 'all, everybody').

> Charles-Edwards continues: 'In view of inscriptions to *Mars Toutatis* and the cult of the war-god *Camulos*, it is possible that **Kori̯onos* was a bye-name of the Celtic war-god, the god by whom this particular people swore, and after whom they called themselves. The whole name, *Corionotatae*, can be interpreted in two ways, either as the name for a group of **tōtās*, or as the name for the inhabitants of a single **tōtā*.... This second interpretation, which makes the *Corionototae* men belonging to a people or kingdom called **Kori̯ono-tota*, seems the more likely.'

IDENTIFICATION. An otherwise unknown people, presumably dwelling north of Hadrian's Wall and perhaps incorporated in one of the major tribes in this area.

*CORIOSOPITUM (?)

SOURCES
AI 464_3 (Iter 1): CORSTOPITUM, vars. CORSTOPILUM, COR STOPITU
Ravenna 107_{18} (= R&C 142); CORIE LOPOCARIUM

Although *Corstopitum* figures in many accounts and maps of Roman Britain, it has long been recognised that the name is corrupt: it is meaningless in British, and the *-rst-* group is an impossibility. *Ravenna*'s name (one word according to R&C, two as above according to Schnetz) is of great importance. It almost certainly belongs here because the Cosmographer is following a main road and places this name at the end of a long section, the road logically leading to Corbridge just short of Hadrian's Wall; the next section of *Ravenna* lists the forts of the Wall. *Ravenna*'s form seems to assure us that we have here a *Corio-* or *Coria* name.

As to the restoration of *AI*'s form, the

preference which R&C stated in their 1949 study, following Holder I. 1127, is surely the best. With minimal restoration we have **Coriosopitum*. *AI*'s form would have arisen via a mistaken **Cortosopitum* (compare *Cortoriacum* for *Corio-* in *ND* v_{96}, and *Cortovallio* of *TP* for **Coriovalium* = Heerlen in Holland), followed by a metathesis of *t-s* to *s*(-)*t*. This is much better than Richmond's revised view, in *Roman and Native in North Britain* (1958), 140, note, that the name might be **corsopitum* 'reedy portion', which can surely be dismissed.

Ravenna's form is less easy to adjust. If we line up

Sopitum
Lopocarium

we have only *-op-* in common. But *c* for *t* is frequent, and it is only the conversion of *s* into *l* that seems to be unparalleled. Endings were often abbreviated: it might be that some scribe finding in his source *Coriosopitum* wrongly suspected an abbreviation and restored a first-declension genitive, *-arum*. Dillemann (p. 69) thinks that *Ravenna*'s form is really for the *Coria* of the Votadini, but this is no more preferable on textual grounds and is unlikely in terms of position, for the Cosmographer has not yet moved north of Hadrian's Wall, clearly perceived on his map source and mentioned in his text.

The question arises, however, despite traditional acceptance, of whether *AI*'s form is really any better than *Ravenna*'s. On the whole *AI* is much more trustworthy than *Ravenna*, but just occasionally the reverse is true, e.g. *Etoceto/Lectoceto*. *AI*'s form is suspect as being the more abbreviated. The grammatical construction of the name may be better represented by *Ravenna* when it gives the name as two words, and this is indicated also by the variant of *AI*. To judge by Continental analogues, **Coriosopites* as an ethnic name would be tolerable, but although the Cosmographer copied such ethnic names from a map as though they were place-names, he did this only north of Hadrian's Wall. For *Corio-* compounded there are a number of parallels, including British *Corionototae*; for *Corio* standing alone there are none. It may therefore be that *Coria* was intended, abbreviated *Cor* in the source of *AI*, in which case the British analogues of *Coria* + ethnic name in the genitive plural are relevant. *Ravenna*, moreover, gives *Corie*, and *e* is sometimes a miscopying of *a* especially in final position (cf. *Vindolande* 107_{12}, *Victorie* 108_{11}). There may well have been, then, a former hosting-place at Corbridge, converted in Roman times into the centre of a *pagus*, called **Coria* plus whatever ethnic name we care to devise from *-stopitum* or *Lopocarium*. The precedent for such a *pagus*-centre is the *Curia* (or *Coria*) *Tectoverdorum* at the *vicus* of Vindolanda, attached to a fort near the Wall. For the moment we leave the name close to its traditionally accepted form, but it merits both asterisk and question-mark.

DERIVATION. In this uncertainty none can be suggested. From about 875 a people of south-west Brittany around Quimper (and so geographically distinct from the *Coriosolites* of Corseul) are referred to as *Cori*(*o*)*sopites*. A possible root for this name is **sopi-* as in the place-name *Sopianae* in Pannonia Inferior (now Pécs); its meaning is unknown. The British name would then have *-*tis* suffix.

IDENTIFICATION. The Roman fort and town at Corchester, Corbridge, Northumberland (NY 9864).

Note. In the Celto-Latin name, *Cor-* at

least is firm, and it survives in the first syllables of Corbridge, Corchester. R&C note the objection of Stevenson in *Northumberland County History*, x, 9, 774, that the ancient name cannot have *Corio-* because this would have produced Anglo-Saxon *Cher-*, not *Cor-*. But there is constant interference, learned or analogical, with the phonetic development of place-names, and this is not a great objection. In the present case the church of Northumbria might well have preserved accurate memory of the old name, with *Cor-* against the tendencies of local speech.

CORITANI

SOURCES

Ptolemy II, 3, 11: Κοριτανοί (= CORITANI)

Ravenna 106_{47} (= R&C 92): RATE CORION

Ravenna's form seems to have arisen from an abbreviation on a map, presumably for **Rate Coritanorum*.

DERIVATION. This is unknown. Their name was associated by Holder I. 1128 with that of the Καρ(ι)τανοί (= *Caritani*) mentioned by Ptolemy II, 11, 6, a people of the *Agri Decumates*, and it has been suggested that the British tribe was related in some way to these, on a basis of pottery types from *Margidunum* and from the region of the Marne in N. France; see F. Oswald in *Ant. J.* XXI (1941), 323–32. An equation between a name in *Ca-* and another in *Co-*, either as a genuine variant or as a scribal matter, should not present an insuperable problem (in view of e.g. *Magontiacum/Moguntiacum*, etc.). Holder's further suggestion of a connection with the *Coriticii*, recorded also in the *Life* of St Briocus as *Coriticiana regio*, is rejected by Jackson *LHEB* 611, who points out that these names are for *Corot-* in view of Welsh *Ceredig* which derives from them (but perhaps *Corit-* could result from a Latin assimilation of *o-o-i* to *o-i-i*?). There can be no relation with the **Qritani* > *Cruithni* 'Picts' as is confidently asserted by N. K. Chadwick in *Celtic Britain* (London, 1963), 20.

IDENTIFICATION. A people of Britain with a capital at *Ratae*, Leicester. Ptolemy also attributes to them *Lindum*, Lincoln which, though separated from them when it became a legionary fortress and later a *colonia*, must have lain in their pre-Roman territory as indicated by the distribution of Coritanian coins.

CORNOVII[1] (England)

SOURCES

Ptolemy II, 3, 11: Κορναούιοι (= CORNAVII), vars. Κορνάβιοι (= CORNABII), and others which all show *-a-*

Inscriptions

RIB 288 (= Burn, 1969, No. 4, pp. 40–41), a dedication to Hadrian in A.D. 129–30 by the CIVITAS CORNOV[IORUM]

RIB 639, the tombstone of a woman at Ilkley, C(IVIS) CORNOVIA

Ravenna 106_{40} (= R&C 79): UTRICONION CORNOVIORUM, var. CORNONINORUM

ND XL_{34}: Tribunus cohortis primae CORNOVIORUM, Ponte Aeli

There can be no doubt that *Cornovii* is the proper form, both for this people and those in Scotland, whose name Ptolemy also spells -αούι- (-ουβ- in one MS only). Holder, Watson and others were prepared to take both *Cornovii* and *Cornavii* as valid forms with different suffixes, since both suffixes are well-recorded and one notes, for example, a duality in

Ausoba, a river of Ireland, and *Ausava*, a river of Germany. However, Jackson after a full discussion in *LHEB* 377–78 concludes that *Cornovii* is the better form, and is that demanded by derivatives in the modern languages; forms with *-a-* are thus simple scribal errors.

DERIVATION. The base of these names is British *corn- 'horn' (Welsh and Irish *corn*; Latin *cornu*) and it has been suggested (Watson *CPNS* 16) that the British peoples were so called because they lived on 'horns' of land, promontories. In the case of Cornwall C. Thomas (*Rural Settlement in Roman Britain* (London, 1966), 86) has plausibly argued that the *Cornovii* there, as Venetic immigrants, might have been given the name by the *Dumnonii* because they dwelt in promontory forts (cliff-castles), but in Cheshire (where the Wirral peninsula would be involved) and in Caithness to interpret the name geographically is probably to use the perception of moderns accustomed to looking at maps. For the people of Shropshire and Cheshire the vertical 'horn' of the Wrekin might conceivably be invoked, but this would not explain those in Caithness. Ross (1967) 143 thinks that peoples do not name themselves in this way and that the *Cornovii* are rather 'worshippers of a horned deity of the *Cernunnos* (stag-god) type', which is surely preferable. For the suffix, compare CANOVIUM.

IDENTIFICATION. A people of Britain with their capital at *Viroconium*, Wroxeter. Ptolemy also attributes to them *Deva*, Chester, which, though sequestered as a legionary fortress, presumably lay originally in their territory.

CORNOVII[2] (Scotland)

SOURCE

Ptolemy II, 3, 8: Κορναούιοι (twice: = CORNAVII), vars. Κουρναούιοι (= CURNAVII), Κορνάβιοι (= CORNABII), Κορνοῦβοι (= CORNUBI)

DERIVATION. See CORNOVII[1].

IDENTIFICATION. A people of Scotland, placed furthest 'east' (i.e. north-east) by Ptolemy and so to be located in Caithness.

Note. The two names *Durocornovium* (qq.v.) indicate the presence of *Cornovii* also in Cornwall and Wiltshire. In Cornwall (to which they ultimately gave its name) they were presumably either a sub-division or a client-tribe of the Dumnonii and the appearance of the place-name in *Ravenna* suggests that they were there before any supposed migration from the Shropshire area in the fifth century (e.g. J. Morris, *The Age of Arthur* (London, 1973), 68–69). The name in Wiltshire is unexplained, but it might represent a group who settled there in the course of an early migration or the early garrison of a fort.

(CORSULA)

SOURCE

Ravenna 109_9 (= R&C 275): CORSULA

This name is a 'ghost'. R&C thought it a good form, and Williams supplied an etymology. However, as Dillemann (p. 72) observes, the 'name' is a corruption of *Insula*. For once the fault was not that of the Cosmographer, but of an early copyist. The name heads *Ravenna*'s first group of islands. Dillemann clinches the argument by noting the introductory phrases to the two groups: to the first, *diverse insule... id est Corsula Mona*; to the second, *Item ad aliam partem dicitur insula Magantia*, from which it is plain that the first should read **id est insula Mona*.

COUNUS (?)

SOURCE

Ptolemy II, 3, 14: Κώουννος νῆσος (= COUNNUS INSULA), vars. Κώουνος (= COUNUS, preferred by Müller), Κωούεννος (= COVENNUS), Κοούηννος (= COVENNUS), etc.

It is unlikely that *Cunis* of *Ravenna* 109_{11} (= R&C 279) belongs here, even though it is listed among the islands; see CENIO

DERIVATION. The correct form is very unsure. Jackson in *JRS* XXXVIII (1948), 56, discusses possibilities: an emendation to Κόουνος (= *COUNUS) as is suggested by a variant could then represent Celtic **counos* or better **caunos* 'harbour', much the best semantically and supported by a number of *Cauno-* names and one *Counos* in Holder. If Κοουίννος is read, British **couinnos* 'chariot' might be intended, but this seems an unlikely name for an island. Holder's listing of the present name as *Covenno-s* seems merely to respond to his wish to identify it with modern 'Convey' island, presumably a misreading of *Canvey* in his notes.

IDENTIFICATION. An island off the coast of south-eastern Britain (see p. 146).

CREDIGONE of *Ravenna* 107_{56} (= R&C 200): see CREONES

CREONES

SOURCES

Ptolemy II, 3, 8: Κρέωνες (= CREONES); in many MSS, there follows mention of the Κέρωνες (= CERONES), but Müller and others regard this as a mistaken duplication; MS U has Κρέωνες only

Ravenna 107_{56} (= R&C 200): CREDIGONE

Ravenna's form has not been previously associated with Ptolemy's. R&C regarded it as a valid name, probably that of the eastern terminal fort of the Antonine Wall (Carriden), but this is now known to have been called *Velunia*. Since a number of other North British names cited by *Ravenna* are now known to be ethnic names misread from a map as though they were place-names (see p. 194), it seems likely that *Credigone* – which is etymologically inexplicable – represents another. In *Ravenna*'s text the name is the last in a section, and after it appears the narrative phrase *Iterum est civitas quae dicitur*... It seems likely that *dic* of this *dicitur*, misread *dig*, was in some MS inserted as a correction over the line and then wrongly incorporated into the name above: **Cre(dig)one-s*. This can be checked in two of the manuscripts. In the Vatican MS (Schnetz's A), *Credigone* appears in a line immediately over *que dicitur* in the next line. In the Paris MS (Schnetz's B) the matter is even clearer: *Credigone* has immediately beneath its *-dig-* the letters *-dr̄-* in the next line, for 'dicitur', and it must have been in expanding an abbreviation of this sort that *-dic-* (misread as *-dig-*) crept up into the line above.

DERIVATION. The name is *Cre-ones*, with *-on-es* suffixes as in many ethnic names. There seem to be no analogues.

Watson *CPNS* 23 cites modern *Crich Cera* in Co. Mayo and *Cerna* in Bregia as possibly having a related root, but this cannot be identified and no meaning is known for it.

IDENTIFICATION. A people of northern Britain placed by Ptolemy between the *Epidii* of Kintyre and the *Carnonacae* and so presumably occupying central and northern Argyllshire.

CROCOCALANA

SOURCE

AI 477_8 (Iter VI): CROCOCALANA, var. CROCAOCALANA
478_{11} (Iter VIII): CROCOCALANO, var. ALANO

DERIVATION. Jackson in *Britannia*, I (1970), 71, was tempted by an emendation **Crocco-calonā* 'loud-calling one', a river-name transferred to a settlement, formed from British **crocco-* (Welsh *croch* 'loud') and **cal-* 'to call', with **-on-ā* suffixes; but this seemed to require too much emendation, and he settled finally on a first element from British **crōco-*, older **crouco-* (Welsh *crug*; Cornish *cruc*; Irish *crúach*, etc.), all meaning 'hill, mound; heap, stack; tumulus.' He noted, however, that this does not make good sense in composition with **calonā*. We can be confident about **croco-* 'tumulus' from related names; in Britain *Croucincum*, *Pennocrucium*; abroad *Crocium* > Cruis (Basses-Alpes, France: Holder I. 1173), Κρουκιάτοννον (Ptolemy II, 8, 2; = *Crouciaconnum* of *TP*) now perhaps Carentan (Manche, France), *Eliocroca AI* 401_6 perhaps > Lorca (Murcia, Spain), etc. A second-century graffito *Ad Craucinam* at La Graufesenque may contain this word (*REA*, LXXVI (1974), 269), though R. Marichal derives the name from a root **crau* 'pierre', following Dauzat. A deity *Crougin-Toudadigoe* (dat.) is recorded in *CIL* II. 2565, from N.W. Spain. The three British names show, if they can be trusted to this extent, different stages of the adoption into Latin usage of original British *ou*, which in British became *ō* by the late first century and *ū* by the end of the third; so that *Croucincum* records the oldest stage, *Crococalana* the intermediate, and *Pennocrucium* the latest (*LHEB* 37, 313).

The second element *-calana* must leave us in doubt. On the analogy of British **Calacum* which contains **cal-* 'to call' and to which Jackson assigns the meaning 'noisy stream', we could guess that the present name has a different suffix but the same sense: 'noisy stream (by the) tumulus' (or 'hillock', etc.), this water-name being transferred to a fort or settlement. However, at Brough (whose identification is certain), there is no stream, and the Trent, more than two miles from it, can hardly be referred to. This being so, it is possible that pre-Indo-European **cala*, discussed under **Calacum*, is present here; as shown in that entry, it was combined with a Celtic element in the two names *Caladuno*, *Caladunum*. For sense, since there is no 'rocky mount' either at Brough, we should have to opt for 'shelter' or perhaps 'habitation', the whole name possibly being 'tumulus-settlement'; but this must be regarded as very tentative, for the name might, after all (as elsewhere) have been transferred from another settlement – where it made different topographical sense – to a new one on a Roman road. For the *-ana* suffix, see Holder I. 134.

IDENTIFICATION. The Roman settlement at Brough, Nottinghamshire (SK 8358).

CROUCINCUM

SOURCE

Ravenna 107_{31} (= R&C 157): CROUCINGO

In the source, *-g-* is miscopied for *c*, as often, or is the result of voicing *c* > *g* in Vulgar Latin; compare *Durotincum*, which is *Durotingo* in *Ravenna* 64_{8}.

DERIVATION. The base is British **crouco-*, later **crōco-* 'mount, tumulus', etc., for which see the previous entry. The suffix **-inco-* is listed by Holder II. 39, with examples in *Agėdincum*, *Durotincum*, *Vapincum*, etc. Dauzat *TF* 181–82 thought the suffix pre-Gaulish in Gaul, since it is found in *Bodincus*, the old name for the river Po, said to be Ligurian, and either borrowed into Gaulish or merging with a cognate there; at a later stage in Gaul the suffix was used to form estate-names, so it may have been equivalent to Celtic **-āco-*, Latin *-ācum*. In Welsh patronymics it appears as *-ing*, e.g. *Coeling*, *Cadelling*. A Germanic origin was debated at one time, but is firmly rejected by Schnetz in *ZONF*, I (1925), 176–78, though by the fifth century confusion with the Germanic suffix was no doubt possible. The sense of the name is presumably 'tumulus-place' or the like.

IDENTIFICATION. Unknown, but apparently in southern Scotland.

CUNETIO

SOURCES

AI 486_{5} (Iter XIV): CUNETIONE

Ravenna 106_{21} (= R&C 46): CUNETZONE

AI has the proper form, an oblique case from which a nominative can be supposed as above; compare *Derventio-ne*, *Navione*, *Verlucio-ne*. *Ravenna*'s form here shows Vulgar Latin assibilation of classical /tj/ (see p. 30). R&C's reading of this name as *Cunetzione* has an extra *-i-* by error.

DERIVATION. This remains uncertain. The long expositions of Williams and of Jackson in *Britannia*, I (1970), 71, should be studied. It is unfortunate that the name seems to have no analogues here or abroad; the *Cunetes* tribe of Spain provide a similarity of form, but they were probably Iberian (non-Celtic). The British name was **Cŭnētịū*, and from this the name of the Wiltshire river, Kennet, is derived; the same may be assumed for several other rivers called Kennet and similar, including the Kent of Cumbria (older *Kenet*), and for the *Cynwyd* of Merioneth (Wales). *Ravenna*'s *Cunia* and *Cunis* rivers are probably not relevant, being referable to *Cenio*. Whether the first element in Countisbury, the name of a Devon hill-fort, belongs here is doubtful; it was in an Old Welsh form (Asser) *Arx Cynuit*, and Jackson thinks this name related to **Cunetiu*, but we seem not to have hill-fort names made from original water-names in other instances. Jackson dismisses the older notion of a Celtic **cuno-* 'high' as non-existent, and a root in well-known **cuno-* 'dog' as most unlikely in a river-name; for the same reason he does not welcome William's proposed root in the **ku-no-* 'point, edge' of Pokorny, and rightly dismisses the consequential argument that in the present case the river might have taken its name from that of the settlement, for we have no evidence that this occurred in Celtic times (though such back-formation is common later). The most recent discussion of the abundant *Cuno*-names, mostly personal names involving *Cuno-* 'dog', is that of H. Birkhan in *Germanen und Kelten*... (Vienna, 1970), 345–79; he mentions British *Cunetio* (p. 348, note), a unique toponym, but without associating it with other *Cuno*-names. The name must be left unresolved.

IDENTIFICATION. The Roman town at Mildenhall, Wiltshire (SU 2169), on the river Kennet.

CUNIA of *Ravenna* 108_{41} (= R&C 270): see CENIO
CUNIS of *Ravenna* 109_{11} (= R&C 279): see CENIO

CURIA TECTOVERDORUM

SOURCE

Inscription: *RIB* 1695 (= Burn, 1969, No. 173, p. 126): an altar set up by the CURIA TEXTOVERDORUM. The stone was found at Beltingham: 'it may have been brought from Chesterholm (*Vindolanda*), or it may have come from a local shrine' (*RIB*).

DERIVATION. For *Curia/Coria*, see CORIA[1]. See also TECTOVERDI.

IDENTIFICATION. Unknown, but apparently near Chesterholm, Northumberland. The people are not otherwise recorded.

DANUM

SOURCES

AI 475_5 (Iter v): DANO
478_8 (Iter VIII): DANO, var. ANO
ND XL_5 (*pictura*): DANO
XL_{20} (text): Praefectus equitum Crispianorum, DANO

DERIVATION. The group of names of which this is a part is much discussed. Jackson in *Britannia*, I (1970), 72, gives the British name as **Dānu*(*n*) and bases this on **dānu*- 'bold'; the name was originally that of the river, in the sense 'rapidly flowing', and was transferred to the settlement. Among ancient river-names having the same base are *Danuvius* (Celtic **Dānou̯ios*, **Dānŭu̯ios*) > Danube and *Rodanus* (Celtic **Rodānos*, with **ro*- intensive prefix) > Rhône; the Russian Don (anciently *Tanais*), the Dnieper, the second element in *Condate*, and in modern Britain the Don of Co. Durham; the Doon of Ayrshire and Donwy in Wales may also belong here. See W. Nicolaisen in *BZN*, VIII (1957), 245–46. Many Gaulish personal names such as *Dannorix*, **Segodannios* show a similar form but are presumably from a different root (*GPN* 189–90). Pokorny 175 would derive some of the above names from **dānu*- 'river' (base **da*- 'flüssig, fliessen'), and in view of the very widespread set of similar names it may be safer to postulate such a base rather than the adjectival one postulated by Jackson, since the application of an adjective not necessarily related to water is harder to explain when repeated so often. Ekwall's linking of Celtic **dānu*- with Sanskrit *danu* 'rain, moisture' seems unwarranted.

IDENTIFICATION. The Roman fort at Doncaster, Yorkshire (SE 5703). This is certainly correct for the *AI* reference and may be so for *ND*, but the possibility remains that this may refer to an unlocated fort near Jarrow, Durham, which is also on a river Don.

Note. The British name survived as *Cair Daun* in Nennius, and via Anglo-Saxon as *Don*caster; on its evolution, see *EPNS*, XXX, 29.

*DARUVEDA

SOURCE

Ravenna 109_{20} (= R&C 295): DAROECLA, var. (2 MSS) DAROEDA

DERIVATION. *Ravenna*'s variant was adopted by R&C as their main form, and gives hope of emendation. For this R&C propose **Daruveda*, arguing a miscopying of letters in Greek at some stage; but this is hardly necessary in view of *Ravenna*'s frequent *o/u* confusions (either scribal or in Vulgar Latin pronunciation) and occasional omission of *-v-*, as in *Segloes* for **Selgoves*. The root is then British **daru- *deru-* 'oak', in Gaulish **deru̯o-* (giving some names in **dru-*; *Druidae* is related) from Indo-European **dereu-* (Greek δρῦς 'oak'; also English *tree*, etc.); cf. Welsh *derw*, Breton *derv*, Cornish *derow*. For its appearance in many simple and compound names, see Holder I. 1270. Of note are the British *Derventio* names, and abroad *Derva* in Pannonia (*Ravenna* 57_{28}) and *Derventum* > Drevant (Cher, France). Of great interest is A. Carnoy, 'Le Chêne dans la toponymie et la linguistique', *RIO*, x (1958), 81–101. The second element is probably *-veda*, one of the possibilities mentioned under *Coccuveda*, here 'slope' rather than 'appearance': hence 'oak-slope (island)' ?

IDENTIFICATION. Unknown, but apparently an island off Scotland.

DECANTAE

SOURCES

Ptolemy II, 3, 8: Δεκάνται (Müller's restoration); MSS have Λεκανται (= LECANTAE), δε Κάντεαι (= DE CANTEAE), Κάνται (= CANTAE)

Ravenna 108_{8} (= R&C 217): DECHA

Müller's restoration seems a natural one. *Ravenna*'s name has not previously been placed in relation with it, and there can be no certainty that this is right; but *Decha* is meaningless and is impossible as a British form, and as we know, a number of North British ethnic names are concealed in the Cosmography as place-names. *Decha* could readily have arisen from **Decante* via an abbreviation *Decāte* which was not understood.

DERIVATION. Watson *CPNS* 18–19 (following Stokes and Holder) finds a base in a root **dec-* 'good, noble', as in Old Irish *dech* 'best, noblest' (cf. Latin *decor*, etc.), with a suffix **-ant-* of participial form as in other ethnic names such as *Novantae*, *Trinovantes*, *Setantii*. He compares Gaulish *Decetia* (Decize, Nièvre), and Goidelic inscriptions of Devon and Anglesey which mention *Decheti*, *Decceti*, *Deceti* (*-t-* in Goidelic representing *-nt-* in equivalent names). See also the *Note* below.

IDENTIFICATION. A people of Scotland placed by Ptolemy 'east' (that is, north) of the *Caledonii* and so apparently inhabiting Easter Ross.

Note. There were other *Decantae* or *Decanti* (for such a variation in declension, cf. *Atrebates*) in N. Wales. They are not recorded in ancient sources, but Degannwy near Llandudno is < **Decantou̯ion* – with suffix as in *Canovium*, etc. – and this place was *Arx Decantorum* in the *Annales Cambriae* (812; see *LHEB* 39) and was *Dygant* in Middle Welsh. Rhys (1904) 295 suggested that Tacitus's *Annals* XII, 32, should be emended *in *Decantos*, supposing **Decanti*, which is by no means impossible even though none of the MS variants suggests this. See our entry for *Deceangli*.

DECEANGLI (?)

SOURCES

Inscriptions on lead pigs: *CIL* VII. 1204 and *EE* VII. 1121, both found at Chester, to be dated to A.D. 74; and *CIL* VII. 1205, found at Hints Common (Staffs.), to be dated to A.D. 76 (also Burn, 1969, No. 25, p. 25). The faint inscription on these has been read in diverse ways, but seems to be DECEANGL, perhaps to be expanded DECEANGL(*icum metallum*); see *JRS*, XII (1922), 283–84, and G. Webster in *Flintshire Historical Society*, XIII (1953), 3 ff.

Tacitus *Annals* XII, 32: in the MSS *inde Cangos*, probably to be adjusted *in Decangos* (acc.)

See also the note to DECANTAE.

For the textual tradition of Tacitus and the various emendations proposed, see the Furneaux text of the *Annals* (2nd edn, Oxford, 1907; II, 99–100), where the passage is very fully annotated, and where possible interpretations of the text on the lead pigs are discussed also. We have preferred to accept the epigraphic evidence (normally the best) and to think that Tacitus's text requires emendation to *in Dec(e)ang(l)os*. See M. G. Jarrett and J. C. Mann, 'The Tribes of Wales', in *Welsh History Review*, IV (1968), 161–74, at 165–66. It has however been argued that there were two adjacent tribes, the *Deceangli* in Flintshire and the *Decangi* (of Tacitus, that is, without emendation) in Herefordshire; see, for example, S. C. Stanford in *Arch. J.*, CXXVII (1970), 124, with a rebuttal by G. Webster in *The Cornovii* (London, 1975), 7–8. The *Gangani* people of north-west Wales (recorded by Ptolemy) are almost certainly not involved here.

DERIVATION. None can be suggested; no root known to us is visible, and there are apparently no similar names elsewhere. The name might just possibly have **dec-* as in *Decantae* and *-ang-* corresponding to *-anc-* as in other British names, but this obviously neglects several other features in the name as recorded. It is always possible that the epigraphic form is itself not merely abbreviated but compressed also; further discoveries – by no means impossible – might give us better forms as in the case of the lead pigs of *Lutudarum*.

IDENTIFICATION. A people of Britain dwelling in the lead-mining area of Flintshire.

DECHA of *Ravenna* 108_8 (= R&C 217): see DECANTAE

DECUÀRIA of *Ravenna* 107_{15} (= R&C 138): see PETUARIA

DELGOVICIA

SOURCES

AI 466_3 (Iter I): DELGOVICIA, var. DELGOVITIA

Ravenna 107_{16} (= R&C 139): DEVOVICIA, var. DEVOVITIA

DERIVATION. *AI*'s form gives a sound basis; *Ravenna*'s is slightly corrupt. The first element is apparently Celtic **delgos* 'thorn' (Old Welsh *dala*, *dal*, Old Irish *delg*). This seems not to enter into any other place-names in ancient sources, but Williams notes that it is common in Scottish names, e.g. Dealginross. It is hard to see any relationship with *delgu* in Gaulish, 'I hold, contain' in a graffito on a vessel from Banassac (Lozère, France), discussed by Vendryes in *EC*, VII (1956),

9–17; the sense is remote, and comparable *-vices* names make us expect as first element a noun, not a verb. The sense and function of the first element of the British name cannot be determined in isolation. Jackson in *Britannia*, I (1970), 72, thinks it possible that *-vic-* corresponded to the British source of Welsh *-wig* 'wood' used as a suffix, as in *coedwig* 'forest', and this was the solution doubtfully favoured by Williams ('thorn-brake' for the complete name); but Jackson points out that **delgos* meant a single thorn, not a bush, so that while Williams's sense is attractive, it is not justified. There is then a possibility of a Celtic **u̯ico-* cognate with, or borrowed from, Latin *vicus* 'town, village, settlement' (Irish *fich* glossed 'municipium'), but Jackson and Ellis Evans *GPN* 281–85 do not think there is good evidence for this; so a meaning 'thorn-town', though possible, is unlikely. (On Latin *vicus* possibly widely used in Roman Britain and borrowed there into Anglo-Saxon, see M. Gelling in *Medieval Archaeology*, XI (1967), 87–104, especially p. 95). Moreover all the British names with *-vic-* have an ending *-ia* or *-ium*, which does not suggest Latin *vicus-vicum* (and a British suffix **-i̯o-* attached to a Latin *vicus* seems unlikely too). The explanation favoured by Jackson and documented in part by Ellis Evans is that the town name is formed with the **-i̯o-* suffix from an ethnicon **Delgou̯ices* 'spear-fighters', with **delgo-* thus in a figurative sense and **u̯ic-* meaning 'fight' (a cognate of Latin *vinco*). This is amply supported by analogues among ethnic names. In Britain were the *Ordovices* 'hammer-warriors' (Welsh *gordd*) and *Gabrantovices* 'horse-riding fighters, cavalrymen'; on the Continent the *Eburovices* 'yew-tree fighters' ('bowmen' ?), *Brannovices* 'raven fighters', etc. (The last two may contain personal names **Eburos*, **Brannos*, however; or refer to some emblem rather than literally to a weapon. This might also apply to the **Delgovices*.) There are two further British place-names which are presumably to be explained in the same way: *Longovicium* 'place of the **Longovices*' ('ship-fighters' ?) and *Vercovicium* 'place of the **Vercovices*' ('effective fighters' ?). A further suggestion made by Pisani in *Archivio Glottologico Italiano*, L (1965), 6–7, is interesting. He suggests that *Visi-* in the name of the Visigoths is a Balto-Slavic or Slavic term corresponding to Celtic **u̯ic-* or **u̯eic-* in ethnic names, also to Sanskrit *viç-* 'tribe', Old Russian *vĭsĭ* 'village'; hence *Visi-* in Visigoth might be simply 'le tribù (assoluto)', or an abbreviation of a compound name analogous to the Celtic names in *-vices*. There may be some significance in the British *-vicia/vicium* variation, although our *Longovicium* records seem to show both as simple alternatives. Whether, without further evidence, we should extend the number of British ethnic names, is doubtful; those mentioned presumably belong to small divisions within larger units.

IDENTIFICATION. Probably the Roman settlement at Wetwang, Yorkshire (SE 9258).

DEMEROSESSA

SOURCE

Ravenna 108_1 (= R&C 203): DEMEROSESA, var. DEMOROSESA

DERIVATION. The only analogue to this name seems to be the *Demĕra* river > Demer (Holland). R&C suggest a relation to the word-family of Greek Θεμερο-, Irish *deim*, Old High German *timbar*, Old

Norse *dimmr*, English *dim*, a group of obscure origin. For the second element, see CAMULOSESSA. R&C's meaning, 'dark seat', 'presumably referring to some awesome hill', seems acceptable enough; however, a comparison with *Camulosessa* might suggest that we have here an unrecorded divine name **Demero-*.

IDENTIFICATION. Unknown, but apparently in Scotland and probably north of the Antonine Wall.

DEMETAE

SOURCE

Ptolemy II, 3, 12: Δημῆται (= DEMETAE), var. Δημηκῆται (= DEMECETAE)

DERIVATION. None can be suggested, and there are apparently no similar names. Ptolemy's forms should have ε-ε (short *ĕ*) not η-η (long *ē*), *Dĕmĕtae*, in view of the modern derivative. The tribal name was known to Gildas (31: *Demetarum*, gen. pl.) and to later writers. The region *Demetia* (in the *Vita Samsonis*, etc.) has in Welsh produced modern *Dyfed*; on this development, see Jackson *LHEB* 278–79, 488.

IDENTIFICATION. A people of south-west Wales, with their capital at *Moridunum*, Carmarthen. Ptolemy also attributes *Luentinum* (q.v.) to them.

DERVENTIO[1]

SOURCES

AI 466_2 (Iter I): DERVENTIONE

ND XL_{16} (*pictura*): DERVENTIONE, var. DERVENCIONE

XL_{31} (text): Praefectus numeri supervenientium Petueriensium, DERVENTIONE

DERIVATION. This name represents British **Deru̯entịū*, based on **daru-* **deru-* 'oak', with **ent-* and **-ịo-(n)* suffixes. For **daru-*, see *DARUVEDA. The sense is thus 'oak-river, river in the oakwood'; here, as seems to be often the case with other tree-names and plant-names used in toponymy, the reference may be partly literal but partly also to some sacred site or religious connotation. This was the name of several British rivers, and by transference, of settlements on their banks without further suffixation; and was the name of various rivers not recorded in our ancient sources, since modern *Derwent*, *Darwen*, *Darent(h)*, *Dart* and Welsh *Derwinni* all derive from it (see map). In British the name had an *-n-* stem, and was taken into Latin with the same as an *-io*, *-ionem* third-declension name. In all but one of the British records of the name it

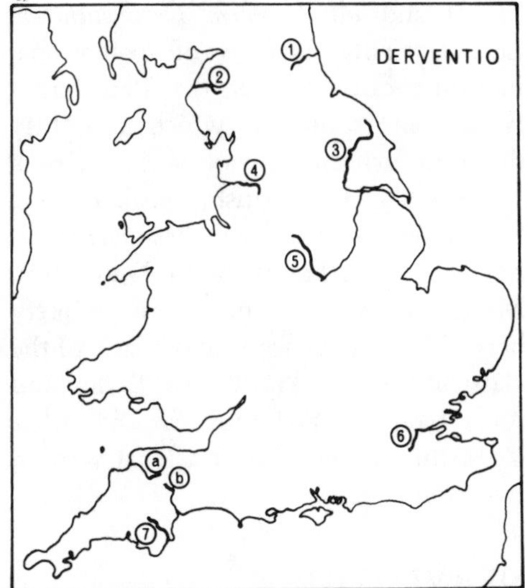

Fig. 28. River-names derived from *Derventio*; 1. Derwent; 2. Derwent; 3. Derwent; 4. Darwen; 5. Derwent; 6. Darent; 7. Dart. Possible examples: (*a*) Little Dart; (*b*) Dart.

is in the oblique-ablative form *Derventi-one*, or in versions which are to be adjusted to this, and it is likely that in these instances the supposed nominative **Derventio* had no real currency; however, *Derventio*[6] appears to offer us a genuine nominative, for a special reason, and therefore all the names are quoted in this form (which has become traditional). The name, common in Britain, seems not to be found on the Continent, though *Derventum* > Drevant (Cher, France) has the same base and one of the suffixes.

IDENTIFICATION. The Roman fort at Malton, Yorkshire (SE 7971), probably covering also the adjacent settlement at Norton. That the *ND* reference is to this place rather than to Papcastle (= *Derventio*[3]) is indicated by the garrison's being derived from *Petuaria* (q.v.).

Note. Bede has two mentions of the original name of the river (the Yorkshire Derwent) from which the fort took its designation: *iuxta amnem Deruventionem* (II, 9) and *ultra amnem Deruventionem* (II, 13). This form is of exceptional interest because it shows that Bede had it from some source in which a slightly different form of the roots was supposed, presumably by British speakers, i.e. **Deru-u̯ent-* (**venta* as in *Bannaventa* ? – but this is not known with *-*i̯o*-suffix). Merely scribal -*vv*- for -*v*- is unlikely here. The name is not found in any of the classical sources known to Bede, and must have reached him – as did other Yorkshire names – from a local written tradition in Latin.

DERVENTIO[2]

SOURCE

Ravenna 106_{46} (= R&C 89): DERBENTIONE, var. DERBENCIONE

DERIVATION. See DERVENTIO[1]. Again, a river-name has been transferred to a settlement; the river is the Derbyshire Derwent.

IDENTIFICATION. The Roman fort and town at Littlechester, Derbyshire (SK 3537).

DERVENTIO[3]

SOURCE

Ravenna 107_{6} (= R&C 122): DERVENTIONE

DERIVATION. See DERVENTIO[1]; for the river from which this fort took its name, see the next entry.

IDENTIFICATION. The Roman fort at Papcastle, Cumberland (NY 1131).

DERVENTIO[4]

SOURCE

Ravenna 108_{31} (= R&C 250): DORVANTIUM

DERIVATION. See DERVENTIO[1]. If this name were isolated, one might be tempted to think *Ravenna*'s *Dor*- a version of *Duro*-, and to think the ending analogous to that of *Derventum* in Gaul. But the association of it with other British *Derventio* names is clear, and the relation to *Derventio*[3] (a fort) clinches the matter. In *Ravenna* the ending is hardly a mistake for nominative -*io*, but a garbled version of -*ion(e)*; or perhaps the compiler, who often wrote Vulgar Latin -*on* for classical -*um*, here mistakenly reversed the process.

IDENTIFICATION. The river Derwent, Cumberland.

Note. Bede in IV, 29, mentions *Deruventionis fluvii primordia* 'sources of the Derwent' (also a large mere, which is Derwentwater). For the form *Deruv-*, see the Note to *Derventio*[1]. In his prose *Life of St Cuthbert* (Migne, *Patrologia*, XCIV, col. 768) Bede has a further mention of river and lake: *Qui in insula stagni illius pergrandis de quo Diorwentionis fluvii primordia erumpunt*..., showing a different source with a greater adaptation, perhaps, to local pronunciation.

*DERVENTIO[5] (?)

SOURCE

Ravenna 105_{50} (= R&C 9): ARDUA RAVENATONE

R&C print this as one continuous name, without suggesting that it is a conflation. It is possible to take *Ardua* as a separate name (see the entry for this), but then *Ravenatone* has no obvious etymology (though Williams suggests a relation with Welsh *araf* 'gentle' and *arafhan* 'to quieten'). It seems likely that the Cosmographer's entry is badly garbled, and that in its second portion he has assimilated a name to that of his own city, Ravenna. There is likely to have been a corruption of another original **Derventione* preceded, if a place, by *A* or *Ad* if read from an itinerary, though there is no close parallel for such usage elsewhere in the British section of *Ravenna*. In a closely following entry at 105_{51} the Cosmographer gives us another *Derventio*, this one being a probable *Statio* and thus clearly a place; hence it seems arguable that the present *Ardua Ravenatone* entry has been misread from a map, as often, and refers to a river. In this event initial *Ar-* represents *Fl* (*Flumen*). Although *Ravenna* has some *Derventione* names accurately, it misrepresents this at 105_{51} (*Deventia*) and 108_{31} (*Dorvantium*), so a further and more serious miscopying here causes no surprise. Furthermore, in its opening section of south-western names, *Ravenna* includes at least two rivers as places (*Eltabo* 105_{46}, *Elconio* 105_{47}), so that again it is unsurprising to find another river in this company.

DERIVATION. See DERVENTIO[1].

IDENTIFICATION. Probably the river Dart, Devon.

*DERVENTIO[6] STATIO

SOURCE

A section of *Ravenna*'s entries reads:

105_{51} (= R&C 10–11): DEVIONISSO STATIO DEVENTIA

105_{52} (= R&C 11): STENE

Statio (see below) is a nominative, in apposition to a place-name. In five Continental inscriptions cited by R&C, *Statio* in every case precedes the place-name (in four of these the name is in adjectival form qualifying *Statio*). But the only analogue in *Ravenna* is *Nemetotacio* 105_{47}, that is *Nemeto Statio* with *Statio* in second place and in simple apposition, and this (with further support from e.g. *Lindum Colonia*, *Eburo *Castellum*) provides the better guide to *Ravenna*'s procedure in the present case. If the analogy holds, we should redivide the above names as *Devionisso Statio* and *Deventia Stene*. This last item is *Steno* in two manuscripts; and since both *Stene* and *Steno* are meaningless in Celtic and Latin, it seems proper to regard this as scribal corruption of **Statio* or **Stacio* and to attach it as an apposition to the previous name. It is much less likely (in view of British *Nemeto Statio*) that

Stene represents a corruption of adjectival *-*iensis*, as R&C proposed.

DERIVATION. Williams suggests that '*dev-entia* is a participial development from **devo-* "bright" or "holy", with the meaning "brilliant". It is probably a stream-name.' This seems shaky (Holder has only one similar name, *Deventia*, which he refers to *Dementia*, a personal name) and places too much trust in *Ravenna*'s text. A simple emendation to **Derventio* seems much better (Schnetz suggests 'fortasse *Statio De[r]ventia*'). For *a/o* alternation, see p. 203. This is a unique example of nominative **Derventio* among the six British names, preserved here, no doubt, because *Statio* is also nominative and was a common noun which went on being declined. See DERVENTIO[1].

IDENTIFICATION. An unlocated *statio* (i.e. posting-station and/or tax-collecting centre) perhaps, like *Nemeto Statio* (q.v.) originating as a Roman fort, on the river Dart; probably near Buckfast (SX 7467) where the Roman road running south-east from Exeter (Margary 491) is likely to have crossed the river.

DEVA[1]

SOURCES

Ptolemy II, 3, 11: Δηοῦα, Λεγίων κ' Νικηφόρος (= DEVA, LEGIO XX VICTRIX), a *polis* of the Cornovii; var. Δηούανα (= DEVANA).

Inscription: *CIL* XIII. 6221 (Worms), a dedication by a man who was ...DEVAS

Inscription: *Année Epigraphique*, 1915, No. 70 (Trier), a dedication by a man who was ...DEVAS

Inscriptions: *EE* IX. 1274ab, tile-stamps which include DE: perhaps to be expanded *De(vensis)* or *De(vae)*, but *De(ciana)* is also possible

Fig. 29. River-names derived from *Deva*: 1. Dee; 2. Dee; 3. Dee (Dent); 4. Dee; 5. Afon Dwyfawr; 6. Afon Dwyfach.

AI 469_2 (Iter II): DEVA LEG. XX VICI
482_5 (Iter XI): DEVAM (acc.)
482_8 (Iter XI): DEVA

Ravenna 106_{44} (= R&C 86): DEVA VICTRIS

These forms hardly call for comment, except DEVAS 'from Chester' in two of the inscriptions; Holder I. 1274 suggested that this is for *Deva(ti)s*. In *Ravenna*'s form, presumably read from a map, it seems that the legionary adjective has transferred itself to the whole settlement (i.e. it is not simply a case of omission of 'Leg. XX'; compare its entry for *Isca Augusta*). *Victris* shows Vulgar Latin *-s* for *-x*; no Greek transcription is involved, as R&C thought.

DERIVATION. The name is British **Dēu̯ā* 'the goddess (par excellence ?)', more properly the name of the river (> Dee) transferred as often to the place. Older Celtic **dei̯o-s* 'god', Indo-European *_deiuōs_ are postulated; cf. Latin _divus_, and cognates in many languages. Jackson mentions derivatives: Old Welsh _duiu_, Welsh _dwy_ as in _Dubrduiu_, _Dyfrdwy_ 'water of Dwy' (= Dee), and discusses the development of the name in Anglo-Saxon (_LHEB_ 375, 629). The name was very widespread: in Britain _Deva_[2] and _Deva_[3], _Devionissum_, _Devona_; abroad, numerous _Deva_ rivers and settlements in Ireland, Gaul and Spain, also in compounds such as _Deobriga_; and in many personal names, especially of Gaul. Many names show _divo-_ rather than _devo-_; there may in some cases have been assimilation to Latin _divo-_, but Ellis Evans _GPN_ 191–93 explains that apart from this, 'Gaulish _ē_ (from Indo-European _ei_) probably had a very close pronunciation, which could account for the _-i-_'; Whatmough _DAG_ 456 thinks that '_ei_ giving _ē_ > _i_ is possibly dialectal' within Gaulish. Many names show _Deo-_, _Dio-_ after loss of _-v-_. The belief of the Celtic peoples in the divinity of water, or more strictly of the presence of a divinity in the water, is widely attested by these names. Other British _Dee_ rivers, not recorded in ancient sources, have the same origin (see map).

IDENTIFICATION. The Roman legionary fortress at Chester (SJ 4066). _Victrix_ reflects the cognomen of the XX Legion, acquired in the suppression of the Boudican Revolt.

Note. Bede in II, 2, gives evidence of a possibly alternative ancient name which continued in use for some centuries: _...ad civitatem Legionum, quae a gente Anglorum Legacaestir, a Brettonibus autem rectius Carlegion appellatur_. If this had endured, it would clearly have produced a *_Caerleon_ like that of Monmouthshire. Watson _CPNS_ 383–84 does indeed mention that Chester was _Caer Lleon_ in Old Welsh. O. G. S. Crawford in _Antiquity_, IX (1935), 287, argues that Arthur's ninth battle as recounted by Nennius, _in urbe Legionis_, took place at Chester, because Caerleon-on-Usk was always so described in Welsh literature, while York – the third and last legionary centre – was never called 'city of the legion'. The proposal is certainly attractive. (Bede's mention of Caerleon by a similar name is taken from Gildas, a different case.)

DEVA[2]

SOURCE

Ptolemy II, 3, 2: Δηούα ποταμοῦ ἐκβολαί (= DEVA FLUVII OSTIA)

DERIVATION. See DEVA[1].

IDENTIFICATION. The river Dee, Stewartry of Kirkcudbright.

DEVA[3]

SOURCE

Ptolemy II, 3, 4: Δηούα ποταμοῦ ἐκβολαί (= DEVA FLUVII OSTIA), var. Διούα (= DIVA)

DERIVATION. See DEVA[1].

IDENTIFICATION. The river Dee, Aberdeenshire.

DEVANA of Ptolemy II, 3, 9: see DEVONA

DEVIONISSUM STATIO

SOURCE

Ravenna 105_{51} (= R&C 10–11): DEVIONISSO STATIO

For discussion of _Statio_ here, see DERVENTIO[6]

DERIVATION. This name belongs ultimately with the *Deva* group, but rather than 'place on the holy stream' as R&C propose – there being no modern *Dee river in these parts – it is probably rather 'place of *Dēu̯i̯os*'. Holder I. 1275 records Celtic *Dēu̯i̯os*, *Dīu̯i̯os*, which is at the base of *Divione* > Dijon (Côte-d'Or, France); it may be noted that *Devione* is a recorded form of this. For **-isso-*, see ABISSUM.

IDENTIFICATION. Unknown, but apparently in south-west Britain.

DEVONA

SOURCES

Ptolemy II, 3, 9: Δηουάνα (= DEVANA), a *polis* of the Taexali

Ravenna 108_7 (= R&C 215): DEVONI

We can be reasonably sure of the correct form. Holder I. 1276 analyses Ptolemy's name as *Dēvănā* and refers *Devoni* to it; and it is true that an *-ana* suffix is known in a few British names, such as *Crococalana*. However, Jackson *LHEB* 34 regards Ptolemy's Δηουάνα (= *Devana*) as an error for *Δηουόνα (= *Devona*), and in view of the fact that *Devona* is strongly paralleled elsewhere (and > Don), while *Devana* is not, he is surely right. Ptolemy may well have associated the place incorrectly with the Dee rather than the Don; see p. 128. *Ravenna* then has the *-o-* correctly but has a miscopying of final *-a* as *-i*: compare *Augusti* 106_{50}, which we know to be for *Augusta*.

DERIVATION. *Devona* is properly a river-name, here transferred as often to the camp on its banks. The formation is as in ABONA, which contains the **-ona* suffix. For the root, see DEVA[1]. Continental analogues include *Devona* (Δηούονα in Ptolemy II, 11, 14) > Dewangen in Würtemburg; *Divona Cadurcorum* (*Cadurcis* > Cahors, Lot, France); a river *Divona* > Divonne (Ain, France); and a goddess *Divona* (text: *Dibona*) in the Gaulish Rom text, Dottin *LG* 43, together with two springs mentioned by Holder I. 1275 and Whatmough *DAG* 455–56 (citing Ausonius).

IDENTIFICATION. The Roman camp at Kintore, Aberdeenshire (NJ 7816), on the river Don.

DICALEDONES (?)

SOURCE

Ammianus Marcellinus XXVIII, 8, 4: DICALYDONAS (acc. pl.)

(Also relevant are the names given in Greek for the 'Oceanus Duecaledonius' by Ptolemy and Marcian: see Chapter II, p. 44)

DERIVATION. The basis of the name is as for the *Calidonii*. The prefix *di-* (= *due-* in the ocean name) implies 'two', and points to the name being an artificial Latin designation, that is, our form is not a latinisation of an original Celtic name and may not have had a basis in native usage. Rhys (1904) 297–98 suggested that the name indicated a 'twin people', perhaps consisting of the Vacomagi and Calidonii proper, but Watson *CPNS* 20 thinks them more the 'double Caledonians' from their position astride the Grampians.

IDENTIFICATION. One of two divisions of the Picts; since the *Verturiones* occupied the region later known as **Fortriu* (gen. *Fortrenn*), the *Dicaledones* were presumably the more northerly group.

*DICTUM

SOURCES

Ravenna 107_{16} (= R&C 140): DIXIO

ND XL_8 (*pictura*): DICTIM

XL_{23} (text): Praefectus numeri Nerviorum Dictensium (var. Dictentium), DICTI

The root and ending of this name are unsure; even the identity of the names in the two sources is not totally certain. It seems best to take *Ravenna*'s form as the usual oblique *-o* case of a masculine or neuter name, and *ND*'s as a locative of the same second declension (the *Dictim* of the *pictura* then being an error for *-um*; but *Dictae* and *Dicti* have also been proposed as nominatives). In equating the sources, we can regard *ND*'s *-ct-* as probably the more correct, and *Ravenna*'s *-xi-* as having developed by miscopying of *-xt-* (for *i* miscopied as *t*, compare *Corto-* for *Corio-* in several instances; also e.g. *Dertum* of *TP* = both *Diriam* and *Dixium* in *Ravenna* – now Monopoli in S. Italy). This *-xt-* was in turn an alternative spelling for the usual Latin *-ct-*, for which see *Tectoverdi*. There is, then, no great problem about regarding the two names as in fact the same.

DERIVATION. The etymology is unknown. It looks Latin but has no suitable meaning in that language. In Celtic, Holder offers only *Dixtus* (genitive: *Dixti*), a personal name of Bordeaux; Holder thinks this is for *Divixtos*, an amply recorded name, itself a shortening of **Dīvo(i)-vixtos*. But a personal name would not simply stand as a place-name in the present instance, since a suffix (e.g. **-i̯o-* or **-āco-*) would be expected.

IDENTIFICATION. An unlocated Roman fort which, from its position in the *Ravenna* list, should lie in north-east England. In *ND* it appears between *Arbeia*, South Shields, and *Concangios*, Chester-le-Street, and on these grounds a site at Wearmouth (as in Frere (1974), 265, map) seems probable: a military base here in the fourth century is certainly to be expected, though none has yet been found.

DOBUNNI

SOURCES

Inscriptions: *RIB* 2250, a milestone of Numerian (A.D. 283–84) inscribed R(es) P(ublica) C(ivitatis) D(obunnorum) (?) from Kenchester, Herefordshire

CIL XVI. 49 (= Burn, 1969, No. 36, p. 34), the military diploma addressed to LUCCONI TRENI F DOBUNN (dat.), 'Lucco son of Trenus, a Dobunnian'; A.D. 105. The man was serving with *cohors I Britannica* in Pannonia

Ptolemy II, 3, 12: Δοβοῦνοι (= DOBUNI); some MSS have -νν- (= -nn-)

II, 3, 13: Δοβούννοις (= DOBUNNIS, dat.)

Cassius Dio LX, 20, 2: Βοδούννων (= BODUNNORUM, gen. pl.)

Ravenna 106_{31} (= R&C 66): CIRONIUM DOBUNORUM

Cassius Dio's form has suffered a scribal metathesis. The equation of '*Bodunni*' with the *Dobunni* was first suggested by Camden, but long resisted; the matter is conclusively resolved by C. F. C. Hawkes in E. M. Clifford (ed.), *Bagendon: a Belgic Oppidum* (Cambridge, 1961), 58–62. The name is further recorded on a tombstone of the mid-sixth century (*CIIC* no. 428): DOBUNNI FABRI FILII ENABARRI (gen.; Tavistock, Devon).

DERIVATION. This is unknown. The name seems to have no parallels except possibly in the divine name **Alanto-dubā* to which Holder draws attention in *CIL* v. 4934, also of unknown meaning.

IDENTIFICATION. A people of Britain with their capital at *Corinium*, Cirencester. Ptolemy attributes no other *polis* to them, but the milestone inscription (if correctly expanded) indicates that their territory extended into Herefordshire, while the distribution of pre-Roman Dobunnic coins (D. F. Allen, in E. M. Clifford, *op. cit.*, 68–149) suggests that they also controlled the area of Gloucestershire, much of Somerset and parts of Oxfordshire and Wiltshire. The territory of the *colonia* of *Glevum* (Gloucester) will have been segregated from them, but on Ptolemy's attribution of *Aquae Calidae* (Bath) and *Ischalis* (Charterhouse?) to the *Belgae* see p. 121.

(DOLOCINDO)

SOURCE
Ravenna 106_{12} (= R&C 38): DOLOCINDO

We prefer to restore this name to *DUROCINTUM, and discuss the reasons under that heading. However, that is tentative, and there is something to be said in favour of a form more closely resembling that preserved by *Ravenna*. R&C took it literally; they and Williams found an etymology in **dolo-* (Welsh *dol*, pl. *dolau*) 'riverside meadow', which is certainly a commonly-used element in modern place-names and which might well be correct in the ancient name, especially as there are a few analogues listed by Holder. The second element proposed by Williams, **cnido-* **nido* 'steam, smoke' (i.e. *cindo* rearranged) seems very forced, and is otherwise unknown in toponymy; the meaning given by R&C and Williams for the whole name, 'misty haugh', is thus unsatisfactory. Possibly a better conjecture is that the second element conceals British **sento-* 'path' (see CLAUSENTUM), which is spelled with a *c* in *Ravenna*'s *Gabrocentio*, though if this is right it might then be preferable to look for an animal name concealed in the first element. These possibilities should be retained.

Dillemann (66) thinks *Dolocindo* a mere ghost-form which arose during copying of *Ravenna* 106_{12-13}:

(Sorbio) doni Vindogladia (...)
Moriduno

represented as

—dolo cindo/clavi
Mo(rionio)

This is attractive and is very much the kind of gross error which *Ravenna* commits, but we do not think it acceptable. Elsewhere we explain that we think **Sorvioduno* is concealed at a slightly earlier stage in *Ravenna*, and that '*Clavimo*' is a corruption of the name of Gloucester. Also, Dillemann's proposal leaves without explanation the disappearance of the long fragments (*Sorbio*) and (*rionio*) from the text. If there is after all something in Dillemann's reasoning, it might be better to consider the *Dolo-* of *Dolocindo* as having arisen not from (*Sorbio*)*doni* but from **Duno*, that is Hod Hill as recorded by Ptolemy, which is in this area and is otherwise omitted from *Ravenna*.

*DUBABISSUM

SOURCE
Ravenna 107_{43} (= R&C 181): DUABSISIS, var. DUABSISSIS

Schnetz, citing instances in *Ravenna* of *s* for *r* and *s* for *v*, observes 'Litterarum ratione habita licet corrigere *Du[r]abrivis* (pro *Durobrivis*)'. In purely scribal terms this is reasonable, if extreme, but it should be noted that (*a*) there are no *Duro-* names in Scotland (this part of *Ravenna*'s list relates to S. Scotland), indeed, none north of Towcester; (*b*) the etymology suggested below is a sound one; (*c*) the possible pairing with *Abissum* linguistically and geographically seems logical enough.

DERIVATION. Making one slight change only in *Ravenna*'s form, R&C propose to read *Dubabissis*, which makes good sense and has analogies. The first element is **dŭbo-* 'black, dark' (Welsh and Breton *du*, Irish *dubh*), found in such ancient names as *Dubis* > Doubs (a tributary of the Saône, France), **Dubo-lindon* > Dublin, *Pennodubus* (Holder I. 1361). The rest is **ab-isso-*, for which see *Abissum*. The whole name is thus 'place on the dark water.' R&C note that this may well be directly associated with *Abissum*, making a pair of contrasting names.

For the ending, *Ravenna*'s *Abisson* clearly suggests *-um*, and *Devionisso* is in line with this. Consequently a notional nominative *-um* ending is here given.

IDENTIFICATION. Unknown, but apparently in southern Scotland.

DUBRIS (place)

SOURCES

AI 473_1 (Iter III): a Londinio ad portum DUBRIS
473_5 (Iter III): Ad portum DUBRIS
Ravenna 106_{35} (= R&C 71): DUBRIS
TP: DUBRIS
ND XXVIII_4 (*pictura*): DUBRIS
XXVIII_{14} (text): Praepositus militum Tungrecanorum, DUBRIS

DERIVATION. It is noteworthy that all records of the name, even those of *AI* set in a grammatical structure, show it as a locative plural in *-is*; like many other names, it had evidently become fossilised in that form (see p. 34). There is no evidence that a notional nominative **Dubrae* had any currency. Possibly the place was sometimes called *Portus Dubris*. The British name was **Dŭbrās* 'waters, stream' (perhaps 'streams'), plural of **dŭbro-* 'water' (Welsh *dwfr*, *dwr*, Cornish *dofer*, *dour*, Breton *dour*; Old Irish *dobur*); see Jackson *LHEB* 577, etc. This is also recorded by *Ravenna* in its river-list (next entry). The word was widely used as a place-name both alone and compounded. In Britain Wendover (Bucks.) and Andover (Hants.) include it; see *LHEB* 629–30. Watson *CPNS* 453–56 lists many Scottish names based on it, of British origin or borrowed by Irish from early Welsh. There are several Douvres in France; also the Dobra river, tributary of the Sella (Oviedo, Spain), and *Dubra* > Tauber, a tributary of the Main (Germany: Whatmough *DAG* 1215); *Vernodubrum* ('alder–water') > Verdouble rivers (Aude and Pyrénées Orientales, France), etc.

IDENTIFICATION. The Roman fort at Dover, Kent (TR 3141).

DUBRIS (*river*)

SOURCE

Ravenna 108_{38} (= R&C 265): DURBIS
There is scribal metathesis, *-rb-* for *-br-* (compare *Condercum*).

DERIVATION. See DUBRIS (place). The present entry records the original water-name, which in the only form known to us seems to have acquired the locative *-is* of the habitation-name even though the latter is secondary.

IDENTIFICATION. The river Dour, Kent.

DUMNA

SOURCES

Pliny *NH* IV, 104: DUMNAM (acc.)

Ptolemy II, 3, 14: Δοῦμνα νῆσος (= DUMNA INSULA); also VIII, 3, 10

DERIVATION. The name is British *dubno- *dumno-, the latter showing an assimilation which was already present at an early stage (in Common Celtic); both forms survived abundantly into classical times (Jackson *LHEB* 484, note). As an adjective the word meant 'deep' (perhaps also 'secret, mysterious') and as a noun 'world' (as in *Dumnorix* 'king of the world'); it is represented in the modern languages by Welsh *dwfn* 'deep', etc., Cornish *down*, Breton *doun*; Irish *domhan* 'world', *doimhin*, *domhain* 'deep', and there are Germanic cognates (*GPN* 196). The word is used alone in *Dumno* of *TP*, an unidentified site in Germany some 35 km from Bingen, and in compounds such as *Dumnissus* > Denzen (?). Of British interest are the compounded personal names *Dumnocoveros*, *Dubnovellaunos* (on a coin, Mack No. 282, with *Dumno-* on others), *Dumnovellaunos* (on a coin of the Coritani, Mack No. 466), *Cogidubnus*, *Togodumnus*, etc. There is also the ethnic name *Dumnonii* (below). For the present name *Dumna* various applications of the basic sense 'deep' might be suggested. Watson *CPNS* 40–41, noting that the name is feminine, proposed 'deep-sea isle'. Ogilvie and Richmond in their edition of the *Agricola* (1967; p. 32) think it may be a divine name and associate it with other deities apparently recorded in *Ravenna* in names of western Scottish islands. It might be 'deep' in the sense of 'furthest out' (as one says 'deep in the countryside').

IDENTIFICATION. The island of Lewis and Harris, or perhaps more properly the whole of the 'Long Island' from the Butt of Lewis to Barra Head; this is *Domon* in Old Irish and Gaelic (Watson *CPNS* 40–41, 72).

DUMNONII[1] (England)

SOURCES

Ptolemy II, 3, 13: Δουμνόνιοι (= DUMNONII), var. Δαμνόνιοι (= DAMNONII)

AI 486_{8-9} and 486_{17} (Iter XV): ISCA DUMNONIORUM; also (by error of the copyist) at 483_8 (Iter XII)

Ravenna 106_2 (= R&C 16): SCADUM NAMORUM, var. SCA DAMNAMORUM; also 106_{6-9} (= R&C 23): Iterum iuxta super scriptam civitatem SCADONIORUM est civitas quae dicitur...

TP: ISCADUMNONIORUM

Inscriptions: *RIB* 1843, a building-stone from Hadrian's Wall near Carvoran: CIVITAS DUM(NO)NI(ORUM)

RIB 1844, a building-stone from Hadrian's Wall near Thirlwall Castle: CIVITAS DUMNONI(ORUM)

(both are probably of A.D. 369)

The name is also present in a passage of Solinus (22, 7) as restored by Mommsen: see SILURA

There can be no doubt that the correct form of this name is *Dumnonii*, precisely as in *Dumnonii*[2], a northern offshoot or related body. The forms in *-a-* are repeated not only in records of *Dumnonii*[2] and *Dumnonium Promontorium*, but also in the case of *Dumnonia* (the region) in Gildas 28, where MS variants include *Damnone, Dannoniae, Domnanie* (gen.). The purely scribal nature of this error can be demonstrated also in the variant with *-a-* in *Ravenna* 106_2 (a text in which *a* for *u* is a common error); its repetition may tell something about the tradition and sources of our texts.

DERIVATION. The basis of the name is British **dubno-* **dumno-*, discussed under DUMNA, with the frequent **-ōn(o)-* suffix (see BREMETENACUM). Related names in Ireland include *Inber Domnann*, the old name of Malahide Bay north of Dublin, *Erris Domnann* in Co. Mayo, in which according to Rhys (1904) 298 *Domnann* is the genitive of an original **Domnū*, she being the goddess who was their eponymous ancestress. This is supported by the people known as the *Fir Domnann*, who were said by the Irish to be of British, not Goidelic, stock. Jackson in *Britannia*, I (1970), 75, interprets their name as meaning 'men (i.e. worshippers) of (the god) **Dumnū* or **Dumnōnū*', since early Irish names in *Fer*, plural *Fir*, are often followed by a divine name in the genitive. The British tribes are thus probably also 'worshippers of (the god) **Dumnōnos*'; perhaps he is 'the mysterious one'. The suggestion of Watson, *CPNS* 26, taking **dubno-* **dumno-* in its basic sense, that both tribes were 'men of the deep', that is 'miners', is not convincing, because although the people of Cornwall produced tin and those in Scotland had iron there is no evidence for true mining as such in the appropriate period in either case.

The name of the region of the present *Dumnonii*, *Dumnonia*, is first known to us in Gildas (see above). From it or from the tribal name derives – via Anglo-Saxon *Defnas* 'men of Devon' – the modern Devon; see *LHEB* 275, 488, 675.

IDENTIFICATION. A people of south-western Britain with their capital at *Isca*, Exeter. Ptolemy also attributes to them *Voliba*, *Uxella* and *Tamara*, all unidentified but all placed in the south-western peninsula, while the name *Dumnonium Promontorium* extends them to the Lizard. They occupied Devon, Cornwall and perhaps part of Somerset.

DUMNONII[2] (Scotland)

SOURCES

Ptolemy II, 3, 7: Δαμνόνιοι (= DAMNONII), var. Δαμνιοι (= DAMNII)
II, 3, 8: Δαμνονίους (= DAMNONIOS, acc.), var. Δαμνίους (= DAMNIOS)

Ravenna 108_{20} (= R&C 235): DAUNONI, var. DANNOM (but R&C read DANNONI)

DERIVATION. For this and for erroneous *-a-* in the sources, see DUMNONII[1]. *Ravenna*'s mention misled R&C. They take it to be 'a name in the list of *loca*, or meeting-places', but like others in this section and elsewhere, it is in fact a tribal name misread from a map as though it were a place-name. *Ravenna*'s main form is to be restored as *Damnoni*, with a further correction to *Dumnoni(i)*.

IDENTIFICATION. A people of southern Scotland. Ptolemy attributes to them *Colania* (Camelon?), *Vindogara* (at or near Irvine), *Coria* (Barochan Hill?), *Alauna* (Ardoch), *Lindum* (Drumquhassle?) and *Victoria* (Inchtuthil?), so that their territory should have extended from Ayrshire and Renfrewshire across the Forth–Clyde isthmus into Dunbartonshire, Stirlingshire and southern Perthshire.

DUMNONIUM PROMONTORIUM

SOURCES

Ptolemy II, 3, 2: Δαμνόνιον τὸ καὶ Ὄκρινον ἄκρον (= DAMNONIUM SIVE OCRINUM PROMONTORIUM)

Marcian II, 45: ...τὸ Δάμνιον ἄκρον (= DAMNIUM cape) τὸ καὶ Ὀκριον καλούμενον (= which is also called OCRIUM)

Marcian's form has lost a syllable through miscopying.

DERIVATION. For this and for the *-a-* in the sources, see DUMNONII[1]. The form is slightly peculiar in that *Dumnonium* looks adjectival, but it could have arisen from a failure by Ptolemy to understand an abbreviated way of writing a genitive plural; one would expect ιων (*-iorum*) here from a comparison with names of other capes which add a tribal designation.

IDENTIFICATION. The Lizard peninsula; for further discussion see OCRINUM.

DUNUM[1]

SOURCE

Ptolemy II, 3, 13: Δούνιον (= DUNIUM), the *polis* of the Durotriges

Ptolemy's form has an apparently intrusive *-i-* not paralleled elsewhere in records of *dunum* names; but compare Ptolemy's writing of the British *Mediolanum* with the same erroneous -ιον (*-ium*), and the same error with the same name twice in Gaul (II, 7, 6; II, 8, 9).

DERIVATION. See BRANODUNUM.

IDENTIFICATION. Probably the Roman fort at Hod Hill, Stourpaine, Dorset (ST 8510); for the reasons for preferring this to Maiden Castle, Dorset, see p. 145.

DUNUM[2]

SOURCE. D. F. Allen in *Britannia*, VII (1976), 96–100, identifies what is almost certainly a further *Dunum* name. Mack No. 313 is a coin of a ruler AMMINVS with the legend DVN on the reverse; its find-spot was not recorded, but another example was found at Folkestone (Kent) in 1965. Allen says: 'It seems probable, therefore, that all three types belong to a ruler with the name *Amminus*, and at least possible that his *oppidum* lay at a place whose name began with the letters *Dun*.' This name can, with near certainty, only have been *Dunum* (or rather, since it may have remained unromanised and is certainly not known in other sources, British **Dūnon*). Moreover, this word does not appear as a first element in compounds, so the name can only have been **Dunon* alone.

DERIVATION. See BRANODUNUM.

IDENTIFICATION. Probably a pre-Roman hill-fort in the area of Kent.

DUNUM SINUS

SOURCE

Ptolemy II, 3, 4: Δοῦνον κόλπος (= DUNUM SINUS)

DERIVATION. For *Dunum*, see BRANODUNUM. κόλπος/*sinus* is 'bay'.

IDENTIFICATION. Tees Bay, Durham.

DURCINATE of *Ravenna* 106_{52} (= R&C 100): see DUROLIPONTE

DURIARNO of *Ravenna* 105_{22} (= R&C 12): see DURNOVARIA

DURNOVARIA

SOURCES

AI 486_{15} (Iter XV): DURNONOVARIA
  483_{6} (copied by error from Iter XV): DURNONOVARIA, var. DURNOVARIA

Ravenna 105_{22} (= R&C 12); DURIARNO

AI's forms show in two cases extra *-no-*, by dittography; the correctness of *Durnovaria* is assured by the Old Welsh and Anglo-Saxon names of the town, respectively *Durngueir* and *Dornwaraceaster* (Jackson, *Britannia*, I (1970), 72). Of *Ravenna*'s form it should be noted that R&C accept it, place it 'In Devon, west of Exeter' and give it an etymology: < *duri* for **duro-* 'fort' plus *-arno-* a common river-name (Holder I. 218), hence 'fort on the river Arnus'. However, it is best regarded as a corruption of *Durnovaria*, as suggested by Miller in 1916. Scribally there is little problem; in the scripts used by the copyists, mistakes involving *a*/*o* and *n*, *v* (*u*) especially when adjacent to *i* are common, and one might conjecture a first stage in which the unfamiliar *Durno-* was reduced to the well-known *Duro-*; compare, perhaps, *Argentovaria* of *AI* 354_{3} and *TP* reduced to *Argentuaria* in Ammianus XXXI, 10, 8. Moreover, mention of *Durnovaria* is to be expected in *Ravenna*, which assiduously lists *civitas*-capitals to the number of ten (twelve, if we include *Petuaria* and *Verulamium*); among those hitherto thought to have been omitted, *Isur(i)um* is possibly concealed in the river-list. It is true that the expected tribal designation **Durotrigum* is not given by *Ravenna* for the present name, but neither is it in *AI*. If *Durnovaria* is placed by the Cosmographer among names that seem rather too westerly for it, the explanation could be that as in other cases (see AQUAE SULIS) he read the name from a map as though it referred to a place at its western rather than its eastern end.

DERIVATION. The name consists of British **durno-* 'fist', perhaps 'stone the size of a fist', found also in Scottish *Dornock*, *Dornoch*, both from **durnāco-* 'site covered with fist-sized pebbles' (Jackson). Modern derivatives include Welsh *dwrn* 'fist', *dyrnaid* 'handful', etc. In place-names abroad we find *Durnomagus* > Dormagen (Germany) and possibly *Durnis > Dorno (N. Italy). A. Carnoy in *RIO*, VI (1954), 5, adds a Dour (*Durnum* in 865) and Baudour (*Baldurnium* in 1010) in France. The **u̯ariā* element is obscure. It is found in *Argentovaria* (above) and may be connected with the base of British *Varar*, *Varis*, in which case it is a water-name. If this is right, the name is a description of the site of Dorchester (low-lying on a river) and could not be – as Watson *CPNS* 488 speculates – the name of Maiden Castle transferred to the new town.

IDENTIFICATION. The Roman city of Dorchester, Dorset (SY 6990), almost certainly the capital of the *Durotriges*. The absence of the tribal suffix from all surviving references may be related to the fact that at some stage the *Civitas Durotrigum* appears to have been divided in two (see LINDINIS).

DUROBRIVAE[1]

SOURCES

Writing-tablet: A tablet found in London in 1959 was published by E. G. Turner and O. Skutsch in *JRS*, L (1960), 108–11. The relevant part is: scito me manẹrẹ aput [Duro]ḅriụas et cabạḅi et...

AI 472_3 (Iter II): DUROBROVIS, var. DUROPROVIS
473_3 (Iter III): DUBOBRIUS
473_8 (Iter IV): DUROBRIVIS

Ravenna 106_{37} (= R&C 74): DUROBRABIS
106_{39} (= R&C 77): BRINAVIS

TP: RORIBIS

Of the writing-tablet, it is argued that *Duro* fits the space available (*Duroco* of *Durocobrivae* would not), and that Rochester rather than Water Newton is the likelier candidate; the letter is addressed to a recipient in London. Forms given by *AI* illustrate a number of the common kinds of miscopying. For *TP*'s form it was suggested by Miller in 1916 that like other names it lost letters by having been written across the join of the sheets (of which the first was later lost), hence in the surviving copy [*Du*]*roribis* with *-b-* omitted and as often *b* for *v*. As for Ravenna's second entry, which R&C took literally and for which Williams provided an etymology, it seems to have arisen from *Duro/brivis* written in two parts, of which the first was neglected when the name was read from a map by the Cosmographer; this was miscopied as **Bravis* or **Brabis*, and a correction *iv* (*iu*) written in over the name was misread *in* and then incorporated into the name; such is the ingenious reasoning of Dillemann (p. 67). There can be little doubt that this is right; the sequence in the Cosmography – *Landini, Tamese, Brinavis* – shows us the direction the compiler's eye was taking as he read his map-source(s), unaware that he was duplicating, as often.

Despite the prevalence of locative forms in records of this name (and in one record of the next name), the writing-tablet with *-as* and *AI*'s form for *Durobrivae*[2] show that the name was or could be declined; we have therefore stated it as a nominative.

DERIVATION. The name is British **Durobrīụās*, a plural. The first element is **dŭro-* 'fort, walled town', apparently usually on low ground (and named in contrast to **dūno-* 'hill-fort'): this is cognate with Latin *fores, forum*, German *Tor, Tür*, English *door*, but is not related to Latin *dūrus* 'hard', which has *ū* (Welsh *dir*, Irish *dúr*). The element was very widely used, always compounded; see the names that follow in this List, and *Lactodurum*, the only British instance in which **dŭro-* appears in second place. The element appears in names all over Gaul and as far east as Moesia, but is rare in Iberia where only two examples are known (*Ocelodurum* now Zamora in W. Spain, and *Octodurum* a *polis* of the Vaccaei in Hispania Tarraconensis, Ptolemy II, 6, 49, an unknown site). This may indicate that **dŭro-* names constitute a somewhat late stratum of Celtic toponymy. Holder I. 1383 has many names; those with the element in second place are perhaps three times as numerous as those that have it in first place. When in second place *-dŭrum* was unstressed, which explains why in the Latin sources its vowel is liable to some variation and even elision, and why names having this element are sometimes wrongly referred to other roots. Often *-doro -dorum* are found, as in British *Lactodoro* of *AI*. Continental instances include *Hicciodero* and *Iciodiro* for *Icciodurum*, *Brivoduorum* for *Brivodurum*, *Autesiodor* for *Autessiodurum*, and *Boiotrum* for *Boiodurum* (mention of these may help in further identifications). The *-durum* names were taken into Latin as neuters (despite early *Octodurus* (Martigny, Switzerland) in Caesar *BG* III, 1).

The second element is British **brīu̯ā* 'bridge', abundantly documented in Gaulish (Vincent 208), rare in Iberia and seemingly unknown in the easterly Celtic regions. It is present in the Vienna Glossary: *brio* = 'ponte'. It is found alone and compounded in both first and second places. In *Brivodurum* > Briare (Loiret, France) the elements of the present British name are reversed. Holder I. 610 lists many names; scribal and spoken variations which appear include *Carobriis* for **Carobrivis* (further reduced in one text to *Gabris*), *Briodurum* for *Brivodurum* (cf. *brio* in the Glossary), and *Bruusara* for *Brivisara* or *Briva Isarae*. *Ravenna* 62_{20} even records *Brivodurum* as *Heliodorum*. It is not easy to see the justification for the two British *-brivae* names being plural in form, but they are clearly so in all our sources, and also in some (by no means all) of the Continental cases (a plural preserved in several French *Brives*, *Brèves*, etc.). Many were small places which can have boasted only one bridge, and this may well have been true also of the British places with a bridge apiece (over the Medway and Nene respectively). Moreover, this plural is reflected in Romano-British *Pontibus* and *Tripontium* (not in *Ad Pontem*, *Pons Aelius*) which might be translations of earlier **briva* names (rather than named in Latin because the bridges were post-Conquest constructions, as *Pons Aelius* certainly was). It may be that the names both Celtic and Latin were plural because rather than a single unified span, a series of stages or spans, or at first no doubt piles of stones in the river, was in question; for *Tripontium* in particular, 'three-stage bridge' seems to be indicated. See also DUROCOBRIVIS.

The name means, then, 'bridge(s)-fort'. The whole question of how these *Duro-* places received their names is discussed in *Britannia*, II (1971), xvi–xvii, and is of interest for many other types of name also. The *Duro-* names seem to have been taken into Latin usage in the early Roman period (they are not found north of Water Newton and Towcester in the Midlands) and can only signify 'fort'; an alternative sense for British **dŭro-*, 'walled town', is certainly possible but is here inapplicable because the towns in question did not receive their walls until long after the naming must have occurred. In some cases pre-Conquest Belgic settlement is known at the sites, but even if these had earthworks they would hardly qualify as **dŭro-* places, and a name in *-dunum* would be expected. That Celtic names should have been adopted for Roman forts is therefore something of a mystery; reasons are suggested in *Britannia*. It has to be remembered, in addition to what is mentioned there, that the Romans were well acquainted with Celtic naming-habits in Gaul, and that names involving latinised *durum* abounded there and had been established in Latin usage for nearly a century when the conquest of Britain was begun. There may thus have been a degree of conventionalism in the process, rather than any direct response to peculiarly British circumstances (compare, perhaps, British *Branodunum*).

IDENTIFICATION. The Roman town at Rochester, Kent (TQ 7468). Rochester was an important centre in the later Iron age and although no pre-Roman fortifications have been positively identified it is likely enough that some existed, but if the 'certain river' referred to by Cassius Dio LX, 20, 2 (p. 60 above) was, as the context suggests, the Medway, there was evidently no pre-Roman bridge. Remains of the Roman bridge over the Medway, on the other hand, have been noted and an early Roman fort to protect the crossing must have existed, probably on the site now occupied by the castle. Since the Roman town walls were not built until after A.D. 200, the name must originally have referred to this fort (perhaps replacing the name of the unit in garrison) and was later transferred to the town which succeeded it.

Note. Bede in II, 3 knew the ancient name, *in civitate Dorubrevi*, presumably through ecclesiastical tradition renewed by Augustine from Rome. Elsewhere he used the Anglo-Saxon form *Hrofi*, etc., which derives from the Romano-British name. For discussion of this, see *LHEB* 267.

DUROBRIVAE[2]

SOURCES

Mortarium stamp: CUNOARUS VICO DURO(BRIVAE); examples are known from Castor and South Shields (Frere, 1974[2], Note 20 to Chapter 10)

Mortarium mark: SENNIΛNUS DUROBRIVIS URI[T], painted on a fragment of a mortarium found in the R. Nene at Water Newton; *JRS*, XXX (1940), 190

AI 475_1 (Iter V): DUROBRIVAS

Ravenna 106_{54} (= R&C 102): DUROBRISIN

In the above, the expanded name in the mortarium stamp could well be *Duro(brivis)*, i.e. '(made by) Cunoarus in the *vicus* at Durobrivae'. *Ravenna*'s form seems to involve *-isin* as a metathesis of *-inis*, in itself a miscopying of *-ivis*.

DERIVATION. See DUROBRIVAE[1].

IDENTIFICATION. The Roman town at Chesterton, Water Newton, Huntingdonshire (TL 1297). Neither air photographs nor small finds indicate any notable Iron Age settlement here and there is no context for a pre-Roman bridge. An early Roman fort is known, however, and the piers of the Roman bridge carrying Ermine Street over the river Nene have been noted. The Roman town walls are of much later construction, so that here, as with *Durobrivae*[1], the name must have been applied in the first instance to the early Roman fort and then transferred to the town which succeeded it.

*DUROCINTUM (?)

SOURCE

Ravenna 106_{12} (= R&C 38): DOLOCINDO

DERIVATION. Under *Dolocindo* we have stated what arguments there are for accepting that as a good form, and have shown what its etymology might be. On balance, however, it seems more likely that *Ravenna* has corrupted another *Duro-* name (see DUROBRIVAE[1]). Examples of *Doro-* for *Duro-* are common in later Latin sources (Vulgar Latin *o* for classical *ŭ*), and *l* for *r* is a simple miscopying (see p. 203). The second element requires little emendation; it is the same as the first element in British **Cintocelum*, and is common in place-names and personal names. A meaning 'chief fort, principal fort' seems indicated.

There is one grave objection. Williams observes that the adjective **cinto-* should come in first place; it does so in all the compound names into which it enters. However, the suggested **Durocintum* receives strong support from an assumed Gaulish **Cintodurum* > Santoyre (*Centoyre*, 1278), now a tributary of the Rue which flows north out of the Massif Central (France), a fort-name evidently transferred at a late stage to a river. If this does in fact make a pair with the British name, such reversals of elements are by no means rare. British **Durocintum* might be for a 'purer' **Cintodurum*; compare *Boioduro* *AI* 249_5, whose variant **Dur(o)boium* > Durbuy (Luxembourg); **Captodurum* whose variant *Dur(o)captum* > Drucat (Somme, France); **Clarodurum* whose variant *Dur(o)clarum* > Duclair (Seine-Maritime, France); and **Tincodurum* whose variant *Dur(o)tincum* > Dourdan (Seine-et-Oise, France). Gaulish **Cintodurum* is thought by Dauzat *TF* 168–69 to have been originally the name of the fort at Dienne.

IDENTIFICATION. Unknown, but apparently not far from Gloucester.

DUROCOBRIVIS

SOURCE

AI 471_2 (Iter II): DUROCOBRIVIS
476_9 (Iter VI): DUROCOBRIUS
479_7 (Iter VIII): DUROCOBRIVIS

For a reason that will be shown, this name (unlike the two *Durobrivae*) has been cited as a fossilised locative in *-is*; see ANICETIS.

DERIVATION. This name is more problematical than might appear at first glance. In form it does not satisfy Jackson, who notes in *Britannia*, I (1970), 73, that *-co-* is hardly British 'with' for this was **com-*, and the name should have been **-combrīu̯ās*. As for the suggested meaning, 'walled town (better, "fort") with the joined bridges', although the second element appears to coincide with *-brivae* in other names, there is no bridge at Dunstable (whose identification is sure) and no river.

On the *-co-* question, it is possible, first, that the infix is not very meaningful. Holder I. 1384 has *Domnoveros* and *Domnocoveros* as apparently forms of the same name (perhaps adjectival, on coins of Volisios in Britain). Rhys (1904) 40 wondered whether *Domnoco-* might not be merely a diminutive of *Domno-*. A diminutive of 'fort' (**duro-*) would be perfectly acceptable, as in Latin *castrum–castellum*.

A better possibility is that there existed a British version of Gaulish *du̯orico-* 'porticus' recorded in an inscription (Holder I. 1390: *Sacer Peroco ieuru dvorico V S L M*), itself a derivative of **duro-* (**du̯oro-n*). Holder thinks that this is present in *TP*'s *Duroico Regum* (for **Durocoregum* > Domqueur, Somme, France; second element Gaulish **rigo-* 'king') and in British *Duroco-brivis*. But 'portico-bridge' does not make good sense, and the possibility arises that we should look for something other than **brīu̯ā* 'bridge' as the second element. It is not open to us to suggest that *AI*'s forms require adjustment, nor that **brīu̯ā* was used for any structure other than 'bridge over water' in any British record. However, there is a possible way forward in the study by M. G. Tibiletti Bruno in the *Rendiconti (Lett.)... Istituto Lombardo*, CI. 3 (1967), 19, of the word *prviam* in a Lepontic–Ligurian funerary text from Vergiate near Sesto Calende. In this word *p* is for *b*, and the word seems identical to Germanic * *bruįō* > **bruggiō*- etc., 'bridge': 'Si tratterà quindi di qualche cosa, forse una cella mortuaria, formata di tavole.' The notion 'plank, board' (*tavola*) seems to be fundamental to other words discussed in the same study, and one wonders whether Celtic **brīųā* in any way retained this primary sense (that of 'bridge' being secondary, though eventually dominant). The example quoted is naturally too remote for there to be any certainty, but there are attractions about it: 'portico-(of)-planks' would not be an impossible name for a fort by any means, and a Celtic **brīųō*- (singular; cf. perhaps *brio* glossed 'ponte' in the Vienna Glossary) might explain why so many of the latinised 'bridge'-names have to have plural form, -*brivae* (see also DUROBRIVAE[1] on this aspect), if they express the idea of 'planks collectively that form a bridge'. In the same paper, Tibiletti Bruno takes up an idea of R. Hertz (1965) on Latin *ponto* 'ferry' being a loan-translation of a lost Celtic (Gaulish) **brīųō*- 'ferry' ('plank-boat'?); there may well be a good deal still to be learned in this area.

IDENTIFICATION. The Roman settlement at Dunstable, Bedfordshire (TL 0121).

DUROCORNOVIUM[1]

SOURCE
AI 485_5 (Iter XIII): DUROCORNOVIO

DERIVATION. For the first element, see DUROBRIVAE[1]; for the second, CORNOVII[1]. The sense is evidently 'fort of the Cornovii people'. The place is distinct from *Durocornovium*[2] in the far south-west, even though Holder thought they were the same. We presumably have here a case in which a *Duro*- name does refer to a native, not a Roman fort, since latinised *Durocornovium* is virtually a transliteration of British **Durocornoųion*; had the name been a new post-Conquest one, we might have anticipated **Durocornoviorum*, but for neither name do our sources suggest this. The pattern *Duro*- plus tribal name seems to be rare, but compare *Durocatalauni* in Gaul (**Catalaunis* > Châlons-sur-Marne, France).

IDENTIFICATION. The Roman settlement at Nythe Farm, Wanborough, Wiltshire (SU 1985). Though some Neronian *terra sigillata* has been found, excavation has not revealed an early Roman fort, and the nearest major Iron Age settlement is at Liddington Castle, 3½ miles to the south. On the second element of the name see the note under *Cornovii*[2].

DUROCORNOVIUM[2]

SOURCE
Ravenna 105_{48} (= R&C 6): PUROCORONAVIS, var. PUROCORONAINS

Here *Ravenna*'s initial *P* for *D* is paralleled in *D* for *P* of *Decuaria* (= *Petuaria*). There is also a scribal assimilation to Latin *corona*. The form on the map which *Ravenna* used as a source may well have had -*cornavio*, with -*a*-, a spelling which is mistaken but found in other records of this people.

DERIVATION. See the previous entry; the same remarks apply.

IDENTIFICATION. Unknown, but apparently in south-west Britain. See the note under *Cornovii*[2] for a possible connection with Cornwall.

DUROLEVUM

SOURCES

AI 472_4 (Iter II): DUROLEVO
Ravenna 108_{37} (= R&C 262): DUROLAVI, vars. DURALAVI, DUROLAM
TP: DUROLEVO

The forms with *-lev-* are correct, and *AI* and *TP* agree on this. For *a/e* miscopying by *Ravenna*, see p. 203. In *Ravenna*, the name appears in the river-list, and it was taken as a river by R&C ('perhaps the Swale'); but it is certainly a habitation-name which the Cosmographer misread from a map as though it were a river, presumably because it was written on the line of a river. *Duro-* indicates the name of a fort, and moreover *Ravenna* cites the name in the locative, which could never be used for rivers.

DERIVATION. For the first element, see DUROBRIVAE[1]. The second element is probably a river-name, perhaps **Levus* when latinised; in Celtic it would have been based on **leu̯i̯o-* 'smooth' (Latin *levis*), present also in British *Leviodunum*, **Levobrinta*, and abroad in the river *Leva* > Lieve, a tributary of the Scheldt, with *Levae Fanum* (*TP*: *Leve Fano*) upon it. The names of two modern Leven rivers, in Lancashire and Yorkshire N.R., are from the same root. The British name *Durolevum* can therefore be interpreted 'fort on the smooth-flowing river'.

IDENTIFICATION. Unknown, but apparently near Sittingbourne, Kent, and so near the river Swale, as R&C noted; Ekwall, *ERN*, regards this as probably of Germanic origin, so this may be the river in question. An early Roman fort here is to be expected and it may even be the place referred to by Cassius Dio LX, 20, 2, where Aulus Plautius left a garrison after receiving the envoys of the *Dobunni*.

DUROLIPONTE

SOURCES

AI 474_8 (Iter V): DUROLIPONTE
Ravenna 106_{52} (= R&C 100): DURCINATE

R&C emend *Ravenna*'s form to **Curcinate* and give an etymology based on the personal name *Curcinus*. But given the frequency of *Duro-* names in southern Britain, the fact that *Duro-* is found as *Dur-* in Continental records, the fact that a name corresponding to *AI*'s *Duroliponte* is otherwise omitted from *Ravenna* (which omits very few road-junctions), and the order Colchester–*Durcinate*–Godmanchester (?) – Water Newton which is being followed, it is very hard to resist the probability that *Durcinate* is a corrupt version of *Duroliponte*. The miscopying is less easy to explain, but a version **Durlipōte* (with *-n-* indicated by a stroke over the preceding letter) at some intermediate stage causes no problem, and *a/o* are often confused also. The equation cannot be absolutely affirmed, but seems likely.

DERIVATION. The name does not have a notional Latin nominative *-pons*, and was not originally connected with *-ponte* in Latin at all, for this would leave the *-li-* unexplained. Jackson in *Britannia*, I (1970), 73, explains the name as involving British **u̯lipo-* 'wet' (Welsh *gwlyb*), from Indo-European **(u̯)leiqᵘ* (cf. Latin *liquidus*, etc.) 'damp; flowing', with **-ont-ī-* or **-ont-iā* suffixes. There was a river *Liquentia* near Venice. Assimilation to Latin *pons*, *pontem* may have occurred early; Jackson notes that the *-ul-* of the Celtic nominative **Durou̯liponti* would be perceived by Romans as *-l-*, who would also take the form as a Latin locative-ablative of *pons*. There is thus a compound of *Duro-* (see DUROBRIVAE[1]) with a river-name **u̯lipontī* 'wet river', perhaps 'overflowing, boggy river'. This is much the most satisfying explanation of this difficult name.

Jackson sees one problem still, in that '**Duro-* does not elsewhere seem to be compounded with *names*, whether of rivers or otherwise'; but we may compare *Durolevum*, also *Ernodurum* of *AI* 460_3 (for **Arnodurum*) 'fort on the *Arno*-river' now St Ambroix-sur-Arnon (Cher, France).

IDENTIFICATION. The Roman town (preceded by an early fort) at Cambridge (TL 4459).

DUROLITUM

SOURCE

AI 480_7 (Iter IX): DUROLITO

DERIVATION. For *Duro-*, see DUROBRIVAE[1]. The second element is probably original **-ritu* 'ford', for which see ANDERITUM; hence 'fort at the ford'. A dissimilation of *r—r* to *r—l* has taken place; this could have occurred either in British (**Duroriton*) or within Latin. H. Birkhan in *Germanen und Kelten*... (Vienna, 1970), note to p. 426, takes the name as having original **litus* 'broad', but this seems less satisfactory.

IDENTIFICATION. Probably the Roman settlement at Little London, Chigwell, Essex (TQ 4596). On the analogy of *Durobrivae* (q.v.) an early Roman fort should await discovery here.

DUROTRIGES (?)

SOURCES

Ptolemy II, 3, 13: Δουρότριγες (= DUROTRIGES)

Inscriptions

RIB 1672, a building-stone from near Cawfields on Hadrian's Wall: C(IVITAS) DUR(O)TR(I)G(UM) [L]ENDIN(I)ESIS

RIB 1673, a building-stone from near Housesteads on Hadrian's Wall: CI(VITAS) DUROTRAG(UM) LENDINIESI[S]

(Both stones are probably of A.D. 369. For the spelling of the adjectival form of the *civitas*-name, see LINDINIS)

It is by no means certain that the name has *-i-*, though it is traditionally cited in this form. While this is present in all the Ptolemy MSS, it could be an error going back to the archetype or to Marinus. *RIB* 1672 omits the vowel, but *RIB* 1673 plainly writes *-a-* (Λ) and it is not likely that a member of the *civitas* literate enough to be given the task of cutting the inscription would mistake the spelling of the name of his own people. For a similar (reverse) error in Ptolemy, compare VINDOGARA, which has Οὐανδο- (= *Vando-*) in all the MSS at II, 3, 7.

DERIVATION. This name is obscure. It might be divided *Duro-triges* or *Durot-riges*. It is tempting to think it another of the many names in **dŭro-* 'fort', although in Britain we know this element chiefly applied to early Roman forts on low ground, so that it could hardly apply particularly in the name of a tribe whose region contains many spectacular hill-forts (which would have had **-dūnon* names). However, this **dŭro-* does enter into a few names such as the two British *Durocornovium* and in Gaul ethnic *Duro-*

casses. Holder suggested (I. 1387) that the name might be a reduction of older **Durot(o)-riges*, that is **dŭro-* 'fort' with some kind of suffix or infix when in composition; but then there is no parallel for this among all the very numerous *Duro-* names.

The second element is possibly *-rīges*, a plural of **rīg-* 'king' which appears in several ethnic names, such as Gaulish *Bituriges* 'kings of the world'. Watson *CPNS* 16, note, identifies an element *-raige* (for older *-rige*?) in Irish ethnic names, e.g. *Dartraige* (*dart* 'year-old bull or heifer') > Dartry, *Cattraige* (*catt* 'wild cat'), *Luchraige* (*luch* 'mouse'), and even though these seem somewhat unheroic names, they may have had totemic significance and are acceptable enough; but we have no evidence that in the present name **durot-* is an animal-name which would fit into this series. If the second element is an unknown *-triges*, the British name might be paralleled by the Ἀλλότριγες (= *Allotriges*: Strabo III, 4, 7; in Ptolemy II, 6, 7 they are the Αὐτριγόνες = *Autrigones*), of Hispania Tarraconensis, with *Allo-* probably as in *Allobroges* of Gaul.

If *-a-* is right, the etymological possibilities are less good. A *-rag-* element is unknown, but *-trag-* is said by Dottin *LG* 193 to be a 'terme de composé' and is related by him to Irish *traig* 'foot' and Welsh *traed* (pl.). But this does not relate well semantically to a first element **duro-*. The name must be left unresolved.

IDENTIFICATION. A people of southern Britain with their capital at *Durnovaria*, Dorchester; for the probability that their *civitas* was at some time subdivided, with a second capital at Ilchester, see *Lindinis*. Ptolemy attributes to them only *Dunum* (= *Dunium*, Hod Hill?), but the distribution of their pre-Roman coins indicates that they occupied Dorset, parts of Wiltshire, Hampshire and Somerset, and perhaps the extreme eastern part of Devon.

DUROVERNUM CANTIACORUM

SOURCES

Ptolemy II, 3, 12: Δαρούερνον (= DARVERNUM), a *polis* of the Cantii: var. Δαρούενον (= DARVENUM)

AI 472_5 (Iter II): DURORUERNO

473_4 (Iter III): DURARUENO

473_9 (Iter IV): DURARUENNO

Ravenna 106_{36} (= R&C 72): DURO AVERNO CANTIACORUM

TP: DUROAVERUS

Ptolemy's form might lead one to think of an etymon in Celtic **daru-* 'oak'; possibly this was in the mind of those who compiled his source. In *AI* it is plain that confusion involving *-r-* set in at an early stage, possibly in the archetype. *Ravenna* shows an attempted rationalisation by compiler or copyist on the basis of classical *Avernus* (perhaps supported by taking *Duro-* as the Latin adjective 'hard, tough'); this form seems to be related to *TP*'s, and may indicate something about a common source (see p. 153).

DERIVATION. For *Duro-*, see DUROBRIVAE[1]. The second element is British **u̯erno-* 'alder; alder-swamp, marsh' (Welsh *gwern* 'alder'; present in such names as *Warrenburn* in Northumberland and *Werneth* in Cheshire). This was taken into Vulgar Latin and survives as *vern* 'alder' in Catalan, with similar words in several dialects of S. France and Italy. The element is found commonly in Gaulish names, e.g. *Vernodubrum* ('alder-water') > Verdouble rivers (Aude and Pyrénées Orientales, France), *Vernetum* > Vernet (many names in France), **Vernomagus* > Vernon (Eure, France); see Dottin *LG* 74, Holder III. 223, Whatmough *DAG* 476–77, etc. The only other British place-name that may contain it is *Vernalis*. There is the divine name or attribute recorded in *RIB* 1102 (Ebchester), *Deo Vernostono Cocidio*. The name is, then, 'alder-fort', or 'walled town by the alder-swamp' (Jackson).

IDENTIFICATION. The Roman city of Canterbury, Kent (TR 1457). The *Duro-* element probably refers here to the important pre-Roman settlement rather than to the suspected Roman fort.

Note. Anglo-Saxon *Cantwaraburg* > Canterbury is recorded from A.D. 754, 'stronghold of the men of Kent' (but see CANTIACI). The Romano-British name survived for a long time beside this. The *Anglo-Saxon Chronicle* under A.D. 604 calls it *Dorwiccaestre*, and a charter of 605 calls one of the roads leading to the town *Drutingstraet*, the first part of this being probably < *Dorwit* (with *-wit* for *-wic*) + *ingas*, from which one may suppose an earlier transitional **Dor-wic* (Latin *vicus*, taken early into Anglo-Saxon). In the important ecclesiastical tradition more learned forms survived also. Bede has *in Doruverni* (I, 26), *in Doruverni civitate* (V, 23), and adjectival forms built on this on several occasions. Innumerable medieval records echo these forms, with variants: *in Dorobernia*, *Dorobernensis archiepiscopus*, etc. The forms are discussed by Zachrisson (1927) 77 and Jackson *LHEB* 259–60; *Doro-* is near-standard in late Latin sources for *Duro-* (in Vulgar Latin *o* is for classical *ŭ*). The name was presumably brought anew from the records of the Roman church by Augustine or his successors, and given definitive form by Bede's authority.

DUROVIGUTUM

SOURCE

Ravenna 106_{53} (= R&C 101): DURO VIGUTO

DERIVATION. For *Duro-*, see DUROBRIVAE[1]. The second element is mysterious and may be corrupt, but no emendation suggests itself. R&C allude hopefully to Holder's *Vegeto(n)*, III. 137, a personal name, and to his *Vigato villa* (*c.* 570) III. 315, concluding that the sense is 'fort of Vigutus'; but in all the abundant records *Duro-* never appears compounded with a personal name.

IDENTIFICATION. Almost certainly the Roman town at Godmanchester, Huntingdonshire (TL 2470), where Ermine Street crosses the river Ouse and is joined by two other roads, from Cambridge and Sandy. Extensive excavation here has produced no evidence of pre-Roman occupation, and the *Duro-* element is most likely to refer to the early Roman fort which preceded the development of the town.

EBIO of *Ravenna* 107_{40} (= R&C 176): see EPIDIUM

EBUDAE

SOURCES

Pliny *NH* IV, 103: XXX HEBUDES

Ptolemy II, 2, 10: Above *Ivernia* lie islands which are called Αἰβοῦδαι (= AEBUDAE), five in number, of which the most westerly is called Αἰβοῦδα (= AEBUDA)...the next towards the east likewise Αἰβοῦδα (= AEBUDA); vars. in MS U Ἔβουδαι (= EBUDAE), Ἔβουδα (= EBUDA)

I, 24, I (table): per EBUDAS insulas

Almagest II, 6, 28: 'Εβούδων (gen.: = EBUDARUM)

Solinus (Additamenta of later date) XXII, 12: EBUDES; ab EBUDIBUS (abl. pl.)

Marcian: a lacuna in his surviving text is filled by Stephanus of Byzantium: 'Αιβοῦδαι (= AEBUDAE), with ethnic Αἰβουδαῖος (= AEBUDAEUS)

The sources, despite appearances, agree about the form. Pliny's *H-* is decorative (it was silent in Latin). The forms with *E-* (rather than *Ae-*) seem to be the more correct, as Jackson explains in *LHEB* 34: 'In Ptolemy's time αι was still a diphthong, but soon after it became an open *ĕ*, and so British *ĕ* is often written αι, as in Αἰβουδαι for 'Εβουδαι.'

DERIVATION. The correctness of *Ebudae* (in the sources, as above) is supported by Watson *CPNS* 38: he cites MacNeill, who thought the *Ibdaig* tribe of Ireland (earlier *Tuath Iboth*, *Fir Iboth*) represented an ancient **Ebudāci* 'men of the *Ebudae*'; their modern Gaelic name – derived from British – is *Ibdach*. No etymology suggests itself within Celtic, and the name of both islands and tribe may well be pre-Celtic.

As mentioned under *Aemodae*, we cannot be entirely sure that the present *Ebudae* are not to be equated with them; but Ptolemy at least associates the present islands with Ireland, and the link with the Irish tribal name is a further indication that the present *Ebudae* are distinct from the *Aemodae*. Modern *Hebrides* derives from an English misreading of Solinus's *Ebudes*, and with reference to the two large groups of outlying islands, is a misapplication of the ancient name.

IDENTIFICATION. The Inner Hebrides excluding Skye but apparently including Rathlin (*Ricina* ?) and perhaps Kintyre (*Epidium*, q.v.); see Chapter III, p. 114.

EBURACUM

SOURCES

(a) Geographical, itineraries, etc.

Ptolemy II, 3, 10: 'Εβόρακον, Λεγίων ς' Νικηφόρος (= EBORACUM, LEGIO VI VICTRIX), a *polis* of the Brigantes

VIII, 3, 7: 'Εβόρακον (= EBORACUM)

AI 466_1 (Iter I): EBURACUM leug. VI Victrix

468_4 (Iter II): EBURACUM

475_7 (Iter V): EBURACO

478_6 (Iter VIII): ab EBURACO

Ravenna 107_{14} (= R&C 137): EBURACUM

ND XL_3 (*pictura*): SEXTAE

XL_{18} (text): Praefectus legionis sextae [addition of editor: victricis, EBURACI]

(b) Inscriptions

JRS, XI (1921), 101–107 (= Burn, 1969, No. 65, pp. 50–51): an altar set up at Bordeaux by M. Aurelius Lunaris, a SEVIR AUG(USTALIS) COL(ONIARUM) EBOR(ACI) ET LIND(I), as a result of a vow taken when he sailed from York, AB EBORACI AVECT(US): A.D. 237

RIB 2274, a milestone of A.D. 251–253 found near Castleford on the road from Tadcaster to Doncaster: EB(ORACO) M P XXII

RIB 648, part of a dedication to Hercules by two men of EBUR, restored as [COL(ONIAE)] EBUR[ACENSIS]

RIB 657, the top of an altar found in York: NUM(INI) AUG(USTI) ET GEN(IO) EḄ[OR(ACI)]

RIB 674 (= Burn, 1969, No. 68, p. 53): a stone coffin found in York, of FL[A]VI BELLATORIS DEC-

(URIONIS) COL(ONIAE) EBORACENS(IS)

RIB 678, a stone coffin found near York: M(ARCUS) VEREC(UNDIUS) DIOGENES SEVIR COL(ONIAE) EBOR(ACENSIS)

CIL XIII. 3162: in the 'Marble of Thorigny' text, AD LEGIONEM SEXT-[AM] occurs meaning 'at York'

(c) Legal, literary and historical

A rescript issued in the Emperor's name on 5 May 210 contains EBORACI (locative); *Codex Justinianus*, III, 32, 1

Aurelius Victor 20, 27: in Britanniae municipio, cui EBORACI nomen

Historia Augusta (Severus), XIX, 1: Periit EBORACI in Britannia

Eutropius VIII, 19, 1: EBORACI (locative); X, 1, 3: EBORACI (locative)

St Jerome, *Interpretatio Chronicae Eusebii*, A.D. 212, A.D. 309: EBORACI (locative)

Excerpta Valesiana, I, 2, 4: EBORACI (locative)

Orosius VII, 17, 8: EBORACUM

Prosper Tiro 764: EBURACI (locative), var. EBORACI
976: EBORACI (locative)

Cassiodorus A.U.C. 893 (A.D. 211): EBORACUM

On these sources, *RIB* p. 215 points out that a distinction should be made between *Eboracum*, the fortress of Legio VI Victrix on the left bank of the Ouse, and *Colonia Eboracensis* on the right bank, but both fortress and Colonia were doubtless currently known by the single name *Eboracum* in ordinary usage. An alternative usage for the fortress is hinted at by *ND* if we take the textual *Sextae* as a sort of locative and regard the text as complete as it stands; the fact that *Sextae* is the caption of *ND*'s *pictura* supports this, as does the reference in the Marble of Thorigny. It could be, then, that *ND* needs no addition; but see the arguments of C. E. Stevens in *Arch.J.*, XCVII (1940), 141.

DERIVATION. The more classical form is *Eburacum* (British **Ebŭrācon*), preserved by *AI*, *Ravenna* and *ND*, but by only one of the inscriptions (*RIB* 648). It is notable that already Ptolemy records *Ebor-*, and that all but one of the literary texts have this too; Prosper Tiro has both. While Ptolemy's form might be open to doubt, the later texts showing *-o-* record the Vulgar Latin process *ŭ* (stressed and unstressed) > *o*, a process which did not occur in British until the sixth century, and then only in the south-west (Jackson); instances from Vulgar Latin in Britain are known. Bede has both forms, according to the source he was following in numerous mentions of the city: with *u*, *Eburaci* (locative) in II, 14, II, 20 and II, 28; also *Eburacum* (acc.) II, 20; with *o*, *apud Eboracum* I, 5 when mentioning the death of Severus. These are references to the old city. When talking of the episcopal see, Bede strangely made the name feminine: *ad Eburacam . . . civitatem* I, 29; *per Eburacae episcopum* I, 29; with *u/o* variation again in the adjectival form, *Eburacensis* II, 18, and *Eboracensis* IV, 3. Already in Roman times ecclesiastical usage had adopted the form with Vulgar Latin *o*, as shown by the name of the bishop who attended the Council of Arles in 314, *Eborius*. For a different explanation of the *u/o* change, with a very full account of the name as a whole, see A. H. Smith in *EPNS*, XIV, 278–80.

Apart from the examples of *Eboraci* properly employed as a locative in the full sentences of literary texts, there is evidence that the fossilised locative *Eboraci* was the name of the city in the third century. The inscription of Bordeaux has *ab Eboraci* (instead of the expected *ab*

Eboraco), and Aurelius Victor writes *Eboraci* as a pseudo-nominative.

British **Ebŭr-āco-n* had one of two possible senses. **Ebŭro-* was 'yew' (Irish *ibhar* glossed 'taxus'; modern Welsh *efwr* 'cow-parsnip', as in *Dinevor* from *Dinefwr*; Breton *evor* 'black alder'); hence, with **-āco-* suffix (see in general BRAVONIACUM) 'place of yews, place abounding in yews'. Jackson and Williams provide many examples of this use of **-āco-* (Welsh *-awc*, *-awg-*, *-og*) with names of trees and plants, e.g. Welsh *rhedynog* 'bracken-patch' < British **ratinăco-* (cf. Radenoc in Brittany), *ceirchog* 'oatfield', *celynnawg* 'holly-thicket'. However, *Ebŭros* is known as a personal name in Gaul, where commonly the **-āco-* suffix was used to denote 'property of, estate of', so that British **Ebŭrācon* could well signify 'estate of *Ebŭros*'. We have no way of knowing which meaning is right, though Jackson (*Britannia*, I (1970), 73–74) regards the first as preferable, because the formation signifying 'estate of' was rare in Britain.

**Ebŭro-* is a common element in Continental toponymy. Similar to the British name are *Eb(u)riacus* > Yvré-le-Polin (Sarthe, France) and Evry (Seine-et-Oise, France). These involve a personal name **Ebŭrios*. The sense 'yew' is presumably (but see P. Aebischer in *RC*, XLIV (1927), 328–35) that present in *Eburodunum* > Brünn (Germany), Yverdon (Switzerland), and Embrun (Hautes-Alpes, France); *Eburobriga* > Avrolles (Yonne, France); *Eburomagus* > Bram (Aude, France); *Eburobrittium* in Lusitania (Pliny *NH* IV, 113). Ethnic names include *Aulerci Eburovices* > Evreux (Eure, France), and the *Eburones* (Caesar *BG* II, 4, etc.) who lived between the Maas and the Rhine; both are 'yew-men' ('bowmen' ?). For a full list, see Holder I. 1395, *GPN* 346–47, *DAG* 721–22.

It is possible that the British name of Roman York was eventually understood by its inhabitants to contain a word for 'boar', and a boar appears as the 'canting badge' of the city on the Bordeaux inscription of A.D. 237; if this was at all common, it might have assisted the Anglo-Saxon interpretation of Romano-British *Eboracum* as *Eoforwic* 'boar-town'. On this and the later history of the name, see *EPNS*, XIV, 275 ff.

IDENTIFICATION. The Roman legionary fortress (SE 6052) and *colonia* (SE 6051) at York, on the left and right banks of the river Ouse respectively. The fortress was occupied by *Legio IX Hispana* from Flavian times until the reign of Hadrian, when it was replaced by *Legio VI Victrix*. The settlement which grew up opposite it appears to have been granted the title of *colonia* by Septimius Severus. The precise location of the *domus palatina* in which Severus (and presumably Constantius Chlorus) died has not been established.

EBURO CASTELLUM

SOURCE

Ravenna 107_{44} (= R&C 184): EBURO CASLUM

The emendation *Cas[tel]lum* is that of Schnetz, and seems obvious, despite the doubts of R&C. Probably the word was abbreviated on the map which *Ravenna* used as a source.

DERIVATION. For **Eburo-*, either 'yew-tree' or a personal name, see the previous entry. In this form and in this area, 'yew-fort' seems the more likely meaning. *Castellum* is 'fort' and is known in other place-names, e.g. in the inscription of the *vicani* at *Velunia* on the Antonine Wall, and in *Princastellum* of *Ravenna* 62_{13}

(for *Perincastellum* > Bernkastel on the Moselle). Rather than being a part of the place-name proper, the Latin word may stand in apposition to *Eburo*, as do other designations in the *Ravenna* list. Schnetz thinks that the name as recorded may stand for original **Eburodunum*, for which three Continental analogues are mentioned in the previous entry.

IDENTIFICATION. Unknown, but apparently in southern Scotland or Northumberland.

EIDUMANIS (?)

SOURCE

Ptolemy II, 3, 4: Εἰδουμανίος ποταμοῦ ἐκβολαί (= EIDUMANIS FLUVII OSTIA), vars. Σιδουμάνιος (= SIDUMANIS), Ἰδουμανίου (= IDUMANII), Εἰδουμανία (= EIDUMANIA), Εἰδουμανίου (= EIDUMANII)

Müller's preferred form is *Sidumanis*, present in six MSS; we follow U and many others.

DERIVATION. This name is mysterious. Bradley suggested that British **dumno-* 'deep' is involved, but this seems impossible when all MSS show -μαν- (*-man-*). If the name does have *Sidu-* there might be an analogue in Gaulish *Sidoloucum* > Saulieu (Côte-d'Or, France) which has been thought to contain **sido-* 'stag'. Ekwall *ERN* 467–68 identifies the river in question with the Lincolnshire Witham (*Wiðma* c. 1025, etc.), a name which he thinks derives without difficulty from a British **Ụidumanios*; to reach this, Ptolemy's entry must be adjusted by supposing initial Οὐ- omitted (for a comparable omission, compare *Votadini* as recorded by Ptolemy) and by supposing that -ει- stands for short *i*, as it sometimes does in Ptolemy (Ekwall compares Ptolemy's Εἴτιος for Ἴτιος, and notes that the variant Ἰδου- supports a reading with short *i*). The restored **Ụidumanios* then has, according to Ekwall, a first element as in *Vidubriga*, *Viducasses*, etc., now represented by Welsh *gwydd* and Old Irish *fid* 'forest', or, if the first vowel is *ei-*, by Welsh *gwydd* and Old Irish *fiad* 'wild'; the second element is perhaps a root cognate with Latin *mānāre* 'to flow'. There are too many uncertainties here, and Jackson *LHEB* 558 thinks the proposed **Ụidumanios* 'a very doubtful form'. In view of the major variations in Ptolemy's forms, the name is best left in the category of the unresolved.

IDENTIFICATION. The major objection to Ekwall's identification with the Lincolnshire Witham is that the position given by Ptolemy places *Eidumanis* south of the River Yare (Norfolk) and below a now unidentifiable coastal 'projection'. To suit his case, Ekwall has to argue that Ptolemy got his points out of order. Bradley thought that Ptolemy's position suited the Essex River Blackwater, and we think this right (p. 138). There is then the curiosity that there is a town of Witham on the Blackwater (recorded as *Witham* in 913, a form which Ekwall in *EPN* finds strange); if it could be shown – which it cannot – that this Witham took its name from the river, it might be possible to transfer Ekwall's argument from Lincolnshire to Essex, as it were. But as remarked above, there are too many uncertainties for this to be possible. See also PENTA in the Appendix.

(EIRIMON)

SOURCE

Ravenna 109_{23} (= R&C 300): EIRIMON

This name is a 'ghost'. It is a Latin transliteration of Greek ἔρημος (= *erēmos*) which had figured on the map which the Cosmographer used as a source. It originated in the Greek adjective which Ptolemy attached to mention of two islands, Ἄδρου (= *Adru*) and Λίμνου (= *Limnu*), both described as ἔρημος 'deserted, uninhabited' and as related geographically to Ireland. On a map the adjective was written a little separated from its island and was taken by the Cosmographer to be the name of an island, and entered in his list accordingly. This is the explanation of Dillemann (p. 71).

EITIS (?)

SOURCES

Ptolemy II, 3, 1: Ἔιτιος ποταμοῦ ἐκβολαι (= EITIS FLUVII OSTIA), vars. Ἐίτυος, Ἴτηου, Ἴτυος
(Müller's Ἴτιος (= ITIS) is a conjecture only)

Ravenna 109_{20} (= R&C 294): ELETE

The form given by *Ravenna* has not previously been associated with Ptolemy's. It occurs in the list of western islands, but we know that this contains anomalies, and the present name could well have been written in the sea on a map and misread by the Cosmographer as though it pertained to an island. Initial *El-* is an almost certain sign of *Fl(umen)*. *Fl Ete* would then be an oblique case, *-e(m)*, of the third declension.

DERIVATION. The form is too unsure to allow speculation. If *It-* is right, *GPN* 356–57 has a number of personal and place-names which may be relevant, including *Ituna* and *Itium Promontorium* (Ἴτιον, Ptolemy II, 9, 1), now Cap Gris Nez (Pas-de-Calais, France); also the *Itius Portus* of Caesar. Holder II. 82 quoted Stokes's derivation of these names from a root *i- as in Latin *ire*, Greek ἰ-έναι, Old Irish *ethaim* 'I go', etc., which Watson *CPNS* 45–46 repeats without conviction. If *Ei-* is right there might be a vague parallel in British *Eidumanis*, but this is in itself a doubtful name. *Eitis* is not related to modern Etive.

IDENTIFICATION. Unknown, but a river of north-west Scotland.

EL- names in *Ravenna*

In the map which the Cosmographer used in part as a source, the abbreviation *Fl* for *Flumen* or *Fluvius* was evidently capable of being misread as *El-* (and sometimes as other letters, such as *Pa-*: *Panovius* for *Fl Novius*, etc.). It can be observed in *TP* – which of course was not the source for *Ravenna* as such – that a similar abbreviation there, *Fl*, could easily be mistaken and then miscopied. Since river-names on the map used by *Ravenna* seem to have been written largely along inland river-courses (not at the mouths), they were further misread as being names of places and were not entered by the Cosmographer in his river-list. The forms, with the entries to which we have referred them, are:

ELAVIANA 109_{14} (= R&C 286)—Abona (river)
ELCONIO 105_{47} (= R&C 3)—Cenio
ELETE 109_{20} (= R&C 294)—Eitis
ELTABO 105_{46} (= R&C 2)—Tavus[2]
ELTAVORI 106_{48} (= R&C 93)—*Tamus

The above reasoning is also that of Dillemann (65) (though he does not make the same identifications); a similar suggestion for the names in Cornwall (though with the *Fl* as a suffix) was earlier made by C. Thomas in *Rural Settlement in Roman Britain*, CBA Research Reports 7 (London, 1966), 86.

EPIACUM

SOURCE

Ptolemy II, 3, 10: Ἐπίακον (= EPIACUM), a *polis* of the Brigantes; var. Ἐπείακον (= EPEIACUM, in U and most MSS)

DERIVATION. This is the personal name whose Latin form is *Eppius* with *-ācu(m)* suffix (see BRAVONIACUM), hence 'property of Eppius, estate of Eppius'. The name *Eppius* is Roman and is abundantly recorded in the Latin Onomasticon, with variants *Epius* and *Aeppius*, and a feminine *Eppia*; also with diverse suffixes, *Eppianus*, *Eppilius*, etc. But it was ultimately of Celtic origin, since it is based on Celtic **epo-s* 'horse' (Welsh *ep*, *eb*, *eb-*, also in Cornish and Breton; Old Irish *ĕch*, Irish *each*, cognate with Latin *equus*). Many names based on this are recorded by Holder and in *GPN* 197–99; for an excellent survey of these names see also H. Birkhan, *Germanen und Kelten*...(Vienna, 1970), 391–416. In Britain the next four names in this List are formed from it, and the goddess (chiefly Gaulish) *Epona* is recorded in a dedication at Auchendavy (*RIB* 2177) and in a graffito *Epon(ae)* on a jar from Alcester (*JRS*, LVI (1966), 224). On the Continent places include *Eporedia* > Ivrea (Aosta, Italy) and *Epomanduodurum* > Mandeure (Doubs, France). There was another *Ep(p)iacum* > Epfig (Bas-Rhin, France: Holder I. 1444), and an *Epiaca* is recorded in the twelfth century in France (Vincent 182). All these are, of course, Latin versions of originally Celtic names, and the same must be true of British *Epiacum*; we should express this as originally British **Epi̯āco-* 'place (or property) of **Epios*'. A man *Eppius M(...)* is recorded in a graffito in a quarry in Cumbria (*RIB* 1015), and he might have been a Roman or a Briton who latinised his Celtic name when writing it. An indication that these names were used in Britain before the Conquest is provided by *Eppillus*, son of Commius, who ruled at Calleva about A.D. 10 and whose name is on coins.

IDENTIFICATION. Probably the Roman fort at Whitley Castle, Kirkhaugh, Northumberland (NY 6948).

EPIDII

SOURCE

Ptolemy II, 3, 8: Ἐπίδιοι (= EPIDII)

DERIVATION. The name is based on British **epo-s* 'horse' (see EPIACUM) with adjectival suffix **-idi̯os*, Latin *-idius*, as in *Lugidius*, *Marcidius* 'horseman', etc. The tribe may have been horse-breeders and horse-breakers (Watson *CPNS* 23–24), but C. Thomas thinks this solution too facile; in *Arch.J.*, CXVIII (1961), 40, he draws attention to the number of N. British tribes with 'animal' names (*Caereni*, *Cornavii*, *Epidii*, *Lugi* if 'raven-people') and thinks that even if the names are not fully 'totemic' they at least indicate animal-cults. Watson recalls that Virgil's tutor in rhetoric had the Gaulish name *Epidius*, and observes that Kintyre is the home of the *Mac Eacherns*, an anglicisation of *Mac Each-thighearna* 'son of horse-lord', which in turn is a Q-Celtic version of the older name.

IDENTIFICATION. A people of Scotland occupying Kintyre.

(EPIDIUM)

SOURCES

Ptolemy II, 2, 10: Ἐπίδιον (= EPIDIUM)

Ravenna 107_{40} (= R&C 176): EBIO

Ptolemy gives the name as that of an island, one of the five *Ebudae*, and he mentions it last in the group (after *Malaia*). In *Ravenna Ebio* (which as it stands suggests no etymon Celtic or Latin) could well be for *Ebi(d)io*, perhaps with Vulgar Latin voicing of *p* > *b* in the Cosmographer's usage; it appears among habitation-names in the region between the two Walls, but as explained in Chapter V there are many illogicalities in the ways the Cosmographer read his North British names from a map, and often his correspondences here with Ptolemy are close; it seems likely that we should make another equation here (but see below).

DERIVATION. The sense seems to be simply 'place inhabited by the Epidii', but it is a most unusual formation, since for a regional name based on a tribal name we would expect **Epidia* (compare *Dumnonia*, *Venedotia*, etc.). The only parallel is Ptolemy's *Brigantium*, which we think a 'ghost' produced by some misunderstanding. The same could well be the case here. The name could be an unconscious duplication by Ptolemy of *Epidium Promontorium*, even though he thinks one an island and the other a cape, and has differing positions for them; but if we are right in equating *Ravenna*'s name with Ptolemy's, the confusion was not Ptolemy's but arose from the map-source which the two ultimately had in common. Bradley thought there was some such confusion; the argument is developed in Chapter III, p. 114. The attempt by Rhys (1904, p. 231) to link this name to that of the *Ebudae* is interesting, but the time of Ptolemy is much too early for *p*/*b* confusions in British or Latin.

IDENTIFICATION. Probably Kintyre.

EPIDIUM PROMONTORIUM

SOURCE

Ptolemy II, 3, 1: Ἐπίδιον ἄκρον (= EPIDIUM PROMONTORIUM) (again in II, 3, 8)

DERIVATION. See *Epidii* and *Epidium*. Watson helpfully notes that the modern Gaelic name for this peninsula is *Ard Echde*.

IDENTIFICATION. The Mull of Kintyre, Argyllshire.

EPOSESSA

SOURCE

Ravenna 106_{28} (= R&C 59, 60): EPOCESSA, YPOCESSA

The two names are obviously of the same place; as often, the Cosmographer tried two spellings and failed to delete one from his final version. The second is inaccurate, and could have resulted from an attempt to associate the name (reasonably) with Greek *hippo-*.

DERIVATION. For **epo-s* 'horse' and names based on it, see EPIACUM. The second element is properly *-sessa*; the Cosmographer's Vulgar Latin speech caused him to represent original *s* as *c*, a hypercorrection (since in V.L. *c* before *e* and *i* was assibilated; compare British *Gabrocentio* in *Ravenna* 107_3 for *-sentio*, and *Brindice* 84_{27} with the more correct *Brendesium* 69_7). For *-sessa*, see CAMULOSESSA. The sense is 'horse-place', perhaps (R&C) 'horse-stalls'; R&C remark that 'The English name "Studfold" or "Steedstalls" is common enough.'

IDENTIFICATION. Unknown, but apparently in the area of the southern Welsh marches.

ESSE (?)

SOURCE

Ravenna 109_{21} (= R&C 296): ESSE

The form is meaningless, and may well be a fragment of another name misread from a map because it was written separately; adjacent names in *Ravenna* or on what we can imagine to have been part of a map do not seem to offer conjectures. The name is listed by the Cosmographer as that of an island, but there is no guarantee that this is right; on the analogy of other names in *E-*, it is possible that we have here a part of a river-name.

'ETSODISINAM'

Ravenna's entry for Ireland (*Scotia*), following a brief general description, occupies 109_{1-5} (= R&C 272–74). We associate one of three rivers mentioned, *Cled*, with Scottish *Clota*, misread from a map as though it related not to Scotland but to Ireland (because the name was written across a much-narrowed Irish Sea). It is probable that the Cosmographer has no information at all for Ireland in his map-source(s) except a coastline labelled *Scotia*, since he mentions no settlements or ethnic or other names. We may assume that the three 'Irish' rivers belong not to the Irish eastern coast but to western Britain. *Etsodisinam* has been thought to conceal the name of the Shannon (in other sources *Sena*, *Scena*), but it is only the *-sinam* part which remotely resembles this, and there is no possibility that the Cosmographer's map-sources included the western portion of Ireland where the Shannon flows.

While *Terdec* remains insoluble, a suggestion can be made about *Etsodisinam*. *Et-* might represent *et* 'also' at the end of the narrative text, but more likely it is a misreading of *Fl*, the abbreviation of *Fl(umen)* or *Fl(uvius)*, as in other cases. Final *-am* is unique in the British section and must be corrupt; the *-m* probably arose from a mark on the British coastline where this name joined it on the map. It is then a question of trying to see which major rivers of western Britain figured on the map which was ultimately the source for Ptolemy and directly the source for the Cosmographer, and which are mentioned by Ptolemy but have not hitherto been identified in *Ravenna*. The obvious candidate is *Belisama*; *Fl Belisama* written across the Irish sea was taken to refer to its western end, in Ireland, and not to its eastern end on the Lancashire coast. There is no great palaeographic problem about

Fl Belisima
Et Sodisina

when we recall that in related documents we find *Isannavantia* with *S* representing *B* of *Bannaventa*[1] (*AI* 477_1) and *Baromaci* for *(Ce)saromagi* in *TP*. For *e/o* and cases of (not precisely relevant) *cl/d*, see p. 202. On the map the name could well have been written – by assimilation of the Celtic superlative to the Latin one – **Belisima*.

The equation seems likely, then, but cannot be absolutely affirmed.

EVIDENSCA of *Ravenna* 107_{47} (= R&C 189): see HABITANCUM

EXOSADES (?)

SOURCE
Ravenna 109_{24} (= R&C 301): EXOSADES, ubi et gemme nascuntur

DERIVATION. The form in *Ravenna* is almost certainly corrupt. Williams took it fairly literally and reasoned that the name might represent **Esocades*, containing *esox* 'salmon'; hence perhaps 'sea-salmon islands'. Schnetz in his 1951 translation of *Ravenna* suggests a mis-copying for *Electrides*, 'Amber Islands', which neatly makes use of *Ravenna*'s gloss about the *gemme*. It is also possible that *Exosades* represents *Orcades*, a paragraph on which follows in the Cosmography. Dillemann (p. 72) suggests a corruption of the *Hebudes* (= *Ebudae*) of Pliny *NH* IV, 103, and explains the note about gems as a misplaced quotation from Jordanes. Within this ample range, one is free to choose.

IDENTIFICATION. Unknown.

FANUM COCIDI

SOURCE
Ravenna 107_{30} (= R&C 155): FANOCODI, var. (2 MSS) FANOCOCIDI

DERIVATION. *Fanum* is Latin, 'temple, shrine'. Similar names are known abroad, e.g. *Fanum Martis* (*AI* 387_1), *Fanum Fortunae* (*AI* 126_{16}) > *Fano* (Pesaro-Urbino, Italy), *Fanum Minervae* (*AI* 364_8), and *Fanum Jovis* (A.D. 1154) > Fanjeaux (Aude, France). Dedications to Cocidius are known in some numbers from the Irthing valley, west of Housesteads and particularly at Bewcastle. He was war-god of the Celts, equated with Mars, and it has been suggested that his idol was painted red and that the name means 'the red one'; R&C thought this could be the case, and Ross (1967), 169–70 marshals other 'red' war-gods in support of the possibility, but the British word for 'red' demands **cocc-* (Welsh *coch*), and since *-cc-* does not appear in any of the numerous dedications to the god, the link must be regarded as very dubious. Other Welsh words in *cog-* cited by Williams do not seem to be relevant either etymologically or semantically. There are many ancient names of various kinds in *Coc-* and it is probably best to regard the root of many of them as for the present unknown. On the god, see Ross, also M. J. T. Lewis, *Temples in Roman Britain* (Cambridge, 1966), 123; and for a map of dedications to him, *Arch. Ael.*[4], XIV (1937), 105.

IDENTIFICATION. Probably the Roman fort at Bewcastle, Cumberland (NY 5674), as argued by E. Birley, *Research on Hadrian's Wall* (Kendal, 1961), 233, following Hodgson.

GABRANTOVICES

SOURCE. See the next entry

DERIVATION. The first part of the name is based on British **gabro-s* 'horse' or 'goat' (Old Irish *gabor* glossed 'caper'; Welsh *gafr* 'goat'; cognate with Latin *caper*). This is well represented in toponymy: in Britain, *Gabrosentum* 'goat-path'; abroad, there is Gaulish **gabro-s* 'goat' in *Gabromagus* (*AI* 276_9) now Windischgarsten (Austria), **Gabrodunum* > Jabrun (Cantal, France) on which Dauzat *TF* 200 remarks 'sans doute avec la valeur d'un surnom de personne'; Holder I. 1511 adds *Gabraeum*, *Gabrega-*

balio, *Gabreta*. Jackson analyses the whole first element of the British name (*JRS*, XXXVIII (1948), 57) as **gabranto-*, a participial stem from a verb **gabrā-* 'to ride a horse'. The second element is that discussed under DELGOVICIA. Hence, for the whole name, 'horse-riding fighters, cavalrymen'. In a note, Jackson thinks none too well of Thurneysen's proposal that *-nt-* is a diminutive suffix, giving a sense 'kid-fighters'; but the idea should be retained, in part because **gabro-* seems so well documented as 'goat' but poorly as 'horse', and in part because the other elements compounded with *-vices* and cognates may have emblematic or totemic connotations rather than literal ones, so that 'kid' is more acceptable than it might be if taken literally. The recent view of H. Birkhan in *Germanen und Kelten*... (Vienna, 1970), 465, is that this tribe consists of 'Ziegenkämpfer' ('goat-fighters').

IDENTIFICATION. An otherwise unrecorded people of Britain, apparently dwelling on the east coast of Yorkshire and presumably included in the federation of the *Brigantes*.

GABRANTOVICUM SINUS

SOURCE

Ptolemy II, 3, 4: Γαβραντουίκων εὐλίμενος κόλπος (= GABRANTVICUM ...SINUS)

In Ptolemy's form the expected composition vowel *-o-* is missing. Jackson explains in *LHEB* 34 that 'Greek ου is used to spell [u̯], and for [ou̯] οου is used; but the first *o* could easily be dropped as in 'Ορδούικες for 'Ορδοούικες' (in a variant in some MSS). Hence it is necessary to restore *-o-* in the present instance. The name is sometimes cited as *Gabrantovicorum*, supposing a nominative **Gabrantovici* for the tribe, but since the other British and Gaulish peoples named with this element seem regularly to show *-vices*, 3rd declension, it seems best to make the present name conform to them with genitive plural *-um*.

DERIVATION. See the previous entry. Ptolemy's entry in full means 'bay of the *Gabrantovices* suitable for a harbour', presumably a description owed to the Roman fleet. This is one of several Ptolemaic names that one may call 'descriptive'; they are artificial and can have had no real currency, though potentially they were true place-names (especially *Novus Portus*, *Ripa Alta*). Others in Britain are *Magnus Portus*, *Prominentia Litoris* (cf. *post Albim Prominentia* in Germania Magna, II, 11, 2) and *Setantiorum Portus*. See p. 116.

IDENTIFICATION. Uncertain: either Filey Bay or Bridlington Bay. In view of Ptolemy's relation of it to the PARISI (q.v.) (II, 3, 10), the latter is more probable.

GABROSENTUM

SOURCES

Ravenna 107_3 (= R&C 117): GABROCENTIO

ND XL_{50}: Tribunus cohortis secundae Thracum, GABROSENTI (var. GUBROSENTI)

DERIVATION. There is no doubt about the correct form of the name. On *Ravenna*'s *c* for *s*, see EPOSESSA; it is not necessary to suppose a Greek archetype, as R&C do. For the first element, see GABRANTOVICES; for the second, see CLAUSENTUM. The sense is 'goat-path', presumably a steep path up sea-cliffs.

IDENTIFICATION. The Roman fort at Moresby, Cumberland (NX 9821), where *Cohors II Thracum* was stationed in the third century (*RIB* 797, 803, 804); for further discussion see ITUNOCELUM.

GALAVA

SOURCES
AI 481_2 (Iter x): GALAVA
Ravenna 107_1 (= R&C 112): CALUNIO, vars. CALUUIO, COLUNIO
107_1 (= R&C 113): GALLUNIO, var. GALLUUIO

Ravenna's duplicated entry (probably a double attempt to spell the same name) is readily restored, since its errors are often found elsewhere (*g* for *c*, *u* for *a*, *n* for *v* or *u*). R&C thought that *Ravenna* was listing two distinct names, and referred the first to their *GALACUM (our *CALACUM), but this is surely to be rejected.

DERIVATION. Jackson in *Britannia*, I (1970), 74, suggests a root **gala* with *-*au̯a* suffix (see ABALLAVA), giving a sense 'vigorous stream', this being transferred to the fort on its banks. Holder I. 1521 offers **galā* 'Tapferkeit' (Irish *gal*, Old Breton *gal* 'force, puissance'; perhaps as in *Galatae* 'viri pugnaces'). In *RIO*, XXVII (1975), 121–22, there is mention of a Galaise stream, a tributary of the Touillon (Doubs, France), and of a river Galaure, a tributary of the Rhône at Saint-Vallier (France).

IDENTIFICATION. The Roman fort at Ambleside, Westmorland (NY 3703), on the river Brathay (a Norse name).

GANGANI

SOURCE. See the next entry

DERIVATION. There were *Gangani* also in Ireland, listed by Ptolemy in II, 2, 4 as Γαγγανοὶ (in all MSS); this unvaried naming in the nominative seems to clinch the right form of the name of the people in Britain (see the next entry). No root is known for the name, which seems to have no analogues anywhere; Bradley suggested a relation to Welsh *cainc* 'branch', with reference to the shape of the Lleyn Peninsula, but this is not, on the whole, the *kind* of name which tribes had. There might just possibly be a connection with the tribe whose name we list as *Deceangli*, but only if the variant Καιαγκανῶν (= *Caeancanorum*, gen. pl.: see the next entry) were taken into account as the true form, which seems unlikely.

IDENTIFICATION. Perhaps a people inhabiting the Lleyn Peninsula, but it is possible that the name has been transferred here in error from Ireland, in which the people referred to above occupied an analogous position (see map, p. 107). It is presumably no more than a coincidence that the peninsula seems later to have drawn its name of Lleyn from immigrant *Lagenii* from Leinster.

GANGANORUM PROMONTORIUM

SOURCE
Ptolemy II, 3, 2: Γαγγανῶν ἄκρον (= GANGANORUM PROMONTORIUM), vars. Καιαγκάνων (= CAEANCANORUM), Ἰαγγάνων (= IANGANORUM), Καγγανῶν (= CANGANORUM), etc. (Καιαγγανῶν is Müller's conjecture; we follow U and many MSS)

DERIVATION. See GANGANI.

IDENTIFICATION. The headland of Braich-y-Pwll, at the end of the Lleyn Peninsula, Caernarvonshire; but see the previous entry.

GARIANNUM

SOURCE

ND xxviii$_{7}$ (*pictura*): GARRIANO
xxviii$_{17}$ (text): Praepositus equitum stablesianorum Gariannonensium (vars. Gariannonenš, Garrianonensis), GARIANNONOR (vars. GARIANONOR, GARRIANONOR)

DERIVATION. The name of this fort is clearly in essence that of its river, the *Gariennus* (next entry). We have no means of knowing if these are both correct or whether both had the same suffix (either might be acceptable). Decisions about *r*/*rr* and *n*/*nn* are less important. The apparently established name for the fort, *Gariannonum*, has the extra syllable suggested by some of *ND*'s forms, but has no clear linguistic basis; *ND*'s extra syllable could have resulted from simple dittography. This may be proved by the listing at *ND* vii$_{99}$ of troops stationed at Blavia (Blaye) in Gaul as the *Garronenses* (var.: *Garionenses*), who took their name from the comparable river *Garunna* (see below).

Holder i. 1985 and Ekwall (*EPN*, s.v. *Yare*) identify a root **gar*- or **ger*- (now Pokorny 352) 'to shout, talk', Celtic **gari̯o*- (cognate with Latin *garrio*, *garrulus*), mentioning as derivatives Welsh *gair* and Breton *ger* 'word', Middle Irish *gairm* 'shout', etc. Hence a meaning 'babbling river' might be appropriate, the fort taking its name from the river, as often. J. Lloyd-Jones supports this for the *Garunna* river, comparing for sense the Welsh river *Llafar* (*llafaraf* 'I speak') ('The Compounds of **Gar*-', *Celtica*, iii (1956), 198–210; at 209). However, since East Anglian rivers in flat country are silent, this etymology should be regarded with caution; there are relations to be considered with other names, such as ethnic *Garunni*, *Gerunda* > Gerona (Catalonia), etc.

An association with the great *Garumna* (as it is commonly spelled, > Garonne) seems likely. This name was probably originally *Garunna* (thus in the best MSS of Caesar, who first mentions it), *Garumna* being a regression. Dauzat *TF* 83 derives this from pre-Indo-European **car*(*r*)- 'stone' plus *onno*- 'river', hence 'rivière caillouteuse'. Hubschmied, who proposes that the name means 'grue' ('crane', the bird) objects to this on various grounds, all good ones; the matter is argued between them anew in *RIO*, vii (1955), 282–84. Since the Garonne is not stony, and would be named first from its broad lower reaches in flat country rather than from **car*(*r*)- 'pic rocheux' near its source (Dauzat's other version), the whole matter must be regarded as still unresolved; but the British name certainly cannot be considered in isolation from its continental cognates.

IDENTIFICATION. The Roman fort of Burgh Castle, Suffolk (TG 4704), on the river Yare.

Note. For the development to modern *Yare*, see Ekwall, s.v., and Jackson *LHEB* 434, 473.

GARIENNUS

SOURCE

Ptolemy ii, 3, 4: Γαριέννου ποταμοῦ ἐκβολαί (= GARIENNI FLUVII OSTIA); vars. Γαρυέννου (= GAR-

UENNI), Γαρυένου (= GARUENI), Γαρρυένου (= GARRUENI)

DERIVATION. See the previous entry.

IDENTIFICATION. The river Yare.

*GELOVIUM (?)

SOURCE
Ravenna 107_{41} (= R&C 178): CELOVION

DERIVATION. The emendation *Gelovium* is that of R&C, and is reasonable given the frequency of *c*/*g* miscopyings. They indicate that **gelov-* is 'sword' (Welsh *gelau* 'sword', used in river-names such as *Aber-Gele(u)*; hence, with *-*i̯o-* suffix, 'place on sword river'. In Middle Welsh *geleu* is recorded in slightly broader senses, 'sword, weapon, spear'. However, it is possible that Welsh *geleu*, *gele*, *gel* 'leech' (possibly connected with the word for 'sword' – the matter is much debated) is pertinent here also, and it cannot be denied that it might make a better sense.

In the general uncertainty about the very form of so many of *Ravenna*'s North British names, this is as much as can be said. Dillemann (p. 70) regards *Celovion* as perhaps a corruption of *Cilurnum*, a fort of Hadrian's Wall; other names of the Wall are indeed duplicated in the Cosmography.

IDENTIFICATION. Unknown, but apparently in southern Scotland.

(GENUNIA: See p. 47)

GLANNOVENTA

SOURCES
AI 481_1 (Iter x): CLANOVENTA
Ravenna 107_2 (= R&C 115): CANTIVENTI, vars. CANTAVENTI, CANTANENTI
ND XL_{52}: Tribunus cohortis primae Morinorum, GLANNIBANTA
The form of *AI* is reasonably accurate, allowing *c*/*g* confusion as often; other miscopyings in the forms of *Ravenna* and *ND* are readily paralleled elsewhere.

DERIVATION. One may readily assume *-nn-*, documented by *ND* and probably present in the source which the Cosmographer miscopied as *-nt-*. For **glanno-* 'bank, shore', see CAMBOGLANNA. This is a much more satisfactory element here than **glano-*, as Jackson notes (*Britannia*, I (1970), 70), and as R&C argue also on topographical grounds. The second element, *-venta*, is discussed under BANNAVENTA[1]. The sense is thus 'shore field', possible 'shore market'.

IDENTIFICATION. The Roman fort at Ravenglass, Muncaster, Cumberland (SD 0895); part of its bath-house survives as Walls Castle.

GLANUM

SOURCE
Ravenna 105_{46} (= R&C 1): GIANO
R&C rightly emend *Ravenna*'s form; for *i* = *l*, see p. 203.

DERIVATION. There are two possibilities:

(*a*) Celtic **glano-s* 'rein, glänzend' (Holder I. 2024), represented by Welsh *glan* 'clean, pure'. This is a common element in hydronyms: *Glanis*, a tributary of the Tiber (Pliny *NH* III, 53); *Glanis*, a river of north Italy (Strabo IV, 6, 9) and two other rivers of the same name, in the Ardennes and in Spain (Holder); *Glane*, a river of the Dordogne (Dottin *LG* 89); *Glanate*, *Civitas Glannativa* > Glandève (Basses-Alpes, France); etc.

(*b*) If the British name is really *Glannum* (with a geminated consonant simplified in *Ravenna*, as often), it could contain British **glanno*- 'bank, shore', for which see CAMBOGLANNA. Rostaing *ETP* 172–73 prefers to explain all the names in our section (*a*) as having this **glanno*- 'bank', since he thinks that **glano*- 'pure' would not suit habitation-names; but this neglects the extent to which river-names were simply transferred to habitations. He speculates further that **gl*- was a pre-Indo-European root in hydronyms, adopted into Celtic; and in view of the geographical spread of these names, this may be a useful idea.

It is impossible to decide which of the two British words, both equally appropriate, enters into the name. We cannot be sure whether this represents a river or a settlement: the fact that the name is not entered in *Ravenna*'s river-list is no bar to its being a river, and it is to be noted that the next two names in the Cosmography, *Eltabo* and *Elconio*, are those of rivers. Two rivers Glen, in Lincolnshire and Northumberland, are derived by Ekwall from British **glano*-. There seems to be no trace of such a name in south-west England.

IDENTIFICATION. Unknown, but evidently in south-west Britian. C. Thomas (*Rural Settlement in Roman Britain*, CBA Research Reports 7 (London, 1966), 86) suggests the possibility that the river Yeo (formerly Nymet) is meant, on the grounds that **glano*- ('pure') could be equated with *nemet*- ('sanctuary'; see under *Aquae Arnemetiae*); but it is difficult to see why the one word should be preferred to the other.

GLEVUM

SOURCES

Inscriptions:

RIB 161 (= Burn, 1969, No. 83, p. 65), the plinth from a monumental tomb at Bath of a man who was DEC(URIO) COLONIAE GLEV(ENSIS)

CIL VI. 3346 (Rome), the tomb of a man who had been *frumentarius* of Legio VI at the (COLONIA) NER(VIA) or NER(VIANA) at GLEVI

JRS, XIX (1929), 216 = *CIL* XVI. 130: the military diploma (found at Colchester) of a soldier of *Cohors I fida Vardullorum*, who is described as GLEVI 'of Gloucester'; A.D. 149–190. (A note in *CIL* says 'pro *Glevi* exspectas *Glevo*')

EE IX. 1283, 1284: tiles stamped R P G, i.e. *Res Publica Glevensium* or *Rei Publicae Glevensium* (see *JRS*, XLV (1955), 68–72)

AI 485_4 (Iter XIII): CLEVO

Ravenna 106_{29} (= R&C 62): GLEBON COLONIA

also possibly *Ravenna* 106_{12} (= R&C 29): CLAVINIO, var. CLAVIMO

(see also *Ravenna*'s *Coloneas* 106_{14} = R&C 33 under COLONIA[2])

The above sources present no problem. *AI* has initial *C* for *G*, a frequent error. See the entry for CLAVINIUM.

DERIVATION. Jackson in *Britannia*, I (1970), 70–71, indicates British **Glēu̯on*, earlier **Glaiu̯on*, to which Welsh *gloyw* or *gloew* 'bright' is related (Holder I. 2026 gives **gleivo-* 'glänzend, klar'; Williams **glevo-*). This is the generally accepted etymology; hence 'bright place, bright town'. Later forms support it: the city is *Cair Gloui* (better, *Gloiu*) in Nennius 49, in modern Welsh *Caer Loyw* or *Loew* (Jackson); Anglo-Saxon *Gleawcaester* > Gloucester. Jackson however raises two doubts: (1) 'It is doubtful whether Welsh *gloyw*, *gloew* "bright" really comes from **glaiu̯o-*, because of the Irish cognate'; (2) 'A town name consisting of a basic adjective alone without any suffix, literally "bright", would be peculiar. This would leave the name unexplained.' The first difficulty perhaps depends upon some irregular phonetic development either within Welsh or Irish, which we no longer perceive. As for the second, it should be said that water-names are not infrequently formed in this way, e.g. British *Leuca* 'shining (one)', *Sena* 'old (one)', and most relevant of all – if it is a place (and adjectival, which is not certain) – *Glanum* 'pure (one)'. Abroad, adjectival formations in late Latin or early Romance are common, for example in Spain Angosto, Frías, Panda, Salientes (*ELH* I. 513). Sometimes a noun no longer expressed has to be assumed, e.g. in Spain *(*Capitias*) *Rubras* > Rubias. *Glevum* is then unusual, but not unique. We can either assume an unexpressed noun, or possibly imagine a metaphorical extension of the basic sense 'bright' to 'noble, famous (place)'.

See also COLONIA[1] and COLONIA[2].

IDENTIFICATION. The Roman *colonia* (succeeding a legionary fortress) of Gloucester (SO 8318); the name *Nervia* or *Nerviana* reflects its foundation in the reign of Nerva (A.D. 96–98).

GOBANNIUM

SOURCES

AI 484_6 (Iter XII): GOBANNIO

Ravenna 106_{25} (= R&C 53): BANNIO

Correction of *Ravenna*'s form has long been agreed; omission of initial letters (perhaps divided from the rest of the name by some mark on the Cosmographer's map-source) occurs occasionally in other sections.

DERIVATION. Jackson in *Britannia*, I (1970), 74, bases the name on British **gobann-* 'blacksmith' (Welsh *gof* 'smith', plural *gofain*(*t*); Irish *goba*, *gobann*), with *-*i̯o*- suffix. The first could be a personal name, therefore 'place of **Gobannos*'. However: 'A different explanation is much more probable, in view of the Roman iron-workings in the neighbourhood. The town is now Welsh *Abergefenni* "mouth of the Gefenni", the river-name being from British **Gobannīā*, and this would be "river of the blacksmiths" or "of the ironworks"; and as so often, the river-name was then applied to the town.' For related personal and place-names, see Holder I. 2030, Dottin *LG* 260 and *GPN* 350–51. *RIB* 45 (Canterbury), a fragmentary text from a dedication or a tombstone, records *Goban*[. . .], the stem of a personal name.

IDENTIFICATION. The Roman fort at Abergavenny, Monmouthshire (SO 3014). Pre-Roman ironworking here is not improbable and might provide a better basis for the name, but the fort seems to have been established early (perhaps in A.D. 50) and the name may have replaced a unit-name (see discussion of this process under *Durobrivae*).

*GRANDINA

SOURCE

Ravenna 109_{21} (= R&C 297): GRADENA, with var. GRANDENA in two MSS

DERIVATION. The variant suggests that *-n-* belongs in the name, and that it has been omitted from other MSS by abbreviation (**Grādina*). *Grandina* in Latin is 'hail'; for other Latin names among the western Scottish islands, see ANAS. Too much trust should not be placed, however, in *Ravenna*'s forms in this section.

IDENTIFICATION. Unknown, but apparently an island, perhaps off the west coast of Scotland.

GRAUPIUS MONS

SOURCE

Tacitus *Agricola* 29, 2: [Agricola] ad MONTEM GRAUPIUM pervenit

DERIVATION. The name in Tacitus is normally taken as an accusative in apposition to *montem*, although notionally it could be the genitive plural of a tribal name. The etymology has been much debated. Holder I. 2040 thought it could be 'Pictish', the root being **graup-* (**grup-* **gruq-*) 'biegen, krümmen', related to Greek γρυπός 'gekrümmt', used especially of the nose, but also 'Hügel, Berg, als der sich wöhlbende, erhebende'. Certainly words pertaining to human physique are often used of geographical features in the way that Holder implies. Watson *CPNS* 55–56 held that the true form was **Craupius*; then **Craup-* > *crup* in Old Welsh, and > *crwb* 'hump, hunch' in modern Welsh, so that 'in form (but not necessarily in place) *Mons* **Craupius* is identical with *Dorsum Crup* of the *Pictish Chronicle*'. This again seems feasible, but Jackson in *PP* 135 was not convinced on phonetic grounds, and preferred to consider the celticity of the name unproven; the Welshness of modern *crwb* has also been doubted. Recently, however, Jackson has revised his view. In an important note to R. Feachem's paper '*Mons Craupius* = Duncrub?', *Antiquity*, XLIV (1970), 120–24, Jackson says that '*Crub* could be from **Craupius* (not *Graupius*), if we suppose that the Pictish descendant **crub* (pronounced *crüb*...) was borrowed by the Gaels with sound-substitution of their own *u*..., as they had no *ü* in their own language. This is quite a familiar thing...Hence *Duncrub* could be *Mons Graupius*, philologically.' (This *Duncrub* is in earlier records the *Dorsum Crup* mentioned by Watson.)

Thus far British scholars. The etymology has been further debated between Pokorny and others. Pokorny in *Vox Romanica*, X (1948–49), 229, also Pokorny 623, has proposed to see in **Croupios* (his adjustment of *Graupius*) a root **kreup-* 'Schorf, sich verkrusten', a further derivative of which is found in Gallic *cruppellarii* 'gepanzerte Gladiatoren der Aedui'. The root has produced words in Germanic, Lithuanian and Slavic, according to Pokorny, but seemingly nothing in Celtic apart from the *cruppellarii* (Tacitus *Annals* III, 43) which Pokorny mentions. The sense of Pokorny's **kreup-* seems to make it an unlikely place-name element, and the lack of Celtic cognates is serious. Pisani doubted whether Pokorny could be right: 'Naturalmente bisogna pensare...que qualche "Veneto" o qualche "Illirio" abbia fatto un viagetto in Britannia per andarvi a battezzare il *Mons* **Croupios*...' (*Paideia*, IX (1954), 101–103). Whatmough in *Lan-*

guage, XXIX (1953), 482, also took a rather jocular view of the matter. Pisani was prepared to think that if textual *Graupius* was right after all, there might be some relation with Greek γρυπός, but he preferred to think the name probably pre-Indo-European.

It seems best, then, to regard the etymology as unknown, but to follow Jackson (in his revised view) about the later development of the name; this, naturally, without prejudice to the discussion of the site of *Mons Graupius*, which is to be argued on quite different lines.

IDENTIFICATION. Probably Bennachie, Aberdeenshire – the suggestion of J. K. St Joseph, *JRS*, LXVII (1977), 141–45; see p. 45 above, with notes 1 and 2. This identification depends on the interpretation of the somewhat vague description of Agricola's campaign by Tacitus and the location at Durno (NJ 699272) of a Roman camp whose size seems to indicate the concentration there of all the Roman forces. The British battle base would then be the hill-fort of Mither Tap of Bennachie (NJ 683224) which, though relatively small, commands a most extensive view.

HABITANCUM

SOURCES

Inscription: *RIB* 1225 (Risingham), an altar whose dedicator was ...HABITANCI PRIMA STAT(IONE) 'on his first tour of duty at Habitancum'

Ravenna 107_{47} (= R&C 189): EVIDENSCA

(The inscription *RIB* 1235, Risingham, a monumental dedication-slab, as restored mentions the EXPL[ORATORES HABITANCENSES]

Although R&C and Williams take *Evidensca* at face-value, discuss it philologically and try to identify it with Inveresk, the name belongs on textual grounds and from its position in the list with *Habitancum*. The suggestion was first made by Holder, and was known to R&C but not argued by them. If **Avitanco* figured in the source used by the Cosmographer, there is no great problem: *H-* is decorative (cf. *Onno/Hunno*, *Ispani* in *RIB* 256, hypercorrect *Have* for *Ave* in *RIB* 1115, etc.); for *d/t* and *a/o*, see p. 203. The only real oddity is intrusive *-s-*. As for position, the Cosmographer is at this point concerned with S.E. Scotland and Northumberland north of the Wall; mention of *Habitancum* is to be expected.

DERIVATION. The base of the name is Latin, well-recorded as the cognomen *Avitus* with many derived forms. It is sometimes written *Abitus*, *Avithus*, *Avittus*, and is found in at least five instances as *Habitus*: *Aulus Cluentius Habitus*, defended by Cicero in 66 B.C., and a man of the same name and family who made a dedication at Carrawburgh, *RIB* 1545; *Q. Iul(ii) Habi(ti)*, *CIL* VII. 1336.525; *Habitus* on a potter's stamp from Gaul, *CIL* XIII. 10010.983; and on the tombstone of a Samnian *sevir*, *CIL* IX. 3097. As for *b/v*, it seems that while *Avitus* was much the commoner, *(H)abitus* has the more classical authority. Confusion of *b/v* began in the first century A.D. in the Vulgar Latin of several Continental provinces, and soon affected writing. As Jackson showed, *b* and *v* remained distinct on the whole in the Latin of Britain, and the very few cases of confusion (e.g. *Vivio* for *Vibio* in *RIB* 17, London; *Vassinus* for *B-* in *RIB* 215, Stony Stratford) are exceptional or due to the presence of people from other provinces. It therefore seems that our place-name is correctly cited with *-b-*.

The *-ancum* suffix (there is no justification for 'Habitanc*ium*') is possibly found in *Concangis* and *Sylinancis*. Holder I. 137 lists Latin *-ac-* from **-anc-*, Germanic *-ing*, *-ang*, Lithuanian *-inka-s*, and finds it in place-names *Almancum*, *Aprianco*, the *nautae Aruranci* (R. *Arura* > Aar), etc.; also in personal names (the most relevant here) *Bellanco*, *Mogiancus*, etc. It is not common and the meaning is unclear. Its use in the other British name(s) suggests that there was a specifically Celtic suffix cognate with those listed by Holder, though he does not indicate one; its function might be that of the similar Celto-Latin suffix **-āco-*, *-ācum*, and the sense of this, often 'property of', might be similar too. As to the race of the person *Habitus* in question, he was more likely a Briton with a Latin name than a Roman (possibly paralleled by the name of the Gaulish potter mentioned above) as the possessor, perhaps, of the land on which the fort was built, for forts were not named after their Roman builders or commanders.

IDENTIFICATION. The Roman fort at Risingham, Northumberland (NY 8986). The archaeological evidence at present available suggests that the fort was not built until Antonine times, in the governorship of Q. Lollius Urbicus (A.D. 139–42), so that a landowner with a Roman name is quite possible.

Note. A. Rutherford in *BBCS*, XXVI (1974–76), 440–44, reverts to an interpretation of *Ravenna*'s *Evidensca* (read erroneously *Eiudensca*, following R&C) in an effort to locate Bede's *Urbs Giudi*. He sees the form as a conflation of this with *Isca* (the Scottish Exe).

HERCULIS PROMONTORIUM

SOURCE

Ptolemy II, 3, 2: Ἡρακλέους ἄκρον (= HERCULIS PROMONTORIUM)

DERIVATION. Presumably, like other names on the coast important to seafarers, this was assigned by Roman or Greek sailors. The name of Hercules is frequent in such names in the ancient world: see indexes to Miller (1916), texts of Pliny, etc. Such places in Britain presumably had native names, not known to us in this case.

IDENTIFICATION. Hartland Point, Devon, but see p. 135.

HORREA CLASSIS[1]

SOURCES

Ptolemy II, 3, 9: Ὄρρεα (= ORREA), the *polis* of the Venicones

Ravenna 108_{10} (= R&C 221): POREO CLASSIS

It has long been recognised that these references are to the same place. *Ravenna*'s initial *P* represents *H-* (a unique but by no means incredible miscopying); *rr* is simplified, and final *o* for *a* is a common error.

DERIVATION. The name is entirely Latin: 'granaries of the fleet, storehouses of the fleet', and was presumably given by the Romans to a newly-built base. Ptolemy's statement that it lay in the lands of the Venicones, north of the Antonine Wall, is important, but his expression '*polis* of' the tribe is purely formulaic. Several other *Horrea* (pl.; the singular is *horreum*, cf. Spanish dialectal *hórreo* 'raised granary') names are known, mainly coastal; see R&C and Miller's (1916) index, etc.

IDENTIFICATION. Probably an unlocated Roman fort near Monifieth, Angus, on the north side of the Tay estuary; see p. 128.

HORREA CLASSIS[2]

SOURCE

Ravenna 107_{46} (= R&C 188): OLEICLAVIS, vars. OLEA CLAVIS, OLECLAVIS

This entry is here identified as another *Horrea* name for the first time. R&C took it literally (*Olcaclavis* on their reading) and provided a meaning 'famous fertile fields'. Yet the new identification is straightforward. It should be noted that one MS has *Olea Clavis* as two words, correctly, and that Latin *horrea* is spelled *Orea* elsewhere in *Ravenna* (64_{48} and 86_{45}); from *Olea Clavis* we need only two miscopied letters to arrive at *Orea Clasis*. The simplification of geminated consonants is frequent in the text.

The *Ravenna* entry is not a mere duplication, but represents a different place from *Horrea Classis*[1]. This can be shown by the fact that *Ravenna* has no discernible repetitions in North Britain other than *Cerma–Cermium*, by the quite different placings and associations of the two *Horrea* names, and also by the fact that the two are miscopied in quite different ways. The Cosmographer seems to have had only one map as a source for North Britain, on which the two names were entered in differing forms (one with *H*-, the other without).

DERIVATION. See HORREA CLASSIS[1].

IDENTIFICATION. As noted above, this should be distinct from the Flavian *Horrea Classis*[1] (last entry) and may refer to a Severan base. From its place in the list it should lie in southern Scotland or Northumberland and both Monifieth and Carpow appear to be too far north, as also does Cramond, but by definition it must be on the coast. Possibly it appeared on the base map as a gloss to South Shields (*Arbeia*, q.v.) which was certainly used as such a base.

HUNNO of *ND* XL_{37}: see ONNUM

IBERRAN (?)

SOURCE

Ravenna 108_4 (= R&C 210): IBERRAN

DERIVATION. This entry is certainly corrupt. The likeliest solution is that it represents (*H*)*ibernia*, written in the sea between Ireland and Britain and misread by the Cosmographer as though it pertained to the west coast of Scotland. It could equally represent *(*Oceanus*) (*H*)*ibern*. (an abbreviated name of the Irish Sea).

IDENTIFICATION. Probably a corrupt form of the name *Ibernia*, Ireland.

ICENI

SOURCES

Coins: The pre-Roman coins of this people are studied by D. F. Allen in *Britannia*, I (1970), 1–33. The legend on a series of coins is ECEN, in a few cases ECENI; others have EC, ECN, ECE; see especially pp. 11–13. 'This must represent the name of the tribe, even though the use of tribal names on Celtic coins is very rare.' (Also Mack, Nos. 424–431.)

Jasper intaglio, set in an iron ring, showing three conjoined heads and legend

CEN, from the river Tas near Caistor St Edmund (*Venta Icenorum*); *Norfolk Archaeology*, XXXIV (1968), 263–71, and *JRS*, LVII (1967), 207; see also Allen, *op. cit.*, 24, and Ross, *Britannia*, III (1972), 293–95.

Caesar *BG* V, 21, 1: CENIMAGNI

Tacitus *Annals* XII, 31 and 32: ICENI

XIV, 31 (twice): ICENI

Ptolemy II, 3, 11: Σιμενοί (= SIMENI, in U and most MSS), vars. Ἰμενοί (= IMENI), Σμενοῖ (= SMENI); Müller's Ἰκενοί (= ICENI) is conjectural

AI 474_6 (Iter V): ICINOS

479_{10} (Iter IX): a VENTA ICINORUM Londinio

Ravenna 106_{54} (= R&C 103): VENTA CENOMUM

TP: AD TAUM

The sources are nearly united in showing ICENI, and the coins also show an initial vowel; only the ring with CEN and *Ravenna*'s form lack this, but in the latter case at least this is due to simple miscopying. On Caesar, see below. In Ptolemy, the error must go back to the archetype.

DERIVATION. Jackson in *Britannia*, I (1970), enters 'meaning and etymology doubtful', as is surely proper. There seem to be very few names which can certainly be related to it: the most relevant is *Iciniaco* (*TP*), now Theilenhofen (Bavaria), whose form suggests *-acum* attached to a personal name. Names in *Icc-* (*Iccauos*, *Iccius*, etc.) are listed by Ellis Evans in *GPN* 351-53; no sure meaning is known for these, and since they often have *-cc-* whereas the name of the British tribe never does, their relevance is doubtful. A. Carnoy in *RIO*, VIII (1956), 98–99, showed a possible way forward by identifying a root **i̯ak-* in Celtic and Indo-European with a sense 'healthy', in Jekker, the Dutch name of the Belgian river Geer, and *Iacca* in Celtiberia > Jaca (Huesca, Spain); also in a weak form **ik-*, in *Icauna* > Yonne (Yonne, France), *Icarus* > Aygues (Vaucluse, France), *Iceavus* in Cote-d'Or, France, and *Icene* (A.D. 701) > R. Itchen of England. Carnoy does not mention the *Iceni* people, but Ekwall *ERN* associated the Itchen rivers of Hampshire and Warwickshire with the *Iceni* etymologically. Since this group (if Carnoy is right) seems to have left no descendants in the Celtic tongues of Britain, the matter must still be left unresolved so far as the *Iceni* are concerned.

The equation of Caesar's *Cenimagni* with the *Iceni* has contextual and linguistic support. Caesar mentions them among the five tribes which submitted to him, perhaps because of their importance, but possibly also because it was against them that the friendly Trinovantes were being defended. In Caesar's text one reads *prohibiti Cenimagni* (in one MS, *Cenimanni*); a confusion and elision of *-i* by an early scribe is by no means impossible (*prohibiti [I]cenimagni*). It is also likely that the reading should be *Iceni magni*, the adjective meaning 'strong' or perhaps 'extensive'; the *Iceni* did indeed occupy much of East Anglia, were a powerful force when Boudica rebelled, and of the five tribes which submitted to Caesar are the only one known to history from other texts. An association of the British tribe by blood or etymology with the Gaulish *Cenomanni* seems unlikely. Records of the Gaulish people, established both in Gallia Cisalpina and in the region of Le Mans (which preserves part of their name), regularly show both *Ceno-* with *-o* and *-manni*, never *-magni*. This *ceno-* might contain the root mentioned under BRANOGENIUM, or that mentioned in *GPN* 177, note 4: '*cen(o)* in the names *Cenabum*, *Cenomani* and *Cenimagni* was equated by

Glück with Irish *cían* "far, distant, long"' with further references; for *-manni*, see Holder II. 408. Had the British people really been associated with these Gauls, it is likely that at least one of the sources (other, that is, than the MS var. in Caesar) would have shown their name with *-manni*.

IDENTIFICATION. A people of Britain with their capital at *Venta Icenorum* (Caistor St Edmund, Norfolk). Ptolemy attributes no other place to them and the distribution of their pre-Roman coins confines them to Norfolk and immediately adjacent parts of Cambridgeshire and Suffolk.

Note. *AI*'s *Icinos* (at 474_6) is of peculiar interest as it here replaces the proper name of the city of *Venta Icenorum*. Apart from the probable case of *Regno* at 477_{10}, this is the only instance in Britain of a practice which was normal in Gaul, both in itineraries and in writers such as Ammianus, and which accounts for the fact that most French cities derive their modern names not from their proper Roman names but from those of the Gaulish tribes whose administrative centres they were.

ICTIS of Diodorus and Pliny. See VECTIS

IENA (?)

SOURCE
Ptolemy II, 3, 2: 'Ιηνᾶ εἴσχυσις (= IENA AESTUARIUM), with many vars., e.g. 'Ικῶα (= ICOA), 'Ικόη (= ICOE)

DERIVATION. The text seems to be too unstable to allow guesses; no roots are visible, and there are no analogues. Some early confusion may have arisen, perhaps with the Dumfries Esk (**Isca*, 'Ισκα), though the position given by Ptolemy does not fit this and it seems best to treat it separately.

IDENTIFICATION. A river of south-west Scotland, west of the Dee; either the Water of Fleet (on which there is a Roman fort at Gatehouse of Fleet) or the river Cree whose name, though Gaelic, means 'boundary' (Watson *CPNS* 182) and so may be of more recent origin.

ILA (?)

SOURCE
Ptolemy II, 3, 4: Ἴλα ποταμοῦ ἐκβολαί (= ILA FLUVII OSTIA), var. Ἴλλα (= ILLA)

DERIVATION. Watson *CPNS* 47–48 thought the name obscure; it seems to have no parallels. He noted that the name produced modern Gaelic *Ilidh*: 'The Gaelic form does not represent *Ila*; it might represent **Ilia*, but it may be on the analogy of the numerous stream-names in *idh*.'

IDENTIFICATION. The river Helmsdale, Sutherland, flowing through *Strath Ilidh* (Strath Ullie); as Watson notes, the strath was renamed Helmsdale by the Norse; Helmsdale town is *Dun Ilidh* and a Helmsdale man is *Ileach*.

INTRAUM (?)

SOURCE
Ravenna 108_{34} (= R&C 256): INTRAUM

This form is corrupt and impossible to restore. It is very likely to be equated with the next name in *Ravenna*, ANTRUM, the latter being an attempt to re-spell a name which even the Cosmographer thought unsatisfactory.

ISSANNAVANTIA of *AI* 477_1: see BANNAVENTA[1]

ISCA[1] (river)

SOURCE

Ptolemy II, 3, 3: Ἴσκα ποταμοῦ ἐκβολαί (= ISCA FLUVII OSTIA), var. Ἴσακα (= ISACA, MS U)

DERIVATION. The name is British **ĭscā* 'water', in the sense of 'river', which underlies not only this and the following names but also Esk and Usk. The word seems to have left few traces in Continental toponymy (see below). Jackson mentions early Irish *esc*, recorded in glossaries but not in texts, explained as meaning 'water'; to this Williams adds Gaelic *easg* 'fen'.

Fig. 30. River-names derived from *Isca*: 1. North Esk; 2. South Esk; 3. Esk; 4. Esk; 5. Esk; 6. Nant Wysk; 7. Usk; 8. Axe; 9. Axe; 10. Exe; 11. Exe Water. (*Isca* appears to mean simply 'water' and it may be that some of these rivers had qualifying names which were not taken into English; see our comment on ALAUNUS[1].)

One must not, however, equate *Isca*[1] (Exe) and *Isca*[3] (Usk) simply and uncritically with **ĭscā* 'water', as has been done in the past. It is best to quote in full the analysis of Jackson in *Britannia*, I (1970), 74–75:

> 'The difficulty is that Caerleon is on the Usk, which is Welsh *Wysg*, Old Welsh *Uisc*, and needs British **Ēscā*, earlier **Ēiscā*; and that Exeter was Old Welsh **Caer Uisc* (Asser: *Cair Uuisc*), from the same British form; though matters are further complicated by the seventeenth-century Cornish *Karêsk*, i.e. *Kar Esk*, given by Lhuyd for Exeter, which must be from **Iscā* not **Ēskā*, in spite of appearances. A British **Eiscā* 'fishy river' can be explained as from Indo-European **peisko-* 'fish', as in Irish *iasc* 'fish' which comes from this; as also, with different ablaut-grade, do Latin *piscis* and English *fish*. But if so, the Romano-British town-names should be *Esca* (i.e. *Ēscā*) not *Isca*; and attempts by Förster, Williams, and others to explain this away, and also to account for the contradiction between *Cair Uuisc* and *Kar Esk*, are not convincing. The question must be left open.'

The etymologies in question are reviewed by Nicolaisen in *BZN*, VIII (1957), 241–42, following in the main differing proposals of Förster. He does not favour the **peiskā* 'fishy water' mentioned by

Jackson (now better *_p(e)ik-sk-ā_, perhaps 'trout' rather than 'fish in general': Hamp in _JIES_, I (1973), 507–11), nor *_peid-skā_ (cf. Greek πῖδαξ 'spring'). As between *_eiskā_ (with _-k-_ suffix well documented in Celtic names) representing Indo-European *_ei-_ 'gehen' and the same representing *_eis-_ '(sich) heftig, ungestüm, schnell bewegen', Nicolaisen favours the latter, because it fits better with other river-names, including the type *_Is-_ found in _Isarā_ and British *_Isurā_. Nicolaisen then separates from all these those names which he thinks directly descend from *_Iscā_: a North and South Esk in Kincardine/Angus, an Esk in Kerry and Lough Easg of Donegal, seeing these as equivalent to Irish _esc_ and Gaelic _easg_ mentioned earlier. With these belong the few Continental names: Isch (a tributary of the Saar: _Isca_ in the eighth century), Ijssche (Brabant; _Isca_ in 822), Ischel (near Traunstein; _Iscala_ in 984), Ischl (a tributary of the Traun; _Iscala_ in 890), and Ischer (Alsace; < *_Iscara_). To these Holder II. 77 adds a further assumed *_Iscara_ and an _Ambiscara_.

The problem to which Jackson drew attention in 1970 is in no way diminished by all this. On the one hand, all our sources for _Isca_-names in Britian (ten, or eleven if we include _Iscalis_) and the Continental examples from medieval documents all show _I-_; on the other hand, the derivatives in the Celtic languages demand original _Ēscā_, from whatever origins (all the etyma proposed have original *_ei-_, which became _ē_ in Common Celtic and continued as _ē_ in British: _LHEB_ 330). Given the certain identity of ancient _Isca_[1] and _Isca_[3] rivers with modern Exe (which has, like Axe, an Anglo-Saxon metathesis) and Usk (without metathesis, like Esk) rivers respectively we may not postulate some exceptional factor such as a Celtic *_Ēscā_ wrongly recorded as Romano-British _Isca_ in the first-century period when native names were becoming established in Latin form. By 1970 Jackson had evidently dropped the explanation which he tentatively gave in _LHEB_ 259: that short _i_ in a British penultimate became _ĕ_ in Late British if the following syllable was final and contained _a_, and that, if Exe, Axe and Esk are from _Isca_ ('which is uncertain'), this explains the _e_ in these; the reason no doubt being that the resulting _ĕ_ is not after all the _ē_ which is demanded by medieval and modern Celtic derivatives in versions of these names. There remains one tenuous possibility, which Jackson in _LHEB_ dismissed. It is that _Ĭscā_ became *_Ēscā_ in the spoken Latin of Britain, just as stressed _ĭ_ regularly became close _ē_ in the speech of most parts of the Empire by the third century. In _LHEB_ 259 there is the uncompromising statement that 'the change to _ę_...emphatically did not occur in British Latin as we know it, though it could presumably have done so in the low-class V.L. which may have been current in the cities'. The basis of this statement is, of course, the fact that most (not all) words having stressed _ĭ_ that were borrowed from Latin retain this _i_ in Welsh (e.g. _fĭde(m)_ > _ffydd_, _cĭppu(m)_ > _cyff_; but as suggested by Smith in _ANRW_ (forthcoming), there may be much learned influence in the arresting of an expected process, and on the contrary, insciptions show examples of _ĭ_ > _e_ (e.g. _ella_ for _ĭlla_ in _RIB_ 154, Bath; _stepibus_ for _stĭpibus_ in the Lydney pavement, _CIL_ VII. 137; _baselicam_ in _RIB_ 978, Netherby, A.D. 222). We then have to suppose that this _Esca_ of spoken Latin influenced the local British pronunciation of the place-names and river-names in question. Since both places are westerly one could argue that

Latin speech continued longer in them than in most other regions, and in the area of the legionary fortress at Caerleon the influence of Latin must have been considerable.

This is certainly special pleading, but is at least a possible explanation of what remains a puzzling situation. The reverse would have to apply to the Gallo-Latin *Isca-* names of the Continent, which against expectation have preserved *I-* in their modern forms (despite a form *Esca* recorded for the river Isch of the Saar in the eighth century: Holder II. 77)

IDENTIFICATION. The river Exe, Devon.

ISCA[2] DUMNONIORUM

SOURCES

Ptolemy II, 3, 13: Ἴσκα, λεγίων δευτέρα Σεβαστή (= ISCA, Legio II Augusta), a *polis* of the Dumnonii

AI 486_{8-9} and 486_{17} (Iter XV): ISCA DUMNONIORUM (and the same at 483_8 (Iter XII), by error of the copyist)

Ravenna 106_2 (= R&C 16): SCADUM NAMORUM, var. SCA DAMNAMORUM

106_{6-9} (= R&C 23): Iterum iuxta super scriptam civitatem SCADONIORUM est civitas quae dicitur...

TP: ISCADUMNONIORUM

In the above, Ptolemy is clearly listing Exeter, but the attachment of Legio II Augusta to it, rather than to ISCA[2] (Caerleon), is probably due to the fact that this was the only place of this name on his map-source. It is now known that the legion had been stationed at Exeter in the early years of the occupation, but by the time that Legio VI was at York and XX at Chester, it was based at Caerleon. In *Ravenna*'s forms the initial *I-* has become attached by error to the end of the previous name, *Melamon-i*.

DERIVATION. See ISCA[1]. As often, an original river-name has been transferred to a military site and so to the town which succeeded it.

IDENTIFICATION. The Roman city of Exeter, Devon (SX 9192), capital of the *Dumnonii*.

ISCA[3] (river)

SOURCE

Ravenna 108_{27} (= R&C 243): ISCA

DERIVATION. See ISCA[1].

IDENTIFICATION. The river Usk, Monmouthshire.

ISCA[4] (legionary fortress)

SOURCES

AI 484_4 (Iter XII): ISCAE LEG. II AUGUSTA, vars. ISCAE LEIA..., ISCAE LEGIS...

484_{10} (Iter XIII): ISCA

485_8 (Iter XIV): ISCA

Ravenna 106_{24} (= R&C 52): ISCA AUGUSTA

DERIVATION. See ISCA[1].

IDENTIFICATION. The Roman legionary fortress at Caerleon, Monmouthshire (ST 3490).

Note. Caerleon derives from well-recorded Old Welsh *Cair*, *Caer* (corresponding to, but not derived from, Latin *castra*) + *Legion*(*is*). Possibly within Roman times, **Castra Legionis* was a popular or alternative name for the place (compare Bede's record of the name *Carlegion* for Chester: see DEVA[1]). Gildas calls Caerleon *Urbs Legionum*, referring to the shrine there of the martyrs Aaron and Julius; this, with the same name for the place, was taken up by Bede I, 7. Since *Urbs* was not a spoken Latin word, it is likely to be in Gildas a literary substitute for another word, which can only have been *Cair* or *Castra.*

ISCALIS (?)

SOURCE

Ptolemy II, 3, 13: Ἴσχάλις (= ISCHALIS), a *polis* of the Belgae; vars. Ἰσκάλις (= ISCALIS), Ἰσκάλλις (= ISCALLIS)

DERIVATION. Despite the fact that most MSS (including U) record the name with χ (*ch*), this is probably another **Isca* 'water' name with a suffix indicating a fort or a settlement. Ptolemy does not use χ in any other British name, and it does not represent a sound of British or of Latin; only in the spelling perhaps first used by Paeanius for the Orkneys does χ appear, and this was imitated by the *-ch-* of some Latin writers (see p. 40). One may assume that original κ was accidentally copied as χ in some early MS of Ptolemy; compare, perhaps, the variations in the Greek and Latin spellings of the *Cauci* people of Germania Magna (Καῦχοι of Ptolemy II, 11, 7 = Καῦκοι of Strabo VII, 13).

**Isca* appears with suffix **-ala* in two early medieval Continental names (see ISCA[1]). The suffix *-alis* is found in British *Vernalis*, if this is taken literally; a sense 'aldery (place)' is suggested in our entry. Holder I. 94 lists two such suffixes, **-ălis* and **-ālis* (as they appear in Latin records), and both of them have left Celtic descendants; the rare analogues quoted by Holder hardly enable us to determine to what kinds of bases the suffixes might be attached, nor what was the force of the latter; and we do not know how the British name might have been pronounced. One cannot go further than a vague guess that the name means 'place on the **Isca* river'.

IDENTIFICATION. Possibly the Roman fort and lead-mining settlement at Charterhouse-on-Mendip, Somerset (ST 3490) (see p. 145). This is some three miles from the old course of the Somerset Axe (when it used to flow through Axbridge), but the waters from here (dammed for use by the Roman miners) would have reached it through the Cheddar Gorge (which they flooded as recently as 1968). The alternative would seem to be an undiscovered early Roman fort actually on the river.

ISURIUM BRIGANTUM

SOURCES

Ptolemy II, 3, 10: Ἰσούριον (=ISURIUM), a *polis* of the Brigantes

AI 465_3 (Iter I): ISURIUM

468_3 (Iter II): ISURIAM

476_1 (Iter V): ISUBRIGANTUM

Ravenna 108_{38} (= R&C 264): COGUVEUSURON

As explained under *Coccuveda*, *Ravenna*'s entry is a conflation. The second part of it, *Usuron*, is for **Isuron*, that is **Isur(i)um*; and although *Coguveusuron* stands in the Cosmographer's river-list and the first part of the conflation does indeed represent a river, it seems best to take *Usuron* as a version of the town-name *Isurium* and not that of its river (see below), because one would expect river-names to be cited – if masculine – either with nominative *-us* or oblique *-o*, but not neuter-seeming *-um* (though there are three instances of this in the river-list). Since the Cosmographer was reading from a map, a conflation of river + town is just as likely to have occurred as a conflation of river + river.

DERIVATION. Jackson in *Britannia*, I (1970), 75, gives the name as British **Isurion*, perhaps derived from British **Isurā*, now the river Ure, 'though this derivation of *Ure* has been doubted'. One may compare *Isara* > Isar, a tributary of the Danube in Bavaria, and > Isère (Isère, France), rivers with a different suffix from the British name; the same suffix is shown in the female name *Isuria* in *CIL* XIII. 5778 (Langres). The meaning of the base is unknown; for discussion, see *LHEB* 473, 523–24, and W. Nicolaisen in *BZN*, VIII (1957), 239–40.

IDENTIFICATION. The Roman city of Aldborough, Boroughbridge, Yorkshire (SE 4066), capital of the *Brigantes*.

ITIS of Ptolemy II, 3, 1 (Müller): see EITIS

ITUNA[1]

SOURCE

Ptolemy II, 3, 2: Ἰτούνα εἴσχυσις (= ITUNA AESTUARIUM)

DERIVATION. To judge by derivatives, the name was *Ítŭnā*. Ekwall *ERN* 142–43 suggests a base **pitunā* (from **pitu-*), cognate with Sanskrit *pitú* 'sap', Greek πιδύω 'to gush', English *fat*, etc.; the meaning may have been simply 'water', used as in other cases as 'river'. On *Ituna* > Eden, see Jackson *LHEB* 554, 578, 673, and our map of these rivers.

IDENTIFICATION. The river Eden, Cumberland.

Note. For the rejection of a proposed new reading in the *Agricola* involving **Ituna*, see p. 45 and note 5.

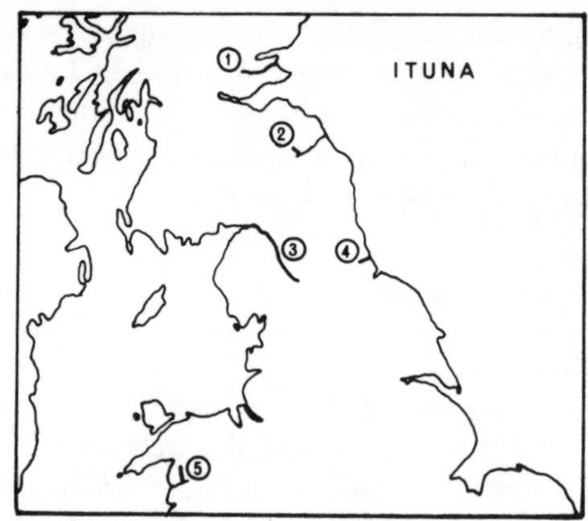

Fig. 31. River-names derived from *Ituna*: 1. Eden; 2. Eden Water; 3. Eden; 4. Eden Burn; 5. Afon Eden.

ITUNA[2]

SOURCE

Ptolemy II, 3, 4: Τίνα ποταμοῦ ἐκβολαί (= TINA FLUVII OSTIA) var. Τίννα (= TINNA)

For reasons given on p. 138, Ptolemy's form is almost certainly a corruption of **Ituna*. Since no variant hints at this, the error must go back to the archetype.

DERIVATION. See ITUNA[1].

IDENTIFICATION. The river Eden, Fife.

ITUNOCELUM

SOURCES

Ravenna 107_3 (= R&C 116): IULIOCENON

ND XL_{51}: Tribunus cohortis primae Aeliae Classicae, TUNNOCELO

The correct form *Itunocelum* was first proposed by Horsley; it, and the equation between the above two forms, have been generally accepted since. *ND*'s form is very close to the true name. *Ravenna*'s was thought by R&C to have developed in the Greek archetype in which they believed: 'The confusion between Ιτυνοκελον and Ιουλιοκενον is very easy, especially in capitals'; but this reasoning is not necessary, for within Latin copying, an unfamiliar first element *Ituno-* was garbled and then assimilated by a scribe to the well-known *Iulio-* (which occurs in a number of Continental place-names). For the second element, compare *Ravenna*'s *Alitacenon* for **Alaunocelon* (*-celum*).

DERIVATION. For *Ituna*, see ITUNA[1]. For *-ocelum* 'head, promontory', see *ALAUNOCELUM.

IDENTIFICATION. Unknown. While he is probably right on the form of the name, Horsley's identification with Bowness (*Britannia Romana* (1733), 103) cannot stand; although Gale's description '*promontorium impendens aestuario*', which he quotes, might be applied to Bowness Hill, the fort below it must be MAIA (q.v.). The order of names in *Ravenna* is *Cantiventi* (= *Glannoventa*, Ravenglass) – *Iuliocenon* – *Gabrocentio* – *Alauna* (certainly Maryport, on the river Ellen). The only forts known between Ravenglass and Maryport are at Moresby and Burrow Walls but, as R&C remark (see also Richmond, *EPNS* XXII, 512), their spacing suggests that another awaits discovery. On the evidence of small finds and the altar from Haile (*RIB* 796) this should be near Beckermet (NY 0104) on the river Ehen. Ekwall *ERN* notes that the common early form of this *Egre* (*Eger*), 'is a back-formation from, Egremont, or rather a modification of the old name under the influence of Egremont, which is a French name'. He suggests *Ehen*, mispronounced *Eger* by Normans, but it seems not impossible that this was another *Ituna*, or Eden. This solution allows the name *Gabrosentum* to be applied to Moresby, thus reconciling its recorded garrisons, but seems to leave Burrow Walls without a name in *Ravenna*.

*ITUNODUNUM

SOURCE
Ravenna 107_{42} (= R&C 179): ITUCODON

R&C recognised the ending as probably corrupt, but did not suggest an emendation; and regarded the first part as correct, relating *Itu-* to Welsh *yd* 'corn'. However, although *c* for *n* is not paralleled elsewhere in the British section of *Ravenna*, it would by no means pass belief. Final *-don* could represent *-dono* (that is, *-dunum*), or perhaps better, *-dum*, a possible form of abbreviation of *-dunum* on a map (cf. *Uxelodum* for *-dunum* on the Rudge Cup).

DERIVATION. For *Ituno-*, see ITUNA[1]. For *-dunum*, see BRANODUNUM.

IDENTIFICATION. Unknown, but from its position in *Ravenna* this should be an unlocated Roman fort on the Fife Eden.

IUCTIUS of *Ravenna* 108_{29} (= R&C 247): see STUCTIA

IULIOCENON of *Ravenna* 107_{3} (= R&C 116): see ITUNOCELUM

IVERNIUM

SOURCE
Ravenna 106_{16} (= R&C 37): IBERNIO

One may assume that here *b* is for *v*, as often.

DERIVATION. This represents British **Iu̯ernio̯-* 'place on the **Iu̯erno-* 'river', the name of the settlement or fort being formed from the river-name with the *-*i̯o*- suffix, as is common. This river (> Iwerne) is identical with the old name of the Kenmore river of Ireland, given by Ptolemy as Ἰέρνου, gen. (= *Iernus*; II, 2, 3), but to be corrected to Ἰουέρνου (= *Ivernus*). Related are the name of Ireland itself, **Īu̯erni̯ā* (*Hibernia*), and personal names such as *Iberna* of *RIB* 377 (Caerleon). The above all seem to have initial *ī*-, which leads Jackson to reject Ekwall's proposed etymology (for the rivers) in Celtic **ĭu̯os* 'yew', for this has *ĭ*-; and equally, then, Williams's sense for the present name of 'yew-tree place' is to be discarded also. O'Rahilly examines various other etymologies that have been proposed for the group, arguing that the names in *Ī*- are by-forms of other names in *Ē*-, and recalling that river-names and divine names often coincide because the river is the manifestation of the deity; hence 'the goddess-names **Ēvernā*, **Ēveriū* would thus appear to mean "she who travels regularly, she who moves in a customary course", from which we infer that the goddess so designated was the sun-goddess...' See O'Rahilly in *Ériu*, XIV (1946), 7–28, and Jackson in *JRS*, XXXVIII (1948), 57; also Holder II. 99.

IDENTIFICATION. Unknown. Apparently a place on the river Iwerne, Dorset, but there is no obvious candidate: the Roman fort on Hod Hill (identified by us as *Dunum*) had a very short life and neither it nor any of the villas in the neighbourhood is related to any known Roman road. Perhaps one of them (such as the celebrated building excavated by Pitt-Rivers south-west of Iwerne Minster) may prove to be part of a larger settlement. Alternatively the reference may be to the river itself.

L—

SOURCE

Inscription: a milestone of Hadrian (A.D. 119–138), *RIB* 2272, found four miles E.N.E. of Lancaster, ends its text with L MP IIII, interpreted as 'from L— 4 miles'.

DERIVATION. Initial *L*— seems natural enough. Lancaster when first recorded in Domesday Book is *Loncastre*. The river Lune is, according to Ekwall *ERN* 271, named from an unrecorded British word cognate with Old Irish *slán* 'health-giving' and found as Welsh *llawn*; as a river-name this is found as Irish *Slaney*.

IDENTIFICATION. The letter apparently represents the beginning of the name of the Roman fort at Lancaster (SD 4762).

LACTODURUM

SOURCES

AI 470_6 (Iter II): LACTODORO

476_{11} (Iter VI): LACTODORO

Ravenna 106_{49} (= R&C 95): IACIO DULMA

For comparable ways of representing *-duro* in *AI*, see DUROBRIVAE[1]. For some of *Ravenna*'s miscopied letters, see p. 203; but the gross confusion at the end of the second element is unmatched.

DERIVATION. The name is more problematical than it might seem at first glance. Jackson in *Britannia*, I (1970), 75, identifies the first element as British **lacto*- 'milk' (Welsh *llaeth*), 'which may be a native word rather than a borrowing from Latin'. Hence 'walled town of the milk-producers, dairymen'. This is phonetically agreeable, semantically less so, though still much better than the effort of R&C to postulate a British word equivalent to Latin *lacio* 'entice' or *laqueus* 'trap, snare', giving a sense 'snare fort', which Jackson rightly thinks unlikely. The problem is that *-durum* names all seem to be those of early forts, not of later walled towns; and it seems unlikely that any area was so uniquely well-populated by dairymen that a fort would be named after them. Since this is the only place in Britain having *-durum* as a second element, we have no local analogues to guide us. Jackson has objected that *duro-* does not seem to be compounded with names, that is with pre-existing proper names, but there are exceptions (see DUROLIPONTE), and the present instance may constitute another. Just as British *Durolevum* seems to have *Duro-* plus a (pre-existing) river-name, *Lactodurum* could have as a first element a pre-existing water-name of a mildly figurative kind, 'milky water' or the like; possibly the old name of the river Tove, which is Anglo-Saxon. The only Continental parallel for this name seems to be *Lactora* (*AI* 462_5, Ravenna, TP, etc.) > Lectoure (Gers, France), which is presumably Gaulish rather than Latin, later *Civitas Lactoratium*, which supposes *Lactorates* as the ethnic name; but this may be a late formation.

IDENTIFICATION. The Roman town at Towcester, Northamptonshire (SP 6948), on the river Tove. There is no pre-Roman hill-fort near here, and while an early Roman fort is to be expected none has yet been located.

LAGENTIUM

SOURCES

AI 475_6 (Iter V): LEGEOLIO
478_7 (Iter VIII): LAGECIO, var. LAIECIO (with *g* written in over the *i*)
Ravenna 107_8 (= R&C 126): LAGENTIUM, var. LAGUENTIUM

The form *Lagentium* seems the best. *Lagecio* of *AI* approaches it if we allow for two simple changes: *c* for *t*, as often, and *n* at some stage represented by an abbreviation (a stroke over the preceding letter) which was subsequently overlooked.

DERIVATION. Jackson in *Britannia*, I (1970), 75, regards the name as unsolved, though he thinks it might relate to early Welsh *llain* '(sword-)blade', '(spear-)blade', hence, with *-*i̯o*- suffix, perhaps 'fort of the swordsmen (or spearmen)'. This seems reasonable. The name is not connected with that of the Aire, on which the place stands; this, though not directly known to us, was probably **Isara* in Ekwall's opinion. Several Continental names listed by Holder II. 121 have *Lag-n-* and could be relevant: *Lagina* > Leine river (a tributary of the Aller, Germany), *Lagnis* (A.D. 632) > Laigne (river of Charente-Maritime, France), *Lagania* (*TP*) = *Laganeos* (*AI* 142_3) in Galatia; in Ireland *Lagina*/*Lagena* > Lein-ster, first mentioned in Adamnan's *Life* of St Columba I, 2, and a *Lagenotus terra* in the same text. To these Williams adds several later Welsh names.

IDENTIFICATION. The Roman fort at Castleford, Yorkshire (SE 4225).

LANDINI of *Ravenna* 106_{38} (= R&C 75): see LONDINIUM

LANUM (?)

SOURCE

Ravenna 107_{58} (= R&C 201): IANO, vars. LANO, LIRIO

The variant *Lano* is adopted by R&C as

their main form, and is certainly preferable. For *i*/*l* miscopyings, see p. 203.

DERIVATION. The word is British **lāno-* 'plain, level ground', cognate with Latin *planus*, etc., which is found also in British *Mediolanum*. To judge by information in Holder II. 142 and *GPN* 215, the present name is the only case of the use of this word uncompounded in toponymy, though *GPN* lists many Gaulish personal names which use it alone (*Lanus*, *Lana*, etc.). It would not be wise to place too much trust in the viability of this name; from experience of *Ravenna* in general, especially of its North British sections, it could be a corruption of something else or a fragment of a longer name misread from a map.

IDENTIFICATION. Unknown, but apparently in Scotland north of the Antonine Wall.

LAVATRIS

SOURCES

AI 468_1 (Iter II): LAVATRIS
476_3 (Iter V): LEVATRIS
Ravenna 107_{13} (= R&C 135): LAVARIS, var. LANARIS
ND XL_{10} (*pictura*): LAVATRES
XL_{25} (text): Praefectus numeri exploratorum, LAVATRES

Lavatris is correct; for the locative plural, see ANICETIS. *E* for *a* and *n* for *v* are common miscopyings. Probably the *-es* of the endings in *ND*'s two forms is a miscopying of *-is*.

DERIVATION. A British **lauatro-* 'water-trough, tub, bath' (plural **lauatrī*), 'possibly referring to a Roman bath-house', is identified by Jackson in *Britannia*, I (1970), 75. This accords with the Celtic bases listed by Holder II. 164: **lautro(n)* 'bath', earlier **loutro-*, **lovatro-*, cognate with Latin *luo*, *lavo*, *lavatorium*, *lavacrum*, etc., and with Greek λουτρόν. As to the sense, Jackson may be right, especially as Gaulish *lautro* is glossed 'balneo' in the Vienna Glossary; but it is hard to see why, if a Roman bath-house were in question, it was not called by Latin *balneum*, which has left abundant traces in Continental toponymy, rather than by a British word. Furthermore, every Roman fort had its bath-house, so one does not see that this could have been a sufficiently distinctive feature to warrant such a naming. This difficulty leads us to look at the senses of related Old Irish *lóathar*, *lóthur*, *lóthor*, for which there appear among glosses the senses 'canalis' (canal) and 'alveus' ('river-bed'). This last is reflected in the river-name *Lautra* cited by Holder. It seems better, then, to think not in terms of a Roman construction but of the latinisation (*Lavatris*) of an existing British name – that given by Jackson – whose sense was 'river-bed' with plural implications. Williams and R&C suggested this, supporting the sense with the note that 'the Greta [river]... brawls over many rock-beds near the fort'.

IDENTIFICATION. The Roman fort at Bowes, Yorkshire (NY 9913), on the river Greta (which is of Norse origin).

LAVOBRINTA of *Ravenna* 106_{40} (= R&C 80): see *LEVOBRINTA

LEGEOLIO of *AI* 475_6: see LAGENTIUM

LEMANA (river)

SOURCE

Ravenna 108_{39} (= R&C 266): LEMANA

DERIVATION. The next name (*Portus*) *Lemanis*, is based on this river-name. Very numerous names either related to this or similar to it in form are listed and discussed by the Celtic philologists, notably Jackson *LHEB* 282, 486, 630, 672–73, and *Britannia*, I (1970), 78; Hubschmid *ELH* I. 490; Whatmough *DAG* x–xi. In ancient times the only other British name recorded and related to this is *Lemannonius Sinus*, but modern derivatives related to the name, now Lympne [lim] (Kent), are listed by Jackson, Ekwall, etc.: the rivers Leam (Northants), Lemon (Devon), Lymn (Lancs), Leven (in Gaelic *Leamhain*: Scotland), Laune (Ireland). Another interesting example is the Lyvennet Beck of Cumbria, *Llwyfenydd* in the poems of Taliesin, for which Förster *FT* 682 postulated British **Leminēta*; this name and Yorkshire Leeming are discussed by A. H. A. Hogg in *Antiquity*, XX (1946), 210–11, and Ifor Williams in *The Poems of Taliesin* (Dublin, 1968), xliv–v. Abroad were *Lemannus Lacus* (Lake Geneva), *Limonum* (Poitiers: Vienne, France), *Lemausum* > Limours (Seine-et-Oise, France), river *Lemane* or *Limane* > Limagne (Puy-de-Dôme and Allier, France), *Lemovices* tribe > Limoges (Haute-Vienne, France); and a wide variety of names such as *Limia*, *Limana*, *Limonia*, extending from Portugal across France and Italy to Serbia and Russia, collected by Hubschmid *ELH* I. 490.

Whatmough attempts to distinguish three possible roots which had sometimes been confused in the past:

(1) **lem*- 'stag', which he hardly follows up except for the possibility that the ethnicon *Lemovices* contains an emblematic animal-name 'stag-fighters', on the analogy of *Branovices*, etc., and that *Limomum* may be the 'source du cerf';

(2) **lem*- **lim*- 'elm' (Welsh *llwyf*; Old Irish *lem*, Irish *leamh*; cognate with Latin *ulmus*);

(3) **lim*- 'marsh', from a root **lei*- 'to pour, flow', cf. Welsh *llif* 'stream, flood' from **limo*-, and Greek λίμνη. Like other British authorities, Jackson unhesitatingly assigns the present name to a British **Leman(n)ā* 'river in the elm-wood', that is **lemo*- 'elm' with *-*an(n)*- suffix, citing *Derventio* 'river in the oakwood' as a parallel. Whatmough equally, after long discussion, appears eventually to conclude that two of his possible roots may be dismissed, and all names assigned to his (2), **lem*- 'elm'; in his view *Lim*- is for *Lem*- in such names as *Limonum*, *lem*- *lim*- being dialectal variations, allophones of a phoneme /i/ which was often written as *e*. L.-F. Flutre in *RIO*, IX (1957), 36–37, reaches the same conclusion about the *Lemovices* as 'combattants de l'orme'. Hubschmid's numerous names all have *Lim*-, so that his distinct etymology, (3) **lim*- 'marsh', could well hold for them.

The above is reasonable. However, it must be doubted whether the elm has ever been sufficiently common, or has ever formed large enough woods, for so many ancient places and especially rivers to be named from it. In this it is surely distinct from the oak (*Derventio*, etc.). This ecological point occurred to A. G. C. Turner in *BBCS*, XXII (1966–68), 116–19, who was not satisfied with the accepted origin of the West Pennine name Lyme in **lem*- 'elm': 'The elm does not seem to have been a particularly common tree in the north of England in early times (any more than it is today)...' Hence 'formally ME *Lime*, OE **Līm* are more easily derived from British **Līm-* identical with Welsh *llif* "stream, flood", found in Dorset R. Lyme; also found as a stream-name in Wales.' But after proposing this interesting idea, Turner appears to settle for the accepted 'elm' meaning or alternatively for 'bare place' (Celtic **lummo-*), which can hardly be a possibility here. If the elm was not common enough to give rise to place-names, the possibility is that a single sacred elm could be a reason for naming; but Alqvist in *Arctos*, VII (1972), 12, discussing Ptolemy's Λίμιος ἄλσος in Silesia (II, 11, 13), remarks that 'Although tree-worship is well attested among the Celts, I have found no specific instance of elms for cult purposes', and the tree does not seem to have the magical or folkloric associations that the oak, for example, still has.

Apart from the *Lemovices* with their emblematic name, all the other names listed could readily – and from a semantic point of view, much more easily – be from **lim-* 3), yet another water-name of the kind so often encountered, with senses 'marsh, flooded area, marshy river', etc. This is the view of Flutre (see above): 'Il est plus probable que ces deux derniers noms [*Limagne*, *Limagnole*, river-names of Lozère], comme celui de la *Limagne*, région du Puy-de-Dôme, dérivent du radical **lim-*/**lem-* "boue, limon", lequel, suivant Dauzat, était latin (et aussi germanique), et a du être aussi gaulois, italo-celtique, sinon celtique, comme l'indique, en face de *Limagne* (évidemment "le bas pays marécageux") le nom *Lemannus* qu'on ne peut expliquer par "lac des ormes". Le radical **lim-* est grec également: λίμνη "marais"...' And Flutre cites British *Lemana* as a further case in the same category of 'marsh' names. Given Whatmough's discussion of *e*/*i* as allophones, and of phoneme /i/ often written *e* (with *e* > *i* in French names of Gaulish origin, *Lemovices* > Limoges, *Lemausum* > Limours, etc.; see further E. Jung in *REL*, XLVII (1969), 451), there seems to be no difficulty about deriving the present name and many related to it from **lim-* 'marsh' (and similar senses). See also Pokorny in *ZCP*, XXI (1940), 119–20.

IDENTIFICATION. The river East Rother (formerly Lympne) of East Sussex and Kent – in preference to other possibilities because it immediately follows *Durbis* in the *Ravenna* list.

LEMANIS, PORTUS LEMANIS

SOURCES

AI 473_{6-7} and 473_{10} (Iter IV): AD PORTUM LEMANIS
Ravenna 106_{35} (= R&C 70): LEMANIS
TP: LEMANIO (possibly LEMAUIO)
ND XXVIII_5 (*pictura*): LEMANNIS
XXVIII_{15} (text): Praepositus numeri Turnacensium, LEMANNIS

DERIVATION. The name is a fossilised locative, for which see ANICETIS; this fixed form was not affected by the use of *portus*, as *AI* shows. The name is based on the river-name in the previous entry. Jackson in *Britannia*, I (1970), 78, examines the process:

'The Anglo-Saxon name of Lympne, *Liminas*, derived from this [*Lemanis*, plural], was also plural; *Lemanis* may therefore represent a British plural, perhaps **Leman*(*n*)*i̯ā*, plural of a derivative **leman*(*n*)*i̯on* or the like, though the force of a plural is less clear here than in the case of Dover. Alternatively, *Lem-*

> *anis* may represent a British *i*-stem nominative singular, as in the Scottish Leven and Irish Laune, from **Lemanis*; but understood by the Romans as a locative plural, and by the Anglo-Saxons following them.'

Perhaps if the base **lim-* with plural termination and a sense 'marshes, flooded areas' (discussed in the previous entry) is borne in mind, the question of the plural to which Jackson alludes is answered.

IDENTIFICATION. The Roman fort of Stutfall Castle, Lympne, Kent (TR 1134). The Royal Military Canal, which runs past it and was constructed during the Napoleonic wars, follows the old course of the East Rother (formerly Lympne) river.

LEMANNONIUS SINUS

SOURCE

Ptolemy II, 3, 1: Λεμαννόνιος κόλπος (= LEMANNONIUS SINUS), vars. Λελααννόνιος (= LELAANONIUS), Λεμααννόνιος (= LEMAANONIUS), Λελμααννόνιος (= LELMAANONIUS)

II, 3, 8: τοῦ Λεμαννονίου κόλπου (= a LEMANNONIO... SINU) (with further vars.)

DERIVATION. The name is based on one of the roots discussed under LEMANA, traditionally **lem-* '*lim-* 'elm' but possibly **lim-* 'marsh' or a further sense connected with water in some form. The closest analogue is *Lemannus Lacus* (Lake Geneva), both having the *-*an*(*n*)- suffix. The present name has a further suffix which is a latinisation of British *-*onio-* (see CANONIUM). Bradley thought the name had left a descendant in that of Loch Lomond, and that both the *sinus* and the Loch reflected a tribal name. Watson *CPNS* 119 supports part of this, observing that 'the name of the river from Loch Lomond is *Leamhain*, genitive *Leamhna*, Leven, meaning "Elm-water". Its plain, the Vale of Leven, was *Magh Leamhna*, and Loch Lomond was of old *Loch Leamhna*.' On p. 71, Watson gives *Argoed Llwyfain* as the Welsh name for a similarly named bay in Scotland (i.e., also originally bearing a name like *Lemannonius*).

IDENTIFICATION. Loch Long which, as Watson *CPNS* 19 points out, bounds Lennox (*Leamhnacht*) on the west.

LETOCETUM

SOURCES

AI 470 (Iter II): ETOCETO

Ravenna 106_{48} (= R&C 94): LECTOCETO

Of *AI*'s form the editor notes 'ante *etoceto* una littera (fortasse *e*) erasa' in one MS. *Ravenna*'s form shows a copyist's assimilation to Latin *lectus* 'bed'.

DERIVATION. Jackson in *Britannia*, I (1970), 74, gives the name as British **Lētocēton*, earlier **Leitocaiton*; the meaning is 'grey wood'. The first element is **leito-* 'grey' (Welsh *llwyd*, Irish *liath*), seemingly not present elsewhere in ancient toponymy. The second is **caito-* 'wood' (Welsh *coed*, Cornish *cûz*, Breton *koat*), cognate with Germanic **haitha*, German *Heide*, English *heath*, and probably with *-cetum* as in Latin *quer*[*cu*]*cetum* 'oakwood', etc. (Holder I. 1002). The element is not common in ancient toponymy: examples are *Cetobriga* > Xetubre > Setúbal (Portugal), **Borvo-cetum* > *Borcetum* > Burtscheid (near Aachen, Germany); but it is found in more recent names in Wales, Scotland, and in England Pencoyd, Penketh, etc. (Ekwall, *EPN*). For the development of the name in Anglo-Saxon (*Lyccid*, later *Lyccid-feld* > Lichfield) see Jackson *LHEB* 332, 563, etc. The Welsh name is *Caer Lwytgoed* (Jackson), but Bede mentions the bishopric under the name of *Licidfelth* (IV, 3) and its bishop as *Alduino Lyccitfeldensi* (V, 23).

IDENTIFICATION. The Roman town at Wall, Staffordshire (SK 0906), 2½ miles south of Lichfield. On the difficult problems surrounding the transfer of the centre of settlement from Wall to Lichfield in post-Roman times see C. C. Taylor, *Transactions of the South Staffordshire Archaeological and Historical Society*, X (1968–69), 43–53.

LEUCA

SOURCE

Ravenna 108_{29} (= R&C 246): LEUCA
108_{30} (= R&C 248): LEUGOSENA

Ravenna's second entry conflates *Leuca* and *Sena*; the latter follows as an independent name in the list at 108_{41} (SENUA), so the muddle involves double duplication as well as conflation. However, it is remotely possible that *Ravenna*'s entries might be correct after all, the two above relating to different rivers: one perhaps the upper reaches or a tributary (*Leuca*), the other a broader or a main stream (*Leucosena* 'senior partner, old one (of the pair)').

DERIVATION. The base is Celtic **leuco-* 'bright, shining, white', documented by Holder II. 195, with derivatives in Welsh *llug* and Irish *luach*. Cognates include Latin *lūx*, *lucēre*, also *lucus* 'small wood', Greek λευκός 'light', etc. From Gaulish **leuca* and from **leuco-* of the Celtic of Spain there was formed in late Latin (St Jerome: *in Ioel* III, 18) *leuco*, which has left Romance descendants: French *lieue*, Spanish dialectal *lleco*, *lieco* 'clearing, clear land, treeless land left uncultivated' (a sense which is important for British *Leucomagus*); one may compare the English cognate *lea*. (See Dottin *LG* 265, J. Hubschmid *ELH* I. 141.)

In addition to the three following British names and *Verlucio*, Celtic **leuco-* is widespread in Continental toponymy: e.g. *Leuciana AI* 438_5 now Santa Cruz del Puerto (Toledo, Spain), Τρίλευκον a promontory in N.W. Spain (Ptolemy II, 6, 4), Λευκάριστος in Germania Magna (Ptolemy II, 11, 13). *Leucus* is known as a personal name. The *Leuci* people of Gallia Belgica had their capital at *Tullum Leucorum* > Toul (Meurthe-et-Moselle, France). The root is also present in the divine name *Leucetios*, god of lightning, equated with Mars in e.g. a Bath inscription to *Loucetio Marti* (*RIB* 140); see Ross (1967)' 174–75. A number of place-names in S. Italy, the Aegean, etc., are formed from Greek λευκός and cognates: *Leucopetra*, *Leucadia*, *Leucae*, etc.

The sense of the British river-name is thus 'shining one'.

IDENTIFICATION. The river Loughor, south Wales.

LEUCARUM

SOURCE

AI 484_1 (Iter XII): LEUCARO

DERIVATION. This name, basically that of a river **Leucara* transferred to a fort on its banks with change of declension, consists of British **leuco-* (as in the previous entry) with the *-*ar*(*a*) suffix. Evidently the Welsh river which is now the Loughor had two slightly different names, *Leuca* (previous entry) recorded by *Ravenna*, and **Leucara* whose fort *Leucarum* was recorded by *AI*. Watson *CPNS* 433 and Jackson in *JRS*, xxxviii (1948), 57, associate with this the Ayrshire river Lugar, from an identical **Leucara*.

A problem of Celtic phonology is pointed out by Williams and by Jackson in *JRS*, xxxviii (1948), 57: Williams notes that Loughor is in Welsh *Casllwchwr*, whose -*ch*- demands original -*cc*-, that is **Luccarum*; Jackson, who spells *Llychwr*, agrees that this cannot come from **Leucara*, for this would have given Welsh **Llugar*, concluding that 'The name Loughor can hardly be the same... The likeness must be due to a coincidence.' But with names so nearly identical in the same area, it would surely be better to assume some disturbance of the normal phonetic process, perhaps by analogy, folk-etymology or the like?

The *-*ăr*(*a*) suffix occurs in British *Leucarum, Lutudarum, Nabarus, Tamarus*, possibly *Metaris, Varar*, and widely abroad. It has long been recognised as a river- or water-suffix, and much studied. A recent summary is that of Dauzat *TF* 131–41. He finds that *Ar*- exists as a root, doubled evidently to mean 'great river' (*Ar-ar*), with suffixes, compounded with other elements, and as a suffix itself. 'Ce suffixe a vécu longtemps en Gaule, où il était très vivant à l'époque gauloise, comme le prouvent certaines formations avec des radicaux celtiques (*Artara, Candara, Isara, Leucara, Samara*)' (*TF* 139); but finally, in view of its antiquity and great extension, '*Ar*- est bien une base hydronymique pre-indo-européenne' (*TF* 141). As a suffix at any rate in Latin usage, and hence presumably in Gaulish and British, *-*ăr*(*a*) had short -*ă*- and was unstressed, hence *Nabarus* > Naver, etc. See also F. G. Diack in *RC*, xxxviii (1920–21), 116–18.

IDENTIFICATION. Probably the Roman fort at Loughor, Glamorgan (SS 5697); but see p. 174.

LEUCOMAGUS

SOURCE

Ravenna 106_{21} (= R&C 45): LEUCOMAGNO, vars. LEUCU MAGNO, LEUCU MAGNA

DERIVATION. For the first element, see LEUCA; for the second (in *Ravenna* with scribal assimilation to Latin *magnus*; cf. *Noviomagus*), see CAESAROMAGUS. Given the diversity of senses of British **leuco*-, the name might be 'clear plain' (i.e. clear of trees and scrub) or 'bright plain, white plain' (i.e. chalky). Williams, though interpreting 'clear plain', provides an analogy for the second sense by mentioning Welsh Gwynfa < **Vindomag* 'white plain, white place'.

IDENTIFICATION. As R&C noted, from its position in the *Ravenna* list (and since Winchester is not in question) this should lie near Andover, and the discovery of buildings associated with the Roman road junction at East Anton, Hampshire (SU 3747), now suggests a likely place.

*LEUCOVIA

SOURCES

Ptolemy ii, 3, 5: Λουκοπιβία (= LOUCOPIBIA), a *polis* of the Novantae; var. Λουκοπιάβια (= LOUCOPIABIA)

Ravenna 107_{37} (= R&C 170): LUCOTION, var. LUCOCION

Müller in editing Ptolemy commented that the second element (meaningless in terms of Celtic roots) could have resulted from a conflation of variants, Λουκοπία and Λουκοβία. This is helpful. *Ravenna*'s entry has not been associated before with Ptolemy's, but its place in *Ravenna* fits in well with this correspondence, and as often noted, most of Ptolemy's north British names do figure in *Ravenna* (since both depended ultimately on the same map-source for this region: see p. 193). The equivalence is suggested also by Dillemann (p. 69). R&C as often took *Lucotion* literally and provided it with an etymology based on **lucot-* 'mouse'; there are indeed names of persons and places based on this (Holder II. 303). One may however suppose that the Cosmographer found a form **Lucovium* on his map (with *u* a more developed stage of earlier *eu*, *ou*) and misread *v* as *t*; his *-on* stands as always for *-um*.

DERIVATION. It has been traditional to interpret Ptolemy's first syllable Λου- as Latin *Lu-*, but as Jackson points out in general terms in *LHEB* 34, the Celtic sound [ou] may be rendered ου in Ptolemy's Greek, though one would expect οου. Since **leuco-* is found in other British names and since **louco-* is the same element with vowels at a different stage of development (compare *Loucetio Marti* and see *LHEB* 306–307, etc.) it seems reasonable to suggest that here we have **leuco-* again; see, then, LEUCA. This was Jackson's suggestion in a note to *LHEB* 307: 'read perhaps Λουκοβια = **Loucou̯i̯ā* < **Leucou̯i̯a*', which we are happy to adopt. Other possibilities such as **luco-* 'marsh' (mentioned by Whatmough *DAG* 512 in discussing the possibility that *Lutecia* – Paris – is for **Lucotecia*), and **loucos* **locos* 'lieu de réunion' (*RIO*, XXV (1973), 203) are less attractive; they take Ptolemy's first syllable at its usual value, but leave the rest unexplained. Pokorny's notion in *Vox Romanica*, X (1948–49), 229, that the name might properly be **Louk-upia* 'Weißbach', **upia* being a word for 'river' with Illyrian connections, seems perverse.

The suffix in our proposed version is *-*ou̯i̯o* (see CANOVIUM), here apparently a kind of feminine as in *Vinovia*. It is curious that in the present case we have evidence of both *-ia* and *-ium* endings, precisely as for *Vinovia–Vinovium*.

IDENTIFICATION. Probably the Roman fort at Glenlochar, Kirkcudbrightshire (NX 7364); since this is on the Dee (DEVA^{2}), the reference would be to a 'shining' reach of the river.

LEVIODUNUM

SOURCE

Ravenna 108_9 (= R&C 220): LEUIODANUM, var. LEVIODANIUM

108_{10} (= R&C 222): LEVIOXAUA, var. LEVIOXANA

Although R&C treated these as two separate names, they seem an obvious duplication resulting from the Cosmographer's attempted correction of his own spelling. R&C adjusted the first to *-dunum* without comment, but for the second sought an etymology in '*-xava* = *-sava*?'. However, the *n* in the variant of the second name should be retained; *a* is for *u* in both forms, a common error. The *-x-* is less readily explained.

DERIVATION. For **leuio-* 'smooth', see DUROLEVUM; for *-dunum*, see BRANODUNUM. The sense is probably 'smooth fort' or 'slippery fort' as indicated by Williams, with reference perhaps to a native rather than a Roman construction, though the name as recorded in the sources is likely to refer to a Roman fort. However, **leuio-* could also be the name of a river, though such a compound would be exceptional. A note of Schnetz in his edition of *Ravenna* should not be overlooked: the form at 108_9 is as readily emended to **Leucodunum* or **Loucodunum*, in which case 'bright fort' (see LEUCA).

IDENTIFICATION. Unknown, but apparently in Scotland north of the Antonine Wall.

*LEVOBRINTA

SOURCE
Ravenna 106_{40} (= R&C 80): LAVOBRINTA

DERIVATION. It seems that *Ravenna*'s form should be corrected as above; compare such spellings as *Durolavi*, *Levatris*. This seems better than Williams's solution, **lavo-* as in Welsh *llawes* 'much, many', which is undocumented in early place-names.

For *Levo-*, see DUROLEVUM. *Brinta* as a river-name has analogues listed by Holder I. 546, e.g. *Brinta* a river of the Venice region, *Brintesia*, etc. Williams suggests that these involve a cognate of Old Irish *brenn-* 'to gush forth'. Hence for the whole name a sense 'smooth gushing one' seems indicated. The name appears among habitation-names in *Ravenna*, but there are several instances in which river-names are so listed, having been misinterpreted from the map-source.

IDENTIFICATION. Unknown, but next to Wroxeter in the list. R&C's tentative attribution to Forden Gaer (SO 2098) depends partly on their identification of Caer Sws with the next name in the list, *Mediomano*, which we equate with MEDIOLANUM (q.v.). No river-name in this area suggests itself, but it may be noted that Vyrnwy is a derivative of *Sabrina* (Ekwall *ERN* 430) or *Sabrinouia* (Jackson *LHEB* 613), and it is perhaps unlikely that both the Severn and its tributary always bore the same name.

LIAR (?)

SOURCE
Ravenna 108_{35} (= R&C 259): LIAR

DERIVATION. The name occurs in *Ravenna*'s river-list. Williams suggested a relation with the root which has given Welsh *llyr* 'sea, flood', hence a possible meaning 'stream'; but the name looks unsatisfactory – perhaps a fragment or a misreading or an abbreviation – and it is unsafe to found any reasoning upon it.

IDENTIFICATION. Unknown, but apparently not far from the river Tyne.

LINDA

SOURCE
Ravenna 108_{36} (= R&C 260): LENDA
The name is more classically *Linda* and is to be associated with the two names following, *Lindinis* and *Lindum*. Of *e* for *i*, R&C remark that 'confusion between *i* and *e* is...common in Roman written

versions of Celtic names' (compare *Lend-* in the two inscriptions under *Lindinis*). However, if the *i* in these names were short, it would have been pronounced (and sometimes written) *e* by the third century in Latin; see p. 26. In the present case the form could have arisen in this country, or could simply reflect the Cosmographer's own speech.

DERIVATION. The name is British **lindo-* 'pool, lake' (Pokorny 674: root **lendh-* 'Naß, Quelle'), now represented by Welsh *llyn* 'pond, lake', also 'liquid, drink', Breton *lenn* 'marsh', Cornish *lyn* 'water'; also Irish *lind* 'drink'. Given this variety of senses in the modern languages, it is plain that *Linda* could have applied to a variety of types of water; R&C thought that 'lake river' was implied, and it might be 'river that forms pools'. Names with this element as listed by Holder II. 227: *Lindesina* now Bourbonne-les-Bains (Haute-Marne, France); *Lindiacum* > Lintgen (Luxembourg); **Lindoduros* > Lindern (near Aachen, Germany); *Diolindum* for **Divo-lindo-n* 'aqua splendens' near Lalinde (Dordogne, France); **Dubo-lindo-n* 'black pool' > Dublin.

IDENTIFICATION. Unknown. From its position in the *Ravenna* list this could possibly be a misunderstood duplication of *Lindum*, but there are several rivers in eastern England whose modern names are of Germanic origin and whose earlier names would have been Celtic.

LINDINIS

SOURCES

Ravenna 106_{11} (= R&C 26): LINDINIS

Inscription: *RIB* 1672, a building-stone from near Cawfields on Hadrian's Wall: C(IVITAS) DUR(O)TR(I)G(UM) [L]ENDIN(I)ESIS

Inscription: *RIB* 1673, a building-stone from near Housesteads on Hadrian's Wall: CI(VITAS) DUROTRAG(UM) LENDINIESI[S]

(Both stones are probably of A.D. 369)

For the *e/i* variation, see LINDA; in the epigraphic evidence above, we certainly have Vulgar Latin *e* < *ĭ*. *RIB* naturally restores the adjectival form of the name in the two inscriptions to classical *-iensis*, but the vulgar *-iesis* is more likely here (see also BANNA, VINDOLANDA).

DERIVATION. For British **lindo-*, see LINDA. Any one of its senses might serve here. Williams says that *-in-* 'suggests a wet place', citing Welsh *gwernin* 'alder-swamp' (from *gwern* 'alder'); R&C think a diminutive possible also; however, **-ina* is a recognised Celtic suffix, perhaps as in British *Sabrina*, here in plural form (see *RIO*, XXV (1973), 217). For locative *-is*, see ANICETIS.

IDENTIFICATION. The Roman town of Ilchester, Somerset (ST 5222), on the river Yeo or Ivel. In addition to the suitability of the name, the identification depends on the fact that Ilchester is the only Roman town of any size in the territory of the *Durotriges* apart from DURNOVARIA, Dorchester (q.v.). C. E. Stevens (*EHR*, LVI (1941), 359, and *Proceedings of the Somerset Archaeological and Natural History Society*, XCVI (1952), 188–92) drew attention to this and argued from the inscriptions that at some stage the *Civitas Durotrigum* was subdivided, with Ilchester becoming the capital of the north-western part. Such subdivision occurred in several cases in Gaul, and Stevens's view has been widely accepted. More recently it has been challenged by

J. E. Bogaers (*JRS*, LVII (1967), 233) who maintains that here *civitas Durotrigum* means simply 'town in the territory of the *Durotriges*', but this does not affect the attribution of the name.

LINDUM[1]

SOURCES

Ptolemy II, 3, 11: Λίνδον (= LINDUM), a *polis* of the Coritani

AI 475_3 (Iter V), 476_7 and 477_9 (Iter VI), 478_{10} (Iter VIII): LINDO

Ravenna 106_{55} (= R&C 104): LINDUM COLONIA

Inscriptions

(*a*) datable

JRS, XI (1921), 101–107 (= Burn, 1969, No. 65, pp. 50–51): an altar set up at Bordeaux by a SEVIR AUG(USTALIS) COL(ONIARUM) EBOR(ACI) ET LIND(I) . . . ; A.D. 237

RIB 2240, a milestone of Valerian, A.D. 253–59, which marked the first mile on the road to Leicester; its inscription ends with R P L (= *Respublica Lindinensis*)

RIB 2241, a milestone of Victorinus, A.D. 268–70, inscribed A L(INDO) S(EGELOCUM) M P XIIII

(*b*) undated

RIB 250, the tombstone of Volusia Faustina, C(IVIS) LIND(ENSIS)

RIB 269, a fragment of a commemorative tablet of which little remains but [L]IND(. . .), rendered 'of Lindum'

CIL VIII. 21669, a tombstone from Ain-Temouchent (ancient Mauretania Caesariensis): D M M IUNIUS CAPITO LINDO ML LEG X G(EMINA)

CIL XIII. 6679: FORTUNAM SUPERAM HONORI AQUILAE LEG XXII PR PF M MINICIUS M FIL QUIR LINDO MAR[CELLINUS ?]

DERIVATION. See LINDA. The particular application suggested by R&C is to the marshes and pools of the Witham, in particular Brayford Mere.

IDENTIFICATION. The Roman *colonia* (succeeding a legionary fortress) of Lincoln (SK 9771). On Ptolemy's attribution of it, see CORITANI.

Note. The name survives in modern Lincoln, while Lindsey (Lincs.) is from **Lindenses*, an ethnicon formed from the name of the *colonia* (plus Anglo-Saxon *ēg* 'island'); on this in turn is based the name Lindisfarne. Bede evidently knew only a garbled form of the ancient name, for he relatinises by a sort of folk-etymology involving *colina* 'hill': *Lindocolinae civitatis* (gen.; II, 16), *in Lindocolino* (ablative; II, 18). For the development of the name in Anglo-Saxon, see Jackson, *LHEB* 247, 258, 309, etc., with a different explanation of Bede's form.

LINDUM[2]

SOURCES

Ptolemy II, 3, 7: Λίνδον (= LINDUM), a *polis* of the D(u)mnonii

Ravenna 107_{32} (= R&C 160): CLINDUM

Ravenna's entry is certainly to be equated with Ptolemy's, though it is hard to see how the copying error with initial *C*- arose.

DERIVATION. See LINDUM[1], and LINDA.

IDENTIFICATION. Probably the Roman fort at Drumquhassle (near Drymen), Stirlingshire (NS 4887), near the south-eastern extremity of Loch Lomond.

LITANA of *Ravenna* 107_{55} (= R&C 198): see ALAUNA[6]

LITANOMAGUS

SOURCE

Ravenna 108_6 (= R&C 214): LITINOMAGO, var. LINTINOMAGO

DERIVATION. There seems no doubt that the proposed emendation is right. British **litano-* (earlier **plitano-*, compare Latin *platanus* from Greek πλατανός) was 'broad, extensive', now represented by Welsh *llydan*, *lledan*, Breton *ledan*; also Irish *leathan*. For *-magus*, see CAESAROMAGUS. The sense is thus 'broad place', perhaps 'place with a wide view'. The adjective was widely used in toponymy: in simple form, *Litana Silva* in Gallia Transpadana, *Littamo AI* 280_1 (?S. Candido, Italy), and as a superlative showing still the primitive consonants *Bletisama* > Ledesma (Salamanca, Spain; Tovar in *ELH* I. 121); in compounds *Litanobriga AI* 380_4 near Chantilly (Oise, France), etc. Holder II. 242 and Ellis Evans *GPN* 216 list personal names compounded with **litano-*.

IDENTIFICATION. Unknown, but apparently in Scotland north of the Antonine Wall, and, from the name, probably in one of the carses, as R&C suggest.

LITUS SAXONICUM

SOURCE

ND L_{36}: [Comes rei militaris] LITORIS SAXONICI per Britannias (again, V_{132})

XXVIII (title): Comes LITORIS SAXONICI per Britanniam (again, XXVIII_{12})

(The relevance of the reference by Ammianus Marcellinus (XXVII, 8, 1) to Nectaridus as *comes maritimi tractus* is disputed.)

DERIVATION. The name is Latin, 'Saxon Shore'. In *ND* the Comes Litoris Saxonici commands units only in Britian, but the description in it of two places in Gaul as *in litore Saxonico* (*Grannona*, XXXVII_{14}, then under the Dux Tractus Armoricani, and *Marcis*, XXXVIII_7, then under the Dux Belgicae Secundae) suggests that the term, and probably the command, once extended to both sides of the Channel. Both the stages in the development of the command and the precise meaning of the term (whether 'coast garrisoned or settled by Saxon mercenaries' or 'coast liable to attack by Saxons' – more probably the latter) are still disputed. For recent discussions see S. Johnson: *The Roman Forts of the Saxon Shore* (London, 1976) and especially D. E. Johnston (ed.): *The Saxon Shore* (CBA Research Report 18, London, 1977).

IDENTIFICATION. So far as Britain is concerned, the forts shown by *ND* as under the command of the Comes Litoris Saxonici are *Othona*, *Dubris*, *Lemanis*, *Branodunum*, *Gariannum*, *Regulbium*, *Rutupiae*, *Anderitum* and *Portus Ardaoni* (qq.v.), showing that it extended from Brancaster, Norfolk, to Portchester, Hampshire.

LOCATREBE

SOURCE

Ravenna 107_{35} (= R&C 166): LOCATREVE

Ravenna has *v* for *b*, as often. It is not possible to guess what the ending should be, but *-e* is unlikely to be right.

DERIVATION. The first element is British **loc-* (**locu-s*, Holder II. 279), 'lake, pool', now represented by Welsh *llwch* 'lake; pool, pond; inlet', Breton *loch* or *louch* 'marsh', etc.; Irish *loch* 'lake, pond'; Latin *lacus* is cognate. This element is found in British *Segelocum*, probably in *Locus Maponi*, and abroad in e.g. Λοκόριτον (= *Locoritum*, Ptolemy II, 11, 14) > Lohr am Main (Germany), *Pennelocus AI* 351_7, *TP*, 'lake-end, head of the lake' now Villeneuve at the east end of Lake Geneva (Switzerland), *Sidoloucum AI* 360_3 = Ammianus XVI, 2, 3 (*Sedelaucum*) > Saulieu (Côte-d'Or, France). The second element *atreb-* is discussed under *Atrebates*. The sense of the name is thus 'lake village', perhaps more strictly 'pool-dwellers' as given by R&C, who add 'as if referring to folk living in crannogs'; but the name could have been given to a Roman fort near a crannog.

IDENTIFICATION. Unknown, but apparently in Scotland south of the Antonine Wall. For a distribution map of crannogs, with list and bibliography, see C. M. Piggott in *PSAS*, LXXXVII (1952–53), 149–50; those dated to the Roman period are all in south-west Scotland.

LOCUS MAPONI

SOURCES

Ravenna 108_{17} (= R&C 228): MAPONI

Inscription: *JRS*, LVIII (1968), 209: A slab found at Birrens fort in 1967: CISTUMUCI LO(CO) MΛbOMI '(gift) of Cistumucus from Locus Maponi'

Before the discovery of the inscription, it could be conjectured (Holder) that *Ravenna*'s genitive form should be completed as **Fanum Maponi* (cf. *Fanum Cocidi*). The existence of *Locus Maponi* on his map-source may well have misled the Cosmographer into forming his small section of *diversa loca* names, in which *Maponi* figures in first place. In the inscription, it is unlikely that *b* represents a voiced *p* (the instance would be unique in Britain in Latin, and could not be British at this date).

DERIVATION. The name is apparently 'place of Maponus', with *Locus* as, or to be taken as, Latin 'place' (but hardly as an officially-designated 'meeting-place of a tribe' as R&C thought about all eight names in *Ravenna*'s section). But some caution is necessary, for there are no analogues anywhere for such a use of Latin *locus* 'place'; and despite the existence of Latin *Fanum* in this region (for *Cocidius*), it is in principle safer to consider that a British word is involved. This can only be **loc-* 'lake, pool' as in the previous entry, which as we see from examples there is represented as *-locus* and similar forms in the Latin records; indeed, inhabitants of such places, or the compilers of the Latin records, may well have assimilated the Celtic word to Latin *locus* 'place' in both Gaul and Britain. In the Birrens inscription, indeed, the restoration of the middle term to *Lo(co)* is only a possibility; **Lo(uco)* with vowels closer to those of British is equally justifiable. The association of Maponus with two Gaulish water-names (see below) allows us still more support for such an association in the present case.

Maponus was the '(divine) youth', a god who enjoyed a cult in northern England and south-west Scotland, and who in four out of five British inscriptions to him is equated with Apollo (Ross,

1967, 368–70). The cult involved 'high Roman military officials and [was] thus of some standing' (Richmond in *Arch. Ael.*[4], XXI (1943), 206–10). His name uses in a special function the common noun **mapo-* of British, represented by Old Welsh *map*, Welsh *mab* 'boy, youth; son'; his name in a proper function is found in Welsh *Mabinogion*, and he is 'in the old Welsh tales *Mabon*, son of Modron' (Williams), that is son of *Matrona* the mother-goddess. In Old Irish *macc*, *mac* retains the consonant of original **maqo-*. There is some evidence of the cult of Maponus in Gaul, in a mention *de Mabono fonte* in a cartulary in about 1090 (Holder II. 414), and in an inscription of Bourbonne-les-Bains (Haute-Marne, France), though in this *Maponus* might be the common rather than the divine name (*DAG* 990).

IDENTIFICATION. R&C, citing Watson *CPNS* 181, say 'Probably the *Clochmabenstane* near Gretna (on the north shore of the Solway Firth), the traditional meeting-place of the Western March and the site of a prehistoric stone circle.' But in that name *Cloch-* is 'stone' (which Anglo-Saxon *-stane* duplicates) and has nothing to do with *locus*. However, there is also in Dumfriesshire the village of *Lochmaben*, also noted by Watson, which is surely a precise derivative of *Locus Maponi*, with *locus* representing British **loc-*, 'lake, pool', here referring to Castle Loch. This is one mile west of the Annan, and a Roman fort to protect its crossing by the Roman road Margary 76 (leading to Nithsdale) might be expected.

LODONE of *Ravenna* 108_6 (= R&C 213): see CALIDONII

LONDINIUM

SOURCES

(*a*) Geographical, itineraries, etc.

Ptolemy I, 15, 7: ...καὶ Λονδινίου (= LONDINII, gen.)
II, 3, 12: Λονδίνιον (LONDINIUM), a *polis* of the Cantii
VIII, 3, 6: Λονδίνιον (= LONDINIUM)

AI 471_5 (Iter II): LONDINIO (and repeatedly in this form)
477_{10} (Iter VII): LUNDINIO (also in 479_{10}, 480_8)

Ravenna 106_{50} (= R&C 97): LONDINIUM AUGUSTI
106_{38} (= R&C 75): LANDINI

(*b*) Inscriptions

JRS, XLIV (1954), 108 (also *Ant.J.*, XXXIII (1953), 206): a letter of Rufus Callusini to Epillicus, on a wooden tablet found in the Walbrook in London in 1927. On the outside of the tablet, the address: LONDINIO

A writing tablet found in London in 1959 was published and discussed by E. G. Turner and O. Skutsch in *JRS*, L (1960), 108–11. In line 3,

Postridie quomodo egṛ[essus?]
LONDINIO...

JRS, XII (1922), 283: A second-century jug with a graffito on the shoulder: LONDINI/AD FANUM ISIDIS 'London: next door to the temple of Isis'

Mint-marks of coins have the name abbreviated as L, LN, LON

(*c*) Literary, historical and ecclesiastical

Tacitus *Annals* XIV, 33: LONDINIUM (acc.)

Panegyric VIII, 17, 1 (A.D. 297–98, Trier?): OPPIDUM LONDINIENSE

Council of Arles, A.D. 314: CIVITATE LONDINENSI (with variants)

Ammianus Marcellinus

xx, I, 3: LUNDINIUM (acc.)

xxvii, 8, 7: ...ad LUNDINIUM, vetus oppidum quod Augustam posteritas appellavit

xxviii, 3, 1: ab Augusta profectus, quam veteres appellavere LUNDINIUM

Stephanus of Byzantium, citing Marcian: Λινδόνιον (= LINDONIUM); the ethnic is Λινδονίνος (= *Lindoninus*)

The sources present no problem. It seems obvious to take *Ravenna*'s *Landini* (read from a map) as a duplication of *Londinium*, as was first proposed by Parthey and Pinder in their edition of 1860, with *a* for *o* as often; we may dismiss Stevens's attempt to relate to it *Lindinis*, and that of R&C to find a place for it 'south of the Thames, on a road leading northwards from Silchester' (with etymology based on Celtic **landa*). See also AUGUSTA[1].

DERIVATION. The sources show that the standard Latin form was *Londinium*, guaranteed by the inscriptions. It was a neuter, as shown by Tacitus's adjectives *insigne*, *celebre*. The sources show three cases in use and two, perhaps three different adjectival forms.

Stephanus's form with *Lind-* is probably a simple miscopying, which stemmed from Marcian; but it does perhaps show that in sixth-century Byzantium direct knowledge of the British city was too weak to produce a correction to the proper form. The records of *Lund-* are another matter. Those in *AI* 477_{10}, 479_{10} and 480_{8} might result from miscopying of *Lond-* or might show that material for the itinera in question was collected or corrected at a late stage, a stage certainly recorded in the late fourth century by Ammianus with his reiterated *Lundinium*. To judge from Anglo-Saxon *Lūndene*, the late Romano-British spoken form was indeed *Lundinium*, this *ū* developing from earlier Romano-British *ō* as it did also in the better-recorded Vulgar Latin of Gaul in some situations. Whether this name with *ū* was taken into Anglo-Saxon speech from the Vulgar Latin pronunciation of the inhabitants, as Zachrisson proposed (p. 80), or from British speakers who also pronounced the name with *ū*, as Jackson prefers (*LHEB* 258, etc.) cannot be resolved, but it is a reasonable supposition that in London more than in most places towards the east of the country some Latin speech would have survived into early Anglo-Saxon times.

Bede's forms regularly show *Lundonia* (II, 3; IV, 6; IV, 12; IV, 22; with adjectival *Lundoniensis*, I, 29, and *Lundonienses* 'Londoners', II, 6, etc.). The fact that he makes the city feminine shows that he is following (as with *Cantia*, Eburaca, and perhaps others) forms probably brought from Rome by Augustine in 597, or that in the letter of Pope Gregory to Augustine in 601 (*Lundoniae civitatis*, gen.; Bede I, 29).

The British etymon is unsure. For long it was customary to give it as 'town of **Londinos*', a personal name based on **londo-* 'fierce'; but this had *ŏ*, and is to be dismissed (*LHEB* 308, note). Jackson in *Britannia*, I (1970), 76, prefers to make no guesses. Various roots known in Ligurian have been proposed, for example by J.-G. Gigot in *RIO*, XXVI (1974), 284–92, but they are unconvincing and have no known cognates in British. There seems to be only one analogue, Λονδοβρίς (= *Londobris*), Ptolemy II, 5, 7, now Berlanga island off Portugal, a name which presumably has as its second element *-bris* for *-brix*, *-briga* (compare Ptolemy's Καιτόβριξ = *Caetobrix* for *Cetobriga*, II, 5, 2). Gigot's three names in Hérault, France, e.g. Saint-Martin-de-Londres, and that of the river Soulondres, are of no value; they are not recorded until 1507, and may go back to an English charter of 1327–63, hence representing the name of *Londres* taken from England.

In the name of London, the suffix regularly recorded as *-inium* poses a problem. The form to be expected is *-onium*, British **-onįon*, and Jackson (*LHEB* 308, note) thinks that **-onįon* was indeed the form heard by Anglo-Saxons. One might suggest that *-inium* early (and wrongly, in a way) became established in Latin usage by dissimilation of *o-o* to *o-i*, or alternatively, by assimilation of the stressed vowel to the *i* of the ending. (It is not quite correct to say, as Jackson does in *Britannia*, I (1970), 76, that 'there is some support for **-onįon* in Greek and Latin sources, including the *AI* itself'; in the Cuntz text, there is no trace of this in the main text nor among variants, and in Greek only the late Stephanus, citing Marcian, has -δον-.)

IDENTIFICATION. The Roman city of London (TQ 3281). Ptolemy's attribution of it to the *Cantii* is plainly an error, since apart from the suburb of Southwark, which developed later, it lay wholly north of the river. See also AUGUSTA[1].

LONGOVICIUM

SOURCES

Inscription: *RIB* 1074, an altar found near Lanchester fort: a dedication to the Germanic goddess *Garmangabis* for the welfare of the VEX(ILLATIONIS) SUEBORUM LON(GOVICIANORUM) GOR(DIANAE)

Ravenna 107_{12} (= R&C 133): LINEOIUGLA, var. LINEONIGLA (R&C read LINCOVIGLA)

ND XL_{15} (*pictura*): LONGOUICIO (var. LONGOUITIO)

XL_{30} (text): Praefectus numeri LONGOUICANORUM, LONGOUICIO (vars. LONGO UICA, LONGOUITIO, etc.)

DERIVATION. *ND*'s main forms seem acceptable; in *Ravenna* the first element is badly miscopied, but the second may have a genuine variant in suggesting *-vicia* (compare *Delgovicia*). The first element is not easy. One may safely dismiss the possibility of Latin *longus* 'long' and of a borrowing of this into British (but see further under the next name), except to note that the earliest recorded form of the modern name is *Langecestr'* in 1196, i.e. 'long ceaster', showing that whatever the origin of the Romano-British name, it was interpreted by Germanic settlers as containing a word meaning 'long'. R&C preferred to see in **longo-* a word connected with the root of Welsh *llong*, 'feminine of *llwng*, used for a pool, as in *Tra-llwng* "Welshpool"', commenting that 'the situation [of Lanchester] makes any connection with Welsh *llong* "ship" out of the question'. It is however this possibility which needs to be retained. As seen under *Delgovicia*, the various elements attached to *-vices* do not have to be literal, but can be symbolic or emblematic. Hence a meaning for *Longovicium* 'place of the **Longovices*', these being 'ship-fighters', seems the best. For further comparisons, see the next entry. One notes also *Longobriga* (*CIL* II. 5564), now Freixo in the Douro province of Portugal, which is on a tributary of the Douro; and the *Longostaletes* people who lived in the Béziers region (Hérault, France), which is coastal.

IDENTIFICATION. The Roman fort at Lanchester, Durham (NZ 1546).

LONGUS

SOURCES

Ptolemy II, 3, 1: Λόγγου ποταμοῦ ἐκβολαι (= LONGI FLUVII OSTIA)

Ravenna 109_{22} (= R&C 299): LONGIS

Ravenna's entry appears in its second set of western islands, but like others in this section, it was a river-name written 'in the sea' of a map and consequently misread by the compiler as though it pertained to an island.

DERIVATION. Bradley took *Longus* as a Latin adjective, 'long', and accepted Skene's identification with the river called in Gaelic *Afon Fhada* 'long river' (in English, the Add); we have said above (p. 133) that the name might perhaps be one conferred by the Roman fleet. However, this would be wholly exceptional for a river-name anywhere in Britain; if the name looks suspiciously Latin, it could be that an existing native name was interpreted as Latin by the fleet. Some association with British **longo-* 'ship', as in the previous entry, seems likely. Watson *CPNS* 44–45 discusses the name at length, drawing attention to modern Loch Long 'Loch of Ships', which the Norsemen called *Skipa fjorðr* 'ship-firth', though thinking it likely that here again this *Long-* was a borrowing from Latin, specifically [*navis*] *longa* 'warship'. Old Irish *long* is explained as a Latin borrowing by Pokorny 197. Loth in *RC*, XLIII (1926), 133–35, thinks the present name genuinely Celtic, though perhaps influenced by Latin in sense, and compares it with the ethnicon *Longostaletes* mentioned in the previous entry, preferring to leave the original Celtic meaning unresolved. This is probably best, for even if we do accept an association with **longo-* 'ship', it is obvious that a river is not named with a simple noun meaning 'ship'; we should expect a compound, or at least a formation by suffix.

IDENTIFICATION. From its position in Ptolemy this should be Loch Linnhe (which, as Watson *CPNS* 79 observes, is a ghost name).

LOPOCARIUM of *Ravenna* 107_{18} (= R&C 142): see *CORIOSOPITUM

LOXA

SOURCES

Ptolemy II, 3, 4: Λόξα ποταμοῦ ἐκβολαί (= LOXA FLUVII OSTIA)

Ravenna 107_{35} (= R&C 165): LOXA

Ravenna's entry occurs in what purports to be a section of habitation-names, but at least two other rivers (misread as settlements from the map) are present in it, and there is no problem about taking this entry as another. However, the identity of *Ravenna*'s name with Ptolemy's cannot be absolutely affirmed, despite appearances; the next name in *Ravenna* is *Locatreve*, and it is not impossible that *Loxa* is a mistaken first attempt to spell the first part of this longer name (compare *Calunio–Gallunio* at 107_1).

DERIVATION. The name is not easy. Ekwall (discussed by Williams) associated it with two Lox rivers of Somerset, *ERN* 267–68, and Williams adds Loxford in Essex. The form *Loxa* with *-x-* seems to be correct, despite Jackson's suggestion (perhaps following Diack: see O'Rahilly

EIHM 381–82) that as with *Taexali*/*Taezali*, *-z-* may be intended (after mis-copying in Greek). *Ravenna*, if it is listing the same name, supports *-x-*. Williams followed Ekwall in proposing a Celtic root cognate with Greek λοξός 'oblique', Latin *luscus* 'one-eyed' and Old Irish *losc* 'crippled'; hence, for a river, 'crooked' or 'winding one'. These meanings are probably applicable to a variety of names abroad. *AI* 456_3 records *Losa* (also *Losa vicus*, *DAG* 248) whose river is now the Losse (Gers, France); personal names include *Lossa* (*DAG* 697, 739, 1283), *Loscius* (*DAG* 706), *Loscus* (*CIL* III. 3059), perhaps *Losagni* (gen.; *CIIC* 236, Iveragh, Co. Kerry); and there is a divine name *Losa*, *Loxa* known on five altars from northern Spain (J. M. Blázquez Martínez, *Diccionario de las religiones prerromanas de Hispania* (Madrid, 1975), 117), though it is of course possible that the *Losa* place in Aquitania and the deity of the Basque Country are of different origin. Jackson in *LHEB* 536–39 (notes) regarded the etymology given above as problematic because of the chronology of sound-changes in British, but we now know that *Ravenna*'s North British information relates not to the fourth century but more to the first, since it was drawn from the military map which was also ultimately a source for Ptolemy. In *PP* 136 (note), Jackson seems disposed to accept the etymology as probable. See *LHEB* 536–39 for the complex phonetic investigation involved. The development of *Loxa* to modern Lossie, if correct, occurred within later Goidelic rather than within British speech, for in Goidelic /ks/ > /s/.

IDENTIFICATION. The river Lossie, Moray.

LUCOTION of *Ravenna* 107_{37} (= R&C 170): see *LEUCOVIA

LUENTINUM

SOURCE

Ptolemy II, 3, 12: Λουέντινον (= LUENTINUM), var. Λουέντιον (= LUENTIUM)

For a suggestion of Dillemann that Ptolemy's entry represents *Aventio*, miscopied, see this name.

DERIVATION. The root seems to be **lou*- **lou̯e*- 'to wash' (Pokorny 692), with which are connected Latin *lavo*, *diluvium*, etc., Gaulish **lautro*- (see LAVATRIS), Welsh *lludw* 'rain', etc. For the formation one might compare the Italian river *Cluentus* (root **clou*- of similar meaning: see CLOTA) with **-ent*- suffix as in *Derventio*, plus **-in*(*a*) perhaps as in *Lindinis*, *Sabrina*. The reference might be literally to washing (if the identification below is right, to the washing of gold-bearing ores); or, if a comparison is again made with *Clota*, *Luentinum* might be 'place on the **Luentina* river' (the *-ina* suffix of *Lindinis* and *Sabrina* being analogous), in which event 'wash' has extended to 'flow' or incorporates (as *Clota* may do) a divine name.

IDENTIFICATION. Probably the Roman fort and gold-mining settlement at Pumpsaint, Carmarthenshire (SN 6640), at the confluence of the Afon Twrch with the Afon Cothi. The suggestion that the reference might be to gold-washing was made to us by Mr G. C. Boon.

LUGI

SOURCE

Ptolemy II, 3, 8: Λοῦγοι (= LUGI), var. Λόγοι (= LOGI); Λούγους (acc. = LUGOS)

DERIVATION. There is an admirable discussion of this name by Anders Ahlqvist in *BBCS*, XXVI (1974–76), 143–46; he had earlier studied the same name applied to a people of Silesia. After discussing numerous possibilities advanced by others, Ahlqvist prefers to connect the ethnicon with the divine name *Lugus* (see the next entry), or with a word meaning 'black' (Celtic **lŭgos* > Irish *loch* 'black') and hence perhaps 'raven' in Gaulish (Gaulish *lougos* recorded as λοῦγος by Clitophon of Rhodes). In the latter case this tribe 'may have been a dark pre-Celtic people, like the Silures' (Watson, quoted by Ahlqvist), though there is general agreement that their name is of Celtic origin. But a sense 'raven-people' may well be preferable, especially since C. Thomas in *Arch.J.*, CXVIII (1961), 40, has drawn attention to the number of North British tribes whose animal names may indicate that they were characterised by animal-cults (see EPIDII). The name *Lugi* may survive in Loth, the name of a parish in south-east Sutherland (older Logh); possibly also in Louth in Ireland. The tribal name *Lugoni* (Λούγονοι, Ptolemy II, 6, 32) in north-west Iberia, and *Luguadici* in an inscription *CIL* II. 2732 from near Segovia (Segovia, Spain), may well contain the same element.

IDENTIFICATION. A people of Scotland, placed by Ptolemy between the *Decantae* and the *Cornovii* of Caithness and so apparently occupying eastern Sutherland, including Loth.

LUGUDUNUM

SOURCE

Ravenna 107_{17} (= R&C 140): LUGUNDUNO, var. LUGUNDINO

The first *n* in *Ravenna*'s entry could have arisen if a copyist mistakenly assumed a tilde (abbreviation for *n*) over the previous letter (*Lugū-*).

DERIVATION. This name was borne by a number of Continental towns, of which much the best-known is (with direct derivation) Lyon (Rhône, France). With elements reversed it is also, as R&C note, the origin of *Dinlleu* in Caernarvonshire (Wales). The name is recorded in a variety of spellings: *Lugudunum*, *Lugidunum*, *Lugdunum*, the best-known (Lyon) almost always in the last form, with early loss of the unstressed vowel; the form of the British name is the most classical. The first element has attracted much study, summarised by Ellis Evans in *GPN* 219–20; the consensus still favours the etymology proposed long ago by D'Arbois de Jubainville, 'fortress of the god *Lugus*'. *Lugus* (*Lug* in later Celtic tradition, *Lleu* as the name of a Welsh hero) was a god equated with Mercury, whose cult had a wide distribution and whose name is found also (via a personal name) in British *Luguvalium*; the basic meaning is 'light' (older Welsh *lleu* 'light', Welsh *goleu*, Breton *goulou*, etc.). Whatmough in *Ogam*, VII (1955), 353–56, suggested that *Lugu-* should be compared with a Celtic *lougeon* (λούγεον) deduced from Strabo, 'marsh, swamp', which is possibly to be seen also in the name of Paris, *Lutecia* if for **Lucotecia* (more usually associated with *Lucotios*, the 'mouse-god'); this **luco–*, **lugo-* then being connected with **locu-* 'lake' as in British *Locatrebe*, *Segelocum*; hence 'marsh-fort' as the sense of *Lug(u)dunum*. But this does not make good sense when applied to the Gallic *Lugdunum* (a hill-site; the low-lying settlement was separately named as *Condate* or *Ad Confluentem*), and there is no reason to suppose that it could have applied to the British *Lugudunum*. Two recent studies of the question are those of P. Flobert in *REL*, XLVI (1968), 264–80, and A. Audin, *Mélanges...J. Tricon* (Lyon, 1972), 11–21. For *-dunum*, see BRANODUNUM; for the formation with a divine name, compare CAMULODUNUM. For *Lugu-* names in Gaul, see Vincent 209.

IDENTIFICATION. Unknown, but apparently in northern England.

LUGUVALIUM

SOURCES

Inscription: *RIB* 2015, an altar found in the foundation of Hadrian's Wall at Old Wall, west of milecastle 59: ...GENIO [...]VALI...The altar is to Mars Cocidius and the Genius of [...]VALI. This last fragment, with single *-l-*, is unlikely to represent the genitive of *vallum*, but could well be for [*Lugu*]*vali*. The space missing on the broken stone seems (from the *RIB* illustration) exactly right for four letters. Milecastle 59 is some six miles from Carlisle; the stone was reused in the foundation of the Wall after being brought from elsewhere.

AI 467_2 (Iter II): LUGUVALLO

474_1, 476_6 (Iter V): LUGUVALIO

Ravenna 107_{10} (= R&C 129): LAGUBALUMI, var. LAGUBALIUM

(*ND*: Seeck's addition to the text is not warranted – see Chapter VI, p. 221)

In these sources, *AI*'s first form shows with its *-ll-* an assimilation to Latin *vallum* 'wall, rampart'. *Ravenna*'s two forms show how readily confusion developed in the copying of these letters. H. Peters's emendation of Severus 22, 4 (*Historia Augusta*), by which the name of Carlisle is read, is not accepted; see p. 65.

DERIVATION. For the first element, see LUGUDUNUM; for the second, see BANNOVALIUM. The name does not mean 'rampart of the god *Lugus*', but is based on a personal British name **Luguualos* with **-io-* derivational suffix, hence **Luguualion* 'town of **Luguualos*' (Jackson in *Britannia*, I (1970), 76). From the British name derive Old Welsh *Cair Ligualid*, Welsh *Caer Liwelydd*, Anglo-Saxon *Luel* (Bede) and modern Carlisle. But Bede also preserved a memory of the official Latin name, as *Lugubalia*, IV, 29; and taking up a reference in the anonymous *Life* of St Cuthbert (*c.* A.D. 698–705) he writes in his own *Vita prosaica* of the Saint (in Migne, *Patrologia*, vol. XCIV) *venit ad Lugubaliam civitatem, quae a populis Anglorum corrupte Luel vocatur* (cols. 766–67), and later *ad eamdem Lugubaliam civitatem* (col. 768). This was taken up by William of Malmesbury in the prologue to Book III of his *Gesta Pontificum Anglorum* (Migne, *Patrologia*, vol. CLXXIX): *Velut est in Lugabalia* (sic) *civitate triclinium lapidum fornicibus concameratum...* (col. 1551).

IDENTIFICATION. The Roman town of Carlisle, Cumberland (NY 4056), probably later promoted to the status of city as the capital of the *civitas Carvetiorum*: see CARVETII.

*LUPANIA

SOURCE

Ravenna 106_{23} (= R&C 49): IUPANIA

DERIVATION. *Iup-* is meaningless as Celtic or as Latin, and R&C very properly emend to **Lupania*; for *i/l* copying errors, see p. 203. Even so, no very obvious meaning suggests itself. The name is not likely to be based on Latin personal names *Lupus, Lupanus*. If Celtic, the name could be that of a settlement based on the name of a **Lupa* river, of which four examples in Gaul are recorded by Holder at II. 347 (> modern Loue, Louve); but then one might more readily expect a **Lupium* settlement, that is British **Lupi̯on*. A group of very widespread *Lup-* names, of rivers, places and persons, assembled by Pokorny in *ZCP*, XXI (1940), 97–98, is classed as deriving from a loan made by Illyrian to Celtic, of unclear meaning; Pokorny does not mention the British name, but it could well belong with this group. Equally, the *Ravenna* entry may be a corruption of some quite different and now unrecognisable name.

IDENTIFICATION. Unknown, but apparently in south Wales.

LUTUDARUM

SOURCES

Inscriptions: lead pigs bearing stamps, of the second and third centuries:

1. IMP CAES HADRIANI AVG MET LVT from Wirksworth (Derbys.); *CIL* VII. 1208 (= Burn, 1969, No. 69 (a), p. 54)
2. C IVL PROTI BRIT LVT EX ARG from Hexgrave Park near Mansfield (Derbys.); *CIL* VII. 1216 (= Burn, 1969, No. 69 (b), p. 54)
3. P RVBRI ABASCANT METALLI LVTVDARES from Tansley Moor near Matlock (Derbys.); *EE* IX. 1266 (= Burn, 1969, No. 69 (c), p. 54)
4. SOC LVT BRIT EX ARG from Ellerker (Yorks.); *JRS*, XLVIII (1958), 152; and another from the same mould, found at Brough-on-Humber (Yorks.), *JRS*, XXXI (1941), 145
5. SOCIOR LVT BR EX ARG from Churchover (Warwicks.); *JRS*, LVII (1967), 206; another from the same mould, found near Broomfleet (Yorks.), *JRS*, LVIII (1968), 210; another from the same mould, found at Belby (Yorks.), *JRS*, XXXI (1941), 146
6. SOCIORUM LVTVD BRIT EX ARG from Ashbourne (Derbys.); *Britannia*, VII (1976), 382–83
7. TI CL TR LVT BR EX ARG from Broomer's Hill, Pulborough (Sussex): *CIL* VII. 1215
8. L ARVCONI VERECVND METAL LVTVD from Matlock Moor (Derbys.); *CIL* VII. 1214

Ravenna 106_{45} (= R&C 88): LUTUDARON, var. LUTUDATON

In the texts on the lead pigs, MET LVT of 1 (with noun not expressed in 2 and 7) is expanded in 3 to METALLI LVTVDARES which can be interpreted *metallis Lutudarensibus* (Burn) or *metalli Lutudaresis*; 7 shows a similar abbreviation. In 4, 5 and 6 the adjective qualifies the 'Lutudarensian partners' in the genitive plural.

DERIVATION. The base seems to be Celtic **lŭtā* (Holder II. 351, Rostaing *ETP* 327) 'mud', 'coenum, palus' (Irish *loth* 'marsh'), cognate with Latin *lŭtum* 'mud, mire', also 'loam, clay, potter's clay'. Among place-names of the same root are *Lutia* of the Arevaci in Spain and *Luteva* > Lodève (Hérault, France), which is also a river-name. It is proposed by R. Schmittlein in *RIO*, XVII (1965), 275–88, to associate with these the ancient name of Paris, *Lutetia* (better than *Lucetia*) as meaning 'marais, rivière marécageuse'. In the British name, for the *-ar-* suffix, see LEUCARUM; the *-d-* is perhaps some kind of compositional consonant. If the identification of the suffix is correct, the basic name is that of a river or water of some kind, presumably 'muddy one'.

IDENTIFICATION. The name clearly belongs to the lead-mining district of Derbyshire, but the precise location of its administrative centre is still unknown, as also is the Roman road system in the Derwent valley. A site near Wirksworth (SK 2854) seems to be indicated (M. Todd, *The Coritani* (London, 1973), 19; the fort at Chesterfield has now been found, but this is too far to the north-east).

MACATONION of *Ravenna* 106_{29} (= R&C 61): see *MAGALONIUM

MAEATAE

SOURCES

Xiphilinus 321 (summarising Cassius Dio LXXVI, 12): Μαιάται (= MAEATAE; twice)

Jordanes 2, 14 (also quoting Cassius Dio): Meatae

DERIVATION. Holder II. 388 thought the name Pictish, and it is discussed by Wainwright *PP* 51–52; it may survive in Dumyat and Myot Hill, near Stirling and thus north of the Antonine Wall. Watson *CPNS* 58 seems to take the name as wholly Celtic, as is surely right in view of the Continental analogues he cites for the second element or suffix: Gaulish *Gais-atai* 'spearmen' (**gaison* 'spear'), *Gal-atai* 'warriors' (**gal* 'valour, prowess'), *Nantu-atai* (*-ates*) 'valley-dwellers'; he notes also the presence in Ireland of the *Magn-atai*. See also ATREBATES, with further references. One might therefore conjecture that in this name at least the force of the suffix is 'those of...'. The first element might be the same as in *Maia*, probably 'larger', in which case a sense 'larger people' or more strictly 'people of the larger part' may be suitable. It is to be noted that Cassius Dio, as quoted by others, seems to say that Britain north of the Antonine Wall was divided between the *Calidonii* and the *Maeatae*, these having subsumed lesser tribes, and it could well be that the *Maeatae* were the 'people of the larger part'. The name was still in use in Adamnan's day: *Miathi* in his *Life* of St Columba, I, 8.

IDENTIFICATION. A confederation of tribes in the southern part of Scotland (the northern part being occupied by a similar confederation of *Calidonii*, q.v.). As noted above, place-names indicate that they extended into Stirlingshire and their northern limit was probably the Mounth, but their southern extent is disputed and depends on the interpretation of the statement of Xiphilinus that they lived 'near the cross-wall which cuts the island in two'. Collingwood (*Roman Britain and the English Settlements* (Oxford, 1937), 157) interpreted it as the Antonine Wall and in this was followed by Richmond (*Roman Britain* (Harmondsworth, 1963), 57–59), but Frere (1974, 188) prefers Hadrian's Wall and attaches the *Selgovae* (q.v.) to them.

*MAGALONIUM

SOURCE

Ravenna 106_{29} (= R&C 61): MACATONION

DERIVATION. R&C propose to emend this to **Magalonion*, reasonably enough (with *c* for *g* by scribal confusion, as often; although *Mac-* may accurately represent the same root, as in Hispanic personal names *Macilo/Magilo*, *ELH* I. 359, and *Macalu*, a divine name in a graffito of Séraucourt (Bourges, France: *DAG* 354). This **Magalonium* they then derive from a river-name **Magalona*, which with British *-*i̯o*- derivational suffix gives for the whole name a sense 'place on the noble river'. Their base is an Indo-European root **mak*- 'to grow' (Holder II. 362), from which Welsh *magu* and Breton *maga* 'to feed' ultimately come, as do Latin *magnus* and Greek μεγάλος. Among place-names closely related are then British *Maglona* and its precise equivalent *Magalona* > Maguelonne (Hérault, France), *Magalonnum* > Moulons (Charente-Maritime, France). The origin of many personal names related to these lies in **maglo-s*, perhaps 'great one', from which derive Old Irish *mál*, Welsh and Breton *mael* 'prince', present in such ancient names as *Magalos*, *Magilos*, *Magilius*; in Britain, *Brigomaglos* on a sub-Roman tombstone at Chesterholm (*RIB* 1722). Based on the *mag-* root are the divine name *Magusanus*, associated with Hercules in a dedication at Mumrills, Stirlingshire (*RIB* 2140); also *DAG* 943 (many); and the Gaulish place-name *Magdunum* > Méhun-sur-Yèvre (Cher, France) and Meung-sur-Loire (Loiret, France), together with British *Magantia*, *Magiovinium* and perhaps *Maia*.

Whether R&C's speculation about **Magalona* river is warranted can be judged from the Continental analogues, for which no such supposition has to be made; and from the fact that no modern river-name derives from this. It seems simplest to see the name as built on **magal-* with suffixes *-*on-i̯o*-, as in CANONIUM; and as meaning 'high, outstanding place' or the like, possibly 'noble place'.

It might turn out that *Ravenna*'s *Macat-* is right after all. A name *Macato* (reading of the first *a* being doubtful) is recorded in *CIL* XIII. 5806 (Langres), and other names, mostly personal, are known with *Mac(c)-*; see *GPN* 364–65.

IDENTIFICATION. Unknown, but apparently not far from Gloucester.

MAGANTIA

SOURCE

Ravenna 109_{18} (= R&C 290): MAGANTIA, var. MAGANCIA

DERIVATION. The name is evidently based on **mag-*, for which see the previous entry, with Celto-Latin suffix. The sense might be 'large island' or 'high, outstanding place'. It is worth noting that the Celto-Roman name of Mainz (Germany), properly *Mogontiacum*, was in the reduced form of late Imperial times *Moguntia*, often spelled *Magontia*, *Magentia*, *Magantia*; the *mog-* root is the same ultimately as *mag-*, and in that form is the base of the divine name *Mogons* (the dative, in dedications, is *Deo Mogonti*). Since the cult of this god seems to have been fundamentally Germanic, and was brought from the middle Rhine by the Vangiones who garrisoned Risingham (thence extending it in the area of Hadrian's Wall), it seems unlikely that a

Celtic cult of a similarly named deity could have given its name independently to a Scottish island (the present *Magantia*) as R&C alternatively propose.

IDENTIFICATION. Unknown, but apparently an island off Britain.

MAGIOVINIUM

SOURCE

AI 471_1 (Iter II): MAGIOVINTO
476_{10} (Iter VI): MAGIOVINIO
479_6 (Iter VIII): MAGIONVINIO

DERIVATION. Jackson in *Britannia*, I (1970), 76, thinks the first element is British **magio-*, as in some Gaulish names, probably meaning 'great'; see *MAGALONIUM. The second element is obscure, but may be paralleled in British *Clavinium* (if this is a valid name); Jackson thinks *Vinovia* may be relevant.

IDENTIFICATION. The Roman town at Dropshort, Little Brickhill, Buckinghamshire (SP 8833).

MAGIS

SOURCES

Inscription: *RIB* 899, an altar set up to Jupiter and Vulcan at Old Carlisle for the welfare of Gordian (A.D. 238–44) by the VIK(ANI) MAG(. . .)
ND XL_{14} (*pictura*): MAGIS
XL_{29} (text): Praefectus numeri Pacensium, MAGIS

Concerning the inscription, M. W. C. Hassall in *Aspects of the ND* (Oxford, 1976), 111, writes that

'One of these sites [*Maglone* and *Magis* of *ND*] must surely be Old Carlisle, which lies west of Kirkby Thore [i.e. the previous fort listed in *ND*, *Bravoniacum*] and from which comes an altar *RIB* 899 set up . . . by the *Vik(ani) Mag(lonenses)* or *Mag(enses)*. The dedicators are usually interpreted as being *Vik(anorum) Mag(istri)*; but against this interpretation and in favour of our own, it can be argued, first, that, normally, *magistri* would precede *vicanorum* (though *vicomagistri* as masters of wards are attested in the *Notitia Urbis Constantinopolitanae*); secondly, *magistri* of *vici* are rare in the western provinces, the officials most commonly mentioned on inscriptions being *curatores*. . . ; thirdly, such semi-official dedications are normally made by the *vicani* themselves, and they usually qualify themselves by a geographical epithet (e.g. the *Vicani Vindolandesses* of the *Vindolanda* inscription).'

DERIVATION. The name is the fossilised Latin locative plural (see ANICETIS) of a name formed on British **magos*, for which see CAESAROMAGUS. The sense then seems to be 'at the plains'.

IDENTIFICATION. Hassall's argument may be supplemented by the observation that the traditional identification of Old Carlisle with *ND*'s *Olenacum* (q.v.) presumes a very odd order in the list. Since we have removed this, it may tentatively be suggested that *Maglona* is Old Carlisle and that *Magis* is the Roman fort at Burrow Walls, Workington, Cumberland (NY 0030), from which we have also removed the name *Gabrosentum* (q.v.).

Note. Seeck's equation of *Magis* with the *Maio*, *Maia* of *Ravenna*, made in his 1876 edition of *ND*, is erroneous. It was taken up by Holder II. 375, who added mention of a *Magia* in Raetia, > Maienfeld (Switzerland) between Chur and Bregenz; this *Magia* of *TP* is also in *CIL* v. 5090 the . . . *stat(ionis) Maiens(is)*, so that a phonetic development of *Magia* to *Maiens(is)* could from this be taken to apply also to the equivalence of British *Magis* with *Maio*, etc. However, as Jackson in *LHEB* 444 makes plain, such a development in British did not occur until after the Roman period; while Continental *Magia* is a precise analogy for British *Magis*, it offers no support for the equivalence of *Magis*/*Maia* in Britain. Moreover, *ND* lists *Magis* in the middle of a section of forts in Yorkshire, Durham and eastern Westmorland, and has not yet gone over to the Cumbrian coast where *Maia* lay.

MAGLONA

SOURCES

Inscription: *RIB* 899, which may belong here: see MAGIS

ND XL_{13} (*pictura*): MAGLOUE

XL_{28} (text): Praefectus numeri Solensium, MAGLONE (var. MAGLOUE)

ND's forms with *u* have a common copying fault of *u* for *n*. Final *-e* may simply be *-a* miscopied, or a first-declension locative.

DERIVATION. *Maglona* belongs with the names listed under **Magalonium*, based on the root **mag-*. Gaulish *Magalona* > Maguelonne (Hérault, France) is an exact equivalent of the British name, which has lost the unstressed vowel by elision. A similar sense, 'high, outstanding place', perhaps 'noble place', is appropriate.

IDENTIFICATION. Probably the Roman fort at Old Carlisle, Cumberland (NY 2646).

MAGNIS[1]

SOURCES

AI 484_7 (Iter XII): MAGNIS

Ravenna 106_{27} (= R&C 57): MAGNIS

DERIVATION. The name is British **magno-* (plural **magnī*), from which comes Welsh *maen* (pl. *mein*) 'stone, rock'. See Jackson in *Britannia*, I (1970), 76. Hamp in *BBCS*, XXVI (1974–76), 157, refines on this by proposing that the British word was neuter **magnon*, collective plural **magnįā*, which, in Latin locative plural guise (see ANICETIS) is naturally *Magnis*. The only Continental parallel seems to be *Magno* of *TP*, in Dalmatia; two places called *Magnacum* in Gaul are probably based on the Latin personal name *Magnus*.

IDENTIFICATION. The Roman town of Kenchester, Herefordshire (SO 4442); for its probable inclusion in the *civitas Dobunnorum*, see DOBUNNI.

MAGNIS[2]

SOURCES

Ravenna 107_{11} (= R&C 130): MAGNIS

ND XL_{43}: Tribunus cohortis secundae Dalmatarum, MAGNIS

Inscription: *RIB* 1825, found in 1766 at Carvoran, now lost:

. . .] Aug(ust. . .)

[. . .|numeri [. . .|Magn⟨c⟩e(n)s(ium)

Of the inscription, *RIB* notes that 'the *c* is intrusive (whether anciently or by a blockmaker's mistake is not clear)'. It is not necessary to suppose *-n-* in *-ensium*, given Vulgar Latin assimilation *ns* > *ss* in comparable forms (see BANNA).

DERIVATION. See MAGNIS[1].

IDENTIFICATION. The Roman fort at Carvoran, Northumberland (NY 6665); its third-century garrison was the *Cohors II Dalmatarum* (*RIB* 1795).

MAGNUS PORTUS

SOURCE

Ptolemy II, 3, 3: Μέγας λιμήν (= MAGNUS PORTUS)
II, 3, 14: Ὑπὸ δὲ τὸν Μέγαν λιμένα νῆσος Οὐηκτὶς (= infra MAGNUM autem PORTUM insula Vectis)

DERIVATION. This is a descriptive Latin name, 'great harbour'; compare GABRANTOVICUM SINUS. There was a Πόρτος Μάγνος (= *Portus Magnus*) in Spain, recorded by Ptolemy II, 4, 7, now Almería. It is to be remarked that whereas Ptolemy translates the British name into Greek, perhaps showing that the name was descriptive rather than that of an established location, he simply transliterates the Hispanic equivalent into Greek as was his practice with most recognised place-names.

IDENTIFICATION. As is argued on p. 116, this is not a place-name properly speaking, but a description of the whole sheltered area between the Isle of Wight and the mainland – including the Solent and Southampton Water.

MAIA or MAIUM

SOURCES

Rudge Cup and Amiens *patera*: MAIS
Ravenna 107_5 (= R&C 120): MAIO
107_{29} (= R&C 154): MAIA
109_{22} (= R&C 298): MAIONA
(*ND*: We propose to read, at XL_{49}, Tribunus cohortis primae Hispanorum, MAIS (or MAIO); for the argument, see p. 221)

In his 1935 study of the Rudge Cup, Richmond noted that Bowness fort was the terminal point of two systems, the Wall and the Cumbrian coastal defences, and was therefore mentioned twice by *Ravenna* (which, he then thought, rarely repeated names). The association of *Ravenna*'s *Maiona* with this place is made here for the first time. Although at 109_{22} it figures in the list of islands *ad aliam partem*, and was taken as a western island by R&C, it is likely that (as is the case with other non-island names in this section) it was written 'in the sea' on a map and wrongly interpreted by the Cosmographer. Final *-na* could have arisen from **Maium* (neuter singular) on the map, written as was the Cosmographer's habit **Maion* and then miscopied.

DERIVATION. It is not sure what the correct form of this name in Latin guise should be. The only epigraphic evidence indicates a locative plural in *-is* (as argued also for the Rudge Cup form of *Camboglanna*). If this is right, the nominative neuter plural of the name is *Maia*, as in *Ravenna* 107_{29}. In that case the neuter singular *Maio* and what we can see in *Maiona* are equally acceptable oblique-case singulars. All may be right; such variation in recorded forms is by no means improbable.

R&C suggests that the base of the name is British **mājōs*, comparative of **māros* (compare Latin *maior*), from which Welsh *mwy* derives; Jackson *LHEB* 357 and 360 appears to accept this. The sense is therefore 'larger (one or ones)', perhaps referring to the size of promontories (Bowness contrasted with Drumburgh). If the name is basically adjectival, it is easy to see how in differing interpretations it could be singular or plural, as the sources appear to show. The root is represented in personal names in Gaul such as *Maiagnus*, *Maianus*, *Maiiona* for **Magiona* (Holder II. 387), perhaps *Maiorix*; in Gaul and Italy a goddess *Maia* was known. The only relevant place-names abroad seem to be *Maio Meduaco* between Brenta Vecchia and Brentella in N. Italy, and the *Statio Maiensis* mentioned under *Magis*. The North British *Maeatae* people may have a first element in their name corresponding to the present name.

IDENTIFICATION. The Roman fort at Bowness-on-Solway, Cumberland (NY 2262).

MAINA of *Ravenna* 108_{25} (= MAVIA of R&C 238): see *MOINA

MALAIA (?)

SOURCES

Ptolemy II, 2, 10: Μαλαῖος (= MALAEUS), vars. Μαλέος (= MALEUS), Μελέος (= MELEUS)

Ravenna 105_{29} (= R&C 304): MALACA

DERIVATION. The correct form of the name is unsure. R&C reasonably conjecture that *Ravenna*'s entry represents *Malaia* or *Malaea*, and this is supported by *Maleam* (acc.) in Adamnan's *Life* of St Columba (I, 22; I, 41; II, 22). The modern Gaelic name of Mull (from the British) is *Muile*. The name is probably to be associated with the numerous *Mal- Mel- Mell-* names which are widespread on the Continent and beyond. Pokorny 721 has a root **mel-* 'hervorkommen, erscheinen, hochkommen; Erhöhung, Wölbung', Dauzat *TF* 75 a pre-Celtic **mala* 'mountain', with a variant **mel(l)-* from which Gaulish **mello-* derived, and there are further representatives such as Breton *mell*, Irish *mell* 'hill'; Rostaing *ETP* 202–205 cites Albanian *mal* and a Ligurian **mel-* which has left several traces in Provence. In ancient names this element is found compounded or with suffix in Μηλόκαβος and Μελιόδουνον (= *Melocabus*, *Meliodunum*: Ptolemy II, 11, 14) in Germania Magna, *Melodunum* > Melun (Seine-et-Marne, France), *Mellosedum* and *Mellosecto* in Gaul; *Meletum* > Meilly-sur-Rouvres (Côte-d'Or, France), *Mellaria* now Fuenteovejuna (Córdoba, Spain). Ptolemy's variant Μελ- (= *Mel-*) may not be unimportant here. For the suffix, compare perhaps British *Arbeia* and other names noted there. A sense 'hill(-island)' seems appropriate, then; there is no reason why the name should not be British, whatever the ultimate origin of **mala* **mel-*. See also *MELETIUM.

IDENTIFICATION. The island of Mull.

MAMUCIUM

SOURCES

AI 468_7 (Iter II): MAMUCIO
482_2 (Iter X): MAMCUNIO, var. MANCUNIO

Ravenna 106_{58} (= R&C 109): MANTIO, vars. MAUTIO, MANCIO

There can be little doubt that *Mamucium* is the correct form; the aberrant forms of both texts are readily explicable as involving letters repeatedly miscopied in medieval scripts. For long *Mancunium* was established, on the basis of the variant reading in *AI*'s Iter X; Holder II. 401 still accepted it, and it is doubtless still firm in popular belief, but it was rejected (and a nearly correct etymology proposed) by Bradley in *EHR*, XV (1900), 495–96.

DERIVATION. Jackson in *Britannia*, I (1970), 76, indicates a compound of British **mammā* 'breast; round, breast-like hill' with the *-*ūc*-*i̯o*- suffixes discussed under our CICUCIUM. The Anglo-Saxon name shows the intermediate stage, *Mameceaster* (A.D. 923). R&C think the 'breast-like hill' was that on which the Roman fort lay. Such naming was not uncommon in several languages. In Moesia was *Trimammio* (*AI* 222_2) = *Trimamion* in *Ravenna* 49_{23}; in Spain, Mamblas (Avila) and Mambrillas (Burgos), and in Portugal Mamos, are based on Latin *mammŭla*. Watson *CPNS* 55 mentions the 'Two Paps of Anu', in Old Irish *dá chích Anann* (hills on the eastern border of Kerry), and Zachrisson (1927) 80–81 mentions modern British names derived from Celtic **mammā*: Mamhead (Devon), Mamble (Worcs.), Mam Tor (Derbys.), Maumbury Rings (Dorset) and Mamhilad (Monmouth).

J. Hind in G. D. B. Jones and S. Grealy (eds.), *Roman Manchester* (Altrincham, 1974), 159–63, has a useful survey of the history of studies of this name, but it is quite unnecessary to suppose with him that the name was properly **Manduvicium* 'pony village', for which there is no justification either textual or semantic.

IDENTIFICATION. The Roman fort at Manchester, Lancashire (SJ 8397).

MANAVIA (?)

SOURCES
Pliny *NH* IV, 103: MONAPIA
Ptolemy II, 2, 10: Μονάοιδα (= MONAOEDA), var. Μοναρίνα (= MONARINA)
Ravenna 108_{19} (= R&C 233): MANAVI
Orosius I, 2, 82: MEVANIA
Julius Honorius 16: MEVANIA, vars. MEBANIA, MEUBANIA
Jordanes I, 8: MEVANIA, var. EVANIA

There are numerous problems here. At least all the sources refer to the Isle of Man (but see Bede, below). Pliny places the island with others *inter Hiberniam ac Britanniam*. The ancient name is usually cited as *Monapia*, following Pliny, apparently from the feeling that since his record is the earliest it is the most likely to be correct. But Holder II. 621, in a note which seems to have been overlooked, already suggested that Pliny's form should be corrected to **Manavia*, and this – as Jackson *LHEB* 376 confirms – is proper, for the Middle Welsh name for Man, *Manau*, demands either **Manău̯i̯ā* or **Manău̯ā* as its British etymon (the first of these is to be preferred, in view of the frequency of the -*ia* termination in the sources). Ptolemy's entry also requires correction; Müller recognised it as corrupt and suggested that the proper form should be *Μονάουα (= **Monava*). *Ravenna*, against custom, has a nearly correct form of the name, but errs in placing it among its *diversa loca*, which as a group was thought by R&C to include tribal meeting-places, of which this was one: 'Presumably connected with *Manau Guotodin* [Nennius], the district at the head of the Firth of Forth', with a reference to Watson *CPNS* 103–104; and perhaps following J. Loth, 'Les deux *Mano* irlandais et les deux *Manau* Brittons', *RC*, LI (1934), 185–95. This was taken further by K. A. Steer in Richmond (ed.), *Roman and Native in North Britain* (1958), 107: '. . . Since well-known megalithic monuments would obviously provide convenient focal points for tribal gatherings, it is tempting to suggest that *Manavi*, which is linked with *Manau*, the district at the head of the Firth of Forth, was located in the vicinity of the *Clack Mannan*, or stone of *Manau*, which originally stood not far from its present position in the centre of

Clackmannan town.' As for derivation, R&C noted that '*Manau* would give a Celtic genitive *Manann*, but a latinised genitive *Manavi*, as here'. This is ingenious but superfluous. A clue to a completely different solution – that which we have adopted – is almost inadvertently given by R&C when they go on to relate their name to various forms given by ancient writers for the Isle of Man; and although there is nothing inherently impossible in R&C's wish to assign *Manavi* to an inland meeting-place (whose name *Manau* must indeed have derived from a similar ancient name, not recorded till Nennius), it is really much more likely that in this entry *Ravenna* is listing the Isle of Man. Probably the name was entered on the map-source stretching across the sea (represented on the map as very narrow) from Man to Scotland, and was misread by the Cosmographer – as in other cases – as though it pertained to the latter. It is to be noted that *Ravenna* otherwise gives no name for Man, which is unlikely to have been overlooked. See further *Ravenna*'s *Manna* 109_{11} (= R&C 280), which we have referred to MONA.

The remaining sources form a group. Presumably it was Orosius or an early copyist who wrote *Mevania* with scribal metathesis of *n-v*, and he was followed by Julius Honorius and Jordanes; also by Bede, who is known to have used Orosius as a source, when he writes (II, 5) that Edwin *Mevanias Brettonum insulas, quae inter Hiberniam et Brittaniam sitae sunt, Anglorum subiecit imperio* (the note about position coming from Pliny). Bede is the only writer to use the name as a plural, presumably for Anglesey + Man jointly.

In looking back at this tangled story, and considering the variant of Julius Honorius in particular, one can see how Pliny's erroneous form arose: **Manavia* with *b* for *v* in some early text, and then perhaps *p* for *b* a little later, giving **Manapia*, with the first *a* still later miscopied as *o*, *Monapia*.

DERIVATION. While *Monapia* was taken seriously, it was tempting to connect the name with the Μαναπία (= *Manapia*) *polis* of the Μανάπιοι (= *Manapii*) people of Ireland (Ptolemy II, 2, 7, etc.), and these with the Μενάπιοι (= *Menapii*) of Gallia Belgica (Ptolemy II, 9, 5, etc.), as does Watson *CPNS* 104. However, if we take *Manavia*, the name seems to be simply **man-*, a variant of **mon-*, with suffix similar to **-au̯a* (see ABALLAVA); hence there is indeed an association with *Mona* (Anglesey) and some logic in Bede's use of the plural name. The sense is 'mountain island' or 'high island'; see also Jackson, etc., above.

IDENTIFICATION. The Isle of Man.

MANDUESSEDUM

SOURCE

AI 470_3 (Iter II): MANDUESEDO, var. MANDUESSEDO

DERIVATION. The name is composed of British **mandu-* 'small horse, pony' and **essedo-* 'war-chariot' (perhaps also 'cart'). The first element was well known in antiquity. Gaulish **mandu-s* or (with assimilation, perhaps dialectal, which did not occur in British until the late fifth century: *LHEB* 512–13) **mannus* was early taken into Latin, as were other Gaulish terms relating to horses, and is first recorded in Lucretius III, 1063 (*mannus*). See Burn, 1969, p. 106. According to Hubschmid in *ELH* I. 143 **mandu-* is probably Illyrian in origin, and related to other words meaning 'horse, mule; sterile'. The element is found in such personal names as *Mandubracius*, chief of the Trinovantes, and *Cartimandua*, queen of the Brigantes; in the Gaulish ethnicon *Viromandui* (> Vermandois) around Saint-Quentin (Aisne, France), and in a number of place-names such as *Epamanduodurum* (> Mandeure, Doubs, France); see Holder II. 409 (with an erroneous sense for **mandu-*) and *GPN* 222–23.

The second element, **essedo-*, was also borrowed early from Gaulish into Latin. There are several mentions in Caesar of the *esseda* 'chariots' and *essedarii* 'charioteers', elsewhere in his text equated with *currus* and *auriga* respectively; also in Virgil and Suetonius. This element is found in *Tarvessedum AI* 278_5 'bull-cart' (near Lake Como in N. Italy). The root is **sed-* 'sit' (Welsh *sedd* 'seat'; Latin *sedeo*, English *sit*, etc.; compare *-sessa* in CAMULOSESSA), as in the ethnicon *Coriosedenses* and place-names *Metlosedum* (> Melun, Seine-et-Marne, France), *Sidoloucum* (> Saulieu, Côte-d'Or, France), etc. See Holder II. 1433, *GPN* 253–54. Jackson in *Britannia*, I (1970), 76, finds the application of a sense 'horse-chariot' to a place obscure, but compares *Marcotaxum* in Scotland and suggests that some local legend may be involved. The first part of the ancient name survives in that of modern Mancetter.

IDENTIFICATION. The Roman settlement at Mancetter, Witherley, Leicestershire (SP 3296).

MANNA of *Ravenna* 109_{11} (= R&C 280): see MONA

MAPORITUM

SOURCE
Ravenna 107_{34} (= R&C 163): MAPORITON

DERIVATION. The name is built on British **mapo-* 'boy, youth; son' (see LOCUS MAPONI) and **ritu-* 'ford' (see ANDERITUM); hence 'the young man's ford' or 'son's ford'. The name is evidently that of a place paired with TADORITUM, adjacent to it and so listed in *Ravenna*; the allusion is lost to us, but if taken literally presumably relates to fords established by, or near land owned by, different generations of a family; but there could be some folkloric reference, or a metaphorical allusion to the size of the stream at these points. See J. Schnetz in *ZONF*, II (1926–27), 231, and III (1927–28), 123. Dillemann (p. 69) challenges the above, thinking both *Maporitum* and *Tadoritum* a mistaken doublet which proceeds from *Carbantoritum* in a complex series of copying errors; but there seems to be no reason to disturb the accepted forms and etymology of these paired names; it is unlikely that such a meaningful pair would have arisen by copying accidents.

IDENTIFICATION. Unknown, but apparently in southern Scotland; in view of the pairing of names noted above it may be wrong to associate this name with *Maponus*, the 'divine youth' often identified with Apollo and much worshipped in the area of Hadrian's Wall (see Ross (1967), 368–70, with distribution map).

MARCOTAXUM

SOURCE
Ravenna 108_{12} (= R&C 225): MARCOTAXON

DERIVATION. The first element is British **marco* (or according to Whatmough **marca*, with *-a* masculine as in *druida*, etc.: *DAG* 574), meaning 'horse', from which derive Welsh *march*, Breton *marc'h*, with cognates in Old Irish *marc*, Old High German *marh* and English *mare*, etc. (Holder II. 419). Watson in *CPNS* 441 cites the same word in Welsh *Marchnant* 'horse-brook' and Gaelic *Marcaidh* 'horse-stream', which occurs several times in Scotland. Ancient names in which this element appears are *Marcodurum* > Düren (Germany) and *Marcomagus* > Marmagen (between Cologne and Trier, Germany), and the personal name *Marcomaro* (Holder II. 422); in Germania Magna was the tribe Μαρκομανοί (= *Marcomani*: Ptolemy II, 11, 11, etc.). See also H. Birkhan, *Germanen und Kelten* ...(Vienna, 1970), 393–416. The second element is identified by Holder II. 1778 with that found in Old Irish *tais* 'soft, gentle', but it seems better for the sense to follow Williams (now Pokorny 1055) in identifying a root **tāg-*, found in Greek ταγέω, τάσσω, τάξις 'to rule, order, array', present in the names of *Taximagulus* who ruled part of Kent (Caesar) and *Tasciovanus*, father of Cunobelinus; also in the place-name *Tasinemetum* in Noricum (a site near Villach). The sense of the British name is thus 'horse-array', 'with evident reference to a historical or legendary event' (R&C); but it might be more mundanely an assembly-point for cavalry, or a horse-trading fair.

IDENTIFICATION. Unknown, but apparently in Scotland north of the Antonine Wall.

MARGIDUNUM

SOURCE

AI 477_6 (Iter VI): MARGIDUNO, var. MARGEDUNO
479_1 (Iter VIII): MARGIDUNO

DERIVATION. Holder II. 424 lists **marga* 'marl', early borrowed into Latin from Gaulish as *marga*, from which derive Spanish and Italian *marga*, etc. For *-dunum*, see BRANODUNUM. The sense thus seems to be 'marly fort', i.e. with an earthwork of marly soil, as is accepted by Jackson in *Britannia*, I (1970), 77. However, R. Coates in a paper in the press (of which we have kindly been given notice) challenges this on the grounds that *Margidunum* with composition-vowel *-i-* cannot have as its first element **marga* 'marl', since Celtic *-a* stems form compounds in either *-a-* (*Bannaventa*) or *-o-* (*Samara–Samarobrivae*). Hence Coates looks for a first element with *-i* stem (cf. **mori-* in *Moridunum*). His view is that this element is **mrogi* 'boundary', preserved in Old Irish *mruig* 'boundary'; so the meaning is 'border fort', the border in question being not that of the Coritani, in whose lands this fort is central, but that of the 'Foss Way on which *Margidunum* stood [as] a temporary *limes* in the Claudian invasion'. In support, Coates cites a *Markedunum* > Marquain (Hainault, Belgium; first recorded in A.D. 902) and another place of the same name > Marquion (Pas-de-Calais, France; first recorded in the tenth century), which he thinks of like origin, and both of which he is able to justify as 'border forts'. There are no obviously analogous names in Holder, but there was a *Margus* river in Moesia (now the Morava) with *Margum* on its bank (*AI* 132_4, *TP*, etc.), now Orašje near Dubravitza (Yugoslavia). These may suggest that there was another Celtic element, neither **marga* nor **mrogi*, used in toponymy. It should be noted that Coates's argument about the possible 'boundary' at *Margidunum* is unsound, for the early boundary lay not on the Foss Way itself but on the Trent,

$1\frac{1}{2}$ miles away; moreover, it is doubtful whether this boundary was conceived as anything sufficiently permanent to warrant a name being based on it, and we know that in practice it represented merely one stage in an advance. It is also possible that *AI*'s composition-vowel is not to be trusted absolutely; the name may well have been **Margadunum* or **Margodunum*, with uncertainty over the unstressed vowel.

IDENTIFICATION. The Roman town (succeeding a presumed fort) at Castle Hill, East Bridgford, Nottinghamshire (SK 7041).

MAROMAGO of *Ravenna* 107_{42} (= R&C 180): see VACOMAGI

MASONA

SOURCE

Ravenna 106_{5} (= R&C 21): MASONA

DERIVATION. It is unwise to found much on a form known from *Ravenna* alone, since the text is often corrupt. If taken literally, the name may have an element *mas-* which occurs in a number of Celtic names but whose meaning is not known. Dottin *LG* 270 gives the Gaulish form as **massa* and cites Irish *mass* 'beau' as perhaps equivalent. *Massava* of *TP* is now Mesves-sur-Loire (Nièvre, France). *RIB* 577, a building-stone from Manchester, records work done by the century of *Masavo*, who according to *RIB*'s note was perhaps German. The suffix *-ona* indicates a river or stream (see ABONA).

IDENTIFICATION. Unknown, but apparently in south-west Britain.

MATOVIUM

SOURCE

Ravenna 107_{58} (= R&C 202): MAULION
108_{3} (= R&C 207): MATOVION

It seems likely that as often *Ravenna* has duplicated a name by following two map-sources. *Maulion* suggests no Celtic root and seems corrupt, but its *-u-* may indicate a form **Matu-* which is then equally valid with *Mato-* (see below).

DERIVATION. **Matu-* is 'bear' in Celtic (Irish *math* 'bear', and *Mathu*, a deity; Welsh *madawg* 'fox'). It is the root of many personal and place-names, for which see Holder II. 479 and *GPN* 228–32. Among personal names are *Matuus*, *Matua*, *Matugenos*, *Toutomatus*. *Matunus* the 'bear-god' had a shrine at Risingham. The closest parallel among place-names is provided by *Matavonium* of *AI* 298_{2}, now Cabasse (Var, France); this is *Matavone* in *TP*, but *Pataum* and *Patavi* in *Ravenna*, which give an idea of the degree of corruption of which this text is capable. The British name may have *-*o̯i̯o*- suffixes (as in CANOVIUM); 'bear-place' seems a possible meaning, whether in a figurative or a literal sense. A personal name **Matuu̯os* with *-*i̯o*- derivational suffix and formation exactly as in *Burrium* and other names, 'place of **Matuu̯os*', may be safer; this personal name being that recorded in Latin sources as *Matuus*, as above.

IDENTIFICATION. Unknown, but apparently in Scotland north of the Antonine Wall; for a very nasty reference to the use of a Caledonian bear in Titus's amphitheatre see Martial, *De Spectaculis* vii.

MEDIOBOGDUM

SOURCE

Ravenna 107_2 (= R&C 114): MEDIBOGDO, var. MEDEBOGDO

DERIVATION. The first element is Celtic **mĕdi̯ŏ-*, cognate with Latin *medius*, English *mid*, etc. It occurs in a few place-names only, including the next two entries, and in the name of the *Mediomatrici* people of the region of Metz. The second element is related by Williams, following Walde-Pokorny, to a root **beugh-* 'bend, curve' (English *bow*); Williams notes that this exactly suits the *Rhobogdii* (Ῥοβόγδιοι, Ptolemy II, 2, 2) people of Ireland, who are thus 'bowmen'. This is then applied by R&C to the topography: *Mediobogdum* means 'place in the middle of the curve', 'which exactly describes Hardknot in relation to the Esk valley'. This seems preferable to Holder's suggestion (I. 454, concerning the Irish *Rhobogdii*) which would involve rather **boc-* (represented by *Ravenna* as *-bog-*, with *g* for *c*, as often) as in British *Bocrandium*, and a sense for the present name of '(place) in the middle of the swelling', or less probably '(place) in the middle of the boggy part'.

IDENTIFICATION. The Roman fort at Hardknot, Cumberland (NY 2101), beside the pass between Ravenglass (*Glannoventa*) and Ambleside (*Galava*).

MEDIOLANUM

SOURCES

Ptolemy II, 3, 11: Μεδιολάνιον (= MEDIOLANIUM), a *polis* of the Ordovices

AI 469_4 (Iter II): MEDIOLANO
481_1 and 482_4 (Iter X): MEDIOLANO

Ravenna 106_{41} (= R&C 81): MEDIOMANO
106_{43-44} (= R&C 84, 85): MEDIOLANO SAUDONIO, vars. MEDIOLANA and SAUDONIE

These sources all refer to the same place. Of *AI* 469_4 the editor, Cuntz, remarks that 'Diversum puto ab *Mediolano* 481_1 & 482_4', but Richmond in reviewing I. D. Margary's *Roman Roads* II in *JRS*, XLVIII 1958), 219, observes that 'The difficulty is almost certain to lie in corrupt numbers [in itinerary mileages] rather than two similar names so near.' As for *Ravenna*'s form with *-mano*, R&C took this literally and assigned a different location to it, but *-mano* has no meaning and this entry is a simple duplication of 106_{43}, with miscopying, both as often. *Ravenna*'s *Mediolano Saudonio* is one of the most startling entries in the whole text. The entry is quite plainly an echo from *Mediolanum Santonum* in Gaul (*Santonis* > Saintes, Charente-Maritime, France); this figures in the Cosmography at 77_{22} in the form *Mediolano Santinis*, where it is, moreover, the only Gallic or Hispanic name to which, in the Cosmography, a tribal adjunct is attached – a distinctive entry whose uniqueness so impressed the compiler when he found it in his map-source that, when he came across another *Mediolano* in Britain, he added the same tribal adjunct to it. *Saud-* for *Sant-* has the common error or *u* for *n*, and a mistaken ending.

For the intrusive *-i-* in Ptolemy's form, compare DUNUM[1] (*Dunium*).

DERIVATION. This name is very common abroad; Holder II. 497 lists no fewer than forty-two *Mediolanum* places, the best-known being Milan, said to have been founded in 396 B.C. In *GPN* 215,

Note 7 gives a bibliography. The name is found as far east as Moesia, in the Rhineland, and is most common in Gaul; it seems not to be known in Iberia. See also Vincent 247–48. For *Medio-*, see the previous name. The second element is probably British **lāno-* 'plain, level ground', for which see LANUM. The present name therefore probably has a sense '(place) in the middle of the plain', perhaps preferable to 'central plain' as suggested by Jackson in *Britannia*, I (1970), 77. However, there are complications. L.-F. Flutre in *RIO*, IX (1957), 39, draws attention to the fact that 'La situation géographique de nombreux *Mediolanum*, situés en plein pays montagneux et souvent juchés sur une hauteur' does not agree with the sense 'plain' usually given to the *-lanum* element; he proposes instead that *-lanum* is not 'plain' but 'lieu consacré', basing himself on the sense of modern Breton *lann*; but this seems unacceptable, for this Breton word supposes an original **landa* (see VINDOLANDA), and no early form shows a trace of this. Ellis Evans in *GPN* 215 points out that there may in fact be two homonymous elements subsumed in **lāno-*, one cognate with Latin *plenus* (Irish *lán* 'full', Welsh *llawn*, Breton *leun*), the other cognate with *planus* 'flat'; while this is undoubtedly so, it remains true that the second offers the better sense in toponymy. C.-J. Guyonvarc'h returns to the question in *Ogam*, XIII (1961), 142–58, listing all known *Mediolanum* names and equating these as a category (not precisely in sense) with *Medionemeton*, holding that they 'ont désigné sans nul doute à l'origine un enclos ou une clairière, au moins un espace libre symbolisant le centre religieux et culturel de la peuplade' (p. 157). The second element in the *Mediolanum* names is for him **lano-s* 'plein' (as Ellis Evans indicates it could be), but 'avec le sens connexe (mais non secondaire) de "parfait, complet"', in an especially religious connotation (for which see further *Ogam*, XII (1960), 532). For this it is presumably necessary to take *Medio-* as a noun, 'centre'. This alternative solution is here explained at length because it is obviously a serious possibility, but that put forward earlier, that **lāno-* in this name is 'plain, level ground' still seems greatly preferable. For one thing, it is very straightforward; for another, the word could well have been used to mean 'small extent of levelled ground' which would take account of those Continental *Mediolanum* places situated in hilly country, with *Medio-* then meaning 'central (to the needs of the community)'.

IDENTIFICATION. The Roman town of Whitchurch, Salop (SJ 5441); on *AI* mileages, see pp. 158 and 171, and on Ptolemy's attribution of the place to the *Ordovices* see p. 121.

MEDIONEMETUM

SOURCE

Ravenna 107_{54} (= R&C 196): MEDIO NEMETON

DERIVATION. For the first element, see MEDIOBOGDUM; for *-nemetum*, see AQUAE ARNEMETIAE. The sense is '(place) in the middle of the sacred grove', or since that seems unlikely for the site of a fort, 'middle grove', perhaps halfway along the length of the Antonine Wall (though there is no certainty that *Ravenna* is defining such a fort despite the heading of its section), or midway between two natural features.

IDENTIFICATION. From its position in the list next to *Colanica* (?Camelon – see COLANIA), it is tempting to identify this with the remarkable shrine of Arthur's O'on, Larbert, Stirlingshire (NS 8782), on which see K. A. Steer, *Arch. J.*, CXV (1958), 99–110, and *RCAHM Stirlingshire* (Edinburgh, 1963), 35 and 118. As is there suggested, this may have been a *tropaeum* or victory monument associated with the campaigns of Antoninus Pius and so would be likely to achieve mention; its Celtic name could have been given by Roman auxiliaries. This seems preferable to the identification with the purely barbarian Cairnpapple suggested by S. Piggott, *PSAS*, LXXXII (1947–48), 118.

MELAMON(I) of *Ravenna* 106_2 (= R&C 15): see MORIDUNUM[1]

*MELETIUM

SOURCE

Ravenna 106_{16} (= R&C 36): MELEZO, var. MEIEZO

Here *-z-* represents *-ti-* with Vulgar Latin assibilation; see AQUAE ARNEMETIAE. It has been the custom to cite this name as **Meletio*, third-declension nominative, but there is no justification for this. If it were so, one would expect in the source **Melezone*, that is, third-declension oblique case, on a par with *Cunetzone* (see CUNETIO). *Ravenna* records only two nominatives (except for names in *-a*, which are in many instances probably oblique cases too), both with Latin *Statio*. It seems best, then, to treat *Melezo* as representing **Meletio*, a second-declension neuter oblique case whose nominative would be **Meletium*. This is further justified by the close analogue *Meletum* (see below).

DERIVATION. Williams favoured a British root cognate with **melisso-s* 'sweet' (Holder II. 537), Old Irish *milis*, Welsh *melys* 'sweet' (compare Latin and Welsh *mel* 'honey'), which R&C accept, giving a sense 'honey place' or 'honey-stream place'. They cite as a semantic parallel *Meduana* (Holder II, 525) > La Mayenne, a tributary of the Loire, a river-name connected with 'mead'. Even if this is phonetically tolerable it is semantically very dubious. A much better base is provided by *mel- mell-* which is found in much Continental toponymy, as detailed in our entry for MALAIA. In particular one notes *Meletum* > Meilly-sur-Rouvres (Côte-d'Or, France), which is the precise equivalent of the British name with slightly different suffix; for **et-i̯o-* compare, perhaps, British *Carvetii*. A simple sense of 'hill-(place)' seems appropriate.

IDENTIFICATION. Unknown, but apparently in southern Britain and perhaps between Gloucester and Badbury.

MEMANTURUM of *Ravenna* 108_7 (= R&C 216): see NOVANTARUM PENINSULA

MESTEVIA of *Ravenna* 106_3 (= R&C 18): see ANTIVESTAEUM

METAMBALA of *Ravenna* 106_{23} (= R&C 50): see *NEMETOBALA

METARIS

SOURCE

Ptolemy II, 3, 4: Μεταρὶς εἴσχυσις (= METARIS AESTUARIUM), var. Μεγαρὶς (= MEGARIS)

DERIVATION. This is obscure, but there are analogous names. Müller in his edition of Ptolemy draws attention to the Μέταυρος (= *Metaurus*) rivers of Umbria and Bruttium, and to a Μέαρος (= *Mearus*; for Μέταρος = *Metarus*) river of Galicia; Pokorny in *ZCP*, XXI (1940), 61, adds the *Metapinum os*, one of the mouths of the Rhone, and the Μέταπα (= *Metapa*) of Anatolia, supposing an Illyrian origin for the last two in **metu*- 'between' and **ap*- 'water'. The British name may be *Met*- with the common *-*ar*(*a*) suffix used in water-names, for which see LEUCARUM.

IDENTIFICATION. In position on Ptolemy's map this clearly represents the Wash and it may be that he misinterpreted what was a *sinus* or gulf in his source as an *aestuarium* or estuary; otherwise one of the rivers flowing into the Wash must be meant and of these the most likely is the Witham, because it gave access to the legionary fortress (and later *colonia*) at Lincoln. Ekwall *ERN* 457–58 provides a Celtic derivation for this, but see our entry EIDUMANIS.

MEVANIA of Orosius, etc.: see MANAVIA

MICTIS of Pliny: see VECTIS

MILIDUNUM of *Ravenna* 106_4 (= R&C 19): see MORIDUNUM[1]

MINERVE of *Ravenna* 109_{10} (= R&C 278): see AQUAE CALIDAE, AQUAE SULIS, and also SILINA

MINOX (?)

SOURCE
Ravenna 108_{18} (= R&C 231): MINOX

DERIVATION. This entry is neither British nor Latin as it stands, and must be corrupt. R&C hopefully think it 'a meeting-place in the miscellaneous list', i.e. of *diversa loca*, but there is no justification for this. Just possibly the name might be **Minax*, Latin, 'threatening (one)', 'dangerous (one)', and might belong with other western Scottish islands named in Latin (see ATINA); but this is speculation only.

IDENTIFICATION. Unknown.

MIO[.]EDUM (?)

SOURCE
Inscription: *RIB* 101, GENIO / SA[CRU]M / MIO[.]EDI / ... 'sacred to the Genius of...' This is probably the base of a statue, found 1 mile south-east of Cirencester, with somewhat rough and now damaged lettering.

DERIVATION. It is usual for such dedications to name a place in the genitive. It seems that only one letter is missing from the place-name; *m* or *r* might be possible, and indeed *Mior*- was read by Baddeley; but neither in British nor in Latin does a restoration suggest itself, and there are no analogous names.

IDENTIFICATION. Unknown, but possibly near Cirencester.

MIXA

SOURCE
Ravenna 108_{17} (= R&C 229): MIXA
What is said under MINOX applies precisely here.

IDENTIFICATION. Unknown.

*MOINA

SOURCE

Ravenna 108_{25} (= R&C 238): MAINA, var. MAVIA

R&C adopted *Mavia* as their main reading, and identified it with the river Meavy of Devon; for this, Williams provided a root **mav-*, which has modern derivatives, and a meaning for the river-name of 'lively one, quick stream'. However, apart from the textual doubt, it is not probable that the Meavy was important enough to figure in *Ravenna*. If we take *Maina* as the proper form, an easy emendation provides immediate analogues and a modern derivative: **Moina* would have involved the common miscopying for *a* for *o*.

DERIVATION. **Moinā* is identical to Gaulish *Moenus* > Main river of Germany and to Middle Irish *Maín*, *Maoin* (< **Moinā*) now the Caragh river of Kerry; probably also related are the *Minius* > Miño river of Galicia (Spain) and the Polish rivers Mién, Mianka. The root is probably Celtic **mei-* as in Latin *meo*, with a sense 'to go' ('moving one, fast-moving one'?). See Holder II. 606, Ekwall *ERN* 288, and Pokorny in *ZCP*, XXI (1940), 55. The name is Meon today, for which Ekwall postulates an ancient *Moenus* or similar as origin.

IDENTIFICATION. Probably the river Meon, Hampshire.

MONA

SOURCES

Caesar *BG* V, 13, 2: MONA
Pliny *NH* II, 187: in MONA
IV, 103: MONA
Tacitus *Agricola* 14, 4 and 18, 4: MONAM INSULAM (acc.)
Annals XIV, 29: MONAM INSULAM (acc.)
Ptolemy II, 2, 10: Μόνα νῆσος (= MONA INSULA)
Xiphilinus, epitome of Cassius Dio:
162 (LXII, 7): Μώνναν (acc.; = MONNAM)
163 bis (LXII, 8): Μώνναν (acc.; = MONNAM)
Μώννης (gen.; = MONNAE)
Ravenna 109_{9} (= R&C 276): MONA
109_{11} (= R&C 280): MANNA, var. MANUA

There is harmony of form and usage in most of these sources. Caesar has been thought to refer to Man (*In hoc medio cursu est insula, quae appellatur Mona*), but we argue in Chapter II (p. 41) that his reference is probably to Anglesey. Pliny says that the island is 200 miles from *Camulodunum*. Tacitus and Cassius Dio clearly refer to Anglesey in connection with Suetonius Paulinus's attack on the island, when the army crossed to it by fording the strait.

Ravenna's second entry has not previously been referred here as a duplication drawn from a second map-source, though Holder suggested it. The emendation is easy, since *a* for *o* is a common copying error; one can see from Xiphilinus's forms that there was a tradition of spelling with *-nn-*. R&C boldly emend to *Man[an]na*, think the reference is to Arran, and provide a picturesque etymology. It is just possible that *Ravenna*'s entry is a garbled version of *Manavia* (Man).

DERIVATION. *Mona* is simply 'mountain' or 'high island', perhaps with special reference to Holyhead mountain, a prominent landmark for voyagers in the Irish Sea (Williams). A British base **mŏn-* is to be observed in **moniịo* or **monido* which has given Welsh *mynydd* 'mountain'; the earlier Welsh name for the island was *Mon-finnid* (= *Mon mynnyd*: Williams), now *Mon*. The base **mŏn-* (also found as *men- min-*, and see MANAVIA) was widespread. Latin *mons* was related to it, but the root may have been pre-Indo-European in origin; Rostaing *ETP* 213–14 cites the British *Mona* (and '*Monapia*') as related to *Monda* or *Munda*, a river of Lusitania (> Mondejo), *Monetium* in Liburnia, *Monaco*, and *Monocaleni*, a people of the Alps.

IDENTIFICATION. The island of Anglesey.

MONAPIA of Pliny: see MANAVIA

MORBIUM (?)

SOURCE
ND XL$_6$ (*pictura*): MORBIO
XL, 21 (text): Praefectus equitum catafractariorum, MORBIO

DERIVATION. None can be suggested, as there seem to be no visible British roots, and no analogues in other provinces. *ND*'s form may be slightly corrupt, but probably not to the extent postulated by Seeck – in a note to his 1876 edition of *ND*, and in *Hermes*, IX (1875), 231 – when he advanced the view that *Morbium* could be a corruption of *Vinovia* (or, as he wrote it, *uĩouium*). Stevens in *Arch. J.*, XCVII (1940), 135, note, thought Seeck's emendation 'wild'.

IDENTIFICATION. The equation with *Vinovia* is followed (with a query) by Frere (1974), 264–65 (map), but without comment. The name appears between *Danum* (Doncaster – or just possibly an unknown fort near Jarrow) and *Arbeia* (South Shields). Since most of the forts in this area have names which are known from other sources, the most likely candidates would be Piercebridge, Durham (NZ 2115) and Greta Bridge, Yorkshire (NZ 0813), from which we have removed the supposed names MAGIS and MAGLONA (qq.v.).

MORICAMBE

SOURCE
Ptolemy II, 3, 2: Μορικάμβη εἴσχυσις (= MORICAMBE AESTUARIUM), var. Μοριακάμβη (= MORIACAMBE)

DERIVATION. The first element is British **mori-* 'sea', cognate with Latin *mare*; Welsh, Cornish and Breton *mor*, Irish *muir*. The element is found in the two British *Moridunum* names, in the personal name of a Briton *Morirex* 'sea-king', the *Morini* people of Gaul, etc. For **cambo-*, see CAMBODUNUM. The sense is thus 'curved sea' or 'curve of the sea', i.e. 'bay', despite Ptolemy's addition of εἴσχυσις.

IDENTIFICATION. In its position on Ptolemy's map the name fits Morecambe Bay and it may be (as in the case of METARIS, q.v.) that he has misinterpreted a *sinus* or gulf as an *aestuarium* or estuary; if not, the reference can hardly be to the estuary of a single river, since, as noted on p. 135, all the major ones here have Celtic names, so that a joint estuary, like that at Cartmel, must be intended. It should be noted that the modern names, Morecambe and Morecambe Bay, are not survivals but antiquarian revivals, following the publication of Whitaker's *History of Manchester* in 1771: the previous name was Poulton. In a similar way the name 'Moricambe Bay' has been attached to an inlet on the southern shore of the Solway Firth.

MORIDUNUM[1]

SOURCES

AI 483_7 (Iter XII, by error of the copyist): MURIDUNO
486_{16} (Iter XV): MORIDUNO
Ravenna 106_2 (= R&C 15): MELAMONI
106_4 (= R&C 19): MILIDUNUM
106_9 (= R&C 23): MORIDUNO
106_{13} (= R&C 30): MORIONIO
TP: RIDUMO

In *TP*, it is evident that initial *Mo-* was written on the first segment of the map, and that when this was lost only the remaining portion on the second sheet could be written when the extant copy was made; compare *Madus* under *Noviomagus*[2]. In *Ravenna*, we have the only case in which a name is not merely duplicated, as often, but given four times. Although R&C seem unaware of this, and provide separate etymologies for two forms in addition to *Moridunum*, the names are inseparable and their unification is readily justified on the grounds of miscopying. However, there must be reasons for this extraordinary repetition. It seems that the Cosmographer had two map sources for Britain to Hadrian's Wall, and a third additional source for south-west England, as argued in Chapter V. This would explain matters to some extent. Perhaps a form of the present name with *-l-* (for *-r-*) figured as such in at least one source. Beyond this, however, it may be pertinent to note that in the surviving *TP*, *Moridunum* is the only south-western place named beside *Isca Dumnoniorum*; although we know that the Cosmographer did not use *TP* as such, he may have had a source related in some way to it, and his eye may have returned mistakenly to this nearly isolated name (*Iterum iuxta super scriptam civitatem Scadoniorum est civitas quae dictur...*).

DERIVATION. For British **mori-* 'sea', see MORICAMBE; for *-dunum*, see BRANODUNUM. The sense is then 'sea-fort'. Jackson in *Britannia*, I (1970), 77, examines other possibilities for the first element, but in view of parallels elsewhere – in addition to *Moridunum*[2] – these hardly need to be followed up. Holder II. 629 notes an assumed **Moridunum* (earlier forms are lacking) > Ortenau (early Mortenau) in Baden (Upper Rhine, Germany), and another > Murten (= Morat in French) on the Murtener See in Switzerland (Freiburg). This semantic extension of **mori-* from 'sea' to extensive inland waters may be significant for another British name that probably contains it, *Vindomora*. One may compare German *See* (masc.) used of inland waters, and *Meer* used for large lakes (e.g. Constance, Balaton) and the cognate English *mere*. There was a *Moridon* in Spain, *Ravenna* 79_{53}, listed among places as *iuxta oceanum*. If this is for **Moridon(um)*, as is likely, it belongs with the present name.

AI's form *Muri-* in the miscopied Iter XII shows a scribal assimilation to Latin *murus* 'wall'; there is an assimilation to another Latin word in one of the forms of *Moridunum*[2].

IDENTIFICATION. Possibly, as argued on p. 180, an unidentified Roman settlement at Sidford, Devon (SY 1389). The possibility that **mori-* might refer to inland waters does not assist alternative identifications, since there are no lakes in the area in question.

MORIDUNUM[2]

SOURCES

Ptolemy II, 3, 12: Μαρίδουνον (= MARIDUNUM), var. Μορίδουνον (= MORIDUNUM, in one MS)

AI 482_9 (Iter XII): MURIDONO

In these we have two conscious or unconscious assimilations: by Ptolemy to Latin *mare* 'sea' (though this could also be a kind of translation), and by *AI* to Latin *murus* 'wall' (as in one record of *Moridunum*[1]). Haverfield conjectured MARI [D]VNO in a text on a milestone from Port Talbot, A.D. 286–305 (*RIB* 2256); the Editor's note rejects this but leaves open the possibility that a recut text may have mentioned the name in adjectival form, MARI [D]VRE(NSIS); but this must be rejected too, for the name has *-dunum* not *-durum* (they were by no means alternative), and *Mori-* not *Mari-* (the latter being no more than a Ptolemaic variation).

DERIVATION. See MORIDUNUM[1].

IDENTIFICATION. The Roman city of Carmarthen (SN 4120), capital of the *Civitas Demetarum* and sited on the Afon Tywi at the head of tidal water. The modern name is a survival (Welsh *Caerfyrddin*).

MUTUANTONIS of *Ravenna* 106_{34} (= R&C 69): see TRISANTONA[1]

NABARUS

SOURCE

Ptolemy II, 3, 1: Ναβάρου ποταμοῦ ἐκβολαί (= NABARI FLUVII OSTIA); vars. Ναβαίου (= NABAEI), Ναυαίου (= NAUAEI)

DERIVATION. Watson *CPNS* 47 suggests a root in **nabh-* as found in Greek νέφος 'cloud, mass of clouds', νεφέλη 'cloud; mist, fog', Latin *nubes* 'cloud' and Sanskrit *nábhas* 'wet cloud', perhaps applied to mist rising from the river. Holder II. 670 adds a mention of Old Irish *nabhanú* 'spring'. This is found not uncommonly in ancient river-names over a wide area. There might be another *Nabarus* in south-west Britain (see *Naurum*). Abroad there were *Nablis* > Naab, a tributary of the Danube in Bavaria; *Nabalia* now the Leck, the northern mouth of the Rhine; *Nabantia* near Coimbra (Portugal); and *Nebrissa* > Lebrija (Sevilla, Spain). The British name is preserved in that of the modern river Naver, in Gaelic *Nabhar*. The name has the common water-suffix **-ar(a)*, for which see LEUCARUM. It is not wholly certain – given *b/v* confusions in Latin sources – that this name and others in *Nab-* are to be separated from *Nav-* in *Navio*, etc., for which a different etymology is proposed.

IDENTIFICATION. The river Naver, Sutherland.

NASSA

SOURCE

Ravenna 108_{33} (= R&C 255): CERTISNASSA

As proposed under CERTIS, this entry looks like a conflation.

DERIVATION. There are a few analogues: the Nassogne river of Belgium, recorded in A.D. 690 as *Nassania fons* (Carnoy in *RIO*, VIII (1956), 102); two rivers Νέστος (= *Nestos*) in Dalmatia and Thrace (Pokorny in *ZCP*, XXI (1940), 121); possibly the second element in British **Raxtonessa*. In Adamnan's *Life* of St Columba the present name is *fluvium Nesam* (II, 19 and II, 21), and its lake is mentioned too (*ad lacum fluminis Nisae*, II, 22), clearly the modern river and Loch Ness. Of the two roots proposed by R&C, that taken from Ekwall *ERN* 119 seems the better: **ned-* as in Sanskrit *nadī* 'river', German *nass* 'wet', Greek νοτέω 'am wet'; Pokorny analyses the name further as from **Nestā* < *Ned-tā*, and thinks the root ultimately Illyrian; Carnoy argues for a root **nat-so*, from Indo-European (*s*)*nat-* 'flowing'.

IDENTIFICATION. The river Ness, Scotland.

NAURUM (?)

SOURCE

Ravenna 108_{26} (= R&C 241): NAURUM

Holder II. 692 and Loth suggest that *Naurum* is an error for **Natrum*, assuming this to be the ancient name of the Wiltshire river Nadder. R&C reject this (and the identification) on the ground that 'There is no sound evidence that the Cosmography mentions inland rivers', and even though it now seems likely that there may be one or two in the text, it is probable that the Nadder was not important enough to warrant mention. An easier emendation would be to **Nau-(a)rum*, with *u* for *b* (via *v*), which has the advantage of producing in **Nabarus*[2] a second instance of a name which we already know existed in Britain. Against this, however, is the fact that in this section of his river-list the Cosmographer seems to be following fairly consistently an order of southern and south-western rivers, and in this region we know of no modern river whose name could derive (as would be expected) from **Nab-* or **Nav-*; moreover it is unlikely that at this point the Cosmographer is listing Ptolemy's Scottish Naver. A further possibility, and perhaps the best, is that *Ravenna* has here a gross corruption for the *Alaunus* recorded in the south-western region by Ptolemy, our *Alaunus*[1]. It is finally always possible that the Cosmographer (working from a map) has put a habitation-name among his river-names, as with *Durolavi* at 108_{37}.

IDENTIFICATION. Unknown, but apparently in southern Britain.

NAVIO

SOURCES

Inscription: *RIB* 2243, a milestone from Buxton, nearly 11 Roman miles south-west of Brough-on-Noe; the last words are A NAVIONE M P XI 'from Navio 11 miles'

Ravenna 106_{56} (= R&C 56): NAVIONE, var. NANIONE

DERIVATION. From the ablative of the inscription and from *Ravenna*'s oblique case we can deduce a notional third-declension nominative *Navio*, without knowing if it had real currency. Williams adopts as a root (now Pokorny 971) **snā-* 'to flow'; from a British derivative come Welsh *nawf*, *nofio* 'swim', and cognates include Latin *no*, *nare*. Two Continental rivers provide analogues: *Nava* > Nahe near Bingen (Germany: Whatmough

DAG 1224) and *Navia* > Navia in N. Spain. The British river-name **Nav-* 'fast-flowing water' (> Noe) has the derivational suffix *-*i̯o*- for the fort on its banks.

IDENTIFICATION. The Roman fort at Brough-on-Noe, Derbyshire (SK 3527).

*NEMETOBALA (?)

SOURCE

Ravenna 106_{23} (= R&C 50): METAMBALA

The form certainly needs emendation; we adopt that of R&C, but there can be no certainty that it is warranted. Loss of one or more letters at the start of a name occurs occasionally in *Ravenna*. We write the new form with medial *-o-* (R&C preserve *-am-*) because the analogues show this in other names which have **nemeto-* as first element.

DERIVATION. For **nemeto-* 'sacred grove', see AQUAE ARNEMETIAE. R&C think that the second element could be **ambala* 'navel', but this is hardly likely in place-names. They speculate also that *-abala* 'apple' might be involved, and cite Nennius on a freak apple-bearing ash-tree which grew at the mouth of the Wye; but on scribal grounds this emendation is hazardous, and the use of such an **abala* as a second element in compounds is nowhere attested. It seems that we should first associate the present name with its only possible British analogue, *Vindobala*. Several roots *bal- ball-* are assembled by Ellis Evans in *GPN* 147–48, mostly in personal names which have *bal(l)-* with suffix or as first element in a compound. Of the various senses of these diverse roots, that in the name *Balista* in Liguria, perhaps 'white-peaked', is the most promising; possibly Celtic **balma* 'pointed rock, peak', which must have existed in British in view of Welsh *bâl* 'peak, summit', Breton *bal* 'steep beach, steep slope'. In the present name 'grove-hill' or 'hill-sanctuary' would make good sense; but there can be no certainty of it.

IDENTIFICATION. The position of the name in the list indicates a location in Monmouthshire or Gloucestershire west of the Severn; a possibility is therefore the sacred site, with a Roman temple in an Iron Age hill-fort, at Lydney, Gloucestershire (SO 6102).

NEMETO STATIO (?)

SOURCE

Ravenna 105_{47} (= R&C 4): NEMETOTACIO, var. NEMETOTATIO

The emendation is that of R&C, among other possibilities they mention. The likelihood of a *Statio* name here is enhanced by that plainly mentioned by the Cosmographer at 105_{51}; the two places cannot have been far apart, and both would have pertained to the same system of administration.

DERIVATION. For **nemeto-*, see AQUAE ARNEMETIAE; and for the second element or word, DERVENTIO[6] STATIO. While this is strongly preferable, another possibility should not be wholly dismissed. Starting from textual *Nemetotatio*, one might suppose scribal removal of a suspected dittography in an original **Nemeto-totatio* or **Nemet(t)otatio*. *Teutates* was an important Celtic deity whose name probably meant 'ruler of the people' (Irish *túath* 'tribe, people'). In Britain he seems to have been mostly a war-god equated with Mars, as in *RIB*

219, 1017. His name was often written *Toutatis*, *Totatis* (examples in Holder II. 1895; *Toutati*, dative, in *RIB* 219). There is, then, nothing unlikely about the appearance of the name of this god in the second place of the present compound, with a meaning for the whole of 'sacred grove of Teutatis'.

IDENTIFICATION. Probably the Roman fort at North Tawton, Devon (SX 6699).

Note. On the Nymet and Nemet names which survive in the area of the present name and may preserve a memory of it, see AQUAE ARNEMETIAE.

NIDUM

SOURCE

AI 484_2 (Iter XII): NIDO

DERIVATION. There are *Nida* rivers listed by *Ravenna* 60_{38} and 62_{34}, now the Nidda (tributary of the Main) and Nied (tributary of the Saar) in Germany. Jackson in *Britannia*, I (1970), 77, notes that Neath in Welsh is *Nedd*, both town and river, which derives from a feminine **Nidā*; hence this was the original name of the river, and derivative *Nidum* that of the fort or settlement. The Nidd river in Yorkshire has the same origin. Pokorny 761 has a root **neid-* **nid-* 'fließen, strömen', and cites Sanskrit *nēdati* 'fließt, strömt' as derived from it, together with the European river-names; but there is a grave lack of derivatives and cognates, and the name remains somewhat obscure.

IDENTIFICATION. The Roman fort at Neath, Glamorgan (SS 7497).

NOVANTAE

SOURCE

Ptolemy II, 3, 5: Νοουάνται (= NOVANTAE), var. Νουάνται (= NUANTAE)
(also in the two following names)

DERIVATION. The base is Celtic **nou̯i̯o-* 'new', found in British *Noviomagus* and the two river-names, and in many names abroad. Old Irish *naue* and Latin *novus* are cognates, and a derivative is Welsh *newydd* 'new'. The present ethnicon can hardly derive from the tribe's dwelling near the river *Novius*, as Rhys (1904) 222 proposed, for the *Trinovantes* with a similarly-formed name had no such river in their lands, and this cannot have been the process involved. Watson *CPNS* 27, following Holder II. 778, thinks that **nou̯i̯o-* had further senses such as 'fresh; lively, vigorous', which applies well to a people and is pertinent also to the river-names. He mentions **Novantium* (> Nogent, many in France) in support, with the meaning 'fresh, green place', but Dauzat and Rostaing (1963) prefer to derive the Nogent names from **Novientum* (**nou̯i̯os* with suffix *-entum*) which 'a désigné à l'époque gauloise les agglomérations nouvelles, correspondant en somme aux Neuville et Villeneuve de l'époque médiévale.' Since there are no really ancient forms for these Gallic names, one can hardly judge between these two opinions. For the suffix **-ant-* in the British ethnicon, see DECANTAE.

IDENTIFICATION. A people of Scotland, occupying Galloway; Ptolemy attributes to them *Rerigonium* (? Stranraer) and *Lucopibia* (? Glenlochar).

NOVANTARUM PENINSULA

SOURCES

Ptolemy II, 3, 1: Νοουαντῶν χερσόνησος (= NOVANTARUM PENINSULA): again in II, 3, 2

Marcian II, 45: Νεουάντων χερσόνησον (acc.; ...Nevantes)

Ravenna 108_7 (= R&C 216): MEMANTURUM

Marcian has evidently translated, or unconsciously adapted, original *Nov-*.

Ravenna's entry has not previously been placed in relation to Ptolemy's. Emendation to initial *N-* seems obvious (compare **Nemetobala*), and is adopted also by R&C for their proposed **Nemanturum*. There are indeed several names analogous to this, including personal *Namanto*, *Namantius* (Holder II. 674), the *Nama(n)turi* people of the Alps (Pliny *NH* III, 137), whom Holder thought Ligurian, and Νεμαντουρίστα (= *Nemanturista*, var. -ισσα/-*issa*) of Ptolemy II, 6, 46, a *polis* in the Spanish central Pyrenees. For these a base in **namo-* **namanto-* is proposed, for which a clue to the meaning is offered by Irish *nama(e)* 'enemy', although it is far from easy to see how such a meaning could be present in the names in question. The **Nemanturum* of R&C may be correct and belong with these, but in principle it is better not to assign to a form recorded in *Ravenna* alone a root which is otherwise not known in Britain and (as shown above) of uncertain filiation. It is also the case that since many of Ptolemy's North British names were taken up by *Ravenna* – often in garbled form – we should consider whether a Ptolemaic entry lies concealed in corrupt form in *Ravenna*, for both drew ultimately from the same map-source. Hence *Novantarum* – which can be readily restored from miscopied *Memanturum* – seems the best possibility here. The second part of the name, **Peninsula* (or possibly **Promontorium*), in abbreviated form and written somewhat apart, was overlooked by the Cosmographer as he read from his map. Such names as can be identified in this part of *Ravenna* are from widely scattered parts of Scotland, and do not bar us from considering the present name as that of a western coastal place.

DERIVATION. See NOVANTAE.

IDENTIFICATION. The Rhinns of Galloway.

NOVANTARUM PROMONTORIUM

SOURCES

Ptolemy II, 3, 1: Νοουαντῶν χερσόνησος καὶ ὁμώνυμον ἄκρον (= NOVANTARUM PENINSULA et eiusdem nominis promontorium)

Marcian II, 45 – repeats Ptolemy

DERIVATION. See NOVANTAE.

IDENTIFICATION. The Mull of Galloway.

NOVIA

SOURCE

Ravenna 106_{34} (= R&C 68): NUBA
108_{40} (= R&C 267): NOVIA

At 106_{34} *Ravenna* is ostensibly listing habitation-names, but there is no guarantee that a few rivers have not been included among them (misread from a map); the next name, also 106_{34}, almost certainly refers to the *Trisantona*[1] river, which gives grounds for taking *Nuba* as a river. It is then inseparable from *Novia*, which figures properly in the river-list. The miscopying of *b*/*v* is very frequent in our texts because of their equation in Continental Vulgar Latin (*Ad Novas AI* 52_3 = *Nobas* of *Ravenna* 80_7, *Ad Novas* of *TP* = *Nobis* of *Ravenna* 73_5). Confusion of *o/u* scribally or in pronunciation was frequent too.

DERIVATION. There is no reason to suppose that this river is to be associated in any way with *Novus Portus*, as R&C tentatively suggest. The name might just possibly be Latin, and refer to a river diverted through a 'new course' (in which event **Nova* might be more correct). But it is safest by far to assume that rivers universally had British names even if unconscious latinisation has affected their recorded forms. If this is correct the name is British **nouịā*, a feminine of **nouịo-* (the base of the river *Novius* in Scotland); the fundamental sense of this is 'new', but better perhaps 'fresh, lively' when applied to water, for as Watson *CPNS* 54–55 says of the *Novius*, 'The reference is most likely to the freshness and verdure of the riverside'. Both Celtic and Latin *Nov-* names are common abroad.

IDENTIFICATION. A river of Britain, placed in the list in the area of Sussex. Arun is TRISANTONA (q.v.) and Rother and Ouse are almost certainly non-Germanic in origin (Ekwall *ERN*, but see Jackson *LHEB* 195, 342), but Adur is more interesting. The modern name appears first in Michael Drayton's *Polyolbion* (1612) and is evidently a learned back-formation from the then-supposed site of *Portus Adurni* in *ND*. Its earlier name was Bramber and this is itself a back-formation from OE *brember*, 'bramble' (whence also the village of Bramber). Adur, then, is the most likely candidate.

NOVIOMAGUS[1] REG(I)NORUM

SOURCES

Ptolemy I, 15, 7: Νοιόμαγον (acc.; = NOEOMAGUM)
II, 3, 13: Νοιόμαγος (= NOEOMAGUS), a *polis* of the Ῥῆγνοι (= REGNI)

Ravenna 106_{17} (= R&C 39): NOVIOMAGNO
106_{20} (= R&C 44): NAVIMAGO REGENTIUM

Ravenna's first form shows a scribal assimilation to Latin *magnus* (compare LEUCOMAGUS); its second form a different assimilation, perhaps, to Latin *navis*. R&C thought *Ravenna* 106_{17} a different place, locating it 'Between *Vindogladia* and *Venta Belgarum*, probably on the Roman road from Wimborne through the New Forest', but there is every reason to regard it as a simple duplication (from a different source, given the lack of tribal attribute) of the other entry at 106_{20}.

DERIVATION. For the first element, see NOVANTAE; for the second, see CAESAROMAGUS. The sense is 'new place', perhaps 'new market'. The name is repeated once in Britain, and Holder II. 790 records no fewer than eighteen on the Continent, mostly in Gaul. Modern names derived directly from it include Nijon, Noyon, Novion (France, with dialectal variation), Neumagen (Germany) and Nijmegen (Holland); see also Vincent 223.

IDENTIFICATION. The Roman city of Chichester, Sussex (SU 8604), capital of the *Civitas Reg(i)norum*.

NOVIOMAGUS[2]

SOURCES

AI 472_1 (Iter II): NOVIOMAGO
TP: MADUS

In *TP*, the name was evidently written across the join between the first two sheets, and when the first was lost, only the final portion of the name could be copied when the extant version was made. Compare the fragments entered under CAESAROMAGUS and DUROBRIVAE[1]. Although at one time *Madus* was taken to be a good name and applied to the Medway, the restoration [*Novio*]*madus* seems entirely acceptable following its suggestion by Miller in 1916.

DERIVATION. See NOVIOMAGUS[1].

IDENTIFICATION. The Roman settlement at Crayford, Kent (TQ 5174), the place where the Britons made a stand against Hengist and Aesc in A.D. 457 according to *ASC*.

NOVIUS

SOURCES

Ptolemy II, 3, 2: Νοουίου ποταμοῦ ἐκβολαί (= NOVII FLUVII OSTIA)
Ravenna 108_{18} (= R&C 230): PANOVIUS, var. PANONIUS
108_{32} (= R&C 253): NOVITIA, var. NOVICIA

It seems probable that these are to be equated. *Ravenna*'s entry at 108_{18} is in the group of *diversa loca*, and was hence thought by R&C to represent a tribal meeting-place. However, one other entry at least (*Taba*, 108_{19}) in this group is very plainly a river-name, and it seems certain enough that -*Novius* is too. The *Pa*- syllable is yet a further version of *Fl*, the abbreviation of *Fl*(*umen*) or *Fl*(*uvius*), misread from a map (see our entry for *EL*- names in *Ravenna*). Dillemann (p. 71) agrees with this proposal, and cites a telling parallel of *Pa*- for *Fl*- in *TP*, whose sheet for Cyrenaica includes a place *Ampaleontes* for **Ad Fl*(*umen*) *Leontes*. As for *Ravenna*'s *Novitia*, both Müller in his edition of Ptolemy and Holder II. 793 suggest that it stands for *Novius*. We cannot tell much from its position in the listing, but such miscopying is perfectly possible; a doubt remains, however, because *Ravenna* seems in general to have had only one map-source for North Britain and does not duplicate names in this region.

DERIVATION. The name is precisely as in NOVIA. Watson *CPNS* 54–55 assesses the possibility that the modern name Nith derives from *Novius*; this seems likely, though 'one cannot be certain, as the name has passed from British through Welsh into Gaelic and thence into English'.

IDENTIFICATION. The river Nith, Dumfriesshire.

NOVUS PORTUS

SOURCE

Ptolemy II, 3, 3: Καινὸς λιμήν (= NOVUS PORTUS)

DERIVATION. The name is Latin, 'new harbour'; compare *Magnus Portus* (which Ptolemy also translates instead of merely transliterating). For similar descriptive names, see GABRANTOVICUM SINUS.

IDENTIFICATION. As argued on p. 116, this almost certainly represents Dover as recorded in an early coastal survey.

OCELUM

SOURCE

Ptolemy II, 3, 4: Ὀκέλλου ἄκρον (= OCELLI PROMONTORIUM), var. Ὀκέλου (= OCELI)

DERIVATION. For **ocelo-* 'headland, promontory, spur', see ALAUNOCELUM. Ptolemy (or more probably, his Latin informants) did not understand the sense of this, which is duplicated by Greek ἄκρον 'promontory'; he should more properly have set *Ocelum* down as a simple nominative to which ἄκρον is in apposition (as he did in the following name). It is however just possible that the genitive is correctly used, in which case we have the divine name *Ocelus* (see ALAUNOCELUM).

IDENTIFICATION. Either Flamborough Head or Spurn Head, Yorkshire. If the literal meaning applied, the former might be preferable, since Spurn, at least in its present state after much erosion, is not physically notable. For reasons discussed above, however, (p. 138) with reference to the river name ABUS (q.v.), Spurn seems more likely.

OCRINUM PROMONTORIUM

SOURCES

Ptolemy II, 3, 2: Δαμνόνιον τὸ καὶ Ὄκρινον ἄκρον (= DAMNONIUM SIVE OCRINUM PROMONTORIUM), var. Ὄκριον (= OCRIUM, preferred by Müller); again in II, 3, 3

Marcian II, 45: ...Δάμνιον ἄκρον (= DAMNIUM cape) τὸ καὶ Ὄκριον καλούμενον (= which is also called OCRIUM)

DERIVATION. Ptolemy here (as for other principal capes which mark the 'corners' of the island) gives alternative names, each of the pairs containing – as argued in Chapter III (p. 115) – an archaic and a more modern name. *Ocrinum* is the more archaic of the present pair, and had probably been preserved in the tradition stemming from Pytheas. The name does not appear elsewhere. It may be an ancient Celtic or even pre-Indo-European name based on a root related to Greek ὄκρις 'rugged point, prominence', or it may be that Pytheas first named it with a form actually derived from the Greek word, which would then have had no currency in Britain. Remote but possible analogues are provided by *Interocrium* > Antrodoco (Rieti, Italy), and by Ὄκρα (= Ocra), a peak in the Julian Alps mentioned by Ptolemy II, 12, I and III, I, I, in whose area Pliny *NH* III, 133, locates a *Subocrini* people.

IDENTIFICATION. The reference is clearly to the Lizard peninsula, Cornwall, but whether to Lizard Point itself is not so certain. Professor C. Thomas has drawn our attention to the fact that what strikes the seafarer is not the headland but the hazardous reef called The Manacles, off the eastern side of the peninsula, which would fit the Greek word admirably. This would be especially true for someone approaching from the east, as Hawkes (*Pytheas: Europe and the Greek Explorers*, Oxford, 1977) argues that Pytheas did on his return journey; and this in turn would also explain why at this corner of the British triangle the names of two headlands (*Belerium* and *Ocrinum*) were preserved in the record.

OCTAPITARUM PROMONTORIUM

SOURCE

Ptolemy II, 3, 2: Ὀκταπίταρον ἄκρον (= OCTAPITARUM PROMONTORIUM), var. Ὀκταπόταρον (= OCTAPOTARUM)

DERIVATION. Little can be offered. Rhys (1904) 231 thought the name non-Celtic. It might have as a first element a form of Celtic **octo-* 'eight' (Old Irish *ocht*, Welsh *wyth*, Breton *eiz*), for which a possible explanation is offered below. The element *Octo-* in two *Octodurum* names (one now Martigny in Switzerland, the other a *polis* of the Vaccaei in Hispania Tarraconensis) has been related to the root which gave Irish *octe*, *ochte* 'angustia', but this again is only a possibility. Pokorny in *ZCP*, XXI (1940), 113–14, after mentioning the Greek mountain name Τίταρος (= *Titaros*) from a root **ku̯it-əro-s* (**ku̯eit-* weiß sein, hell sein') and the fact that this is not represented in Celtic, speculates about an Illyrian root **pit-* 'Fichte, Harzbaum', perhaps present in the Corsican river-name Πιτανός (= *Pitanos*), with cognates in Greek πίτυς, Albanian *piše* 'Fichte'. In this case a Mediterranean connection of this kind is perhaps attractive, if the name were given (like that of other British promontories) by a seafaring people, and then preserved in Greek tradition; a reference to a promontory by its 'fir-trees' (or others) would be natural enough.

IDENTIFICATION. St David's Head, Pembrokeshire. The figure of eight might conceivably refer to the group of islets known collectively as the Bishops and Clerks; alternatively the narrow passage between them and Ramsey Island, or that between Ramsey and the mainland (Ramsey Sound), might be in question.

OLENACUM (?)

SOURCES

Ptolemy II, 3, 10: Ὀλίκανα (= OLICANA), a *polis* of the Brigantes; var. Ὀλόκανα (= OLOCANA)

Ravenna 107_5 (= R&C 121): OLERICA

ND XL_{55}: Praefectus alae primae Herculeae, OLENACO (var. ELENACO)

Ravenna 106_{59} (= R&C 110) is hardly in question here. Although R&C give this as *Alicuna*, var. *Alunna*, Schnetz in his text reads *Alūna*, which he notes is easily emended to *Alauna*; and gives as the only variant *Alicinca*, but nowhere mentions R&C's '*Alicuna*'. We refer this to ALAUNA[8].

It can be taken as fairly certain that the above three entries refer to the same place. They agree on *Ol-*; there are no other *Ol-* names in Britain and very few abroad, so it is highly unlikely that we have two (or much less, three) different *Ol-* places in a limited area of north-west England where the texts place them. What we know of the texts allows us to say that *ND* is likely to be nearly right, *Ravenna* generally the most corrupt, and Ptolemy less wholly trustworthy than has hitherto been believed. If we start with the possibility that *ND*'s *Olenaco* is nearly right, *Ravenna*'s *Olerica* is easily corrected to agree with it; *-ri-* is a miscopying of *-na-*, and final *-a* is an error for *-o*, as often. As for Ptolemy, one observes that at II, 14, 4 (Pannonia Superior) he has Ὀλίμακον (= *Olimacum*), which Müller and others think is for *Alicano* of *AI* 261_9 or *Halicano* of *AI* 262_4 (now Dolnja Lendava, Yugoslavia); if this is so, Ptolemy has produced a metathesis of *c...n* to *n...c*, misread in turn (in a Latin text) as *m . . . c*, giving his *Olimacum*. This name is *Ligano* in *Ravenna* 57_6, which assures us of *c . . . n* (represented as *g . . . n*) being correct in this name. It is then at least possible that Ptolemy in listing British *Olenacum* made the same metathesis, producing *Olicana*. This is a further – scribal – reason for thinking that the three names are inseparable. That *Olicana* has been traditionally accepted and that Ilkley has been derived from it (despite objections) is a tribute to Ptolemy's authority, but need not weigh with us.

DERIVATION. If *Olenacum* is right, it has no easy etymology. The *-ācum* suffix (see BRAVONIACUM) suggests that we should look for a personal name as a base; as in *Epiacum*, *Sulloniacis* and possibly *Eburacum*, the suffix conveys 'estate of, property of'. *GPN* 239–40 offers a number of personal names based on *Ollo-* (always with *-ll-*), including e.g. *Ollecnos*, but there seem to be no place-names related to these. Tacitus in *Annals* IV, 72 (concerning A.D. 28) mentions a centurion *Olennius*. The most one can say is that the name possibly means 'property of' a man whose name was **Olen-*.

If it should be thought that *Ravenna*'s *Olerica* has some merit, there is an analogue to hand in Gaulish *Olericium* > Lirey (Aube, France), on which see Holder II. 843 and Whatmough *DAG* 607; this name might contain a Celtic **oler(i)ca* 'swan', as R&C think, though it is not easy to see how a simple noun like this could be a place-name (strictly, a fort-name) without suffix.

IDENTIFICATION. As noted above, the identification of Ptolemy's *Olicana* with Ilkley has no etymological basis and we have suggested another name for it (see VERBEIA). The position given by Ptolemy suits the Roman fort at Elslack, Yorkshire (SD 9249) equally well, and this also provides a site with a fort of suitable size and late occupation for *ND*'s *Olenacum*. This immediately follows *Bremetenacum* in the list (and is only three places from it in *Ravenna*) and so is unlikely to represent Old Carlisle, for which we suggest MAGLONA (q.v.).

OMIRE of *Ravenna* 106_{10} (= R&C 25, conflated with the next entry, TEDERTIS): for *-omi* as the last syllables of another name, see SORVIODUNUM

ONNA

SOURCE
Ravenna 106_{18} (= R&C 40): ONNA

DERIVATION. This name is inseparable from the next, *Onnum* (*Onno*), and may well be **Onno* too, since *Ravenna* often confuses *a/o*; or *Onna/Onnum* might represent Latin plural and singlular forms of the same name, as in *Maia/Maio*. Several etymologies have been proposed for the northerly *Onnum*. That favoured by Jackson in *JRS*, XXXVIII (1948), 57, is British **onno-* 'ash-tree', citing Gaulish *onno* glossed 'fraxinus', Welsh *onn* (to which Williams adds Cornish *onnen*, Breton *ounnen* and Old Irish *huinn*). Williams notes the frequency with which trees are associated with river-names. This etymology for both British names is, therefore, possible; the ash grows both on Hadrian's Wall and in Hampshire; and the tree is commonly used in Anglo-Saxon toponymy. However, we have no clear evidence of the use of a name for 'ash' in Celtic toponymy in other regions in ancient times; and rivers and places are not named in Celtic with a tree-word used alone, since we usually find such words compounded (*Daruveda*) or with suffix (*Aballava*, *Derventio*, *Vernalis*). Jackson's view must therefore be regarded as unsubstantiated. A second possibility, mentioned by Williams, is that a root **ond*- 'stone, rock' is in question (Irish *ond*, *onn*), and for the topography of both places R&C cite rocky features which might justify this meaning; but again, there are no other traces of this in toponymy, and it is clear from *LHEB* 513 that the assimilation *-nd-* > *-nn-* in British began in the late fifth century, hence much too late for it to be shown in Romano-British names (see, however, VINDOLANDA for a possible example of such an assimilation in Latin).

The best solution may be to turn to *onno*- **onna* 'stream, water', despite the objections of Celtic authorities. This word appears in the Vienna Glossary as *onno* = 'flumen'. *GPN* 370–71 lists personal names *Onna*, *Onnio*, etc., and there is *Onna*...(presumably the owner's name) as a graffito cut before firing on a jar from Sutton Courtenay (Berkshire) reported in *JRS*, LVI (1966), 224. While only one other place-name (see below) has *Onna* as an independent name, Whatmough *DAG* 578 draws attention to the large number of place-names, especially river-names, which end in *-onna*. The objection of Ellis Evans, Whatmough and others to accepting that all these contain *onno* 'flumen' of the Glossary is that Celtic cognates are lacking; but this problem seems to have been resolved by Dauzat in *TF* 118–21. Of *onno*, **onna* 'cours d'eau, source' he says that it was not originally a Celtic word, but a Gaulish borrowing from an earlier language that was not only pre-Celtic but perhaps pre-Iberian too (that is, with respect to regions occupied), in view of the river One < *Onna* (Louchon, France; a Gascon area). Since it was used as a second element especially, in e.g. Valdone, Vallone, it came to be taken as a mere suffix, as in *Bebronna* 'beaver-river', *Calonna* > Chalonnes, *Sauconna* > Saône; and often appears as *-umna* in river-names such as *Vultumna*, *Garumna*, since there is hesitation between *o* and *u* (*ŭ*) in inscriptions (*-mn-* spellings represent hypercorrection, since it is known that *Garonna* is an earlier form than *Garumna*). This root might still be Indo-European, says Dauzat, if **onna* represents a more ancient **wonda*, from the same root as Latin *ŭnda*. He regards *onna* as a simple variation of basic *onno*. If this root was borrowed into Gaulish from an earlier language and widely used for naming purposes, its presence in British toponymy should cause no surprise. See also *EC*, XIV (1975), 445.

IDENTIFICATION. Unknown. The name is listed between *Noviomagus* (Chichester) and *Venta Belgarum* (Winchester), so that the possibilities include the Roman defended site at Iping, Sussex (SU 8426), on the river Rother, and the settlement at Neatham, Hampshire (SU 7340), on the Wey. Either of these is more likely, both in position and in importance, than R&C's suggestion of Nursling, Hampshire (SU 3616), on the Test (which was where Crawford lived).

ONNUM

SOURCE

ND XL_{37}: Praefectus alae Sabinianae, HUNNO

DERIVATION. See the previous entry. *H*- is intrusive, a mere learned decoration by a scribe; *-u-* is miscopied for *-o-*, as often in our texts.

IDENTIFICATION. The Roman fort at Halton Chesters, Northumberland (NY 9968), whose garrison in the third century was the *Ala Sabiniana* (*RIB* 1433). If the reference is to water, it may be noted that this is the only place where a stream (the Fence Burn) actually touches the line of Hadrian's Wall in the 10-mile stretch from Whittledean to the North Tyne.

OPPORTUNUS SINUS

SOURCE
Ptolemy II, 3, 10: Εὐλίμενον κόλπον (acc.), which repeats the entry of II, 3, 4 where the same bay is related to the Gabrantovices. In the medieval Latin translation of Ptolemy the adjective εὐλίμενος 'suitable for a harbour' is represented as *opportunus* at II, 3, 10, and as *portuosus* at II, 3, 4. See GABRANTOVICUM SINUS.

ORCADES

SOURCES
These are numerous. The islands are first mentioned by Mela II, 6, 85, and next by Pliny *NH* IV, 103; then by most writers down to Bede. The name is regularly *Orcades*, accusative *Orcadas*. The spelling is normally with *-c-*, but Eutropius has *-ch-*, and so do several later writers who perhaps followed Paeanius's Greek spelling with -χ-. See the discussion in Chapter II, p. 40.

DERIVATION. The base is also that of the next name, *Orcas*: Celtic **orco-s* from Common Celtic **porko-s*, cognate with Latin *porcus* 'pig, boar'. A related word is Latin *orca*, thought to have resulted from a contamination of two originally different words, Greek ὄρυγα and ὕρχα; its sense is apparently somewhat variable, 'whale, narwhal, dolphin', perhaps 'sea-monster' also, and this may not have been without influence in the way that the islands' name was interpreted (if not upon the original naming); see C.-J. Guyonvarc'h in *Ogam*, XIX (1967), 233–39. Celtic **orco-s* has left no Brittonic descendants, but Old Irish *orc* is recorded as meaning 'piglet, young boar'; there is also Irish *erc* 'salmon', and this, according to Guyonvarc'h, is a word related to *orc* because in form they continue a well-attested alternation of Indo-European, **perk-/pork-*. For the possible extension of the sense 'pig' in Celtic, Williams helpfully notes Welsh *mor-hwch* 'dolphin', literally 'sea-pig'. We thus have several possibilities. The name might mean literally 'whale islands' or refer to a sea-monster or to some large creature such as seals or porpoises (Williams), or it might mean 'îles de saumon' (Guyonvarc'h); it can scarcely refer literally to pigs or boars. But it is also possible, according to Watson *CPNS* 28–30, that the name derives from a tribal designation, **Orcoi* 'boars', which as Watson notes was a noble animal in Celtic folklore; this is supported by Jackson *PP* 135, who thinks **Orci* Celtic and 'doubtless a totemistic appellation'. This notion is supported by C. Thomas in *Arch.J.*, CXVIII (1961), 40, in view of the strong evidence of such totemistic references in the names of N. British tribes.

Both *Orcas* and *Orcades* seem to be treated in our texts as very Greek names (especially in the termination *-ades*), which may indicate that they were already old when they came to Mela, and had been first set down in the Greek of Pytheas. Watson thinks both names adjectival, without quite explaining how he thought they functioned. He also observes that when the name became known to

Pytheas, a Celtic people must already have been established in the islands. See also Holder II. 869 and Whatmough *DAG* 466.

IDENTIFICATION. The Orkney Islands.

ORCAS PROMONTORIUM

SOURCES

Diodorus Siculus V, 21: Ὄρκαν (= ORCADEM)

Ptolemy II, 3, 1: Ταρουεδοὺμ ἢ καὶ Ὀρκὰς ἄκρα (= TARVEDUM SIVE ORCAS PROMONTORIUM)
II, 3, 4: Μετὰ τὸ Ταρουεδοὺμ ἄκρον ἢ τὴν Ὀρκάδα (= POST TARVEDUM PROMONTORIUM SIVE ORCADEM)
II, 3, 14: Κατὰ τὴν Ὀρκάδα ἄκραν (= AD ORCADEM PROMONTORIUM)

Marcian II, 45: Ὀρκάδος (= ORCAS)

DERIVATION. See the previous entry. The name, like that of other 'corner' capes, is presented in the sources as the more archaic of a pair; it existed in Greek tradition but probably had no real local currency, being perhaps originally a deduction from the name of the *Orcades* because this mainland cape faced the islands.

IDENTIFICATION. As used by Ptolemy the name applies to Dunnet Head, but see p. 115.

ORDOVICES

SOURCES

Tacitus *Annals* XII, 33: ORDOVICAS (acc. pl.)
Agricola 18, 2: ORDOVICES

Ptolemy II, 3, 11: Ὀρδοούικες (= ORDOVICES), var. Ὀρδούικες (= ORDVICES)

DERIVATION. The first element is British **ordo*- 'hammer', from which derives Welsh *gordd* 'hammer'; there is also *órd*, *ordd* in Irish. For the second element, see DELGOVICIA. The sense is thus 'hammer-fighters', with reference either literally to a weapon or to an emblem. The name survived: a fifth-century tombstone from Penbryn (Cardiganshire) bears the inscription *Corbalengi iacit Ordous*, the last word representing a late form of British **Ordouix* 'Ordovican tribesman' (*ECM* 126 = *CIIC* 354; see Jackson *LHEB* 619, etc.), and there are modern place-names *Dinorwig* or *Dinorddwig* 'fortress of the Ordovices' between Caernarvon and Bangor, and *Rhyd Orddwy* 'ford of the Ordovices' near Rhys in Flintshire.

IDENTIFICATION. A people of north Wales. Ptolemy attributes *Mediolanium* and *Brannogenium* to them, but see p. 121 and entries for BRANOGENIUM and MEDIOLANUM.

OTHONA

SOURCE

ND XXVIII$_3$ (*pictura*): OTHONA, var. OTHANA
XXVIII$_{13}$ (text): Praepositus numeri Fortensium, OTHONAE

DERIVATION. This is a very problematic name. The evidence of *ND* is supplemented, exceptionally, by a later form in Bede, who (III, 22) writes of St Cedd preaching to the East Saxons *maxime in civitate quae lingua Saxonum Ythancaestir* _appellatur_. St Cedd built his church at Bradwell in about 654, at the Roman fort and using its materials. It is usually assumed that Bede's _Ythan-_ represents a continuation in Anglo-Saxon of _Othōna_, perhaps of a variant *_Othōnia_ (Zachrisson (1927), 83), but Ekwall _EPN_ (s.v. Bradwell) thinks it likely that _Yþþan_ is the genitive of a personal name *_Yþþa_ or *_Yþþe_ (fem.). It seems, however, that when we have such a degree of phonetic similarity, the fact that the two locations coincide (the church at the fort), a _caestir_ name, and no more than a hypothetical Anglo-Saxon personal name (not commonly associated with _caestir_), there is every reason to postulate a probability of the continuation of the Romano-British name to Bede's time; and this probability is enhanced by the strong survival-rate of the names of the Saxon Shore forts. The phonetic difficulty is resolved by Förster _FT_ 597 (note), at least for the vowels. He starts from an assumed British *_Ottōna_, Latin _Othōna_, whose stressed vowel would have evolved via *_Oþün_ to Anglo-Saxon *_Uþīn_ > *_Yþin_, then to the form recorded by Bede; he cites the development of Latin _colōnia_ to Anglo-Saxon _-cylen_ (_Lindcyln_) in support. This seems to accord with Jackson's discussion of the development of _ọ̄_ in _LHEB_, although at 568–69 he seems to doubt Förster's *_Ottōna_ on other grounds, that it has no clear etymology and leaves the _-th-_ of the Latin form unexplained.

There are other possibilities. A British *_Ottōna_, of unknown etymology, might have been assimilated by Latin speakers to the Roman personal name _Otho_. This was a _cognomen_ of the _gens Salvia_, its best-known member being M. Salvius Otho, briefly Emperor in A.D. 69. This name has been related to Greek ὄθομαι, whence the _-th-_ spelling, though it is often written _Otto_ also. British had no _-th-_ [θ] sound, and may not have entered into the later part of the transmission process at all; the name could have been made known by Latin speakers to early Germanic mercenaries, or could have survived among Latin speakers of south-east Britain and been transmitted to Anglo-Saxon settlers, its _-th-_ being heard naturally by the latter as their _þ_.

If British is involved, we have noted that _-th-_ [θ] was not a sound which existed in it. The name cannot have had _-t-_ written _-th-_ by a medieval scribe (_Othona_), as did often happen, because original British _-t-_ lenited (as Latin _t_ was voiced to _d_ in late Vulgar Latin) and is represented as _d_ in Anglo-Saxon borrowings, e.g. *_Anderitum_ > Andred, *_Rutuna_ > Roden, which is not the case with the present name. However, original British _-tt-_ does appear as _-th-_ in later forms (_LHEB_ 565), and could explain why a British *_Ottōna_ (scribally represented as _Othona_) would give, in the evolution of the sounds of British, an Anglo-Saxon _Ythan-_ as Bede has it, though according to Jackson (_LHEB_ 568) the dating of such a borrowing remains a problem.

IDENTIFICATION. The Roman fort at Bradwell-on-Sea, Essex (TM 0308).

PANOVIUS of _Ravenna_ 108_{18} (= R&C 230): see NOVIUS

PARISI

SOURCE

Ptolemy II, 3, 10: Πάρισοι (= PARISI), var. Παρείσοι (= PAREISI)

(The appearance of the letter C on the left side-panel of _RIB_ 707 has suggested that it was matched by a P on the missing right side-panel, the two standing for C(_ivitas_)

P(*arisorum*). This is conjectural, and not universally accepted, but has an important bearing on the vexed question of the status of PETUARIA (q.v.)).

DERIVATION. The name is identical with that of the Gaulish *Parisii*, which survives as that of the capital of France: for a discussion of the connection, see I. M. Stead, *The La Tène Cultures of Eastern Yorkshire* (York, 1966), and H. G. Ramm, *The Parisi* (London, 1978). Holder II. 932 explains their name by comparison with an assumed **Quār-īsii* in Q-Celtic, based on a verb-stem **qari-* **qariu-*, citing as a derivative Old Irish *cuirim* 'ich setze, stelle', a cognate being Old Welsh *peri*, infinitive of *param*, *paraf* 'würke'; with suffixes *-*is-i̯o*-. To this O'Rahilly *EIHM* 147–48 adds the parallel of the *Quariates* people of the Alps, whose name in P-Celtic would be **Pariatis*, a precise forerunner of Welsh *peiriad* 'one who causes'. Senses suggested for the ethnic name are 'efficaces, strenui' (Zeuss) and 'gens dont les actes produisent des effets' (d'Arbois de Jubainville); but O'Rahilly thinks the *Quariates* have the name of a deity which means 'the shaper, maker'. Any one of these might have applied to the *Parisi*; the suggestion about a base in a divine name is that most in accord with modern thinking about many ethnic names.

IDENTIFICATION. A people of eastern Yorkshire to whom Ptolemy, placing them next to the *Brigantes* and near *Gabrantovicum Sinus*, ascribes only *Petuaria* (q.v.).

PENNOCRUCIUM

SOURCE

AI 470_1 (Iter II): PENNOCRUCIO

DERIVATION. The first element is British **pĕnnŏ-* 'head, hill; end; (as adj.) chief', represented now by Welsh *penn*, Cornish and Breton *pen*, and presumably related to **pen-* of wide Mediterranean (Ligurian?) currency, in names all meaning 'hill, height'. In Q-Celtic **quenno-s* gave Irish *cend*, *cen*, *ceann*. Older **penno-* or Welsh and Cornish *pen*(*n*)- is abundantly represented in the toponymy of modern Wales, Cornwall and adjoining areas. Zachrisson (1927) 49 collected many of them; he has interesting early forms for Pentridge (Dorset), evidently identical in origin to the present name. Ancient place-names include *Pennelocos* of *AI* 351_7 (= *Pennolucos* of *TP*) 'head of the lake' (Lake Geneva) now Villeneuve (Switzerland), and a **Pennovindos* (= Welsh Penwyn) 'white hill' > Pavant (Aisne, France), noted by Dottin *LG* 75. The second element is British **crōco-*, older **crouco-*, for which see CROCOCALANA; with *-*i̯o*- suffix. *AI*'s form with -*u*- (-*crucio*) might show that the name was adopted from British not earlier than the late third century, or that the recorded Latin form reflects the late third-century evolution of the British vowel (*ou* > *ō* > *ū*); but it is more likely that *AI*'s form is not altogether trustworthy, and that the *u* represents *o*, as often.

The sense presents a problem. 'Chief mound' or perhaps 'tumulus on the hill' seems obvious, but M. Gelling (1978, p. 41) finds this 'inexplicable in terms of the modern topography', since the crossroads at which the Romano-British settlement stands is not on a hill, and there is no trace of a tumulus. G. Webster in Wacher (1966), 44, thought that the name 'may originally have derived from a native hill-fort on the higher ground to the south-west' (for a similar transference, compare perhaps BANNAVENTA[1]), and in *The Cornovii* (1975, p. 78) speculates that alternatively the name 'could signify a special assembly point for the tribe, or a place of some local importance'. Gelling suggests 'that there might have been a great tumulus called "the chief mound" on the site of the town, of which no trace remains, or that the name was that of a large district and the mound lay elsewhere'. These views seem to cover all the diverse possibilities.

IDENTIFICATION. The Roman settlement (succeeding forts) at Water Eaton, Staffordshire (SJ 9010), on the river Penk and 2½ miles south of modern Penkridge. The nearest *known* hill-fort to the south-west is Chesterton Walls, 10 miles distant; Castle Ring (9 miles to the east) is nearer to *Letocetum* than to *Pennocrucium* and even the nearest hill-fort, Berry Ring (6½ miles to the north), is too remote. No tumulus is known near here.

Note. The name survives in that of the village of Penkridge, via Anglo-Saxon *Pencric* (A.D 958); this was taken from speakers of Brittonic with the second *c* intact as a velar (*LHEB* 260). The name of the river Penk derives by back-formation (with wrongly perceived division) from that of the village.

PETRIANIS

SOURCE

ND XL_{45}: Praefectus alae Petrianae, PETRIANIS (thus in Seeck's edition)

This name is a 'ghost'. See Chapter VI, p. 221.

PETUARIA

SOURCES

Ptolemy II, 3, 10: Πετουαρία (= PETUARIA), the *polis* of the Parisi

Inscription: *RIB* 707, the dedication-slab of the theatre at Petuaria, the new stage being presented by an AEDILIS VICI PETU[AR(IENSIS)], A.D. 140–44.

Ravenna 107_{15} (= R&C 138): DECUARIA

ND XL_{31} gives an adjectival form for the unit stationed at *Derventio*[1]: Praefectus numeri supervenientium Petueriensium ...

Ravenna's form is explained as simple miscopying; compare the reverse, *P* for *D*, in its *Purocoronavis* at 105_{48}.

DERIVATION. The name is a feminine of British **petu̯ari̯o-* 'fourth' (Welsh *pedwerid* (*pedwyr-yd*)), based on **petor-* 'four', in compounds *petru-*, cognate with Latin *quattuor*. The element is found abroad in the place-names *Petromantalum* *AI* 382_5, 384_{10} 'four roads, crossroads'; *Pedeverius* (A.D. 979) perhaps for earlier **Petuarios* > Pithiviers (Loiret, France); and in the ethnic names *Petrucorii* 'four hosts' (*BG* VII, 75, etc.) > Périgueux (Périgord, France), *Petranioi* at Lamas de Moledo (Pontevedra, Spain; *ELH* I. 120). For the formation *Petrucorii* Whatmough *DAG* 402 compares *Tricorii*, *Tetrapolis*, *Novempopuli*, etc. The suggested sense of *Petuaria* is, then, 'fourth (part)', the Parisi being perhaps divided into four *pagi*; for a discussion of the similarly organised *Petrucorii*, see C. E. Stevens in his chapter 'Roman Gaul' in J. M. Wallace-Hadrill (ed.), *France* (2nd ed. 1970), 22. See further on the ordinal forms of '4' in Celtic E. P. Hamp in *BBCS*, XXVI (1974–76), 309–11.

IDENTIFICATION. This is usually taken as Brough-on-Humber, Yorkshire (SE 9326), and if the *Praetorio* of *AI* 466_5 (Iter I) is accepted as a corruption of the name this is the easiest identification, since the roads lead there; see discussion in Chapter IV, p. 156. However the most recent excavator of Brough, J. Wacher (in *The Towns of Roman Britain* (London, 1974), 394–97), points out that the occupation of the place seems always to have been military and naval rather than civil and suggests that the *Vicus Petuariensis* may have been located not at Brough itself but some three miles downstream at North Ferriby; the stone bearing *RIB* 707 was not found in situ but re-used in a fourth-century building in the naval base, and the theatre referred to has not been identified.

There is also the vexed question of the town's status. Unless the C in the left side-panel of *RIB* 707 can be taken to imply a P in the missing right side-panel, thus giving C(*ivitas*) P(*arisorum*), there is no evidence that *Petuaria* was the capital of the *Parisi*, nor that the *civitas*, as opposed to the individual *vicus*, had a fully romanised form of government. It is, therefore, uncertain whether the place was ever known as *Petuaria Parisorum*.

PEXA of *Ravenna* 107_{53} (= R&C 193): see PICTI
(R&C suggest that the name should have *D*- (there are indeed cases of this error in *Ravenna*), drawing attention to *Dixio* (see *DICTUM), but in terms of geography that is not helpful. R&C's suggested equivalence with *Decha* of *Ravenna* 108_{8} is slightly more promising; however, we have taken that as a garbled version of *Decantae*.)

PICTI

SOURCES
The *Picti* are first (but see below) mentioned by two of the Panegyrici Latini: VIII (V), 11, 4 (A.D. 297–98), and VI (VII), 7, 2 (A.D. 310). Ammianus Marcellinus mentions them in connection with events respectively of A.D. 360 (XX, 1, 1), 365 (XXVI, 4, 5) and 368 (XXVII, 8, 4), on the third occasion writing an important note on the fact that they were divided into two nations (*Dicalydones*, *Verturiones*). There are then several references in Claudian, in the *Chronica Gallica* of A.D. 452, in Apollinaris Sidonius, and others. All sources write the name as *Picti*, with the exception of Ammianus, who at XXVI, 4, 5 calls them *Pecti* (but *Picti* in his other two mentions).

It is possible that *Ravenna*'s *Pexa* at 107_{53} (= R&C 193) is for *Pecti* or, even more interestingly, **Pectia* 'Pictland'. The Cosmographer lists the name as that of an Antonine Wall fort, but we already know that this section contains several names that are nothing of the sort, including two that are probably tribal names misread from a map as though they were forts (*Volitanio* = *Votadini*, *Credigone* = *Creones*). *Pexa* could well come into this category; the original map-source could have carried **Pecti* or **Pexti* (for *-ct-*/*-xt-*, compare *Tectoverdi*, and see below), whose *-e-* would be important beside that recorded by Ammianus, or possibly **Pect(i)a* or **Pext(i)a*. Whether the tribal name or a regional name is in question, the record is (if accepted) of importance, because it would in effect be the earliest known to us; for the Cosmographer's map-source for N. Britain was, as argued on pp. 193–97, a Severan modernisation of the early military map.

DERIVATION. It is uncertain whether *Picti* is truly and solely Latin, or simply a convenient latinisation of an existing native name, presumably British. What is sure is that this people was always known as *Picti* 'painted ones' to the Romans. It is not known what the Picts called themselves at any time in their long history. Suggestions about a native Celtic word are recorded by Holder II. 993, citing **picto-s* as 'soigneux, diligent' according to Ernault, and mentioning the cognate **Quicti*, with several derivatives; and are made by Förster *FT* 119 on the basis of a plural **Peχtās*, older **Piχtas* with vowel-affection causing *ĭ* > *e*. If Förster is right, Ammianus's form *Pecti* (possibly with that of *Ravenna*) assumes great importance, and there is support for it in the fact that the people was known in Old Norse as *Pettr*, in Anglo-Saxon as *Peohtas*, in Old Scots as *Pecht*, and in Middle Welsh as *Peith-wyr* (Watson *CPNS* 67–68), all forms which demand original *Pect-*. However, Jackson in *LHEB* 576–77 is inclined to dismiss Ammianus's *Pecti* as merely erratic, a scribal confusion (he naturally did not take account of *Ravenna*'s *Pexa*), and in his more recent discussion in Chapter VI, 'The Pictish Language', of F. T. Wainwright's (ed.) *The Problem of the Picts* (1956), he doubts more strongly whether there was a native word subsequently latinised, concluding 'The probability is that it [*Picti*] was always simply the Latin verbal adjective *picti*', with the interesting addition that 'It is not impossible that it was first used as a translation of *Priteni* ("people of the designs", i.e. tattoos).' One can support this in a small way by recalling that there are literary analogies for such naming of peoples in Latin, in texts likely to have been known to many educated Romans: Virgil has *picti Agathyrsi* (*Aeneid* IV. 146) and *pictosque Gelonos* (*Georgics* II. 115), both placed somewhere in the North.

On the *i*/*e* question, we do not necessarily have to think in terms solely of British speech. In spoken Latin, stressed *ĭ* > *e* in most parts of the Empire by the third century, including Britain (as a good deal of epigraphic evidence shows), and in Gaul the related name *Pictavi* is recorded as *Pectavi*. Hence the Severan map of North Britain may well have given the name with *e*. Ammianus could have received from a British source a report on the events of A.D. 368 which mentioned *Pecti* in the spoken Latin of the day, and adopted it unquestioningly. The further implication is that other languages (Old Norse, Anglo-Saxon, Welsh, etc.), whose forms all demand *Pecti*, received it in spoken or written (ecclesiastical?) Latin in this form, adopting it from Latin and not from British. Since the name was not necessarily one which the Picts ever used among themselves or which others learned from them, this seems a tenable proposition.

Since, however, account must be taken of the Gaulish ethnic names *Pictavi* and *Pictones* (cf. Poitou, Poitiers), which must be related to *Picti–Pecti* and which have standard Celtic suffixes, there may after all be a native Pictish word from which the Picts were named. The best recent studies of this are those of W. F. H. Nicolaisen in *Studia Celtica*, VII (1972), 1–11, and in his book *Scottish Place-names* (London, 1976), 150–58. Nicolaisen does not think that Latin *Picti* is primary. He draws attention, as others have done, to the abundance of *pett-* place-names in Pictish lands; and since Gaulish **pĕtį̯a* was borrowed into Latin as *pettia* in the sense 'piece of land' (in fact *pĕttia* > Romance *pièce*, *piece*), it is certain that such was also the meaning of **pett-* in Pictish. The matter is very important for discussion of the whole question of the linguistic affinities of the Picts with P-Celtic, and of their boundaries. It is not altogether easy to see how the sense could enter into an ethnic name, and Nicolaisen does not affirm it, but the people could be simply 'those of whom *pett-* is typical, those who call their lands *pett-*'. If this is right, clearly Latin *Picti* is secondary, a sort of Latin folk-etymology (perhaps aided by Virgilian echoes); moreover, *e* is primary and *i* secondary.

IDENTIFICATION. A collection of peoples in northern Scotland, as perceived by Roman writers from the third century onwards. For their origins, extent and culture see especially F. T. Wainwright (ed.), *The Problem of the Picts* (Edinburgh, 1956) and C. Thomas, 'The Animal Art of the Scottish Iron Age and its Origins', *Arch. J.*, CXVIII (1961), 14–64, and 'The Interpretation of the Pictish Symbols', *ibid.*, CXX (1963), 31–97.

PILAIS

SOURCE

Ravenna 105_{49} (= R&C 7): PILAIS

DERIVATION. The entry is meaningless as it stands, and must be corrupt. It is not possible to suggest emendations.

IDENTIFICATION. Unknown, but apparently in south-west Britain.

PINNATA CASTRA

SOURCES

Ptolemy II, 3, 8: Πτερωτὸν στρατόπεδον, a *polis* of the Vacomagi; again in VIII, 3, 9. Ptolemy's Greek name was at one time rendered as *Alata Castra*; the rendering *Pinnata Castra* is Müller's, consequent upon his equation of this place with the *Pinnatis* of *Ravenna*.

Ravenna 108_5 (= R&C 211): PINNATIS, var. PUMATIS

There is a further highly interesting pair of entries in *Ravenna* at 107_{31-32} (= R&C 158, 159): *Stodoion* (var.: *stodoyon*) and *Sinetriadum*. If we set these in the same order beside a transcription of Ptolemy's entry, we have

Pteroton Stratopedon
Stodoion Sinetriadum

The equation can by no means be affirmed, but it should be noted that (*a*) no explanation for *Ravenna*'s two names has ever been advanced, and they have seemed hopelessly corrupt; (*b*) the number of letters gives a precise 'fit'; (*c*) certain parts of *Ravenna*'s two entries already correspond closely with those in the transliteration of Ptolemy (such as *-oion*/*-oton*), and other features – by no means all – are within the range of common mistakes. It is not easy to envisage the process by which, if this notion is right, a Latin transliteration of this Ptolemy entry reached the Cosmographer (as a duplication of *Pinnatis* which he had from another source); our discussion of the points involved is on p. 197.

Ravenna's *Pinnatis* has *-is* miscopied for *-a*, as occasionally elsewhere (e.g. *Uxelis* 106_1 for *Uxela*).

DERIVATION. The name appears to be wholly Latin, 'winged camp', but the sense in which this is intended is not clear. Richmond's suggestion, 'camp with merlons', made when he was arguing for its attribution to Inchtuthil (*PSAS*, LVI (1921–22), 299), seems unlikely, because this would not distinguish it from many other Roman camps and forts. A camp at a place where there was an unusual number of birds might be more probable – or even possibly one where there were many pearl-bearing *pinnae* or fan-mussels (see Rivet in *Studien zu den Militärgrenzen Roms*, II (Köln and Bonn, 1977), 60 and n. 32).

IDENTIFICATION. This is attributed by Ptolemy to the *Vacomagi* and, as argued on p. 128, must lie near the coast of the Moray Firth west of the mouth of the river Spey and probably near the mouth of the river Findhorn, perhaps in the area of Culbin Sands, where small finds of all periods are recorded. Its appearance in the list in Book VIII of Ptolemy is accounted for by the fact that it was the furthest place in Britain to which he could give a name: presumably the furthest encampment of Agricola's army.

PONS AELII or PONS AELIUS

SOURCE

ND XL_{34}: Tribunus cohortis primae Cornoviorum, PONTE AELI

DERIVATION. This is Latin, 'Hadrian's Bridge'. *Aelius* was the gentile name of Hadrian. *ND*'s form with locative *Ponte* seems to show that *Aeli* is a no longer variable genitive, so that *Pons Aeli(i)* seems the more likely form for the name in the nominative. However, adjectival *Aelius* is possible, and was used elsewhere: the Roman name given to Jerusalem was *Aelia*, and there was another in north Africa (*AI* 554, *TP*); also *Aeliana* in Armenia (*ND Or.* XXXVIII_{24}). We are fortunate in knowing the precise origin of the *pons* at Newcastle. *RIB* 1319 and 1320 are a pair of altars dedicated respectively to Neptune and Oceanus by Legio VI, apparently on their arrival from Germany: 'The bridge... named after Hadrian and designed as the original starting-point of Hadrian's Wall, must belong to the inception of the Wall in A.D. 122.'

IDENTIFICATION. The Roman fort at Newcastle upon Tyne, Northumberland (NZ 2563).

PONTIBUS

SOURCE

AI 478_4 (Iter VII): PONTIBUS

DERIVATION. The name is Latin, '(at) the bridges'. For the possible force of the plural in this name, see the discussion of Celtic and Latin usages under DUROBRIVAE[1]. For ablative-locative *-ibus*, see ANICETIS. There was another *Pontibus* in Gaul, *AI* 363_1.

IDENTIFICATION. The Roman settlement at Staines, Middlesex (TQ 0371), at the crossing of the river Thames.

PORTUOSUS SINUS of Ptolemy II, 3, 4: see OPPORTUNUS SINUS

*PORTUS ARDAONI or *ARDAONIUM(?)

SOURCES

Ravenna 106_{19} (= R&C 43): ARDAONEON

ND XXVIII_{11} (*pictura*): PORTUM ADURNI

XXVIII_{21} (text): Praepositus numeri exploratorum, PORTUM ADURNI

DERIVATION. There can be no certainty of the correct form of this name. *ND*'s has long been known and has become established, but it has no special authority. The association of it with *Ravenna*'s *Ardaoneon*, first suggested by Holder but seemingly not considered by British scholars, seems logical both textually and by position in *Ravenna*'s list. However, the two texts are evidently citing the name in different or alternative forms: *ND* has *Portus* plus an apparent genitive *Adurni* ('port of...') or locative case ('port at...'), whereas *Ravenna* dispenses with 'port' and has a neuter nominative (*-on* representing *-um*, as always). For other instances of such different usage, see *Abona*, *Dubris*, *Lemanis*, all of which have *Portus* in some texts. Although in general *ND* is more trustworthy than *Ravenna*, the latter's number of letters must (despite probable miscopying of them) be taken into account.

Although the other British names involving *Portus* involve what are ultimately river-names, this is not necessarily the case here, and *Ravenna*'s *-on* (for *-um*) does not indicate a river. It is then likely that, as R&C proposed for *Ardaoneon*, British **ardu*– 'height' is involved, for which see ARDOTALIA, the reference being (if the identification, below, is right) to the hill behind the harbour. *Ravenna*'s form then hints at a suffix, perhaps British **-on-i̯o-*, for which see CANONIUM, this appearing much compressed in *ND*'s record. But all this is very tentative.

The modern river-name Adur (W. Sussex) is not relevant either for etymology or for location. It was probably coined by Drayton in 1612 on the basis of *ND*'s entry; before that, the river was called the Bramber (see NOVIA).

IDENTIFICATION. If the reference to a height is correct, this must be the Roman fort at Portchester, Hampshire (SU 6204), below Portsdown, since the alternative sometimes suggested (Walton Castle, now under the sea off Felixstowe, Suffolk, TM 3235) can have had no such notable hill near it. There are no inscriptions recording the garrison in either case.

PORTUS LEMANIS of *AI* 473_{6-7} and 473_{10}: see LEMANIS

PRAESIDIUM

SOURCE

ND XL_4 (*pictura*): PRAESIDIUM
XL_{19} (text): Praefectus equitum Dalmatarum, PRAESIDIO

DERIVATION. *Praesidium* is a Latin military term, 'fort, fortlet, post'; also 'garrison'. See CAMULOSESSA PRAESIDIUM.

IDENTIFICATION. Unknown. The name itself might suggest that the unit was attached to the provincial governor (*praeses* in fourth-century usage) and in that case *Praesidium* would mean York and serve both for *Legio VI* (which here has no named station) and for the *Equites Dalmatae*; a possible analogy might be provided by *ND Or.* XXXIV_{35}, where, under the *Dux Palaestinae*, the *Ala II Felix Valentiana* is listed as '*apud Praesidium*' (the '*apud*' is unique in the text, but there is another entry *Praesidio* at *Or.* XXXIV_{41} and these three are the only places where *Praesidium* appears in the whole *ND*). But the illustration shows two forts, one for *Legio VI* and another for the *Equites*, and unless the former were in the legionary fortress and the latter billeted in the *colonia* this should indicate a separate site. A further possibility is that *Praesidium* really refers to the legion and that the name of the station of the *Equites* has been lost, perhaps because it resembled *Praesidio* in form (for a similar confusion see PRAETORIUM). Frere (1974) 265 (map), tentatively attaches the name to Newton Kyme, Yorkshire (SE 4545), but apparently only on the grounds that here there was a fort newly built in the fourth century which is not otherwise listed.

PRAETORIUM

SOURCE

AI 464_1, 466_4 (Iter I): PRAETORIO

DERIVATION. This is Latin, 'army headquarters, commandant's house, official residence'. A number of places in the Continental provinces bore this name.

IDENTIFICATION. For reasons argued on pp. 155–57 this is probably a mis-copying of PETUARIA (q.v.).

PROCOLITIA of *ND* XL_{39}: see BROCOLITIA

PROMINENTIA LITORIS

SOURCE

Ptolemy II, 3, 4: 'Εξοχή (= PROMINENTIA LITORIS)

DERIVATION. For similar 'descriptive' names, see GABRANTOVICUM SINUS. This is another seafarers' term, presumably, but hardly one that can have had real currency; the Latin above is simply a translation of the Greek, 'prominent feature of the coast', not a genuine British place-name.

IDENTIFICATION. Unknown. Though placed by Ptolemy between the rivers GARIENNUS and EIDUMANIS (qq.v.) it is unlikely to be identifiable because of the erosion to which this coast has been subjected.

PUROCORONAVIS of *Ravenna* 105_{48} (= R&C 6): see DUROCORNOVIUM[2]

RATAE CORITANORUM

SOURCES

Inscriptions

CIL XVI. 160 (= Burn, 1969, No. 71, pp. 55–56): A.D. 106, the decree of Roman citizenship to Marcus Ulpius Novantico who had served with the 1st Cohort of Britons, found in Dacia; the soldier was ... RATIS 'from Leicester'

RIB 2244, a milestone of Hadrian, A.D. 119–20: A RATIS M(ILIA PASSUUM) II

Ptolemy II, 3, 11: 'Ράτε (= RATE), a *polis* of the Coritani; some MSS have 'Ράχε (= RACHE), 'Ράγε (= RAGE); Müller's 'Ράται (= RATAE) is conjectural

AI 477_4 (Iter VI): RATAS
479_3 (Iter VIII): RATIS

Ravenna 106_{47} (= R&C 92): RATE CORION

DERIVATION. This is an unusually well-recorded name which shows itself fully declined as a plural. It is a latinised form of British **rātis* (probably feminine) 'earthen rampart, fortification, fort', > Welsh *rhawd* in *beddrawd* 'grave-mound, tomb; cemetery'; cognates are Irish *rá(i)th* 'earthen rampart surrounding a chief's residence, fort' and Latin *pratum* 'meadow'. Gaulish *ratin* (acc.) is recorded on *CIL* XIII. 1171 (Vieux-Poitiers, Vienne, France). The Gaulish place-names in which this word occurs for certain as a second element are *Argentorate* now Strasbourg (Bas-Rhin, France), *Corterate* > Coutras (Gironde, France) and *Carpentorate* (*Meminorum*) > Carpentras (Vaucluse, France). Other names possibly based on the same word are *Ratis* island > Île de Ré (Charente-Maritime, France), *Ratiatum* > Retz in St-Pierre and Ste-Opportune-de-Retz (Orne, France),

Ratiaria of the XIV Legion in Moesia. However, some of these and further names in *Rat-* may involve not the word for 'fort' but Celtic **ratis* (masculine) 'fern, bracken', found in Welsh *rhedyn*, Breton *raden*, Irish *raith*, and by borrowing Basque *iratze*; see Whatmough *DAG* 467. There was a *Dea Ratis*, perhaps 'goddess of the fort', worshipped at Chesters and Birdoswald (*RIB* 1454, 1903); possibly the *Dea Latis* at Birdoswald and Fallsteads (*RIB* 1897, 2043) is the same, with *L-* resulting from mishearing. Romano-British *Ratae* is plural, presumably, because a plural sense 'ramparts (which collectively make up the fort)' was retained. For discussion and further analogues, see Jackson in *Britannia*, I (1970), 78; Holder II. 1075; *GPN* 240–41; Vincent 228. At Leicester there is evidence of one and possibly one other Roman fort; there was a pre-Roman settlement, but seemingly no pre-Roman fortification; hence the naming process (British name used for new Roman fort) is the same as that discussed for the *Duro-* names under DUROBRIVAE[1].

Gelling (1978) 47 mentions a Ratby parish near Leicester, containing the enigmatic earthwork called Bury Camp; the parish name might preserve a memory of a British **Rat-* name, though Ekwall's evidence in *EPN* would not support this.

IDENTIFICATION. The Roman city of Leicester (SK 5804), capital of the *Civitas Coritanorum*.

RATOSTABIUS (?)

SOURCE

Ptolemy II, 3, 2: Ῥατοσταθυβίου ποταμοῦ ἐκβολαί (= RATOSTATHYBII FLUVII OSTIA), var. Ῥατοσταβίου (= RATOSTABII, preferred by Müller)

Müller has an explanation for what he regards as the intrusion of θυ (= THY) into the majority of MSS

DERIVATION. This is a difficult name. It is possible that the first element is one of the words discussed under *Ratae* (British **rātis-* 'fort' or **ratis* 'fern, bracken'), but neither of these goes well as part of a river-name, since forts are usually named from rivers and not vice-versa; moreover, compounds of these do not show *-o*. A Gaulish **ratou-* 'port' was suggested by Müller, but there seems to be little evidence for it; it would suit the present name (Ptolemy's full reference then being to 'the estuary of the river of **Stabi̯os*-port'), but it will not suit places in France which derive from a recorded or assumed *Ratumagus*, *Ratomagus*, such as Ruan (Loir-et-Cher), Ruan (Loiret), Pont-de-Ruan (Inde-et-Loire), Pondron (for Pont-de-Ron, Oise) (*Rotomagus* > Rouen seems to have a different root), for these have no harbours. It probably has to be recognised that we have a Celtic **rato-* **ratu-* of unknown meaning in these and other names.

If the second element is **stabi̯o-*, Holder at II. 1078 lists a number of names having *stab-*, again of unknown meaning; these include a personal name *Stabius* which would be equivalent to a British **Stabi̯os*, but it seems most unlikely that a personal name should enter into a river-name. The name might just possibly be *Rato-s-tabius*, with *-s-* as a composition-consonant, but this seems to have no parallels; however, the prospect is attractive, because an element **Tabi̯os*, that is **Taba* with **-i̯o-* suffix, is one possible origin of the name of the river Taff (Welsh *Taf*). See also TAMIUS.

IDENTIFICATION. Whatever the correct form of the name, from its position in

Ptolemy, between the Towy and the Severn, this must represent the river Taff, Glamorgan, since the names of the Loughor, Neath, Ewenny and Usk are otherwise accounted for. A reference to Cardiff is most unlikely, for although finds of pottery indicate the possibility of a Flavian fort there, this would probably be too late for incorporation in the coastal survey on which Ptolemy's list is based.

RAVATONIUM (?)

SOURCE
Ravenna 108_4 (= R&C 209): RAVATONIUM

DERIVATION. Williams compares this name with that of the rivers *Ravius*, *Ravina*, and relates the name to a root found in Sanskrit *sravat* 'stream', Old Irish *sruaim* 'stream', Welsh *ffreu* 'to flow' (*gwaedffreu* 'slaughter'), alternatively **sruta-* 'flowing' which is represented in Welsh *ffrwd* 'brook' and Old Irish *sruth* 'brook'. Hence the British name would have been **Ravatonā* for the river or stream and **Ravatonįon* (with *-*on-įo-* suffixes, as in CANONIUM) for the place. This is obviously most acceptable, if *Ravenna*'s entry is to be trusted.

IDENTIFICATION. Unknown, but apparently in Scotland north of the Antonine Wall.

RAVENATONE of *Ravenna* 105_{50} (= R&C 9): see DERVENTIO[5]

RAXTOMESSA (?)

SOURCE
Ravenna 108_{40} (= R&C 268): RAXTOMESSA

DERIVATION. *Ravenna* lists this as a river-name. Its form is too unsure to allow suggestions about roots and meanings. The first element might properly be *Rato-* with a sense discussed under *Ratostabius*, including that of a British equivalent to a tentatively assumed Gaulish **ratou-* 'port'; in this case the formation would closely parallel that of *Ratostabius*. The *-xt-* of *Ravenna*'s form is unlikely to be correct, since the various Celtic words discussed in other entries have *rat-* but not original *ract-* or *raxt-* in any of their recorded forms, while *rectu-* 'right, law', etc. (*GPN* 241–42), which does show *-xt-* in addition to *-ct-*, always has *-e-* and is in any case unfitted by its sense for use in toponymy. The second element might be a true river-name, perhaps **Nessa* or better *Nassa* (see NASSA).

IDENTIFICATION. Unknown, but apparently in southern Britain.

REGINI, later REGNI

SOURCES
Ptolemy II, 3, 13: 'Ρῆγνοι (= Regni), vars. 'Ρίγνοι (= RIGNI), 'Ρηγινοί (= REGINI)
AI 477_{10} (Iter VII): A REGNO LUNDINIO
Ravenna 106_{20} (= R&C 44): NAVIMAGO REGENTIUM
(The name is not found in *CIL* VII. 45, now *RIB* 152, as was at one time conjectured.)

There has been much discussion of the interpretation of these sources, and several confusions. One was caused by association of *AI*'s form with the *regnum* ('kingdom') of Cogidubnus allowed to him after the Conquest, and with the title of *rex* granted to him (*RIB* 91 and Tacitus, *Agricola* 14). Another was produced by Haverfield's suggestion that in *Ravenna* the tribal name should be emended to *Reg[n]ensium* (gen. pl.), nominative **Regnenses* 'people of the Kingdom', a suggestion adopted by R&C in their 1949 study, and by others. Further, *AI*'s form was often cited as *Regnum* (a nominative deduced from *AI*'s seeming ablative *Regno*), whereas it is best to adopt Holder's suggestion (II. 1112) that the entry should be emended to *a Regnis*.

DERIVATION. We go therefore to Ptolemy's forms in the hope of enlightenment. Jackson in *Britannia*, I (1970), 78–79 (also *JRS*, XXXVIII (1948), 58) takes the form Ῥηγινοί (= *Regini*), even though this is found in only one inferior MS, as closest to the truth; and regards the forms with *-gn-* as assimilations to Latin words having *regn-*. This is surely right, since it enables Jackson to postulate as the British ethnic name **Reginī* 'proud ones, stiff ones' (for the semantic aspect, compare *Belgae*), the plural of **regin-* 'stiff, stark' (Old Irish *rigin*, etc.), from a base **reg-* 'to stretch, stiffen', A number of personal names such as *Rigina*, *Rigenus*, are listed by Ellis Evans in *GPN* 373; they include *[R]egin[i]* of *CIIC* 359 and the Old Welsh name *Regin* (later *Rein*; see *LHEB* 445).

AI's form as emended, *a Regnis*, is therefore a latinised version of the tribal name, with, again, assimilation to Latin *-gn-*. *Ravenna*'s entry requires emendation to *Reginorum* or perhaps *Regenorum*. In all this, it should be noted that the assimilations in both Ptolemy and *AI* to Latin *regn-* were probably genuine enough in local usage (i.e. not the work of Continental scribes at later date), being assisted by the existence of Cogidubnus's *regnum* for a long time after A.D 43.

For the use of a tribal name as an indication in an itinerary, compare *Icinos* (see ICENI).

IDENTIFICATION. A people of southern Britain with their capital at *Noviomagus*, Chichester; Ptolemy attributes no other place to them. *RIB* 91 shows that they were indeed one of the *quaedam civitates Cogidumno regi donatae* (*Agricola* 14), but the plural implies others and the identity of the others is disputed. The name adopted here implies their previous existence as a tribe, but the distribution of pre-Roman coins of the house of Commius suggests that they may have been clients of the *Atrebates* and gives no clue to their extent.

REGULBIUM

SOURCE

ND XXVIII$_8$ (*pictura*): REGULBI
XXVIII$_{18}$ (text): Tribunus cohortis primae Baetasiorum, REGULBIO

DERIVATION. The name is a compound of British **ro-* 'great' (a prefix, strictly **rəo-*, rendered in Latin as heard or adapted by Latin speakers, *re-*, a common prefix) and **gulbi̯o-* 'beak', metaphorically 'headland'. On this and on the development to Reculver see Jackson *LHEB* 559, with discussion of views of Förster and Ekwall, 661, etc.; this development is not without problems, and the persistence of unlenited *g-* and *-b-* suggest an early adoption of the name in Anglo-Saxon, before British lenition and perhaps before the Anglo-Saxon occupation of Kent. Derivatives and cognates of **gulbi̯o-* cited by Jackson and by Dottin *LG* 261 include Gaulish *gulbia* 'bec' in texts of Vegetius and Isidore, Old Irish *gulba* and Middle Welsh *gylf* 'beak', and Breton *golvan* 'passereau'. See also Pokorny in *Vox Romanica*, x (1949), 263–64. There seem to be no other examples of the use of the word in ancient toponymy. The attempt of D. A. White (citing Taylor and Haig) in *Litus Saxonicum* (Madison, 1961), 80–81, to avoid the seeming difficulties of a Celtic etymon by proposing to derive Reculver from a Germanic personal name *Raculf* is not to be entertained.

IDENTIFICATION. The Roman fort at Reculver, Kent (TR 2269).

RERIGONIUM

SOURCES

Ptolemy II, 3, 5: Ῥεριγονιον (= RERIGONIUM), a *polis* of the Novantae; var. Ῥετιγόνιον (= RETIGONIUM)

Ravenna 107_{39} (= R&C 174): BRIGOMONO

Ravenna's entry has not previously been equated with Ptolemy's. As argued in Chapter V, the correspondence between Ptolemy's and *Ravenna*'s North British names is close, and where the former has a name which seems to be lacking in the latter, we should seek it there concealed in a corrupt form. The placing of the name in *Ravenna*'s sequence suits the identification well. The miscopying of *ni* as *m* was common, and loss of an initial letter is paralleled (**-erig* for **Rerig-*, the surviving and now initial *e-* being further miscopied as *B-*). Dillemann (69) supports this equation.

DERIVATION. The name is to be analysed (following Watson *CPNS* 34–35 and Jackson *LHEB* 661–62) as a latinisation of British **ro-rigoni̯o-* 'very royal (place)', presumably the royal seat of the Novantae. For **ro-*, again adapted as Latin *re-*, see the previous entry. The rest of the name is British **rig-* **rigon* 'king' (Indo-European **reik-*, from which Latin *rex*, *regem*, Gaulish **-rix*, **rigo-*, Welsh *rhi*, *rhion*, Irish *rí*, derive); with **-i̯o-* derivational suffix. The element is abundantly present in Continental place-names, ethnic and personal names, many of them assembled by Ellis Evans in *GPN* 243–49. British *Rigodunum* contains it, and the ethnicon *Durotriges* may do so. It is present in two British divine names, *Mars Rigisamus* (superlative, 'most kingly') in *RIB* 187 (West Coker, Somerset; see Ross, 1967, 175), and *Mars Rigonemetos* ('king of the grove' or 'sanctuary') at Nettleham, Lincs. (*JRS*, LII (1962), 192; Ross, 176). On coins of Tasciovanus, who ruled from about 20 B.C. to A.D. 10, is the legend *Tascio Ricon* or *Riconi*, this being the equivalent of *-rigon-* in the present name (Mack Nos. 184, 185). Watson notes that *Rerigonium* survived in an early Welsh triad as *Penrionyd*, later Welsh *Rhionydd* and eventually English *Ryan*.

IDENTIFICATION. An unlocated Roman fort, or possibly camp, near Loch Ryan (see next entry) and perhaps under the modern town of Stranraer, Wigtownshire (NX 0660).

RERIGONIUS SINUS

SOURCE

Ptolemy II, 3, 1: Ῥεριγόνιος κόλπος (= RERIGONIUS SINUS)

DERIVATION. See the previous entry. The form here may indicate a Latin-seeming adjective, or an appositional noun (British **-ios*?).

IDENTIFICATION. Loch Ryan, Wigtownshire, whose name is a survival (see the previous entry).

RIGODUNUM

SOURCE

Ptolemy II, 3, 10: Ῥιγόδουνον (= RIGODUNUM), a *polis* of the Brigantes

DERIVATION. For the first element, see RERIGONIUM; for the second, see BRANODUNUM. The sense is 'king-fort', 'royal fort', similar in formation to Kingston, Königsburg, etc. Compounds of this kind involving *rigo-* are listed by Holder II. 1187, Ellis Evans *GPN* 243–49; they are numerous on the Continent.

IDENTIFICATION. From its position in Ptolemy, probably the Roman fort at Castleshaw, Yorkshire (SD 9909).

RIPA ALTA

SOURCE

Ptolemy II, 3, 4: Ὄχθη ὑψηλή (= RIPA ALTA)

DERIVATION. The name is Latin, 'high bank', Ptolemy's entry being a Greek version of this. For similar descriptive names, see GABRANTOVICUM SINUS. Such names could become place-names in the full sense: *Alta Ripa* of *ND* XLI$_{7,19}$ > *Altrip* (Germany); and *Ripa Alta* of *AI* 244$_5$ (= *Alta Ripa* of *TP*) is now Tolna in Yugoslavia.

IDENTIFICATION. Tarbat Ness, Easter Ross.

RUMABO of *Ravenna* 107$_{47}$ (= R&C 190): see ABUS

RUTUNIUM

SOURCE

AI 469$_5$ (ITER II): RUTUNIO

DERIVATION. Ekwall *ERN* 345 and Jackson in *Britannia*, I (1970), 79, indicate a probable base in a British word derived from Indo-European **reu̯-* 'to move swiftly' (Latin *ruo*, Old Irish *rúathar*, Welsh *rhuthr* 'rush, attack', English *rush*?, etc.). This is then a classic case of a settlement-name based on the name of a river, which would have been British **Rutūnā* (for the form, compare *Ituna*) > Roden; hence, with the derivational suffix **-i̯o-*, British **Rutuni̯on* for the settlement.

Names in *Rut-* are frequent in Continental sources, especially personal names; see Holder II. 1252–57, Ellis Evans *GPN* 466–67. The *Rŭtēni* people of Gallia Narbonensis had a capital at *Segodunum*, known in the fourth century as *Civitas Rutenorum*; this, as *Rutenos*, > Rodez (Aveyron, France). These people were perhaps 'swift ones'.

IDENTIFICATION. The Roman settlement or posting-station which, though ill-attested archaeologically, must have existed near where the Roman road from Whitchurch to Wroxeter (Margary 6a) crossed the river Roden; so Harcourt Mill, Salop (ST 5525).

RUTUPIAE

SOURCES

Ptolemy II, 3, 12: Ῥουτουπίαι (= RUTUPIAE), a *polis* of the Cantii

AI 463$_4$ (before Iter I): A Gessoriaco de Gallis RITUPIS in portu Brittaniarum

466$_5$ (Iter II): ad portum RITUPIS (again 472$_6$)

IM 496$_4$: ad portum RITUPIUM

Ravenna 106$_{36}$ (= R&C 73): RUTUPIS

TP: RATUPIS

ND XXVIII$_9$ (*pictura*): RUTUPIS, var. RITTUPIS

XXVIII$_{19}$ (text): Praefectus legionis secundae Augustae, [RUTUPIS – editor's addition to the text]

Ammianus Marcellinus XX, I, 3: ad RUTUPIAS (*concerning event of* A.D. *360*)

XXVII, 8, 6: defertur RUTUPIAS, stationem ex adverso tranquillam (*concerning event of* A.D. *368*)

Orosius I, 2, 76: RUTUPI PORTUS, vars. RUTHUBI, RUTUBI.

As an elegant variation on *Britannicus*, an adjective *Rutupinus* was used by the Latin poets: Lucan *Pharsalia* vi, 67: *Rutupinaque litora*; Juvenal iv, 141: *Rutupino*. . .*fundo* (vars. *Ruptupino*, *Ritupino*); Ausonius *Parentalia* vii, 2: *tellus*. . .*Rutupina*; *Parentalia* xviii, 8: *Rutupinus ager;* and *Ordo Nobilium Urbium* vii, 9: *Rutupinum*. . .*latronem*.

We give the name in nominative plural form, following Ptolemy, because it is clear that in the usage of literary Latin writers it was declinable (Ammianus); but it is also clear that in ordinary usage (reflected in *AI*, *Ravenna*, *TP* and ND) the name had settled like many others into a locative-ablative plural in *-is*, no longer declinable. E. P. Hamp in *BBCS*, XXVI (1974–76), 395–98, wishes to see behind each of the main recorded forms a Latin version of a different British morphological formation, in terms of number and case. The result is elegant and convincing, but it would seem to imply that Ammianus and Orosius, for example, had first-hand information from contemporary British-speaking informants and were simply latinising the results anew. This can hardly have been so; the name was well established in Latin usage and was well known, as that of the main port of entry. Alone among literary men after Ptolemy, Ammianus gave it a full declensional form. Orosius's *Rutupi Portus* is best explained as a mildly unsatisfactory form within Latin, rather than as a genuine singular which represents a hitherto unrecorded and meaningful syntactical formation (after all, it requires only loss of one letter from *AI*'s *Ritupis* to produce this, and is surely the simplest explanation).

DERIVATION. It is clear that the best form is *Rutupiae*, *Rutupis*; the scansion in Latin verse was *Rŭtŭpīnus*, whose long *ī* leads Jackson to think that the British name was **Rutupīā* or plural **Rutupīās*, rather than **Rutupi̯ā-s*. The Latin verse scansion could be artificial or conventional, as the meaning certainly is; however, the first two short vowels suit Hamp's view that the British name was **Rŭtŭpii̯ās* (nominative plural). If the name properly has *Ru-*, as is clear, *AI*'s forms in diverse itinera which regularly have *Ri-* are probably due to an assimilation to the more familiar Celtic word **ritu-* 'ford'; and **ritu-* was in fact taken as the etymon by Zachrisson (1927) 81–82, which must be dismissed on various grounds. For further discussion of the recorded forms, with confirmation of initial *Rutu-*, see the study of Hamp mentioned above.

The name has been thought a difficult one. There is a possible analogue in *Rutuba* mentioned by Pliny *NH* III, 48, a river of N. Italy near the present French border; there is another *Rutubis*, a port of Mauretania (Pliny *NH* II, 9), which then suggests that both correspond to an old Mediterranean level of naming; but in another study in *EC*, XI (1966–67), 413–14, Hamp took the N. Italian *Rutuba* to be Gaulish and hence equivalent to the British name. Williams associated initial *Rŭt-* with Welsh *rhwd*, now meaning 'rust' but earlier 'filth' in general, which

R&C then applied as meaning 'mud-flats, muddy creek(s)'. Jackson in *Britannia*, I (1970), 78, following study in *LHEB*, passim, took Anglo-Saxon *Repta-Caester* as indicating that the British name had a base **tup-* of unknown meaning, with the prefix **ro-* 'great', 'or at least that it had become interpreted as such in popular etymology by the late British period'. However, Jackson did not entirely dismiss Williams's suggestion, which has been taken up by Hamp in the two papers mentioned, and in another in *BSL*, LXVIII (1973), 79–80. Hamp prefers initial **rŭtŭ-* 'mud', with an Indo-European suffix represented by the *-b-* in the Gaulish name and *-p-* in the British; hence **Rŭtŭpii̯ās*, plural in form. For the sense, Hamp suggested 'muddy (estuary, waters, shallows, or similar)', adding that 'Perhaps the plural referred to the branching of the water around the island'; here R&C are perhaps better, since they observe that more than one stream does in fact run into Richborough creek and that this might explain the plural. Jackson's **ro-* perhaps need not be retained in view of Hamp's comprehensive explanation; an objection to it is that in the other names in which this appears – *Regulbium, Rerigonium* – it was taken into Latin as *re-*, no doubt because of association with the common Latin prefix *re-* (with some similarity of sense too), and the same might be expected in this surely very latinised port and area of Kent; but *Re-* nowhere appears in the numerous sources for the name.

There are problems too in following the Romano-British name into its Anglo-Saxon and modern forms. Bede I, I has the statement that *civitas quae dicitur Rutubi portus, a gente Anglorum nunc corrupte Reptacaestir vocata*, his Romano-British name being taken from a text of Orosius in which the *-b-* resulted from a Vulgar Latin voicing of *-p-* in the speech of one of Orosius's scribes. On this development, with a full survey, see Jackson *LHEB* 661–62, and suggestions by Hamp in his 1974–76 study.

IDENTIFICATION. The Roman fort at Richborough, Kent (TR 3260).

SABRINA

SOURCES

Tacitus *Annals* XII, 31 (as emended by Bradley): cis TRISANTONAM et SABRINAM fluvios

Ptolemy II, 3, 2: Σαβρίνα ἔισχυσις (= SABRINA AESTUARIUM)

Ravenna 108_{25} (= R&C 239): SARVA, var. SARNA
109_{15} (= R&C 287): SOBRICA

Ravenna's *Sarva* or *Sarna* is properly placed in the river-list, among names which we recognise as belonging to south-west Britain. The Severn is otherwise omitted from *Ravenna*, and it is logical to expect mention of it at this point; the equivalence of this entry with *Sabrina* was suggested by Müller and Holder, and such miscopying can be paralleled elsewhere in the text. It is fair to note, however, that R&C thought *Sarna* another south-western river, citing Italian *Sarnus* and *Sarnis* in support of its independent existence. *Sobrica* has not hitherto been associated with the Severn. In *Ravenna* it figures in a list of islands, but several of these are already suspect, and this name is probably also *Sabrina* read from a map in which it had been written in the western sea. R&C took it as a good name whose second element was *-brica* for *-briga*, though doubting whether initial *So-* could be correct. Duplication in *Ravenna*, from different map-sources, causes no surprise.

DERIVATION. No clear Celtic etymon is identifiable. The name is doubtless connected with other river-names such as *Saba*, *Sabis* > Sambre (Belgium), **Savara* > Sèvre (Niortaise, Nantaise) and > Sèvres (Seine-et-Oise, France), *Sabatus* (a river of Bruttium); also **Sabrona* > Old Irish Sabrann, the river of Cork (see O'Rahilly, *EIHM* 4). There has recently appeared at La Graufesenque a graffito *Ad Sabros*, perhaps the name of the river there now known as the Dourbie (*REA*, LXXVI (1974), 269). Rostaing *ETP* 243 thinks the root **sab-* a pre-Indo-European water-name, but it is clear that it was taken into Celtic (British), for in addition to the present name, Savernake (Wilts.) has the same origin, and there are a few others listed by Pokorny in *ZCP*, XXI (1940), 121; furthermore, **-ina* is a recognised Celtic suffix (see LINDINIS). According to Ross (1967) 21, *Sabrina* is a divine name which underlies the river-name. Pokorny in *ZCP*, XXI (1940), 79, proposes that the root **sab-*, common in water-names, means 'Saft' and has Illyrian connections, and suggests more specifically (p. 121) an adjectival **sabro-* as a basis for some of the names. This seems an entirely reasonable approach.

Accurate memory of the Romano-British name long survived. Gildas (3) writes *Sabrinae* (gen.), and Bede (V, 23) *ultra amnem Sabrinam*. This was so for some time still when Welshmen wrote Latin, even though during the later sixth century initial *s-* became *h-* (the Welsh name of the river is *Hafren*); on this and on reasons why the Anglo-Saxons took over the name still with *S-* (*Saefern*), see the very detailed discussion of Jackson in *LHEB* 516–19 and passim; also D. Jenkins in *BBCS*, XXV (1973), 114–16, with a riposte by Jackson in *Studia Celtica*, X/XI (1975–76), 44, note 1.

IDENTIFICATION. The river Severn.

SALINAE[1]

SOURCES

Ptolemy II, 3, 11: Σαλῖναι (= SALINAE), a *polis* of the Catuvellauni; var. Σαλῆναι (= SALENAE)

Ravenna 106_{31} (= R&C 65): SALINIS, var. SALMIS

DERIVATION. The name is Latin, 'salt-works'. Several places so named are known in the Continental provinces.

IDENTIFICATION. In position on Ptolemy's map this should be sited near the Wash (which would in any case put it outside the area normally attributed to the *Catuvellauni*), but for reasons discussed on p. 120 it is probably to be identified with Droitwich, Worcestershire (SO 8963).

SALINAE[2]

SOURCE

Ravenna 106_{46} (= R&C 90): SALINIS

DERIVATION. See the previous entry.

IDENTIFICATION. The Roman town of Middlewich, Cheshire (SJ 7066).

SAPONIS (?)

SOURCE

Ravenna 109_{13} (= R&C 283): SAPONIS

DERIVATION. *Ravenna*'s form might be a genitive, i.e. (*insula*) *Saponis*, or it might be a garbled version of **Sapo Ins.* (for *insula*), since other garbled renderings of *insula* appear in this section of the Cosmography. The latter explanation is the more likely, since an island name based on late Latin *sapo–saponis* (third declension) 'soap' is hardly possible, while one based on a late Latin **sapus* 'fir, pine' would be acceptable. Holder II. 1362 identified a word **sapo-s* 'fir', and if this existed in British, **Sapo* (with Latin *insula*) would have meant 'fir-tree (island)'. Williams notes Middle Breton *sap*, etc., as a surviving derivative. The same word taken into Latin left Romance descendants, Old French *sap*, Provençal *sap-s*, while **sap-pinus* > French *sapin*. Some western Scottish islands do seem to have Latin names (see ANAS), but if the map-source used by the Cosmographer for North Britain was ultimately of first-century date, even with Severan revisions, this seems too early for a Latin **sapus* and the name should more readily be regarded as Celtic. There is no semantic problem, since trees are often used in toponymy; but it is unwise to found precise arguments on a form recorded by *Ravenna* alone, whose entries – especially for North Britain – are so often corrupt.

IDENTIFICATION. Unknown, but apparently an island off Britain.

SARNA, SARVA of *Ravenna* 108_{25} (= R&C 239): see SABRINA

SAUDONIO of *Ravenna* 106_{44} (= R&C 85): see MEDIOLANUM

SCITIS

SOURCES

Ptolemy II, 3, 14: Σκητὶς νῆσος (= SCETIS INSULA), vars. Σκιτίς (= SCITIS), Ὄκιτις (= OCITIS)

Ravenna 109_{15} (= R&C 288): SCETIS

DERIVATION. It is likely that *Scitis* is the better form; the name is twice written *Scia* in Adamnan's *Life* of St Columba (I, 33 and II, 26). Watson *CPNS* identified a Celtic root now represented by Gaelic *sgian* 'knife', *sgiath* 'wing', related to Latin *scindo* and Greek σκίζω 'I cut', and assigned a sense 'divided isle' to the name; the reference might be to the numerous deep indentations in its coastline, or less probably to the two major 'constrictions' of its shape. There seem to be no other instances of the use of this root in toponymy.

IDENTIFICATION. The Isle of Skye.

SEGEDUNUM

SOURCES

Ravenna 107_{24} (= R&C 143): SERDUNO

ND XL_{33}: Tribunus cohortis quartae Lingonum, SEGEDUNO (var.: SEDUNO)

DERIVATION. The first element in this and the three following names has a base in Indo-European **segh-*, with many derivatives including British **sĕgŏ-* perhaps 'power, force', Irish *seg*, *segh* 'strength, vigour', Welsh *hy* 'daring, bold'; and in Gothic *sigis*, German *Sieg* 'victory'. For names based on it, see in general Holder II. 1444 ff., *GPN* 254–57. Place-names based on *Seg-* with suffix or in compounds (always as first element) are widespread all over Gaul, Spain, W. Germany and N.

Italy, and may extend more widely still: Rostaing *ETP* 246–50 (following Trombetti) thinks the root too widely extended for it to be reckoned as Celtic and Germanic only. In personal names a sense 'strong, bold' is an obvious one. This may apply to place-names also, though scholars familiar with Gothic and German senses of *Seg-* have often attributed the meaning '(place of) victory' to these, so that e.g. *Segobriga* > Segorbe (Castellón, Spain) either 'strong fort' or 'victory-fort'.

Abroad, four places called *Segodunum* are known, three in Gaul and one in Germany (*RIO*, XIV (1962), 180), the best-known being *Segodunum Rutenorum* now Rodez (Aveyron, France). For *-dunum*, see BRANODUNUM. The name is thus 'strong fort' or possibly 'victory-fort'. Since this is a purely Roman fort, the naming-process is the same as that outlined in discussion under DUROBRIVAE[1].

This name should perhaps be more classically *Segodunum*, with *-o-*, and the following should in the same way be *Segolocum*; the better-recorded Continental analogues normally show *-o-* in compounds. However, *-e-* is shown both by *ND* above, and twice by *AI* in the next name. As Jackson in *LHEB* 645 notes, this is a matter of the slurring or relaxation of the unstressed vowel, well documented as time went on (in post-Roman inscriptions) and normal also in Latin speech documented in Romano-British epigraphy.

IDENTIFICATION. The Roman fort at Wallsend, Northumberland (NZ 3066), whose third-century garrison was *Cohors IV Lingonum* (*RIB* 1299–1301).

SEGELOCUM

SOURCES

AI 475_4 (Iter V): SEGELOCI

478_9 (Iter VIII): AGELOCO

Inscription: *RIB* 2241 (= Burn, 1969, No. 209, p. 155): a milestone of Victorinus (A.D. 268–70) with A L S MP XIIII, presumably to be expanded as AL(INDO)S(EGELOCUM)MPXIIII 'from Lindum to Segelocum, 14 miles'.

DERIVATION. For *Sege-*, see SEGEDUNUM; for *-locum*, see LOCATREBE. Hence perhaps 'violent pool'; Jackson in *Britannia*, I (1970) 79, notes that 'This could refer to a pool on the Trent with a rapid current'.

IDENTIFICATION. The Roman settlement at Littleborough, Nottinghamshire (SK 8282), where the Roman road from Lincoln to Doncaster (Margary 28a) crossed the Trent.

SEGONTIACI

SOURCE

Caesar *BG* V, 21, 1: SEGONTIACI

DERIVATION. For the root, see SEGEDUNUM. Here it is part of a divine or personal name **Segontịos* (latinised *Segontius*, male cognomen, and female *Segontia*, are in fact documented: Holder II. 1450); compare the next entry. The suffix latinised as *-ăcu-* (see BRAVONIACUM) is adjectival and is paralleled in the British name *Cantiaci* and in others abroad. The French place-name Segonzac (Cher) and another Sonzay-en-Touraine (Indre-et-Loire) derive from an assumed **Segontiacum* with the same suffix, used in the special sense so abundantly documented in Gaul and known in Britain, 'estate of'. In an ethnic name such as the present one the suffix presumably implies 'people of' a chieftain (rather than of a region, as is the case with *Cantiaci*); or if a divine name is in question, 'devotees of'. This last is possible: Rhys (1904) 29 associated the tribe with Silchester on the grounds of an inscription – now *RIB* 67 – which is a dedication to *Deo Her*[*culi*] *Saegon*[. .], this last word being completed by Stukeley as *Saegontiaco* (though *Saegontio* seems more likely in view of the available space).

IDENTIFICATION. A British tribe mentioned only by Caesar and presumably later absorbed in a larger confederation. They are likely to have been situated in south-eastern Britain, so that any direct connection with the next name is very improbable.

SEGONTIUM

SOURCES

AI 482_5 (Iter XI): SEGUNTIO

Ravenna 106_{42} (= R&C 82): SEGUNTIO

To these may be added the adjectival form of *ND* v_{65} and v_{213}, vii_{49}: a unit of *Seguntienses* (var.: *Saguntienses* in v_{213}) was serving near Aquileia (it appears to be agreed that these originated at, or in the area of the British fort, not in one of the similarly named Hispanic places)

DERIVATION. For the base **sego-*, see SEGEDUNUM. Jackson in *Britannia*, I (1970), 79, thinks that the fort-name was taken from a river-name, this being British **Segontī* 'vigorous river'; in British the fort-name was (with *-*i̯o*- suffix) **Segonti̯on*, recorded in Old Welsh as *Caer Segeint*, Middle Welsh *Caer Seint*. The river is *Saint* in modern Welsh; Williams observes that *Seoint* is 'an antiquarian and incorrect version'. The retention of initial *S*- in the modern name of the river has caused disagreement. Williams suggested a process by which the river-name derived from the ancient fort-name, since original *s*- usually > Welsh *h*- (thus **Haint*); but *s*- is by no means abnormally retained in a number of Welsh words, according to Jackson, who cites further his *LHEB* 513 and Lewis & Pedersen 17. The latter source, however, lists no proper names among its examples, and one wonders whether after all Williams may not have been right: in view of the importance of *Segontium* in its region, and its connection with the stories of Maximus, the name might have retained its *S*- long through learned influence. Although forts and settlements usually take their names from rivers in Celtic times, and not vice-versa, there are exceptions; we discuss a probable example under COLONIA[1] (Colchester). In later periods such back-formation is of course common.

There are parallels to this name abroad, in no case based on river-names. There are two *Segontia* places in Spain, the better-known > Sigüenza (Guadalajara), which shows the same variation in spelling in the sources: *Segontia AI* 436_5 and 439_3, *Seguntia* in *Ravenna* 80_{16}. Also in Spain, *Saguntum* (e.g. *Ravenna* 79_6) is now *Sagunto* (Valencia; by learned revival, the medieval name being *Murviedro* 'old wall'), well-known in classical history as the *casus belli* of the Second Punic War.

IDENTIFICATION. The Roman fort at Caernarvon (SH 4862).

SELGOVAE or SELGOVES

SOURCES

Ptolemy II, 3, 6: Σελγοοῦαι (= SELGOVAE), vars. Σελγοῦαι (= SELGVAE), Λελγοῦαι (= LELGVAE), Ἐλγοοῦαι (= ELGOVAE); II, 3, 10: Σελγοούας (= SELGOVAS, acc.)

Ravenna 108_{20} (= R&C 234): SEGLOES

R&C took *Ravenna*'s entry as a place-name, restoring it from an assumed corrupted state to *(LOCUS) SELGO[V]E[N]S[IS] (assuming also an abbreviation of the kind illustrated by *Lutudares* for *Lutudarensis*) and defining it as tribal meeting-place. However, as we now know (p. 212), *Ravenna*'s list of *diversa loca* is not to be taken so literally. As with *Dumnonii*[2] – mention of whom follows the present entry in *Ravenna* – this is a tribal name read from a map by the Cosmographer as though it were a place-name; it is to be restored as *Selgoves*, with scribal metathesis of *-lg-* and with *-v-* omitted.

DERIVATION. The name means 'hunters', being based on British **selg-* 'hunt' (Old Welsh *helgha ti* glossed 'venare', *in helcha* glossed 'in venando'; Old Irish *selg* 'hunting'); with **-ou̯-* suffix, for which Gaulish parallels such as *Comedovae* exist. See Holder II. 1461, Rhys (1904) 375, and Jackson *LHEB* 467. The alternative declensional forms in *-ae* and *-es* may both be valid; see ATREBATES.

IDENTIFICATION. A people of southern Scotland to whom Ptolemy attributes *Carbantorigum*, *Uxellum*, *Corda* and *Trimontium*; he places them 'below' (i.e. east of) the *Novantae*, 'west' (i.e. south) of the *Damnonii* and north of the *Brigantes*, so that they presumably occupied the upper Tweed basin.

SENA

SOURCE

Ravenna 108_{30} (= R&C 248): LEUGOSENA

108_{41} (= R&C 269): SENUA

As argued under LEUCA, *Ravenna*'s first form is a conflation; and the name is duplicated, from a second map-source. In *Ravenna*'s second form, the *u* probably arose from a mistake in copying **Senna* (compare *TP*'s *Caunonio* under CANONIUM).

DERIVATION. The name is the feminine of the British adjective **seno-* 'old' (Welsh *hĕn* , Cornish and Breton *hēn*; Old Irish *sen*, later *sean*; Latin cognates are *senex*, *senior*, *Seneca*, etc.). Applied here to a river, 'no doubt the word was a title of reverence' (Williams); indeed, 'Old Man River' is a parallel. Watson *CPNS* 474 finds the same word probably in the name of a Sutherland river, *Abhainn Sin* 'old river', and it is the basis of the name of the Shannon in Ireland, Σήνου (gen., = *Senos*; nominative **Seni*), Ptolemy II, 2, 3. Holder II. 1464 cites *Sena* as a river of Umbria and as the name of a town upon it, in the land of the *Senones* (now Sinigaglia). The word is found compounded in a number of place-names, notably **Senomagus* in our next entry and similar names abroad; also in personal names such as *Cantosenus*, and either alone, adjectivally, or as part of a compound, in the legend of a coin of the Coritani (Mack No. 461; also D. F. Allen, *The Coins of the Coritani* (London, 1963), p. 29 and note 3).

IDENTIFICATION. Unknown, but apparently a river on the south coast of Britain.

*SENOMAGUS

SOURCES

AI 480_1 (Iter IX): SITOMAGO
TP: SINOMAGI

DERIVATION. It seems to be traditional to take *AI*'s entry as the better, but there is no reason to do so. Accepting it, Jackson in *Britannia*, I (1970), 79, indicates that the first element could be British **sito-* 'long, wide'; but this appears to be a unique case of this word in ancient toponymy (compare perhaps for sense **litano-*). This being so, it is preferable to reckon *AI*'s entry as a slight miscopying (compare *t* for *n* in *AI* 483_8, MS B, *dumnuntiorum* for *dumnonniorum*). If **Senomagus* is right, as in *TP*, the etymology is British **seno-* 'old' (see the previous entry) + **magos*, for which see CAESAROMAGUS, the whole name meaning 'old market'. There are no fewer than four precise analogues for this in Gaulish *Senomagus* places, three in France and one in Belgium; the best-recorded of these is *Senomago* of *TP* > St-Pierre-de-Senos (Drôme, France), which was succeeded by a nearby *Noviomagus* > Nyons (Drôme). It is true that in East Anglia we have no trace of a **Noviomagus* which could have been the successor to our **Senomagus*; but in the case of the two other British *Noviomagus* places, we find no trace of either *Senomagus* which may have preceded them, so this is not a counter-argument.

IDENTIFICATION. As stated on p. 170, the mileages should indicate a site near Yoxford, Suffolk (TM 3968), but there is no concentration of Iron Age coins or other material in this area.

SETANTII

SOURCE. See the next entry

DERIVATION. This ethnic name is mysterious; there seem to be no British roots visible, and very few analogues anywhere of names in *Set-*. It is tempting, in view of Ptolemy's variants which show *Seg-* (Σεγ-) both for the port-name and the river-name, to suspect some confusion with the *Seg-* of *Segontium*, a possibility that occurred to Rhys (1904) 315 with regard to the river, though eventually he seems to wish to maintain *Setantii* as a proper form. The strongest argument for so doing is provided by Watson *CPNS* 25, who points out that the first name of the Irish hero Cuchulainn was *Setanta* (from an earlier **Setantios*): 'the *Setantii* were an ancient British tribe near Liverpool...the inference is that *Setanta* means "a Setantian" and that Cuchulainn was of British origin'. But the relation between these two names has been questioned. There is a full exposition of the problem by Guyonvarc'h in *Ogam*, XIII (1961), 587–98, with discussion of views of Mac Neill, Osborne, and others, including Brittonic-Goidelic transferences in both historical and phonetic aspects. The essence of the matter is that it is tempting to see in this name Irish *sét* ('path'; = British **sento-*, for which see CLAUSENTUM), but **-ant-* suffix (as in DECANTAE) is Brittonic only, for *-nt-* does not exist in Goidelic. The name might be based on a divine name **Setantios*. not otherwise known, and he in turn might be related etymologically and by sense to the goddess *Sentona*, perhaps 'wayfarer' (see further TRISANTONA[1]). Clearly there is an additional problem in reconciling the *a*/*e* vowels in these forms (*Trisantona*, Gaulish *Santones*) if they are indeed connected. There, for the present, the matter rests; but it is as well to reiterate that one cannot base too much speculation on forms recorded by Ptolemy alone, particularly when, in numbers, the MSS of his work record attractive variants.

IDENTIFICATION. Presumably a minor tribe, but since they appear only as part of a 'descriptive' name in the coastal list (next entry) and not in their own right in the full list of tribes, they probably formed part of the Brigantian confederacy. If the river name *seteia* is directly connected with them, they should have stretched along the Lancashire coast from the Mersey to Fleetwood.

SETANTIORUM PORTUS

SOURCE

Ptolemy II, 3, 2: Σεταντίων λιμήν (= SETANTIORUM PORTUS), vars. Σεγαντίων (= SEGANTIORUM), Γεσαντίων (= GESANTIORUM)

DERIVATION. See the previous entry. This is one of Ptolemy's 'descriptive' names.

IDENTIFICATION. From its position on Ptolemy's map probably a harbour at or near Fleetwood, Lancashire, at the mouth of the river Wyre. Since it occurs only in the coastal list and is not called a *polis*, no permanent establishment need be implied.

SETEIA

SOURCE

Ptolemy II, 3, 2: Σετηία ἔισχυσις (= SETEIA AESTUARIUM), vars. Σεγηία (= SEGEIA). Σεγηίαις (= SEGEIAIS), Σεγηιατίς (= SEGEIATIS)

DERIVATION. See SETANTII. Evidently the river-name is the basic one of the trio; it might, as often, enshrine a divine name, but this possibility does not help towards an etymology or a meaning. The name has the *-*e̯ia* suffix as in ARBEIA.

IDENTIFICATION. From its position south of *Belisama* (q.v.), and since the Dee would be *Deva*, this is almost certainly the river Mersey.

(SICILIA: see Chapter II, p. 49)

SILINA (?)

SOURCES: These are unusually complicated, and it is best to consider each in turn:

1. Pliny *NH* IV, 103: SILUMNUS, inter Hiberniam ac Britanniam; var. (in three MSS) SILIMNUS

As a geographical location, Pliny's 'between Ireland and Britain' is too vague to tell us much; in the group, *Silumnus* appears after *Vectis* (Wight) and before *Andros* (probably Howth, near Dublin), which at least does not inhibit us from postulating that the name refers to the Scillies. If we take Pliny's variant *Silimnus* and recall that *-mn-* is often a hypercorrect rendering of *-nn-* (as in *Garumna* for original *Garonna*, because in spoken Latin *colŭmna* was sounded *colonna*, etc.), we can restore **Silinnus* and then **Silin*(*n*)*a*.

2. Solinus 22, 7: SILURAM quoque insulam ab ora quam gens Brittana *Dumnonii tenent turbidum fretum distinguit.

Dumnonii is Mommsen's restoration of a corrupt passage. *Siluram* in the text has a variant *Sillinas quoque insulas* (in three inferior MSS) which Mommsen discusses, thinking it more of an interpolation produced by someone who was aware of *Sylina* in Sulpicius Severus (see below), knew that the Scillies were intended by that and also knew that they were to be associated with the Dumnonii; yet this seems to show an unusual knowledge – in a Continental scribe – of British geography, moreover of a little-known region, and it may be better to regard *Sillinas* in Solinus as an entirely genuine and potentially superior variant. *Silura* has been thought (p. 41) to refer to Lundy Island, but this is not separated from the mainland by a 'strait' and can hardly have had a population large enough to produce anything for barter or to bring its 'ancient customs' to the attention of a writer; this objection applies also to Steep Holm and Flat Holm. For *Silura* to refer to the land of the Silures, we have to explain away the *insula(s)* of both text and variant. Hence the variant *Sillinas quoque insulas*, or better, a singular (in keeping with the main text, and for a reason to be mentioned below), **Sillinam quoque insulam*, is worth retaining and associating with the Scillies.

3. Sulpicius Severus II, 51, 3–4: [Instantius was] in SYLINANCIM insulam, quae ultra Britannias sita est, deportatus;...[Tiberianus was] in SYLINANCIM insulam datus (var. of the first mention: SYLINAM)

Here again, the variant *Sylinam* could be preferable, and can be placed in immediate relation to the forms isolated earlier. For a conjecture about the very strange *Sylinancim* (acc.; nominative **Sylinancis*) we revert to Solinus. If we take his variant, **Sillinam quoque insulam*, we can see that in some early text there could have appeared, with standard abbreviations, **Silinamq in*; which, with only minor miscopying of a name that must have seemed obscure, could produce *Silinancim* in a tradition known to Sulpicius Severus.

DERIVATION. It may seem from the above that risky methods have been used to isolate **Sil(l)ina*; but to propose this as the possibly correct form does not rob any place of a name, for the entries of Pliny and Solinus have never been clearly assigned by etymology or location to any surviving place, and to select variants does no injustice to the main texts whose forms are dubious enough.

In what follows we depend heavily upon the generosity and expert knowledge of Professor Charles Thomas, who has very kindly communicated to us materials assembled for his forthcoming study of the place-names of Scilly.

It should first be noted that the singular form upon which our sources more or less agree is to be expected; in classical times Scilly consisted of one large island (with a few outliers), and assumed its present form of many islands in a phase of submergence during the eighth to twelfth centuries.

In post-Roman times there have been three main forms of the name of the islands, which should provide clues to the correct ancient form:

(*a*) The commonest version is *Sully* (from 1193), which is the Scilly/Scillies of today, fully documented by K. Sisam in *The Scillonian*, No. 129 (1957), 51–55.

What is presumably a variant of this, *Sullia*, *Sulleya*, etc., is found from the twelfth to fourteenth centuries, and may have a Norse or English termination expressing 'isles'.

(*b*) Beside a tradition in English, there has naturally also been a Cornish tradition of the name. This is found in an alleged charter of Athelstan about A.D. 925–930, *Sillanes insulae*, and surfaces again in a number of records of the late sixteenth and seventeenth centuries, e.g. *a Sillinis insulis* (Camden), *Sillane islands*, etc. This Cornish name has *-n-* (an essential feature) in a type *S^{v}L-əN* (**Sillan*) and presumably represents an authentic spoken tradition, i.e. it is not due to a learned revival of the sixteenth century as one might suspect if Camden's, within his Latin text, were the only example. On this, see Professor Thomas's paper in *Devon and Cornwall Notes and Queries*, XXXIII (1977), 352–54 (though since that was written he has found other examples, including that of 925–30).

(*c*) The form *Syllingar* and its relatives is Scandinavian and is found from about 1150. The *-ingar* ending implies something like 'place of the inhabitants of', as in other island names in Norse, etc. French *Sorlingues* was based on this and propagated among Continental navigators by Mercator's map of 1564. This is hardly relevant to our inquiry.

The only proposal about an etymology of which we are aware is that of Rhys (1904) 316–17. On a reading *Silulanus* of a name in a Lydney (Goucestershire) inscription, now *RIB* 306, he envisaged a connection of the *Silures* and of Solinus's *Silura* with the Scillies (the latter, through the variant, we now favour); but the Lydney name is now read as *Silvianus*.

The Cornish form documented in (*b*) above is clearly the most important for us, and rather than having originated at an early stage within Cornish (where it is hard to explain), it is best regarded as a continuation of an original British name which was latinised probably as *Sil(l)ina*, on our reading of the sources. In British the stress would have been *Silína*. For this to suit the variety of later forms it seems that the first *i* was short (see *LHEB* 282–86, and Sisam's paper, 52, on *Sully/Scilly* and *Syllingar*). The name might have **-ina* suffix as in *Lindinis*, *Sabrina*, but the base seems to be unknown. It is tempting to think that a religious site on the early island might have contained the name of the goddess *Sūlis*, as at Bath, and in this name *ū* would (via *ü*) have produced *i* in Cornish (*Sill-*), but of course all three classical sources are firm in showing original *Sil-*. If there is some connection with *Sulis*, it is just possible that the *Minerve* which *Ravenna* lists as an island at 109_{10} (= R&C 278) belongs here rather than to Bath, in whose entry (AQUAE CALIDAE, AQUAE SULIS) we discuss the matter.

IDENTIFICATION. The Scilly Isles.

SILURES

SOURCES

Pliny *NH* IV, 103: SILURES

Tacitus *Agricola* 11,2 and 17,3; *Annals* XII, 32, 38, 39 (twice) and 40; XIII, 33; XIV, 29; with the name in a variety of cases, SILURES, SILURAS (acc. pl.), SILURUM (gen. pl.)

Ptolemy II, 3, 12: Σίλυρες (= SILURES), var. Σύληρες (= SULERES)

AI 485_9 (Iter XIV): VENTA SILURUM

Ravenna 106_{22} (= R&C 48): VENTASLURUM

Jordanes 2, 13 (quoting Tacitus): SILORUM (gen. pl.)

Inscriptions
CIL II. 5923, found at La Longuera Alta, near Albanchez (Almería, Spain): L CORNELIUS L FIL(IUS) L N(EPOS) SILUR
RIB 311 (= Burn, 1969, No. 67, p. 52): RES PUBL(ICA) CIVIT(ATIS) SILURUM (shortly before A.D. 220)
(Note: Frontinus *Strategemata* I, 5, 26, has been quoted as containing this name; the possibility is seductive, since he did campaign against the Silures, but the texts have *Ligures*)

DERIVATION. This is unknown. It is very doubtful whether *Silura* island is textually sound (see the previous entry). In view of the remarks of Tacitus about the possible relationship of this people to the Iberians, it is noteworthy that a *Silurus Mons* is recorded somewhere in Spain by Avienius 433. Apart from this, the name seems to have no analogues.

IDENTIFICATION. A people of south Wales and Monmouthshire, with their capital at *Venta*, Caerwent. Ptolemy does not list this place and attributes only *Bullaeum* (= *Burrium*), Usk, to them, but on this see p. 115.

SINETRIADUM of *Ravenna* 107_{32} (= R&C 159): see PINNATA CASTRA

SITOMAGO of *AI* 480_{1}: see *SENOMAGUS

SMERTAE or SMERTI

SOURCES
Ptolemy II, 3, 8: Σμέρται (= SMERTAE), var. Μέρται (= MERTAE)
Ravenna 107_{36} (= R&C 168): SMETRI
Ravenna's form has scribal metathesis of *-tr-* for *-rt-*, as in several other entries. The final *-i* might mean *-e* (a common Vulgar Latin rendering of *-ae*), or it might be that the tribe had an alternative second-declension form; for such variation, see ATREBATES. R&C took *Ravenna*'s entry as the name of a place ('suggests the centre of a tribal sept'), but it is evidently a tribal name not recognised as such by the Cosmographer when he read it from a map, as in other cases.

DERIVATION. There are two possible roots. One, **smeru-* (now Pokorny 970) 'Schmer, Fett', has produced Welsh *mer* and Irish and Gaelic *smior* 'marrow', Old Irish *sméraim* 'j'enduis' (d'Arbois de Jubainville, cited by Holder II. 1593; he also postulated **smertus* 'l'acte d'enduire d'un corps gras et brillant'), German *Schmer* and English *smear*, etc. This was the root favoured by Holder for the present ethnic name and other proper names, and by Watson *CPNS* 17 when he identified *Smertae* as a participial formation; the tribal name (on this view) means 'smeared people', the reference evidently being to smearing with enemy or sacrificial blood. The other root is more innocent: *(*s*)*mer-*, Pokorny 969, 'gedenken, sich erinnern, sorgen', from which come Latin *memor*, Welsh *armerth* 'preparation', Old Irish *airm*(*mert*) 'prohibition', together with personal names related to this root by Zeuss, Dottin *LG* 287, and others: e.g. *Smertrios* (a Gaulish god) 'le pourvoyeur', *Rosmerta* (a goddess) 'la grande purvoyeuse', the man *Smertrius* whose tombstone at Moresby is *RIB* 804, etc. The best exposition of this view is that of Vendryes in *EC*, III (1937), 133–36, who also discusses interference by popular etymology in post-classical developments in Irish and Welsh. This was taken further by P.-M. Duval in *EC*, VI (1953–54), 219–38, who (following

Loth) argues specifically against the Holder–Watson etymology, with a full survey of all the personal and divine names in *Smert-*. Pokorny agrees with this analysis, listing all the proper names under his **(s)mer*-root. This, applied to the British tribe, would presumably make them 'providers' or 'far-sighted ones'. There seems to be no means, phonetic or semantic, of deciding the issue; but the opinions of the recent Continental scholars have great weight in this case. Watson notes that the tribal name survives in modern *Carn Smeart* on the ridge between the Carron and the Oykel (Sutherland).

IDENTIFICATION. A people of northern Scotland, placed by Ptolemy 'above' (i.e. west of) the *Lugi* and so in the central parts of southern Sutherland and northern Ross.

SOBRICA of *Ravenna* 109_{15} (= R&C 287): see SABRINA

SOLILII or SOLILIORES: See CORIA SOLILIORUM

SORVIODUNUM

SOURCES

AI 486_{13} (Iter XV): SORBIODONI
483_4 (Iter XII, by error of the copyist): SORVIODUNI

Ravenna 106_{9-10} (= R&C 24, 25): (ALAUNA) SILVA ... OMI(RE)

The name has hitherto seemed to be omitted from *Ravenna*, which is unexpected for a road-junction in an area (the south-west) for which the Cosmographer's information seems in general rich. The entries above at 106_{9-10} offer a prospect. In no province does *Ravenna* mention *silvae* (several are present on *TP*, but although the Cosmographer is known to have used a map related to this, it was not *TP* as such), so this is a likely corruption. *Omire* and the following entry (*Tedertis*) are manifestly corrupt. It is likely that confusion developed here at an early stage of textual transmission. One may suggest that **Sorvio doni* was written as two words on the map-source, perhaps one above the other (see p. 191; compare *Camulo dono* at 106_{59}, and for the locative in *-i*, compare *AI*'s forms, above). The unfamiliar **Sorvio* was misread as Latin *silva*, the next element *doni* as (*d*)*om* or (*d*)*omi* and conflated with a following name. Later development of the name (see below) demands *-v-*; the scribal confusion resulting from Vulgar Latin equivalence of *b*/*v* is illustrated by *AI*'s two forms.

DERIVATION. Jackson in *Britannia*, I (1970), 79, and more fully in *JRS*, XXXVIII (1948), 58, indicates a British * *soruio*-of unknown meaning; this, via later British **serw*, was taken into Anglo-Saxon as **Seru-*, and, by 'breaking', **Seoru-* and *Searo-* (*Searobyrg*, 552). Ekwall *EPN* s.v. sees a possible association with Anglo-Saxon *searu* 'armour', and notes the later Norman dissimilation of *l-r*. Anglo-Saxon *burh* appears to translate the second element *-dunum* of the original name (see BRANODUNUM). There is a single analogue for the British name, *Sorviodurum* (*Sorvioduro*, *TP*) in Raetia, near modern Straubing on the Danube (Germany).

IDENTIFICATION. The Roman settlement at Old Sarum, Wiltshire (SU 1332), the name being taken from the Iron Age hill-fort.

SPINIS

SOURCE

AI 485_6 (Iter XIII): SPINIS
486_6 (Iter XIV): SPINIS

DERIVATION. The name is Latin (singular *spina*) 'at the thorn-bushes', and seems to represent, surprisingly, an original Latin naming, presumably because it was a new road-station and not an existing native settlement. *Spina* enters into a number of Latin names in Gaul such as Epinay, Epineau. For the locative *-is*, see ANICETIS.

IDENTIFICATION. The presumed Roman settlement at Woodspeen, Berkshire (SU 4562); although the nucleus has not been found, Roman finds are plentiful in this area and, as explained on p. 176, the *AI* mileages indicate that it lay here, west of the modern village of Speen.

Note. The name survives in that of modern Speen and Woodspeen. Both Ekwall and Jackson comment that there must have been interference in the development of the name (recorded as *Spene* in 821, etc.). Jackson in *Britannia*, I (1970), 79, objects to Ekwall's indications of possible Celtic words which could so have interfered, and suggests that a Primitive Welsh **spīn* (equivalent to the Latin name and spoken in the area after Roman times) was related by folk-etymology to Anglo-Saxon *spēne* 'chips, shingles'. Gelling (1978) 58 has a similar argument. Certainly the place cannot have been important enough for written tradition in Latin to have had any effect, e.g. in reviving the Latin name by antiquarian or ecclesiastical interest.

STENE of *Ravenna* 105_{52} (= R&C 11): see DERVENTIO[6] STATIO

STODOION of *Ravenna* 107_{31} (= R&C 158): see PINNATA CASTRA

STUCTIA

SOURCES

Ptolemy II, 3, 2: Στουκκία ποταμοῦ ἐκβολαί (= STUCCIA FLUVII OSTIA), vars. Στουκία (= STUCIA), Σουκκία (= SUCCIA), Τουκκία (= TUCCIA), Στουλκία (= STULCIA)
Ravenna 108_{29} (= R&C 247): IUCTIUS

DERIVATION. In view of the modern form (below) there can be no hesitation in supporting Müller's choice of his preferred name. Müller also seems to have been the first to associate *Ravenna*'s entry with Ptolemy's. *Ravenna*'s form has lost initial *S*-, and then seems to have had the first *t* miscopied as *i*. The ending might show that the river was known in both masculine and feminine forms, as is possible since the name was adjectival.

The base is British **stuctį̯o*- 'bent, curved' (Welsh *ystwyth* 'supple'; cf. Breton *stoui* 'to bend oneself'). The modern name of the river, *Ystwyth*, is a direct and natural descendant of the ancient one; R&C note its appropriateness, for the river 'has many notable windings and falls'. There is apparently no need to postulate in the ancient name an initial *ex*- or *es*- (as Williams did) in order to produce the modern name. The etymology has been clear from the time of Holder (II. 1640).

IDENTIFICATION. The river Ystwyth, Cardiganshire.

SUBDOBIADON (?)

SOURCE

Ravenna 107_{55} (= R&C 197): SUBDOBIADON

DERIVATION. The entry is grossly corrupt, and none can be suggested. *Ravenna*'s *-on* indicates *-um*, and *-iadon* strongly hints at *-iadunum*. The first syllable is possibly a scribal assimilation to Latin *sub-*.

IDENTIFICATION. Unknown, but either a fort on the Antonine Wall or a place not far from it.

SULLONIACIS

SOURCE

AI 471_{4} (Iter II): SULLONIACIS

DERIVATION. This seems to be an estate-name based on the personal name of an owner, **Sulloniҫos* (to be latinised as **Sullonius*, but not in fact known as a Latin name), on which see *GPN* 471. It has the *-ācu-* suffix so common in estate-names of Gaul, on which see BRAVONIACUM. For locative plural *-is*, see ANICETIS. The plural may indicate 'the family of' or 'the descendants of' Sullonios.

IDENTIFICATION. The Roman settlement at Brockley Hill, Middlesex (TQ 1793).

SUSURRA

SOURCE

Ravenna 109_{13} (= R&C 284): SUSURA

DERIVATION. The name is (with others of its group of islands: see ANAS) Latin, a feminine version of *susurrus* 'whisper'. R&C suggest that the name implies 'whispering island', perhaps in connection with an oracle (observed by the Roman fleet?); they cite *Mercurius Susurrio* in *CIL* XIII. 12005 at Aachen, to be understood as either an oracular god or a wind-god, as a parallel. However, there might be a more mundane explanation, e.g. the sound of surf.

IDENTIFICATION. Unknown, but apparently an island off Britain.

TABA of *Ravenna* 108_{19} (= R&C 232): see TAVA

TADORITUM

SOURCE

Ravenna 107_{33} (= R&C 162): TADORITON

DERIVATION. This name is paired in *Ravenna* with MAPORITUM, as mentioned in the entry for the latter (see there also Dillemann's view, that both are scribal corruptions). Assumed British **tata-* is 'grandfather' (Welsh *tad*); for **ritu-* 'ford', see ANDERITUM.

IDENTIFICATION. Unknown, but apparently in southern Scotland and presumably at a river crossing.

TAEXALI

SOURCE

Ptolemy II, 3, 9: Ταιξαλοι (= TAEXALI; in U and most MSS), vars. Ταίζαλοι (= TAEZALI: Müller's preferred form), Ταξάλοι (=TAXALI), Τεξάλοι (=TEXALI)

See also the forms of the next name.

DERIVATION. This is obscure. Jackson *PP* 136 thinks the name 'cannot be said to be Celtic with any confidence'. However, the one *polis* with Ptolemy assigns to the tribe – *Devana* (better, *Devona*) – has a thoroughly Celtic name, so the possibility must be left open. As between *x* (ξ) and *z* (ζ), the former has the better authority. If *-ae-* is right, representing Celtic *-ai-*, the only suggestion about a root is that made by O'Rahilly in *EIHM* 382, note, that the name might contain a word related to Celtic **taisto-* 'dough' (Welsh *toes*, Irish *taes*); but this seems an unlikely word to enter into an ethnic name. If the variant *Tax-* (present in four MSS) can be considered – and we recall that ι (*i*) does occasionally intrude into Ptolemy's text, as in Δούνιον (*Dunum*[1]) and Μεδιολάνιον (*Mediolanum*) – we are within range of the *Taxi-* element which is found in two names. In Britain was *Taximagulus*, one of the rulers of Kent (Caesar *BG* v, 22, 1), whose name is interpreted by Holder and others as 'slave of the god *Taxis*' (but see *GPN* 116–17), and in Noricum was a place *Tasinemetum* (*TP*), the 'sanctuary of the god *Tasis* or *Taxis*' (Holder). One wonders whether these forms with *-x-* may not be metathesised forms (*-ks-* for *-sk-*) of the numerous names of persons and places in *Tasco- Tasgo-* (which may or may not be the same, and whose meaning is somewhat unsure: see *GPN* 263–65). On attempts to spell in Latin Celtic /χs/, which may also be relevant here, see Jackson in *LHEB* 536–39 (with some mention of the present name).

IDENTIFICATION. A people of Scotland related by Ptolemy to their promontory (see the next entry) and, by the attribution to them of *Devana*, to the Dee or Don, and so occupying Aberdeenshire.

TAEXALORUM PROMONTORIUM

SOURCE

Ptolemy II, 3, 4: Ταιζάλων ἄκρον (= TAEZALORUM PROMONTORIUM). All MSS have ζ (*z*). This in itself does not mean that we should adopt it; one finds, for example, that *Uxela*[1] in Ptolemy II, 3, 6 is spelled with ζ (*z*) in several MSS, when we can be sure from other occurrences of this name that it had *x*.

DERIVATION. See the previous entry.

IDENTIFICATION. Evidently the north-east point of Aberdeenshire and so Kinnairds Head (or just possibly Rattray Head).

TAGEA of *Ravenna* 108_{12} (= R&C 226): see TAMEIA

TAMARA

SOURCES

Ptolemy II, 3, 13: Ταμάρα (= TAMARA), a *polis* of the Dumnonii

Ravenna 105_{48} (= R&C 5): TAMARIS

Ravenna's final *-is* is probably for *-a*, as in its *Uxelis* for *Uxela*.

DERIVATION. See the next entry. As often, the settlement takes its name from the river on which it stands.

IDENTIFICATION. An unidentified place on the River Tamar. From its listing by Ptolemy, who attributes it to the *Dumnonii*, it is most likely to be an early Roman fort, which may perhaps await discovery under the town of Launceston, Cornwall (SX 3384).

TAMARUS

SOURCES

Ptolemy II, 3, 3: Ταμάρου ποταμοῦ ἐκβολαί (= TAMARI FLUVII OSTIA)
Ravenna 108_{26} (= R&C 240): TAMARIS

DERIVATION. The name is British **Tamaros* (alternatively **Tamarā*), made up of a base **tam-* with **-ar(a)* suffix found in many other names (see LEUCARUM). The root is present in the British names which follow in this List, *Tameia*, *Tamesa* or *Tamesis*, *Tamius*, *Tamus*, and in many modern names (not recorded in ancient sources) which are listed by Jackson *LHEB* 487 and by W. Nicolaisen in *BZN*, VIII (1957), 256–57: Thame, Team, Teme, etc.; also with *-v-* or *-w-* (showing British lenition), Tavy, Teviot, Tawy. Abroad the root was widespread too in river-names: *Tamaris* (Mela III, 11) or *Tamara* (Ptolemy II, 6, 2) > Tambre (Coruña, Spain), *Tamarici Fontes* in Cantabria (Spain; Pliny *NH* XXXI, 23), *Tamarus AI* 103_1 > Tammaro, a tributary of the Calore near Benevento (Italy), **Tamira* or **Tamera* > Demer, a tributary of the Dyle (Belgium), and modern Tamaran, a tributary of the Bourbince (Saône-et-Loire, France: Dauzat *TF* 138).

**Tam-* is usually interpreted as 'dark', in view of cognates cited under *Tamesa*, *Tamesis*, but modern opinion among Continental scholars would regard these as illusory. The most comprehensive recent survey is that of Nicolaisen (above), 256–62, who boldly unites a very large number of names as based on the Indo-European root **ta-* **tə-* 'fließen' ('to flow'). Three consonantal formations are differentiated: the first with *-m-*, which accounts for all the names mentioned above; the second with *-n-*, which explains modern British Tone, Tain, Tean, and several Continental names; the third with *-u̯-*, which embraces ancient *Tau̯ā* (or *Tau̯i̯ā*), modern Taw, Tay, and again Continental examples. This is amply convincing as to forms, and semantically also, since it is easier to think that so many rivers over a vast area were named simply 'flowing one, river' than that they were called 'dark', a more particular and subjective designation.

IDENTIFICATION. The River Tamar, along the boundary between Devon and Cornwall.

TAMEIA

SOURCES

Ptolemy II, 3, 8: Τάμεια (= TAMEIA, in most MSS), a *polis* of the Vacomagi; var. Ταμία (= TAMIA)
Ravenna 108_{12} (= R&C 226): TAGEA

Ravenna's form has not hitherto been equated with Ptolemy's, but as explained in Chapter V, there is some logic in supposing that a Ptolemy N. British name should be sought in *Ravenna* if it is not immediately apparent in the text, and the placing of *Tagea* in the Cosmography suits the equation with Ptolemy well enough. Williams took *Tagea* literally and derived it from **tegesa* 'houses' (Welsh *tai*).

DERIVATION. This fort-name is in essence that of a river, for which see the root **tam-* under TAMARUS; it has **-ei̯a* suffix as in ARBEIA.

IDENTIFICATION. Probably the Roman fort at Cardean, Angus (NO 2846).

TAMESA or TAMESIS

SOURCES

Caesar *BG* v, 11, 8: flumen ... quod appellatur TAMESIS
v, 18, 1: ad flumen TAMESIM (acc.)

Tacitus *Annals* xiv, 32: in aestuario TAMESAE (gen.)

Ptolemy ii, 3, 4: Ταμήσα εἴσχυσις (= TAMESA AESTUARIUM)
ii, 3, 11: Ταμήσα (= TAMESA)
(All the MSS have initial 'I- (= I-); T- is Müller's natural conjecture. At ii, 3, 4 there is a var. 'Ιάμισσα (= IAMISSA))

Cassius Dio xl, 21, 3: Ταμέσαν (acc.; = TAMESAM)
lx, 2, 5: Ταμέσαν (acc.; = TAMESAM)
lx, 21, 3: Ταμέσᾳ (dat.; = TAMESAE)
(also Xiphilinus lxii, 2; Ταμέσᾳ (dat.; = TAMESAE))

Ravenna 106_{38} (= R&C 76): TAMESE

OROSIUS vi, 9, 6: TAMENSEM (acc.), vars. TAMENSIM, THAMESIM

It appears from the above that both a first-declension *Tamesa* and a third-declension *Tamesis* had authority in Latin. The British form of the name supports the former. It was the *Tamesis* tradition – presumably owed to Orosius – that was known to later writers in Britain: Gildas 3 has *Tamesis* (gen.), with var. *Tamensis*, and in 10–11 *Tamesis* (gen.). Bede has four mentions, at i, 2; ii, 3; iii, 22 and iv, 6, in various cases – *Tamensim* and *Tamensem* (acc.), *Tamensis* (gen.) and *Tamense* (abl.). The forms in *-ns-* from Orosius onward have no authority, and presumably arose from association with Latin adjectives in *-ensis*, or by hypercorrection (because classical *-ensis* was *-esis* in Vulgar Latin). *Ravenna*'s entry is not in the river-list (the name is missing there, oddly enough) and was taken by R&C to refer to a settlement, 'probably Dorchester-on-Thames' (Oxfordshire), but like other river-names it was misread by the Cosmographer from a map on which *Tamese* was written along the river's inland course.

DERIVATION. The British name was **Tamēssā*, perhaps for older **Tamēstā*; it was long thought to be built on a base **tam-* 'dark' (see TAMARUS), particularly as Ekwall was able to mention as close parallels Sanskrit *Tamasa*, a tributary of the Ganges, Sanskrit *tamasá* 'dark', and as a cognate Latin *tenebrae*. However, it now seems more probable that the name is one of a very large number of names based on the root **ta-* **tə-* 'to flow', discussed under TAMARUS. On the name and its associates see M. Förster, *Der Flussname Themse* (Munich, 1942), Jackson *LHEB*, passim, and Nicolaisen in *BZN*, viii (1957), 258–59; on the later development of the name, *LHEB* 331. The Anglo-Saxon forms were *Temis*, *Temes*, etc.; the modern spelling with *-a-* is probably due to learned influence from knowledge of the classical spelling.

IDENTIFICATION. The river Thames.

TAMIUS (river) or TAMIUM (fort)

SOURCE

Ravenna 108_{28} (= R&C 244): TAMION, vars. TANISON, TAIMON

DERIVATION. The name is British **Tam-i̯o-*, that is **tam-* (see TAMARUS) with **-i̯o-* derivational suffix. This is an entry in *Ravenna*'s river-list, but this is no guarantee that it refers to a river (as even R&C realised), and we know that at least one other entry in this section (*Durolavi* 108_{37}) is a place-name misread from a map. There are two other relevant criteria. One is that for a river-name one would expect *-us* (nominative) or *-o* (oblique) for a masculine name such as this, not the *-um* which *Ravenna* here shows with its *-on*; but several other entries in the river-list show *-um-*, and are certainly rivers. The other is that the *-*i̯o*- suffix is normally used to form names of forts and settlements derived from water-names; but a few river-names are also formed with it (e.g. *Derventio*). Neither of these criteria, then, helps towards a solution in this case. As to position, the entry in *Ravenna* falls between mentions of the rivers Usk and Ewenny in S. Wales, and there is no reason to doubt that the present name belongs there geographically. Already under *Ratostabius* we have suggested that if **Tabi̯os* (**Taba* with *-*i̯o*- suffix) is in question, it might represent the river Taff (Welsh *Taf*); but also the present **Tami̯os* (*Tamius*) could be the origin of Taff/*Taf*, since British *-b-* and *-m-* by lenition both > Welsh *-f-*. But both cannot be right. For *Ratostabius* all Ptolemy MSS show β (*b*), and are inherently more likely to be right than the single MS of *Ravenna* with *-m-*; on the other hand, it is unlikely that *Ravenna*'s entirely acceptable *-m-*would have arisen as a copying accident. We have, then, a genuine conflict of evidence which neither linguistic nor geographical analysis can resolve; only an epigraphic discovery would do so. All that is clear is that Ptolemy's *Ratostabius* is, or at least incorporates, a river-name, while *Ravenna*'s entry might refer to a river or to a fort/settlement.

IDENTIFICATION. Possibly a Roman fort at Cardiff, Glamorgan (ST 1876), but if so presumably the one which, on the evidence of pottery, is believed to have preceded the known fort, which is not earlier than the late third century (V. E. Nash-Williams, *The Roman Frontier in Wales* (2nd edn, revised by M. G. Jarrett, Cardiff, 1969), 71).

TAMPIUM

SOURCE

H. G. Pflaum, 'Le Marbre de Thorigny', *Bibliothèque de l'Ecole des Hautes Etudes*, No. 292 (Paris, 1948), p. 9 (also *CIL* XIII. 3162). The text is on three sides of a statue-base found at Vieux and now at Thorigny in Normandy (France). The relevant part of the text on the left side reads in expanded form:

Exemplum epistulae Claudii Paulini legati Augusti pro praetore provinciae Britanniae ad Sennium Sollemnem. A TAMPIO.

The inscription (of A.D. 238) records a letter which Tiberius Claudius Paulinus, governor of Lower Britain, sent from *Tampium* to his friend Sennius Sollemnis.

DERIVATION. *Tampium* appears to be a proper form, recorded in this unique source. It has no analogues and it is impossible to conjecture an etymology or meaning.

IDENTIFICATION. Unknown. Though Paulinus is here recorded simply as governor of *Britannia*, his date (established by *RIB* 1280) and the mention in the present inscription of *Legio VI* (stationed at York) combine to show that his province was actually *Britannia Inferior.* This included York and Lincoln (*JRS*, XL (1921), 102: the dedication at Bordeaux by M.

Aurelius Lunaris) and this restricts the area in which the name should be sought. Any connection with the *Ala* (*I Pannoniorum*) *Tampiana* is unlikely, since the author of this boastful inscription would surely have insisted on accuracy in the transcription of the letter.

*TAMUS

SOURCE

Ravenna 106_{48} (= R&C 93): ELTAVORI, var. ELTANORI

R&C read *Eltanori* as their main form, as have other editors except Schnetz, noting *Eltavori* as a variant only; it seems best, partly in view of the identification suggested below, to accept their form, as in one or two other cases. As with other corrupt *Ravenna* names, *El-* here represents *Fl*, the abbreviation for *Fl(umen)* or *Fl(uvius)*. Final *-ri* is written for *m* or *n* (compare perhaps *Ravenna*'s *Enmidion* 91_1 for *Erimidion*); the resulting **Tanom* or **Tanon* is more classically **Tanum*, as always. If we add that *n* is often in *Ravenna* a miscopying of *m*, we have **Tamum*. The steps in the restoration are numerous, but all are supported by evidence from within this text.

DERIVATION. **Tamus* is a British river-name **Tamos*; for the root **tam-*, see TAMARUS. Like several other inland river-names which figured on his map-source, it was misread by the Cosmographer as though it were a place, and was entered in his list of habitation-names.

IDENTIFICATION. From its position in the list between Leicester and Wall, evidently the river Tame, an important tributary of the Trent (which might, in Roman times, have been taken as the boundary between the *Coritani* and the *Cornovii*).

TANATIS or TANATUS

SOURCES

Ptolemy II, 3, 14: Τολιάτις νῆσος (= TOLIATIS INSULA), var. Τολιάπις (= TOLIAPIS)

Solinus 22, 8: TANATUS

Ravenna 105_{30} (= R&C 306): TANIATIDE, var. TAMATIDE

Isidore XIV, 6, 3: THANATOS, insula Oceani, freto Gallico a Britannia aestuario tenui separata

The correct form is that of Solinus and Isidore. Müller thinks that Ptolemy's version arose from a misreading of N as ΛΙ (*LI*), and there is a further error of *o* for *a*. *Ravenna*'s entry indicates an oblique case in *-ide(m)*, which is not to be despised in view of Ptolemy's nominative in *-is*; perhaps, as often, the name was declined in two ways.

DERIVATION. Förster *FT* 579 suggests that the Latin name is a version of a British **Tannēton*, from a root **tanet-* known in that form in Old Welsh as 'feurig, glänzend' (Welsh, Cornish and Breton *tan* 'fire', Old Irish *tene*, gen. *tened*). Watson *CPNS* 443 mentions the river Teinntidh near Callander (Perthshire), a Gaelic name with which he compares Old Irish *tentide*; the river would have been called 'fiery, from its rapid boiling course', though it is probably easier to retain Förster's sense 'glänzend' ('shining') for a river-name, since we have semantic parallels such as *Leuca*. Ekwall thinks the precisely comparable Shropshire river Tanat the 'brilliant river'. To these W. Nicolaisen in *BZN*, VIII (1957), 260, who also discusses the etymology, adds mention of the Scottish rivers Tennet (Angus) and Tynet or Tynot (Banff). Ekwall *EPN* thinks that the present name 'may mean "bright island" or "fire island" (from a beacon or lighthouse)'. We would then have a literal meaning for the island-name, and a slightly metaphorical one for the rivers. If the etymology is right, **tanet-* in British has undergone an assimilation of vowels (*a-e* > *a-a*) in being latinised, perhaps by association with Greek θάνατος; this association is entirely clear in Isidore's version with *Th-*, and he explains the name *a morte serpentum* 'from the death of snakes', the earth of the island when transported elsewhere being fatal to them (as recorded by Solinus). The Anglo-Saxon name was *Tenid*, *Tanet*, etc.; presumably modern *Th-* is due to learned influence (but not from Bede, who at I, 25, has *Tanatos*). A possible analogue abroad, Taneto near Parma (Italy), is mentioned by Nicolaisen; other apparently similar names probably have Gaulish **tann-* 'oak', which sometimes appears with the *-ētum* suffix indicating 'wood of...'.

IDENTIFICATION. The Isle of Thanet, Kent (which was then separated from the mainland by the Wantsum Channel).

Note. Nennius hints at an alternative British name when he writes (31) of the *insulam, quae in lingua eorum* [i.e., Saxons] *vocatur Tanet, Brittanico sermone Ruoihm* (again simply *Tanet* in 36, 43). Variants include *Tanett*, *Thanet*, *Tenet*; and for the British name, *Ruichum*, *Ruoichim*, *Ruoichin*, *Roihin*, *Ruimh*. The name is also found in line 31 of the Welsh prophetic poem *Armes Prydein* of about 900, as *Danet* (see Ifor Williams's edition, English version by R. Bromwich (Dublin, 1972), p. 31).

TARVEDUNUM

SOURCES

Ptolemy II, 3, 1: Ταρουεδούμ ἡ και Ὀρκας ἄκρα (=TARVEDUM SIVE ORCAS PROMONTORIUM), vars. Ταρουηδούμη (= TARVEDUME), Ταρουιδούμ (= TARVIDUM), Ταρουέδα (= TARVEDA)

II, 3, 4: Ταρουεδούμ (= TARVEDUM)

Marcian II, 45: Ταροαιδούνου (gen.; = TAROAEDUNUM) ? recte Ταρουεδούνον (= TARVEDUNUM)

DERIVATION. Though none of the Ptolemy MSS shows *-dunum*, Marcian preserves a form close to this, and the restoration is undoubtedly correct. On Ptolemy's spelling, see Chapter III, p. 133. On the first element, see Holder II. 1742 and *GPN* 261–63: British **taru̯o-* 'bull', now represented by Welsh *tarw*, Cornish *tarow*, Breton *taro*, *tarv*; and in Irish, *tarb*, cognate with Latin *taurus*. The corresponding Gaulish word occurs in such place-names as *Tarvenna AI* 376_3, etc., > Thérouanne (Pas-de-Calais, France), *Tarvessedum AI* 278_5 near Lake Como (N. Italy), and others perhaps assimilated to Latin *taurus*. For *-dunum*, see BRANODUNUM. The sense is thus 'bull-fort', presumably named from the resemblance of the headland to a bull; Watson *CPNS* 36 mentions a similar name with elements reversed, Duntarvie in Lothian (Scotland), and points out that Thurso Bay, opposite Dunnet Head, is Norse *Thjórsá* 'Bull's Water'. The name is given by Ptolemy as a contemporary alternative to the traditional *Orcas*.

IDENTIFICATION. Dunnet Head, Caithness. On the equation with *Orcas*, see p. 115.

TAVA or TAVUS[1]

SOURCES

Tacitus *Agricola* 22, 1: vastatis usque ad TAUM (aestuario nomen est) nationibus... (var.: ad TANAUM)

Ptolemy II, 3, 4: Ταούα ἔισχυσις (= TAVA AESTUARIUM)

Ravenna 108_{19} (= R&C 232): TABA

There can be little doubt that *Ravenna*'s entry, included in the section of *diversa loca*, is a river-name (*Panovius* for *Fl Novius* at 108_{18} is another). Presumably on the map-source, *Taba* – with Vulgar Latin *b* for *v*, as often – was written along the inland course of the river and misread as a habitation-name; and was accepted as such ('a *locus* or tribal meeting-place') by R&C. The name is then omitted from *Ravenna*'s list of rivers.

DERIVATION. Authorities both on toponymy and on Tacitus agree in dismissing the *Tanaum* variant and in thinking that *Taum* is written for *Tavum* (and it is easy to see how *Tanaum* arose via **Tauum* in copying, since *n/u* are readily confused in some medieval scripts). The name seems to have both masculine and feminine forms; *Tavus*[2] shows a masculine in the single record. The root is British **tau̯o-* **tau̯ā*. This has traditionally been taken (since at least Holder II. 1774) to mean 'silent, peaceful', in line with the senses of Welsh *taw* 'silent, silence', Irish *toi*, etc. But Ekwall objected that the Tay and Taw (then associated etymologically with this) are not calm or peaceful rivers (*ERN* 394); and Watson *CPNS* 50–51, while accepting the etymology, added that the Gaelic name of the Tay, *Tatha* from older *Toē*, could not have arisen from *Tava* but presupposes a form **Tau̯i̯ā*. Pokorny in *ZCP*, XXI (1940), 83, followed by W. Nicolaisen in *BZN*, VIII (1957), 260–61, altogether dismiss a root meaning 'silent' and derive the name – one of a very large family – from the Indo-European root **ta-* **tə-* 'fließen', with the third type of consonantal development in Nicolaisen's classification (see TAMARUS) in *-u̯-*; this Celtic *Tau̯ā* or *Tau̯i̯ā* > Tay, Taw, meaning simply 'flowing one, river'. Continental parallels include **Tau̯ā* > Thève, a tributary of the Oise (France); *Tavia IM* 503_2, *TP*, a river of Liguria > Taggia (N. Italy); *Tabia*, a settlement in Dalmatia (*Ravenna* 55_{23}); and *Tavium*, an *oppidum* of Galatia (Pliny *NH* V, 146) = *Tavia* (*AI* 201_8, etc.), now Nefez Köi in Turkey, which shows the same gender variation as the present British name. These forms were thus extraordinarily widespread.

IDENTIFICATION. The river Tay, Scotland.

TAVUS[2]

SOURCE

Ravenna 105_{46} (= R&C 2): ELTABO

As with **Tamus* and several other names, *El-* is here a misreading of *Fl*, the abbreviation of *Fl(umen)* or *Fl(uvius)* on a map. *Tabo* has Vulgar Latin *b* for *v*, as often, and is the oblique case of *Tavus*.

DERIVATION. See TAVA (TAVUS[1]).

IDENTIFICATION. The river Taw, Devon (as observed by C. Thomas, *Rural Settlement in Roman Britain* (London, 1966), 87).

TECTOVERDI

SOURCE

Inscription: *RIB* 1695 (= Burn, 1969, No. 173, p. 126): an altar set up by the CURIA TEXTOVERDORUM. The stone was found at Beltingham; 'it may have been brought from Chesterholm (*Vindolanda*), or it may have come from a local shrine' (*RIB*)

DERIVATION. The name, not documented elsewhere, is problematic. Whatmough *DAG* 666 is doubtful whether the text is accurate, conjecturing that the name was really **Texuandruorum* or the like (the *Texuandri* of Germania Inferior are mentioned by Pliny *NH* IV, 106, and are *Texandri* in an inscription *EE* III. 103, *Toxiandria* in Ammianus XVII, 8, 1, etc.; their name may survive in Tessenderloo or Testerup in Holland). But this is to assume that the *curia* was incapable of spelling its name on an important occasion, in what looks like a carefully cut text.

Jackson *LHEB* 407 points out that the *-xt-* spelling 'is a Gallo-Latin spelling habit, the *x* being taken over from the Greek alphabet, and used to spell the Gallo-Latin and British χ... But the British χ*t* is regularly spelt *ct* in Latin sources, as is natural, the Romans substituting their own *ct* for the foreign χ*t*.' (Jackson *LHEB* 404 explains that Indo-European *-kt-* (*ct*) was /χt/ already in Common Celtic, and in British remained so throughout the Roman period. /χ/ is a guttural, the sound which is spelled *ch* in Welsh *bach*, Scots *loch*, etc.). Thus *-ct-* as a Latin spelling is found in *Lactodurum*, *Octapitarum*, *Vectis*, etc. The exceptional 'false' *-xt-* spelling is found in Britain in the present name, in the divine name *Anextiomaro* (*EE* VII. 1162: South Shields), and in the river-name *Raxtomessa* of *Ravenna* 108_{40} (which is not very trustworthy). The equivalence of *xt* and *ct* can be seen when the same name is written both ways on Gaulish territory: *Rectugenus*, *Rextugenos* and also *Reitugenus* (Dottin *LG* 42, 64, 94), this last representing a phonetic development of Gaulish at a late stage (in British, /χt/ > /i̯th/ about A.D. 600).

The above enables us to equate the first element in the name with that of the *Volcae Tectosages* (Τεκτοσάγες, Ptolemy II, 10, 6) of Gallia Narbonensis, and that of the *Tectosages* of Galatia. At one time a meaning 'cover' was suggested, in line with Latin *tego*, *tectum*. Holder II. 1780 notes **tecto-* in this and related names and defines it via a gloss on Irish *techt* 'itio, aditus' and Welsh *taith* 'journey'. This has been challenged, for example by L. H. Gray in *EC*, VI (1953–54), 68. In Gaulish *Contextos*, *Atextorigi*, etc., she discerns a root **tege-* 'engendrer, enfanter', present in Sanskrit *tákman* 'postérité', Greek τίκτω, and cognate with Anglo-Saxon *þegn*, Old High German *degen* 'servant'. These and other possibilities are reviewed by Ellis Evans in *GPN* 265–66, with the suggestion that the assembled names are of multiple origin but with a preference for the early suggestion of a meaning 'cover', and approval for Schmidt's interpretation of *Tectosages* as 'die auf den Besitz losgehen'. The latest view seems to be that of C.-J. Guyonvarc'h in *Ogam*, XIX (1967), 231–33, who discusses the ethnic names (but not the present one) and that of the Irish ruler *Techtmar*, concluding that he is a 'possessor' rather than a 'procreator': 'Tout confirme donc l'etymologie "souveraine" et "légitime" de *techt*; et c'est en ce sens qu'il conviendra d'interpréter les thèmes gaulois en *tecto-* ou ceux, plus tardifs, en *text-*', thinking furthermore that all Ellis Evans's names can be explained in this way. Unfortunately, the second element of the British name is wholly unknown, and no conjectures can be offered.

IDENTIFICATION. The *Tectoverdi*, perhaps a people within the confederation of the Brigantes, seem to have lived in the area of Chesterholm, Northumberland. See CURIA TECTOVERDORUM and VINDOLANDA.

TEDERTIS

SOURCE

Ravenna 106_{10} (= R&C 25): TEDERTIS

This entry is a gross corruption or a fragment. R&C print it conflated with the previous entry, *Omire*, whose first two or possibly three letters we have removed to form the ending of a version of SORVIODUNUM. It is thus possible that we have to do not with *Tedertis* but with *Retedertis* or *Iretedertis*; which hardly improves matters, unless *Re-* stands for *Fl-* 'river' on a map. In any event, no conjectures can be made.

IDENTIFICATION. Unknown, but apparently in southern Britain.

TERDEC (?)

SOURCE

Ravenna 109_5 (= R&C 274): TERDEC

Ravenna's section for *Scotia* (Ireland) consists of three names, all rivers. As explained in Chapter v (p. 214), *Ravenna* may well have had no information at all for Ireland, and these three river-names may relate to western Britain rather than to Ireland, being written in the Cosmographer's map-source across a much-narrowed Irish Sea. We have postulated that *Cled* 109_4 is for *Clota*, the Clyde; it seems likely that *Terdec* is a now unrecognisable western British river-name, but no guesses can be made. See also 'ETSODISINAM'.

*TERMINUS

SOURCE

Ravenna 106_3 (= R&C 17): TERMONIN

It is likely that scribal metathesis has operated in this entry, and that **Terminon* was intended; this, with *Ravenna*'s common *-on* for classical *-um*, gives us **Terminum*, nominative *Terminus*. For a similar vowel metathesis, compare *Cironium* for *Corinium* at 106_{31}. Dillemann's effort (p. 65) to see in this entry **Lemanio* seems far-fetched; it is palaeographically complicated, and there is no sign that *Ravenna*'s names in this first part of the list belong anywhere other than in south-west England.

DERIVATION. The Latin word is probably used in the sense 'boundary, boundary-stone'. From *terminus* as a common noun was derived Welsh *terfyn*, not necessarily in Romano-British times. The river *Tarvin* (Cheshire) is likely to represent an early naming and is similarly from *terminus*, with the lenited *m* of British, from which one can see that the Latin word was in real use. The objection of R&C that the loan of Latin *terminus* seems too late to be present in *terfyn* and Tarvin, and that 'the normal Latin word used in political boundaries is *fines*, *terminus* being an agrimensorial word', is hardly proper; not only can we assume that an agrimensorial use is here being made of the word, but we find it also on *RIB* 325, a boundary-stone from near Caerleon inscribed *Termin*, which the editor expands as *Termin(us)*. Similar namings are known in Spain, modern Término (Santander) and Termens (Lérida) being from *terminus* (*ELH* I. 511).

IDENTIFICATION. Unknown, but apparently in south-west Britain.

THULE, THYLE

SOURCES

These are numerous. The earliest surviving mention is that by Virgil, who also began the literary topos: *tibi serviat ultima Thule* (*Georgics* I. 30). Among the geographers the name is first cited by Strabo (recalling Pytheas), in four places: Θούλης, Θούλην (=THULES, THULEN); then by Mela II, 6 (57): THYLE. Greek initial *Th-* and a Greek-style declension in Latin were maintained by most writers, and both *-u-* and *-y-* spellings are found. Variants in the MSS of Orosius embrace most possible forms: *Thyle, Tyle, Tylae, Thulae, Thola, Tholae.*

DERIVATION. The name is obviously very ancient; no origin or meaning can be suggested for it. In usage it was both a geographical term (of varied application) and a semi-mythical and literary commonplace.

IDENTIFICATION. This is not, properly speaking, a British island. The application of the name to Shetland by Tacitus, *Agricola* 10, and by Ptolemy II, 3, 14, means not that it ever really bore the name but merely that the furthest land seen to the north would automatically be identified as *Thule*. See the discussion on pp. 42–43 and our entry AEMODAE.

TINA (Τίνα) of Ptolemy II, 3, 4: see ITUNA[2]

TINEA

SOURCE

Ravenna 108_{35} (= R&C 258): TINOA, var. TINEA

R&C give *Tinea* as their main form, as is surely right.

DERIVATION. Williams cites a root **tā-* **tĭ-* (now Pokorny 1053) 'to melt, flow', with *-na* formation; the root is ultimately related to that of *Tamarus* and other names mentioned in that entry. (R&C associate *Ravenna*'s name with Ptolemy's Τίνα II, 3, 4, but for this see now our ITUNA[2]). As parallels with this *Tin(e)a* Williams mentions Old Bulgarian and Russian *tina* 'mud, mire'. Continental analogues suggest that *Tinea* is more likely than *Tina* to be the correct form of the British name: Pliny *NH* III, 53, mentions a *Tina* river, tributary of the Tiber, and there was a *Tinias* (*TP*) on the Black Sea coast, now Iniada in Bulgaria; there was also a *Tinna* river (*TP*) which flowed into the Adriatic in Central Italy, now the Tenna. Bede has forms which point rather to *Tina*: he has *Tina* at V, 21, but also a masculine *Tinus* (*Tini* gen. at V, 6; *Tino* abl. at V, 2). Not recorded in ancient sources but derived from the same name, evidently widespread in Britain, are the Tyne of East Lothian (Scotland), Tyne Brook (Herefords.), Tynebec in Craven (Yorks.) and Tindale (Cumberland), and ultimately from the same root are the Till river of Northumberland and the Tille, a tributary of the Saône (France), etc. See further Ekwall *ERN* 426 and Nicolaisen in *BZN*, VIII (1957), 262.

IDENTIFICATION. The river Tyne, Northumberland.

TOESOBIS (?)

SOURCE

Ptolemy II, 3, 2: Τοισόβιος ποταμοῦ ἐκβολαί (=TOESOBIS FLUVII OSTIA), var. Τισοβίου (= TISOBIS)

DERIVATION. This is wholly unknown; possibly the form is corrupt.

IDENTIFICATION. Uncertain. From its position in Ptolemy this should apply to a river flowing into Tremadoc Bay by way of Traeth Bach, that is, Afon Glaslyn or Afon Dwyryd, but the forms do not correspond and it may be that Ptolemy has taken the name of the bay as that of a river mouth (cf. METARIS).

TOLIATIS (Τολιάτις) of Ptolemy II, 3, 14: see TANATIS

TOVIUS

SOURCE

Ptolemy II, 3, 2: Τουβίου ποταμοῦ ἐκβολαί (= TUBII FLUVII OSTIA), vars. Τοβίου (= TOBII; MS U, and preferred by Müller), Τοιβίου (= TOEBII), Τουβούα (= TUBUA)

DERIVATION Jackson *LHEB* 351 thinks the British name was **Touịos*, presumably a root plus the common *-*ịo*- suffix; from this derives modern Welsh *Tywi* (English Towy). Our preferred form of the old name represents this. Holder II. 1900 lists a single parallel, an assumed **Toviacum* based on **Touịos*, > Tubize (Brabant, Belgium). A possible root in 'Ligurian' is mentioned by Rostaing *ETP* 260: **tob*- **tov*-, variants of **teba* 'pierre, roche, motte de terre', with **tob*- by an evolution of sense passing perhaps from 'pente, ravin' to a meaning 'creux', which might then presumably apply to a river-bed and then suit the present name. Whether this **tob*-/**tov*- variation could explain the *b*- in all Ptolemy's forms is hard to say; *b* and *v* were not confused in British, and the period of Ptolemy's sources (first century A.D.) is probably too early for *b*/*v* confusion in Vulgar Latin. In any case we must regard the relationship with a 'Ligurian' root as most tenuous when there seem to be no representatives of it in Insular Celtic words and a single uncertain place-name of Gaulish origin, so the etymology and meaning are best left unresolved.

IDENTIFICATION. The river Tywi (Towy), Carmarthenshire.

TRAJECTUS

SOURCE

AI 486_2 (Iter XIV): TRAIECTUS

DERIVATION. The name is a Latin common noun, 'crossing', perhaps more specifically 'crossing-point' or 'ferry'. There are several Continental examples, and the name survives in modern Maastricht and Utrecht (Holland), etc. The word seems to have been used solely for the Roman transport system, and has nothing to do with possible Celtic names (such as the word which is now Welsh *traeth* 'sands').

IDENTIFICATION. The reference is probably to the crossing of the Severn; see the discussion in Chapter IV, pp. 117–18.

TRAXULA

SOURCE

Ravenna 108_{24} (= R&C 236): TRAXULA

DERIVATION. Williams has reason to dismiss the proposal of Ekwall *ERN* 401 of a derivative from the root **treg*- (now Pokorny 1090), represented by Welsh *trenn* 'impetuous, strenuous' and Irish *trén* 'strong, swift'. Williams prefers a root in **trenq*- 'to wash, bathe' (now Pokorny 1094), which has given Welsh *trwnc* 'urine' ('used for washing by the Celts') and *trochi* 'to wash, bathe', whose *-ch-* represents earlier *-nk-s*, and whose original British form might then have had *-(n)ks-* represented by Latin *-x-*. This root seems to have derivatives only in Lithuanian, which could explain its rarity in ancient toponymy. Williams's sense for the river-name is, then, tentatively, 'washing-pool or river'; R&C compare names such as English Washbrook. The ending *-ula* looks like a Latin diminutive, but cannot in fact be that; possibly some other British suffix was assimilated to this during copying. The above, though satisfactory up to a point and the best that can be offered, should be regarded as conjectural in view of the unreliability of names recorded by *Ravenna* alone. Any equation with the Test (*Terstan* 877: Ekwall), whose name is probably British, is phonetically impossible to establish unless one supposes several irregular developments.

IDENTIFICATION. Unknown, but apparently a river in southern Britain.

TRIMONTIUM

SOURCES

Ptolemy II, 3, 6: Τριμόντιον (= TRIMONTIUM), a *polis* of the Selgovae

Ravenna 107_{44} (= R&C 183): TRIMUNTIUM, var. TRIMINITIUM

Inscription: *RIB* 2313, part of a milestone found at Ingliston (Scotland):... [TRI]MONTI(O) M P [... (dated to A.D. 140–44)

DERIVATION. The name is Latin, '(place of the) three hills', in this case the three Eildon Hills, which are visible from a great distance. Pliny *NH* IV, 41, mentions a *Trimontium* in Thrace, now Plovdiv (Bulgaria). The present name could well be a Latin version (applied to the Roman fort) of an equivalent British name earlier applied to the hill-fort of the Selgovae on the northernmost of the Eildon Hills, where also a Roman signal-station was erected.

IDENTIFICATION. The Roman fort at Newstead, Roxburghshire (NT 5734), at the foot of the three Eildon Hills.

TRINOVANTES

SOURCES

Caesar *BG* V, 20, 1 (also V, 21, 1 and V, 22, 5): TRINOBANTES

Tacitus *Annals* XIV, 31: TRINOBANTES

Ptolemy II, 3, 11: Τρινόαντες (= TRINOANTES), var. Τρινοούαντες (= TRINOVANTES, one MS)

II, 3, 14: Τρινόαντας (acc., = TRINOANTAS), var. Τρινώαντας (= TRINOANTAS)

Orosius VI, 9, 8: TRINOBANTUM (gen.), var. TRINOVANTUM

DERIVATION. There can be no doubt that the proper form has *-v-*, despite the appearance of *-b-* in seemingly authoritative texts of Caesar and Tacitus; their forms would be due to the *b/v* equivalence in the spoken Latin of copyists of late Antiquity whose texts were used by the medieval scribes of the surviving MSS. Orosius was following Caesar, and Bede (*Trinovantes* at I, 2) was following Orosius, evidently using a text having the *-v-* variant. The name has the intensive prefix **trĭ-* (cognate with Latin *trans*), now represented by Welsh *try*, Breton *tri-*; and present in Old Irish as *tri*, *tré*, etc. The rest of the name is identical to that of the *Novantae*, here in a different declension (see ATREBATES); the sense is thus 'most lively, very vigorous' or the like. For the formation, compare the ethnic names *Cassi* (British) and *Tricassii, Tricasses* (of Gaul).

IDENTIFICATION. A people of Britain inhabiting Essex and adjoining areas. Ptolemy attributes only *Camulodunum* to them, and whether they were attributed to the *colonia* or had a separate capital of their own (possibly *Caesaromagus* = Chelmsford) is disputed; see discussions in R. Dunnett, *The Trinovantes* (London, 1975), 63–64, and J. Wacher, *The Towns of Roman Britain* (London, 1975), 196–98.

TRIPONTIUM

SOURCE

AI 477_2 (Iter VI): TRIPONTIO

DERIVATION. The name is Latin, '(place of the) three bridges' (but see below), formed in the same way as *Trimontium*. Jackson in *Britannia*, I (1970), 79, takes an extreme Celticist view when he says that the name is a 'compound of **tri-* "three" and **pontịo-* from Latin *pont-* and the *-*ịo-* suffix. The Latin word was borrowed into British, whence Welsh *pont*, so that this is not a hybrid.' This seems unnecessarily complicated in view of the Latin name *Pontibus* in Britain, and of the fact that Latin *tres tri-* regularly enters into such compounds in other provinces, e.g. *Tresarbores, Tres Tabernae, Tricornia Castra*; compare other numerals in *Ad Duos Pontes, Septem Arae*, etc. The name is best regarded as purely Latin, whether or not it translates an earlier Celtic **briụa* name. For the force of the plural in such names, see DUROBRIVAE[1]. At the Roman settlement identified below there is, however, no river such as to warrant any kind of 'bridge'; it may be necessary to suggest a sense for the present name of 'causeway, raised passage over wet ground', or similar.

IDENTIFICATION. The Roman settlement at Cave's Inn Farm, Churchover, Warwickshire (SP 5379).

TRISANTONA[1]

SOURCES

Ptolemy II, 3, 3; Τρισάντωνος ποταμοῦ ἐκβολαί (= TRISANTONIS FLUVII OSTIA)

Ravenna 106_{34} (= R&C 69): MUTUANTONIS, var. MANTUANTONIS

Ravenna's entry might be a conflation with another name beginning or ending in *Mu-*, but more probably *Mu-* represents a garbled abbreviation of *Fl* for *Fl(umen)* or *Fl(uvius)*, as often. There is a further serious miscopying in the first syllable of the name proper. As often, the Cosmographer took the name – written inland along the course of the river on his map source – as a habitation-name.

DERIVATION. The first element is the intensive British prefix **trĭ-*, for which see TRINOVANTES. The second is problematic. Ekwall *ERN* 417–18 proposed a base in **santōn-*, present also in the name of the Gaulish *Santones* people and as British **sento-* 'path' (see CLAUSENTUM), the word which gave Welsh *hynt* 'path, road' and whose Old Irish cognate is *sét* 'journey'; this root, applied to a river, might mean 'trespasser', that is 'one liable to flood'. One might suggest alternatively 'wanderer, meanderer'. But Williams objected that Welsh *hynt* demands **sento-* (as is clear) with *-e-*, not

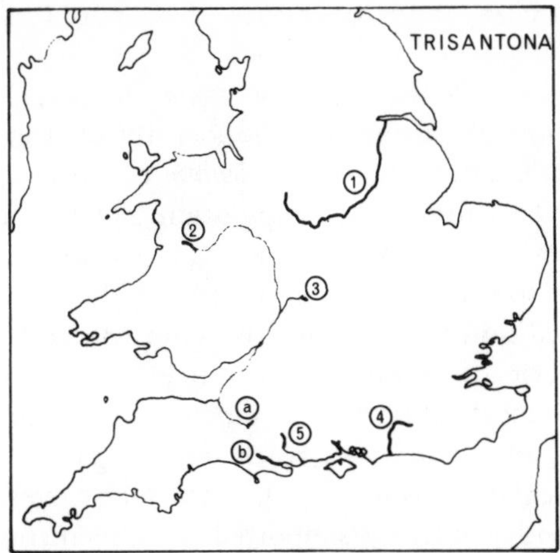

Fig. 32. River-names derived from *Trisantona*: 1. Trent; 2. Trannon; 3. Trent; 4. Tarrant (Arun); 5. Tarrant. Possible examples: (*a*) Trent; (*b*) Trent (Piddle).

from a root having *-a-* as in our river-names. He therefore proposed to seek a root **sem-* (now Pokorny 901: 'schöpfen, gießen') 'to draw water', with *-sant-* in the British river-names representing *-sn̥t-*, found in Old Irish words and in Latin *sentina* 'bilge', etc.; Williams's sense for the river-names would then be (with the intensive prefix) 'water pouring out, i.e. flooding strongly' or perhaps 'draining thoroughly'. More recently Guyonvarc'h in *Ogam*, XIII (1961), 592–98 (especially 596), in a study of the British ethnicon *Setantii* upon which we have already drawn in that entry (but without mention of the British river-names) makes one think that Ekwall could have been right after all. The key reference of Guyonvarc'h is to a goddess *Sentona* perhaps 'déesse-route, maîtresse de la route', recorded in a dedication at Fiume (now Rijeka, Yugoslavia), *CIL* III. 3026, and known also as a female name; with quotation of O'Rahilly *EIHM* 295 on the same matter, more or less in agreement with Ekwall. British *Trisantona* might then be 'great wanderer, great wayfarer', that is a description of a long and winding river (or possibly, again, one liable to variable meanders and to flooding); or the name might contain, or actually be, a divine name, as in many other instances. There remains, of course, the problem to which Williams drew attention: that *-sant-* is not *-sent-*. The two are not known as dialectal variations one of the other, and in any case British **sento-* is well-established; so there must remain a considerable doubt about meaning and etymology.

The proper form of the two British names is unsure. For the next name Tacitus seems to assure us of a first-declension *-ona*. Ptolemy here gives us a third-declension genitive in *-is*, which supposes a nominative **Trisanto*; *Ravenna*, though often unreliable, offers *-is*, but is not likely to be giving us a nominative, and final *-is* in this text is sometimes a mis-copying of *-a* (as in *Uxelis* 106_1 for *Uxela*). The two British rivers could have identical elements but differing Latin declensional forms.

For later developments of *Trisantona* in Welsh, and when taken from British into Anglo-Saxon, see *LHEB* 524–25. The present *Trisantona* > Tarrant (*Tarente*, *c.* 725), the former name of the Sussex Arun (this modern name being by back-formation from Arundel), which is identical to Trent and several other names, including Welsh *Tarannon* (Montgomeryshire).

IDENTIFICATION. The river Arun, Sussex, which is especially liable to flooding in the area of Amberley Wild Brooks.

TRISANTONA[2]

SOURCE

Tacitus *Annals* XII, 31 (as emended by Bradley): cis TRISANTONAM et SABRINAM fluvios

DERIVATION. See TRISANTONA[1].

IDENTIFICATION. The river Trent, flowing from Staffordshire to the Humber.

Note. Bede had no record of a classical tradition for this name. He calls the Trent *Treenta* (II, 16) and *Treanta* (III, 24 and IV, 21), and does not decline the name.

TRUCCULENSIS PORTUS (?)

SOURCE

Tacitus *Agricola* 38, 4: TRUCCULENSEM PORTUM (acc.), var. TRUTULENSEM PORTUM

This name presents a much-discussed problem. In either form it is unlikely to be correct as it stands. Students of Tacitus have speculated about it, including, in recent years, the following:

(1) Ogilvie and Richmond in their 1967 edition of the *Agricola* think (as was first suggested by Lipsius) that **Rutup(i)ensem* may have been intended, adding that this makes an easy change palaeographically, since the var. *(T)rutulensem* needs only one further emendation to produce *Rutupensem*. They support this possibility by adding that *proximo* might mean 'the shore adjacent or nearest to Rome, that is the south coast', which suits Richborough. **Rutupensem* is indeed an easy emendation. The objection that the adjectival form of *Rutupiae* was *Rutupinus* may not matter much; the latter may have been a literary convention (from Lucan onward) rather than common usage.

(2) N. Reed in *Britannia*, II (1971), 147–48, argues for the identity of Tacitus's name with *Ugrulentum* of *Ravenna* 108_3, following a suggestion of Hübner in *Hermes*, XVI (1881), 545. He argues from the critical apparatus of the 1967 edition that *Truccu-* has better MS authority than *Trutu-*, but in that case rather considerable textual emendation is required before we reach *Ravenna*'s *Ugrulentum*. The case is, however, independently supported by Dillemann (p. 70) who, after seeming to deny the equation, none the less remarks that 'The change from *Trutulensis* to *Ugrulentum* in a poor text can be explained by three common errors: a metathesis *Tutru* for *Trutu*, the omission of the initial letter, and a misreading of *c* for *g* or *t*.' This is most reasonable so far as *Ravenna*'s methods are concerned, and argues for the correctness of *Trutulensis*. It is as well to observe here that *Ugrulentum* is almost certainly an untrustworthy form, as so often in *Ravenna* (especially with North British names); Reed's further argument, based on the order of names in the Cosmography, rests on an unwarranted assumption – derived from R&C in 1949 – about the logic followed in the text.

(3) J. G. F. Hind in *Britannia*, V (1974), 285–88, challenges both the above suggestions on palaeographic and other grounds, and offers the possibility of a corruption of **Tun(n)ocelensis*, that is an adjectival form of *Itunocelum* (*Tunnocelo* being the version in *ND*). He supports this with the possibility that the corruption in Tacitus's text could have come about by association with Latin *trucculum*, giving a sense 'rough, stormy port'. However, there is no such word (? ad-

jective *truculentus*); *ND*'s form is irrelevant, and one must start from accurate early *Itunocelum*, the process of miscopying then being a more difficult one to envisage.

The form of the name in Tacitus is puzzling. Why the apparent circumlocution, with adjectival form plus *portus*? It can hardly be a question here of elegant periphrasis as a rhetorical figure. The reason is probably that this *portus* was based like other British *portus*-names ultimately on a river-name (*Portus Dubris*, *Portus Lemanis*); but whereas the other port-names refer directly to existing settlements – so that *Portus Lemanis*, for example, is 'port-at-the-settlement-*Lemanis*- (which-is-on-the-river-*Lemana*)' – in the present case in the remote northwest no settlement existed, and *Trucculensis Portus* is probably the 'Trucculan harbour' at the mouth of a river **Truccula* or **Trucculus*. This argument may dispose of the suggestion of Ogilvie and Richmond, for if Richborough were intended, one would expect simply **portum Rutupias* in Tacitus's text.

As we have said, *Ravenna*'s *Ugrulentum* is in itself an untrustworthy form with no visible etymology; there is no point in taking it as a base and arguing from it. Reed and Dillemann seem to assume that the Cosmographer was miscopying *Trucculensis* from Tacitus's text, but there is no evidence that the Cosmographer knew him. The only statement one can make is that Tacitus's text is far more accurately preserved than *Ravenna*'s; and that the Cosmographer took *Ugrulentum* – as he did his other N. British names – from the modernised Severan military map. If the equation of *Ugrulentum* with Tacitus's name is correct, *Ugrulentum* must have figured on the first (Flavian) version of this map, which was that known to Marinus and through him to Ptolemy; but Ptolemy does not mention it, nor any name resembling it. We can proceed, then, on the basis that Tacitus's two forms are a better guide. Yet *Ravenna*'s entry may serve in one way, because its *-ulen(t)-* coincides with Tacitus's, and we can take it as nearly certain – if we accept the equation – that the Flavian map had an entry which was adjectival (and nominative: see p. 196, note), perhaps after all *(*Portus*) *Truculensis* or *Trutulensis*. Tacitus's main form then has *-cc-* for *-c-* or *-ct-*, and his variant has *t* for *c*, a common error in medieval scripts; while *Ravenna*'s *Ugrulentum* has the changes noted by Dillemann.

DERIVATION. Since we cannot, from the above, be sure of the original form, we have no prospect of a solution. It is tempting to think that the name is based on Celto-Latin *tructa* 'trout', probably an early borrowing (already in Pliny) from Gaulish into Latin; a river **Tructula* 'little trout' is just conceivable as a half-joking name conferred by the Roman fleet, which we know gave Latin names to some of the western isles at this same time; and even though no other Latin names appear on the western Scottish seaboard, and fish-names do not normally enter into river-names, the exception might be tolerable in this exceptional case (that is, the fleet called at a hitherto unnamed place). There is no evidence that *tructa* existed in British; the words for 'trout' in the modern Celtic languages are quite different. Alternatively, Burn suggested in T. A. Dovey (ed.) *Tacitus* (London, 1969; p. 59) that *Truccu-* derived from a Celtic root identical to that which has given *twrch* 'boar' in Welsh (**turco-*, Holder II. 1995; Breton *tourch*, Irish *torc*), observing that this does in fact exist as a Welsh river-name (Watson *CPNS* 232). This would then involve a metathesis of **Turc-* to **Truc-* for Tacitus's forms, and another metathesis for *Ravenna*'s of *(*T*)*urc-* to **Ucr-* **Ugr-*. There is unfortunately no evidence for the use of this 'boar' name in ancient toponymy in any region, nor of a deity with such a name who might have been present in water. The question must be left entirely open.

IDENTIFICATION. In addition to the possibilities mentioned by others, we indicate in Chapter II (p. 49 and notes) that an attractive identification might be with Sandwood Loch (Sutherland).

TUEROBIS (?)

SOURCE

Ptolemy II, 3, 2: Τουερόβιος ποταμοῦ ἔκβολαι (= TUEROBIS FLUVII OSTIA)

DERIVATION. Ptolemy's form suggests no Celtic roots. The MSS show no variants of note. Bradley in 1885 suggested that the modern *Teifi* river was intended, 'but this is phonologically impossible unless we read Τουεγόβιος instead of Τουερόβιος.' The point of this remark is that whereas *r* of British remains in Welsh, *g* of British is in many phonetic contexts lenited or altogether lost in Welsh, so that a form **Tuegobis* could indeed have produced Welsh *Teifi*. Certainly this identification suits the position which Ptolemy gives. Perhaps Bradley was right; however, although at first glance confusion of γ with ρ (*g* with *r*) would seem very likely, this is not common in Ptolemy MSS and there is no case of it in his British section; moreover, **Tuegobis* offers no ready analysis in Celtic terms, and *Teifi* could have derived from a variety of possible forms (though not from *Toesobis*, as Jackson makes clear in *LHEB* 523, note, in rejecting this suggestion by Förster). It is likely that the identification is right but that Ptolemy's entry is more corrupt than has been hitherto thought.

IDENTIFICATION. Probably the river Teifi, Cardiganshire.

TUESIS[1] (river)

SOURCE

Ptolemy II, 3, 4: Τούεσις εἴσχυσις (= TUESIS AESTUARIUM), var. Τούαισις (= TUAESIS), etc.

(Possibly *Ravenna* 108_5 belongs here; the entry is among habitation-names, but *Ravenna* often misreads an inland river-name from the map-source as a habitation-name; and *Tuesis* is not repeated among the entries in *Ravenna*'s river-list. See the next entry)

DERIVATION. Jackson in *PP* 151 thinks the root 'not demonstrably Celtic', no doubt because its root cannot be recognised in the modern languages derived from British, and has no cognate in Irish. It could indeed be pre-Celtic or even non-Indo-European. Watson *CPNS* 49 thought it constructed like *Tamesis* (*Tam-es-is*), and cited *Atesis* (*At-es-is*) > Adige, suggesting a root in **tu-* 'to swell' as in Latin *tumeo*. Ekwall *ERN* 423 indicates a base in **teu̯ā*, **tu-* as in Sanskrit *tavás* 'powerful' and *távisi* 'power'. Either of these roots would naturally make the name Indo-European. It is tempting to suggest an error on the map which was ultimately the source for both Ptolemy and *Ravenna* (with regard to North Britain) for a form **T(a)vesis*, that is British **Tau̯es-*, would make the name in structure an echo of *Tamesis* (above) and would be connected to the **ta-* **tə-* root from which so many river-names were formed in Britain and elsewhere (see TAMARUS, and more specifically TAVA); but the recorded versions give no hint which would justify this. There seem, otherwise, to be no analogues anywhere which would help to solve the problem. The Spey has a Gaelic name which does not derive from the ancient one (Watson *CPNS* 474).

IDENTIFICATION. The river Spey, Inverness-shire and Moray.

TUESIS[2] (place)

SOURCES

Ptolemy II, 3, 8: Τούεσις (= TUESIS), var. Τούαισις (= TUAESIS), a *polis* of the Vacomagi

Ravenna 108_5 (= R&C 212): TUESSIS

As mentioned in the previous entry, *Ravenna* may here have taken a river-name as a habitation-name.

DERIVATION. See the previous entry. As in other cases, a camp has simply taken the name of the river on which it stands.

IDENTIFICATION. The Roman camp at Bellie, Fochabers, Moray (NJ 3561), near the mouth of the Spey.

TUNNOCELO of *ND* XL_{51}: see ITUNOCELUM

UGRULENTUM (?)

SOURCE

Ravenna 108_3 (= R&C 208): UGRULENTUM

DERIVATION. None can be suggested; the entry is probably highly corrupt, and there are no analogues anywhere of names in *Ugr-*. The possibility of some connection with the *Trucculensis Portus* of Tacitus is attractive; see the discussion in that entry.

IDENTIFICATION. None, beyond the possible equation with *Trucculensis Portus* (itself uncertain), can be suggested.

UGUESTE

SOURCE

Ravenna 108_9 (= R&C 219): UGUESTE

DERIVATION. It is likely that this name, like the preceding, is corrupt, perhaps in similar ways. If taken more or less literally, it might have a first element related to that in such names as *Uggate* (*AI* 384_3, *TP*) now Pont de l'Arche near Rouen (Seine-Maritime, France), *Ugernum* (*TP*) now Beaucaire (Gard, France), *Ugernica insula* > Guernègues (Bouches-du-Rhône, France), and *Ugia* (*AI* 410_1 or *Ugium* (*Ravenna* 81_{52}) now Las Cabezas (Sevilla, Spain). However, the closest parallel is that provided by the Gaulish divine name *Ucuetis* (in the dative, *Deo Ucueti*, *Ucuete* in inscriptions: *EC*, VI (1953–54), 67; also *RIO*, XIV (1962), 178, and *Ogam*, XV (1963), 225) and the place-names *Ucetia* > Uzès (Gard, France: Holder III. 13) and *Ucesia* of the Cantabri now Villaviciosa (Avila, Spain), mentioned by Ptolemy II, 6, 6. The relationship and meaning of these are unknown.

If the name is corrupt, several possibilities suggest themselves. Initial *U-* could be a mistake for *Vi-*, as when *Virgaba* appears as a variant for *Urgapa* in *Ravenna* 81_{48}, or when *Vibisco* of *AI* 352_1 is written *Ubisco* in one MS. It is also the case that in Celtic speech reductions of the type *Uirdorix* > *Urdorix* occurred; see our discussion of this under VIROCONIUM. Then, since *b/v* are regularly confused in *Ravenna* and other texts, the present *Ugueste* could well be *Begesse* (via **Vigesse*) and be a duplication of this name at 107_{35}; the latter, if correct, has at least a reasonable etymology, and there is a related name, *Bigeste* in Dalmatia, not too remote from that under discussion. It should finally be noted that since *c* in *Ravenna* is often miscopied as *g*, a possible initial *Vic-* would open up other comparisons. Some of these corrections might apply to the previous name also.

IDENTIFICATION. Unknown, but apparently in Scotland north of the Antonine Wall.

UXACONA

SOURCE

AI 469_7 (Iter II): UXACONA

DERIVATION. The name is built up of British **uxo-* (earlier **ux-s-*from **up-s-*) 'high', perhaps by extension 'noble', with suffixes *-*āco-* (see BRAVONIACUM) and *-*ōno-* (see BREMETENACUM). Hence 'high place', perhaps 'noble place'. The **uxo-* element has cognates in Greek ὕψος, ὕψι, ὑψηλός, and in Latin *summus*; see also *Uxela*, etc., and Holder III. 59–67 for a rich documentation of it in ancient names. Among Continental place-names containing it are *Uxantis* > Ouessant (= Ushant; Finistère, France), **Oxone* > both Usson and Isson (Puy-de Dôme, France), and *Uxama* or *Uxamo* > Huémoz (Vaud, Switzerland), Exmes (Orne, France) and Osma (Soria, Spain). A Gaulish word containing it has been identified in the graffiti of La Graufesenque: *summa uxsedia* 'somme la plus élevée, total général' (tally of pots made), and *uxsedi*, *uxsedias*, etc., as a type of pot 'à bords plus élevés que les autres' (R. Marichal in *REA*, LXXVI (1974), 95–96 and 101, following Loth, Thurneysen, Whatmough, etc.).

IDENTIFICATION. The Roman settlement at Red Hill, Lilleshall, Salop (SJ 7210).

UXELA[1] (river: England)

SOURCE

Ptolemy II, 3, 2: Οὐεξάλλα εἴσχυσις (= VEXALLA AESTUARIUM), vars. Οὐξέλλα (= UXELLA, preferred by Müller), Οὐζέλλα (= UZELLA), etc.

It is possible that *Uxelis* of *Ravenna* 106_1 belongs here; the Cosmographer sometimes misread a river-name, written along an inland river-course on a map, as though it were a habitation-name (next entry).

DERIVATION. The name (single *-l-* in British and Latin) was adjectival and agreed with an unstated feminine noun, obviously 'water' or 'river'. It is based on **uxo-* 'high' (see UXACONA) and has left derivatives in Welsh *uchel* 'high', in Cornish and in Breton; there is also Irish *uasal* 'noble, high-born'. Applied to a river, the adjective is probably 'noble', but could, as often, be the name of the divinity of the stream (there is a dedication to a *Deo Uxello* in *CIL* III. 387).

IDENTIFICATION. From its position in Ptolemy this should be a Somerset river, either the Axe or the Parrett. Both of these names are of Celtic origin (for the later, see the discussion in Ekwall *ERN* 320–22), but in the case of the former it is perhaps possible that, as is suggested for ALAUNUS[1], the Anglo-Saxons adopted the generic name *Isca* in error for the proper name *Uxela*. Against this is the probable relation of Ptolemy's ISCALIS (q.v.) to the Axe. Unsolved.

UXELA[2] (fort: England)

SOURCES

Ptolemy II, 3, 13: Οὔξελλα (= UXELLA), a *polis* of the Dumnonii; vars. Οὐζέλα (= UZELA), Οὐεζέλα (= VEZELA)

Ravenna 106_1 (= R&C 13): UXELIS

As noted under *Uxela*[1], *Ravenna* could here be citing the river erroneously in the list of habitation-names (compare TUESIS for a similar case). *Ravenna*'s entry in *-is* can hardly mean a locative; *-is* for *-a* is a not uncommon error.

DERIVATION. See UXELA[1] and UXACONA. Here as often a habitation-name is simply that of the river on which the place stands.

IDENTIFICATION. Unknown, but apparently an early Roman fort in Devon or Cornwall.

UXELODUNUM

SOURCES

Rudge Cup: UXELODUM

Amiens patera: UXELODUNUM

Ravenna 107_{28} (= R&C 152): UXELLUDAMO, var. UXELODIANO

ND XL_{49}: Tribunus cohortis primae Hispanorum, AXELODUNO (var.: AXDODUNO)

DERIVATION. For the first element, see UXELA[1] and UXACONA; for the second, see BRANODUNUM. The sense is plainly 'high fort'. The miscopyings in the sources, of a name of which we are entirely certain, exemplifies a range of scribal processes. The Rudge Cup form results, however (like its *Camboglans*) from the need to abbreviate as the engraver squeezed names in round its rim. The name is of frequent occurrence in Gaul and has there given rise to problems of identification. Derivatives show varying degrees of development, e.g. the more popular Puy d'Issolu (Lot, France) and Issoudun (Indre, France), with learned interference.

IDENTIFICATION. The Roman fort at Stanwix, Cumberland (NY 4057), apparently garrisoned in the fourth century by the *Ala Augusta Gallorum Petriana Milliaria C.R.* This unit is not epigraphically attested here, and before A.D. 98 (when it is first called C.R. in diplomas) a standard-bearer of it was buried at Corbridge (*RIB* 1172). See discussion on p. 221.

UXELUM

SOURCES

Ptolemy II, 3, 6: Οὔξελλον (= UXELLUM), a *polis* of the Selgovae; vars. Οὔζελλον (= UZELLUM), Οὔξελον (= UXELUM)

Ravenna 107_{37} (=R&C 169): UXELA

DERIVATION. See UXELA[1] and UXACONA. Here the name is again adjectival, presumably corresponding to British **Uxelon* neuter; hence 'high (place)' or perhaps 'noble (place)'. In the endings,

Ptolemy is more likely to be right than *Ravenna*; the latter's form could have arisen via **Uxelo*, oblique case, with final *-o* miscopied as *-a*, as often; but it is always possible that the Cosmographer misread from a map the name of an unrecorded river *Uxela*, on which the fort *Uxelum* may have stood.

IDENTIFICATION. Perhaps the Roman fort at Ward Law, Caerlaverock, Dumfriesshire (NY 0266).

VACOMAGI

SOURCES

Ptolemy II, 3, 8: Οὐακομάγοι (= VACOMAGI)

Ravenna 107_{42} (= R&C 180): MAROMAGO

Ravenna's entry has not previously been associated with Ptolemy's. The proposal may seem extreme, but has its logic.

(*a*) As explained in Chapter V (p. 194), *Ravenna* takes up all Ptolemy's North British ethnic names except for very minor tribes which had probably been absorbed into larger groups by the time of the Severan revision of the military map; the sole exception among larger tribes has been the *Vacomagi*, and it is logical that they should figure in *Ravenna*.

(*b*) Their position in the list suits this equation well.

(*c*) The etymology assigned to *Maromago* by R&C and Williams, 'great plain', is superficially attractive but not sound. The adjective **maro-* 'great' is always a second element when compounded, in very numerous names of places and persons; one or two apparent exceptions, with *Maro-* in first place, turn out to have other etymologies, as is made clear by Schmidt in *ZCP*, XXVI (1957), 237–38.

(*d*) Other ethnic names of North Britain are already known to be listed as places in *Ravenna*.

(*e*) For the miscopying, compare initial *M-* for V- in *Mestevia* 106_3 for (*Anti*)*Vestaeum*. For *c* rendered as *r* there is no direct parallel, but it could have arisen via **Vatomagi* (*c*/*t* confusions are common) with *t* then copied as *r*, as in *Lutudaton* 106_{45} in one MS.

DERIVATION. Jackson *PP* 136 observes that this name 'cannot be said to be Celtic with any confidence', but in view of the Continental analogues, some of them with typically Celtic suffixes and formation, we need not be in doubt. Rhys (1904) 321 thought **vaco-* a borrowing from Latin *vacuus*, later *vacus* (the borrowing > *gwag* 'empty' does in fact exist in Welsh), giving a sense '(people of the) open plains', but Watson *CPNS* objected that this could not have been borrowed at an early enough stage to be present in Ptolemy; more fundamentally, it is not credible that the name of a tribe in Scotland should be formed with a Latin borrowing. The root is now widely accepted among Continental scholars as **u̯ek-* **u̯ak-* (Pokorny 1135) 'gebogen sein', the *Vacomagi* being 'die Bewohner der gekrümmten Felder'. From the same root comes Latin *vaccilare* and (via **u̯ek-to-*) Welsh *gwaeth*, a comparative, 'schlechter'. Ancient river-names include *Vacalus*, *Vacua*, and there are place-names *Vacontium* (Ptolemy II, 15, 4) in Pannonia Inferior, perhaps *Vagoritum* (Ptolemy II, 8, 7) of the Arvii in Gallia Lugdunensis, and ethnic names *Arevaci*, *Bellovaci*, *Vaccaei*, etc.; together with divine names and personal names listed by Ellis Evans

GPN 475–76. Whether all belong in effect to Pokorny's root, and whether the sense proposed fits them all, must remain in some doubt, which Ellis Evans expresses by listing the names in his Appendix. For *-magi*, see CAESAROMAGUS. This is recorded, though not frequently, in other ethnic names such as *Vehomagi*, *Vercomagi* (Holder II. 375). 'Crooked' or 'bent fields', as Pokorny expresses the sense of the *Vacomagi*, is not a particularly transparent concept; if the tribe typically had small, 'irregular fields' in hilly country, the sense might just fit, but one feels it to be unlikely that **magos* 'field, plain' would have been used for fields small enough to be perceived as 'crooked'. Ellis Evans's caution seems perfectly justified.

IDENTIFICATION. A people of Scotland of uncertain location. Ptolemy places them '*below the Caledonii*' and attributes to them *Bannatia*, *Tameia*, *Pinnata Castra* and *Tuesis*; there is no other evidence for their position and, as noted above (pp. 121 and 141), Ptolemy is not always reliable in his tribal attributions. Watson *CPNS* 22 says that they 'like the Caledonians appear to have occupied both sides of the Grampians, including Speyside and East Perthshire', but Ogilvie and Richmond, 43, rightly reject this: 'The Vacomagi of Strathmore are placed both there and in Banffshire, clean against topographical likelihood.' Their confidence in Strathmore, however, was based on their identification of *Pinnata Castra* with Inchtuthil, which weighted the balance three to one in favour of the southern area, and our restoration of the place to the southern shore of the Moray Firth makes the odds equal.

VAGNIACIS

SOURCE

AI 472_2 (Iter II): VAGNIACIS

DERIVATION. In a recent study in *BBCS*, XXVI (1974–76), 30–31 and 139–40, E. P. Hamp resolves the problem of what had seemed a mysterious name. He postulates a British **u̯āgnā* meaning probably 'marsh', the ancestor of Old Welsh *guoun* and Welsh *gwawn* 'moor, meadow', Breton *geun*, *yeun* 'marsh'; also Irish *fán* 'slope, valley'. To its yod-stem is added the suffix **-āco-* (see BRAVONIACUM) to give a sense 'marshy place', perhaps 'marshy-place estate'. For locative *-is*, see ANICETIS. There seem to be no other uses of this word in ancient toponymy.

IDENTIFICATION. The Roman settlement at Springhead, Southfleet, Kent (TQ 6172).

VARAR

SOURCES

Ptolemy II, 3, 4: Οὐάραρ εἴσχυσις (= VARAR AESTUARIUM), var. Οὐαράρις χύσις (= VARARIS...); again, II, 3, 8

Ravenna 108_{13} (= R&C 227): VORAN

It seems likely that *Ravenna*'s entry, otherwise unexplained, belongs with Ptolemy's; it has two errors of a common kind.

DERIVATION. The name could be either *Varar* or *Vararis*; Müller suggested that in both Ptolemy's entries Οὔραρις (= *Var-aris*) should be read, a syllable having been missed from the end of this in some MSS because of the similarity to the start of the following εἴσχυσις. If *Ravenna*'s

Voran belongs with this, however, it probably indicates a spelling with five letters. The origin of modern Gaelic *Farrar* in this is certain.

Older etymologies included Latin *varus* or *varius*, perhaps 'winding' of a river (MacBain), and it was suggested that in form the name was similar to the Gaulish *Arar* 'noted for its slowness and supposed to be connected with Welsh *araf* "slow"' (Watson *CPNS* 48). But the obvious solution is a root as in the next name, *Varis*. For this **u̯ara* is proposed, perhaps related to the second element in *Durnovaria* which is otherwise unexplained. Jackson in *Britannia*, I (1970), 79, says (of **u̯aro-* as found in Gaulish river-names) that 'The meaning "water" is often proposed, chiefly because it is so often the name of rivers, but the evidence for such a meaning in western Indo-European is poor, and in Celtic it is nil.' With regard to derivatives in the medieval and modern Celtic languages, that is obviously correct. Continental scholars, however, see the matter differently. Dauzat *TF* 115–18 remarks that Celticists long denied that there could be a Celtic **u̯ara* 'water', but thinks it now widely accepted that there was an Italo-Celtic word of that form and sense, corresponding to Sanskrit *var vari* 'water' and perhaps represented in Latin by *urina*. There is now an extensive bibliography of studies which agree with this; see e.g. Pokorny in *ZCP*, XXI (1940), 62; Nicolaisen in *BZN*, VIII (1957), 235; Krahe in *BZN*, XIII (1962), 275. Rostaing *ETP* 297–99 thinks the name pre-Indo-European, since it is found widely round the Mediterranean; he perceives a sense-development 'rocher > ravin > ruisseau'. Krahe also sees the name as one which 'aus einem Fl.N. der großen und weitbreiteten alteuropäischen Sippe stammt'. The most recent discussion of *Varar* along these lines is that of Nicolaisen in his book *Scottish Place-names* (London, 1976), 181–83; he thinks the name pre-Celtic but Indo-European, of a kind with such elements as **kar*(*r*)- (see VINDOGARA) and those in the river-names *Nassa*, *Nabarus*, etc.

Names known from ancient sources (Holder III. 104, etc.) include Ligurian *Varus* > Var (Var, France) and Venetian *Varanus* (Pliny *NH* III, 126; now the Stella?), and the following, all with recognised Celtic suffixes: **Varantia* or **Verentia* > Wernitz (Wörnitz) in Bavaria, a tributary of the Danube; *Vareia*, a settlement of the Celtic Berones, > Varia near Logroño (Spain); *Varenae* > Varennes-le-Grand (Saône-et-Loire, France); *Varenna* > Varenne (river of Orne, France; and several other places of the same name in France). In addition to these, there are scores of more recent names in *Var-* and *Ver-* (for which an ancient variation **u̯era* is supposed) in France and elsewhere, and many of these are in lands which were Gaulish-speaking; they are listed by Rostaing and Dauzat.

It seems, then, that we must accept the fact that the word was not originally Celtic, since Celtic forms and derivatives are lacking; but that a non-Celtic word was early adopted into Gaulish and also into British, if not as a common noun then at least for place-name formation (with Celtic suffixes, as shown above). The parallel is perhaps with words like *ville* and *polis*, which without at any time existing as common nouns in English are widely used in place-name formation in modern Britain and America respectively.

The present name then presumably has the *-*ar*(*a*) suffix found commonly in Celtic water-names; see LEUCARUM.

IDENTIFICATION. Here the Beauly Firth or more probably (since Ptolemy does not list the river Ness) the inner part of the Moray Firth as far as Chanonry Point (as observed by Watson *CPNS* 48). The name Beauly is a back-formation, and above Struy the river Beauly is still known as the Farrar (in Glen Strathfarrar).

VARIS

SOURCE
AI 482_7 (Iter XI): VARIS

DERIVATION. See the previous entry. For locative *-is*, see ANICETIS. A sense 'at the streams' would be appropriate. *TP* records a *Varis* (now Povija) in Dalmatia.

IDENTIFICATION. Almost certainly an unlocated Roman fort at St Asaph, Flintshire (SJ 0374), on the river Clwyd or its tributary the Elwy.

VEB...

SOURCE
Lead pigs originating in Somerset, seven in all, recorded as follows: *EE* III. 121a; *PSA*[2], XXXI (1918), 37; *JRS*, XXI (1931), 256; and a group of four found in 1956 at Rookery Farm, Green Ore, Wells (Somerset), *JRS*, XLVII (1957), 230–31. They are dated to A.D. 60–79 (Vespasian), and all bear the same text: BRIT(ANNICUM) EX ARG(ENTARIIS) VEB. There can be no doubt that VEB is a short form of the name of the mining district or of its centre.

DERIVATION. Since LVT on comparable lead pigs from Derbyshire contains the first three letters of *Lutudarum*, it is likely that VEB is the true start of the Somerset name. This makes it a rarity; the only place-name with these letters recorded in Holder III. 130 is *Vebritum* > Vebret (Cantal, France), but a variety of personal names is known, including *Vebro*, *Vebrius*, *Vebrumaros*, *Vebrumna*, all of normal Celtic form; for a complete list and references, see *GPN* 272. In view of our place-name, it is likely that a British cognate of this Gaulish **u̯ebro-* existed, and that it produced Welsh *gwefr* 'amber'; in Gaulish, the element was evidently used to signify 'fair-headed' in personal names. If this is the basis of our toponym *Veb-*, the reference to amber can hardly be literal, but presumably refers to the colouring of a geological feature; or it might be a personal name of the possessor of an estate with suffix, such as **Vebriacum*, for which there would be many analogies. This seems a better proposition (because of its vowel) than a derivation from a British cognate of Gaulish **u̯oberna* 'ruisseau plus ou moins caché' (Vincent 251–55), much used in toponymy; there are no ancient forms, but names derived from it in *Vabr- Vavr- Vévr- Voivr-* are common in France, and the root is represented by Welsh and Cornish *gover*, Irish *fobar*, etc., and possibly also by Latin *vepres* 'bush, thicket'.

IDENTIFICATION. Evidently the name of the lead-mining district in the Mendips, Somerset. For a possible name for the settlement at Charterhouse see ISCALIS.

VECTIS

SOURCES
Diodorus Siculus V, 22: Ἴκτιν (acc.; = ICTIM)
Pliny *NH* IV, 103: VECTIS

IV, 104: insulam MICTIM (acc.)

Suetonius VIII, 4, 1: insulam VECTEM (acc.)

Suetonius VIII, 4, 1: insulam VECTEM (acc.)

Ptolemy II, 3, 14: Οὐηκτίς (= VECTIS), var. Οὐικτίς (= VICTIS)

IM 509_2: VECTA

Ravenna 105_{29} (= R&C 303): VECTIS

Panegyric VIII (V), 15, 1: apud VECTAM insulam (acc.)

Eutropius/Paeanius: Βέκτην (acc.; = BECTEM)

Several problems arise in connection with these sources. There can be little doubt that the correct form is *Vectis*; this is nominative and singular, its accusative being **Vectim* or *Vectem*. However, first-declension *Vecta* seems to have existed also, since both *IM* and the Panegyric have it independently; it is moreover the standard form in Bede, who in seven mentions gives *Vectam* acc. (I, 3; I, 15; IV, 13; IV, 16), *Vectae* gen. (Preface; V, 23) and *Vectae* dat. (V, 19), and also names the inhabitants as *Victuarii, hoc est ea gens quae Vectam tenet insulam* (I, 15). Bede's source for this is not known; he knew Pliny, but did not follow him in this instance; he can hardly have known the *IM*, and there is no evidence that he was acquainted with the Panegyric.

Some have held that the *Ictis* of Diodorus is a separate name, and have identified it with St Michael's Mount (Cornwall). It is likely that Pliny's second mention, *Mictim*, should also be *Ictim* (nom. *Ictis*), its initial *M-* having arisen scribally by dittography, repeating final *-m* of *insulam*, or from a garbled transcription of *Οὐικτιν of Timaeus. It is true that Pliny seems unconscious of any duplication, but he is very vague about his first mention of *Vectis*, placing this with other islands *inter Hiberniam ac Britanniam*, and for his second mention he specifically says he is following Timaeus who was also the source for Diodorus. We need suppose, then, only one original version of (*V*)*ictis* for *Vectis*, in the Greek of Timaeus. W. Ridgeway in *JRS*, XIV (1924), 123–36, defending the equation *Ictis* = *Vectis*, cited a parallel: Greek 'Ικτούμουλαι = Latin *Victimulae*, among other arguments. There is further support for this from R. Schmittlein in *RIO*, XVII (1965), 279, and recently from C. F. C. Hawkes in *Pytheas: Europe and the Greek Explorers* (Oxford, 1977), 29–32. For a contrary view, see R. Dion in *REA*, LXXIII (1971), 403, citing a congress paper of 1968.

DERIVATION. One may suppose a British name **Ueχta* (hence *Vecta* in Latin, the forms in *-is* then being perhaps influenced by the Latin noun *vectis*, acc. *vectim*, on which see below). The best etymology of several that have been suggested is that of Förster *FT* 118, who sees the name as based on British **u̯ekto-*, cognate with Latin *vectis* 'lever' (and *vexo vexare* rather than the partial homonym *veho vehere*, according to Ernout & Meillet); a root represented by Irish *fecht* and Welsh *gwaith* (fem.), 'turn; time, occasion; course, journey, expedition'. These modern senses leave us still somewhat short of a sense applicable to an island, but Förster quotes an interpretation of the name of Wight in a thirteenth-century MS of Nennius: 'quam Britones insulam *Gueid* vel *Guith*, quod latine "divorcium" dici potest', noting that Latin *divortium* is 'fork in a road; watershed', and that British **u̯ekto-* could have developed a secondary sense similar to this; R&C add the useful gloss that this being so, the name could refer to the situation of the island 'in the fork of the Solent'. This may be right, if the unaided eye of early man could take in so much; possibly it is better to see in the name the idea of 'watershed', bearing in mind the currents and peculiar tidal habits of the Solent.

See *GPN* 281–85 for the third category of a large assemblage of names in *Vic-* *Vict-* *Vect-* which are probably related to the present name; among places, the closest analogue is perhaps the river *Victium* near Vercellae in Piedmont (Italy).

IDENTIFICATION. The Isle of Wight.

Note. Irish *Muir n-Icht* 'the English Channel' (a name which appears in the Irish Nennius) cannot, it appears, derive from *Vectis* or *Victis* – which would have given **Ficht* – but must come from *Ictis*. This does not mean, however, that we have to concede *Ictis* a true separate existence (and support the identification with St Michael's Mount). The obvious suggestion is that *Icht* derived from a learned tradition in Ireland, not from spoken British forms. All the early names of seas around Britain seem to be learned (Graeco-Latin), not British ones, and can have had no popular currency. The learned tradition in Ireland probably knew *(M)Ictim* in Pliny, just as he was known to Bede.

VEDRA

SOURCES

Ptolemy II, 3, 4: Οὐέδρα ποταμοῦ ἐκβολαί (= VEDRA FLUVII OSTIA)

Ravenna 108_{33} (= R&C 254): ADRON

The association of *Ravenna*'s entry with Ptolemy's was made by Pinder & Parthey, Holder, Müller, etc., and is repeated by Schnetz, who makes a correction to *U[e]dron*; *a* for *u* is a common copying error. Ptolemy's ending is the more likely to be correct, and his name has -α (*a*) in all but one of the MSS, which has -ου (*u*); but it is just possible that *Ravenna*'s *-on* (for *-um*, giving nominative **-us* as for other rivers) is correct also, the name being adjectival (see below).

DERIVATION. This name is inseparable from *Virvedrum*, a cape. Both have been explained as containing a Celtic **u̯edro-* 'clear', here feminine (if *Vedra*), presumably agreeing with 'water', and in *Virvedrum* a neuter qualifying 'cape' (Watson *CPNS* 36). But there seems to be no hard evidence for such a word in Celtic, and only Old Slavonic *vedru* 'clear' in support, first noted by Holder. Ekwall *ERN* 442 thinks the analogy doubtful, and prefers to derive the name from a root **u̯ed-* 'wet' (Walde-Pokorny I. 252), found with *r*-formation in *Vedra*, in Greek ὕδωρ, ὕδρα, Umbrian *utur* 'water', Anglo-Saxon *wæter*, *otr*, etc. The German river-name Wetter is then a precise equivalent of present *Vedra*. See also E. P. Hamp in *EC*, XII (1971), 547–50, on primitive **u̯odr/n* 'water'; and for further discussion of the group, Nicolaisen in *BZN*, VIII (1957), 236. There seems to be no reason to follow Ekwall into speculation that modern Wear (Anglo-Saxon *Wiur*) derives not from *Vedra* but from an unrecorded **U̯isur-*; see Jackson *LHEB* 362. A parallel is noted for the Wear (known in Welsh as *Gweir*) by Watson *CPNS* 360, when deriving the second part of the name of the river Traquair of Peeblesshire from another assumed *Vedra*: *-quair* corresponds to that same Welsh *Gweir*.

Jackson *LHEB* 431 remarks that *Adron* of *Ravenna* is a fossilised form, since *-dr-* > *-i̯r-* 'comparatively early in British'; but *Ravenna* was not necessarily using late Romano-British sources, and for rivers may have used the same map-source as that which was (ultimately) in Ptolemy's hands.

IDENTIFICATION. The river Wear, Durham.

VELOX (?)

SOURCE

Ravenna 108_{42} (= R&C 271): VELOX

DERIVATION. R&C doubtfully take this as the Latin adjective, 'swift'; but there are no Latin river-names in Britain, and the name is hardly likely to be a translation of a British adjective. Nor is it likely that it is a Latin adjective attached to the previous name, for this would be unparalleled in this text. The name is probably a corruption, with scribal assimilation to a well-known Latin word. The original cannot be conjectured, though Holder guessed *Uxelo*.

IDENTIFICATION. Unknown, but apparently a river in southern Britain.

VELUNIA or VELUNIATE

SOURCES

Inscription: *JRS*, XLVII (1957), 229–30 (= Burn, 1969, No. 135, pp. 104–105): an altar set up by the VIKANI CONSI[S]TENTES CASTEL[LO] VELUNIATE, found at Carriden in 1956

Ravenna 107_{52} (= R&C 191): VELUNIA

DERIVATION. It is unsure which of the two forms is preferable. The inscription naturally takes precedence, for *Ravenna* sometimes abbreviates, but it is not clear precisely what the inscription is expressing: a locative (Wright) or an ablative of place (nominative **Velunias*: Salway, *The Frontier People of Roman Britain* (Cambridge, 1965), 220), perhaps an adjective in abbreviated form, **Veluniate(nsi)*; possibly the name was – on the analogy of *Arelate* in Gaul – *Veluniate* in nominative, ablative and locative cases (Richmond and Steer, *PSAS*, XC (1956–57), 1).

In etymology the name is probably related to British **u̯ellaun-* perhaps 'good', for which see BOLVELLAUNIUM; hence perhaps 'goodly (place)'; if there is *-ate* suffix, see ATREBATES. The notable aspect of the name, whose vowel is guaranteed by the inscription (not later than the end of the second century) and not simply by *Ravenna*, is that whereas other Romano-British names based on **u̯ellaun-* all retain the *-au-* in fossilised form, here this diphthong has evolved not merely to *-ō-* as in *Alone*, *Alione*, but beyond that to *-ū-*, a development which Jackson *LHEB* 306 & 313 says occurred by the end of the third century. It thus records a second-century form taken from British speakers at the time of the occupation of the *vicus* at the fort, and represents a later stage than first-century names taken into official Latin usage with *-au-*. See also ALAUNA[1].

IDENTIFICATION. The Roman fort at Carriden, West Lothian (NT 0280).

VENICONES

SOURCES

Ptolemy II, 3, 9: Οὐενίκωνες (= VENICONES), vars. Οὐενίκωμες (= VENICOMES), Οὐεννίκωνες (= VENNICONES), etc.

Ravenna 107_{43} (= R&C 182): VENUTIO

Ravenna's entry has not hitherto been

associated with Ptolemy's, but it is in the right place in the list for mention of the tribe to be logical (in garbled form among place-names, as in other cases), and there is no great palaeographic problem, given frequent *t* for *c* and possibly an abbreviation *Venico* on a map, *ni* being misread as *nu* (compare in *Ravenna* 107_{17} *Lugunduno*, for which two MSS have *Lugundino*). R&C provide a picturesque etymology for *Venutio*, taken literally, citing the Brigantian chieftain *Venutius* mentioned by Tacitus; and are followed by Eric Birley, *Roman Britain and the Roman Army* (1961), 45–46.

RIB 1543, an altar *Die Minerve Venico*..., possibly contains the name of 'a Veniconian tribesman', but more likely it is a personal name formed on the same root, like others listed by Holder III. 169. *RIB* 639 (Ilkley) is not now read as containing *Venico-*.

DERIVATION. For the Indo-European root **u̯en-*, originally 'strive' then 'wish, love', and with further complex semantic changes, see Pokorny 1146. Derivatives include Latin *Venus*, *venia*, *venerari*, Anglo-Saxon *wine* 'friend', and in Old Irish *fine* 'tribe, stock, family'. For British and Gaulish, proper names are listed by Ellis Evans in *GPN* 277–79 (*Venicarus*, *Veniclutius*, *Venimarus*, etc.); see also L. H. Gray in *EC*, VI (1953–54), 64, and K. H. Schmidt in *ZCP*, XXVI (1957), 289–90. Jackson in *Britannia*, I (1970), 80, discussing British *Venonis*, thinks the base in British was **u̯eni-* with the probable sense 'family, kindred' for personal names, a sense preserved by Breton *gwenn* 'race'. In the present tribal name and in *Venedotia* > Gwynedd (N. Wales) the same sense might apply, but the suffixes of *Venicones* do not help us to elucidate it exactly. There is certainly a relationship of this name to that of the Οὐεννίκνιοι (= *Vennicnii*) people of Ireland, Ptolemy II, 2, 2, who are 'descendants of the tribe' with a second element as in BRANOGENIUM, but that second element is hardly present in that of *Venicōnes*, for its various reflexes seem never to show *-o-*.

IDENTIFICATION. A people of Scotland, placed by Ptolemy 'below' the *Vacomagi* and 'west' (i.e. south) of the *Taexali* of Aberdeenshire, with *Orrea* attributed to them. While this was identified as Carpow it was natural to locate them in Fife, but a position north of the Tay, in Strathmore, seems more likely.

VENONIS

SOURCES

AI 470_4 (Iter II): VENONIS
477_3 (Iter VI): VENONIS
479_4 (Iter VIII): VENNONIS

DERIVATION. For locative *-is*, see ANICETIS. For the base **u̯eni-*, see the previous entry. In the present name an older semantic content may survive in addition to senses listed there; Jackson in *Britannia*, I, 1970), 80, says that 'Interpretations of this sort [i.e. "family, kindred"] could only apply to *Venonis* if we assume a goddess-name **U̯enonā*, something like "the lovable one", used as a river-name and, with formative suffix, this applied to a town, perhaps **U̯enoni̯on*.' He adds that this is 'very hazardous', presumably because of the lack of analogies among place-names and lack of evidence for such a divine name. For **-on(o)-*, see BREMETENACUM. The name does not seem to have **-on-i̯o-n* as Jackson suggests, for that would be represented as latinised *-onium* as in other cases (see CANONIUM). As for the sense, we cannot suppose a river-name, for there is no river at the site, and we hardly need to suppose a divine name either; perhaps simply 'place of the family/tribe' is intended.

IDENTIFICATION. The Roman settlement at High Cross, Sharnford, Leicestershire (SP 4788).

VENTA BELGARUM

SOURCES

Ptolemy II, 3, 13: Οὐέντα (= VENTA), a *polis* of the Belgae

AI 478_2 (Iter VII): VENTA BELGARUM
483_2 (Iter XII, by error of the copyist): VENTA BELGARUM
486_{11} (Iter XV): VENTA VELGARUM, var. VELLGARUM

Ravenna 106_{18} (=R&C 41): VENTA VELGAROM, var. VELGARONI

ND XI_{60}: Procurator gynaecii in Britannis Ventensis (var.: bentensis)

ND's reference to the 'manager of the state weaving-works of *Venta* in Britain' is usually taken to refer to Winchester, following Haverfield (*VCH, Hampshire*, I, 292); on the possibility that it might refer to Caistor St Edmund, see W. H. Manning in *Antiquity*, XL (1966), 60–62, but for a full assessment see J. P. Wild, 'The *Gynaeceum* at *Venta* and its Context', *Latomus*, XXVI (1967), 648–76, with reference to other studies.

DERIVATION. See BANNAVENTA[1]. The sense is probably 'market of the Belgae'. *Venta* survives as the first syllable of Winchester. A memory of the Romano-British name survived accurately in Bede's time: *in civitate Venta, quae a gente Saxonum Uintancaestir appellatur* (III, 7), and again in III, 7; IV, 15 and V, 23; also an adjective *Ventanus* (V, 23). His source for this was probably ecclesiastical tradition, presumably continuous in this instance from late Romano-British times.

IDENTIFICATION. The Roman city of Winchester, Hampshire (SU 4829), capital of the *Belgae*.

VENTA ICENORUM

SOURCES

Ptolemy II, 3, 11: Οὐέντα (= VENTA), the *polis* of the Iceni

AI 474_6 (Iter V): ICINOS, var. ICIANOS
479_{10} (Iter IX): A VENTA ICINORUM Londinio

Ravenna 106_{54} (= R&C 103): VENTA CENOMUM

TP: AD TAUM

On the possibility that a mention in *ND* might refer to this *Venta*, see the previous entry, together with Wild's rebuttal. *TP*'s AD TAUM was long thought to refer to a distinct place, but G. H. Wheeler in *EHR*, XXXV (1920), 377–82, analysed it as *Ad (Ven)ta (Icenor)um*, the missing portions of this having been written on the lost first sheet of the map, and the remainder having been wrongly united when the surviving first sheet was copied; this reasoning has been generally accepted.

DERIVATION. For *Venta*, see BANNAVENTA[1], and for discussion of the use here of *Icinos*, see ICENI. The sense is probably 'market of the Iceni'.

IDENTIFICATION. The Roman city at Caistor St Edmund, Norfolk (TG 2303), capital of the *Iceni*.

VENTA SILURUM

SOURCES

AI 485_9 (Iter XIV): VENTA SILURUM

Ravenna 106_{22} (= R&C 48): VENTA-SLURUM

DERIVATION. See BANNAVENTA[1]. The sense is probably 'market of the Silures'. The name survives in part: it was *Cair Guent* in Nennius, and the name *Gwent* is now applied to a large administrative area of S. Wales.

IDENTIFICATION. The Roman city at Caerwent, Monmouthshire (ST 4690), capital of the *Silures*.

VENUTIO of *Ravenna* 107_{43} (= R&C 182): see VENICONES

VERATINO of *Ravenna* 106_{45} (= R&C 87): see VERNEMETUM

VERBEIA

SOURCE

Inscription: *RIB* 635, an altar set up at Ilkley (Yorks.) VERBEIAE SACRUM ... 'sacred to Verbeia'

Verbeia in this text is clearly the goddess of the river Wharfe, but given the equation elsewhere in Celtic lands of the divinity with the river, and identity of names, we are justified in taking *Verbeia* as a record of the river-name.

DERIVATION. Ekwall *ERN* 455 identifies a British base **Ụerb-* 'to turn, twist', cognate with that found in Anglo-Saxon *weorpan* 'to throw', Latin *verbena*, etc. It is probably the same root as that found in some Gaulish names such as *Verban(n)-os*, the old name of Lago Maggiore, perhaps in personal names *Verbacius*, *Verbigenus*, etc. (Holder III. 181). To this is added the suffix **-eịa*, for which see ARBEIA, of uncertain function. Hence 'winding river'. Ekwall goes on to note that the British name was later interpreted as containing Scandinavian *hverfr* 'winding', whence *Weorf* (963), *Werf* (1158) and modern Wharfe.

IDENTIFICATION. The name of the river Wharfe, and hence very probably also that of the Roman fort at Ilkley, Yorkshire (SE 1148), which (apart from the fourth-century fort at Newton Kyme) is the only important Roman foundation on it.

VERCOVICIUM

SOURCES

Inscription: *RIB* 1594 (Housesteads; = Burn, 1969, No. 147, pp. 113–14): an altar set up by the GER(MANI) CIVES TUIHANTI CUNEI FRISIORUM VER(COVICIANORUM); it dates to the reign of Severus Alexander, murdered in A.D. 225

Ravenna 107_{27} (= R&C 149): VELURTION (Schnetz lists no variants; R&C read VELURCION)

ND XL_{40}: Tribunus cohortis primae Tungrorum, BORCOUICIO (vars. BORCOUITIO, BOREOUITO)

There can be no doubt of the correct form of the name. It was long quoted as *Borcovicium*, following *ND*; the inscription, discovered in 1883, was not at first read as above, but it now provides evidence of the first syllable. In *ND*'s forms *b/v* is a common Vulgar Latin confusion, and *o* for *e* is a not uncommon copying error. *Ravenna*'s seriously confused entry has less reason behind it.

DERIVATION. *u̯erco- *u̯ergo- is listed by Holder III. 213 and Dottin *LG* 297 as a noun, 'work' (it is cognate with English 'work'), as found adjectivally when Latin *efficax* is glossed by Breton *guerg*, and as present in the Irish verbs *do(f)airci* 'efficit, parat' and *fairged* 'faciebat'. Its best-known appearance is in *vergobretus* (Caesar I, 16, 5: *vergobretum*, acc.), chief magistrate of the Aedui of Gaul, in other tribes, and attested on an inscription of Saintes (*CIL* XIII 1048) and on Gaulish coins; the title means 'judicio efficax' according to Zeuss. This has been very generally accepted, but is challenged by Guyonvarc'h in *Ogam*, XI (1959), 66–80; he does not think the Breton gloss satisfactory and notes that there are no modern descendants of the word *guerg*, but does not quite reach a conclusion about a new meaning. The element is known in a few personal names but in no other place-names. The second element is that discussed under DELGOVICIA, but the parallel of LONGOVICIUM is closer. The full sense is probably 'place of the **Vercovices*', and they are (despite Guyonvarc'h's reservation) 'effective fighters'. This need not imply the existence of an unknown tribe, for the name could be one applied by the British to the first Roman garrison of the fort, hypothetically British **U̯ercou̯ices*, with *-*i̯o*- (-*ium*) derivational suffix.

IDENTIFICATION. The Roman fort at Housesteads, Northumberland (NY 7968).

VERLUCIO

SOURCE

AI 486_4 (Iter XIV): VERLUCIONE

DERIVATION. The name represents British **U̯erlūci̯ū* for older **U̯erleuci̯ū*, nominative, accommodated in the Latin third declension; its sense is 'very bright place'. The Celtic prefix *u̯er- has as cognates *super* (*s-uper*), ὑπέρ, English *over*, etc.; in Gaulish *u̯er-, in British *u̯er- and later *u̯or-, represented in modern derivatives such as Welsh *gwor-*, *gor-*; in Cornish and Breton; also Irish *for*, *for-* 'on, over'. Its sense is thus intensive, 'very', and augmentative, 'great'. See for many names into which it enters Holder III. 179 and *GPN* 279–81. It is present in British *Vernemetum* 'fanum ingens' and *Virvedrum* (for **Ver*-), *Verturiones*, *Verubium*, also in the name of the famous Vortigern, **Vertigernos* 'superbus tyrannus' = 'great prince'. The base *luc*- is as in *Leuca* and related names (see LEUCA); the original diphthong is here reduced via *ō* to *ū* (see ALAUNA[1] and references there to *LHEB*). The name is completed by the derivational suffix *-*i̯o*-.

IDENTIFICATION. The Roman settlement at Sandy Lane, Calne, Wiltshire (ST 9667).

VERNALIS(?)

SOURCE

Ravenna 105_{49} (= R&C 8): VERNALIS, var. VERNILIS

DERIVATION. The name probably has British *u̯erno- 'alder', for which see DUROVERNUM. R&C thought the second part was a whole element related to Ptolemy's *Ila*, perhaps with a sense 'hasten, flow', hence for the whole name 'flowing amid alders'; but Continental analogues which have *Vern*- plus suffix make it much more likely that this is the case here. Examples are (Holder III. 217):

**Vernacum* 'alnetum', origin of three places on the Continent and of Fernagh, etc., in Ireland; *Vernate* > Verna (Isère, France); *Vernetum* > Vernet and similar in no fewer than 91 instances in France (also *vernetum* > *vernet*, a common noun in Provençal). For the rare suffix *-alis*, here Celtic rather than Latin, see ISCALIS; the sense is not known, but presumably has an adjectival force; thus for the whole name 'aldery (place)'. However, there can be no certainty of this; *Ravenna*'s forms are scarcely to be trusted to this extent, and this one is suspicious because it seems to be a nominative (hardly a locative plural) and nominatives are rare in *Ravenna*.

IDENTIFICATION. Unknown, but apparently a place in south-west Britain.

VERNEMETUM

SOURCES
AI 477_5 (Iter VI): VEROMETO
479_2 (Iter VIII): VERNEMETO
Ravenna 106_{45} (= R&C 87): VERATINO

The entry in *Ravenna* has not previously been associated with *AI*'s. But its eight letters correspond to the short form of the name in Iter VI, and if the latter figured on a map resembling *TP* and was read from that by the Cosmographer, there is no problem. The Cosmographer's eye was following road-stations in the Midlands in this section, but as usual, not in any wholly logical way; all the adjacent names can be identified with confidence, and it is natural that *Vernemetum*, otherwise omitted from *Ravenna*, should be mentioned here. There is no difficulty in supposing textual corruption at an early stage.

DERIVATION. For the prefix **u̯er-*, see VERLUCIO; for *nemeton*, see AQUAE ARNEMETIAE. The sense in British is thus 'very sacred grove' or 'great sacred grove'; but the reference may be to a construction (shrine or temple), since in Venantius Fortunatus I, 9, a Gaulish *Vernemetis* is glossed 'fanum ingens' (site unknown: near Agen, Lot-et-Garonne, France). There are several other Gaulish names of precisely this form, including a *Vernemetas* on Merovingian coins > Vernantes (Maine-et-Loire, France); see *RIO*, XIV (1962), 179, *DAG* 477–78. Whatmough thinks that *Augustonemetum* (now Clermont-Ferrand, Puy-de-Dôme, France) is probably a translation or renaming of another *Vernemetum*, and the same may be true of *Lucus Augusti* (Tacitus *Hist.* I, 66) > Luc-en-Diois (Drôme, France).

IDENTIFICATION. The Roman settlement near Willoughby on the Wolds, Nottinghamshire (SK 6425).

VEROMO (?)

SOURCE
Ravenna 108_2 (= R&C 206): VEROMO

DERIVATION. The name is corrupt, perhaps by misreading an abbreviation of a second part from a map. The first part might by **u̯er-* as in VERLUCIO, or perhaps better, *Vero- Viro-* as in many names. As R&C note, *-mo* might represent *-mago* (*magus*), and they cite records from Gaul in which this is certainly the case. Equally it might represent *-dono* (*dunum*), as in *Morionio* of *Ravenna* 106_{13} which requires only one further miscopying (*m* for *ni*, not uncommon) to produce *-mo*. Moreover, *Virodunum* is recorded elsewhere (e.g. > Verdun, France).

IDENTIFICATION. Unknown, but apparently a place in Scotland north of the Antonine Wall.

VERTERIS

SOURCES
AI 467_5 (Iter II): VERTERIS
476_4 (Iter V): VERTERIS
Ravenna 107_9 (= R&C 127): VALTERIS
ND XL_{11} (*pictura*): UERTERIS
XL_{26} (text): Praefectus numeri directorum, UERTERIS

DERIVATION. For locative *-is*, see ANICETIS. Jackson in *Britannia*, I (1970), 81, largely agrees with Williams in seeing here a British **u̯ertero-* meaning 'upper part, summit', built up from **u̯er-* (see VERLUCIO) and a contrastive-comparative formant **-tero* (as in Latin *alter*, English *either*), found also in the second part of *rhacter* (Welsh 'summit'). This has given a Welsh word *gwarther* 'summit' recorded in medieval verse and two personal names cited by Williams. Cognate formations are Sanskrit *vartra* 'dyke, dam' and German *Werder* 'embankment'. There seem to be no analogues in ancient toponymy elsewhere. The name is not related to that of the *Verturiones* of Scotland as was suggested by Holder, Rhys and Watson.

IDENTIFICATION. The Roman fort at Brough Castle, Westmorland (NY 7914).

VERTEVIA of *Ravenna* 106_1 (= R&C 14): see ANTIVESTAEUM

VERTIS (?)

SOURCE
Ravenna 106_{30} (= R&C 64): VERTIS

DERIVATION. R&C accept the entry and attempt an etymology. However, the name is almost certainly corrupt; it might well have the intensive prefix **u̯er-* (see VERLUCIO), but after that it seems too short by at least one syllable, probably when misread from a map-source. Another *Verteris* hardly seems possible here. The name might have locative plural *-is* (see ANICETIS), or *-is* might be a miscopying of *-a*, as often.

IDENTIFICATION. Possibly the Roman town of Worcester (SO 8554).

Note. Whatever its correct form, *Vertis* can have nothing to do with the name Worcester, which is first recorded in 691 as *Weogornaceaster*; the first element of this may be a genitive of an ethnic name, **Weogoran*, this deriving ultimately from a British equivalent of the Gaulish river-name *Vigora* perhaps 'winding river' (whose name survives in Wyre); it is uncertain which river in the area is referred to. See M. Gelling in *Transactions of the Worcestershire Archaeological Society*[3], II (1968–69), 26.

VERTURIONES

SOURCE
Ammianus Marcellinus XXVII, 8, 4: VERTURIONES (acc. pl.), var. VECTURIONES; a people who with the *Dicaledones* made up the *Picti*.

DERIVATION. The older etymology (Stokes, Holder, Rhys, Watson *CPNS* 68–69) connected the name with a supposed Welsh *gwerthyr* 'fortress', but Williams and others have doubted if such a word existed. It is found in local names but without early attestation, and seems not to be recorded in literature until 1753

(Thomas Richards's dictionary), after which it was used by antiquarians (*GPC*, s.v., without reference to the present name for an etymology). F. G. Diack in *RC*, XXXVIII (1920–21), 121–22, had already indicated a division *Ver-turiones* 'very powerful', with intensive prefix **u̯er-* (see VERLUCIO) and *Turiónes*, a tribal name equivalent to *Turoni-Turones* of Gaul (> Tours). O'Rahilly *EIHM* 463–64 accepts this. The base is then **trēno-* (earlier **trexno-*) 'strong', now represented by Welsh *trenn* 'impetuous, strenuous' (briefly mentioned under our *Traxula*), with a form of development shown by many Gaulish personal names such as *Tŭros Tŭrus* (from which came *Turones*) and *Tŭrio- Tŭria* (from which **Turiones*); Holder II. 2006, etc. The British name was taken into Gaelic as *Fortrenn*, the name of a region, a genitive of a notional nominative **Fortriu* (dative *Fortrinn*), on which see Wainwright *PP* 21; this name has British **u̯or-*, a later stage of **u̯er-*. It may be significant for the history of the North British tribes that the place Dumyat, which preserves the name of the *Maeatae*, is in Fortrenn.

IDENTIFICATION. A people of Scotland, not recorded earlier than the fourth century, who inhabited Fortrenn (i.e. Strathearn and Menteith, Perthshire).

VERUBIUM PROMONTORIUM

SOURCE

Ptolemy II, 3, 4: Οὐερουβίουμ ἄκρον (= VERUBIUM PROMONTORIUM), var. Βερουβίουμ (= BERUBIUM)

Note that here, and for *Tarvedu(nu)m* and *Virvedrum*, Ptolemy exceptionally transmits the termination as *-um* (not *-on*)

DERIVATION. Holder III. 249 marked the name 'Pictish', but went on to list what are evidently related names of fully Celtic kind, especially *Verubius* > Verebbio (Italy). The name might contain **u̯eru-* 'broad', which some have seen in *Verulamium*, as proposed by Holder; but since the existence of this in Celtic seems doubtful, it is better to retain the suggestion of Watson *CPNS* 36–37, that the name is *Ver-ub-ium*, from British **u̯er-*, intensive prefix (see VERLUCIO), together with an element **ub-* later represented by Irish *ubh* 'point'; with the common **-i̯o-* suffix. Hence 'pointed cape'. Watson draws attention to the *Ubii* people of the Rhineland.

IDENTIFICATION. Noss Head, Caithness.

VERULAMIUM

SOURCES

Coins of Tasciovanus, who ruled from about 20 B.C. to about A.D. 10, have the legends VER, VERL, VERO, VERLAMIO and VIR (Mack Nos. 152–92 *passim*).

Inscription: A monumental inscription of the governorship of Agricola, A.D. 79, was found in fragmentary state in 1955, and published in *JRS*, XXXVI (1956), 8–10 (also Burn, 1969, No. 40, pp. 39–40). In line 6 there survives VEỊ: 'from the letter which follows VE there remains a vertical with the left portion of two serifs. Either L or R is readable, so VEỊ may be part of CIVITAS CATU]VEL [LAUNORUM] or RES PUBLICA] VER [ULAMIENSIUM] or MUNICIPIUM] VER[ULAMIUM].' The last version is that quoted by several authorities, including Frere, *Britannia*[2] (1974), 232.

Tacitus *Annals* XIV, 33: Municipio VERULAMIO (dative)

Ptolemy II, 3, 11: Οὐρολάνιον (= UROLANIUM), a *polis* of the Catuvellauni

AI 471_3 (Iter II): VEROLAMIO

476_8 (Iter VI): VEROLAMI

479_8 (Iter VIII): VEROLAMO

Ravenna 106_{50} (= R&C 96): VIROLANIUM

The name is recalled by Gildas (11), in connection with the martyrdom of St Alban in A.D. 286: he calls the saint adjectivally *Verolamiensem* (acc.), with many vars. (see Chapter II). In connection with the same martyrdom Bede also knew the name through ecclesiastical tradition: *Passus est autem beatus Albanus ... iuxta civitatem Verolamium, quae nunc a gente Anglorum Uerlamacaestir sive Uaeclingacaestir appellatur* (I, 7).

The sources show, then, *Ver-* on the whole, with *Vir-* among the early coins when, in writing British names for the first time, some uncertainty about Latin letters was natural. *Ravenna*'s *Vir-* is probably of little account; it might be accidental, or an unconscious assimilation to British *Viroconium* and numerous Continental names having *Viro-*. Records with the second vowel *-o-* may state a genuine variant (already present in the coin-legends), or in later instances may show the Vulgar Latin development *ŭ* > *o* (as in *Camoloduno AI* 480_4, *Eboracum*, etc.). Ptolemy's form is curious. Müller indicated that one should read for it Οὐερολάμιον (= VEROLAMIUM), but it is worth noting that a reduction of Celtic **U̯er-* to **U̯r-* in initial position can take place (see VIROCONIUM), so that Ptolemy may be recording a genuine phonetic variant.

It seems safe, on balance, to take the tradition *Verulamium* as the correct Romano-British form.

DERIVATION. This has been much discussed, without a consensus emerging. Jackson after analysing opinions in *Britannia*, I (1970), 80–81, thinks the name 'unsolved'. R&C's proposal of **u̯er-* intensive prefix plus **lāmo-* **ulāmo-* 'slimy' is not satisfactory on various grounds, especially (Jackson) that this word is not documented in Celtic. Similarly Jackson rules out a formation **U̯erulāmi̯on* based on a personal name **U̯erulāmos* 'broad-hand' (**u̯eru-* 'broad' plus **lāmā* 'hand'), partly because Celtic **u̯eru-* is undocumented, partly because Anglo-Saxon *Werlame-* could not have derived from a British name having *-ā-* (but *-a-* could have been retained by Latin influence? – see the forms of Gildas and Bede). The coin evidence is inconclusive, since although it shows *Ver* (suggesting a first element) it also shows *Vero*.

It seems however that we should retain the possibility of a British **u̯eru-* 'broad'. With some doubt, Ellis Evans in *GPN* 124 thinks it could have existed, citing cognates in Sanskrit *urú* 'wide, far' and Greek εὐρύς. Some such element needs to be postulated in order to explain the personal names with **u̯eru-* and not **u̯er-*, which are certainly Celtic, such as *Verucloetius* perhaps 'far-famed'. In toponymy the only parallel is *Verulani*, an *oppidum* in the region of Rome mentioned by Pliny *NH* III, 64. See also, perhaps, the previous entry. The Belgic site is large and too diverse in topography for this to be called in with hints about the meaning of *-lam-*. Possibly both elements were very ancient ones, still used traditionally in name-formation but no longer present in the spoken languages of post-Roman Celtic Britain when written records began.

IDENTIFICATION. The Roman city on the west side of St Albans, Hertfordshire (TL 1307). The status of the place is disputed. That Tacitus is using the term *municipium* in its technical sense is made probable by the fact that in the same chapter he has remarked that London did not hold the title of *colonia*, though he may have been writing anachronistically. The text of the inscription is uncertain (see above), but a further indication that the town did achieve municipal rank is the absence of a tribal suffix in any of the itinerary references, and perhaps the erection in it of two commemorative arches. On the other hand the *Catuvellauni*, of whose *civitas* it should be the capital, continue to be referred to as such (*RIB* 1065, 1962), and not as *Verulamienses*. On the complicated questions surrounding the legal status of such communities see A. N. Sherwin White, *The Roman Citizenship* (2nd edn, Oxford, 1973), Chapters XIV and XV.

Note. It was the Anglo-Saxon *Væclingas*, referred to by Bede, who gave their name to Watling Street (Anglo-Saxon *Wæclingastræt*). Originally it described only the Roman road from London to St Albans, and the extension of the name to other Roman roads in England was a later development.

VICTORIA

SOURCES

Ptolemy II, 3, 7: Οὐικτωρία (= VICTORIA), a *polis* of the D(u)mnonii

Ravenna 108_{11} (= R&C 224): VICTORIE

It is to be noted that Ptolemy transliterates without translating. *Ravenna*'s form is possibly a locative, with Vulgar Latin *e* representing classical *ae*, as often; but it may be a simple miscopying of nominative *-a*. It is not necessary to suppose it a genitive, as R&C do, postulating a missing noun such as *castellum* (with Continental analogues).

DERIVATION. The name is Latin, 'victory'. No actual Roman victory need be in question (R&C); still less should the name be related to a rescue of the IX Legion as Ogilvie and Richmond think in their edition of the *Agricola* (1967), 243–44. The naming is probably due to the fact that the XX Legion *Victrix* garrisoned the fortress.

IDENTIFICATION. The Roman legionary fortress at Inchtuthil, Caputh, Perthsire (NO 1239).

VILLA FAUSTINI

SOURCE

AI 474_5 (Iter v): VILLAFAUSTINI

DERIVATION. The name is Latin, 'estate of Faustinus'. Eight other villas are included in the *AI*, one in Italy and seven in Africa (see Chapter IV, note 1, p. 163); but of these only one, *Minna Villa Marsi* 63_1, has the form *villa* + personal name in the genitive. The present name is to be grouped with other Romano-British estate-names having locative plural versions of the personal name, listed under ANICETIS; see also *ALBINIANO.

IDENTIFICATION. Uncertain. Either the Roman settlement at Scole House, Scole, Norfolk (TM 1478), or that near Stoke Ash, Suffolk (TM 1170); see the discussion in Chapter IV, p. 163.

VINDOBALA

SOURCES

Ravenna 107_{25} (= R&C 145): VINDOVALA

ND XL$_{36}$: Tribunus cohortis primae Frixagorum, VINDOBALA

DERIVATION. The first element is British **ụindo-* 'white', also 'bright, fair' and 'happy, fortunate', now represented by Welsh *gwyn*; also Old Irish *find*, Irish *finn*, *fionn* (English *winter* 'white time'). This is a first element in the five following names, and is frequently represented in Continental toponymy from Illyria and Pannonia to Spain; it is also present in many personal names, e.g. British *Vindomorucus* (*RIB* 2053, Drumburgh). In some Continental regions Celtic **ụindo-* is to be distinguished from an element of similar appearance, **vin-* **vin-t-*, a pre-Indo-European word meaning 'mountain' (Rostaing *ETP* 290). Examples of names with **ụindo-* which survive include *Vindobona* > Vienna, *Vindonissa* > Windisch (Switzerland) and *Vindobriga* > Vendoeuvre (eight in France and one in Switzerland).

The second element requires us to trust *ND*'s *-bala* rather than *Ravenna*'s *-vala* (*ND* is in any case the more trustworthy of the two texts). The name hardly contains the root **ụal-* 'strong', as R&C thought, for if it did, we should expect it to appear as *-valium* (or *-vallum*) in the present name, as in other British examples (see BANNOVALIUM). Moreover, R&C's meaning 'white strength' seems unnatural. Nor is it likely that both *ND* and *Ravenna* have committed identical errors in miscopying *r* as *l*, despite the temptation to make an association with a **Vindovara* 'eau blanche' postulated by Dauzat in Gaul (*TF* 116–17), and there is no consonant present in the British name which could have provoked an *r–l* metathesis. If we take *-bala*, it seems right to associate this with the root **bal-* discussed under **Nemetobala*; a meaning for the whole of 'white peak', perhaps 'bright peak', seems proper.

IDENTIFICATION. The Roman fort at Rudchester, Northumberland (NZ 1167). *ND*'s unit name is evidently a garbled form of *Cohors I Frisiavonum*, whose earlier presence in Britain is attested by diplomas and who probably formed the garrison of Rudchester in the third century (see *RIB* 1395, note).

VINDOCLADIA

SOURCES

AI 483_5 (Iter XII: by error of the copyist): VINDOGLADIA

486_{14} (Iter XV): VINDOCLADIA

Ravenna 106_{17} (= R&C 38): BINDOGLADIA

Confusions of *c/g* are common in our texts; it is noteworthy that the copyist of *AI* was not consistent even within his own work. *Ravenna* also has this error, and has Vulgar Latin *b* for *v*, as often.

DERIVATION. The name is British **Ụindocl̄adiā*. For **ụindo-*, see VINDOBALA. The second element has a base in British **clad-* 'to dig' or **clādo-* 'ditch' (Welsh *clawdd* 'ditch'), literally 'that which is dug'; hence for the whole name, 'white ditches', with reference to defences cut in chalk (Jackson, *Britannia*, I (1970), 81).

IDENTIFICATION. The Roman settlement at the road-junction beside the Iron Age hill-fort of Badbury Rings, Dorset (ST 9603), from which the name was derived.

VINDOGARA (?)

SOURCES

Ptolemy II, 3, 7: Οὐινδόγαρα (=VINDOGARA), a *polis* of the D(u)mnonii; this form is not present in any of the MSS, which have Οὐανδόγαρα (= VANDOGARA), Οὐανδούαρα (= VANDUARA), but is required by analogy with the form in II, 3, I (next entry)

Ravenna 107_{30} (= R&C 156): BROCARA

Ravenna's entry has not hitherto been associated with Ptolemy's. Superficially it looks like another *Broc-* name. As argued in Chapter V (p. 194), however, almost all Ptolemy's North British *poleis* were taken up by *Ravenna*, logically, since both ultimately depended on the same map. *Brocara* is in the right part of *Ravenna*'s list for it to be equated confidently with *Vindogara*. For the palaeography, one must suppose a seriously garbled first part of the name in the archetype, probably with *-n-* abbreviated, and of course Vulgar Latin *B-* for *V-*.

DERIVATION. For **u̯indo-*, see VINDOBALA. The second element does not correspond to any obvious Celtic root. Watson *CPNS* 32 alludes hopefully to Gaelic *gar*, *garan* 'thicket', and to the possibility that the place called *Girvan* (older *Garvane*) continues the ancient name. No element resembling *-gara* is attached to *Vindo-* in any of the numerous Continental names. The possibility then is that Ptolemy's form is corrupt in a further way. His *Vindo-* (from II, 3, I) is to be retained, but for a second element *-mara* (for *-mora*?: suitable for a coastal site) or *-bara* (for *-vara*) are possibilities, and there are others; however, errors of copying involving γ and μ (*g* and *m*), γ and β (*g* and *b*) are not common and not present elsewhere in Ptolemy's British section. In any case, since all the MSS have -γαρα (*-gara*), the error, if there is one, goes back to the archetype and perhaps to Ptolemy's source of information.

There is a possibility that *Ravenna* with its *-cara* could be right. If this is so, none of the purely Celtic **caro-* roots documented by Ellis Evans in *GPN* 162–63 (much more common as the first element in compounds than as the second) seems to fit for sense, but it may be worth following up one – two? – root(s) additionally mentioned there, Indo-European **kar-* 'hard', etc., Pokorny 531, and possibly pre-Indo-European **kar(r)-* 'stone, rock', which may be related to it. There is now an ample bibliography on this theme, including, for example, Dauzat *TF* 81–90 on **car(a)* in Gaul, and Nicolaisen in *BZN*, VIII (1957), 247–50, with very numerous water-names in *Car-* from modern Britain; see also the references in *GPN*. It is Dauzat's view that if this root was in origin non-Celtic, it 'a dû être adopté par le celtique commun' (83); and if the word was as fully present in Gaulish as Dauzat implies, there is no reason why it should not have been present also in British. In some regions of the Continent this **car(a)* appears as **gar(a)*, which might mean that both Ptolemy and *Ravenna* are correct in their spellings, at least of this element. Plainly a sense 'white rock, bright rock' would be straightforward for *Vindogara* or **Vindocara*, and is precisely paralleled by Gaulish *Caralba*.

In view of textual uncertainties, there can be no confident assertion of any etymology, but that adduced in the preceding paragraph is the most attractive. See also *CALACUM.

IDENTIFICATION. An unlocated Roman fort or camp near Irvine Bay, Ayrshire.

VINDOGARA SINUS

SOURCE

Ptolemy II, 3, 1: Οὐινδόγαρα κόλπος (= VINDOGARA SINUS), vars. Οὐιδόγαρα (= VIDOGARA), Οὐιδόταρα (= VIDOTARA), Οὐινδόχαρα (= VINDOCHARA)

DERIVATION. See VINDOGARA. None of the variants for the present name is attractive in helping us to solve the problem, but they do at least point to uncertainty about the second element.

IDENTIFICATION. Irvine Bay, Ayrshire.

VINDOLANDA

SOURCES

Inscription: *RIB* 1700 (= Burn, 1969, No. 172, p. 125), an altar dedicated by the VICANI VINDOLANDESSES (late second or early third century), found at Chesterholm

Ravenna 107_{12} (= R&C 132): VINDOLANDE

ND XL_{41}: Tribunus cohortis quartae Gallorum, VINDOLANA

For the Vulgar Latin assimilation *-ns-* > *-ss-* in the inscription, compare RIB 1905 under BANNA. *Ravenna*'s entry might show V.L. *-e* for *-ae*, locative, but this case does not appear in its records of Hadrian's Wall forts having singular form, and the *-e* is probably a simple miscopying of *-a*. *ND*'s form in *-lana* might just show V.L. assimilation of *-nd-* > *-nn-*, of which sporadic instances are known in Imperial times in some regions, including Britain; the assimilation could not be a British one, for this did not occur until the end of the fifth century (Jackson).

DERIVATION. For **u̯indo-*, see VINDOBALA. British **landā* may have meant originally, if the Gaulish equivalent is a guide, 'terrain plat, peu fertile, couvert de broussailles et de plantes sauvages' (*RIO*, IX (1957), 35), a sense which survives in French *lande* 'heath' and the well-known Les Landes. The Welsh and Breton derivatives, *llan* (Irish *land*), etc., have senses which have evidently evolved via 'rough meadow' > 'small enclosed meadow' > 'enclosure' > 'churchyard, church, monastery'. The complete name is unlikely to have had a sense 'white' in it, but was perhaps 'bright moor' (with heather in flower?) or 'fair moor'.

IDENTIFICATION. The Roman fort at Chesterholm, Northumberland (NY 7766), garrisoned in the third century by *Cohors IIII Gallorum* (*RIB* 1685–1688, 1705–1706, 1710).

Note. *Vindolanda vicus* may have continued, or replaced, a native *Curia Textoverdorum*. See the entry for this.

VINDOMORA

SOURCE

AI 464_4 (Iter I): VINDOMORA

DERIVATION. For **u̯indo-*, see VINDOBALA. The second element is (if *AI*'s entry is to be trusted) the plural of British **mori-* 'sea', for which see MORICAMBE. As mentioned under MORIDUNUM[1], this word could apply to inland waters, though it is documented only of extensive ones; if it is present here, it would apply to a broadening of river-waters or to a small lake. Ellis Evans in *GPN* 233 accepts this as a *mori- name, but if this is too strained semantically, it is possible that there was a British equivalent to Gaulish *mori- '*fanum*, temple' (*GPN* 103, 232; by allusion only); or such a word could have been imported by Gaulish troops. It is always possible that a name recorded in a single source, as here, is corrupt; one notes, for example, that even such a well-known city as *Vindobona* (Vienna) can appear in *AI* 233_8 as *Vindomona*, in *ND* xxxiv_{25} as *Vindomara*, in *ND* xxxiv_{28} as *Vindomana*, and in Jordanes as *Vindomina*, so that on such analogies a very different second element could be envisaged in the present instance. However, the probability is still that *Vindomora* 'bright waters' is correct. The man who was in charge of building a stretch of wall or doing repairs at or near Drumburgh, and who recorded the fact as *Pedatura Vindomoruci* (*RIB* 2053; A.D. 369?) has a name which presumably means 'man of *Vindomora*', or which is at least formed in the same way; for suffixes *-ūc-i̯o-, see CICUCIUM.

IDENTIFICATION. The Roman fort at Ebchester, Durham (NZ 1055).

*VINDONIUM (?)

SOURCE
AI 486_{10} (Iter xv): VINDOMI
483_1 (Iter XII, by error of the copyist): VINDOMI

DERIVATION. The entry may be taken fairly literally (i.e. without supposing that a second element has been abbreviated) in view of parallels in Gaul, e.g. personal names *Vindonio*, *Vindonius*, and the divine name *Vindonnus*; see Holder III. 349. *Vindinum* was the old name of Le Mans. These assure us that we may legitimately postulate a name formed from British *u̯indo- 'white' (see VINDOBALA) and suffixes *-on-i̯o- as in CANONIUM, presumably with a sense 'white place', i.e. one on chalky ground. The correction to *-oni* in *AI*'s entry is easy; the name appears to be a locative like *Sorvioduni AI* 483_4.

IDENTIFICATION. Probably the Roman settlement at the Wheatsheaf Inn, North Waltham, Hampshire (SU 5645).

VINION (?)

SOURCE
Ravenna 109_{12} (= R&C 282): VINION

DERIVATION. The name might have any one of a number of roots *u̯in- *u̯en-, discussed for preceding names; superficially an association with *Vinovia*/*Vinovium* seems attractive. But *Ravenna*'s forms are hardly to be trusted to the point of warranting speculation in a case like this, especially as the uncorroborated form may be corrupt. Dillemann (p. 72) suggests it may represent Cape *Vennicnion* of Ptolemy II, 2, 1, that is, part of the Irish coast misread by the Cosmographer from a map as though the name were that of a Scottish island. Equally, the name might represent, as do others in the two sections of island-names, a western Scottish river.

IDENTIFICATION. Unknown. Though it appears in the island list, it is not certain that this is an island, for reasons given above.

VINOVIA or VINOVIUM

SOURCES

Inscription: *RIB* 1036, an altar set up by a soldier who was EX C FRIS VINOVIE, expanded by *RIB* as *ex c(uneo) Fris(iorum) Vinovie(nsium)*

Ptolemy II, 3, 10: Οὐιννοούιον (= VINNOVIUM, in U and most MSS), var. Οὐινοούιον (= VINOVIUM, preferred by Müller)

AI 465_1 (Iter I): VINOVIA

Ravenna 107_{13} (= R&C 134): VINOVIA, var. VINONIA

In the inscription, *RIB* expands to give an adjectival form of the name; but it is perfectly possible that *Vinovie*, which occupies a full line, is complete in itself as a Vulgar Latin locative of the place-name.

DERIVATION. As between *-nn-* (Ptolemy) and the other texts with *-n-* it is impossible to judge. The difference in endings, neuter *-ium* (British **-i̯on*) in Ptolemy and feminine *-ia* in the other texts (the inscription, if adjectival, could be based on either), is curious; possibly there was an early and a later form of the name. In any case British suffixes together making up **-ou̯i̯o-* are involved (compare CANOVIUM). Jackson in *Britannia*, I (1970), 81, thinks the **u̯in-* element obscure, dismissing R&C's proposal of **u̯en-* (as in Welsh *gwen* 'smile') on the grounds that the name would need to be **Venovia* at the early date of the texts, and this form nowhere appears; moreover, it is hard to see how such a meaning could be used in place-name formation. Pre-Indo-European **vin-* 'mountain' can hardly be in question. There is one exact parallel in an inscription which mentions *Vinovie[nses]* in Germania Inferior, at a place now called Vein; see Whatmough *DAG* 933. The name must be regarded as unsolved.

IDENTIFICATION. The Roman fort at Binchester, Durham (NZ 2131).

Note[1]. See MORBIUM for an emendation to the text of *ND*, which is not acceptable.

Note[2]. Jackson in *Britannia* rightly notes that the name Binchester cannot come directly from the British **U̯inou̯i̯a* or **U̯inou̯i̯on*, giving detailed reasons in *LHEB* 89 (note 2) and 260 (note 5): principally that a British initial *U̯-* is taken into Anglo-Saxon as *W-*, so that if there had been direct derivation one would expect *Winchester. Ekwall *EPN* thought the first element of Binchester was perhaps Anglo-Saxon *binn* 'manger', later 'stall', adding that 'The old fort may have been used as a shelter for cattle'. Jackson seems to prefer this explanation, but is prepared to allow that 'At most, influence of Anglo-Saxon *binn* "manger" on **Win-ceaster* might be postulated.' This seems right; when we have a Romano-British *Vin-*, and an Anglo-Saxon settlement on the same spot called *Bin-*, it would seem obvious to admit the folk-etymology as an influence in the continuation of the old name – a continuation surely indicated by the *-chester*.

Note[3]. A further interesting survival is discussed by O. G. S. Crawford in *Antiquity*, IX (1935), 287. Arthur's eighth battle was fought, according to Nennius (56), *in castello Guinnion*. Crawford notes that objection had been made to the indentification of this with *Vinovia* on phonetic grounds, rightly; but Crawford seems not to have noted that Ptolemy's alternative *Vinnovium* (British **U̯innou̯i̯on*) brings us very close to the later name set down by Nennius. There is still a problem, however, in that *Vinnovium* should have given in Old Welsh at this stage a form in *-wy*, or similar; but it could be that *-ion* has been maintained as a learned form. Crawford, even without this support, thought that the identification should not be entirely rejected, and he was surely right (Holder III. 354 supported the equation too).

VIROCONIUM CORNOVIORUM

SOURCES

Ptolemy II, 3, 11: Οὐιροκόνιον (= VIROCONIUM), a *polis* of the Cornovii

AI 469_6 (Iter II): URIOCONIO, var. URIOCUNIO

482_{9-10} (Iter XII): VIROCONIORUM

484_9 (Iter XII): VIRICONIO, vars. UIROCONIO, UIRICONIO

Ravenna 106_{40} (= R&C 79): UTRICONION CORNOVIORUM

Coins: of Carausius, seven (including two found at Wroxeter) have the mintmark BRI, possibly for BRICONIUM, but see N. Shiel, *The Episode of Carausius and Allectus* (BAR 40, Oxford, 1977), 177–180, dismissing this interpretation.

The form in *AI* 482_{9-10} perhaps results from a conflation of the city-name with the tribal name, even though the latter is not present in the other itinera. *Ravenna*'s entry *Utri-* could be a miscopying of *Viri-*, but could also result from a scribal assimilation to Latin *utri-*.

DERIVATION. In its strict form the name probably had *Viro-*, but *Viri-* could be a spoken form, by assimilation. The etymology has been much debated and remains unsure. If we divide the name *Viroconium*, the second element is as in British *Ariconium*, and is unknown. The first element however then has numerous Continental analogues, in addition to British *Virosidum*: *Virodunum* > Verdun (Meuse, France), Verduno (Piedmont, Italy), Verdú and Berdún (Spain), Wirten (Germany), etc.; *Virovesca* > Briviesca (Burgos, Spain); *Viromagus* = Oron or Promasens (Switzerland); *Viroviacum* > Werwick, Vervicq (Belgium); and the *Viromandui* people of Gaul (> Vermandois; *Augusta Viromanduorum* = St Quentin). In listing these and other names in *GPN* 286–88, Ellis Evans allows that they may contain either Celtic **u̯iro-* 'man' (Latin *vir*, Welsh *gwr*, Irish *fear*) or **u̯iro-* 'true' (Latin *verus*, Welsh *gwîr*, Old Irish *fír*). It is certainly possible to interpret *Virodunum*, as French scholars naturally do, 'vraie forteresse', but in other names it is hard to see that either meaning, 'man' or 'true', makes much sense or gives a natural compound, and it is likely that a third, unknown **u̯iro-* element is involved in them, possibly in the present name also.

It could be, however, that despite the attractive analogues above, we have in *Viroconium* a personal name plus suffix. Names such as *Viriatus*, *Virius*, *Virinius* are frequent in Spain (*ELH* I. 367), and *Viricius*, *Vericius* are widely recorded (Holder III. 379). In Britain *Verica*, ruler of the Atrebates, is named on coins as *Verica* and *Ver* but also as *Vir*, *Viri* (Mack Nos. 109–131B). In *CIL* V. 4594 (Brescia, Italy) there appears *Virico*. It is easy to analyse these names as *Viric-* (of unknown meaning; hardly **u̯iro-* 'man') with various suffixes. The place-name *Viroconium* might therefore more properly be *Viriconium*, to be analysed in British terms as **U̯irico-* with suffixes **-on-i̯o-* as in CANONIUM, etc.; a meaning 'town of **U̯irico-*' is likely, and is one of the possibilities admitted by Jackson in his study of the name in *Britannia*, I (1970), 81. The name presumably applied originally to the hill-fort on the Wrekin, and was transferred to the Roman fortress and the town which grew from it.

Jackson in *LHEB* 601–602 and again in *Britannia* draws attention to other problems. The Anglo-Saxon derivative *Wreocen*, *Wrocen*, and Old Welsh *Guricon*, *(G)ureconn* (Middle Welsh *Gwrygon*) demand an initial **Uric-* and a final **-on* in the Romano-British name; but these are not found in the ancient sources. Hence Jackson supposes that there was a British by-form **Uriconon* from which the Anglo-Saxon and Welsh forms were taken, and that (as Williams suggested) Romano-British *Viroconium* was no more than an official Latin version, lacking spoken currency in British, the *Viro- Viri-* forms being Latin substitutes for the 'rare and peculiar' British *Uri-; although final *-ium* could represent a British spoken variant **-ion*. If this is right, the coins with *Bri-* could represent a further and later attempt to render the British sound in Latin letters, though the mint-mark could also be explained in Vulgar Latin terms as showing loss of unstressed *-i-* (which happened especially when in association with *r*) and as showing *b/v* equivalence; cf. *Virovesca* > Briviesca, above; but there are strong numismatic arguments against associating the mint-mark with Wroxeter.

It is however possible that both *Viroconium* and **Uricon(i)on* are right, perhaps at different stages. Dottin *LG* 358 and Tovar *ELH* I. 117 (quoting Palomar Lapesa) draw attention to the tendency of initial **Uer-* to reduce to **Ur-* in various Celtic regions. Examples are *Ueramos-Vramus*, *Virincis AI* 349_5 = *Uruncis AI* 252_2, *Vitricium AI* 345_2 = *Utricio TP*, etc., and possibly Ptolemy's Οὐρολάνιον (= *Urolanium*, for *Veru-*); in personal names, *Verbigenus-Urbigenus*, *Virdorix-Urdorix*, etc.; see also British *Ugueste* in this List, and for further discussion, *EC*, XIV (1974), 61. The uncertainties of this process may also explain in part the numerous *Vir- Ver-* spelling variations on the coins of *Verica* (above) and of Tasciovanus (see VERULAMIUM), British *Virvedrum* for **Ver-*, *Viromandui/Veromandui*, *Virovesca/Verovesca*, etc.

IDENTIFICATION. The Roman city at Wroxeter, Salop (SJ 5608), capital of the *Cornovii* and succeeding a legionary fortress on the same site; the Wrekin with its hillfort is 4 miles to the east.

VIROSIDUM

SOURCE

ND XL_{56}: Tribunus cohortis sextae Nerviorum, VIROSIDO

DERIVATION. The first element is one of those listed under *Viroconium*, but it is impossible to say which. The second could be a variant of, or miscopying of, the **sed-* 'sit' root discussed under *Manduessedum* and *Camulosessa*, for which close parallels in its present application are provided by *Metlosedum* > Melun (Seine-et-Oise, France) and *Sidoloucum* (*Sedelaucum*) > Saulieu (Côte-d'Or, France), the latter also providing support in one of its forms for present *-sidum*. A sense of 'seat', vaguely 'place', is therefore appropriate. For the formation as a whole the Continental analogues *Virodunum*, *Viromagus*, etc., are then illustrative.

IDENTIFICATION. Almost certainly the Roman fort at Brough by Bainbridge, Yorkshire (SD 9390), garrisoned in Severan times by *Cohors VI Nerviorum* (*RIB* 722) and still occupied in the fourth century. Since this is the last name in

ND's list it is impossible to be certain, but the order which we propose (*Bremetenraco*/Ribchester – *Olenaco*/Elslack – *Virosido*/Bainbridge) is geographically logical.

VIRVEDRUM PROMONTORIUM

SOURCE

Ptolemy II, 3, 4: Οὐιρουεδροῦμ ἄκρον (= VIRVEDRUM PROMONTORIUM) vars. Οὐιερ- (= VIER-), etc.

Note that here, and for *Tarvedu(nu)m* and *Verubium*, Ptolemy exceptionally transmits the termination as *-um* (not *-on*). See also the next entry.

DERIVATION. For *Vir-*, a latinised form of British **u̯er-*, see VERLUCIO; for *-vedrum*, see VEDRA. If we apply Ekwall's etymology to the present name, it means something like 'very wet (cape)' or 'great wet (cape)', presumably with reference to waves crashing at its foot and sending up spray.

IDENTIFICATION. Duncansby Head, Caithness.

VIVIDIN (?)

SOURCE

Ravenna 108_{36} (= R&C 261): VIVIDIN

DERIVATION. The name is taken literally by R&C and given a root in **biu̯o-* (Welsh *byw*, Breton *biu* 'lively'; cognate with Latin *vivus*); hence 'lively water'. There is then a possible analogue in *Vibisco* . *AI* 352_1 = *Bibiscon Ravenna* 63_{14} > Vevey (Switzerland). This seems too trusting textually; the fact that a name figures in *Ravenna*'s river-list is no guarantee of its nature. Possibly the name represents *Virvedrum* (see the previous entry), miscopied as **Virvidron* > **Vividon* > *Vividin*; or (less probably) a coastal name in *-dunum*.

IDENTIFICATION Unknown, but apparently a river or place between Northumberland and Kent.

VOLAS SINUS (?)

SOURCE

Ptolemy II, 3, 1: Οὐάλας κόλπος (= VOLAS SINUS), vars. Οὐάλσος (= VALSOS), Οὔόλσας (= VOLSAS)

DERIVATION. None can be suggested. Ptolemy's name with *-s* is strange in appearance, and the variants suggest a corrupt or doubtful archetype. *Vol-* however may be right, as it is paralleled: **Volisama* (*Volesma* 1195) > Voulême (Vienne, France), **Volodurum* > Vollore (Puy-de-Dôme, France), Οὐολόβριγα (= *Volobriga*, Ptolemy II, 6, 40) on the north-west coast of Spain. There is also *Volisios*, the name of two rulers of the Coritani on coins (Mack Nos. 463–65 and 466–68). The root of these names is not known.

IDENTIFICATION. An inlet in northern Scotland, west of the mouth of the Naver, and perhaps Loch Eriboll, Sutherland. See p. 132.

VOLIBA (?)

SOURCE

Ptolemy II, 3, 13: Οὐολίβα (= VOLIBA), a *polis* of the D(u)mnonii

DERIVATION. None can be suggested; *Vol-* may well be right, but the ending is probably corrupt. For names in *Vol-*, see the previous entry. There is no Celtic suffix **-iba*; perhaps British **-eu̯a* written *-eva* in Latin was mistakenly transcribed as *-eba*, *-iba*, before reaching Ptolemy, though this is early for *b/v* confusions; the suffix might then be as in *Calleva*. The name has been thought to be modern Golden in Probus parish, Cornwall, but this is fanciful; see *VCH Cornwall*, Part V (1924), 35. The most authoritative discussion of Roman Cornwall, that by C. Thomas in C. Thomas (ed.), *Rural Settlement in Roman Britain* (1966), 74–98, has a mention of *Voliba* but none of a possible modern representative of the name.

IDENTIFICATION. An unlocated early Roman fort in Cornwall or Devon. Recent discoveries of an early legionary fortress at Exeter and of forts elsewhere show that the south-western peninsula was not, as previously supposed, exempt from military occupation so that, *pace* Thomas, there is no reason to suppose that Ptolemy here departed from his normal practice and named purely native settlements.

VOLITANIO of *Ravenna* 107_{52} (= R&C 192): see VOTADINI

VORAN of *Ravenna* 108_{13} (= R&C 227): see VARAR

VOREDA

SOURCES

Inscription: *RIB* 920, an altar from Old Penrith or Brougham dedicated by the VEX(ILLATIO) GERMA[NO]-R(UM) V[O]R[E]D(ENSIUM)

AI 467_{3} (Iter II): VOREDA

Ravenna 107_{10} (= R&C 128): BEREDA

DERIVATION. Jackson in *Britannia*, I (1970), 82, gives a British **U̯orēdā* 'horse-stream', based on **u̯orēdo-* 'horse' (Welsh *gorwydd* 'horse'). This was one of the meanings offered by Williams, though not quite in this form. Jackson dismisses Williams's other proposal, a meaning 'path, way' like that of Spanish *vereda*, but it is interesting to note that the two are in fact connected. It seems that Gaulish **u̯erēdos* (identical with the British word) was borrowed into Latin as *verēdus* 'post-horse' (*veredarius* 'courier', *paraveredus* > palfrey); in Hispanic Low Latin *vereda* (first recorded A.D. 757) was taken from this in the sense of 'path', and is known in Spanish, Catalan and Portuguese (with place-names derived from it: *Vereia*, *Brea*, *Breda*, etc.). *Ravenna*'s form *Bereda* is hardly likely to show knowledge of this Hispanic word, but results from scribal assimilation of the vowels, together with Vulgar Latin *b* for *v*.

IDENTIFICATION. The Roman fort at Old Penrith, Plumpton Wall, Cumberland (NY 4938), beside the river Petteril (whose name is of uncertain origin, Ekwall *ERN*).

VOTADINI

SOURCES

Ptolemy II, 3, 7: Ὠταδινοὶ (= OTADINI), vars. Γαδινοί (= GADINI), Ὠταδηνοί (= OTADENI), Ὠταλινοί (= OTALINI, favoured by Müller), Ταδινοὶ (= TADINI) II, 3, 10: Ὠταδινούς (acc., = OTADINOS), vars. Ὠταλινούς (= OTALINOS), Ὠταδηνούς (= OTADENOS)

Ravenna 107_{52} (= R&C 192): VOLITANIO

In Ptolemy's forms, it is to be noted that δ for λ (*d* for *l*) and vice versa is not uncommon in his text, hence *Otalini*. To explain the omission of initial Οὐ- (*V*-), Williams suggested that a blank was left in the archetype for a capital to be decorated with penwork, and that this was never filled. This is possible, as the name begins a paragraph, but such an error does not appear to affect precisely comparable names. *Ravenna*'s entry is as usual accepted as trustworthy by R&C, both as a form and as a fort of the Antonine Wall (in whose section it occurs). Their etymology is: British **vo*- (Old Irish *fo*- glossed 'sub', Old Welsh *guo*, *go* 'rather, somewhat') plus **litan*- 'broad', hence 'rather broad place', with reference to a small plateau. This is acceptable up to a point, but it is very likely that (as first suggested by Holder) *Volitanio* is simply a rendering of *Votadini*, with metathesis of vowels of a kind paralleled elsewhere in the text.

DERIVATION. There can be no doubt that the proper form is *Votadini*, given the Welsh derivative *Guotodin*, later *Gododdin*. On the latter, important in the history of Welsh verse, see Jackson, *The Gododdin* (Edinburgh, 1969), especially 69–75, on the location of the *Manau Guotodin* of Nennius (62). Watson *CPNS* 28 says that in an eleventh-century Gaelic poem there appears *Fotudain*, which corresponds exactly to the Welsh forms. According to Watson the name can be compared with early Irish *fothad* 'support' ('*Fothad*, a mythical ancestor of an Irish people, perhaps derived from **Vo-tādos*': O'Rahilly *EIHM* 10, note), with a suffix *-in-* as in many ethnic names. The sense is not entirely clear, but seems preferable to others suggested by Holder II. 887. See also I. Williams, *Canu Aneirin* (Cardiff, 1938), xviii.

IDENTIFICATION. A people of Britain placed by Ptolemy 'south' (i.e. east) of the *Damnonii*, with *Curia* (?Inveresk), *Alauna* (?Learchild misplaced, or in Fife?) and *Bremenium* (High Rochester) attributed to them. It thus appears that they stretched from the Wear or the Tyne through Northumberland and the Lothians (including Traprain Law) to the Forth. *Manau Gododdin* (spanning the mouth of the Forth from Slamannan to Clackmannan and including Stirling), from which Cunedda and his sons were transferred to north Wales in the fifth century, was presumably their most northerly district.

ZERDOTALIA of *Ravenna* 106_{58} (= R&C 108): see AQUAE ARNEMETIAE and *ARDOTALIA

APPENDIX

DOUBTFUL NAMES, GHOST-NAMES AND INVENTIONS

It would be a pointless task to collect and discuss the numerous Romano-British names which, since the sixteenth century, have been added to the exiguous stock of names conveyed to us in the sources we have defined. Some result from the spurious *De Situ Britanniae* of 'Richard of Cirencester' (see pp. 182–84), and still turn up occasionally in local histories, provincial magazines, etc. Some have been generated by antiquarian enthusiasm as names which, in a retrospectively idealised Romano-British world, ought to have existed; some stem from misreadings of true sources, others from speculation in modern scholarly studies. These are not, of course, to be in any way grouped with names that we can assume with total certainty to have existed but which had not the fortune to be recorded in sources ancient enough for our purposes, such as **Isca* and **Alauna* names of several rivers, and scores of other British water-names whose modern derivatives give us equal assurance. Nor are they to be confounded with ghost-names which are respectable to the extent that they appear to exist in our texts and have long been accepted as names, but now seem to result from errors or corruptions in those texts: such are *Corsula*, *Eirimon* and *Petrianis*, for which see the entries in the Alphabetic List. The names below are offered as a selection only, which illustrates the various considerations involved:

ANTONA, AVONA

The MSS of Tacitus's *Annals* at XII, 31, read *cunctaque castris Antonam et Sabrinam fluvios*... Mannert emended *Antonam* to *Avonam*, Heinsius inserted *inter* after it, and others suggested *usque* or *contra*. In *The Academy* for 28 April and 13 May 1883, Henry Bradley put forward the suggestion *cunctaque cis Trisantonam et Sabrinam*, which was supported by Haverfield and has been accepted by most Romano-British scholars since. It involves the alteration of only one letter (*cas-* to *cis*), makes excellent geographical sense, and is confirmed archaeologically by the distribution of early Roman forts. (See also TRISANTONA[2].)

AUGUSTA[2]

Latin *Augusta* is traditionally held to be the origin of Aust (Gloucestershire). The first record is *Aetaustin* (691–92), the next *æt/to Austan* (794); *Augusta* appears about 1105. The name can hardly have anything to do with any **Traiectus Augustus* notionally ascribed to the influence of Legio II *Augusta*, though there are certainly Roman remains at Aust and the crossing by the Aust passage existed (A. H. Smith in *EPNS*, XL, 127–28). The other possibility, also mentioned by Smith, is that there was a connection with *Augustinaes Ac* mentioned by Bede (II, 2) as the place where Augustine in 602–603 met the British bishops, but 'It is doubtful... whether the intelligible compound *Augustinaes Ac* would have been reduced to *Auste* by the eleventh century' (Smith). Other objections to this are the fact that the meeting with Augustine took place, says Bede, 'on the borders of the Wiccii and West Saxons'; if it had been at a place on the Severn Bede would probably have said so, for he knew the Romano-British name of this (V, 23) and mention of it would have made a more natural description. Moreover, the meeting ended in anything but harmony, and neither side can have had a motive for celebrating its location with a new name. The earliest form of the name, *Austin*, does however suggest a connection with a name *Augustinus*, with loss of *-g-* in this situation typical of Vulgar Latin usage (cf. *Austalis* for *Augustalis* in a London graffito). The *Augusta* of 1105 is then a latinisation of the kind which is common in medieval legal documents. To conclude: the place does seem to involve a Latin personal name, which in the seventh century can only have been an ecclesiastical one; there is no evidence whatsoever that it was called *Augusta* in Roman times.

BANNAVENTA[2]

The bibliography on St Patrick is immense. A good text of his *Confessio* in the *Libri Epistolarum* is that edited by L. Bieler in *Classica et Mediaevalia*, XI (1950), 1–150. Interesting and reliable accounts are those of J. B. Bury, *The Life of St Patrick* (London, 1905), and L. Bieler, *The Life and Legend of St Patrick* (Dublin, 1949), with discussion of his birthplace on pp. 51–53, or more recently R. P. C. Hanson, *St Patrick* (Oxford, 1968) and J. T. McNeill, *The Celtic Churches: A History, A.D. 200 to 1200* (Chicago & London, 1974), esp. pp. 56–57. Born in about 389, the boy Patrick was carried off to Ireland by raiders in about 405 from his parents' home near *uico bannauem taburniae* (var.: *taberniae*), 'where three roads meet', this in turn being, according to Muirchú, 'near the western sea' and otherwise known as *Nemtrie* (vars.: *Nentriae*, *Ventre*, etc.). Patrick's father was a decurion and a deacon, so the place must have been (or was close to a larger town which was) substantial enough to have its *ordo* of decurions.

Bannavem is scarcely a possible form of a Romano-British name, and *taberniae* (preferable to *taburniae*) is not right either. As Bury (1905, Appendix C) saw, the proper division is no doubt *Bannaventa Berniae*. We already know *Bannaventa*[1] as a place in Northamptonshire, not near the western sea; St Patrick's home was another place of the same name, and it probably carries *Berniae* as an adjunct to distinguish it from the first. The identifications that have been made are detailed by Bieler. Those that are worth retaining include that of Collingwood & Myres, who thought the place in the region of the Bristol Channel; of G. H. Wheeler in *EHR*, L (1935), 109–13, who though restoring the place-name in an extravagant way thought that the region of Carlisle might be indicated; and that of Bury, who first suggested that *Berniae* was for **Berni[c]iae*, though ultimately preferring a site in the south-west (? Banwen in Glamorgan). It is possible that Wheeler, and Bury's hint, could be right. Jackson devotes a whole Appendix of *LHEB* to upsetting the traditional view that the *Bernicia* of post-Roman England derived from **Brigantia*; he replaces this by a base in Celtic **berna* or **birna*, represented by Old Irish *bern* 'gap, mountain pass'. If we can be allowed a **Bernia* which preceded **Bernicia* (names built on the same base, with different suffixes) and applied to the same region, and if – which is by no means sure – the English kingdom extended to the western seaboard at the Solway Firth, then the region of Carlisle could indeed be the home of St Patrick. *Bannaventa* we know to have been a Romano-British name; *Bernia* does not have to be a Romano-British name contemporary with St Patrick, but could have been added by an early scribe concerned to distinguish the place. Many early medieval documents about saints are full of pious fictions, but there seems every reason to accept St Patrick's as wholly genuine; the very strength of what he says about his home is that it is unknown, since if a larger and identifiable place had been mentioned, one would be tempted to think it an interpolation in the interests of local pride. Nothing, it seems, can be made of *Nemtrie/Ventre*.

BERONIACUM

S. Applebaum in 'A Note on Three Romano-British Place-Names', *JBAA*[3], XVII (1954), 77–79, notes this name – *decimam de Beroniaco* – in a document of Pope Adrian IV of 1154. Ekwall, consulted by Applebaum, thought the name might apply to Ludlow Deanery (Shropshire), part of the diocese of Hereford at the time. Applebaum concludes: 'It seems probable, then, that we are faced with a lost Romano-British place-name which we may add to our toponymy. If it was near Ludlow, a possibility is Caynham Camp, two miles south-east of the town...' Certainly *Beroniaco* looks Celtic, but it may be no more than a latinisation of a somewhat different vernacular name made *ad hoc* for legal purposes in 1154. Even if it is comparatively ancient, it need not be Romano-British, for Herefordshire and parts of Shropshire were Celtic-speaking still in the early seventh century.

BERTHA

This name, now applied to a farm and the Roman fort on it in Redgorton parish, Perthshire (NO 0926), was invented by John Fordoun in the fourteenth century to supply a plausible antecedent for the city of Perth, which stands 2½ miles downstream from it. The fort was earlier called Rath-inver-Amon, or 'fort at the mouth of the Amon', i.e. Almond, which joins the Tay at this point. See O. G. S. Crawford, *The Topography of Roman Scotland North of the Antonine Wall* (Cambridge, 1949), 59–61, with the suggestion, which the name-form contradicts, that it might be *Tamia*.

BIERIUM

This name was extracted from a difficult inscription, *CIL* VII. 268 (now *RIB* 721, a late fourth-century text from Ravenscar, Yorkshire) by C. E. Stevens in *Arch. J.*, XCVII (1940), 151–54, with some adventurous philological juggling as to form and sense. The name is now read as an official title, *magister*.

BIRILA

This name appears in *Ravenna* 109_{14} (= R&C 295), with var. RIRILA; it appears in the list of islands, but as we know from experience, it may well not be an island at all, and might be non-

British. Dillemann (72) thinks it could represent the *Berrice* of Pliny *NH* IV, 104. Certainly the name as it stands has no visible etymology and is corrupt.

BURGODUNUM

This is a name that one finds occasionally applied to the Roman settlement at Adel near Leeds (Yorkshire), e.g. in local publications of quite recent date. It has no ancient warrant and seems to have arisen among antiquarians of the early nineteenth century, being based on nothing more solid than the name *Burhedurum* by which Adel is designated in Domesday Book.

CAII COLLIS

This is a picturesque invention by G. M. Hughes in his book *Roman Roads in South-east Britain* (1936) in order to explain the name Key Coll Hill near Newington in Kent. The *Collis* would have been 'of Caius', that is, of Julius Caesar.

DOROCINA

In the modest popularising book *Roman Britain* by R. R. Sellman (1956), there is mention on p. 61 that Dorchester-on-Thames was *Dorocina* in Roman times. There is no record of this place in our sources, although it is known that there was a small Roman town there and although interesting early names for the Saxon town are known, such as *Dorcic* in Bede. Since the root of the name seems to be the British one found in *Condercum* (Ekwall), one could conjecture various Romano-British forms which would account for the river Dorce also (as 'bright river') and be based on this; but equally, a Romano-British fort-name in **Dŭro-c-* would fit, the river-name then being by back-formation. In any case, *Dorocina* is fanciful, and derives from 'Richard of Cirencester' (see p. 183).

MADUS

From its appearance on *TP*, this was taken at one time as a valid name, and applied to the Medway. It is however a fragment, as explained in our entry for *Noviomagus*[2].

MELANDRA

This name was coined comparatively recently for the Roman fort at Melandra Castle, near Glossop (Derbyshire). In I. D. Margary's book *Roman Roads*, revised one-volume edition (London, 1967), p. 364, *Melandra* appears italicised as though an authentic Romano-British name.

PENTA

Bede III, 22, says of Ythancaestir (Bradwell, Essex) that it lay *in ripa Pentae* (var.: *Paente*) *amnis*, that is, on the River Blackwater. This could well be a comparatively ancient name. It has been cited usually as *Panta*, without MS authority, probably in order to connect it with Welsh *pant* 'hollow, depression'; a British root of this could conceivably have made an ancient river-name, but there is no evidence anywhere of its having done so. Bede could have had no reason to invent such a name, which would have come to him in the story of St Cedd.

RICINA, RIGINA

This is listed by Pliny *NH* IV, 103 (RIGINIA, *inter Hiberniam ac Britanniam*; vars. *Ricnea, Rignea*), Ptolemy II, 2, 10 ('Ρικίνα = *Rhicina*, with vars.), and *Ravenna* 109_{10} (= R&C 277: REGAINA, var. *Regama*). There are several Continental parallels for the name, which probably contains Celtic **ric-* **rig-* 'king'; see *GPN* 248. But it might have a pre-Indo-European root meaning 'height' as certain *Ric- Reg-* names seem to do in non-Celtic areas of the Continent, as is not impossible for a northerly island which was a landmark for early seafarers; see Rostaing *ETP* 238–39. The name has been identified with Rathlin Island off the north coast of Ireland (which is Irish *Rachra*, gen. *Rechrann*; in Adamnan's *Life* of St Columba, *Rechru* I. 5 and *in Rechrea insula* II. 41). For the island to figure in three ancient sources it was doubtless a prominent one, and on this score the identification suits.

TAUM, AD TAUM

Some have been misled by the *Taum* which appears in the East Anglian portion of *TP*, and by *Ad Taum* which appears in the *Agricola* of Tacitus, 22, 1. See respectively our entries for *Venta Icenorum* and *Tava/Tavus*[1].

VENANTODUNUM

This name, which is simply a Latin translation of English Huntingdon, was coined by John Leland, as is specifically stated by Camden (*Britannia*, 1586, 280): 'Huntersdune: Mons venatorum ... et novum vocabulum *Venantodunum* Lelandus noster nobis excudit.' Huntingdon was not a Roman town, its Roman equivalent being across the river at Godmanchester (DUROVIGUTUM?, q.v.).

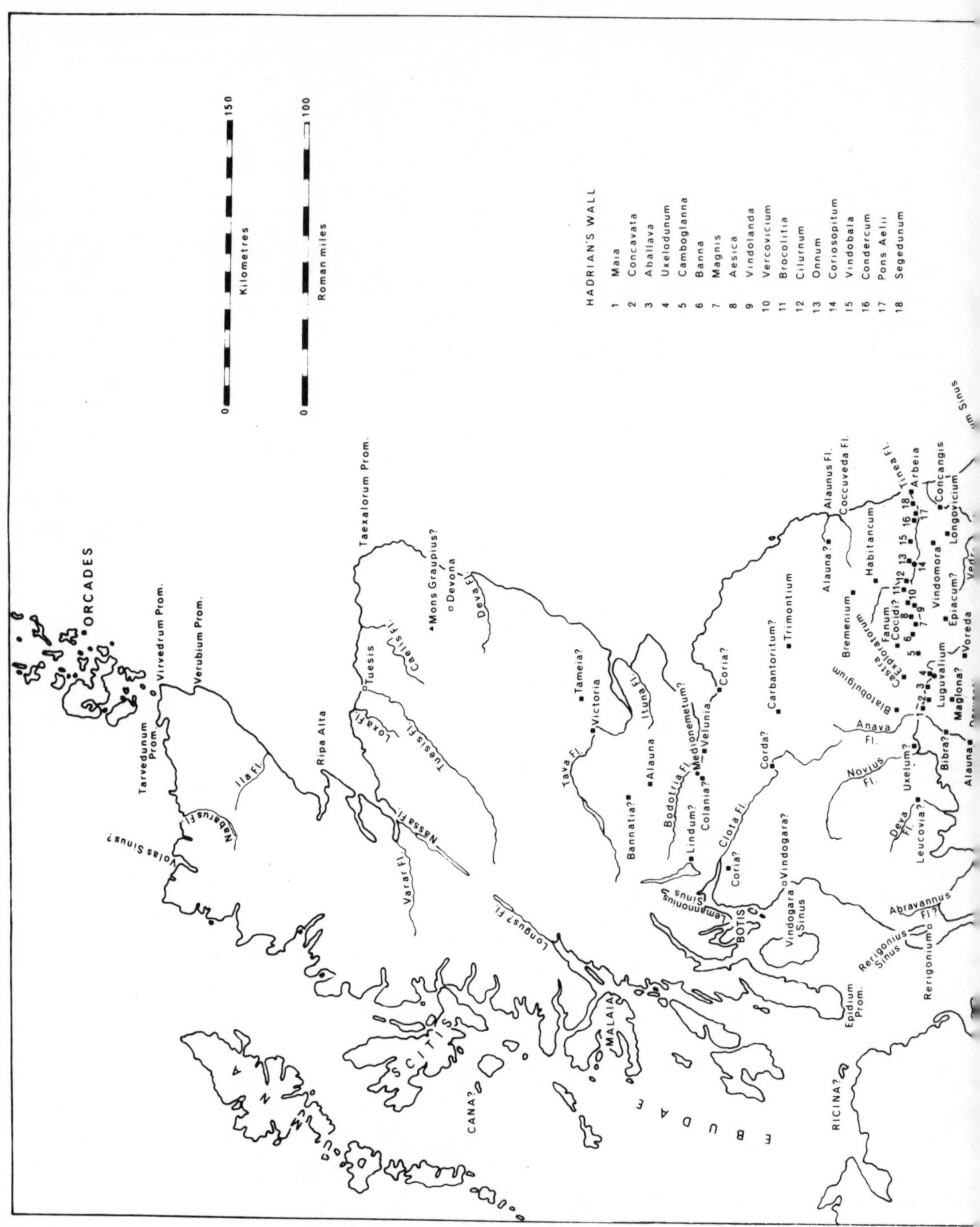

Fig. 33. Map of Great Britain showing name

which can be located with certainty or probability.

INDEX

of modern names in England, Wales, and Scotland

(References in bold type are to the principal entries in the Alphabetic List)

Abergavenny 173, 207, **369**
Add R. 399
Adel 279, 513
Adur R. 207, 213, **427**, 442
Afon Alun 243
Afon Alyn 243
Afon Brefi 277
Afon Cothi 400
Afon Dwyfach 336
Afon Dwyfawr 336
Afon Dwyryd 135, 474
Afon Eden 380
Afon Fhada 399
Afon Glaslyn 135, 474
Afon Mawddach 135
Afon Teifi 277
Afon Twrch 400
Afon Tywi 422
Aire R. 159, 293, 383
Alan R. 243
Alcester (Dorset) 244
Alcester (Warwickshire) 207, **244**, 360
Aldborough 119, 120, 142, 155, 157, 162, 279, **380**
Ale Water 243
Alham R. 243
Allan Water 128, 243, 245
Allen R. (Cornwall) 243
Allen R. (Dorset) 136, 243, 247
Allen R. (Hampshire) 136, 243, 247
Almond R. 512
Almondbury 295
Aln R. (Northumberland) 138, 140, 210, 213, 243, **245**, **247**
Alne R. (Warwickshire) 243, 244
Alsh, Loch 133
Ambleside 170, 171, 208, 222, **365**, 415
Ancaster 164
Andover 341, 389
Anglesey 40, 42, 57, 117, 132, 214, 215, 411, 419, **420**
Annan R. 45, 213, **250**, 396
Archenfield 258
Ardoch 125, 126, 128, 140, 211, **245**
Arran 133, 419
Arthur's O'on 211, **417**
Arthur's Seat 320
Arun R. 45, 136, 207, 427, **477**
Arundel 477
Ashbourne 403
Ashley (Hampshire) 178, 179, **278**
Auchendavy 360
Auchinhove 45
Aust 177, 410
Avon R. (Devon) 239
Avon R. (Gloucestershire) 177, 178, 212, 214, 239, **240**
Avon R. (Hampshire) 136, 247
Avon R. (Stirlingshire) 239
Avon R. (Warwickshire) 239
Avon Water (Hampshire) 239
Avon Water (Lanarkshire) 239
Axbridge 379
Axe R. (Devon) 136, **246**, 247, 376
Axe R. (Somerset) 21, 135, 145, 261, 376, 379, 483
Axminster 180
Ayle Burn 243

Badbury Rings 178, 206, 417, **500**
Bagendon 321
Baggy Point 135
Bain R. 265
Bainbridge 223, 507
Banbury 252
Bane R. 7
Banwen 511
Bapchild 162
Bar Hill 295
Barochan Hill 125, 126, 140, 211, **319**, 343

Bath 12, 22, 48, 119, 121, 176, 177, 197, 206, 230, 249, 252, 253, 254, 255, **256**, 306, 340, 368, 377, 388, 459
Baylham House 170, **314**
Beam R. 170
Beauly R. 138, 487
Beauly Firth 138, 141, **487**
Beckermet **381**
Beckfoot 208, **268**, 284
Belby 403
Bellie 126, 128, 141, 211, **481**
Beltingham 318, 319, 329, 470
Bennachie 45, **371**
Benwell 209, 220, **316**
Berry Ring 437
Bewcastle 26, 209, **363**
Binchester 119, 120, 142, 155, 208, 231, 312, 314, **504**
Birdoswald 209, 221, 261, **262**, 444
Birrens 157, **269**, 279, 395
Bitterne 166, 227, **309**
Bitton 177, 178
Blackmore Forest 243
Blackwater R. 138, 297, 358, 513
Blebo 269
Boroughbridge 380
Borough Hill 265
Bourne (Lincolnshire) 164
Bowes 157, 162, 208, 220, 316, **384**
Bowness 208, 209, 214, 221, 381, 408, **409**
Bowness Hill 381
Bradwell 48, 219, **435**, 513
Braich-y-Pwll 135, **366**
Braint R. 279
Brancaster 29, 219, **275**, 312, 394
Brathby R. 365
Braunton 135
Brayford Mere 393
Brecon Gaer 207, **307**
Brent (Devon) 279
Brent (Somerset) 279
Brent R. (Middlesex) 279
Bridlington Bay 138, **364**
Brockley Hill 158, **463**
Broom, Loch 133
Broomer's Hill 403
Broomfleet 403
Brough (Nottinghamshire) 165, 167, **327**
Brough (Westmorland) 157, 162, 164, 208, 220, **496**
Brougham 162, **284**, 301, 508
Brough by Bainbridge 221, 223, **506**, 507
Brough-on-Humber 119, 120, 142, 155, 156, 157, 208, 403, **437**, 438
Brough-on-Noe 208, 254, 423, **424**
Broughton (Hampshire) 179
Buckfast **336**
Bull Point 135
Burgh-by-Sands 209, 220, **238**
Burgh Castle 219, **366**
Burrow-in-Lonsdale 119, 120, 142, 170, 172, 223, **288**
Burrow Walls 220, 381, **406**
Burwens **276**
Bury Camp (Leicestershire) 444
Bute 133, 214, **273**
Buxton 208, 230, **255**, 423

Cae'r Castell **277**
Caerhun 172, 207, **297**
Caerlaverock **484**
Caerleon 13, 36, 48, 114, 115, 122, 173, 174, 175, 176, 198, 199, 220, 222, 229, 268, 337, 376, **378**, 382, 472
Caernarvon 172, 207, **454**
Caer Sws 391
Caerwent 16, 115, 176, 177, 206, 228, 246, 272, 460, **493**
Cairnpapple 417
Caistor (Lincolnshire) **265**
Caistor St Edmund 119, 150, 162, 169, 208, 209, 229, 374, 375, **492**
Callender 468
Calne **494**
Cam Beck 294
Cambridge 5, 162, 208, **352**, 354
Camelon 125, 126, 140, 211, **312**, 343, 417
Canna 214, **296**
Canterbury 48, 57, 119, 150, 158, 160, 161, 162, 191, 207, 229, **354**, 369
Canvey Island 146, 326
Caputh 499
Cardean 126, 141, 212, **466**
Cardiff 445, **467**
Carlisle 27, 46, 48, 57, 157, 162, 208, 209, 221, 234, 242, 246, 265, 301, 302, **402**, 511, 512
Carmarthen 22, 119, 173, 174, 198, 333, **422**
Carpow 109, 110, 373, 491
Carrawburgh 209, 220, **285**, 371
Carriden 196, 211, 326, **490**
Carron R. 461
Cartmel 420
Carvoran 208, 220, 232, 342, 407, **408**
Cashio Hundred 302
Castledykes 125, 140, 210, **317**
Castleford 162, 167, 208, 279, 355, **383**
Castle Hill (East Bridgford) 165, 167, **414**
Castle Loch 396
Castle Ring (Staffordshire) 437
Castleshaw 119, 120, 142, 158, **448**
Castlesteads 208, 210, 220, **294**
Castor (Huntingdonshire) 348

Catterick 19, 48, 57, 119, 120, 142, 155, 157, 162, 164, 208, **304**
Catterick (near Settle, Yorkshire) 303
Catterick Moss (Co. Durham) 303
Cave's Inn 25, 164, 165, 320, **476**
Cawfields 352, 392
Caynham Camp 512
Chanonry Point 487
Charterhouse 119, 145, 340, **379**, 487
Cheddar Gorge 379
Chelmsford 150, 162, 168, 170, 208, **288**, 476
Chester 13, 36, 48, 119, 120, 122, 123, 128, 135, 142, 157, 172, 207, 220, 227, 229, 325, 331, **337**, 378
Chesterfield 207, 404
Chesterholm 208, 220, **329**, 405, 471, 472, **502**
Chester-le-Street 208, 220, 231, **314**, 316, 339
Chesters 209, 220, **308**, 444
Chesterton (Huntingdonshire) **348**
Chesterton Walls (Staffordshire) 437
Chichester 22, 115, 117, 119, 166, 167, 206, 209, 229, **427**, 432, 446
Chigwell 168, 170, **352**
Chollerford 307
Chollerton 307
Christchurch Harbour 136
Churchover 403, **476**
Churn R. 321
Cirencester 46, 48, 118, 119, 175, 198, 207, 308, **321**, 340, 418
Clackmannan 411, 509
Clochmabenstane 396
Clun 312
Clwyd R. 172, 487
Clyde R. 45, 133, 181, 214, **310**, 472
Cockermouth Castle 238
Coddenham 150, 168, 170, **314**
Colchester 12, 19, 31, 48, 117, 119, 146, 150, 162, 164, 168, 169, 208, 229, 230, 241, 290, **295**, **312**, 313, 351, 368, 454
Colne R. 312
Cong Burn 315
Conway R. 297
Conwy R. 297
Coquet R. 210, 213, **311**
Corbridge 115, 208, 322, **323**, 324, 483
Corchester **323**, 324
Corryvrechan 42
Countisbury 328
Cowbridge 173, 175, **273**
Crake R. 135
Cramond 373
Crayford 150, 158, 161, **428**
Cree R. 135, **375**
Crick 177
Cromarty Firth 138
Culbin Sands 441
Cullen 285
Cynwyd R. 328

Dalginross 109, 126, 141, **262**
Dane R. 316
Darent(h) R. 333
Dart R. (Devon) 205, 333, **335**, 336
Darwen R. 333
Daventry 265
Dee R. (Aberdeenshire) 138, 141, 336, **337**, 338, 464
Dee R. (Cheshire) 135, 336, 457
Dee (Dent) R. (Lancashire) 336
Dee R. (Kircudbright) 135, 336, **337**, 375, 390
Degannwy 330
Derwent R. (Cumberland) 45, 57, 213, 333, **335**
Derwent R. (Derbyshire) 333, 334, 404
Derwent R. (Northumberland) 333
Derwent R. (Yorkshire) 45, 57, 155, 333, 334
Derwentwater 335
Derwinni R. 333
Deveron R. 138, **286**
Dinlleu 401
Dinor(dd)wig 434
Dolaucothi 119, 145
Don R. (Aberdeenshire) 128, 141, 338, 464
Don R. (Co. Durham) 329
Doncaster 162, 167, 220, **329**, 355, 420, 453
Donwy R. 329
Doon R. 329
Dorce R. 513
Dorchester (Dorset) 22, 115, 178, 180, 205, 206, **345**, 353
Dorchester-on-Thames 48, 57, 466, 513
Dornoch 345
Dornock 345
Dour R. 213, **342**
Dover 23, 36, 116, 117, 136, 150, 160, 207, 219, **341**, 386, **428**
Droitwich 119, 120, 143, 207, **451**
Dropshort 158, 164, 167, **406**
Drumburgh 220, 221, 222, **315**, 408, 500, 503
Drumquhassle 126, 128, 140, 209, 343, **393**
Drymen 393
Dumyat 46, 404, 497
Duncansby Head 137, **507**
Duncrub 45, 370
Dunkeld 289
Dunnett Head 133, 137, **434**, **469**
Dunstable 158, 164, 167, 349, **350**
Duntarvie 469
Durno 45, 371

Earn R. 258
East Anton 179, 206, **389**
East Bridgford **414**

Easter Happrew 125, 128, 139, 210, **301**
East Rother R. **386**, 387
East Stoke 165, **241**
Ebchester 155, 354, **503**
Eden R. (Cumberland) 45, 114, 135, **380**, 381
Eden R. (Fife) 138, **380**, 381
Eden Burn 380
Eden Water 380
Edgeworth 170, 172, **310**
Egremont 381
Ehen R. 381
Eildon Hills 19, 475
Ellen R. 243, 245, 381
Ellerker 403
Elmet 57
Elslack 119, 120, 142, 221, **431**, 507
Elwy R. 487
Eriboll, Loch 133, **507**
Erme R. 206, 258, **259**
Esk R. (Cumberland) 376, 415
Esk R. (Dumfries) 375, 376
Esk R. (Yorkshire) 376
Etive, Loch 133, 359
Ewell 117
Ewenny R. 175, 213, 260, **261**, 445, 467
Ewenydd R. 260
Exe R. (Devon) 122, 136, 376, **378**
Exe R. (Scotland) 372
Exeter 22, 114, 119, 122, 150, 178, 180, 197, 198, 200, 204, 205, 206, 209, 229, 255, 336, 343, 376, **378**, 508
Exe Water 376

Fal R. 136, **306**
Farley Mount **278**
Farrar R. 138, 212, **487**
Faversham 162
Felixstowe 441
Fence Burn 433
Fenni Fach 307
Filey Bay 138, **364**
Findhorn R. 128, 138, 441
Flamborough Head 138, **429**
Flat Holm 41, 458
Fleetwood 135, **457**
Folkestone 344
Forden Gaer **391**
Foreland Point 135
Forres 47
Forth R. 45, 138, 213, 270, **271**, 272
Forth, Firth of 410, 509
Fortrenn 47, 497
Foulness 146
Froxfield 232
Fyne, Loch 133

Gartree Road 117
Gatehouse of Fleet 375
Gefenni R. 369
Gidea Park 170
Gitting R. 170
Gittisham 179, 180
Glastonbury 238
Glen R. (Lincolnshire) 368
Glen R. (Northumberland) 368
Glenlochar 125, 139, 210, **390**, 425
Glossop 257, 513
Gloucester 12, 175, 206, 207, 209, 227, 229, 231, 252, 257, **313**, 340, 368, **369**, 405, 417
Godmanchester 208, 351, **354**, 514
Golden 508
Grange, Pass of 45
Great Chesters 209, 220, 221, 233, **242**
Green Ore 487
Greta R. 384
Greta Bridge 278, **420**
Gretna 396
Gwynfa 389

Haile 381
Halton Chesters 209, 220, **433**
Harcourt Mill 157, 160, **448**
Hardknot 208, **415**
Harris 40, **342**
Hartland Point 135, **372**
Hayshaw Moor 279
Hebrides 40, 41, 114, 131, 132, 146, **355**
Helmsdale R. 137, **375**
Hendy 174
Hereford 258, 512
Hexgrave Park 403
Hexham 242
Hexham Abbey 322
Higham 150, 168, 169, **241**
High Cross 157, 165, 167, **492**
High Peak 180
High Rochester 125, 139, 155, 210, **276**, 509
Highveer Point 135
Hints Common 331
Hod Hill 145, 340, **344**, 353, 382
Holt 157, 160, **274**
Holyhead 419
Horncastle 7, 208, **265**
Housesteads 209, 220, 352, 363, 392, 493, **494**
Humber R. 138, **241**
Huntingdon 514

Icklingham 164
Ilchester 180, 206, 353, **392**
Ilkley 324, 431, 491, **493**
Inchtuthil 109, 110, 128, 140, 212, 343, 440, 485, **499**

Inveresk 125, 140, **320**, 371, 509
Iping **432**
Irthing R. 363
Irvine 125, 140, 209, 343
Irvine Bay 123, 133, **502**
Itchen R. (Hampshire) 374
Itchen R. (Warwickshire) 374
Ivel R. 392
Iwerne R. **382**
Iwerne Minster **382**

Jarrow 220, 282, **329**, 420
Jura 42

Keer R. 135
Keith 45
Kelk 289
Kelvedon 150, 168, **297**
Kenchester 173, 207, 209, 339, **407**
Kennet R. (Wiltshire) 177, 328, 329
Kennet R. (Westmorland) 244
Kent **300**
Kent R. 135, 171, 310, 328
Kenwyn 307
Kenwyn R. 136, **306**
Key Coll Hill 513
Kinnairds Head 138, **464**
Kintore 126, 128, 211, **338**
Kirkby Thore 157, 208, 220, **276**, 291, 406
Kirkhaugh 360
Knock Hill 45
Kyle of Durness 133
Kyle of Tongue 133

Lackford 162, 163, 164, **294**
Lancaster 10, 142, 171, 172, 223, 228, 229, 259, **382**
Lanchester 208, 220, 312, 398, **399**
Land's End 115, 135, 198, 205, 249, **253**, **267**
Larbert 417
Lark R. 163, 294
Launceston **464**
Leam R. 385
Learchild 140, 509
Leeds 57, 157, 159, 208, **293**
Leeming 385
Leicester 16, 26, 117, 118, 119, 165, 167, 207, 229, 232, 312, 324, 393, 443, **444**, 468
Leintwardine 119, 120, 143, 173, 207, **275**
Leire R. 312
Lemon R. 385
Lennox 133, 387
Leven R. (Lancashire) 135, 351
Leven R. (Scotland) 385, 387
Leven R. (Yorkshire) 351
Leven, Vale of 387
Lewis 40, 114, 146, **342**
Lichfield **388**
Liddington Castle 350
Lilleshall 482
Lincoln 12, 17, 19, 46, 48, 119, 120, 138, 153, 162, 164, 165, 167, 208, 209, 227, 228, 229, 313, **393**, 417, 453, 467
Lindisfarne 393
Lindsey 393
Linnhe, Loch 133, 141, 214, **399**
Little Avon R. 239
Littleborough 162, 167, **453**
Little Brickhill **406**
Littlechester 207, **334**
Little Dart R. 333
Little London (Chigwell) 170, **352**
Little Ponton 305
Lizard, The 115, 135, 343, **344**, **429**
Llandewi Brefi 277
Llandovery 207, **242**
Llandudno 330
Llanfair-ar-bryn **242**
Llanio 207, **277**
Lleyn Peninsula 365, **366**
Lochmaben **396**
Lomond, Loch 128, 387, 393
London 6, 19, 36, 46, 48, 57, 118, 122, 123, 142, 143, 145, 153, 158, 160, 161, 162, 164, 166, 168, 170, 192, 207, 208, 209, 225, 230, 231, 255, **260**, 285, 299, 345, 396, **398**
London Bridge 117
Long, Loch 133, 141, **387**, 399
Long Island 40, 114, 146, **342**
Lossie R. 138, 210, **400**
Loth 401
Loughor 173, 174, **389**
Loughor R. 174, 213, **388**, 389, 445
Low Borrow Bridge 120, 171, 222
Low Learchild **245**
Lox R. 399
Loxford 399
Luce Bay 135
Ludlow 512
Ludlow Deanery 512
Lugar R. 389
Lundy Island 41, 458
Lune R. 135, 288, 382
Lydney 26, 207, 377, **424**, 459
Lyme R. 386
Lymn R. 385
Lympne 150, 160, 207, 219, 229, 385, 386, **387**
Lympne R. 213, 252, **386**, 387
Lyne 139, **301**
Lyne Water 301
Lyvennet Beck 385

Maiden Castle (Dorset) 22, 145, 344, 345
Maidstone 161
Malton 155, 156, 157, 220, **334**
Mamble 410
Mamhead 410
Mamhilad 410
Mam Tor 410
Man, Isle of 40, 57, 132, 212, 215, 410, **411**
Mancetter 157, **412**
Manchester 157, 158, 160, 170, 172, 208, 209, 246, 312, **410**, 414
Mansfield 403
Marlborough 232
Maryport 208, 221, **245**, 381
Matlock 403
Maumbury Rings 410
Meavy R. 419
Medway R. 347, 348, 428, 513
Melandra Castle 208, **257**, 513
Menai Bridge 297
Meon R. 212, **419**
Mersea Island 146
Mersey R. 135, **457**
Middleton 301
Middlewich 207, **451**
Mildenhall 176, 177, 206, **329**
Millington 156, 157
Mither Tap of Bennachie 45, **371**
Mole R. 255
Monifieth 126, 128, 141, **373**
Monmouth 175, **269**
Moray Firth 116, 441, 485, **487**
Morecambe 420
Morecambe Bay 135, **420**
Moresby 208, 220, **365**, 381, 460
Moricambe Bay 421
Morte Point 135
Mounth, The 404
Mull 132, **409**
Mull of Galloway 133, **426**
Mull of Kintyre 133, **361**
Mumrills 405
Muncaster **367**
Myot Hill 404

Nadder R. 423
Nant Alun 243
Nant Wysk 376
Naver R. 133, 389, **422**, 423, 507
Nayland 169
Neath 173, 174, 175, **425**
Neath R. 445
Neatham 179, **432**
Nemet R. 255, 425
Nene R. 138, 347, 348
Ness R. 213, **423**, 487
Ness, Loch 423
Netherby 26, 157, 221, **302**, 377
Nettleham 255, 447
Newcastle upon Tyne 220, **441**
Newington 513
Newstead 125, 139, 210, **475**
Newton Kyme 442, 493
Nidd R. 425
Nith R. 135, 212, 213, **428**
Nithsdale 396
Normandykes 128
Nor'nour 253
North Esk R. 376
North Ferriby 156, **438**
North Foreland 136
North Tawton 205, **425**
North Tyne R. 307, 308, 433
North Uist 41
North Waltham 180, **503**
Northwich 157, 170, 207, **316**
Norton 334
Noss Head 137, **497**
Nursling 432
Nymet R. 255, 368, 425
Nythe Farm **350**

Old Carlisle 220, 406, **407**, 431
Old Lindley Moor 295
Old Penrith 157, 208, 223, 301, **508**
Old Sarum 178, 179, 206, **461**
Old Wall 402
Orkney Islands 40, 42, 57, 114, 137, 146, 181, 215, **434**
Orsett 170
Ouse R. (Cambridgeshire) 354
Ouse R. (Sussex) 427
Ouse R. (Yorkshire) 138, 210, 211, **241**, 356
Overborough 172, 223, 259, **288**
Oykel R. 461

Papcastle 208, 223, **334**
Parrett R. 135, 483
Passinford Bridge 170
Penbryn 434
Pencoyd 388
Penk R. 437
Penketh 388
Penkridge **437**
Penmachno 298
Penrith 251
Pentland Firth 137
Pentridge 436
Penwith **267**
Petteril R. 508
Pevensey 207, 209, 219, 222, 230, 250, **251**
Piercebridge 316, **420**

Plumpton Wall 508
Pontardulais 174
Popplechurch 176
Porlock 135
Portchester 206, 219, 222, 394, **442**
Port Talbot 422
Poulton Bay 135
Prestatyn 172
Probus 508
Pulborough 403
Pumpsaint **400**

Raedykes 45
Ramsey Island 430
Ramsey Sound 430
Ratby 444
Rattray Head 138, **464**
Ravenglass 170, 171, 208, 221, **367**, 381, 415
Ravenscar 512
Reculver 219, 230, **447**
Redgorton 512
Red Hill (Lilleshall) 157, **482**
Redwick 177
Rhinns of Galloway 133, 211, **426**
Rhydd 251
Rhyd Orddwy 434
Ribble R. 135, **268**, 277
Ribchester 170, 171, 172, 208, 221, 223, **277**, 507
Richborough 48, 49, 58, 116, 119, 150, 154, 158, 160, 207, 219, 222, 228, 229, **450**, 478, 479
Ridware 251
Risingham 210, 234, 269, 371, **372**, 405, 414
Rochester 48, 57, 150, 158, 160, 161, 207, 231, 285, 312, 346, **348**
Roden R. 160, 448
Roding R. 170
Rohallion 289
Rom R. 170
Romford 169, 170
Rother R. (East Sussex) 427
Rother R. (West Sussex) 432
Rudchester 209, 220, **500**
Ryan, Loch 123, 133, 139, **447**

Saint R. 20, 454
St Albans 49, 58, 119, 158, 164, 167, 207, 228, 229, 230, 305, **499**
St Asaph 172, **487**
St David's Head 135, **430**
St Lythans 273
St Mary Bourne 179
St Michael's Mount 488, 489
Salisbury 209
Saltersford 162, 164, **305**
Sandwood Loch 49, **480**
Sandy 354
Sandy Lane 176, 177, **494**
Sapperton 162, 164, **305**
Scarba 42
Schiehallion 289
Scilly Isles 41, 253, 255, 457, 458, **459**
Scole 162, 163, **499**
Sea Mills 176, 177, 206, **240**, 262
Seaton 180, 247
Seiont R. 20, 454
Selsey 22
Severn R. 45, 58, 135, 177, 178, 212, 214, 239, 391, 445, 450, **451**, 511
Shaftesbury 244
Sharnford 492
Sheepscar Beck 293
Sheppey 146
Shetland Isles 41, 42, 117, 146, **241**, **473**
Sid R. 180
Sidbury Castle 180
Sidford 150, 178, 180, 205, 206, **422**
Silchester 16, 119, 166, 175, 176, 178, 179, 180, 199, 207, 209, 227, 230, 260, 291, **292**, 397
Sills Burn 276
Sittingbourne 150, 158, 162, **351**
Skye 40, 114, 132, 146, 214, 355, **452**
Slack 23, 119, 120, 142, 157, 158, 159, 208, 279, **295**
Slamannan 509
Snipeshill 162
Solent, The 136, **408**, 489
Solway Firth 396, 421, 512
Southampton Water **408**
South Esk R. 376
Southfleet 485
South Foreland 136, **300**
South Shields 220, **256**, 305, 339, 348, **373**, 420, 471
Southwark 398
Speen 19, 176, **462**
Spey R. 128, 138, 141, 441, **481**
Springhead 158, 161, **485**
Spurn Head 138, **429**
Staines 166, **441**
Stanwix 10, 36, 209, 220, 221, **483**
Steep Holm 41, 458
Stirling 509
Stoke Ash 162, 163, **499**
Stoneham 48
Stour R. (Dorset) 136, 247
Stour R. (Suffolk) 169, 241
Stourpaine 344
Strageath 128
Stranraer 123, 125, 139, 210, 425, **447**
Stratford St Mary 169, 170
Strathmore 128
Strathnaver 137
Strath Ullie 137, 375
Struy 487

Stutfall Castle **387**
Sudbrook 177
Swale R. (Kent) 351
Swale R. (Yorkshire) 57, 303, 304

Tadcaster 48, 57, 157, 158, 159, 208, **289**, 355
Taff R. 135, 213, 444, **445**, 467
Tain R. 465
Tamar R. 119, 136, 145, 212, **464**, 465
Tame R. 207, **468**
Tanat R. 468
Tansley Moor 403
Tarbat Ness 138, **448**
Tarrant R. 45, 136, **477**
Tarvin R. 472
Tas R. 374
Tavistock 339
Tavy R. 465
Taw R. 205, 465, **470**
Tawy R. 465
Tay R. 45, 128, 138, 141, 212, 373, 465, **470**, 491, 512
Team R. 465
Tean R. 465
Tees Bay 138, **345**
Teifi R. 135, **480**
Teinntidh R. 468
Teme R. 465
Tennet R. 468
Test R. 432, 475
Teviot R. 465
Thame R. 465
Thames R. 45, 58, 116, 138, 207, 397, 441, **466**
Thanet, Isle of 41, 58, 136, 146, 150, 300, **469**
Thirlwall Castle 342
Thorpe (Nottinghamshire) 241
Thruxton 230
Thurso Bay 133, 469
Till R. 473
Tindale 473
Tomen-y-Mur 229
Tone R. 465
Tove R. 383
Towcester 158, 164, 207, 341, 347, **383**
Towy R. 445, **474**
Traeth Bach 135, 474
Traprain Law 509
Traquair R. 489
Tremadoc Bay 474
Trent R. 45, 327, 413, 453, 468, 477, **478**
Tweed R. 128, 139, 301, 455
Tyne R. (Northumberland) 45, 58, 114, 138, 213, 391, **473**, 509
Tyne R. (East Lothian) 138, 473
Tynebec 473
Tyne Brook 473
Tynet (Tynot) R. 468
Tywi R. 135, **474**

Uphall Camp 170
Ure R. 213, 380
Usk 115, 119, 145, 173, 175, **285**, 460
Usk R. 213, 376, **378**, 445, 467

Vyrnwy R. 391

Wall (Staffordshire) 157, 207, **388**, 468
Walls Castle **367**
Wallsend 209, 220, **453**
Walton Castle 221, 442
Wanborough 175, 176, **350**
Ward Law 125, 140, 210, **484**
Waring R. 7
Warrenburn 353
Wash, The 120, 138, 143, **418**, 451
Washbrook 475
Watercrook, 170, 171, 172, 223, **244**
Water Eaton 157, **437**
Water Newton 153, 162, 164, 208, 231, 346, 347, **348**, 351
Water of Fleet **375**
Water of Luce 135, **240**
Wear R. 109, 112, 114, 138, 213, 253, 489, **490**, 509
Wearmouth 208, 220, **339**
Weaver R. 316
Wells 487
Wendover 341
Werneth 353
West Coker 447
Western Isles 249 (and see Hebrides)
Weston under Penyard 175, **258**
West Stow 164
Wetwang 155, 156, 157, 208, **332**
Wey R. 432
Wharfe R. **493**
Wheatsheaf Inn (North Waltham) 178, 180, **503**
Whilton Lodge 157, 164, 165, 167, **265**
Whitchurch 119, 120, 121, 143, 157, 170, 207, **416**, 448
Whitley Castle 119, 120, 142, **360**
Whittledean 433
Whitton Cross-roads (Glamorgan) 273, 274
Wickham 166, **309**
Wigan 171, 172
Wight, Isle of 41, 57, 58, 116, 117, 150, 181, 408, 457, 488, **489**
Wigtown Bay 135
Willoughby 165, 167, 207, **495**
Wilton 163
Wimborne 427
Winchester 5, 36, 48, 58, 119, 120, 166, 178, 179, 180, 206, 209, 229, 267, 312, 389, 432, **492**

Winster R. 135
Wirksworth 403, **404**
Witham (Essex) 138, 358
Witham R. (Lincolnshire) 138, 305, 358, 393, **418**
Witherley 412
Woodspeen 175, 176, **462**
Worcester 207, **496**
Workington 406
Wrath, Cape 112, 133
Wrekin 505, 506
Wroxeter 119, 120, 128, 157, 173, 198, 199, 207, 209, 227, 325, 391, 448, 505, **506**
Wye R. 424
Wyre R. 457, 496

Yare R. 138, 358, 366, **367**
Yartleton 258
Yeo R. 255, 368, 392
Ynis Gaint 297
York 12, 13, 18, 24, 28, 36, 46, 48, 57, 119, 122, 123, 142, 155, 156, 157, 162, 167, 192, 208, 209, 219, 220, 225, 228, 229, 233, 282, 355, 356, **357**, 442, 467
Yoxford 150, 168, 170, **456**
Ystwyth R. 135, 213, **462**